MODERN GUNS

Identification & Values

11th Edition

Russell Quertermous
Steve Quertermous

COLLECTOR BOOKS
A Division of Schroeder Publishing Co., Inc.

The current values in this book should be used only as a guide. They are not intended to set prices, which vary from one section of the country to another. Auction prices as well as dealer prices vary greatly and are affected by condition as well as demand. Neither the Authors nor the Publisher assumes responsibility for any losses that might be incurred as a result of consulting this guide.

Searching For A Publisher?

We are always looking for knowledgeable people considered to be experts within their field. If you feel that there is a real need for a book on your collectible subject and have a large comprehensive collection, contact Collector Books.

Front cover: Remington 788 rifle, Taurus Model 689 revolver, Smith & Wesson Model 60 revolver

Cover design: Beth Summers
Layout design: Karen Geary

Contents

I. Shotguns 7

AYA	Ithaca	Remington
Armalite	Iver Johnson	Richland
Baikal	Kessler	Ruger
Baker	Kleinguenther	SKB
Beretta	L.C. Smith	Sarasqueta
Bernardelli	Lefever	Sauer
Breda	Mannlicher	Savage
Browning	Marlin	Sears
Charles Daly	Mauser	Smith & Wesson
Colt	Maverick	Stevens
Darne	Mitchell Arms	Universal
Davidson	Mossberg	Valmet
Fox	New England	Weatherby
Franchi	New Haven	Western
Greifelt	Noble	Western Field
Harrington & Richardson	Parker	Winchester
High Standard	Pedersen	Zoli
Hunter	Premier	

II. Rifles 149

Anschutz	Kimber	Remington
Armalite	Kleinguenther	Ruger
Browning	Mannlicher	Sako
BSA	Mark X	Savage
Carl Gustaf	Marlin	Sears
Charles Daly	Mauser	Sedgley
Charter Arms	Military	Smith & Wesson
Colt	Mitchell Arms	Standard
FN	Mossberg	Stevens
Harrington & Richardson	Musketeer	Thompson Center
Heckler & Koch	New England	Universal
High Standard	New Haven	Valmet
Husqvarna	Newton	Walther
Ithaca	Noble	Weatherby
Iver Johnson	Pedersen	Western Field
Johnson	Plainfield	Winchester

III. Handguns 359

AMT	Glock	Rossi
American	Great Western	Ruger
Astra	Harrington & Richardson	Sauer
Auto Mag	Hartford	Savage
Bauer	Heckler & Koch	Sheridan
Bayard	High Standard	Smith & Wesson
Beretta	Iver Johnson	Star
Browning	Japanese	Sterling
Browning, FN	Lignose	Stevens
CZ	Llama	Steyr
Charter Arms	MAB	Taurus
Colt	Mauser	Thompson Center
Dardick	Mitchell Arms	Walther
Desert Eagle	New England	Webley
Detonics	North American Arms	Wesson
Fiala	Remington	

Introduction

Since the first edition of *Modern Guns* was released in the fall of 1978, the firearms industry has witnessed many changes. We've seen years of rapidly escalating prices and periods of relative calm in the market place. We've watched trends come and go, but generally quality and reliability have been determining factors for value.

The past couple of years have seen a resurfacing of some guns that had been previously discontinued and manufacturers continue to adapt their line to the changing trends and needs of sportsmen and collectors. Most have held prices down to a reasonable level.

There does seem to be a sort of cautious watchfulness toward legislation and a general concern that the right to keep and bear arms might be gradually eroded away by a well meaning but frustrated group of lawmakers. Their solution to crime and violence in our society leans toward disarming its citizenry.

This eleventh edition of *Modern Guns* is set up in the same way as previous editions. It is divided into three broad sections: Shotguns, Rifles, and Handguns and then divided alphabetically within each section by manufacturer. There is a contents page at the beginning of each section. Within the manufacturers' listings the guns are grouped where possible into like kinds; that is single shots are grouped together, bolt action arms are together, lever actions are together, slide actions are together, and finally semi-automatics. In the case of handguns, single shots are followed by semi-automatics then revolvers.

The guns included are those made from the turn of the century to the present. This is by no means an exhaustive work on all firearms. You won't find extremely rare examples of exotic firearms or custom guns that demand thousands of dollars. Hopefully, you will find a comprehensive overview of the firearms market today with examples of the majority of guns that can commonly be seen changing hands.

Keep in mind that prices will vary in different parts of the country. What is popular in one area might be slighty less so in another. Also keep in mind that, ultimately, the value of a gun as in any item is determined by the seller's eagerness to sell and the purchaser's willingness to buy. As always we encourage you to do more research on particular items that are of interest to you and to use this book as a guideline to establish the relative worth of your guns. There are no hard fast rules, no absolutes. Don't be afraid to use this book, take it along to auctions, garage sales, flea markets, and gun shows and use it as a guide. But don't let the figures in a book dictate whether or not you will make a trade on something you might really want.

Values

For the purpose of estimating values, the firearm's condition is the first and foremost consideration. Conditions of guns evaluated in this guide are considered to be in accordance with the National Rifle Association (NRA) definitions, taken from its magazine, *The American Rifleman*. This evaluation system is generally accepted in the firearms trade.

New Discontinued – same as new, but discontinued model. The following definitions will apply to all second-hand articles.

Perfect – in new condition in every aspect.

Excellent – new condition, used little, no noticeable marring of wood or metal, bluing perfect (except at muzzle or sharp edges).

Very Good – in perfect working condition, no appreciable wear on working surfaces, no corrosion or pitting, only minor surface dents or scratches.

Good – in safe working condition, minor wear on working surfaces, no broken parts, no corrosion or pitting that will interfere with proper functioning.

Fair – in working condition, but well worn, perhaps requiring replacement of minor parts or adjustments, no rust but may have corrosion pits which do not render article unsafe or inoperable.

Values in this guide are for guns in the following conditions:

New (retail) – suggested retail prices still in production.

Excellent and Very Good or Very Good and Good – second-hand items.

The illustrations included are from gun manufacturer's promotional photos, advertisements, catalogs, and brochures. Since they are from a number of sources, relative size cannot be determined by comparing photos.

Acknowledgments

The companies included for the use of catalogs, advertisements, and promotional material.

A special thanks to the following gun manufacturers for additional photos, information, and assistance: Beretta Arms Co., Inc. for material on Beretta handguns and shotguns; Browning for material on Browning handguns, rifles, and shotguns; Charter Arms Corporation for material on Charter Arms handguns; Colt Industries, Firearms Division for material on Colt handguns and rifles; Commercial Trading Imports, Inc. for material on Baikal shotguns; Harrington & Richardson, Inc. for material on Harrington & Richardson handguns, rifles, and shotguns; Heckler & Koch for material on Heckler & Koch rifles and handguns; Interarms for material on Mark X rifles, Valmet rifles, Whitworth rifles, Walther handguns and rifles, Star handguns, and Astra handguns; Ithaca Gun Co. for material on Ithaca shotguns; Iver Johnson Arms, Inc. for material on Iver Johnson handguns; Kleinguenther, Inc. for materials on Kleinguenther rifles; Mannlicher for materials on Mannlicher rifles and shotguns; Marlin for material on Marlin and Marlin-Glenfield rifles and shotguns; O.F. Mossberg & Sons, Inc. for material on Mossberg and New Haven rifles and shotguns; Remington for material on Remington rifles, shotguns, and handguns; Richland Arms Co. for material on Richland shotguns; Savage Arms for material on Savage rifles and shotguns, Stevens rifles and shotguns, Fox shotguns, and Anschutz rifles; Sears, Roebuck & Co. for material on Sears rifles and shotguns and Ted Williams rifles and shotguns; Smith & Wesson for material on Smith & Wesson handguns, rifles, and shotguns; Speer Inc. Advertising for material on Mossberg firearms; Sterling Arms Corporation for material on Sterling handguns; Universal Firearms for material on Universal rifles; Weatherby, Inc. for material on Weatherby rifles and shotguns; Winchester-Western for material on Winchester rifles and shotguns; U.S. Repeating Arms for material on Winchester rifles and shotguns.

Petersen Publishing Company for the use of the following photographs from *Guns and Ammo Annual*, 1977, 1982 and *Hunting Annual* 1983:

Shotguns:

Beretta BL4, 680 Trap, 685, MKII Trap, GR-2; 410, AL-2; Bernardelli Game Cock; Browning Super Light, Citori Trap, B-SS, BPS, 2000; Charles Daly Field III, Auto Superior; Fox FA-1; Franchi Standard; Harrington & Richardson 176, 1212; Ithaca 37 Standard, 37 DV Deluxe, 37 Bicentennial, 51 Deluxe Trap, 51 Magnum, 51 Deerslayer; Mannlicher Oxford, Mossberg 500 ATP8, 500 AHTD, Slugster, Richland 200; Smith & Wesson 916, 1000, 3000; Valmet 412K; Weatherby Orion, Athena, 92, 82; Winchester 1200 Defender

Rifles:

Anschutz 1422D, 520/61; Browning BAR; Harrington & Richardson 750; Heckler & Koch 770, 940; Mossberg 321K, 341, 353, 800, 810; New Haven 453T; Remington 541 S, 700 ADL; Salo Classic, Safari; Stevens 35, 125; Valmet 412, M62/S, M71/S; Walther KKJ, KKM, UIT, Moving Target; Winchester 70 XTR Featherweight, 70 Western, 70XTR Sporter Magnum, Super Xpress

Handguns:

Beretta 951; Browning Challenger II, Challenger III; Charter Arms Explorer II, Bulldog Tracker; Colt S-4 Targetsman, Target S-3; Dan Wesson 9-2, 44V; Heckler & Koch HK4, P9S; Iver Johnson TP22; Llama Comanche; Ruger Redhawk; Smith & Wesson 30, 1953 22/32, 25-1955, 10, 31, 27, 28, 58, 38, 547 M & P, 586; Sterling MKII 400

Stackpole Books for the use of the following photographs from W.H.B. Smith's *Book of Pistols and Revolvers* and *Book of Rifles*: Astra 1911-Patent, 1915 Patent, 1924, 300, 600, 400; Bayard 1908, 1923, 1930; Beretta 1915, 1923, 1931; Browning, FN, 1900, 1903 Military, 1910, 1922; CZ 22, 1945; Colt 1900, 1902, 1905, Model M, 1911; Fiala Single Shot; Harrington & Richardson 32; Japanese Military pistols; Lignose 2A, 2 Pocket; MAB C; Mauser 2; Sauer 1913, WTM, H; Savage 1907, 1915, 1917; Smith & Wesson 32 & 35, No. 3 Frontier, Doubled Action Frontier, Military & Police 32-20, New Century; Star 1919; Steyr Solothurn, Vest Pocket; Walther 5, 4, 7, 9; Webley & Scott 1906, Mark I; Military rifles

Shotguns

AYA 8
Armalite 8
Baikal 9
Baker 11
Beretta 11
Bernardelli 20
Breda 21
Browning 21
Charles Daly 31
Colt 33
Darne 34

Davidson 35
Fox 35
Franchi 38
Greifelt 42
Harrington & Richardson 42
High Standard 47
Hunter 50
Ithaca 50
Iver Johnson 56
Kessler 57
Kleinguenther 58
L.C. Smith 59
Lefever 60
Mannlicher 60
Marlin 61

Mauser 68
Maverick 70
Mitchell 71
Mossberg 72
New England 80
New Haven 81
Noble 82
Parker 85
Pedersen 86
Premier 88
Remington 89
Richland 100
Ruger 101
SKB 102
Sarasqueta 105
Sauer 105
Savage 106
Sears 113
Smith & Wesson 114
Stevens 116
Universal 128
Valmet 129
Weatherby 130
Western 134
Western Field 134
Winchester 136
Zoli 148

AYA

AYA Matador
Gauge: 10, 12, 16, 20, 20 magnum
Action: Box lock; top lever break-open; hammerless; selective single trigger & automatic ejector
Magazine: None
Barrel: Double barrel, 26", 28", 30" any choke combination
Finish: Blued; checkered walnut pistol grip stock & beavertail forearm
Approximate wt.: 7 lbs.
Comments: Made from 1953 until 1963. Replaced by Matador II.
Estimated Value: Excellent: $485.00
                       Very good: $390.00

AYA Matador II
Same as the Matador except ventilated rib. Produced from about 1963 to 1970.
Estimated Value: Excellent: $540.00
                       Very good: $430.00

AYA Bolero
Same as the Matador except non-selective single trigger & extractors; 28 & 410 gauges. Made from the mid 1950's until 1963.
Estimated Value: Excellent: $420.00
                       Very good: $335.00

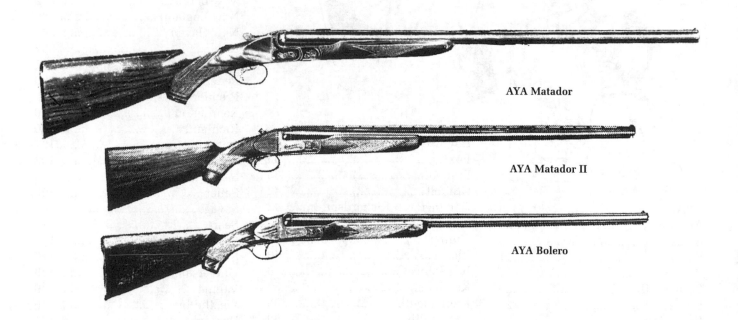

AYA Matador

AYA Matador II

AYA Bolero

Armalite

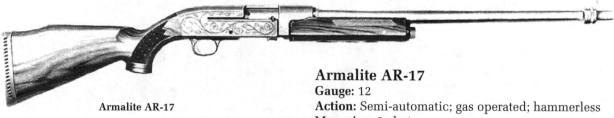

Armalite AR-17

Armalite AR-17
Gauge: 12
Action: Semi-automatic; gas operated; hammerless
Magazine: 2-shot
Barrel: 24" aluminum alloy; interchangeable choke tubes; improved modified & full chokes
Finish: Gold anodized or black anodized; plastic stock & forearm
Approximate wt.: 5½ lbs.
Comments: Barrel & receiver housing made of high-tensile aluminum alloy. Made from about 1963 to 1965. Approximately 2,000 manufactured.
Estimated Value: Excellent: $730.00
                       Very good: $540.00

Baikal

Baikal Model IJ-27 and IJ-27EIC

Gauge: 12
Action: Box lock; top lever break-open; hammerless; double trigger
Magazine: None
Barrel: Over & under double barrel; 26" or 28" improved cylinder & modified or modified & full chokes; ventilated rib
Finish: Blued; engraved receiver; hand checkered walnut pistol grip stock & forearm
Approximate wt.: 7½ lbs.
Comments: Made in Soviet Union; IJ-27EIC has single trigger and automatic ejectors; add $40.00.
Estimated Value: Excellent: $320.00
  Very good: $260.00

Baikal Model IJK-27EIC Silver

Same as the Model IJ-27EIC except: silver inlays and fancy engraving.
Estimated Value: Excellent: $535.00
  Very good: $425.00

Baikal Model IJ-12

Less fancy but similar to the IJ-27. No engraving, no recoil pad; 28" barrel only. Imported in the early 1970's.
Estimated Value: Excellent: $270.00
  Very good: $215.00

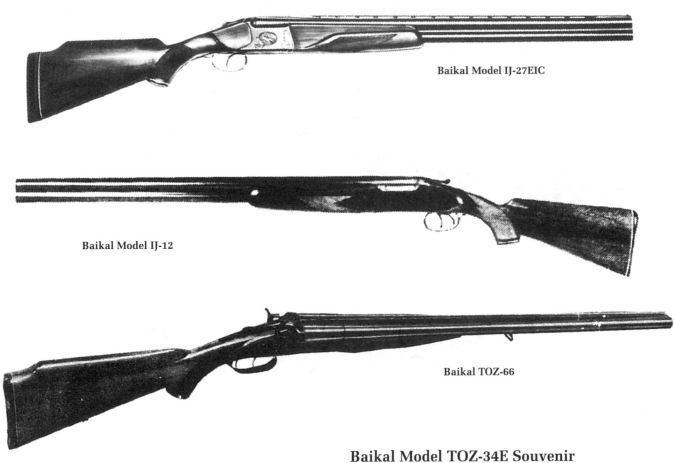

Baikal Model IJ-27EIC

Baikal Model IJ-12

Baikal TOZ-66

Baikal TOZ-66

Gauge: 12
Action: Box lock; top lever break-open; exposed hammers
Magazine: None
Barrel: Side by side double barrel; 28" chrome lined, variety of chokes
Finish: Blued; checkered wood pistol grip stock & short tapered forearm; engraving
Approximate wt.: 8 lbs.
Comments: Imported during the 1970's.
Estimated Value: Excellent: $280.00
  Very good: $220.00

Baikal Model TOZ-34E Souvenir

Gauge: 12, 20, 28
Action: Box lock; top lever break-open; hammerless
Magazine: None
Barrel: Over and under double barrel; 26" or 28" improved cylinder & modified or modified & full; ventilated rib on 12 and 20 gauge; solid rib on 28 gauge
Finish: Blued; select walnut, hand checkered and pistol grip stock and forearm; engraved receiver
Approximate wt.: 7 lbs.
Comments: Imported from the Soviet Union. It features selective ejectors and cocking indicators.
Estimated Value: Excellent: $650.00
  Very good: $485.00

Baikal Model IJ-18

Gauge: 12, 20, 410
Action: Box lock; top lever break-open; hammerless; single shot; cocking indicator
Magazine: None
Barrel: 26", 28" modified, 30" full choke
Finish: Blued; checkered walnut-stained hardwood, pistol grip stock and tapered forearm; engraved receiver
Approximate wt.: 6 lbs.
Comments: Imported from the Soviet Union.
Estimated Value: Excellent: $70.00
                                    Very good: $60.00

Baikal IJ-58MA and 58MAE

Gauge: 12, 20 magnum
Action: Box lock; top lever break-open; hammerless
Magazine: None
Barrel: side by side double barrel; 26" improved cylinder & modified, 28" modified & full chokes; chrome lined
Finish: Blued; checkered walnut pistol grip stock and short tapered forearm; engraved receiver. IJ-58MAE has selective ejectors, add $28.00.
Approximate wt.: 7 lbs.
Comments: Imported in 1970's.
Estimated Value: Excellent: $300.00
                                    Very good: $235.00

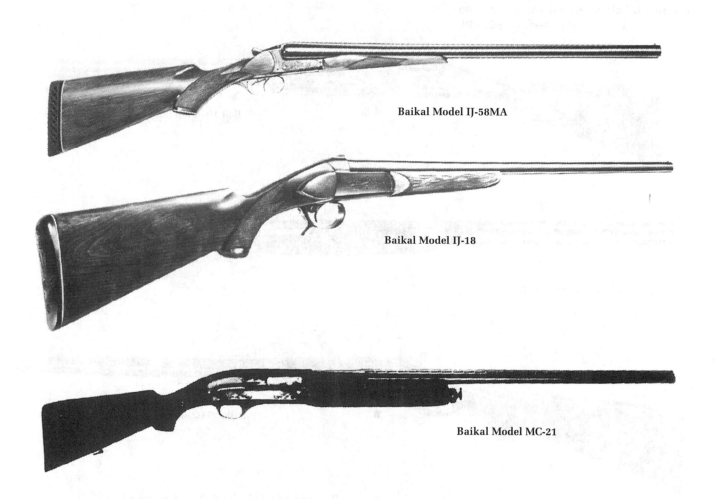

Baikal Model IJ-58MA

Baikal Model IJ-18

Baikal Model MC-21

Baikal Model IJ-43

Gauge: 12
Action: Box lock; top lever break-open; hammerless
Magazine: None
Barrel: Side by side double barrel; 20", 26," or 28", barrels
Finish: Blued; checkered walnut stock and forearm; engraved receiver
Approximate wt.: 8½ lbs.
Comments: Imported from the Soviet Union.
Estimated Value: Excellent: $260.00
                                    Very good: $210.00

Baikal Model MC-21

Gauge: 12
Action: Semi-automatic; hammerless; side ejection
Magazine: 5-shot tubular
Barrel: 26" improved cylinder; 28" modified; 30" full chokes; ventilated rib
Finish: Blued; checkered walnut, pistol grip stock and forearm; engraved receiver
Approximate wt.: 7½ lbs.
Comments: Imported in the 1970's.
Estimated Value: Excellent: $350.00
                                    Very good: $270.00

Baikal Model MC-5

Baikal Model MC-5
Gauge: 20
Action: Box lock; top lever break-open; hammerless; double triggers
Magazine: None
Barrel: Over and under double barrel; 26" or 28" improved cylinder & modified or skeet chokes; ribbed
Finish: Blued; checkered walnut pistol grip or straight stock and forearm; engraved receiver
Approximate wt.: 5¾ lbs.
Comments: Imported during the 1970's.
Estimated Value: Excellent: $920.00
Very good: $700.00

Baker

Baker Batavia Leader

Baker Black Beauty Special
Similar to Baker Batavia Leader except higher quality wood and finish. Add $75.00 for automatic extractors.
Estimated Value: Excellent: $750.00
Very good: $575.00

Baker Black Beauty Special

Baker Batavia Leader
Gauge: 12, 16, 20
Action: Box lock; top break-open; hammerless
Magazine: None
Barrel: 26", 28", 30", or 32" side by side double barrel; any standard choke combination
Finish: Blued; walnut pistol grip stock and forearm.
Approximate wt.: 7 to 8 lbs.
Comments: Made from about 1900 to 1930. Add $75.00 for automatic extractors.
Estimated Value: Excellent: $500.00
Very good: $400.00

Beretta

Beretta Companion FS-1
Gauge: 12, 16, 20, 28, 410
Action: Underlever; hammerless; single shot
Magazine: None
Barrel: 26", 28" full choke
Finish: Blued; checkered walnut pistol grip stock and forearm
Approximate wt.: 5 lbs.
Comments: A folding shotgun made from about 1960 to the late 1970's.
Estimated Value: Excellent: $140.00
Very good: $110.00

Beretta Model 412
Gauge: 12, 20, 24, 28, 32, 410
Action: Underlever, break-open, hammerless, single shot
Magazine: None
Barrel: 28" full or modified choke
Finish: Blued; checkered or smooth walnut semi-pistol grip stock and forearm
Approximate wt.: 5 lbs.
Comments: A lightweight folding shotgun designed for beginners, campers, and backpackers. Made from early 1980's to mid 1990's.
Estimated Value: Excellent: $160.00
Very good: $130.00

Beretta Companion FS-1

Beretta Mark II Trap

Beretta Mark II Trap
Gauge: 12
Action: Box lock; top lever break-open; hammerless; single shot
Magazine: None
Barrel: 32", 34" full choke; ventilated rib
Finish: Blued; checkered walnut Monte Carlo pistol grip stock and forearm; recoil pad; engraving
Approximate wt.: 8 lbs.
Comments: Made from the mid 1970's to early 1980's.
Estimated Value: Excellent: $610.00
                        Very good: $485.00

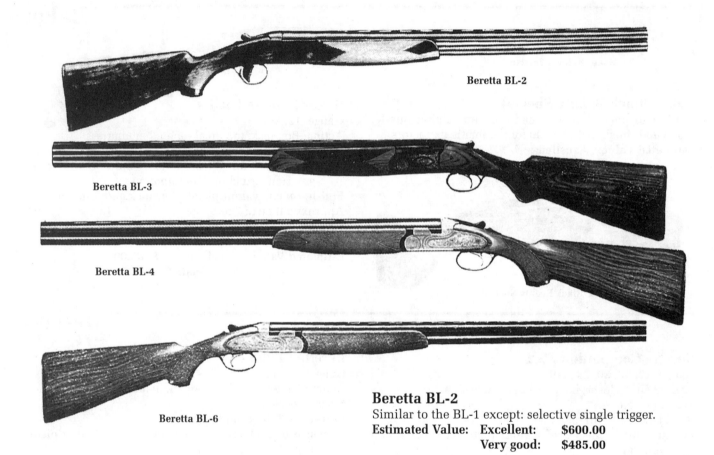

Beretta BL-2

Beretta BL-3

Beretta BL-4

Beretta BL-6

Beretta BL-1
Gauge: 12
Action: Box lock; top lever break-open; hammerless; double triggers
Magazine: None
Barrel: Over and under double barrel; chrome steel; 26"-30" improved cylinder & modified or modified & full chokes
Finish: Blued; checkered walnut semi-pistol grip stock and forearm
Approximate wt.: 7 lbs.
Comments: Made from about 1969 to early 1970's.
Estimated Value: Excellent: $535.00
                        Very good: $425.00

Beretta BL-2
Similar to the BL-1 except: selective single trigger.
Estimated Value: Excellent: $600.00
                        Very good: $485.00

Beretta BL-3
Similar to the BL-2 except: ventilated rib; engraving.
Estimated Value: Excellent: $700.00
                        Very good: $560.00

Beretta BL-4 and BL-5
Similar to the BL-3 except: deluxe engraving and checkering; automatic ejectors. Add $200.00 for BL-5.
Estimated Value: Excellent: $810.00
                        Very good: $650.00

Beretta BL-6
The finest of the BL line. Highest quality checkering and engraving. Similar to the BL-4.
Estimated Value: Excellent: $1,400.00
                        Very good: $1,135.00

Beretta Silver Snipe

Gauge: 12, 20, regular or magnum
Action: Box lock; top lever break-open; hammerless
Magazine: None
Barrel: 26"-30" improved cylinder & modified, modified & full, full or skeet chokes; ribbed; over and under double barrel
Finish: Blued; nickel receiver; checkered walnut pistol grip stock and forearm
Approximate wt.: 7½ lbs.
Comments: Made from mid 1950's to late 1960's. Add $25.00 for single selective trigger.
Estimated Value: Excellent: $640.00
Very good: $510.00

Beretta Silver Snipe

Beretta Golden Snipe

Similar to the Silver Snipe except: ventilated rib; automatic ejectors. Discontinued in the mid 1970's.
Estimated Value: Excellent: $755.00
Very good: $605.00

Beretta Asel

Gauge: 12, 20
Action: Box lock; top lever break-open; hammerless; automatic ejector; single trigger
Magazine: None
Barrel: Over and under double barrel; 25", 28", 30" improved cylinder & modified or modified & full chokes
Finish: Blued; checkered walnut semi-pistol grip stock and forearm
Approximate wt.: 7 lbs.
Comments: Made from late 1940's to mid 1960's.
Estimated Value: Excellent: $1,430.00
Very good: $1,135.00

Beretta Model S56E

Beretta Model S56E

Similar to Model S55B except: scroll engraving on the receiver; selective automatic ejectors.
Estimated Value: Excellent: $875.00
Very good: $710.00

Beretta Model S55B

Gauge: 12, 20, regular or magnum
Action: Box lock; top lever break-open; hammerless
Magazine: None
Barrel: Over and under double barrel; chrome lined; ventilated rib; 26" improved cylinder and modified; 28" or 30" modified & full; 30" full in 12 gauge
Finish: Blued; checkered walnut pistol grip stock and beavertail forearm; recoil pad on magnum
Approximate wt.: 6 to 7 lbs.
Comments: Made from late 1970's to early 1980s.
Estimated Value: Excellent: $780.00
Very good: $625.00

Beretta Model 680 Trap

Beretta Model 680 Trap

Similar to the Model 680 Skeet except: Monte Carlo stock, recoil pad; 30" or 32" improved modified & full choke barrels.
Estimated Value: Excellent: $1,520.00
Very good: $1,215.00

Beretta Model 680 Mono Trap

Similar to the Model 680 Trap except: a single high-ventilated rib barrel; 32" or 34" full choke barrel.
Estimated Value: Excellent: $1,445.00
Very good: $1,160.00

Beretta Model 680 Competition Skeet

Gauge: 12
Action: Top lever, break-open; hammerless; automatic ejector; single selective trigger
Magazine: None
Barrel: Over and under double barrel; 26" or 28" skeet choke barrels; ventilated rib
Finish: Blued; checkered walnut pistol grip stock and forearm; silver grey receiver with engraving; gold-plated trigger
Approximate wt.: 7 lbs.
Comments: Interchangeable barrel; price includes luggage-style case.
Estimated Value: Excellent: $1,500.00
Very good: $1,200.00

Beretta Model 625

Gauge: 12, 20, regular or magnum
Action: Box lock; top lever break-open; hammerless; double barrel; mechanical extractor
Magazine: None
Barrel: 26" improved cylinder/modified; 28" or 30" modified/full; double barrel
Finish: Blued; grey receiver; checkered walnut pistol grip or straight stock and tapered forearm
Approximate wt.: 6 to 7 lbs.
Comments: Produced in the mid 1980's.
Estimated Value: Excellent: $890.00
                       Very good: $710.00

Beretta Model 685

Gauge: 12, 20, regular or magnum
Action: Top lever, break-open; hammerless; single selective trigger
Magazine: None
Barrel: Over and under double barrel; 26" improved cylinder & modified, 28" or 30" modified & full, 30" full & full; ventilated rib
Finish: Blued; checkered walnut pistol grip stock and fluted forearm; silver grey receiver with light engraving
Approximate wt.: 8 lbs.
Comments: Discontinued in late 1980's.
Estimated Value: Excellent: $850.00
                       Very good: $680.00

Beretta Model 626; 626 Onyx

Similar to the Model 625 except: selective automatic ejectors. Deduct 30% for Regular Model 626 (discontinued 1990). Produced from late 1980's to early 1990's.
Estimated Value: Excellent: $1,400.00
                       Very good: $1,125.00

Beretta Model 627EL, 627EELL

Similar to the Model 626 with higher grade finish and engraved sideplates. Add 70% for EELL Model.
Estimated Value: Excellent: $2,450.00
                       Very good: $1,960.00

Beretta Model 686 & 686 Essential

Gauge: 12, 20, 28, regular or magnum
Action: Top lever, break-open; hammerless; single selective trigger; selective automatic ejectors
Magazine: None
Barrel: Over and under double barrel; 26" improved cylinder & modified, 28" or 30" modified & full, or 30" full & full; ventilated rib; multi-choke tubes
Finish: Blued; checkered walnut pistol grip stock and fluted forearm; silver grey receiver with engraving or plain black receiver
Approximate wt.: 7 lbs.
Comments: Add 25% for Ultralight Onyx Model, 26% for Silver Perdiz, 6% for Sporting Clays Model, 30% for Silver Pigeon Model
Estimated Value: New (retail): $1,186.00
                       Excellent: $ 890.00
                       Very good: $ 715.00

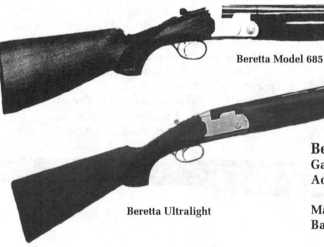

Beretta Model 685

Beretta Ultralight

Beretta Ultralight

Gauge: 12 (2¾" chamber)
Action: Low profile, improved box lock; automatic safety; single selective trigger
Magazine: None
Barrel: Over and under double barrel; 28" with MC3 choke tube; ventilated rib
Finish: Blued with game scene engraved nickel finish receiver; select walnut checkered pistol grip stock and schnabel forearm
Approximate wt.: 6 lbs.
Comments: Introduced in the early 1990's.
Estimated Value: New (retail): $1,716.00
                       Excellent: $1,290.00
                       Very good: $1,030.00

Beretta Model 687L Silver Pigeon

Gauge: 12, 20, regular or magnum
Action: Top lever, break-open; hammerless; selective automatic ejectors; single selective trigger
Magazine: None
Barrel: Over and under double barrel; 26" or 28" with interchangeable choke tubes; ventilated rib
Finish: Blued; greyed receiver with engraving; checkered walnut pistol grip stock and forearm
Approximate wt.: 6 to 6¾ lbs.
Comments: Add 25% for Golden Onyx Model; 20% for Sporting Clays Model.
Estimated Value: New (retail): $2,031.00
                       Excellent: $1,524.00
                       Very good: $1,220.00

Beretta Model 687EL Gold Pigeon

Similar to the Model 687L except: higher quality finish, extensive engraving on receiver and sideplate. Add 6% for Sporting Clays Model.
Estimated Value: New (retail): $3,446.00
                       Excellent: $2,585.00
                       Very good: $2,065.00

Beretta GR-2

Beretta GR-2
Gauge: 12, 20
Action: Box lock, top lever, break-open; hammerless
Magazine: None
Barrel: Side by side double barrel; 26"-30"; variety of choke combinations
Finish: Blued; checkered walnut semi-pistol grip stock and forearm
Approximate wt.: 6 to 8 lbs.
Comments: Made from the late 1960's to mid 1970's.
Estimated Value: Excellent: $650.00
                    Very good: $515.00

Beretta GR-3
Similar to the GR-2 except: single selective trigger.
Estimated Value: Excellent: $690.00
                     Very good: $550.00

Beretta GR-4
Similar to the GR-3 except: automatic ejector engraving and deluxe wood work.
Estimated Value: Excellent: $850.00
                     Very good: $680.00

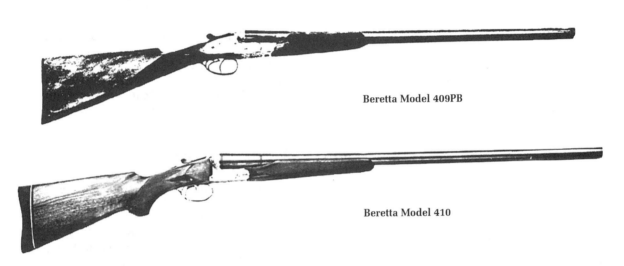

Beretta Model 409PB

Beretta Model 410

Beretta Model 409PB
Gauge: 12, 16, 20, 28
Action: Box lock, top lever, break-open; hammerless; double triggers
Magazine: None
Barrel: Side by side double barrel 27½", 28½", 30" improved cylinder & modified or modified & full chokes
Finish: Blued; checkered walnut straight or pistol grip stock and small tapered forearm; engraved
Approximate wt.: 6 to 8 lbs.
Comments: Made from mid 1930's to mid 1960's.
Estimated Value: Excellent: $720.00
                    Very good: $575.00

Beretta Model 410E
Similar to the 409PB except: higher quality finish and engraving; automatic ejector.
Estimated Value: Excellent: $900.00
                     Very good: $725.00

Beretta Model 411E
Similar to 410E with higher quality finish.
Estimated Value: Excellent: $1,190.00
                     Very good: $ 950.00

Beretta Model 410
Gauge: 10 magnum
Action: Box lock; top lever, break-open; hammerless; double triggers
Magazine: None
Barrel: Side by side double barrel; 27½", 28½", 30" improved cylinder & modified or modified & full chokes
Finish: Blued; checkered walnut pistol stock & short tapered forearm
Approximate wt.: 10 lbs.
Comments: Made from the mid 1930's to early 1980's.
Estimated Value: Excellent: $1,200.00
                    Very good: $ 975.00

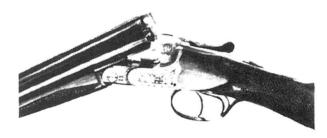

Beretta Model 410E

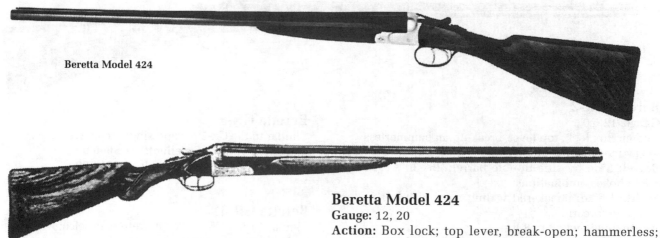

Beretta Model 424

Beretta Silver Hawk Featherweight

Beretta Silver Hawk Featherweight

Gauge: 12, 16, 20, 28
Action: Box lock; top lever, break-open; hammerless
Magazine: None
Barrel: Side by side double barrel; 26"-32" variety of chokes; matted rib
Finish: Blued; checkered walnut pistol grip stock and forearm
Approximate wt.: 7¼ lbs.
Comments: Made from the mid 1950's to late 1960's.
Estimated Value: Excellent: $650.00
                        Very good: $520.00

Beretta Silver Hawk Featherweight Magnum

Similar to the Silver Hawk Featherweight in 10 or 12 gauge magnum; chrome lined 30" or 32" barrels; ventilated rib; recoil pad.
Estimated Value: Excellent: $750.00
                        Very good: $600.00

Beretta Model 424

Gauge: 12, 20
Action: Box lock; top lever, break-open; hammerless; double trigger
Magazine: None
Barrel: Side by side double barrel; chrome lined; matted rib; 26" or 28" improved cylinder & modified or modified & full chokes
Finish: Blued; checkered walnut straight grip stock and forearm
Approximate wt.: 6 lbs.
Comments: Produced from the late 1970's to mid 1980's.
Estimated Value: Excellent: $855.00
                        Very good: $680.00

Beretta Model 426

Gauge: 12, 20, magnum
Action: Top lever, break-open; hammerless; single selective trigger; selective automatic ejector
Magazine: None
Barrel: Side by side double barrel; 26" improved cylinder & modified or 28" modified & full; solid rib
Finish: Blued; checkered walnut pistol grip stock and tapered forearm; silver grey engraved receiver; silver pigeon inlaid
Approximate wt.: 8 lbs.
Comments: Discontinued mid 1980's.
Estimated Value: Excellent: $1,080.00
                        Very good: $ 865.00

Beretta Silver Pigeon

Beretta Silver Pigeon

Gauge: 12
Action: Slide action; hammerless
Magazine: 5-shot tubular
Barrel: 26"-32", various chokes
Finish: Blued; engraved and inlaid with silver pigeon; chrome trigger; checkered walnut pistol grip stock and slide handle
Approximate wt.: 7 lbs.
Comments: Made from about 1960 for 6 years.
Estimated Value: Excellent: $400.00
                        Very good: $320.00

Beretta Gold Pigeon

Similar to the Silver Pigeon except: heavy engraving; gold pigeon inlaid; ventilated rib; gold trigger.
Estimated Value: Excellent: $745.00
                        Very good: $595.00

Beretta Ruby Pigeon

Similar to the Gold Pigeon except: deluxe engraving and ruby eye in inlaid pigeon.
Estimated Value: Excellent: $900.00
                        Very good: $720.00

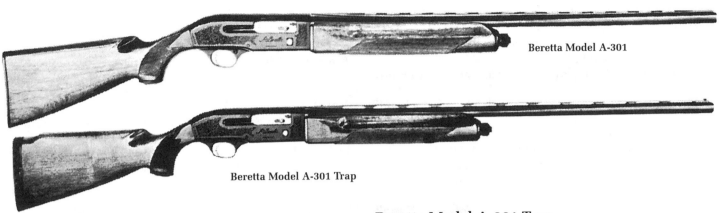

Beretta Model A-301

Beretta Model A-301 Trap

Beretta Model A-301

Gauge: 12, 20, regular or magnum
Action: Gas operated, semi-automatic; hammerless
Magazine: 3-shot tubular
Barrel: 26" improved cylinder; 28" modified or full; 30" full in 12 gauge; ventilated rib; chrome molybdenum
Finish: Blued; checkered walnut pistol grip stock and forearm; decorated alloy receiver; recoil pad on magnum model
Approximate wt.: 6¼ to 7 lbs.
Comments: Made from the late 1970's to early 1980's. Add 10% for magnum.
Estimated Value: Excellent: $450.00
Very good: $360.00

Beretta Model A-301 Trap

Similar to the A-301 except: Monte Carlo stock, recoil pad & gold plated trigger; 12 gauge only; 30" full choke.
Estimated Value: Excellent: $465.00
Very good: $370.00

Beretta Model A-301 Skeet

Similar to the A-301 Trap except: 26" skeet choke barrel.
Estimated Value: Excellent: $460.00
Very good: $365.00

Beretta Model A-301 Deer Gun

Similar to the A-301 except: 22" slug barrel; adjustable open sights.
Estimated Value: Excellent: $440.00
Very good: $350.00

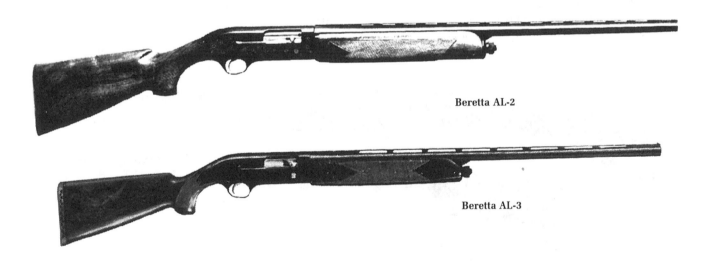

Beretta AL-2

Beretta AL-3

Beretta AL-1

Gauge: 12, 20 regular or magnum
Action: Gas operated, semi-automatic; hammerless
Magazine: 3-shot tubular
Barrel: 26"–30" skeet, improved cylinder, modified or full chokes; ventilated rib
Finish: Blued; checkered walnut pistol grip stock and forearm
Approximate wt.: 6½ to 7¾ lbs.
Comments: Made from the late 1960's to mid 1970's.
Estimated Value: Excellent: $375.00
Very good: $300.00

Beretta AL-2

Similar to the AL-1 except: ventilated rib; recoil pad; chrome lined bores.
Estimated Value: Excellent: $400.00
Very good: $320.00

Beretta AL-3

Similar to the AL-2 with light engraving.
Estimated Value: Excellent: $450.00
Very good: $360.00

Beretta Silver Lark

Gauge: 12
Action: Gas operated, semi-automatic; hammerless
Magazine: 5-shot tubular
Barrel: 26"-32", improved cylinder, modified or full chokes
Finish: Blued; checkered walnut pistol grip stock and forearm
Approximate wt.: 7 lbs.
Comments: Made from the early to late 1960's.
Estimated Value: Excellent: $375.00
                       Very good: $300.00

Beretta Gold Lark

Similar to the Silver Lark with high-quality engraving and ventilated rib.
Estimated Value: Excellent: $485.00
                       Very good: $390.00

Beretta Ruby Lark

Similar to the Silver Lark with deluxe engraving and a stainless steel barrel.
Estimated Value: Excellent: $650.00
                       Very good: $520.00

Beretta Model A302 Mag-Action

Beretta Model A302 Mag-Action

Gauge: 12, 20, regular or magnum
Action: Gas operated, semi-automatic
Magazine: 3-shot tubular
Barrel: 26" improved cylinder; 28" modified or full; 30" full; ventilated rib
Finish: Blued; checkered walnut pistol grip stock and fluted forearm
Approximate wt.: 7 lbs.
Comments: Interchangeable barrel, 2¾" or 3" chambering. Produced from 1982 to 1987; add 5% for multi-choke model with four choke tubes.
Estimated Value: Excellent: $515.00
                       Very good: $410.00

Beretta Model A302 Skeet

Similar to the Model A302 Mag-Action except: 26" skeet choke barrel.
Estimated Value: Excellent: $540.00
                       Very good: $430.00

Beretta Model A302 Trap

Similar to the Model A302 Mag-Action except: Monte Carlo stock & 30" full choke barrel.
Estimated Value: Excellent: $550.00
                       Very good: $435.00

Beretta Model A302 Slug

Similar to the Model A302 Mag-Action except: 22" slug barrel; adjustable front sight, folding leaf rear sight; swivels.
Estimated Value: Excellent: $530.00
                       Very good: $420.00

Beretta Model 1200

Beretta Model 1201 FP Riot

Beretta Model 1201 FP Riot

Gauge: 12 (3" chambers)
Action: Inertia operated, semi-automatic, short recoil
Magazine: 5-shot (3" shells); 6-shot (2¾" shells); tubular magazine
Barrel: Matte black 20" barrel, chrome plated interior; blade front sight and adjustable rear sight
Finish: Matte black polymer pistol grip stock and forearm
Approximate wt.: 6½ lbs.
Comments: Introduced in the early 1990's; available with optional pistol grip
Estimated Value: New (retail): $683.00
                       Excellent: $520.00
                       Very good: $400.00

Beretta Model 1200, 1200 Riot, & 1201

Gauge: 12 and 12 magnum
Action: Inertia operated, semi-automatic, short recoil
Magazine: 3-shot tubular; 7-shot in riot model
Barrel: 24", 26", 28" modified, full, or changeable choke tubes; 20" cylinder bore on Riot Model
Finish: Blued; non-glare; synthetic stock & forearm
Approximate wt.: 7 lbs.
Comments: Made from 1988 to mid 1990's. Add 5% for Riot Model.
Estimated Value: Excellent: $490.00
                       Very good: $400.00

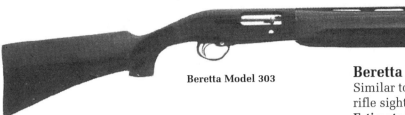

Beretta Model 303

Beretta Model 303

Gauge: 12, 20, regular or magnum
Action: Gas operated, semi-automatic
Magazine: 3-shot tubular
Barrel: 26", 28", 30" or 32" in a variety of chokes or inter-changeable choke tubes; 24" barrel on youth model
Finish: Blued; checkered walnut pistol grip stock & fore-arm; recoil pad on youth model
Approximate wt.: 6 to 7 lbs.
Comments: Replaced the 302 series in late 1980's. Deduct 6% for shotguns without interchangeable choke tubes; add 10% for Sporting Clays Model.
Estimated Value: New (retail): $772.00
Excellent: $580.00
Very good: $465.00

Beretta Model 303 Slug

Similar to the Model 303 except: 22" cylinder bore barrel, rifle sights. Discontinued in 1992.
Estimated Value: Excellent: $575.00
Very good: $460.00

Beretta Model 303 Skeet

Similar to the Model 303 except: 26" skeet choke barrel.
Estimated Value: New (retail): $822.00
Excellent: $620.00
Very good: $495.00

Beretta Model 303 Trap

Similar to the Model 303 except: 30" or 32" full choke barrel or interchangeable choke tubes. Add 6% for inter-changeable choke tubes.
Estimated Value: New (retail): $822.00
Excellent: $620.00
Very good: $495.00

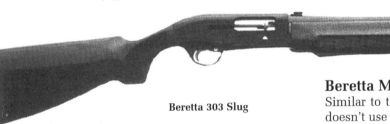

Beretta 303 Slug

Beretta Model A 304 Lark

Similar to the Model A 390 except: 12 gauge 2 3/4 only; doesn't use the self compensating gas system; inertia oper-ated only; introduced in 1990's. Add 20% for gold lark.
Estimated Value: New (retail): $735.00
Excellent: $550.00
Very good: $440.00

Beretta Model A 390 Mallard

Gauge: 12, regular or magnum; 3" chamber
Action: Gas operated, semi-automatic; self-compensating gas operating system performs with any 12 gauge factory load
Magazine: 3-shot tubular
Barrel: 24", 26", 28", or 30" with mobilchoke screw-in choke tubes; ventilated rib
Finish: Black; checkered walnut or synthetic pistol grip stock & forearm; a new stock drop system and cast-off spacer allows stock adjustment.
Approximate wt.: 7 to 8 lbs.
Comments: Introduced in 1992. Add 20% for gold mal-lard, add 15% for ported sport trap.
Estimated Value: New (retail): $822.00
Excellent: $620.00
Very good: $490.00

Beretta Model A 304 Slug

Same as A304 Lark except: 20" or 22" barrel with rifle sights (adjustable rear).
Estimated Value: New (retail): $735.00
Excellent: $550.00
Very good: $440.00

Beretta Pintail

Gauge: 12, regular or magnum; 3" chamber
Action: Inertia operated, semi-automatic; falling block locking breech bolt
Magazine: 3-shot tubular
Barrel: 24", 26", or 28", nickel/chromium/molybenum steel with mobilchoke changeable tubes
Finish: Semi-matte black; checkered pistol grip stock and forearm
Approximate wt.: 7lbs.
Comments: Introduced in 1994.
Estimated Value: New (retail): $743.00
Excellent: $560.00
Very good: $450.00

Beretta Model A 390 Slug

Same as Model A 390 except: 20" or 22" barrel; fixed choke; plain barrel with hook-in bases for scope mount-ing; blade front sight and adjustable rear; introduced in 1992.
Estimated Value: New (retail): $822.00
Excellent: $620.00
Very good: $490.00

Beretta Model Pintail Slug

Same as Pintail except: 24" barrel with rifle sights (adjustable rear).
Estimated Value: New (retail): $743.00
Excellent: $560.00
Very good: $450.00

Bernardelli

Bernardelli Game Cock Deluxe

Bernardelli Game Cock

Gauge: 12, 20
Action: Box lock; top lever break-open; double trigger; hammerless
Magazine: None
Barrel: Double barrel, 25" improved & modified or 28" modified & full chokes
Finish: Blued; checkered walnut straight stock & forearm; light engraving
Approximate wt.: 6½ lbs.
Comments: Produced in the early 1970's.
Estimated Value: Excellent: $810.00
                        Very good: $650.00

Bernardelli Game Cock Deluxe

Same as the Game Cock except: light scroll engraving; single trigger; automatic ejector.
Estimated Value: Excellent: $865.00
                        Very good: $690.00

Bernardelli Italia

Gauge: 12, 16, 20
Action: Top lever break-open; exposed hammers; double trigger
Magazine: None
Barrel: Double barrel; chrome lined 30" modified & full chokes
Finish: Blued; engraved receiver; checkered walnut straight grip stock & forearm
Approximate wt.: 7 lbs.
Comments: Produced into the early 1990's.
Estimated Value: Excellent: $1,065.00
                        Very good: $ 850.00

Bernardelli Holland

Gauge: 12
Action: Slide lock; top lever break-open; hammerless; double trigger; automatic ejector
Magazine: None
Barrel: Double barrel, 26" to 32" any choke combination
Finish: Blued; straight or pistol grip stock & forearm; light engraving
Approximate wt.: 7 lbs.
Comments: Imported from the mid 1940's to the early 1990's.
Estimated Value: Excellent: $3,160.00
                        Very good: $2,528.00

Bernardelli Game Cock Premier

Same as the Game Cock except: more engraving; selective single trigger; automatic ejector.
Estimated Value: Excellent: $1025.00
                        Very good: $820.00

Bernardelli Roma

Gauge: 12, 16, 20, 28
Action: Anson & Deeley type; top lever break-open; hammerless; double trigger; automatic ejector
Magazine: None
Barrel: Double barrel; 27½" or 29½" modified & full choke
Finish: Blued; checkered walnut straight or pistol grip stock & forearm
Approximate wt.: 5 to 7 lbs.
Comments: Imported in three grades from the mid 1940's to late 1980's. Add $50.00 for single trigger.

Estimated Value:	Roma 3	Roma 4	Roma 6
Excellent:	$865.00	$1,080.00	$1,120.00
Very good:	$650.00	$ 865.00	$ 895.00

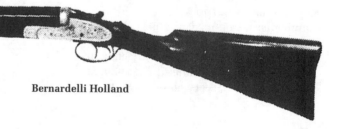

Bernardelli Italia

Bernardelli Brescia

Similar to the Italia except: 28" barrels or 20 gauge in 26" barrels; modified & improved cylinder bore.
Estimated Value: Excellent: $850.00
                        Very good: $675.00

Bernardelli Holland

Bernardelli Holland Deluxe

Same as the Holland with engraved hunting scene.
Estimated Value: Excellent: $3,700.00
                        Very good: $2,960.00

Bernardelli St. Uberto 1

Gauge: 12, 16, 20, 28
Action: Box lock; top lever break-open; double triggers; hammerless
Magazine: None
Barrel: Double barrel, 26" to 32", any choke combination
Finish: Blued; checkered walnut straight or pistol grip stock & forearm
Approximate wt.: 7 lbs.
Comments: Made from the mid 1940's to the 1990's.
Estimated Value: Excellent: $985.00
Very good: $790.00

Bernardelli St. Uberto 1

Breda Autoloading

Breda

Breda Autoloading

Gauge: 12, 12 magnum
Action: Semi-automatic; hammerless
Magazine: 4-shot tubular
Barrel: 25½" or 27½"
Finish: Blued; checkered walnut straight or pistol grip stock & forearm; available with ribbed barrel; engraving on grades 1, 2 & 3
Approximate wt.: 7¼ lbs.
Comments: Engraved models worth more, depending on grade & quality of engraving. Add 30% for magnum.
Estimated Value: Excellent: $375.00
Very good: $300.00

Browning

Browning BT-99 Trap

Browning BT-99 Trap

Gauge: 12
Action: Top lever break-open; automatic ejector; hammerless; single shot
Magazine: None
Barrel: 32" or 34" full, modified or improved modified choke; high post ventilated rib; later models have choke tubes
Finish: Blued; wide rib; checkered walnut pistol grip stock & forearm, or Monte Carlo stock; recoil pad; Pigeon Grade is satin grey steel with deep relief hand engraving
Approximate wt.: 8 lbs.
Comments: Produced from the early 1970's to mid 1990's. Add 17% for Pigeon Grade; 35% for stainless; 117% for Golden Clay.
Estimated Value: Excellent: $ 1,050.00
Very good: $ 840.00

Browning Model BT-99 Plus

Gauge: 12
Action: Top lever, break-open; automatic ejector; single shot
Magazine: None, single shot
Barrel: 32" or 34", choke tubes; high post, ventilated, tapered target rib with matted sight plane; front & center sight beads; ported barrel or stainless steel available
Finish: Blued; receiver engraved with rosette & scrolls; select walnut, checkered pistol grip stock & modified beavertail forearm; Monte Carlo style comb with recoil reducer system; adjustable for drop, cant, cast & length of pull; recoil pad
Approximate wt.: 8¾ lbs.
Comments: A trap shotgun with adjustable stock & patented recoil reduction system. Produced from 1989 to mid 1990's. Add 1% for ported barrel; 30% for stainless steel; 13% for Pigeon Grade; 75% for Golden Clay.
Estimated Value: Excellent: $1,480.00
Very good: $1,190.00

Browning Model BT-100

Gauge: 12

Action: Top lever, break-open; hammerless; single shot; adjustable trigger pull; ejector-selector

Magazine: None, single shot

Barrel: 32" or 34", high ramp tapered rib; invector-plus choke tubes

Finish: Stainless steel or blued steel barrel and receiver; checkered walnut pistol grip stock and forearm; optional thumb hole stock; adjustable or Monte Carlo style stock.

Approximate wt.: 8¾ lbs.

Comments: Introduced in the mid 1990's. Add 21% for stainless steel barrel receiver and trigger guard; add 14% for thumb hole stock; add 10% for adjustable comb stock.

Estimated Value:
New (retail): $1,995.00
Excellent: $1,500.00
Very good: $1,200.00

Browning Superposed

Gauge: 12; 20 added following World War II; 28 & 410 added in early 1960's

Action: Non-selective trigger; twin single triggers; selective trigger

Magazine: None

Barrel: Browning over & under double barrel; 26½", 28", 30", 32" choice of chokes; ventilated or matted rib

Finish: Blued; hand-checkered European walnut pistol grip stock & forearm; fluted comb; recoil pad; engraving

Approximate wt.: 6 to 8 lbs.

Comments: This gun first appeared in 1931 & has been made in a dozen different grades. More inlays & engraving is added on higher grades. Some expensive, highly decorative grades were produced. Belgium-made until 1973.

Estimated Value:
Excellent: $1,080.00 - $5,300.00
Very good: $ 820.00 - $3,900.00

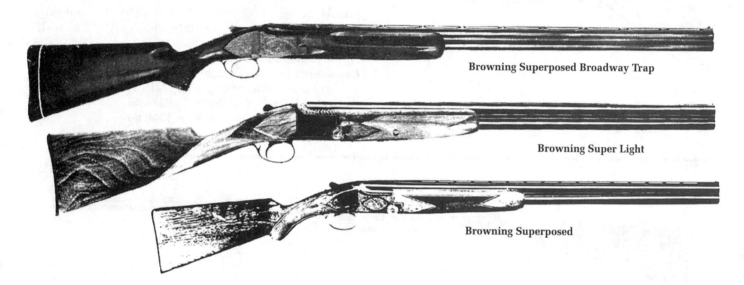

Browning Superposed Broadway Trap

Browning Super Light

Browning Superposed

Browning Super Light

Similar to Superposed except: lightweight; 26½" barrel; straight grip stock. Introduced in the late 1960's in many grades.

Estimated Value:
Excellent: $2,150.00 - $5,400.00
Very good: $1,750.00 - $4,325.00

Browning Superposed Broadway Trap Grade I

Similar to Superposed but with wide ventilated rib. Introduced in 1960 in many grades.

Estimated Value:
Excellent: $1,945.00 - $4,320.00
Very good: $1,510.00 - $3,450.00

Browning Superposed Magnum Grade I

Same gun as the Superposed except chambered for 3" magnum 12 gauge & with recoil pad.

Estimated Value:
Excellent: $1,725.00 - $3,875.00
Very good: $1,295.00 - $3,025.00

Browning Citori Grade I

Gauge: 12, 20, 28, 410; regular & magnum

Action: Top lever break-open; hammerless; single selective trigger; automatic ejector

Magazine: None

Barrel: Over & under double barrel; 26" or 28", variety of choke combinations in 420, 28 or 20 gauge; 26", 28" or 30" variety of choke combinations in 12 gauge; ventilated rib; some models have choke tubes

Finish: Blued; checkered walnut stock & forearm; Hunting Model has pistol grip stock & beavertail forearm; Sporter has straight stock & lipped forearm; engraved receiver; high-polish finish on Hunting Model, oil finish on Sporter; Upland Special has straight stock; Lighting Model has rounded pistol grip

Approximate wt.: 6½ to 7¾ lbs.

Comments: Produced from the early 1970's to present. In 1982 a Superlight Model was added with straight stock & scaled-down lipped forearm. Add 3% for 410 or 28 gauge; 4% for Superlight or Upland Special.

Estimated Value:
New (retail): $1,334.00
Excellent: $1,000.00
Very good: $ 800.00

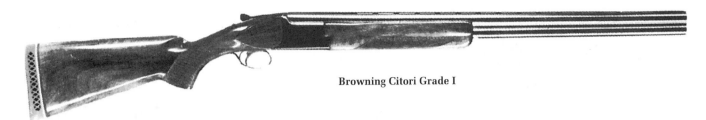

Browning Citori Grade I

Browning Citori Grade II

Similar to the Citori Grade I except: select walnut stock, satin grey receiver engraved with Canada Goose & Ringneck Pheasant scenes. Add 5% for 410 or 28 gauge.
Estimated Value: Excellent: $1,050.00
                    Very good: $ 790.00

Browning Citori Grade III

Similar to the Grade II except: greyed receiver, scroll engraving & mallards & ringnecks decoration; 20 gauge, 28 gauge & 410 bore have quail & grouse. Add 10% for 28 or 410 guage.
Estimated Value: New (retail): $2,006.00
                    Excellent: $1,545.00
                    Very good: $1,200.00

Browning Citori Grade V

Similar to the Citori Grade III except: hand-checkered wood, hand-engraved receiver with Mallard Duck & Ringneck Pheasant scenes. Add 5% for 410 or 28 gauge; 3% for "Invector" choke tubes.
Estimated Value: Excellent: $1,590.00
                    Very good: $1,190.00

Browning Citori Sideplate

Similar to the Citori Grade V in 20 gauge Sporter style only; 26" improved cylinder & modified or modified & full choke; sideplates & receiver are decorated with etched upland game scenes of doves, Ruffed Grouse, quail, pointing dog; trigger guard tang is decorated & engraved. Introduced in 1981. Discontinued in 1984.
Estimated Value: Excellent: $1,595.00
                    Very good: $1,200.00

Browning Citori Skeet

Similar to the Citori except: 26" or 28" skeet choke barrels; high post target rib. Add 15% for Grade II, 36% Grade III, 75% for Grade VI, 105% for Golden Clay.
Estimated Value: New (retail): $1,586.00
                    Excellent: $1,190.00
                    Very good: $ 950.00

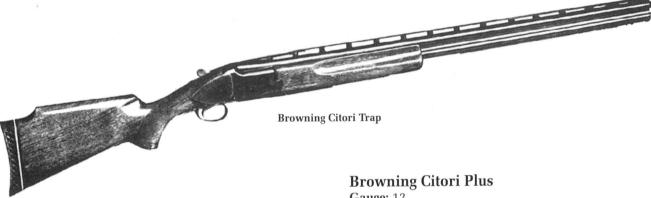

Browning Citori Trap

Browning Citori Trap

A trap version of the Citori in 12 gauge only; high post target rib; 30", 32" or 34" barrel; Monte Carlo stock. Add 15% for Grade II, 36% Grade III, 75% for Grade VI, 105% for Golden Clay.
Estimated Value: New (retail): $1,586.00
                    Excellent: $1,190.00
                    Very good: $ 950.00

Browning Citori Grade VI

Similar to the Grade V Citori with greyed or blued receiver, deep relief engraving, gold plating & engraving of ringneck pheasants, mallard drakes & English Setter.
Estimated Value: New (retail): $2,919.00
                    Excellent: $2,190.00
                    Very good: $1,750.00

Browning Citori Plus

Gauge: 12
Action: Top lever, break-open; hammerless; automatic ejectors
Magazine: None
Barrel: 30" or 32" over & under double barrel with high post, ventilated, tapered target rib; matted sight plane; choke tubes; front & center sight beads; ported barrel available
Finish: Blued; receiver engraving; select walnut checkered pistol grip stock & modified beavertail forearm; Monte Carlo style comb with recoil reduction system adjustable for drop, recoil pad cant, cast & length of pull
Approximate wt.: 9¼ to 9½ lbs.
Comments: A trap shotgun with adjustable stock & patented recoil reduction system. Introduced in 1990. Add $30.00 for ported barrel, 10% for Pigeon.
Estimated Value: Excellent: $1,600.00
                    Very good: $1,285.00

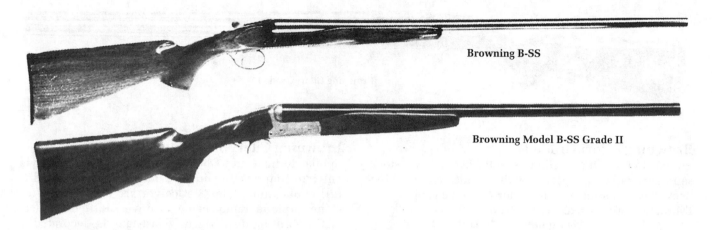

Browning B-SS

Browning Model B-SS Grade II

Browning B-SS

Gauge: 12, 20
Action: Top lever break-open; hammerless; automatic ejector
Magazine: None
Barrel: Side by side double barrel; in 12 gauge, 30" full & full or modified & full chokes; in 12 & 20 gauge, 28" modified & full chokes; 26" modified & full or improved cylinder & modified chokes
Finish: Blued; checkered walnut pistol grip stock & forearm
Approximate wt.: 7 to 7½ lbs.
Comments: Made from the early 1970's to 1988. Add 5% for barrel selector.
Estimated Value: Excellent: $625.00
**   Very good: $470.00**

Browning Model B-SS Grade II

Similar to the B-SS except: engraved satin grey frame featuring a pheasant, duck, quail & ducks. Discontinued 1984.
Estimated Value: Excellent: $850.00
**   Very good: $650.00**

Browning B-SS Sidelock

Similar to the Model B-SS except: sidelock action, engraved grey receiver, double triggers, small tapered forearm & straight grip stock.
Estimated Value: Excellent: $1,380.00
**   Very good: $ 985.00**

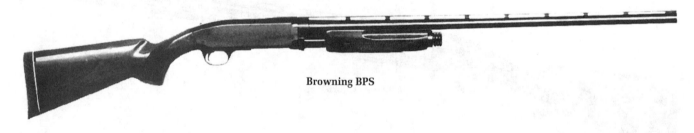

Browning BPS

Browning A-Bolt

Gauge: 12 (slugs), 3" chambers
Action: Bolt action, repeating
Magazine: 2-shot detachable box with hinged floor plate
Barrel: 22" rifled, 23" invector with rifled tube; adjustable rifle sights for rifled barrel
Finish: Checkered walnut, one-piece pistol grip stock and forearm on Hunter model; no glare graphite-fiberglass stock on Stalker model
Approximate wt.: 7 lbs.
Comments: Introduced in the 1990's. Add 11% for sights; add 12% for walnut stock (Hunter model); add 8% for rifled barrel.
Estimated Value: New (retail): $720.00
**   Excellent: $540.00**
**   Very good: $430.00**

Browning BPS

Gauge: 12, 20; 2¾" or 3"; 10 Ga. (added 1988); 12 Ga. 3½" magnum (added 1989)
Action: Slide action; concealed hammer; bottom ejection
Magazine: 4-shot; 3-shot in magnum
Barrel: 26" improved cylinder bore, 28" modified choke, 30" or 32" full choke; ventilated rib; 20 gauge added in 1982 with variety of chokes; choke tubes on later models
Finish: Blued; checkered walnut pistol grip stock & slide handle. Trap Model has Monte Carlo stock; Stalker Model has graphite-fiberglass composite stock, matte finish
Approximate wt.: 7½ lbs., 9 lbs. magnum
Comments: Produced since the late 1970's. Add 26% for 3½" magnum; add 5% for Trap Model (discontinued).
Estimated Value: New (retail): $535.00
**   Excellent: $400.00**
**   Very good: $320.00**

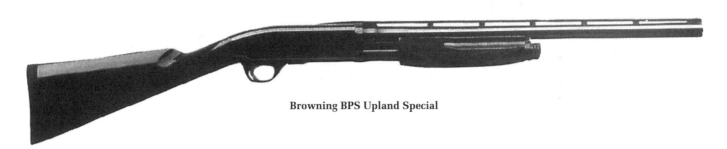

Browning BPS Upland Special

Browning BPS Upland Special
Similar to the BPS except: straight grip stock, 22" barrel and "Invector" choke tubes. Introduced in 1984.
Estimated Value: New (retail): $535.00
                Excellent: $400.00
                Very good: $320.00

Browning BPS Youth and Ladies
Similar to the Model BPS in 20 gauge only with 22" barrel, compact stock & recoil pad. Introduced in 1986.
Estimated Value: New (retail): $535.00
                Excellent: $400.00
                Very good: $320.00

Browning BPS Pigeon Grade Hunting
Same as the BPS except: 12 gauge only; select, high-grade stock and gold trim receiver; introduced in 1992; Invector chokes.
Estimated Value: New (retail): $714.00
                Excellent: $535.00
                Very good: $430.00

Browning BPS Deer Special
Similar to the BPS except: 12 gauge only; 20" barrel with 5" rifled slug choke tube; screw-adjustable rear sight; scope mount base; introduced in 1992.
Estimated Value: New (retail): $604.00
                Excellent: $450.00
                Very good: $360.00

Browning BPS Turkey Special
Similar to the BPS except: 12 gauge only; 20" barrel with newly designed extra full choke tube; receiver drilled and tapped for scope base; introduced in 1992.
Estimated Value: New (retail): $572.00
                Excellent: $430.00
                Very good: $345.00

Browning BPS Buck Special
Similar to the BPS except: 24" barrel for slugs, rifle sights. Add 5% for strap & swivels, 30% for 10 gauge.
Estimated Value: New (retail): $520.00
                Excellent: $390.00
                Very good: $310.00

Browning Model 12

Browning Model 42, Grades I & V
Same as Browning Model 12, Grades I & V except: 410 gauge with 3" chamber; Produced in the early 1990's; add 70% for Grade V.
Estimated Value: Excellent: $600.00
                Very good: $480.00

Browning Model 12, Grades I & V
Gauge: 20, 28 (added 1990)
Action: Slide action, repeating; concealed hammer
Magazine: 5-shot tubular; 2-shot with plug
Barrel: 26" modified, high ventilated rib
Finish: Blued; checkered walnut pistol grip stock & slide handle; steel grip cap. Grade V has engraved receiver with gold plated scenes.
Approximate wt.: 7 lbs.
Comments: A reintroduction of the popular Winchester Model 12 designed by John Browning. Produced from1988 to the early 1990's. Add 60% for Grade V.
Estimated Value: Excellent: $550.00
                Very good: $440.00

Browning B.A.A.C. No. 1 Regular
Gauge: 12
Action: Semi-automatic, hammerless
Magazine: 4-shot
Barrel: 28"
Finish: Blued; walnut straight stock & grooved forearm
Approximate wt.: 7¾ lbs.
Comments: This gun was sold in the U.S. from 1902 to 1905. Made in Belgium.
Estimated Value: Excellent: $380.00
                        Very good: $300.00

Browning B.A.A.C. No. 2 Trap
Trap Grade version of the No. 1 with some checkering.
Estimated Value: Excellent: $425.00
                        Very good: $340.00

Browning B.A.A.C. Two Shot
Similar to the No. 1 in 2-shot model.
Estimated Value: Excellent: $325.00
                        Very good: $260.00

Browning B.A.A.C. No. 0 Messenger
A short, 20" barrel, version of the No. 1, made for bank guards, etc.
Estimated Value: Excellent: $360.00
                        Very good: $290.00

F.N. Browning Automatic
Similar to the B.A.A.C. No. 1 sold only overseas. Some models carried swivels for sling. Produced until Browning's American sales began in 1931.
Estimated Value: Excellent: $400.00
                        Very good: $325.00

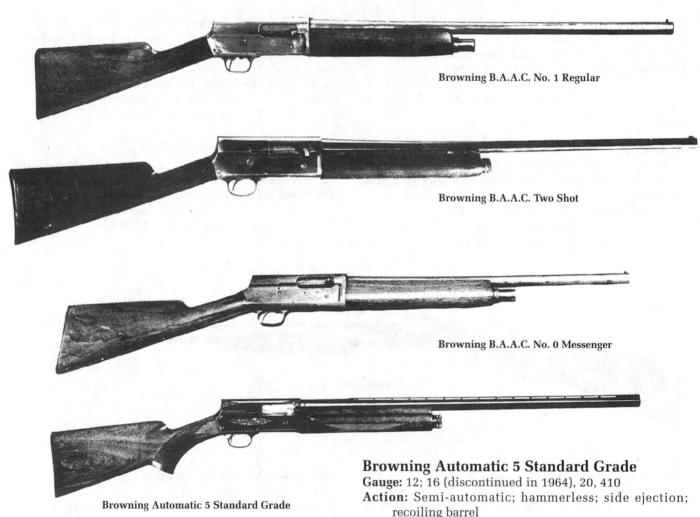

Browning B.A.A.C. No. 1 Regular

Browning B.A.A.C. Two Shot

Browning B.A.A.C. No. 0 Messenger

Browning Automatic 5 Standard Grade

Browning Automatic 5 Standard Grade
Gauge: 12; 16 (discontinued in 1964), 20, 410
Action: Semi-automatic; hammerless; side ejection; recoiling barrel
Magazine: 4-shot, bottom load; 3-shot model also available
Barrel: 26"-32" full choke, modified or cylinder bore; plain, raised matted rib or ventilated rib
Finish: Blued; checkered walnut, pistol grip stock & forearm
Approximate wt.: 7 to 8 lbs.
Comments: Made from about 1931 to 1973 in Belgium. Add 13% for ventilated rib.
Estimated Value: Excellent: $695.00
                        Very good: $560.00

Browning Automatic 5 Grades II, III, IV
Basically the same shotgun as the Standard Grade with engraving & improved quality on higher grades. Discontinued in the early 1940's. Add $50.00 for rib.
Estimated Value: Excellent: $865.00 to $2,160.00
                        Very good: $700.00 to $19,500.00

Browning Automatic-5 Light 12

Browning Automatic-5 Light 20

Browning Auto-5 Light 20
Basically the same as the Standard Grade except: 20 gauge only; a lightweight 26" or 28" barrel. Made from the late 1950's to present. Add 25% for Belgian-made; rounded pistol grip reintroduced in 1987.

Estimated Value: New (retail): $840.00
Excellent: $630.00
Very good: $500.00

Browning Auto-5 Trap
Basically the same as the Standard Grade except 12 gauge only; trap stock; 30" full choke; ventilated rib; made in Belgium until 1971. Add 25% for Belgian-made.

Estimated Value: Excellent: $600.00
Very good: $480.00

Browning Auto-5 Light 12
Basically the same as the Standard Grade except 12 gauge only & lightweight. Made from about 1948 to present. Add 25% for Belgian-made; rounded pistol grip reintroduced in 1987. Stalker model has graphite composite stock and non-glare finish.

Estimated Value: New (retail): $840.00
Excellent: $630.00
Very good: $500.00

Browning Auto-5 Light Skeet
Similar to the Light 12 & Light 20 excep: 26" or 28" skeet choke barrel. Add 25% for Belgian-made.

Estimated Value: Excellent: $550.00
Very good: $445.00

Browning Automatic-5 Magnum 20

Browning Automatic-5 Magnum 12

Browning Automatic-5 Light Buck Special

Browning Auto-5 Light Buck Special
Similar to the Standard Model, 12 or 20 gauge; special 24" barrel choked & bored for slug. Made from the early 1960's to present. Add 4% for strap & swivels; add 25% for Belgian-made.

Estimated Value: New (retail) $829.00
Excellent: $620.00
Very good: $500.00

Browning Auto-5 Buck Special Magnum
Same as the Buck Special, for 3" magnum shells, in 12 & 20 gauge. Add 4% for strap & swivels; add 25% for Belgian-made.

Estimated Value: New (retail): $855.00
Excellent: $640.00
Very good: $515.00

Browning Auto-5 Magnum 20
Similar to the Standard Model except 20 gauge magnum; 26" or 28" barrel. Made from the late 1960's to present. Add 25% for Belgian-made; rounded pistol grip reintroduced in 1987.

Estimated Value: New (retail): $866.00
Excellent: $650.00
Very good: $520.00

Browning Auto-5 Magnum 12
Similar to the Standard Model except 12 gauge magnum, equipped with recoil pad. Made from the late 1950's to present. Also equipped with a 32" full choke barrel. Add 25% for Belgian-made; rounded pistol grip reintroduced in 1987. Stalker model has graphite composite stock and non-glare finish.

Estimated Value: New (retail): $866.00
Excellent: $650.00
Very good: $520.00

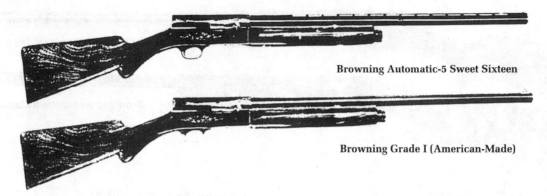

Browning Automatic-5 Sweet Sixteen

Browning Grade I (American-Made)

Browning Auto-5 Sweet Sixteen
A lightweight 16 gauge version of the Standard Model with a gold plated trigger. Made from about 1936 to 1975 in Belgium. Reintroduced from 1987 to early 1990's; add 25% for Belgium-made.

Estimated Value: Excellent: $550.00
                        Very good: $440.00

Browning Grade I (American-Made)
Similar to Browning Standard Grade. Made by Remington from 1940 until about 1948. World War II forced the closing of the Fabrique Nationale plant in Belgium.

Estimated Value: Excellent: $375.00
                        Very good: $300.00

Browning Special (American-Made)
Similar to Grade I with a matted or ventilated rib.

Estimated Value: Excellent: $420.00
                        Very good: $335.00

Browning Special Skeet (American-Made)
Same as the Grade I with a Cutts Compensator.

Estimated Value: Excellent: $400.00
                        Very good: $325.00

Browning Utility (American-Made)
Similar to Grade I with Poly-Choke.

Estimated Value: Excellent: $325.00
                        Very good: $260.00

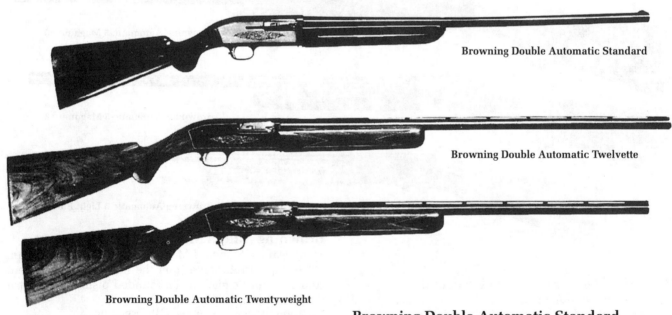

Browning Double Automatic Standard

Browning Double Automatic Twelvette

Browning Double Automatic Twentyweight

Browning Double Automatic Twelvette
Basically the same as the Standard except: lightweight aluminum receiver. Made until the early 1970's.

Estimated Value: Excellent: $490.00
                        Very good: $390.00

Browning Double Automatic Twentyweight
A still lighter version of the Standard with 26½" barrel. Made until the early 1970's.

Estimated Value: Excellent: $500.00
                        Very good: $395.00

Browning Double Automatic Standard
Gauge: 12
Action: Semi-automatic; short recoil, side ejection; hammerless; 2-shot
Magazine: 1-shot
Barrel: 30" or 28" full choke; 28" or 26" modified choke; 28" or 26" skeet; 26" cylinder bore or improved cylinder
Finish: Blued; checkered walnut pistol grip stock & forearm
Approximate wt.: 7¾ lbs.
Comments: Made from the mid 1950's to the early 1960's. Add 8% for ventilated rib.

Estimated Value: Excellent: $430.00
                        Very good: $350.00

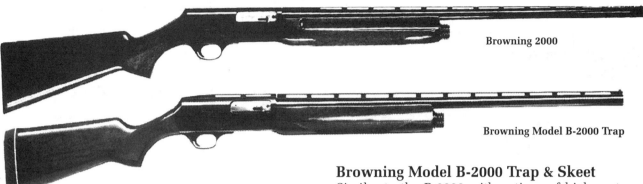

Browning 2000

Browning Model B-2000 Trap

Browning Model B-2000 Trap & Skeet
Similar to the B-2000 with options of high-post ventilated rib & recoil pad on Trap Model.

Estimated Value:	Excellent:	$430.00
	Very good:	$325.00

Browning 2000 or B-2000
Similar to the Automatic 5 shotgun except gas operated. Introduced in the early 1970's in 12 & 20 gauge regular or magnum. Discontinued about 1981.

Estimated Value:	Excellent:	$400.00
	Very good:	$300.00

Browning 2000 Buck Special
Similar to the 2000 except: 24" barrel; adjustable rifle sights; swivels.

Estimated Value:	Excellent:	$460.00
	Very good:	$375.00

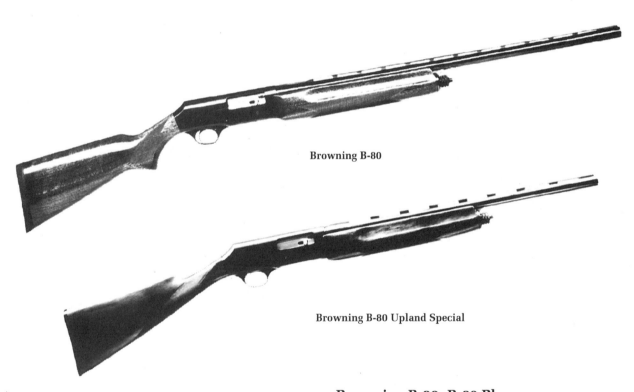

Browning B-80

Browning B-80 Upland Special

Browning B-80 Buck Special
Similar to the B-80 with 24" slug barrel, rifle sights. Add $20.00 for strap & swivels.

Estimated Value:	Excellent:	$460.00
	Very good:	$365.00

Browning B-80 Upland Special
Similar to the Model B-80 with a straight grip stock & 22" barrel. Introduced in 1986. Discontinued in 1991.

Estimated Value:	Excellent:	$450.00
	Very good:	$360.00

Browning B-80, B-80 Plus
Gauge: 12, 20; 2¾" or 3"
Action: Semi-automatic; gas operated
Magazine: 3-shot, 2-shot in magnum
Barrel: 26", 28", 30" or 32" in a variety of chokes; internally chrome plated; ventilated rib; choke tubes available
Finish: Blued; checkered walnut semi-pistol grip stock & fluted, checkered forearm; alloy receiver on Superlight Model
Approximate wt.: 6 to 8 lbs.
Comments: Introduced in 1981. Superlight Model (B-80 plus) added in 1982. Discontinued in 1991.

Estimated Value:	Excellent:	$450.00
	Very good:	$360.00

Browning Model A-500

Browning Model A-500G

Browning Model A-500

Gauge: 12, regular or magnum
Action: Short recoil operated semi-automatic
Magazine: 4-shot tubular; 3-shot in magnum; plug included; magazine cut-off allows chambering of shell independent of magazine
Barrel: 26", 28", 30" choke tubes; ventilated rib; 24" Buck Special barrel available
Finish: Blued; checkered walnut pistol grip stock & forearm; recoil pad
Approximate wt.: 7¼ lbs.
Comments: Made from 1987 to 1991.
Estimated Value: Excellent: $445.00
                       Very good: $355.00

Browning Model A-500G

Gauge: 12, regular or magnum
Action: Gas operated, semi-automatic
Magazine: 4-shot; 3-shot with magnum shells; 2-shot with plug installed
Barrel: 26", 28" or 30" barrel; ventilated rib with matted sighting surface; choke tubes
Finish: Blued; gold accents on receiver; select checkered walnut, pistol grip & forearm; recoil pad; gold trigger
Approximate wt.: 7¾ to 8½ lbs.
Comments: Produced from 1990 to 1994.
Estimated Value: Excellent: $480.00
                       Very good: $385.00

Browning Model A-500G Buck Special

Similar to the Model A-500G with a 24" slug barrel & adjustable rear, ramp front sights.
Estimated Value: Excellent: $500.00
                       Very good: $400.00

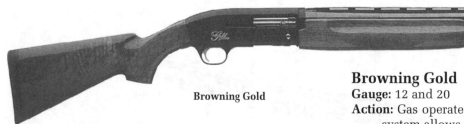

Browning Gold

Browning Model A-500R

Gauge: 12, regular or magnum
Action: Recoil operated, semi-automatic
Magazine: 4-shot; 3-shot with magnum shells; 2-shot with plug installed
Barrel: 26", 28" or 30" with choke tubes; ventilated rib with matted sighting surface
Finish: Blued; red accents on receiver; select checkered walnut pistol grip stock & forearm; gold trigger
Approximate wt.: 7¾ to 8 lbs.
Comments: Produced from 1990 to 1994.
Estimated Value: Excellent: $420.00
                       Very good: $335.00

Browning Model A-500R Buck Special

Similar to the Model A-500R with a 24" slug barrel, adjustable rear & ramp front sights. Discontinued in mid 1990's.
Estimated Value: Excellent: $450.00
                       Very good: $360.00

Browning Gold

Gauge: 12 and 20
Action: Gas operated, semi-automatic; self-regulating gas system allows all loads to be shot interchangeably
Magazine: 3-shot for 3" shells; 4-shot for 2¾" shells; tubular
Barrel: 26", 28" or 30" with invector choke tube system; ventilated rib; the Sporting Clays models have a tapered rib and barrel ports
Finish: Non-glare black receiver; checkered walnut, pistol grip stock and forearm
Approximate wt.: 6¾ lbs. for 20 gauge; 7½ lbs. for 12 gauge
Comments: Introduced in the mid 1990's. Add 4% for Sporting Clays model.
Estimated Value: New (retail): $735.00
                       Excellent: $550.00
                       Very good: $440.00

Browning Gold 10

Similar to the Browning Gold except: 10 gauge; 3½" chamber; approximate wt.: 10¾ lbs.; extra full choke turkey tube; the Stalker has a composite stock with a dull matte finish.
Estimated Value: New (retail): $1,008.00
                       Excellent: $ 755.00
                       Very good: $ 600.00

Charles Daly

Charles Daly Single Barrel Trap

Charles Daly Commander 100

Gauge: 12, 16, 20, 28, 410
Action: Box lock; top lever, break-open; hammerless; automatic ejector
Magazine: None
Barrel: Over & under double barrel; 26", 28", 30" improved cylinder & modified or modified & full chokes
Finish: Blued; checkered walnut straight or pistol grip stock & forearm; engraved
Approximate wt.: 5 to 7½ lbs.
Comments: Made from the mid 1930's to about 1939.
Estimated Value: Excellent: $650.00
Very good: $520.00

Charles Daly Commander 200

This is a fancier version of the Commander 100 with select wood, more engraving & a higher quality finish.
Estimated Value: Excellent: $835.00
Very good: $670.00

Charles Daly Single Barrel Trap

Gauge: 12
Action: Box lock; top lever, break-open; hammerless; automatic ejector
Magazine: None
Barrel: 32" or 34" full choke; ventilated rib
Finish: Blued; checkered walnut Monte Carlo pistol grip stock & beavertail forearm; recoil pad
Approximate wt.: 8 lbs.
Comments: Made from late 1960's to mid 1970's. This model should not be confused with the Single Barrel Trap Models made in the 1930's that are worth several times more.
Estimated Value: Excellent: $550.00
Very good: $440.00

Charles Daly Hammerless Double

Gauge: 10, 12, 16, 20, 28, 410
Action: Box lock; top lever, break-open; hammerless; automatic ejector (except Superior)
Magazine: None
Barrel: Double barrel; 26", 28", 30", 32"; choice of choke combinations
Finish: Blued; checkered walnut pistol grip stock & short tapered forearm; engraving
Approximate wt.: 4 to 8 lbs.
Comments: Manufactured in differing grades, alike except for quality of finish & amount of engraving. Made from 1920 to 1935.
Estimated Value: Excellent: $1,600.00 to $4,500.00
Very Good: $1,300.00 to $3,500.00

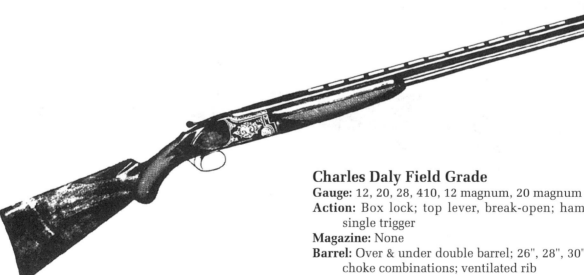

Charles Daly Field Grade

Charles Daly Field Grade

Gauge: 12, 20, 28, 410, 12 magnum, 20 magnum
Action: Box lock; top lever, break-open; hammerless; single trigger
Magazine: None
Barrel: Over & under double barrel; 26", 28", 30", various choke combinations; ventilated rib
Finish: Blued; engraved; checkered walnut pistol grip stock & forearm; 12 gauge magnum has recoil pad
Approximate wt.: 6 to 8 lbs.
Comments: Manufactured from the early 1960's to mid 1970's.
Estimated Value: Excellent: $600.00
Very good: $475.00

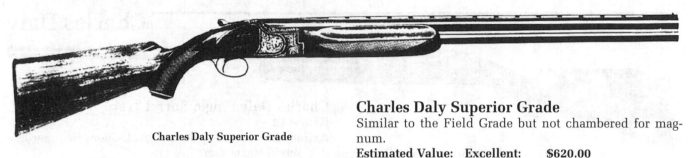

Charles Daly Superior Grade

Charles Daly Superior Grade

Similar to the Field Grade but not chambered for magnum.

Estimated Value: Excellent: $620.00
                       Very good: $485.00

Charles Daly Diamond Grade

Charles Daly Diamond Grade

Similar to the Superior with select wood & fancier engraving.

Estimated Value: Excellent: $750.00
                       Very good: $600.00

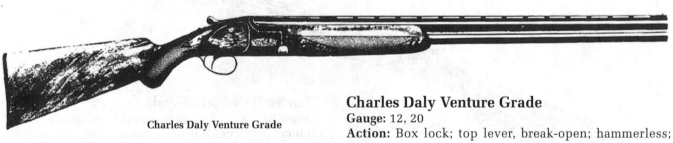

Charles Daly Field III

Charles Daly Field III

Similar to the Field Grade with some minor changes; double trigger.

Estimated Value: Excellent: $400.00
                       Very good: $320.00

Charles Daly Superior II

Similar to the Field III but higher quality.

Estimated Value: Excellent: $560.00
                       Very good: $450.00

Charles Daly Venture Grade

Charles Daly Venture Grade

Gauge: 12, 20
Action: Box lock; top lever, break-open; hammerless; automatic ejector
Magazine: None
Barrel: Over & under double barrel; 26", 28", 30", various chokes; ventilated rib
Finish: Blued; checkered walnut pistol grip stock & forearm
Approximate wt.: 7 to 8 lbs.
Comments: Made since the early 1970's to mid 1980's. Add $25.00 for Skeet Model; $35.00 for Trap Model.
Estimated Value: Excellent: $490.00
                       Very good: $395.00

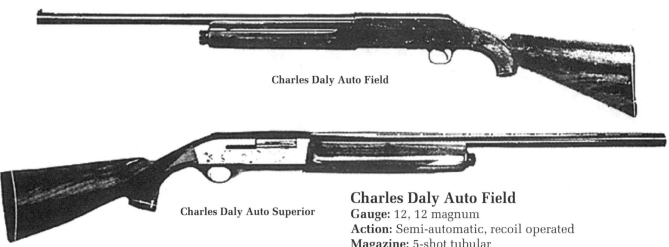

Charles Daly Auto Field

Charles Daly Auto Superior

Charles Daly Auto Field
Gauge: 12, 12 magnum
Action: Semi-automatic, recoil operated
Magazine: 5-shot tubular
Barrel: 26" improved cylinder or skeet, 28" modified or full, 30" full, chokes; ventilated rib
Finish: Blued; checkered walnut pistol grip stock & forearm
Approximate wt.: about 7½ lbs.
Comments: Made from the mid 1970's to 1990's.
Estimated Value: Excellent: $325.00
Very good: $260.00

Charles Daly Auto Superior
Similar to the Auto Field but higher quality.
Estimated Value: Excellent: $350.00
Very good: $280.00

Colt

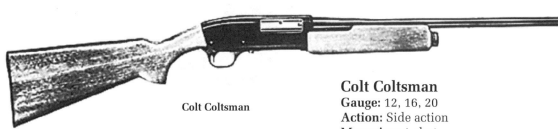

Colt Custom

Colt Coltsman

Colt Custom
Gauge: 12, 16
Action: Box lock; top lever, break-open; hammerless; double trigger; automatic ejector
Magazine: None
Barrel: Double barrel; 26" improved & modified, 28" modified & full or 30" full chokes
Finish: Blued; checkered walnut pistol grip stock & tapered forearm
Approximate wt.: 7 to 8 lbs.
Comments: Produced in the early 1960's.
Estimated Value: Excellent: $450.00
Very good: $360.00

Colt Coltsman
Gauge: 12, 16, 20
Action: Side action
Magazine: 4-shot
Barrel: 26" improved, 28" modified, 30" full chokes
Finish: Blued; plain walnut pistol grip stock & slide handle
Approximate wt.: 6½ to 7 lbs.
Comments: Made from the early to mid 1960's in takedown models.
Estimated Value: Excellent: $300.00
Very good: $240.00

Colt Coltsman Custom
A fancier version of the Coltsman with checkering & a ventilated rib.
Estimated Value: Excellent: $340.00
Very good: $275.00

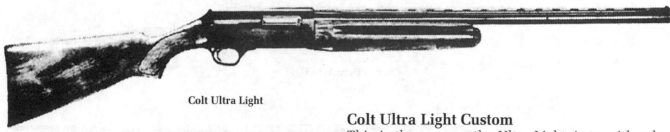

Colt Ultra Light

Colt Ultra Light

Gauge: 12, 20
Action: Semi-automatic
Magazine: 4-shot
Barrel: Chrome lined, 26" improved or modified, 28" modified or full, 30", 32" full chokes; rib available
Finish: Blued; checkered walnut pistol grip stock & forearm; alloy receiver
Approximate wt.: 6½ lbs.
Comments: A takedown shotgun produced during the mid 1960's. Add $15.00 for solid rib; $25.00 for ventilated rib.
Estimated Value: Excellent: $325.00
                       Very good: $260.00

Colt Ultra Light Custom

This is the same as the Ultra Light Auto with select wood, engraving & ventilated rib.
Estimated Value: Excellent: $350.00
                       Very good: $280.00

Colt Magnum Auto

Same as the Ultra Light Auto in magnum gauges & of heavier weight. Add $15.00 for solid rib; $25.00 for ventilated rib. Made in the mid 1960's.
Estimated Value: Excellent: $375.00
                       Very good: $300.00

Colt Magnum Auto Custom

Same as Magnum Auto with select wood, engraving & ventilated rib. Produced in the mid 1960's.
Estimated Value: Excellent: $400.00
                       Very good: $320.00

Darne

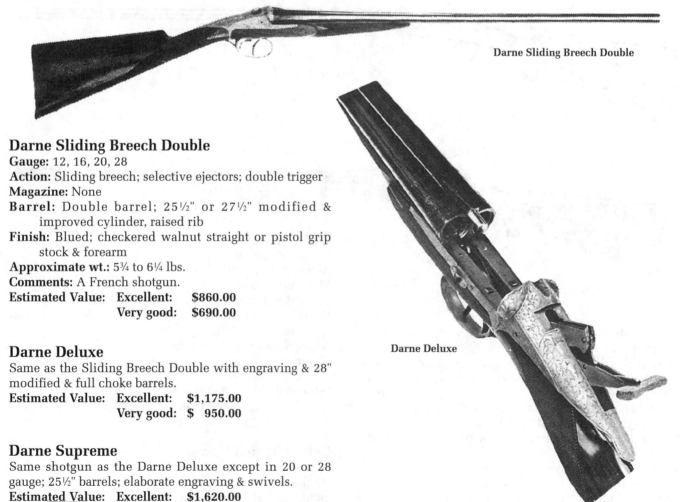

Darne Sliding Breech Double

Darne Deluxe

Darne Sliding Breech Double

Gauge: 12, 16, 20, 28
Action: Sliding breech; selective ejectors; double trigger
Magazine: None
Barrel: Double barrel; 25½" or 27½" modified & improved cylinder, raised rib
Finish: Blued; checkered walnut straight or pistol grip stock & forearm
Approximate wt.: 5¾ to 6¼ lbs.
Comments: A French shotgun.
Estimated Value: Excellent: $860.00
                       Very good: $690.00

Darne Deluxe

Same as the Sliding Breech Double with engraving & 28" modified & full choke barrels.
Estimated Value: Excellent: $1,175.00
                       Very good: $ 950.00

Darne Supreme

Same shotgun as the Darne Deluxe except in 20 or 28 gauge; 25½" barrels; elaborate engraving & swivels.
Estimated Value: Excellent: $1,620.00
                       Very good: $1,300.00

Davidson

Davidson Model 69 SL

Davidson Model 73 Stagecoach
Gauge: 12, 20 magnum
Action: Box lock; top lever break-open; exposed hammers
Magazine: None
Barrel: Double barrel; 20" improved cylinder & modified or modified & full chokes; matted rib
Finish: Blued; checkered walnut pistol grip stock & forearm; sights; engraved receiver
Approximate wt.: 7 lbs.
Comments: Made from early to late 1970's.
Estimated Value: Excellent: $260.00
                       Very good: $210.00

Davidson Model 69 SL
Gauge: 12, 20
Action: Side lock, hammerless
Magazine: None
Barrel: Double barrel; 26"-30", variety of chokes
Finish: Blued or nickel; checkered walnut pistol grip stock & forearm; gold trigger; bead sights; engraved
Approximate wt.: 6 to 7 lbs.
Comments: Made from early 1960's to late 1970's.
Estimated Value: Excellent: $350.00
                       Very good: $280.00

Davidson Model 63B

Davidson Model 63B
Gauge: 12, 16, 20, 28, 410
Action: Box lock; top lever break-open; double triggers
Magazine: None
Barrel: Double barrel; 26", 28"; 25" in 410; 30" in 12 gauge; improved cylinder & modified, modified & full, full & full chokes
Finish: Blued or nickel; checkered walnut pistol grip stock & forearm; bead sights; some engraving
Approximate wt.: 6 to 7 lbs.
Comments: Produced in Spain.
Estimated Value: Excellent: $300.00
                       Very good: $235.00

Davidson Model 63B Magnum

Davidson Model 63B Magnum
Same as Model 63B in 10, 12 or 20 gauge magnum. Available with 32" barrel in 10 gauge.
Estimated Value: Excellent: $320.00
                       Very good: $255.00

Fox

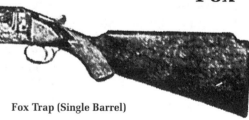

Fox Trap (Single Barrel)
Gauge: 12
Action: Box lock; top lever break-open; hammerless; automatic ejector; single shot
Magazine: None
Barrel: 30", 32" trap bore; ventilated rib
Finish: Blued; checkered walnut half or full pistol grip stock & large forearm; some with recoil pad; decorated receiver; after 1931 Monte Carlo stock. Grades differ in quality of craftsmanship & decoration. ME Grade was made to order with inlaid gold & finest walnut wood.
Approximate wt.: 7 to 8 lbs.
Comments: Made until the early 1940's. Prices for grades made before 1932 are about 20% less.

Fox Trap (Single Barrel)

Estimated Value:	Grade	Excellent	Very Good
	JE	$2,000.00	$1,600.00
	KE	$2,800.00	$2,200.00
	LE	$3,600.00	$3,000.00
	ME	$7,000.00	$6,000.00

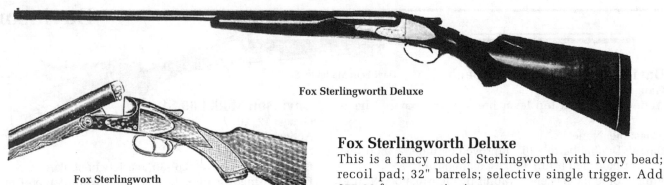

Fox Sterlingworth Deluxe

Fox Sterlingworth

Fox Sterlingworth

Gauge: 12, 16, 20

Action: Box lock; top lever break-open; hammerless; double trigger or selective single trigger; some with automatic ejector

Magazine: None

Barrel: Double barrel; 26"-30"; full & full, modified & full, cylinder & modified chokes

Finish: Blued; checkered walnut pistol grip stock & fore-arm

Approximate wt.: 5¾ to 8 lbs.

Comments: Made until the early 1940's. Add $50.00 for selective trigger; $75.00 for automatic ejector.

Estimated Value: **Excellent:** **$800.00**
                          Very good: **$650.00**

Fox Sterlingworth Deluxe

This is a fancy model Sterlingworth with ivory bead; recoil pad; 32" barrels; selective single trigger. Add $75.00 for automatic ejector.

Estimated Value: **Excellent:** **$900.00**
                          Very good: **$725.00**

Fox Sterlingworth Skeet

Basically the same as the Sterlingworth with skeet bore; 26" or 28" barrels; straight grip stock. Add $75.00 for automatic ejector.

Estimated Value: **Excellent:** **$1,000.00**
                          Very good: **$ 800.00**

Fox Skeeter

Similar to Sterlingworth with 28" skeet bored barrels; ventilated rib; ivory bead; recoil pad, 12 or 20 gauge; automatic ejector.

Estimated Value: **Excellent:** **$1,075.00**
                          Very good: **$ 865.00**

Fox Model B

Fox Hammerless Doubles

These are very similar to the Sterlingworth models, in varying degrees of increased quality. All have automatic ejectors except Grade A. Add $50.00 for selective single trigger; $125.00 for ventilated rib.

Estimated Value:	Grade	Excellent	Very Good
	A	$1,000.00	$ 800.00
	AE	$1,400.00	$1,150.00
	BE	$2,000.00	$1,600.00
	CE	$2,200.00	$1,750.00
	DE	$4,000.00	$3,200.00

Fox Super Fox

Gauge: 12

Action: Box lock; top lever break-open; hammerless; double trigger; automatic ejector

Magazine: None

Barrel: Double barrel; 30" or 32" full choke

Finish: Blued; checkered walnut pistol grip stock & fore-arm

Approximate wt.: 7¾ to 9¾ lbs.

Comments: This is a long range gun produced from the mid 1920's to early 1940's.

Estimated Value: **Excellent:** **$700.00**
                          Very good: **$565.00**

Fox Model B & BE

Gauge: 12, 16, 20, 410

Action: Box lock; top lever break-open; hammerless; double triggers; plain ejector

Magazine: None

Barrel: Double barrel; 24"-30" full & full, modified & full, cylinder & modified chokes; ventilated rib

Finish: Blued; checkered walnut pistol grip stock & fore-arm; case hardened receiver on current model

Approximate wt.: 7½ lbs.

Comments: Made from the early 1940's to 1988. 16 gauge discontinued in the late 1970's. Model BE has auto-matic ejector.

Estimated Value: **Excellent:** **$315.00**
                          Very good: **$250.00**

Fox Model B Lightweight

Same as the Model B with 24" cylinder bore & modified choke barrels in 12 & 20 gauge.

Estimated Value: **Excellent:** **$300.00**
                          Very good: **$240.00**

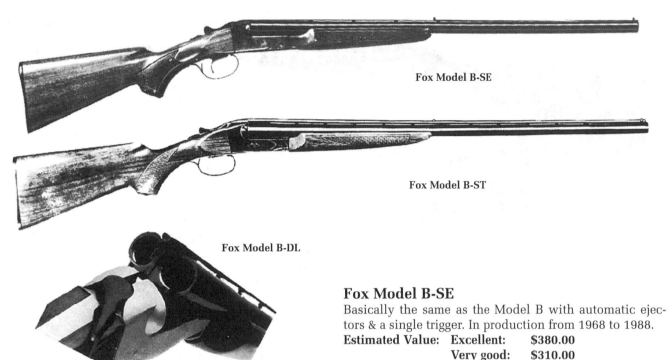

Fox Model B-SE

Fox Model B-ST

Fox Model B-DL

Fox Model B-DL & B-DE
Similar to the B-ST with chrome frame & beavertail forearm. Made from the early 1960's to early 1970's.
Estimated Value: **Excellent:**   **$375.00**
                        Very good: **$300.00**

Fox Model B-SE
Basically the same as the Model B with automatic ejectors & a single trigger. In production from 1968 to 1988.
Estimated Value: **Excellent:**   **$380.00**
                        Very good: **$310.00**

Fox Model B-ST
This is the same as Model B with gold plated nonselective single trigger. Made from the mid 1950's to mid 1960's.
Estimated Value: **Excellent:**   **$350.00**
                        Very good: **$280.00**

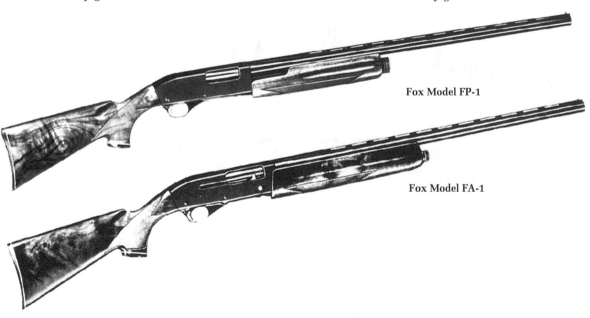

Fox Model FP-1

Fox Model FA-1

Fox Model FP-1
Gauge: 12; 2¾" or 3"
Action: Slide action, hammerless
Magazine: 4-shot tubular; 3-shot with 3" shells
Barrel: 28" modified, 30" full choke; ventilated rib
Finish: Blued; checkered walnut pistol grip stock & slide handle; rosewood cap with inlay
Approximate wt.: 7¼ lbs.
Comments: Produced from 1981 to 1983.
Estimated Value: **Excellent:**   **$300.00**
                        Very good: **$240.00**

Fox Model FA-1
Gauge: 12; 2¾"
Action: Semi-automatic; gas operated
Magazine: 3-shot tubular
Barrel: 28" modified; 30" full choke; ventilated rib
Finish: Blued; checkered walnut pistol grip stock & forearm; rosewood cap with inlay
Approximate wt.: 7½ lbs.
Comments: Produced from 1981 to 1983.
Estimated Value: **Excellent:**   **$310.00**
                        Very good: **$250.00**

Franchi ――――――――――――――――

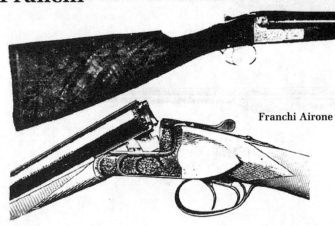

Franchi Astore

Franchi Airone

Franchi Airone
Gauge: 12
Action: Box lock; top lever, break-open; hammerless; automatic ejector
Magazine: None
Barrel: Double barrel; several lengths & choke combinations available
Finish: Blued; checkered walnut straight grip stock & short tapered forearm; engraved
Approximate wt.: 7 lbs.
Comments: Made from the mid 1940's to late 1950's.
Estimated Value: Excellent: $945.00
                    Very good: $755.00

Franchi Astore
Gauge: 12
Action: Box lock; top lever, break-open; hammerless; double triggers
Magazine: None
Barrel: Double barrel; several lengths & choke combinations available
Finish: Blued; checkered walnut straight grip stock & short tapered forearm
Approximate wt.: 7 lbs.
Comments: Made from the mid 1950's to late 1960's.
Estimated Value: Excellent: $920.00
                    Very good: $735.00

Franchi Astore 5
Same as the Astore with higher quality wood & engraving.
Estimated Value: Excellent: $1,450.00
                    Very good: $1,160.00

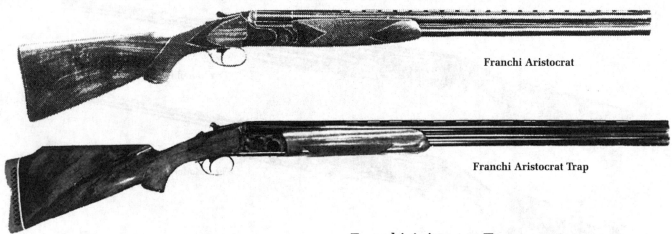

Franchi Aristocrat

Franchi Aristocrat Trap

Franchi Aristocrat
Gauge: 12
Action: Box lock; top lever, break-open; hammerless; automatic ejector; single trigger
Magazine: None
Barrel: Over & under double barrel; 24" cylinder bore & improved cylinder; 26" improved cylinder & modified, 28", 30" modified & full chokes; ventilated rib
Finish: Blued; checkered walnut pistol grip stock & forearm; engraved
Approximate wt.: 7 lbs.
Comments: Made from the early to late 1960's.
Estimated Value: Excellent: $635.00
                    Very good: $510.00

Franchi Aristocrat Trap
Similar to the Aristocrat with Monte Carlo stock; chrome lined barrels; case hardened receiver; 30" barrels only.
Estimated Value: Excellent: $700.00
                    Very good: $560.00

Franchi Aristocrat Skeet
Same as the Aristocrat Trap with 26" skeet barrels.
Estimated Value: Excellent: $730.00
                    Very good: $585.00

Franchi Aristocrat Silver King
Similar to the Aristocrat with higher quality finish; select wood; engraving.
Estimated Value: Excellent: $780.00
                    Very good: $625.00

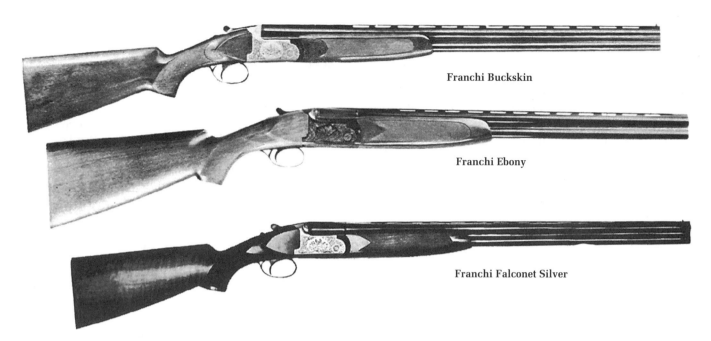

Franchi Buckskin

Franchi Ebony

Franchi Falconet Silver

Franchi Falconet Buckskin & Ebony
Gauge: 12, 20
Action: Box lock; top lever, break-open; hammerless
Magazine: None
Barrel: Over & under double barrel; 24"-30" barrels in several choke combinations; ventilated rib; chrome lined
Finish: Blued; colored frame with engraving; epoxy finished checkered walnut pistol grip stock & forearm
Approximate wt.: 6 to 7 lbs.
Comments: Made from about 1970 to late 1970's. Buckskin & Ebony differ only in color of receiver & engraving.
Estimated Value: Excellent: $635.00
                                  Very good: $510.00

Franchi Falconet Silver
Same as the Buckskin & Ebony except: 12 gauge only; pickled silver receiver.
Estimated Value: Excellent: $675.00
                                  Very good: $540.00

Franchi Falconet Super
Similar to the Falconet Silver except: slightly different forearm; 12 gauge only; 27" or 28" barrels.
Estimated Value: Excellent: $700.00
                                  Very good: $560.00

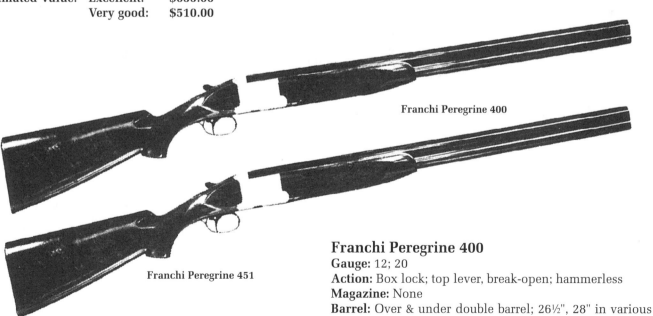

Franchi Peregrine 400

Franchi Peregrine 451

Franchi Peregrine 451
Similar to the 400 except: alloy receiver; lightweight.
Estimated Value: Excellent: $595.00
                                  Very good: $475.00

Franchi Peregrine 400
Gauge: 12; 20
Action: Box lock; top lever, break-open; hammerless
Magazine: None
Barrel: Over & under double barrel; 26½", 28" in various chokes; chrome lined; ventilated rib
Finish: Blued; checkered walnut pistol grip stock & forearm
Approximate wt.: 7 lbs.
Comments: Made from the mid to late 1970's.
Estimated Value: Excellent: $630.00
                                  Very good: $500.00

Franchi Diamond

Gauge: 12
Action: Box lock; top lever, break-open; hammerless; single selective trigger; automatic extractors
Magazine: None
Barrel: Over & under double barrel; 28" modified & full choke; ventilated rib
Finish: Blued; checkered walnut pistol grip stock & forearm; silver plated receiver
Approximate wt.: 6¾ lbs.
Comments: Produced in Italy.
Estimated Value:　Excellent:　　$800.00
　　　　　　　　　　　Very good:　　$650.00

Franchi Alcione

Gauge: 12, 3" magnum
Action: Box lock; top lever, break-open; hammerless; single selective trigger; automatic split selective ejectors
Magazine: None
Barrel: Over & under double barrel; 26" improved cylinder & modified; 28" modified & full choke; ventilated rib
Finish: Blued; coin-finished steel receiver with scroll engraving; checkered walnut pistol grip stock & forearm; recoil pad
Approximate wt.: 7 lbs.
Comments: Produced in Italy.
Estimated Value:　Excellent:　　$600.00
　　　　　　　　　　　Very good:　　$480.00

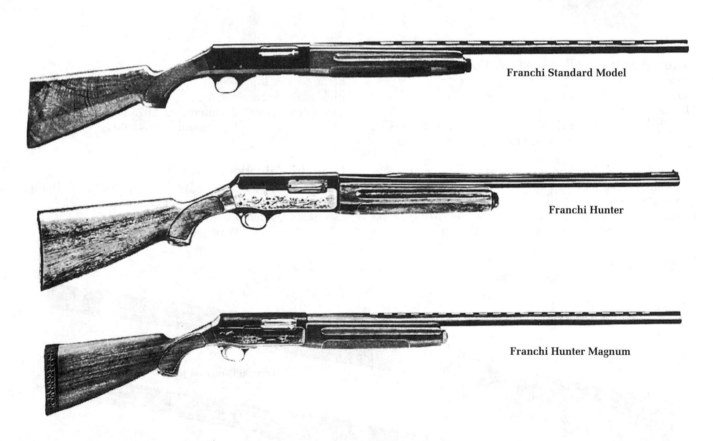

Franchi Standard Model

Franchi Hunter

Franchi Hunter Magnum

Franchi Standard Model, 48AL

Gauge: 12, 20, 28
Action: Semi-automatic; recoil operated
Magazine: 5-shot tubular
Barrel: 24"or 26" improved cylinder, modified or skeet, 28" modified or full chokes; ventilated rib on some models; chrome lined
Finish: Blued; checkered walnut pistol grip stock with fluted forearm
Approximate wt.: 5 to 6¼ lbs. One of the lightest autoloaders available.
Comments: Manufactured in Italy from about 1950 to 1990; 28 gauge discontinued.
Estimated Value:　Excellent:　　$375.00
　　　　　　　　　　　Very good:　　$300.00

Franchi Hunter, 48AL

Similar to the Standard Model; 12 or 20 gauge; higher quality wood; engraving; ventilated rib.
Estimated Value:　Excellent:　　$420.00
　　　　　　　　　　　Very good:　　$335.00

Franchi Hunter Magnum

Same as the Hunter with recoil pad & chambered for magnum shells.
Estimated Value:　Excellent:　　$430.00
　　　　　　　　　　　Very good:　　$345.00

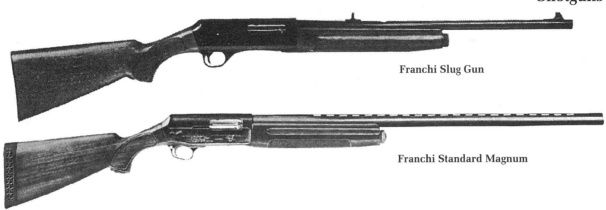

Franchi Slug Gun

Franchi Standard Magnum

Franchi Standard Magnum, 48AL
Similar to the Standard with recoil pad; chambered for magnum shells; 12 or 20 gauge.
Estimated Value: Excellent: $405.00
Very good: $325.00

Franchi Slug Gun, 48AL
Similar to the Standard Model with a 22" cylinder bore barrel; sight; swivels; alloy receiver. Made from the mid 1950's to early 1980's; 12 or 20 gauge.
Estimated Value: Excellent: $380.00
Very good: $300.00

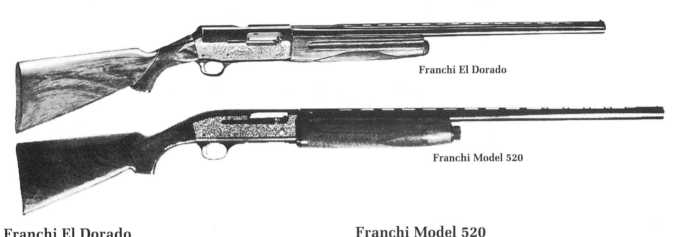

Franchi El Dorado

Franchi Model 520

Franchi El Dorado
Similar to the Standard Model with heavy engraving; select wood; gold trigger; ventilated rib.
Estimated Value: Excellent: $510.00
Very good: $410.00

Franchi Model 520
Similar to the Model 500 with deluxe features.
Estimated Value: Excellent: $400.00
Very good: $320.00

Franchi Model 500
Similar to the Standard except: gas operated; 12 gauge only; made for fast takedown.
Estimated Value: Excellent: $375.00
Very good: $300.00

Franchi Model 530 Trap
Similar to the Model 520 except: Monte Carlo stock; high ventilated rib; 3 interchangeable choke tubes.
Estimated Value: Excellent: $595.00
Very good: $475.00

Franchi Prestige

Franchi Prestige, PG 85MA
Gauge: 12, regular or magnum
Action: Gas operated, semi-automatic
Magazine: 5-shot tubular (2¾" shells)
Barrel: 24" slug, 26" improved cylinder or modified, 28" modified or full, 30" full; chrome lined; ventilated rib
Finish: Blued; checkered walnut pistol grip stock & fluted forearm; sights on slug barrel
Approximate wt.: 7½ lbs.
Comments: Introduced in the mid 1980's to early 1990's.
Estimated Value: Excellent: $405.00
Very good: $325.00

Franchi Elite
Similar to the Prestige with higher quality finish. Receiver has acid-etched wildlife scenes.
Estimated Value: Excellent: $440.00
Very good: $350.00

Greifelt

Greifelt Model 22
Gauge: 12, 16
Action: Box lock; top lever, break-open; hammerless; double trigger
Magazine: None
Barrel: Side by side double barrel; 28" or 30" modified or full choke
Finish: Blued; checkered walnut straight or pistol grip stock & forearm; cheekpiece
Approximate wt.: 7 lbs.
Comments: Made from the late 1940's.
Estimated Value: Excellent: $1,600.00
                       Very good: $1,295.00

Greifelt Model 22E
Same as Model 22 with automatic ejector.
Estimated Value: Excellent: $1,750.00
                       Very good: $1,400.00

Greifelt Model 103
Gauge: 12, 16
Action: Box lock; top lever, break-open; hammerless; double triggers
Magazine: None
Barrel: Double barrel; 28" or 30" modified & full
Finish: Blued; checkered walnut straight or pistol grip stock & forearm; cheekpiece
Approximate wt.: 7 lbs.
Comments: Maded from the late 1940's.
Estimated Value: Excellent: $1,475.00
                       Very good: $1,185.00

Greifelt Model 103E
Same as the Model 103 with automatic ejector.
Estimated Value: Excellent: $1,595.00
                       Very good: $1,275.00

Greifelt Model 22

Harrington & Richardson

Harrington & Richardson No. 3
Gauge: 12, 16, 20, 410
Action: Box lock; top lever, break-open; hammerless; single shot; automatic extractors
Magazine: None
Barrel: 26"-32" full choke
Finish: Blued; walnut semi-pistol grip stock & tapered forearm
Approximate wt.: 5½ to 6½ lbs.
Comments: Made from about 1908 until World War II.
Estimated Value: Excellent: $110.00
                       Very good: $ 85.00

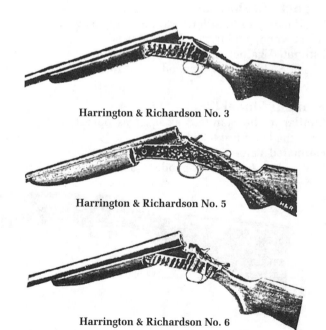

Harrington & Richardson No. 3

Harrington & Richardson No. 5

Harrington & Richardson No. 6

Harrington & Richardson No. 5
Gauge: 20, 28, 410
Action: Box lock; top lever, break-open; exposed hammer; single shot; automatic extractors
Magazine: None
Barrel: 26", 28" full choke
Finish: Blued; walnut semi-pistol grip stock & tapered forearm
Approximate wt.: 4½ lbs.
Comments: Made from about 1908 until World War II.
Estimated Value: Excellent: $115.00
                       Very good: $ 75.00

Harrington & Richardson No. 6
Similar to the No. 5 in 10, 12, 16 & 20 gauge; heavier design & barrel lengths of 28"-36". Weighs 5 to 8 lbs.
Estimated Value: Excellent: $120.00
                       Very good: $ 95.00

Harrington & Richardson No. 8

Similar to the No. 6 with different style forearm & in 12, 16, 20, 24, 28 & 410 gauges.

Estimated Value: **Excellent:** $90.00
Very good: $75.00

Harrington & Richardson No. 8

Harrington & Richardson No. 7 or No. 9

Similar to the No. 8 with smaller forearm & more rounded pistol grip. Not available in 24 gauge.

Estimated Value: **Excellent:** $95.00
Very good: $80.00

Harrington & Richardson No. 7

Harrington & Richardson Topper No. 48

Harrington & Richardson Topper No. 48

Similar to the No. 8. Made from the mid 1940's to the late 1950's.

Estimated Value: **Excellent:** $100.00
Very good: $ 80.00

Harrington & Richardson Topper No. 488 Deluxe

Similar to the No. 48 with chrome frame; recoil pad; black lacquered stock & forearm.

Estimated Value: **Excellent:** $105.00
Very good: $ 85.00

Harrington & Richardson Topper Jr. 480

Youth version of the No. 48; 410 gauge; 26" barrel; smaller stock. Made from 1959 to 1962.

Estimated Value: **Excellent:** $100.00
Very good: $80.00

Harrington & Richardson Topper Jr. 580

Similar to the Topper Jr. 480 with color finish similar to 188 Deluxe. Made from 1958 to 1962.

Estimated Value: **Excellent:** $95.00
Very good: $80.00

Harrington & Richardson Folding Model

Harrington & Richardson No. 148

Gauge: 12, 16, 20, 410
Action: Box lock; top lever, break-open; hammerless; single shot; automatic extractor
Magazine: None
Barrel: 28"-36" full choke
Finish: Blued; walnut semi-pistol grip stock & forearm; recoil pad
Approximate wt.: 5 to 6½ lbs.
Comments: Made from the late 1950's to early 1960's.
Estimated Value: **Excellent:** $95.00
Very good: $80.00

Harrington & Richardson Folding Model

Gauge: 28, 410 with light frame; 12, 16, 20, 28, 410 with heavy frame
Action: Box lock; top lever, break-open; exposed hammer; single shot
Magazine: None
Barrel: 22" in light frame; 26" in heavy frame; full choke
Finish: Blued; walnut semi-pistol grip stock & tapered forearm; sight
Approximate wt.: 5½ to 6¾ lbs.
Comments: This shotgun has a hinged frame; barrel folds against stock for storage. Made from about 1910 until World War II.
Estimated Value: **Excellent:** $140.00
Very good: $115.00

Harrington & Richardson Topper 188 Deluxe

Similar to the No. 148 with black, red, blue, green, pink, yellow or purple lacquered finish; chrome plated frame; 410 gauge only.

Estimated Value: **Excellent:** $100.00
Very good: $ 80.00

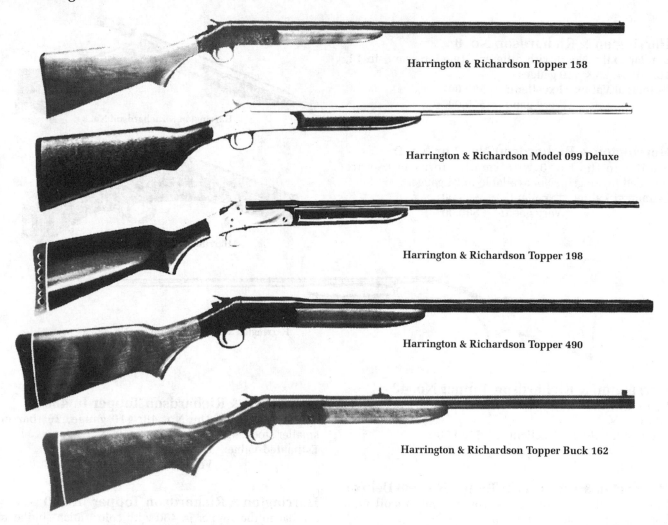

Harrington & Richardson Topper 158

Harrington & Richardson Model 099 Deluxe

Harrington & Richardson Topper 198

Harrington & Richardson Topper 490

Harrington & Richardson Topper Buck 162

Harrington & Richardson Topper 158 or 058

Gauge: 12, 16, 20, 28, 410
Action: Box lock; side lever, break-open; exposed hammer; single shot
Magazine: None
Barrel: 28"-36", variety of chokes
Finish: Blued; plain wood, straight or semi-pistol grip stock & tapered forearm; recoil pad on early models
Approximate wt.: 5½ to 6½ lbs.
Comments: Made from the early 1960's to mid 1970's as Model 158, mid 1970's to 1985 as 058. Also available is 058 combination with 22" rifle barrel in 22 Hornet or 30-30 Win. (Add 20%.)
Estimated Value: Excellent: $110.00
                        Very good: $ 85.00

Harrington & Richardson Model 099 Deluxe

Similar to the Model 158 with electro-less matte nickel finish. Introduced in 1982, discontinued in 1984.
Estimated Value: Excellent: $105.00
                        Very good: $ 85.00

Harrington & Richardson Topper 198 or 098

Similar to the Model 158 or 058 except: 20 or 410 gauge only; black lacquered stock & forearm; nickel plated frame. Discontinued in 1982.
Estimated Value: Excellent: $100.00
                        Very good: $ 80.00

Harrington & Richardson Model 258 Handy Gun

Similar to the Model 058 combination shotgun/rifle with nickel finish, 22" barrel; 20 gauge with 22 Hornet, 30-30, 44 magnum, 357 magnum or 357 Maximum rifle barrel; includes case. Produced in the mid 1980's.
Estimated Value: Excellent: $200.00
                        Very good: $160.00

Harrington & Richardson Topper 490 & 490 Greenwing

A youth version of the Model 158 & 058 with 26" barrel; shorter stock; 20, 28 & 410 gauges only. Greenwing has higher quality finish (1980-86). Made from early 60's to 1986.
Estimated Value: Excellent: $100.00
                        Very good: $ 80.00

Harrington & Richardson Topper 590

Similar to the 490 with chrome plated frame & color lacquered stock & forearm. Made from 1961 to 1963.
Estimated Value: Excellent: $95.00
                        Very good: $75.00

Harrington & Richardson Topper Buck 162

Similar to the Model 158 & 058 with a 24" cylinder bore barrel for slugs; equipped with sights.
Estimated Value: Excellent: $110.00
                        Very good: $ 85.00

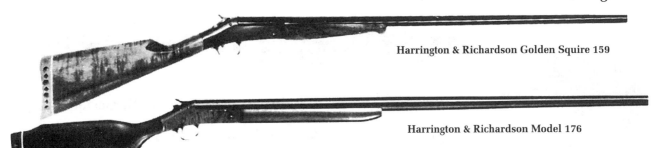

Harrington & Richardson Golden Squire 159

Harrington & Richardson Model 176

Harrington & Richardson Golden Squire 159
Gauge: 12, 20
Action: Box lock; top lever, break-open; exposed hammer; single shot; automatic ejectors
Magazine: None
Barrel: 28", 30" full choke
Finish: Blued; wood, straight grip stock & lipped forearm; recoil pad
Approximate wt.: 6½ lbs.
Comments: Made in the mid 1960's.
Estimated Value: Excellent: $110.00
                        Very good: $ 85.00

Harrington & Richardson Golden Squire Jr. 459
Similar to the 159 with a 26" barrel & shorter stock.
Estimated Value: Excellent: $105.00
                        Very good: $ 80.00

Harrington & Richardson Model 176
Gauge: 10, 12, 16, 20 magnum
Action: Box lock; top push lever, break-open; exposed hammer; single shot
Magazine: None
Barrel: 32" or 36" full choke in 10 or 12 gauge; 32" full choke in 16 or 20 gauge
Finish: Blued; case hardened frame; plain hardwood Monte Carlo pistol grip stock & forearm; recoil pad
Approximate wt.: 8 to 10 lbs.
Comments: Produced from the late 1970's to mid 1980's. All guns except 10 gauge discontinued in 1982.
Estimated Value: Excellent: $110.00
                        Very good: $ 85.00

Harrington & Richardson Model 176 Slug
Similar to the Model 176 with a 28" cylinder bore slug barrel; rifle sights; swivels. Produced from 1982 to 1985.
Estimated Value: Excellent: $120.00
                        Very good: $ 95.00

Harrington & Richardson Model 088

Harrington & Richardson 404

Harrington & Richardson Model 088 Jr.
Similar to the Model 088 with a scaled-down stock & forearm; 25" barrel in 20 or 410 gauge.
Estimated Value: Excellent: $110.00
                        Very good: $ 85.00

Harrington & Richardson Model 088
Gauge: 12, 16, 20, 410, regular or magnum
Action: Box lock; top lever, break-open; exposed hammer; single shot
Magazine: None
Barrel: 28" modified or full in 12 gauge; 28" modified in 16 gauge; 26" modified or full in 20 gauge; 25" full in 410
Finish: Blued; case hardened frame; plain hardwood semi-pistol grip stock & forearm
Approximate wt.: 6 lbs.
Comments: An inexpensive line of all purpose shotguns produced from the late 1970's to mid 1980's.
Estimated Value: Excellent: $105.00
                        Very good: $ 85.00

Harrington & Richardson Model 404
Gauge: 12, 20, 410
Action: Box lock; side lever, break-open
Magazine: None
Barrel: Double barrel; 26", 28" variety of choke combinations
Finish: Blued; checkered wood semi-pistol grip stock & forearm
Approximate wt.: 5¾ to 7½ lbs.
Comments: Made from the late 1960's to early 1970's.
Estimated Value: Excellent: $210.00
                        Very good: $170.00

Harrington & Richardson Model 404C
Similar to the 404 with Monte Carlo stock.
Estimated Value: Excellent: $220.00
                        Very good: $180.00

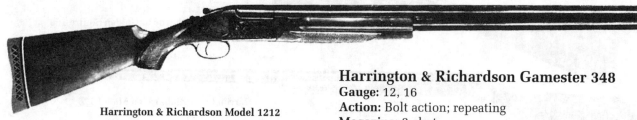

Harrington & Richardson Model 1212

Harrington & Richardson Model 1212
Gauge: 12
Action: Box lock; top lever, break-open; single selective trigger
Magazine: None
Barrel: Over & under double barrel; 28" improved modified over improved cylinder; ventilated rib
Finish: Blued; decorated frame; checkered walnut pistol grip stock & forearm
Approximate wt.: 7 lbs.
Comments: Introduced in the mid 1970's. Manufactured in Spain for H & R. Discontinued in 1980.
Estimated Value: Excellent: $375.00
                        Very good: $300.00

Harrington & Richardson Model 1212 Waterfowl
Similar to the Model 1212 in 12 gauge magnum; 30" full choke over modified barrel; ventilated recoil pad.
Estimated Value: Excellent: $400.00
                        Very good: $320.00

Harrington & Richardson Gamester 348
Gauge: 12, 16
Action: Bolt action; repeating
Magazine: 2-shot
Barrel: 28" full choke
Finish: Blued; plain wood, semi-pistol grip stock & forearm
Approximate wt.: 7 lbs.
Comments: Made from about 1950 to 1954.
Estimated Value: Excellent: $100.00
                        Very good: $80.00

Harrington & Richardson Gamester 349 Deluxe
Similar to the 348 Model with adjustable choke; 26" barrel; recoil pad.
Estimated Value: Excellent: $105.00
                        Very good: $ 90.00

Harrington & Richardson Huntsman 351
Gauge: 12, 16
Action: Bolt action; repeating
Magazine: 2-shot tubular
Barrel: 26" adjustable choke
Finish: Blued; plain Monte Carlo semi-pistol grip stock & forearm; recoil pad
Approximate wt.: 7 lbs.
Comments: Made from the mid to late 1950's.
Estimated Value: Excellent: $110.00
                        Very good: $ 85.00

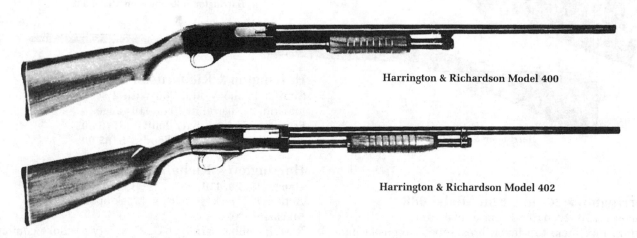

Harrington & Richardson Model 400

Harrington & Richardson Model 402

Harrington & Richardson Model 400
Gauge: 12, 16, 20
Action: Slide action; hammerless; repeating
Magazine: 5-shot tubular
Barrel: 28" full choke
Finish: Blued; semi-pistol grip stock & grooved slide handle; recoil pad on 12 & 16 gauges
Approximate wt.: 7½ lbs.
Comments: Made from the mid 1950's to the late 1960's.
Estimated Value: Excellent: $175.00
                        Very good: $140.00

Harrington & Richardson Model 401
Similar to the 400 with adjustable choke. Made to the early 1960's.
Estimated Value: Excellent: $190.00
                        Very good: $150.00

Harrington & Richardson Model 402
Similar to the 400 in 410 gauge only.
Estimated Value: Excellent: $200.00
                        Very good: $160.00

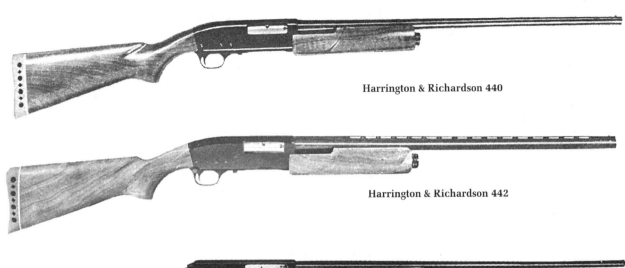

Harrington & Richardson 440

Harrington & Richardson 442

Harrington & Richardson 403

Harrington & Richardson Model 403
Gauge: 410
Action: Semi-automatic
Magazine: 4-shot tubular
Barrel: 26" full choke
Finish: Blued; wood semi-pistol grip stock & fluted forearm
Approximate wt.: 5¾ lbs.
Comments: Made from the mid 1960's.
Estimated Value: Excellent: $250.00
Very good: $200.00

Harrington & Richardson Model 440
Gauge: 12, 16, 20
Action: Slide action; hammerless; repeating
Magazine: 4-shot clip
Barrel: 24"-28" variety of chokes
Finish: Blued; walnut semi-pistol grip stock & forearm; recoil pad
Approximate wt.: 7 lbs.
Comments: Made from the early to mid 1970's.
Estimated Value: Excellent: $190.00
Very good: $150.00

Harrington & Richardson Model 442
Similar to the 440 with a ventilated rib & checkering.
Estimated Value: Excellent: $200.00
Very good: $160.00

High Standard

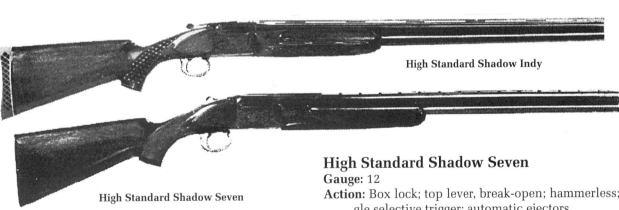

High Standard Shadow Indy

High Standard Shadow Seven

High Standard Shadow Indy
Similar to Shadow Seven with higher quality finish; chrome lined barrels; engraving; recoil pad.
Estimated Value: Excellent: $725.00
Very good: $580.00

High Standard Shadow Seven
Gauge: 12
Action: Box lock; top lever, break-open; hammerless; single selective trigger; automatic ejectors
Magazine: None
Barrel: Over & under double barrel; 27½", 29½", variety of chokes; ventilated rib
Finish: Blued; checkered walnut pistol grip stock & forearm; gold plated trigger
Approximate wt.: 8 lbs.
Comments: Made to the late 1970's.
Estimated Value: Excellent: $595.00
Very good: $475.00

High Standard Flite-King Field

High Standard Flite-King Special

High Standard Flite-King Deluxe Rib

High Standard Flite-King Trophy

High Standard Flite-King Brush

High Standard Flite-King Skeet

High Standard Flite-King Trap

High Standard Flite-King Field

Gauge: 12, 16, 20, 410
Action: Slide action; hammerless; repeating
Magazine: 5-shot tubular; 4-shot tubular in 20 gauge
Barrel: 26" improved cylinder; 28" modified; 30" full chokes
Finish: Blued; plain walnut semi-pistol grip stock & grooved slide handle
Approximate wt.: 6 to 7¼ lbs.
Comments: Made to the early 1960's to late 1970's.
Estimated Value: Excellent: $180.00
                       Very good: $140.00

High Standard Flite-King Special

Similar to Flite-King Field with an adjustable choke & 27" barrel. No. 410 gauge.
Estimated Value: Excellent: $185.00
                       Very good: $145.00

High Standard Flite-King Deluxe Rib

Similar to the Flite-King Field with ventilated rib & checkered wood.
Estimated Value: Excellent: $195.00
                       Very good: $155.00

High Standard Flite-King Trophy

Similar to the Deluxe Rib model with an adjustable choke & 27" barrel. No 410 gauge.
Estimated Value: Excellent: $205.00
                       Very good: $165.00

High Standard Flite-King Brush

Similar to Flite-King Field with an 18" or 20" cylinder bore barrel; rifle sights. 12 gauge only.
Estimated Value: Excellent: $210.00
                       Very good: $170.00

High Standard Flite-King Skeet

Similar to the Deluxe Rib model with a skeet choke; 26" ventilated rib barrel. Not available in 16 gauge.
Estimated Value: Excellent: $215.00
                       Very good: $175.00

High Standard Flite-King Trap

Similar to the Deluxe Rib model with a 30" full choke barrel; ventilated rib; recoil pad; trap stock. 26" barrel on 410 gauge.
Estimated Value: Excellent: $220.00
                       Very good: $180.00

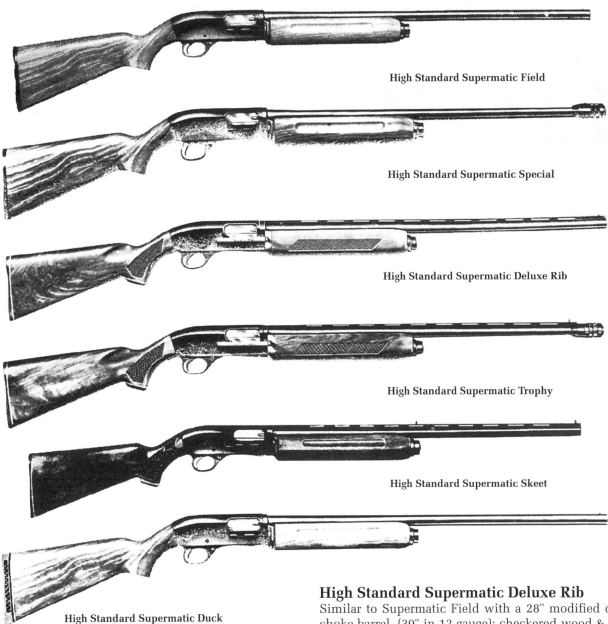

High Standard Supermatic Field

High Standard Supermatic Special

High Standard Supermatic Deluxe Rib

High Standard Supermatic Trophy

High Standard Supermatic Skeet

High Standard Supermatic Duck

High Standard Supermatic Field

Gauge: 12, 20, 20 magnum
Action: Semi-automatic, gas operated; hammerless
Magazine: 4-shot tubular; 3-shot tubular in 20 magnum
Barrel: In 12 gauge: 26" improved; 28" modified or full,
  30" full chokes. In 20 gauge: 26" improved; 28"
  modified or full chokes
Finish: Blued; plain walnut semi-pistol grip stock &
  fluted forearm
Approximate wt.: 7 to 7½ lbs.
Comments: Available from about 1960 to late 1970's; 20
  gauge magnum from 1963 to late 1970's.
Estimated Value: Excellent: $235.00
  Very good: $190.00

High Standard Supermatic Special

Similar to the Supermatic Field with adjustable choke &
27" barrel.
Estimated Value: Excellent: $245.00
  Very good: $195.00

High Standard Supermatic Deluxe Rib

Similar to Supermatic Field with a 28" modified or full
choke barrel, (30" in 12 gauge); checkered wood & ventilated rib.
Estimated Value: Excellent: $250.00
  Very good: $200.00

High Standard Supermatic Trophy

Similar to the Supermatic Field with a 27" barrel;
adjustable choke; ventilated rib; checkering.
Estimated Value: Excellent: $270.00
  Very good: $215.00

High Standard Supermatic Skeet

Similar to Field Model with a 26" ventilated rib barrel;
skeet choke; checkered wood.
Estimated Value: Excellent: $280.00
  Very good: $225.00

High Standard Supermatic Duck

Similar to the Supermatic Field in 12 gauge magnum
with a 30" full choke barrel & recoil pad. Made from the
early 1960's to mid 1960's.
Estimated Value: Excellent: $260.00
  Very good: $210.00

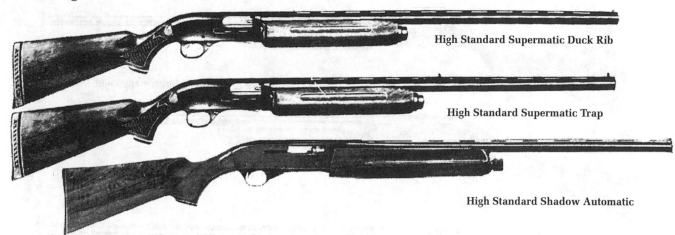

High Standard Supermatic Duck Rib

High Standard Supermatic Trap

High Standard Shadow Automatic

High Standard Supermatic Duck Rib
Similar to the Supermatic Duck with checkered wood & ventilated rib.

| Estimated Value: | Excellent: | $270.00 |
| | Very good: | $215.00 |

High Standard Supermatic Trap
Similar to the Supermatic Field in 12 gauge only; 30" full choke; ventilated rib; checkered trap stock & forearm; recoil pad.

| Estimated Value: | Excellent: | $265.00 |
| | Very good: | $210.00 |

High Standard Shadow Automatic
Gauge: 12, 20, regular or magnum
Action: Semi-automatic; gas operated; hammerless
Magazine: 4-shot tubular
Barrel: 26", 28", 30"; variety of chokes; rib
Finish: Blued; walnut pistol grip stock & forearm; sights; recoil pad available
Approximate wt.: 7 lbs.
Comments: Made in the mid 1970's.

| Estimated Value: | Excellent: | $280.00 |
| | Very good: | $225.00 |

Hunter

Hunter Fulton
Gauge: 12, 16, 20
Action: Box lock; top lever, break-open; hammerless; double or single trigger
Magazine: None
Barrel: Double barrel; 26" to 32" any choke
Finish: Blued; checkered walnut pistol grip stock & forearm
Approximate wt.: 6½ to 7½ lbs.
Comments: Made from the early 1920's until shortly after World War II in the United States. Add $50.00 for single trigger.

| Estimated Value: | Excellent: | $540.00 |
| | Very good: | $430.00 |

Hunter Fulton

Hunter Special
Similar to Hunter Fulton but higher quality. Add $50.00 for single trigger.

| Estimated Value: | Excellent: | $700.00 |
| | Very good: | $560.00 |

Ithaca

Ithaca Victory
Gauge: 12
Action: Box lock; top lever, break-open; hammerless; single shot
Magazine: None
Barrel: 34" full choke; ventilated rib; trap grade
Finish: Blued; engraving; checkered pistol grip stock & forearm
Approximate wt.: 8 lbs.
Comments: Made from the early 1920's to World War II. Other grades in higher quality available, valued up to $4,000. Prices here are for Standard Grade. Made in 5 grades.

| Estimated Value: | Excellent: | $1,185.00 |
| | Very good: | $ 950.00 |

Ithaca Victory

Ithaca Hammerless Double Field Grade
Gauge: 12, 16, 20, 28, 410
Action: Box lock; top lever, break-open; hammerless
Magazine: None
Barrel: Double barrel; 26"-32"; various chokes
Finish: Blued; checkered walnut pistol grip stock & short tapered forearm
Approximate wt.: 6 to 10 lbs.
Comments: Made in this style from the mid 1920's to late 1940's. Add $50.00 for automatic ejector, magnum or ventilated rib. Made in 8 various grades differing in quality, with values up to $5,000. Prices here for Standard Grade.
Estimated Value: Excellent: $590.00
                       Very good: $475.00

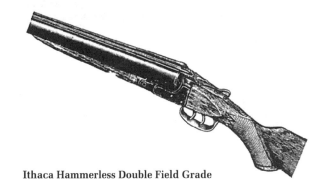

Ithaca Hammerless Double Field Grade

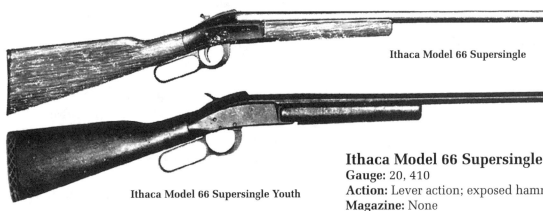

Ithaca Model 66 Supersingle

Ithaca Model 66 Supersingle Youth

Ithaca Model 66 Supersingle
Gauge: 20, 410
Action: Lever action; exposed hammer; single shot
Magazine: None
Barrel: 26" full choke; 28" full or modified choke, 30" full choke
Finish: Blued; plain or checkered straight stock & forearm
Approximate wt.: 7 lbs.
Comments: Made from 1963 to late 1970's.
Estimated Value: Excellent: $110.00
                       Very good: $ 90.00

Ithaca Model 66 Supersingle Youth
Similar to the 66 with shorter stock; 410 gauge; 25" barrel; recoil pad.
Estimated Value: Excellent: $100.00
                       Very good: $ 80.00

Ithaca Model 37 Standard

Ithaca Model 37 Standard, 37 Featherlight, 37 Field Grade Standard
Gauge: 12, 16, 20, 28
Action: Slide action; hammerless; repeating; bottom ejection
Magazine: 4-shot tubular
Barrel: 26"-30" various chokes
Finish: Blued; walnut, semi-pistol grip stock & grooved slide handle; some with checkering
Approximate wt.: 6 to 7 lbs.
Comments: Made from 1937 to 1985; add 25% for magnum with interchangeable choke tubes.
Estimated Value: Excellent: $275.00
                       Very good: $215.00

Ithaca Model 37V, 37 Featherlight Vent, 37 Field Grade Vent
Similar to the Model 37 with ventilated rib. Manufactured with three interchangeable choke tubes; discontinued in late 1980's.
Estimated Value: Excellent: $345.00
                       Very good: $275.00

Ithaca Model 37D Deluxe
Similar to the 37 with checkered stock & slide handle. Made from the mid 1950's to 1970's.
Estimated Value: Excellent: $280.00
                       Very good: $225.00

Ithaca Model 37DV Deluxe Vent
Similar to the 37D with ventilated rib.
Estimated Value: Excellent: $390.00
                       Very good: $310.00

Ithaca Model 37R

Ithaca Model 37R
Similar to the 37 with a solid raised rib. Slightly heavier. Discontinued in the late 1960's.
Estimated Value: **Excellent:**   **$300.00**
                 Very good: **$240.00**

Ithaca Model 37R Deluxe
Similar to the 37 Deluxe with a raised solid rib. Made to the early 1960's.
Estimated Value: **Excellent:**   **$325.00**
                 Very good: **$260.00**

Ithaca Model 37T Trap
Similar to the 37S with trap stock; recoil pad; choice wood.
Estimated Value: **Excellent:**   **$350.00**
                 Very good: **$280.00**

Ithaca Model 37 Supreme, 37 Featherlight Supreme,
Similar to the 37T Target. Discontinued in 1987.
Estimated Value: **Excellent:**   **$400.00**
                 Very good: **$320.00**

Ithaca Model 37S Skeet
Similar to the 37 with extended slide handle & ventilated rib. Made to the mid 1950's.
Estimated Value: **Excellent:**   **$340.00**
                 Very good: **$270.00**

Ithaca Model 37T Target
Available in skeet or trap version with high-quality finish & select wood. Replaced the 37S & 37T Trap. Made from the mid 1950's to about 1961.
Estimated Value: **Excellent:**   **$360.00**
                 Very good: **$290.00**

Ithaca Model 37 Deerslayer,
Similar to the Model 37 with a 20" or 25" barrel & rifle sights. Made from the 1960's to 1987; 12 or 20 gauge.
Estimated Value: **Excellent:**   **$345.00**
                 Very good: **$275.00**

Ithaca Model 37 Deerslayer Super Deluxe
Similar to the Model 37 Deerslayer with higher quality finish. Discontinued 1985.
Estimated Value: **Excellent:**   **$375.00**
                 Very good: **$300.00**

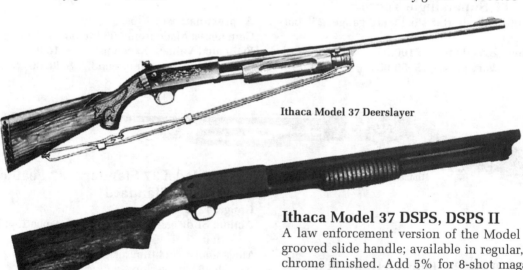

Ithaca Model 37 Deerslayer

Ithaca Model 37 M&P

Ithaca Model 37 M&P, 87 M&P
Similar to the Model 37 for law enforcement use; 18" or 20" cylinder bore barrel; non-glare tung oil finish; parkerized or chrome finish metal; 5- or 8-shot magazine. Add 10% for chrome (discontinued 1985); 7% for hand grip. Discontinued in 1987.
Estimated Value: **Excellent:**   **$270.00**
                 Very good: **$215.00**

Ithaca Model 37 DSPS, DSPS II
A law enforcement version of the Model 37 Deerslayer; grooved slide handle; available in regular, parkerized, or chrome finished. Add 5% for 8-shot magazine; 15% for chrome finish (discontinued 1985); 5% less for DSPS II; discontinued in 1987.
Estimated Value: **Excellent:**   **$275.00**
                 Very good: **$220.00**

Ithaca Bear Stopper
A short barrel version of the Model 37; 18½" or 20" barrel; 12 gauge; one-hand grip & grooved slide handle; 5- or 8-shot magazine; blued or chrome finish. Add 5% for 8-shot; 10% for chrome. Produced in early 1980's.
Estimated Value: **Excellent:**   **$325.00**
                 Very good: **$260.00**

Ithaca Model 37 Camo Vent

Similar to the Model 37 Field Grade Vent with a rust-resistant camo finish in spring (green) or fall (brown); sling & swivels; 12 gauge, 26" or 28" full choke barrel. Introduced in 1986. Discontinued in 1987.

Estimated Value: Excellent: $440.00
                  Very good: $350.00

Ithaca Model 37 Ultra Deerslayer

Similar to the Ultra Featherlight with a 20" barrel for slugs; sights; recoil pad; swivels. Discontinued in 1987.

Estimated Value: Excellent: $340.00
                  Very good: $275.00

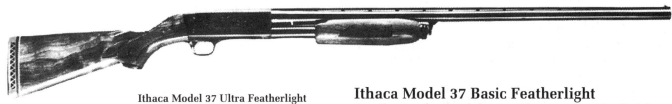

Ithaca Model 37 Ultra Featherlight

Ithaca English-Ultra Featherlight

Gauge: 12, 20
Action: Slide action; hammerless; repeating; aluminum receiver
Magazine: 3-shot tubular
Barrel: 25" full, modified or improved cylinder bore; ventilated rib
Finish: Blued; checkered walnut straight grip stock & slide handle; waterfowl scene on receiver
Approximate wt.: 4¾ lbs.
Comments: A lightweight English stock version of the Model 37 series. Made from 1982 to 1987.

Estimated Value: Excellent: $395.00
                  Very good: $315.00

Ithaca Model 37 Basic Featherlight

Similar to the Model 37 without cosmetic finish; no checkering; finished in non-glare tung oil; grooved slide handle; "vapor blasted" metal surfaces with a non-glare finish; add 2% for ventilated rib, 30% for magnum. Introduced in 1979, discontinued in the mid 1980's.

Estimated Value: Excellent: $280.00
                  Very good: $225.00

Ithaca Model 37 Ultra Featherlight

A 20 gauge lightweight version of the Model 37; 25" ventilated rib barrel; recoil pad, gold trigger; special grip cap. Introduced in 1979. Currently available with interchangeable choke tubes. Renamed Model 87 in 1987.

Estimated Value: Excellent: $345.00
                  Very good: $275.00

Ithaca Model 87 Field

Ithaca Model 87 Field

Gauge: 12, 20
Action: Slide action; hammerless; repeating
Magazine: 3-shot tubular
Barrel: 26", 28" or 30"; 3 choke tubes; 3" chamber; ventilated rib
Finish: Blued; pressed checkered American walnut stock & side handle
Approximate wt.: 6¾ lbs. (20 ga.); 7 lbs. (12 ga.)
Comments: Introduced in 1987 to replace Model 37.

Estimated Value: Excellent: $355.00
                  Very good: $285.00

Ithaca Model 87 Deluxe

Same as Model 87 Field except: cut checkered stock & slide handle with a high gloss finish & gold trigger.

Estimated Value: Excellent: $400.00
                  Very good: $320.00

Ithaca Model 87 Ultra Field

Same as Model 87 Field except: aluminum receiver; discontinued in 1991.

Estimated Value: Excellent: $345.00
                  Very good: $275.00

Ithaca Model 87 M&P & 87DSPS

Same as Model 87 Field except: 12 gauge with 20" plain barrel; dull oil finished wood; parkerized or nickel finish; 5- or 8-shot magazine; fixed cylinder choke; add 25% for nickel finish.

Estimated Value: Excellent: $320.00
                  Very good: $255.00

Ithaca Model 87 Supreme

Same as Model 87 Field except: high grade finish & checkering; gold trigger; Raybar irridescent orange sight.

Estimated Value: Excellent: $610.00
                  Very good: $490.00

Ithaca Model 87 Turkey

Same as Model 87 Field except: 12 gauge with 24" or 22" barrel; smooth stock & slide handle; fixed full choke barrel or full choke tube; matte blue barrel with oil finished wood or camouflaged finish; add 9% for choke tube or camouflaged finish.

Estimated Value:	Excellent:	$350.00
	Very good:	$280.00

Ithaca Model English 87

Same as English Ultra Featherlight except: 20 gauge 24" or 26" barrel; 3 changeable choke tubes; weighs 6¾ lbs.; steel receiver; introduced in 1987.

Estimated Value:	Excellent:	$405.00
	Very good:	$325.00

Ithaca Model 87 Camo Field

Same as Model 87 Field except: 12 gauge with 24", 26", or 28" barrel; smooth American walnut stock & grooved slide handle; camouflaged finish.

Estimated Value:	Excellent:	$400.00
	Very good:	$320.00

Ithaca Model 87 Deerslayer

Same as Model 87 Field except: 20" or 25" special bore plain barrel for rifled slugs; 12 or 20 gauge; smooth oil finished stock & grooved slide handle; plain matte finished barrel.

Estimated Value:	Excellent:	$320.00
	Very good:	$255.00

Ithaca Model 87 Deerslayer II

Ithaca Model 87 Deluxe Deerslayer

Same as Model 87 Field except: 20" & 25" barrel length; cut checkering with high gloss finish; plain barrel with Raybar front sight & adjustable rear; gold trigger; special bore slug barrel or rifled barrel; add 8% for rifled barrel.

Estimated Value:	Excellent:	$350.00
	Very good:	$280.00

Ithaca Model 87 Deerslayer II

Same as Model 87 Deluxe Deerslayer except: Monte Carlo stock; rifled barrel is permanently screwed into the receiver.

Estimated Value:	Excellent:	$425.00
	Very good:	$340.00

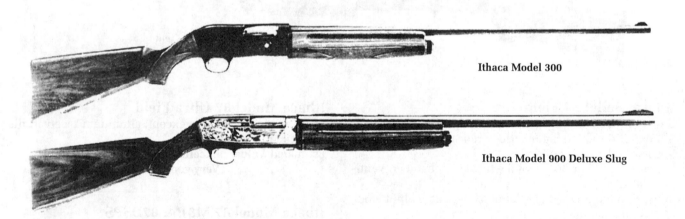

Ithaca Model 300

Ithaca Model 900 Deluxe Slug

Ithaca Model 900 Deluxe

Similar to the 300 except: ventilated rib; gold filled engraving; nameplate in stock; gold trigger.

Estimated Value:	Excellent:	$325.00
	Very good:	$260.00

Ithaca Model 900 Deluxe Slug

Similar to the 900 Deluxe with a 24" barrel for slugs; rifle sights.

Estimated Value:	Excellent:	$335.00
	Very good:	$265.00

Ithaca Model 300

Gauge: 12, 20
Action: Semi-automatic; recoil operated; hammerless
Magazine: 3-shot tubular
Barrel: 26" improved cylinder; 28" modified or full, 30" full chokes
Finish: Blued; checkered walnut pistol grip stock & forearm
Approximate wt.: 6½ to 7 lbs.
Comments: Made from 1970 to 1973. Add $10.00 for ventilated rib.

Estimated Value:	Excellent:	$275.00
	Very good:	$215.00

Ithaca Model 51 Standard

Ithaca Model 51 Deluxe Skeet

Ithaca Model 51 Deluxe Trap

Ithaca Model 51 Magnum

Ithaca Model 51 Deerslayer

Ithaca Model 51A Waterfowler

Ithaca Model 51 Standard, 51 Featherlight, 51A
Gauge: 12, 20
Action: Gas operated, semi-automatic
Magazine: 3-shot tubular
Barrel: 26"-30", various chokes; some with ventilated rib
Finish: Blued; checkered walnut pistol grip stock & forearm; decorated receiver
Approximate wt.: 7½ lbs.
Comments: Manufactured from 1970 to 1986.
Estimated Value: Excellent: $350.00
                  Very good: $260.00

Ithaca Model 51 Magnum
Similar to the 51 but chambered for magnum shells; ventilated rib.
Estimated Value: Excellent: $390.00
                  Very good: $310.00

Ithaca Model 51 Deerslayer
Similar to the Model 51 with 24" barrel for slugs; sights; recoil pad; 12 gauge only.
Estimated Value: Excellent: $350.00
                  Very good: $260.00

Ithaca Model 51 Deluxe Skeet, 51A Supreme Skeet
Similar to the 51 with recoil pad; ventilated rib; 28" or 29" skeet choke barrel, 26" after 1985. Discontinued in late 1980's.
Estimated Value: Excellent: $645.00
                  Very good: $480.00

Ithaca Model 51 Deluxe Trap, 51A Supreme Trap
Similar to the Model 51 except: 12 gauge only; select wood; 28" or 30" barrel; recoil pad. Add 5% for Monte Carlo stock. Discontinued in late 1980's.
Estimated Value: Excellent: $650.00
                  Very good: $490.00

Ithaca Model 51A Waterfowler, 51A Turkey Gun
Similar to the Model 51A with matte-finish metal & flat-finish walnut. The Turkey model has a 26" ventilated rib barrel, the Waterfowler has a 30" ventilated rib barrel. Introduced in 1984. Add 10% for camo finish. Discontinued in late 1980's.
Estimated Value: Excellent: $465.00
                  Very good: $350.00

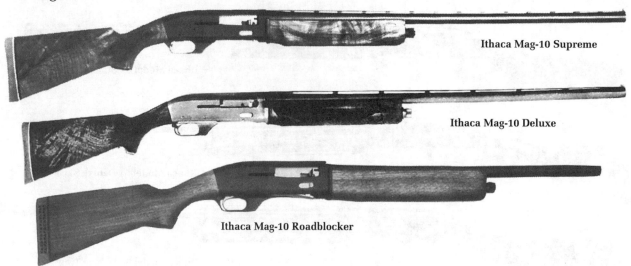

Ithaca Mag-10 Supreme

Ithaca Mag-10 Deluxe

Ithaca Mag-10 Roadblocker

Ithaca Mag-10 Deluxe

Gauge: 10 magnum
Action: Semi-automatic; gas operated
Magazine: 3-shot tubular
Barrel: 32" full choke; ventilated rib
Finish: Blued; checkered walnut pistol grip stock & fore-
    arm; recoil pad; swivels
Approximate wt.: 11½ lbs.
Comments: Deduct 15% to 20% for Ithaca Mag-10
    Standard. Produced from mid 1970's to mid 1980's.
Estimated Value: Excellent: $700.00
                       Very good: $525.00

Ithaca Mag-10 Supreme

Similar to the Magnum 10 Deluxe with higher quality
finish & select wood.
Estimated Value: Excellent: $840.00
                       Very good: $630.00

Ithaca Mag-10 Roadblocker

A law enforcement version of the Mag-10 with a 20" barrel; plain stock; "vapor blasted" metal finish. Add 5% for
ventilated rib.
Estimated Value: Excellent: $560.00
                       Very good: $420.00

Iver Johnson

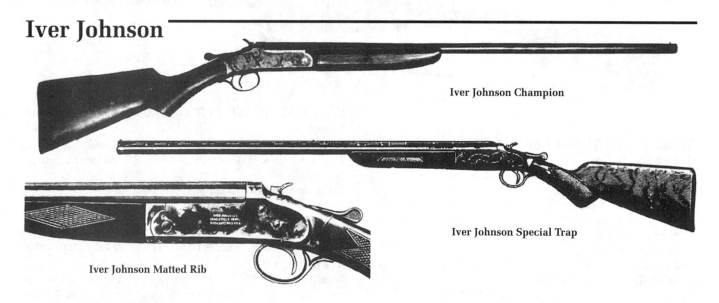

Iver Johnson Champion

Iver Johnson Special Trap

Iver Johnson Matted Rib

Iver Johnson Matted Rib

Similar to the Champion with a matted rib & checkering.
Discontinued in the late 1940's.
Estimated Value: Excellent: $145.00
                       Very good: $120.00

Iver Johnson Special Trap

Similar to the Champion with a 32" ribbed barrel; checkered stock; 12 gauge only. Manufactured until the early
1940's.
Estimated Value: Excellent: $200.00
                       Very good: $160.00

Iver Johnson Champion

Gauge: 10, 12, 16, 20, 410
Action: Box lock; top lever, break-open; hammerless; sin-
    gle shot; automatic ejectors
Magazine: None
Barrel: 26"-30", full choke
Finish: Blued; hardwood semi-pistol grip stock & short
    tapered forearm
Approximate wt.: 7 lbs.
Comments: Made from about 1910 to the late 1950's.
Estimated Value: Excellent: $120.00
                       Very good: $ 90.00

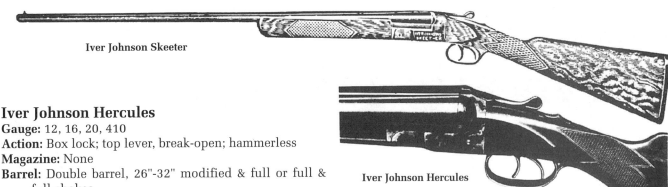
Iver Johnson Skeeter

Iver Johnson Hercules

Iver Johnson Hercules
Gauge: 12, 16, 20, 410
Action: Box lock; top lever, break-open; hammerless
Magazine: None
Barrel: Double barrel, 26"-32" modified & full or full & full chokes
Finish: Blued; checkered walnut pistol grip stock & tapered forearm
Approximate wt.: 6 to 8 lbs.
Comments: Made from about 1920 to 1949. Available with some extras. Prices are for Standard Grade. Add $75.00 for single trigger or automatic ejectors.
Estimated Value: Excellent: $430.00
Very good: $345.00

Iver Johnson Skeeter
Similar to the Hercules with addition of 28 gauge; 26"-28" barrels; wide forearm. Add $75.00 for automatic ejectors; $75.00 for single selective trigger.
Estimated Value: Excellent: $600.00
Very good: $475.00

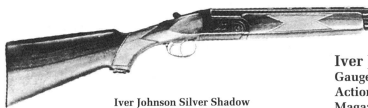
Iver Johnson Silver Shadow

Iver Johnson Silver Shadow
Gauge: 12
Action: Box lock; top lever, break-open; hammerless
Magazine: None
Barrel: Over & under double barrel; 28" modified & full choke; ventilated rib
Finish: Blued; checkered walnut pistol grip stock & forearm
Approximate wt.: 8¼ lbs.
Comments: Manufactured in Italy for Iver Johnson. Add $75.00 for single trigger. Made from the early 1970's to late 1970's.
Estimated Value: Excellent: $400.00
Very good: $325.00

Iver Johnson Super Trap
Gauge: 12
Action: Box lock; top lever, break-open; hammerless
Magazine: None
Barrel: Double barrel; 32" full choke; ventilated rib
Finish: Blued; checkered walnut pistol grip stock & forearm; recoil pad
Approximate wt.: 8½ lbs.
Comments: Production stopped during World War II. Available with some extras. Prices for Standard Grade; add $35.00 for non-selective single trigger; $75.00 for selective single trigger or automatic ejectors.
Estimated Value: Excellent: $595.00
Very good: $475.00

Iver Johnson Super Trap

Kessler

Kessler 3-Shot
Gauge: 12, 16, 20
Action: Bolt action; hammerless; repeating
Magazine: 2-shot detachable box
Barrel: 26", 28", full choke
Finish: Blued; plain pistol grip stock & forearm; recoil pad
Approximate wt.: 6 to 7 lbs.
Comments: Made for a few years only in the early 1950's.
Estimated Value: Excellent: $100.00
Very good: $ 85.00

Kessler Lever Matic
Gauge: 12, 16, 20
Action: Lever action
Magazine: 3-shot
Barrel: 26", 28", 30", full choke
Finish: Blued; checkered walnut straight stock & forearm; recoil pad
Approximate wt.: 7 lbs.
Comments: Produced for only a few years in the early 1950's.
Estimated Value: Excellent: $190.00
Very good: $150.00

Kleinguenther

Kleinguenther Condor

Kleinguenther Condor

Gauge: 12, 20
Action: Double lock; top lever break-open; hammerless; selective single trigger; automatic ejectors
Magazine: None
Barrel: Over & under double barrel; ventilated rib; 26" improved & modified or skeet; 28" modified or modified & full; 30" modified & full or full in 12 gauge
Finish: Blued; checkered walnut pistol grip stock & forearm; recoil pad
Approximate wt.: 7½ lbs.
Comments: An Italian shotgun produced in the 1970's.
Estimated Value: Excellent: $645.00
                       Very good: $515.00

Kleinguenther Condor Skeet

A skeet version of the Condor with a wide rib.
Estimated Value: Excellent: $680.00
                       Very good: $545.00

Kleinguenther Condor Trap

A trap version of the Condor with a Monte Carlo stock, wide rib; available in 32" barrel.
Estimated Value: Excellent: $690.00
                       Very good: $550.00

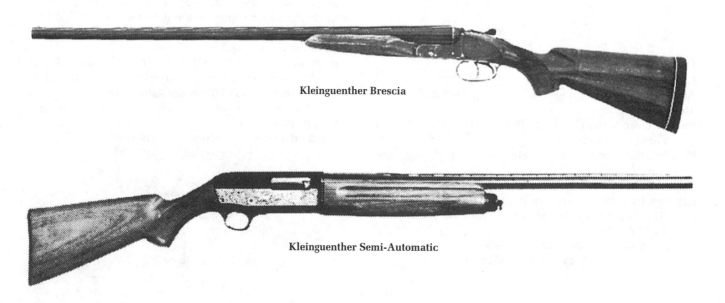

Kleinguenther Brescia

Kleinguenther Semi-Automatic

Kleinguenther Brescia

Gauge: 12, 20
Action: Box lock; top lever, break-open; hammerless; double trigger
Magazine: None
Barrel: Double barrel; chrome lined, 28" improved or modified or modified & full chokes
Finish: Blued; checkered walnut pistol grip stock & tapered forearm
Approximate wt.: 7½ lbs.
Comments: Manufactured in Italy.
Estimated Value: Excellent: $350.00
                       Very good: $275.00

Kleinguenther Semi-Automatic

Gauge: 12
Action: Semi-automatic; hammerless; side ejection
Magazine: 3-shot tubular
Barrel: Chrome lined; 25" skeet, 26" improved cylinder, 28" & 30" full chokes; ventilated rib
Finish: Blued; smooth walnut pistol grip stock & grooved forearm; engraved
Approximate wt.: 7½ lbs.
Comments: Made from the early to mid 1970's.
Estimated Value: Excellent: $375.00
                       Very good: $300.00

L.C. Smith

L.C. Smith Single Barrel

Gauge: 12
Action: Box lock; top lever, break-open; automatic ejectors, hammerless
Magazine: None, single shot
Barrel: 32", 34" choice of bore; ventilated rib
Finish: Blued; checkered walnut pistol grip stock & forearm; recoil pad
Approximate wt.: 8 lbs.
Comments: Produced by Hunter Arms from about 1917 to 1945 & Marlin from about 1946 to 1951.
Estimated Value:

	Olympic	Specialty	Crown
Excellent:	$1,450.00	$2,000.00	$3,200.00
Very good:	$1,050.00	$1,450.00	$2,500.00

L.C. Smith Single Barrel

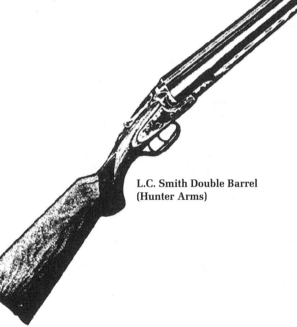

L.C. Smith Double Barrel
(Hunter Arms)

L.C. Smith Double Barrel (Hunter Arms)

Gauge: 12, 16, 20, 410
Action: Side lock, top lever break-down; hammerless; automatic ejectors; double or single trigger
Magazine: None
Barrel: 26"-32" double barrel, any choke
Finish: Depending on grade, checkered walnut pistol, semi-pistol or straight grip stock & forearm; blued barrels
Approximate wt.: 6½ to 8½ lbs.
Comments: Produced by Hunter Arms from about 1890 to 1945 & Marlin from 1946 to 1951. Prices for Hunter Arms in Field Grade. Other grades higher due to higher quality of workmanship & finish. Add $50.00 for single trigger.
Estimated Value: **Excellent:**   **$850.00**
               Very good: **$680.00**

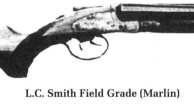

L.C. Smith Field Grade (Marlin)

L.C. Smith Deluxe (Marlin)

Gauge: 12, regular or magnum
Action: Top lever break-open; hammerless; side lock; double triggers
Magazine: None
Barrel: Double barrel; 28" modified & full chokes; floating steel ventilated rib
Finish: Top quality, hand-fitted, hand-checkered walnut pistol grip stock & beavertail forearm; blued; case hardened side plates
Approximate wt.: 6¾ lbs.
Comments: Made from about 1968 to mid 1970's.
Estimated Value: **Excellent:**   **$600.00**
               Very good: **$475.00**

L.C. Smith Field Grade (Marlin)

Same as the Deluxe Model with standard checkered walnut pistol grip stock & forearm & extruded ventilated rib. Made from about 1951 to 1968.
Estimated Value: **Excellent:**   **$560.00**
               Very good: **$450.00**

Lefever

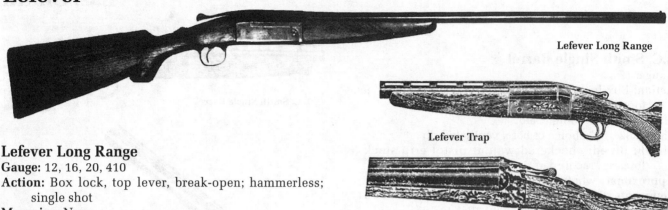

Lefever Long Range

Lefever Trap

Lefever Nitro Special

Lefever Long Range
Gauge: 12, 16, 20, 410
Action: Box lock, top lever, break-open; hammerless; single shot
Magazine: None
Barrel: 26", 28", 30", 32"; any choke
Finish: Blued; plain or checkered walnut pistol grip stock & forearm; bead sight
Approximate wt.: 5 to 7 lbs.
Comments: Made from the early 1920's to the early 1940's.
Estimated Value: Excellent: $250.00
                      Very good: $200.00

Lefever Trap
Gauge: 12
Action: Box lock; top lever break-open; hammerless; single shot
Magazine: None
Barrel: 30" or 32" full choke; ventilated rib
Finish: Blued; checkered walnut pistol grip stock & forearm; recoil pad
Approximate wt.: 8 lbs.
Comments: Made from the early 1920's to the early 1940's.
Estimated Value: Excellent: $485.00
                      Very good: $385.00

Lefever Nitro Special
Gauge: 12, 16, 20, 410
Action: Box lock; top lever, break-open; hammerless; double triggers
Magazine: None
Barrel: Double barrel; 26", 28", 30", 32"; any choke
Finish: Blued; checkered walnut pistol grip stock & forearm
Approximate wt.: 5½ to 7 lbs.
Comments: Made from the early 1920's to late 1940's. Add $75.00 for single trigger.
Estimated Value: Excellent: $595.00
                      Very good: $475.00

Lefever Excellsior
Similar to Nitro-Special with light engraving & automatic ejector. Made from the early 1920's to the late 1940's.
Estimated Value: Excellent: $620.00
                      Very good: $495.00

Mannlicher

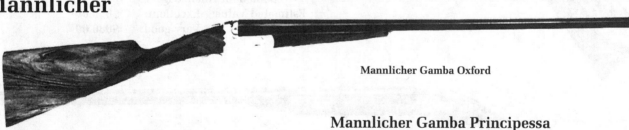

Mannlicher Gamba Oxford

Mannlicher Gamba Oxford
Gauge: 12, 20, 20 magnum
Action: Top lever break-open; hammerless; single or double trigger
Magazine: None
Barrel: Double barrel; 26½" improved cylinder & modified or 27½" modified & full
Finish: Blued; engraved receiver; checkered walnut straight grip stock & tapered forearm
Approximate wt.: 5½ to 6½ lbs.
Comments: Add $140.00 for single trigger.
Estimated Value: Excellent: $1,400.00
                      Very good: $1,150.00

Mannlicher Gamba Principessa
Gauge: 28
Action: Top lever break-open; hammerless; single or double trigger
Magazine: None
Barrel: Double barrel; 26" improved cylinder & modified or 28" modified & full
Finish: Blued; case hardened receiver with engraved scrollwork; checkered walnut straight grip stock & tapered forearm; beavertail forearm available; recoil pad
Approximate wt.: 5½ lbs.
Comments: Add $130.00 for single trigger.
Estimated Value: Excellent: $1,270.00
                      Very good: $1,000.00

Marlin

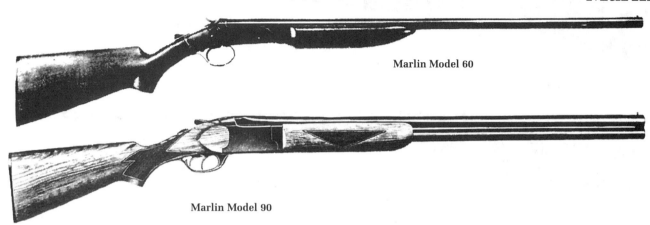

Marlin Model 60

Marlin Model 90

Marlin Model 60

Gauge: 12
Action: Box lock; take down breech-loading; exposed hammer; single shot
Magazine: None
Barrel: 30" or 32" full choke; matted top; 2¾" chamber
Finish: Blued; walnut pistol grip stock & beavertail forearm
Approximate wt.: 6½ lbs.
Comments: This shotgun was made in 1923, a combination of Marlin & Hopkins & Allen parts. Less than 1,000 were manufactured.
Estimated Value: Excellent: $200.00
                     Very good: $160.00

Marlin Model 410

Gauge: 410
Action: Lever action; exposed hammer
Magazine: 5-shot tubular
Barrel: 22" or 26", 2½" chamber
Finish: Blued; walnut pistol grip stock & beavertail forearm
Approximate wt.: 6 lbs.
Comments: A solid frame lightweight shotgun produced from about 1929 to 1932.
Estimated Value: Excellent: $550.00
                     Very good: $440.00

Marlin Model 90

Gauge: 12, 16, 20, 410 (also .22 caliber & .222)
Action: Top lever break down; box lock; double trigger (single trigger available prior to World War II); hammerless; non-automatic extractors
Magazine: None
Barrel: Over & under double barrel, 26", 28" or 30" rifle; shotgun barrels available in 26"; 2¾" chamber, 3" chamber in 410; full, modified, skeet or improved cylinder bore
Finish: Blued; plain or checkered walnut pistol grip stock & forearm; recoil pad
Approximate wt.: 6 to 7½ lbs.
Comments: This shotgun or combination was manufactured from about 1937 to 1958. Add $40.00 for 410 gauge; $50.00 for single trigger.
Estimated Value: Excellent: $475.00
                     Very good: $380.00

Marlin Model 55 Hunter

Gauge: 12, 16, 20
Action: Bolt action; repeating
Magazine: 2-shot detachable box
Barrel: 26" or 28" full choke; "Micro Choke" available; 2¾" or 3" chamber
Finish: Blued; walnut pistol grip stock & forearm; recoil pad optional
Approximate wt.: 7¼ lbs.
Comments: Made from about 1950 to 1965.
Estimated Value: Excellent: $110.00
                     Very good: $ 90.00

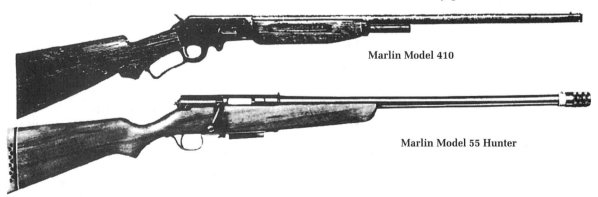

Marlin Model 410

Marlin Model 55 Hunter

Marlin Model 55G

Marlin Glenfield 50

Marlin Model 55 Swamp Gun

Marlin Model 55S Slug Gun

Marlin Model 55 Goose Gun

Marlin Model 55S Slug Gun
Basically the same as Model 55, this gun has rifle sights & a 24" barrel that is chambered for 2¾" & 3" shells. It has swivels & a recoil pad. Produced from 1973 to the late 1980's.

| Estimated Value: | Excellent: | $110.00 |
| | Very good: | $ 90.00 |

Marlin 55G, Glenfield 55G & Glenfield 50
The same basic shotgun as the Marlin Model 55 Hunter. It was produced from about 1961 to 1966 as the 55G & Glenfield 55G & in 1966 it became the Glenfield 50.

| Estimated Value: | Excellent: | $100.00 |
| | Very good: | $ 80.00 |

Marlin Model 55 Swamp Gun
Same as the Model 55 except barrel is shortened with "Micro Choke," recoil pad is standard & it has swivels. It weighs about 6½ lbs. & is chambered for 3" 12 gauge magnum shells. Produced for two years beginning in 1963.

| Estimated Value: | Excellent: | $110.00 |
| | Very good: | $ 90.00 |

Marlin Model 55 Goose Gun
Same as the Model 55 except: swivels; recoil pad; extra long 36" full choke barrel; 12 gauge magnum only; weighs 8 lbs.; introduced in 1966.

Estimated Value:	New (retail):	$308.00
	Excellent:	$230.00
	Very good:	$185.00

Marlin Model 59

Marlin Model 59, 60G, 61G
Gauge: 410
Action: Bolt action; self-cocking
Magazine: None; single shot
Barrel: 24" full coke; chambered for 2½" or 3" shells
Finish: Blued; walnut pistol grip or semi-pistol grip stock & forearm
Approximate wt.: 5 lbs.
Comments: This takedown model was produced from about 1959 to 1961. It was replaced by Model 61G in 1962 which was replaced by the Model 60G in 1963 & discontinued in 1970.
Estimated Value: Excellent: $120.00
Very good: $ 95.00

Marlin Model 5510 Supergoose 10

Marlin Model 5510 Supergoose 10
Gauge: 10 gauge magnum
Action: Bolt action
Magazine: 2-shot detachable box (2⅞" shells must be loaded singly)
Barrel: 34" full choke; chambered for 2⅞" or 3½" shells
Finish: Blued; black walnut semi-pistol grip stock & forearm; swivels; recoil pad
Approximate wt.: 10½ lbs.
Comments: This is a more powerful version of the Marlin Goose Gun. Produced from 1976 to 1986.
Estimated Value: Excellent: $220.00
Very good: $175.00

Marlin Model 512 Slugmaster
Gauge: 12 (3" chamber)
Action: Bolt action; repeating
Magazine: 2-shot detachable box
Barrel: 21" rifled (one turn in 28" for sabot slugs or Foster-type rifled slugs); adjustable folding semi-buckhorn rear and ramp front sight with removable hood
Finish: Blued; checkered walnut finish, birch one-piece pistol grip stock & forearm with recoil pad and swivel studs
Approximate wt.: 8 lbs.
Comments: Introduced in 1994.
Estimated Value: New (Retail): $353.00
Excellent: $265.00
Very Good: $210.00

Marlin Model 1898

Marlin Model 19

Marlin Model 1898
Gauge: 12 (2¾")
Action: Slide action; exposed hammer; side ejection
Magazine: 5-shot tubular
Barrel: 26", 28", 30" or 32"
Finish: Blued; walnut pistol grip stock & grooved slide handle
Approximate wt.: 7¼ lbs.
Comments: This shotgun was produced in many grades from 1898 to 1905. Price for grade A (Field Grade).
Estimated Value: Excellent: $400.00
Very good: $320.00

Marlin Model 19 & 19G
Similar to the Model 1898 with improvements. Made from 1906 to 1907; 19G produced until 1915.
Estimated Value: Excellent: $350.00
Very good: $280.00

Marlin Model 24

Marlin Model 21 "Trap Model"

Marlin Model 26

Marlin Model 16

Marlin Model 16

Gauge: 16 (2¾")
Action: Slide action; exposed hammer
Magazine: 5-shot tubular
Barrel: 26" or 28"
Finish: Blued; walnut pistol grip stock & forearm; some checkered, some with grooved slide handle
Approximate wt.: 6¼ lbs.
Comments: This takedown model was made from about 1904 to 1910.

Estimated Value:	Excellent:	$380.00
	Very good:	$300.00

Marlin Model 24

An improved version of the Model 19 made from 1908 to 1915.

Estimated Value:	Excellent:	$375.00
	Very good:	$300.00

Marlin Model 21 "Trap Model"

Similar to the Model 24 with trap specifications. Made from 1907 to 1909.

Estimated Value:	Excellent:	$380.00
	Very good:	$290.00

Marlin Model 26

Very similar to the Model 24 except: stock is straight grip; solid frame. Made from about 1909 to 1915.

Estimated Value:	Excellent:	$350.00
	Very good:	$280.00

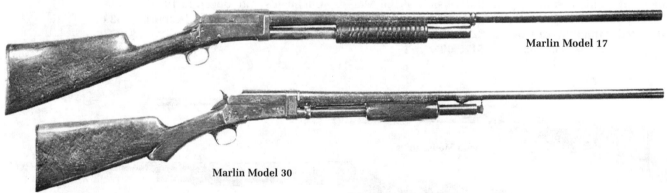

Marlin Model 17

Marlin Model 30

Marlin Model 30 & 30G

Gauge: 16 & 20
Action: Slide action; exposed hammer
Magazine: 5-shot tubular
Barrel: 25", 26", 28" modified choke, 2¾" chamber
Finish: Blued; checkered walnut straight or pistol grip stock, grooved or checkered slide handle
Approximate wt.: 6¾ lbs.
Comments: Made from about 1910 to 1915. In 1915 it was called the Model 30G.

Estimated Value:	Excellent:	$320.00
	Very good:	$250.00

Marlin Model 17 & 17G

Gauge: 12
Action: Slide action; exposed hammer
Magazine: 5-shot tubular
Barrel: 30" or 32" full choke; others available by special order
Finish: Blued; walnut pistol grip stock & grooved slide handle
Approximate wt.: 7½ lbs.
Comments: This solid frame shotgun was made from about 1906 to 1908; from 1908 to 1915 as Model 17G.

Estimated Value:	Excellent:	$350.00
	Very good:	$285.00

Marlin Model 28

Marlin Model 28T

Marlin Model 28A

Marlin Model 31

Marlin Model 31A

Marlin Model 28, 28T, 28TS

Gauge: 12

Action: Slide action; hammerless; side ejection

Magazine: 5-shot tubular

Barrel: 26" or 28" cylinder bore or modified choke; 30" or 32" full choke

Finish: Blued; checkered walnut pistol grip stock & slide handle

Approximate wt.: 8 lbs.

Comments: This takedown shotgun was produced from about 1913 to just before World War I. The Model 28T & 28TS were Trap Grade guns with an available straight stock. Add $100.00 for 28T, 28TS.

Estimated Value: Excellent: $375.00

Very good: $300.00

Marlin Model 28A

Basically the same as the Model 28. Made from about 1920 to 1922; replaced by the Model 43A.

Estimated Value: Excellent: $350.00

Very good: $285.00

Marlin Model 31

This shotgun is much like the Model 28 except: 20 or 16 gauge. Made from about 1915 to 1917 & 1920 to 1922.

Estimated Value: Excellent: $385.00

Very good: $310.00

Marlin Model 31A

Very similar to the Model 28A in 20 gauge only. Replaced by the Model 44A.

Estimated Value: Excellent: $375.00

Very good: $300.00

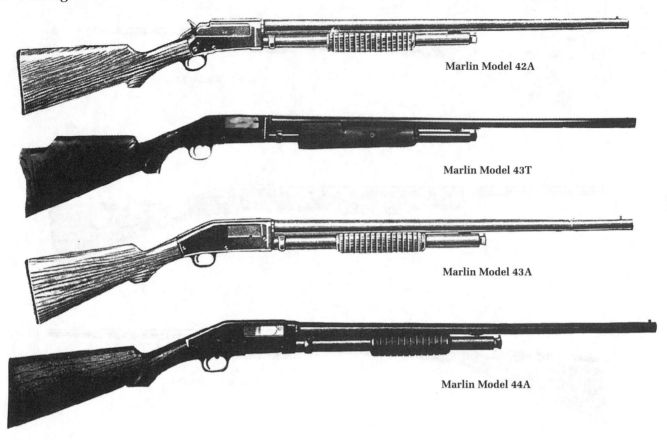

Marlin Model 42A

Marlin Model 43T

Marlin Model 43A

Marlin Model 44A

Marlin Model 42A

Gauge: 12
Action: Slide action; exposed hammer; side ejection
Magazine: 5-shot tubular; bottom load
Barrel: 26" cylinder bore, 28" modified, 30" & 32" full choke; 2¾" chamber; round matted barrel
Finish: Blued; black walnut semi-pistol grip stock, grooved slide handle
Approximate wt.: 7½ lbs.
Comments: A takedown shotgun manufactured from about 1922 to 1934.
Estimated Value: Excellent: $310.00
                      Very good: $250.00

Marlin Model 49

This shotgun is similar to the Model 42A. It was given away with stock in the corporation. It was produced from about 1925 to 1928.
Estimated Value: Excellent: $400.00
                      Very good: $320.00

Marlin Model 43A

Gauge: 12
Action: Slide action; hammerless; side ejection
Magazine: 5-shot tubular
Barrel: 26" cylinder bore, 28" modified, 30" & 32" full choke; 2¾" chamber
Finish: Blued; walnut pistol grip stock & grooved slide handle
Approximate wt.: 8 lbs.
Comments: Made from about 1923 to 1930. It was a new style takedown. Replaced by Model 53.
Estimated Value: Excellent: $270.00
                      Very good: $215.00

Marlin Model 43T & 43TS

Same basic shotgun as the Model 43A except: checkered Monte Carlo stock & forearm with recoil pad. The Model 43TS had a choice of many options & the value is dependent on the number & type of extras.
Estimated Value: Excellent: $400.00
                      Very good: $320.00

Marlin Model 53

Similar to Model 43A. Made in Standard Grade only, from 1929 to 1931 & replaced by Model 63A.
Estimated Value: Excellent: $375.00
                      Very good: $300.00

Marlin Model 44A

Gauge: 20
Action: Slide action; hammerless; side ejection
Magazine: 4-shot tubular; bottom load
Barrel: 25" or 28" cylinder bore, modified or full choke; 2¾" chamber
Finish: Blued; walnut pistol grip stock & grooved slide handle
Approximate wt.: 6 lbs.
Comments: A takedown model produced from about 1923 to 1935.
Estimated Value: Excellent: $385.00
                      Very good: $310.00

Marlin Model 44S

Same basic shotgun as the Model 44A except: either straight or pistol grip checkered stock & forearm.
Estimated Value: Excellent: $400.00
                      Very good: $320.00

Marlin Model 63A

Gauge: 12
Action: Slide action; hammerless; side ejector
Magazine: 5-shot tubular
Barrel: 26" cylinder bore, 28" modified choke, 30" or 32" full choke
Finish: Blued; plain walnut pistol grip stock & grooved slide handle
Approximate wt.: 8 lbs.
Comments: An improved version of the Model 43A. Made from about 1931 to 1935.
Estimated Value: **Excellent:**   **$300.00**
                         Very good: **$240.00**

Marlin Model 63T & 63TS

The Model 63T was basically the same shotgun as the Model 63A except it was only produced in 30" or 32" barrel & had a checkered straight stock. The Model 63TS could be ordered to the buyer's specifications. Prices are for Standard Trap gun.
Estimated Value: **Excellent:**   **$350.00**
                         Very good: **$280.00**

Marlin Model Premier Mark I

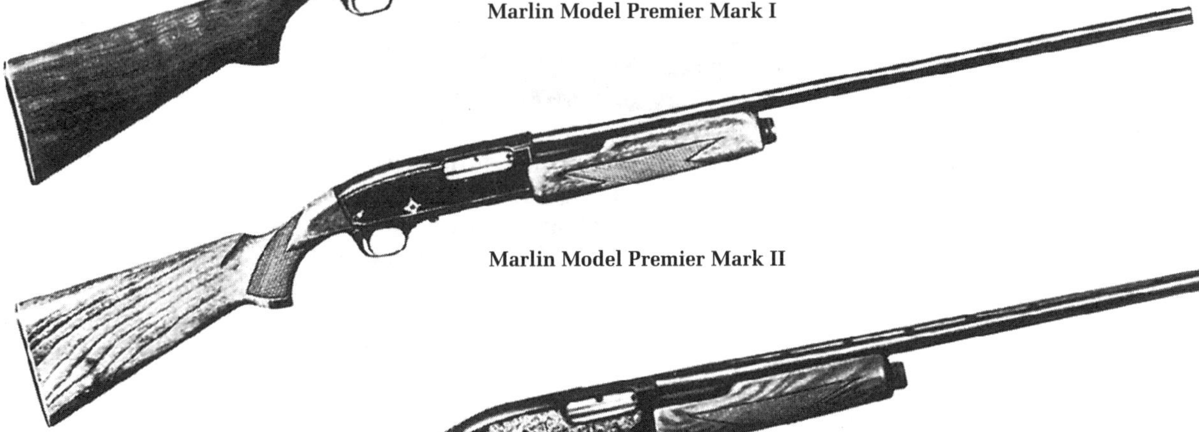

Marlin Model Premier Mark II

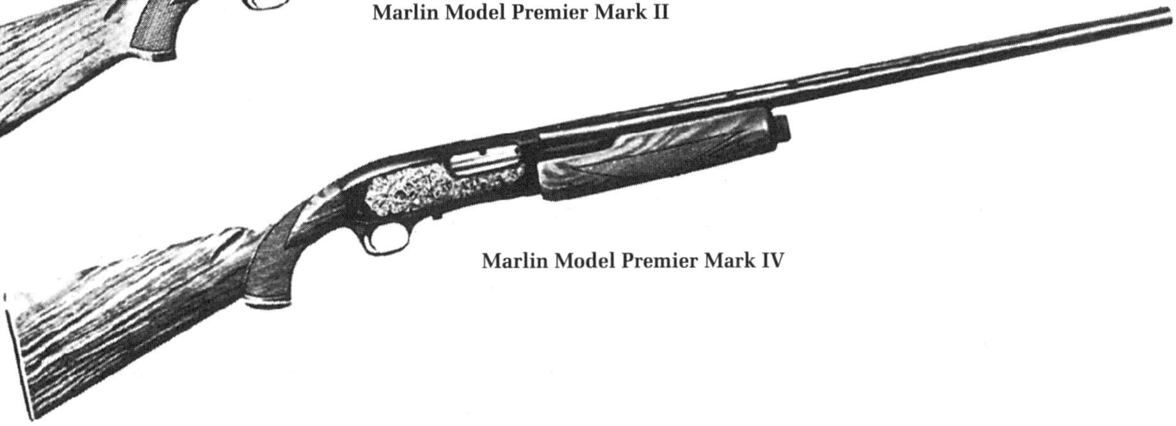

Marlin Model Premier Mark IV

Marlin Model Premier Mark I

Gauge: 12
Action: Slide action; hammerless; side ejection
Magazine: 3-shot tubular
Barrel: 26" cylinder bore, 28" modified, 30" full choke; ventilated rib available; 28" slug barrel with rifle sights available; 2¾" chamber
Finish: Blued; walnut pistol grip stock & forearm; recoil pad optional
Approximate wt.: 7 lbs.
Comments: Made from about 1960 to 1963.
Estimated Value: **Excellent:**   **$185.00**
                         Very good: **$145.00**

Marlin Model Premier Mark II

This is basically the same shotgun as the Premier Mark I except the stock & forearm are checkered & the receiver is engraved.
Estimated Value: **Excellent:**   **$225.00**
                         Very good: **$180.00**

Marlin Model Premier Mark IV

This is basically the same shotgun as the Mark II except the wood is more elaborate & the engraving heavier.
Estimated Value: **Excellent:**   **$310.00**
                         Very good: **$250.00**

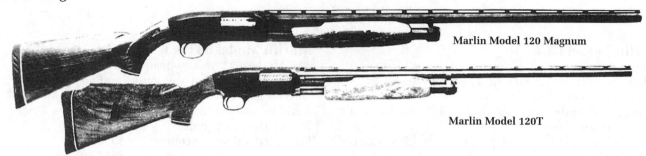

Marlin Model 120 Magnum

Marlin Model 120T

Marlin Deluxe 120 Slug Gun

Similar to the Marlin 120 with a 20" slug barrel & rifle sights. Produced from the late 1970's to 1986.

| Estimated Value: | Excellent: | $315.00 |
| | Very good: | $250.00 |

Marlin Model 120T

This is basically the same shotgun as Model 120 with a Monte Carlo stock & 30" full choke or 30" modified trap choke barrel. This gun was offered from 1973 to the late 1970's.

| Estimated Value: | Excellent: | $325.00 |
| | Very good: | $260.00 |

Marlin Model 120 Magnum

Gauge: 12 gauge magnum
Action: Slide action; hammerless
Magazine: 5-shot tubular (4-shot with 3" shells)
Barrel: 26" cylinder bore, 28" modified or 30" full choke
Finish: Blued; ventilated rib; checkered walnut, pistol grip stock & forearm; recoil pad
Approximate wt.: 7¾ lbs.
Comments: This gun was first offered in 1971. In 1973 a 40" MXR Magnum barrel & a choked 26" slug barrel were offered for the first time. Discontinued in 1986.

| Estimated Value: | Excellent: | $300.00 |
| | Very good: | $240.00 |

Marlin Glenfield 778

Marlin Glenfield 778

Gauge: 12, regular or magnum
Action: Slide action; hammerless; repeating
Magazine: 5-shot tubular; 4-shot with 3" magnum
Barrel: 26" improved cylinder; 28" modified; 30" full choke; ventilated rib available; 38" MXR full choke barrel available without rib
Finish: Blued; checkered hardwood, semi-pistol grip stock & fluted slide handle; recoil pad
Approximate wt.: 7¾ lbs.
Comments: Made from about the late 1970's to early 1980's. Add $50.00 for ventilated rib or MXR barrel.

| Estimated Value: | Excellent: | $195.00 |
| | Very good: | $155.00 |

Marlin Glenfield 778 Slug

Similar to the Glenfield 778 with a 20" slug barrel & rifle sights.

| Estimated Value: | Excellent: | $215.00 |
| | Very good: | $175.00 |

Mauser

Mauser Model 496 Trap

Mauser Model 496 Competition

Mauser Model 496 Competition

Similar to the Model 496 with select wood; higher ventilated rib.

| Estimated Value: | Excellent: | $675.00 |
| | Very good: | $540.00 |

Mauser Model 496 Trap

Gauge: 12
Action: Box lock; top lever, break-open; hammerless; single shot
Magazine: None
Barrel: 32" modified or 34" full chokes; ventilated rib
Finish: Blued; checkered walnut Monte Carlo pistol grip stock & tapered forearm; engraved; recoil pad
Approximate wt.: 8½ lbs.
Comments: Imported in the 1970's.

| Estimated Value: | Excellent: | $550.00 |
| | Very good: | $440.00 |

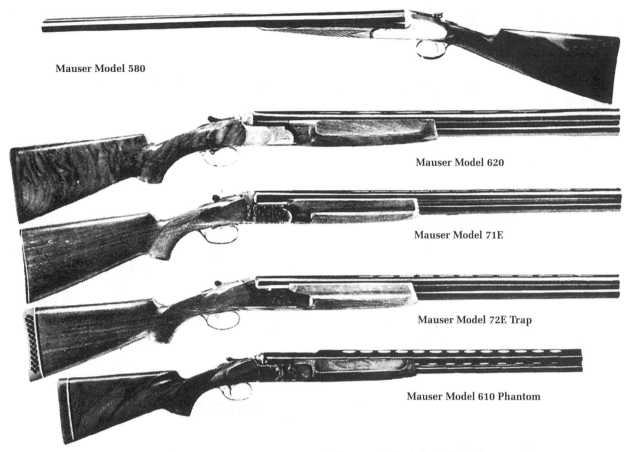

Mauser Model 580

Mauser Model 620

Mauser Model 71E

Mauser Model 72E Trap

Mauser Model 610 Phantom

Mauser Model 580
Gauge: 12
Action: Side lock; top lever break-open; hammerless
Magazine: None
Barrel: Double barrel; 28"-30", various chokes
Finish: Blued; checkered walnut straight stock & tapered forearm; engraved
Approximate wt.: 7¾ lbs.
Comments: Imported in the 1970's.
Estimated Value: Excellent: $900.00
Very good: $720.00

Mauser Model 620
Gauge: 12
Action: Box lock; top lever, break-open; hammerless; automatic ejectors; single trigger
Magazine: None
Barrel: Over & under double barrel; 28", 30" improved cylinder & modified or modified & full or skeet chokes; ribbed
Finish: Blued; plain walnut pistol grip stock & forearm; recoil pad
Approximate wt.: 7½ lbs.
Comments: Imported from the early to mid 1970's.
Estimated Value: Excellent: $950.00
Very good: $760.00

Mauser Model 71E
Similar to the Model 620 with double triggers & no recoil pad; 28" barrel.
Estimated Value: Excellent: $475.00
Very good: $380.00

Mauser Model 72E Trap
Similar to the Model 71E with large recoil pad; engraveing; wide rib; single trigger.
Estimated Value: Excellent: $625.00
Very good: $500.00

Mauser Model 610 Phantom
Gauge: 12
Action: Box lock; top lever, break-open; hammerless
Magazine: None
Barrel: Over & under double barrel; ventilated rib between barrels & on top barrel; 30", 32" various chokes
Finish: Blued; case hardened frame; checkered walnut pistol grip stock & forearm; recoil pad
Approximate wt.: 8 lbs.
Comments: Made in the mid 1970's.
Estimated Value: Excellent: $975.00
Very good: $780.00

Mauser Contest
Gauge: 12
Action: Top lever break-open; automatic ejectors; single selective trigger
Magazine: None
Barrel: Over & under double barrel; 27½" improved cylinder & improved modified
Finish: Blued; engraved grey sideplates; checkered walnut pistol grip stock & lipped forearm
Approximate wt.: 7½ lbs.
Comments: Add $500.00 for trap model.
Estimated Value: Excellent: $1,050.00
Very good: $ 840.00

Maverick (Mossberg)

Maverick Model 88 Field

Maverick Model 88 Field
Gauge: 12 (3" chamber)
Action: Slide action; hammerless; repeating
Magazine: 5-shot tubular
Barrel: 28" or 30" plain or ventilated rib; full, modified, or accu-choke tubes
Finish: Blued; smooth black synthetic pistol grip stock and grooved slide handle
Approximate wt.: 7¼ lbs.
Comments: Produced in mid 1990's; add 5% for ventilated rib; add 5% for accu-choke tubes; add 10% for accu-choke tube set (full, modified, and improved cylinder).
Estimated Value: **Excellent:** **$165.00**
                Very good: **$135.00**

Maverick Model 88 Deer
Same as the Model 88 Field except: 24" plain cylinder bore barrel with rifle sights.
Estimated Value: **Excellent:** **$175.00**
                Very good: **$140.00**

Maverick Model 88 Security

Maverick Model 88 Bullpup
Gauge: 12 regular or magnum
Action: Slide action; hammerless; repeating, using the basic Mossberg 500 action
Magazine: 5-shot or 7-shot tubular
Barrel: 18½" or 20" cylinder bore with top carrying handle and heat shield; rifle sights
Finish: Blued; black synthetic housing stock and pistol grips (2); pistol grip at trigger with grip safety and pistol grip slide handle
Approximate wt.: 9½ lbs.
Comments: Same as the Mossberg Model 500 Bullpup except: introduced in 1994 as Maverick.
Estimated Value: **Excellent:** **$260.00**
                Very good: **$200.00**

Maverick Model 88 Security
Same as the Model 88 Field except: 18½" or 20" cylinder bore barrel; 5 or 7 shot magazine; available with pistol grip kit and/or heat shield; add 6% for 7 shot; add 6% for pistol grip kit or heat shield.
Estimated Value: **Excellent:** **$165.00**
                Very good: **$135.00**

Maverick Model 91

Maverick Model 91
Gauge: 12 (3½" chamber)
Action: Slide action; hammerless; repeating
Magazine: 4-shot tubular
Barrel: 18½" or 20" with ventilated rib and accu-mag choke tube or cylinder bore
Finish: Blued; black synthetic pistol grip stock and grooved slide handle
Approximate wt.: 7¾ lbs.
Comments: Produced in mid 1990's.
Estimated Value: **Excellent:** **$195.00**
                Very good: **$160.00**

Mitchell

Mitchell High Standard

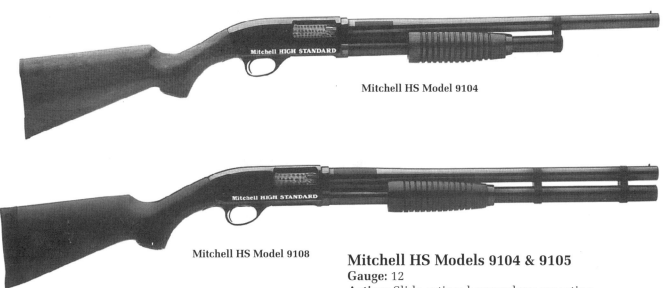

Mitchell HS Model 9104

Mitchell HS Model 9108

Mitchell HS Models 9104 & 9105
Gauge: 12
Action: Slide action; hammerless; repeating
Magazine: 5-shot tubular
Barrel: 20" plain barrel; bead sight (Model 9104)
Finish: Blued; plain smooth walnut semi-pistol grip stock & grooved slide handle
Approximate wt.: 6½ lbs.
Comments: Produced in mid 1990's; add 7% for rifle sights (Model 9105).

Estimated Value:	Excellent:	$200.00
	Very good:	$160.00

Mitchell HS Models 9108, 9109, 9111, & 9113
Same as Models 9104 & 9105 except: 7 shot magazines (9108, 9109); 6-shot magazine and 18½" barrel on Model 9111 & 9113; military green or brown stock & slide handle. Add 7% for rifle sights.

Estimated Value:	Excellent:	$200.00
	Very good:	$160.00

Mitchell HS Model 9114

Mitchell HS Model 9115

Mitchell HS Model 9115
Same as Model 9104 except: 7-shot magazine; 18½" barrel; ventilated steel heat shield on barrel; Parkerized finish; Stealth grey synthetic stock & slide handle; butt stock has 4-shot storage capacity.

Estimated Value:	Excellent:	$250.00
	Very good:	$200.00

Mitchell HS Models 9114 & 9114FS
Same as Model 9104 except: 7-shot magazine; removable synthetic butt stock, "one hand" pistol grip and slide handle (Model 9114); Model 9114FS has a special folding steel butt stock which can be used folded or extended and a "one hand" pistol grip.

Estimated Value:	Excellent:	$245.00
	Very good:	$195.00

Mossberg

Mossberg Model 83D

Mossberg Model 183K

Mossberg Model 83D, 183D
Gauge: 410
Action: Bolt action; repeating
Magazine: 2-shot, top loading; fixed magazine
Barrel: 23" on 83D, 24" on 183D; interchangeable choke fittings
Finish: Blued; hardwood Monte Carlo semi-pistol grip one-piece stock & forearm
Approximate wt.: 5½ lbs.
Comments: Made as the 83D from about 1940 to 1947 & as the 183D from 1948 until the early 1970's.
Estimated Value: Excellent: $120.00
                      Very good: $100.00

Mossberg Model 183K
Similar to the 183D with adjustable choke & recoil pad. Made from the early 1950's to mid 1980's.
Estimated Value: Excellent: $125.00
                      Very good: $105.00

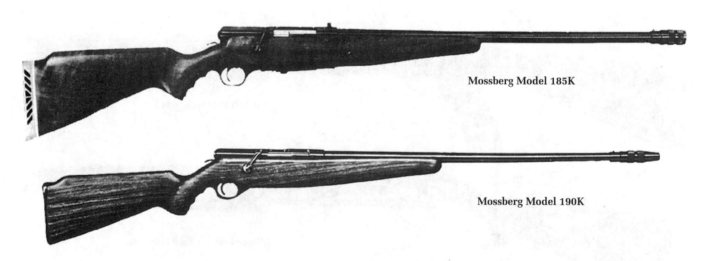

Mossberg Model 185K

Mossberg Model 190K

Mossberg Model 190K
Similar to the 183K in 16 gauge. Made from the mid 1950's to early 1960's.
Estimated Value: Excellent: $105.00
                      Very good: $ 85.00

Mossberg Model 185K
Similar to the 183K in 20 gauge. Made from about 1950 to early 1960's.
Estimated Value: Excellent: $110.00
                      Very good: $ 90.00

Mossberg Model 195K
Similar to the 183K in 12 gauge. Made from the mid 1950's to early 1960's.
Estimated Value: Excellent: $115.00
                      Very good: $ 90.00

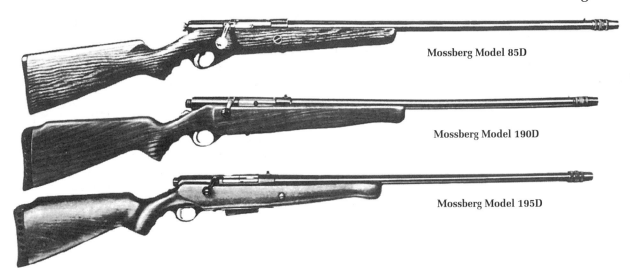

Mossberg Model 85D

Mossberg Model 190D

Mossberg Model 195D

Mossberg Model 85D, 185D
Gauge: 20
Action: Bolt action; repeating
Magazine: 2-shot detachable box
Barrel: 25" on 85D, 26" on 185D; interchangeable choke
fittings
Finish: Blued; hardwood pistol grip one-piece stock &
forearm
Approximate wt.: 6½ lbs.
Comments: Made as the 85D from about 1940 to 1948 &
as the 185D from 1948 to the early 1970's.
Estimated Value: **Excellent:**   **$110.00**
                      Very good: **$ 90.00**

Mossberg Model 190D
Similar to the 185D in 16 gauge. Made from the mid
1950's to early 1960's.
Estimated Value: **Excellent:**   **$100.00**
                      Very good: **$ 80.00**

Mossberg Model 195D
Similar to the 185D in 12 gauge. Made from the mid
1950's to early 1970's.
Estimated Value: **Excellent:**   **$115.00**
                      Very good: **$ 95.00**

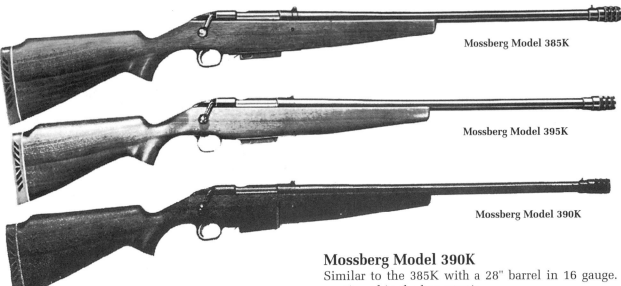

Mossberg Model 385K

Mossberg Model 395K

Mossberg Model 390K

Mossberg Model 385K
Gauge: 20
Action: Bolt action; repeating
Magazine: 2-shot detachable box
Barrel: 26" adjustable choke
Finish: Blued; wood Monte Carlo semi-pistol grip one-
piece stock & tapered forearm; recoil pad
Approximate wt.: 6½ lbs.
Comments: Made from the early 1960's to early 1980's.
Estimated Value: **Excellent:**   **$115.00**
                      Very good: **$ 95.00**

Mossberg Model 390K
Similar to the 385K with a 28" barrel in 16 gauge. Dis-
continued in the late 1970's.
Estimated Value: **Excellent:**   **$110.00**
                      Very good: **$ 90.00**

Mossberg Model 395K
Similar to the 385K in 12 gauge. Weighs 7½ lbs.
Estimated Value: **Excellent:**   **$110.00**
                      Very good: **$ 90.00**

Mossberg Model 585
Similar to the Model 385K with improved safety. Pro-
duced in mid 1980's.
Estimated Value: **Excellent:**   **$130.00**
                      Very good: **$105.00**

Mossberg Model 595

Similar to the Model 395K with improved safety. Introduced in 1984. Available with 28" adjustable choke barrel or 38" Waterfowl barrel. Add $20.00 for Waterfowl model.

Estimated Value: Excellent: $125.00
                       Very good: $100.00

Mossberg Model 395 SPL

Similar to the Model 395K with a 38" full choke barrel for Waterfowl; swivels. Introduced in 1982.

Estimated Value: Excellent: $120.00
                       Very good: $100.00

Mossberg Model 695 Bolt Action

Gauge: 12, 3" chambers
Action: Bolt action, repeating
Magazine: 2-shot detachable
Barrel: 22" smooth bore with Accu-choke or rifled bore; rifle sights and "Weaver-style" scope bases
Finish: Synthetic stock and forearm in matte or woodland finish; pistol grip stock with lipped fore end
Approximate wt.: 7 lbs.
Comments: Introduced in 1996; add 6% for rifled barrel

Estimated Value: New (retail): $276.00
                       Excellent: $210.00
                       Very good: $165.00

Mossberg Model 695 Bolt Action

Mossberg Model 3000 Field

Gauge: 12, 20; regular or magnum
Action: Slide action; hammerless; repeating
Magazine: 4-shot tubular, 3-shot in magnum
Barrel: 26" improved cylinder, 28" modified or full, 30" full; ventilated rib; "Multi-choke" available
Finish: Checkered walnut pistol grip stock & slide handle
Approximate wt.: 6¼ to 7½ lbs.
Comments: Produced in the mid 1980's. Add $25.00 for "Multi-choke."

Estimated Value: Excellent: $290.00
                       Very good: $230.00

Mossberg Model 3000 Waterfowler

Similar to the Model 3000 with 30" full choke barrel & Parkerized, oiled finish or camo finish with "Speedfeed" storage stock (add 10%). Add 10% for "Multi-choke."

Estimated Value: Excellent: $320.00
                       Very good: $260.00

Mossberg Model 3000 Slug

Similar to the Model 3000 with a 22" slug barrel & rifle sights. Add $35.00 for black finish with "Speedfeed" storage stock.

Estimated Value: Excellent: $280.00
                       Very good: $220.00

Mossberg Model 200D

Gauge: 12
Action: Slide action; hammerless; repeating; slide handle is metal cover over wood forearm
Magazine: 3-shot detachable box
Barrel: 28" interchangeable choke fittings
Finish: Blued; wood Monte Carlo semi-pistol grip one-piece stock & forearm
Approximate wt.: 7½ lbs.
Comments: Made from the mid to late 1950's.

Estimated Value: Excellent: $140.00
                       Very good: $110.00

Mossberg Model 200K

Similar to the 200D with adjustable choke.

Estimated Value: Excellent: $145.00
                       Very good: $115.00

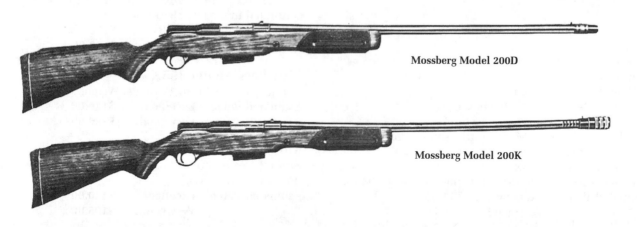

Mossberg Model 200D

Mossberg Model 200K

Mossberg Model 500 Field

Mossberg Model 500 Super

Mossberg Model 500 AHTD

Mossberg Model 500 Slugster

Mossberg Model 500 Field

Gauge: 12, 16, 20, 410
Action: Slide action; hammerless; repeating
Magazine: 5-shot tubular
Barrel: 24" cyl. or rifle bore; 26" adjustable choke or improved cylinder; 28" modified or full; 30" full choke in 12 gauge only; available with "Accu-Choke" after 1984; vent rib available
Finish: Blued; walnut finish or synthetic pistol grip stock & grooved slide handle; recoil pad; camo finish & "Speedfeed" stock available after 1985
Approximate wt.: 6 to 8 lbs.
Comments: Manufactured from about 1960 to present. Add 15% for rifled barrel; add 20% for camo finish
Estimated Value: New (retail): $278.00
                Excellent: $210.00
                Very good: $165.00

Mossberg Model 500 Super

Similar to the 500 Field with checkered stock & slide handle & ventilated rib. 12 gauge magnum.
Estimated Value: Excellent: $220.00
                Very good: $175.00

Mossberg Model 500 Hi-Rib Trap AHTD, AHT

Similar to 500 with high rib barrel & Monte Carlo stock. AHT full choke; AHTD had adjustable choke; 28" or 30" barrel.
Estimated Value: Excellent: $290.00
                Very good: $235.00

Mossberg Model 500 Slugster

Similar to 500 with 18" or 24" slug barrel & rifle sights. Add 20% for removable choke; add 15% for Trophy Model; add 12% for rifled barrel.
Estimated Value: New (retail): $288.00
                Excellent: $215.00
                Very good: $175.00

Mossberg Model 500 ALDR, CLDR, ALDRX

Similar to 500 in 12 gauge (ALDR) & 20 gauge (CLDR) with removable choke. Add $50.00 for additional slugster barrel (ALDRX).
Estimated Value: Excellent: $215.00
                Very good: $170.00

Mossberg Model 500 ALMR Duck Gun

Similar to 500 in 12 gauge with 30" or 32" vent rib barrel for 3" magnum. Discontinued in the early 1980's.
Estimated Value: Excellent: $225.00
                Very good: $180.00

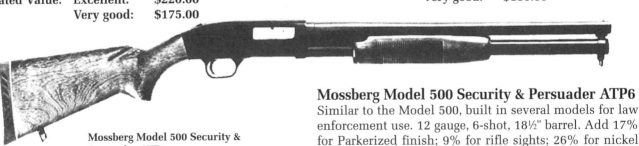

Mossberg Model 500 Security & Persuader ATP8

Mossberg Model 500 Viking

Same as the Mossberg Model 500 Field except: 12 and 20 gauge only; matte blue finish with green synthetic stock and slide handle; add 5% for 24" rifled barrel with rifle sights. Introduced in 1996.
Estimated Value: New (retail): $266.00
                Excellent: $200.00
                Very good: $160.00

Mossberg Model 500 Security & Persuader ATP6

Similar to the Model 500, built in several models for law enforcement use. 12 gauge, 6-shot, 18½" barrel. Add 17% for Parkerized finish; 9% for rifle sights; 26% for nickel finish; 13% for "Speedfeed" stock; 22% for camo finish.
Estimated Value: Excellent: $200.00
                Very good: $160.00

Mossberg Model 500 Security & Persuader ATP8

Similar to the Model 500 ATP6 series with a 20" barrel, 8-shot capacity. Add 8% for rifle sights; 16% for Parkerized finish; 24% for nickel finish; 12% for "Speedfeed" stock; 20% for camo finish. Discontinued in mid 1990's.
Estimated Value: Excellent: $205.00
                Very good: $165.00

Mossberg Model 500 Mariner

Similar to the Persuader series except it has a special Teflon & metal coating that is resistant to salt water spray. Stock & slide handle are synthetic. Available in 6- or 9-shot version. Add 3% for 9-shot model, 10% for "Speedfeed" stock, add 15% for ghost ring sight. Introduced in 1987.

Estimated Value: New (retail): $403.00
                    Excellent: $300.00
                    Very good: $240.00

Mossberg Model 500 Camper

Similar to the Model 500 Cruiser in 12 gauge, 20 gauge or 410 bore; 18½" barrel; synthetic grip & slide handle; camo carrying case. Introduced in the late 1980's.

Estimated Value: Excellent: $225.00
                    Very good: $180.00

Mossberg 500 Security & Persuader CTP6, ETP6

Similar to the other 500 series law enforcement shotguns in 20 gauge (CTP6) or 410 bore (ETP6); 18½" barrel; 6-shot.

Estimated Value: Excellent: $200.00
                    Very good: $160.00

Mossberg Model 500 Persuader Cruiser

Similar to the Model 500 ATP6 and ATP8 series law enforcement shotguns with "one-hand" grip. Add 26% for nickel finish, add 3% for 410 gauge.

Estimated Value: New (retail): $272.00
                    Excellent: $205.00
                    Very good: $170.00

Mossberg Model 500 ER

Mossberg Model 500 APR Pigeon

Similar to the 500 Field except: engraving; ventilated rib. Made from the late 1960's to the late 1970's.

Estimated Value: Excellent: $280.00
                    Very good: $225.00

Mossberg Model 500 ARTP Trap

Similar to the 500 APR with a 30" full choke barrel; Monte Carlo stock. Discontinued in the late 1970's.

Estimated Value: Excellent: $295.00
                    Very good: $235.00

Mossberg Model 500 ER, ELR

Similar to the 500 Field in 410 gauge; 26" barrel; skeet version has checkering & ventilated rib. Discontinued in the early 1980's.

Estimated Value: Excellent: $215.00
                    Very good: $175.00

Mossberg Model 500 Regal

Similar to the Model 500 with deluxe finish, crown design on receiver. Produced in mid 1980's. Add $20.00 for "Accu-Choke."

Estimated Value: Excellent: $225.00
                    Very good: $180.00

Mossberg Model 500 Sporting

Mossberg Model 500 Bullpup

Gauge: 12 regular or magnum
Action: Slide action, hammerless; repeating, using the basic Mossberg 500 action
Magazine: 5-shot or 7-shot
Barrel: 18½" or 20" cylinder bore with top carrying handle and heat shield; rifle sights
Finish: Blued; black synthetic housing stock and pistol grips (2); pistol grip at trigger with grip safety and pistol grip slide handle
Approximate wt.: 9½ lbs.
Comments: Made from mid 1980's to early 1990's.
Estimated Value: Excellent: $250.00
                        Very good: $190.00

Mossberg Model 500 Sporting

Gauge: 12, 20, 410; regular or magnum
Action: Slide action, hammerless; repeating; double slide bars
Magazine: 5-shot tubular with 3-round field plug
Barrel: 20", 24", 26", 28" "Accu-Choke" tubes or fixed choke; plain or ventilated rib
Finish: Blued or camo with checkered walnut finish stock and slide handle or synthetic stock and slide handle
Approximate wt.: 6.8 to 7.2 lbs.
Comments: Introduced in 1990; add 18% for ghost ring sights; add 8% for camo finish.
Estimated Value: New (retail): $281.00
                        Excellent: $210.00
                        Very good: $170.00

Mossberg Model
HS 410 Home Security

Mossberg Model 590 Special Purpose

Gauge: 12 regular
Action: Slide action, hammerless; repeating; double slide bars
Magazine: 9-shot tubular
Barrel: 20" cylinder bore metal heat shield, bayonet lug, and sling swivels; optional ghost ring sight
Finish: Blued or Parkerized with synthetic stock and slide handle. Speed-feed stock available. Also, laser sight built into forearm is available
Approximate wt.: 7 lbs.
Comments: Introduced in 1990; add 10% for speed-feed stock or ghost ring sight.

Estimated Value:	New (retail):	$329.00
	Excellent:	$245.00
	Very good:	$200.00

Mossberg 835 Field Grade Ulti-Mag

Gauge: 12 (3½" chamber); regular or magnum
Action: Slide action, hammerless; repeating; double slide bars
Magazine: 4- or 5-shot tubular
Barrel: 24" or 28" with ventilated rib and Accu-Mag Choke tube or 24" with rifle sights and fixed cylinder bore choke
Finish: Blued, walnut-finish, checkered stock and slide handle
Approximate wt.: 7.3 to 7.7 lbs.
Comments: Introduced in 1990; Add 4% for 24" fixed cylinder bore choke barrel with rifle sights.

Estimated Value:	New (retail):	$313.00
	Excellent:	$235.00
	Very good:	$185.00

Mossberg Model HS 410 Home Security

Gauge: 410; 3" chamber; 20 gauge after 1995
Action: Slide action, hammerless; repeating
Magazine: 4-shot tubular
Barrel: 18½" with muzzle brake and spreader choke (the spreader choke delivers almost twice the size circle of a regular shotgun pattern)
Finish: Blued; synthetic stock and slide handle also vertical slide kit available; the laser sight model has a vertical hand grip slide which contains the light and battery
Approximate wt.: 6¼ lbs.
Comments: Introduced in 1990; add 82% for laser light model.

Estimated Value:	New (retail):	$293.00
	Excellent:	$220.00
	Very good:	$175.00

Mossberg 835 Regal or Crown Grade Ulti-Mag

Same as 835 Field Grade Ulti-Mag except: walnut stock and slide handle; dual-comb stock (stock comb height can be changed by removing one bolt); 24" rifle bore barrel with scope base available; add 5% for 24" rifle bore barrel.

Estimated Value:	New (retail):	$412.00
	Excellent:	$310.00
	Very good:	$245.00

Mossberg 835 Camo Ulti-Mag

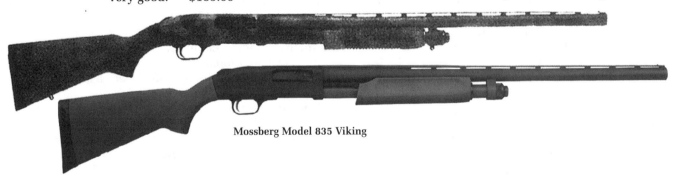

Mossberg Model 835 Viking

Mossberg Model 835 Viking

Similar to the Model 835 Field Grade except: matte blue finish with Viking green synthetic stock and slide handle; 28" ventilated rib barrel with modified choke tube. Introduced in 1996.

Estimated Value:	New (retail):	$301.00
	Excellent:	$225.00
	Very good:	$180.00

Mossberg 835 Camo Ulti-Mag

Same as 835 Regal Ulti-Mag except: camo finish; the National Wild Turkey Federation (NWTF) Model has synthetic stock (without dual comb feature) and slide handle with Realtree Camo pattern and 24" barrel with x-full tube Accu-Mag choke; add 7% for the NWTF Model.

Estimated Value:	New (retail):	$493.00
	Excellent:	$370.00
	Very good:	$295.00

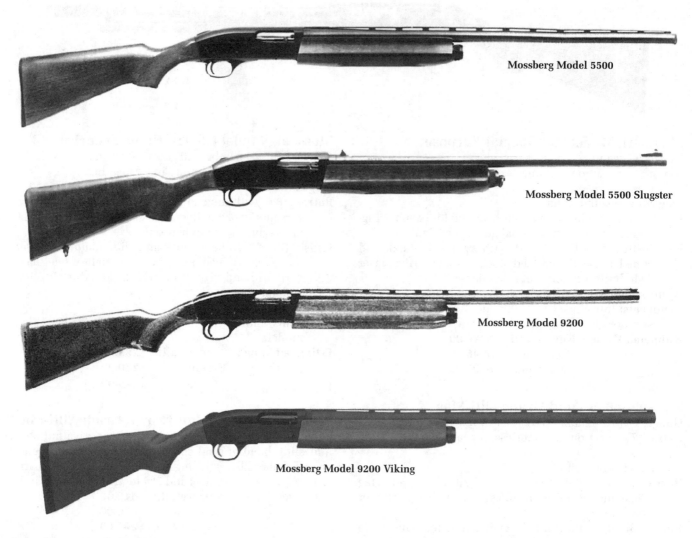

Mossberg Model 5500

Mossberg Model 5500 Slugster

Mossberg Model 9200

Mossberg Model 9200 Viking

Mossberg Model 5500

Gauge: 12, regular or magnum
Action: Gas operated semi-automatic
Magazine: 4-shot tubular
Barrel: 26" improved cylinder, 28" modified, 30" full; 28" "Accu-Choke" with interchangeable tubes; ventilated rib available; 25" on youth model
Finish: Blued; checkered hardwood or synthetic semi-pistol grip stock & forearm; aluminum alloy receiver; small stock on youth model
Approximate wt.: 7½ lbs.
Comments: Produced from the early 1980's to early 1990's. Deduct 20% for synthetic stock; Add 5% for magnum.

| Estimated Value: | Excellent: | $325.00 |
| | Very good: | $260.00 |

Mossberg Model 5500 Slugster

Similar to the Model 5500 with 18½" or 24" slug barrel, rifle sights & swivels.

| Estimated Value: | Excellent: | $360.00 |
| | Very good: | $290.00 |

Mossberg Model 9200

Gauge: 12 regular and magnum, interchangeably
Action: Gas operated semi-automatic; a gas regulating system compensates for varied pressures from normal to 3" magnum loads.
Magazine: 4-shot; 3-shot in magnum
Barrel: 24" rifled bore; 24" or 28" smooth bore with Accu-Choke tubes; wide ventilated rib, white front bead and brass midpoint bead
Finish: Blued or camo; checkered pistol grip walnut stock and forearm; camo finish has synthetic stock and forearm; the 24" rifled bore has walnut finish dual-comb stock in blued finish.
Approximate wt.: 7½ lbs.
Comments: Introduced in 1992; add 17% for camo finish; add 5% for 24" rifled bore with dual comb stock.

Estimated Value:	New (retail):	$478.00
	Excellent:	$360.00
	Very good:	$285.00

Mossberg Model 9200 Viking

Same as the Mossberg Model 9200 except: 28" ventilated rib barrel with modified choke tube; matte blue finish; green synthetic stock and forearm. Introduced in 1996.

Estimated Value:	New (retail):	$404.00
	Excellent:	$300.00
	Very good:	$245.00

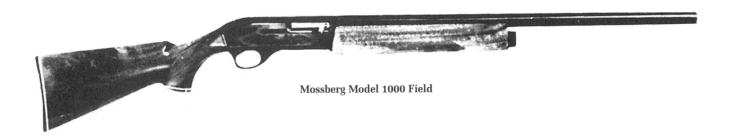

Mossberg Model 1000 Field

Mossberg Model 1000 Super
Gauge: 12 or 20, regular or magnum
Action: Gas operated semi-automatic
Magazine: 3-shot tubular
Barrel: 26", 28", 30" "Multi-choke"; ventilated rib
Finish: Blued; checkered walnut pistol grip stock & forearm; recoil pad; scrolling on receiver
Approximate wt.: 6¾ to 7¾ lbs.
Comments: Produced in the mid 1980's in Japan.
Estimated Value: Excellent: $400.00
                       Very good: $300.00

Mossberg Model 1000 Super Waterfowler
Similar to the Model 1000 Super with dull wood & Parkerized finish; 12 gauge only. Made in Japan.
Estimated Value: Excellent: $420.00
                       Very good: $315.00

Mossberg Model 1000 Super Slug
Similar to the Model 1000 Super with 22" slug barrel.
Estimated Value: Excellent: $395.00
                       Very good: $295.00

Mossberg Model 1000 Super Skeet
Similar to the Model 1000 Super with 25" barrel.
Estimated Value: Excellent: $495.00
                       Very good: $370.00

Mossberg Model 1000 Field
Similar to the Model 1000 Super with alloy receiver; various chokes available including a 26" skeet barrel; add $30.00 for "Multi-choke"; Junior model has 22" barrel with "Multi-choke" (add $25.00). Made in Japan.
Estimated Value: Excellent: $330.00
                       Very good: $245.00

Mossberg Model 1000 Slug
Similar to the Model 1000 Field with 22" slug barrel, rifle sights. Made in Japan.
Estimated Value: Excellent: $320.00
                       Very good: $240.00

Mossberg Model 1000 Trap
Similar to the Model 1000 Field with a 30" "Multi-choke" barrel, recoil pad, Monte Carlo stock & high-rib barrel. Made in Japan.
Estimated Value: Excellent: $420.00
                       Very good: $315.00

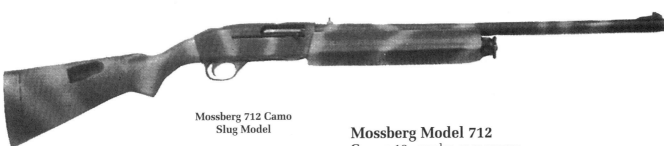

Mossberg 712 Camo
Slug Model

Mossberg Model 712 Camo Slug Model
Similar to the Model 712 with camo finish & "Speedfeed" storage stock. Add $20.00 for "Accu-Choke." Produced in mid 1980's. Made in Japan.
Estimated Value: Excellent: $320.00
                       Very good: $250.00

Mossberg Model 712 Regal
Similar to the Model 712 with deluxe finish, crown design on receiver. Produced in mid 1980's. Add $20.00 for "Accu-Choke." Made in Japan.
Estimated Value: Excellent: $310.00
                       Very good: $245.00

Mossberg Model 712
Gauge: 12, regular or magnum
Action: Gas operated semi-automatic
Magazine: 4-shot tubular, 3-shot in magnum
Barrel: 30" full, 28" modified, 24" "Accu-choke," 24" slug; ventilated rib available
Finish: Alloy receiver with anodized finish; checkered walnut finish semi-pistol grip stock & forearm; recoil pad; Junior Model has 13" stock
Approximate wt.: 7½ lbs.
Comments: This shotgun was designed to handle any 12 gauge shell interchangeably. Produced from 1986 to late 1980's; add $15.00 for slug model with rifle sights; $15.00 for ventilated rib; $40.00 for "Accu-choke." Made in Japan.
Estimated Value: Excellent: $300.00
                       Very good: $240.00

New England

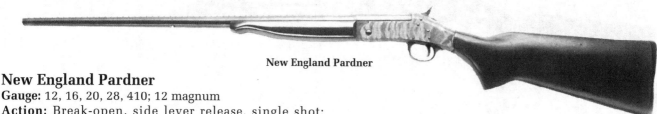

New England Pardner

New England Pardner

Gauge: 12, 16, 20, 28, 410; 12 magnum
Action: Break-open, side lever release, single shot; exposed hammer
Magazine: None, single shot
Barrel: 24", 26" or 28"; full, modified or cylinder bore
Finish: Blued with color case hardened frame; hardwood walnut finish pistol grip, smooth stock & lipped forearm
Approximate wt.: 5 to 6 lbs.
Comments: Introduced in 1989.
Estimated Value: New (retail): $124.95
                       Excellent: $ 95.00
                       Very good: $ 75.00

New England Youth Pardner

Same as the Pardner except: 20, 28, or 410 gauge only with 22" barrel & straight grip, shorter stock with recoil pad. Introduced in 1989.
Estimated Value: New (retail): $134.95
                       Excellent: $100.00
                       Very good: $ 80.00

New England Deluxe Pardner

Same as the Pardner except: 12 or 20 gauge only with special double back-up butt stock (holds two spare shells) & recoil pad. Introduced in 1989 & discontinued in 1992.
Estimated Value: Excellent: $120.00
                       Very good: $ 95.00

New England Mini-Pardner

Same as the Pardner except: 20 or 410 gauge only, 18½" barrel with short butt stock; weighs 4¾ lbs.; equipped with swivel studs. Introduced in 1989 & discontinued in 1992.
Estimated Value: Excellent: $110.00
                       Very good: $ 90.00

New England Protector

Gauge: 12
Action: Break-open, side release, single shot exposed; hammer
Magazine: None, single shot
Barrel: 18½"
Finish: Blued or nickel; smooth hardwood walnut finish; pistol grip stock & lipped forearm; recoil pad; special double back-up butt stock holds two spare shells; swivels
Approximate wt.: 5¾ lbs.
Comments: Made from 1990 to 1992. Add 8% for nickel finish.
Estimated Value: Excellent: $125.00
                       Very good: $100.00

New England 10 Gauge Magnum, Turkey & Goose Gun

Gauge: 10 gauge, 3½" chamber
Action: Break-open, side lever release, single shot; exposed hammer
Magazine: None, single shot
Barrel: 32" full choke; 28" (in 1992) turkey & goose gun
Finish: Blued; hardwood walnut finish, smooth, pistol grip stock & forearm; recoil pad; also camo matte finish stock & forearm
Approximate wt.: 10 lbs.
Comments: Introduced in 1989. Add 12% for camo finish.
Estimated Value: New (retail): $169.95
                       Excellent: $130.00
                       Very good: $105.00

New England Turkey

Similar to the 10 gauge magnum turkey & goose gun except: 24" barrel; mossy oak or bottom land camo finish.
Estimated Value: New (retail): $135.95
                       Excellent: $100.00
                       Very good: $ 80.00

New England 10 Gauge Magnum

New England Handi-Gun Combination

See Handi-Gun Combination in Rifle section.

New Haven (Mossberg)

New Haven Model 273

New Haven Model 290

New Haven Model 290
Gauge: 16
Action: Bolt action; hammerless; repeating
Magazine: 2-shot detachable box
Barrel: 28" removable full choke
Finish: Blued; walnut Monte Carlo pistol grip one-piece stock & tapered forearm
Approximate wt.: 6½ lbs.
Comments: Made in the early 1960's.
Estimated Value: Excellent: $100.00
Very good: $ 80.00

New Haven Model 283, 283T
A 410 gauge version of the 290 with a 24" barrel. Currently called 283T. Discontinued early 1980's.
Estimated Value: Excellent: $110.00
Very good: $ 90.00

New Haven Model 295
A 12 gauge version of the 290.
Estimated Value: Excellent: $105.00
Very good: $85.00

New Haven Model 285
A 20 gauge version of the 290 with 24" barrel.
Estimated Value: Excellent: $100.00
Very good: $ 80.00

New Haven Model 495

New Haven Model 600

New Haven Model 273
Gauge: 20
Action: Bolt action; hammerless; single shot
Magazine: None
Barrel: 24" full choke
Finish: Blued; plain walnut Monte Carlo semi-pistol grip one-piece stock & forearm
Approximate wt.: 6¼ lbs.
Comments: Made in the early 1960's.
Estimated Value: Excellent: $85.00
Very good: $70.00

New Haven Model 495, 495T
Gauge: 12
Action: Bolt action; hammerless; repeating
Magazine: 2-shot detachable box
Barrel: 28" full choke
Finish: Blued; walnut Monte Carlo semi-pistol grip stock & tapered forearm
Approximate wt.: 7½ lbs.
Comments: Made from the mid 1960's to early 1980's.
Estimated Value: Excellent: $120.00
Very good: $ 95.00

New Haven Model 485T
A 20 gauge version of the Model 495; 26" barrel.
Estimated Value: Excellent: $125.00
Very good: $100.00

New Haven Model 600
Gauge: 12, 20, 410
Action: Slide action; hammerless; repeating
Magazine: 6-shot tubular
Barrel: 26" improved cylinder, 28" modified or full, 30" full chokes. Ventilated rib, adjustable choke & interchangeable choke available
Finish: Blued; walnut semi-pistol grip stock & slide handle
Approximate wt.: 7½ lbs.
Comments: Made from the early 1960's to early 1980's. Add $30.00 for ventilated rib; $20.00 for adjustable choke; $10.00 for interchangeable choke.
Estimated Value: Excellent: $200.00
Very good: $160.00

New Haven Model 600 AST
Similar to Model 600 except: 24" barrel & rifle sights.
Estimated Value: Excellent: $210.00
Very good: $170.00

Noble

Noble Model 420

Noble Model 420

Gauge: 12, 16, 20
Action: Box lock; top lever, break-open; hammerless; double triggers
Magazine: None
Barrel: Side by side double barrel, 28" modified & full
Finish: Blued; checkered walnut pistol grip stock & forearm
Approximate wt.: 6¾ lbs.
Comments: Made from the late 1950's to the early 1970's.
Estimated Value: Excellent: $275.00
                  Very good: $220.00

Noble Model 420 EK

A fancy version of the Model 420 with automatic ejectors; select walnut; recoil pad; engraving; sights; gold inlay. Made in the late 1960's.
Estimated Value: Excellent: $340.00
                  Very good: $275.00

Noble Model 450E

Very similar to Model 420 EK. Made from the late 1960's to the early 1970's.
Estimated Value: Excellent: $350.00
                  Very good: $275.00

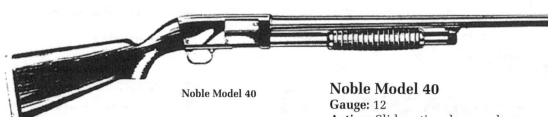

Noble Model 40

Noble Model 40

Gauge: 12
Action: Slide action; hammerless
Magazine: 5-shot tubular
Barrel: 28" with multi-choke
Finish: Blued; plain walnut pistol grip stock & grooved slide handle; recoil pad
Approximate wt.: 7½ lbs.
Comments: Made from the early to mid 1950's.
Estimated Value: Excellent: $160.00
                  Very good: $130.00

Noble Model 50

Basically the same gun as the Model 40 without recoil pad or "Multi-Choke."
Estimated Value: Excellent: $150.00
                  Very good: $120.00

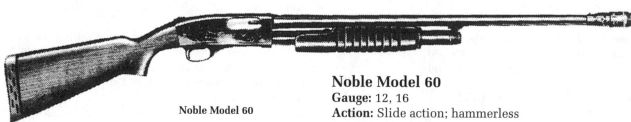

Noble Model 60

Noble Model 60

Gauge: 12, 16
Action: Slide action; hammerless
Magazine: 5-shot tubular
Barrel: 28" with variable choke
Finish: Blued; plain walnut pistol grip stock & grooved slide handle; recoil pad
Approximate wt.: 7½ lbs.
Comments: Manufactured in takedown version from the mid 1950's to late 1960's.
Estimated Value: Excellent: $160.00
                  Very good: $130.00

Noble Model 60 ACP

Very similar to Model 60 with a ventilated rib. Made from late 1960's to early 1970's.
Estimated Value: Excellent: $170.00
                  Very good: $140.00

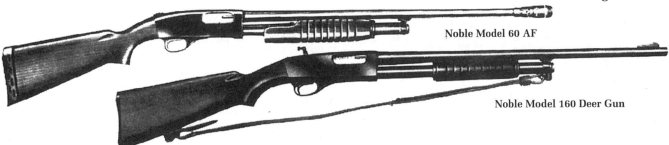

Noble Model 60 AF

Noble Model 160 Deer Gun

Noble Model 60 AF

A fancier version of the Model 60 with special steel barrel; select wood; fluted comb. Made only during the mid 1960's.

Estimated Value: Excellent: $175.00
Very good: $145.00

Noble Model 160 Deer Gun, 166L Deer Gun

Very similar to the Model 60 with a 24" barrel; sights; swivels. Made in the mid 1960's as 160 & from late 1960's to early 1970's as 166L.

Estimated Value: Excellent: $170.00
Very good: $160.00

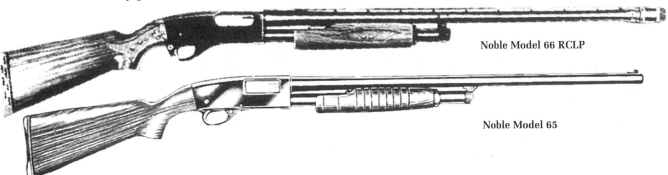

Noble Model 66 RCLP

Noble Model 65

Noble Model 65

Basically the same as the Model 60 without the recoil pad or adjustable choke.

Estimated Value: Excellent: $150.00
Very good: $125.00

Noble Model 66 RCLP

Similar to the Model 60 ACP with a fancier checkered stock.

Estimated Value: Excellent: $175.00
Very good: $150.00

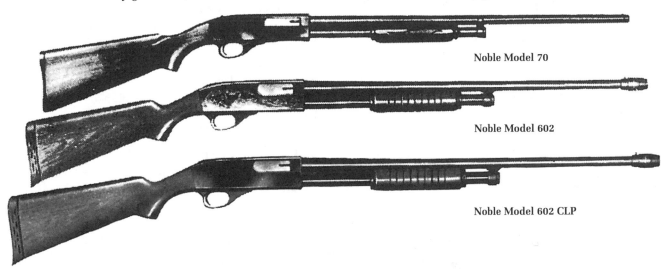

Noble Model 70

Noble Model 602

Noble Model 602 CLP

Noble Model 70 & 70X

Gauge: 410
Action: Slide action; hammerless
Magazine: 5-shot tubular
Barrel: 26" modified or full choke
Finish: Blued; checkered walnut pistol grip stock & slide handle
Approximate wt.: 6 lbs.
Comments: Made from the late 1950's to late 1960's as Model 70 & from the late 1960's to early 1970's as 70X.

Estimated Value: Excellent: $175.00
Very good: $145.00

Noble Model 602

Similar to the Model 70 in 20 gauge & 28" barrel; weighs 6½ lbs. Grooved slide handle.

Estimated Value: Excellent: $180.00
Very good: $145.00

Noble Model 602 CLP, 602 RCLP, 602 RLP

The 602 CLP is same as 602 with adjustable choke & recoil pad; 602 RCLP is same as 602 with recoil pad; 602 RLP is same as 602 with recoil pad & ventilated rib. Add $20.00 for ventilated rib.

Estimated Value: Excellent: $190.00
Very good: $150.00

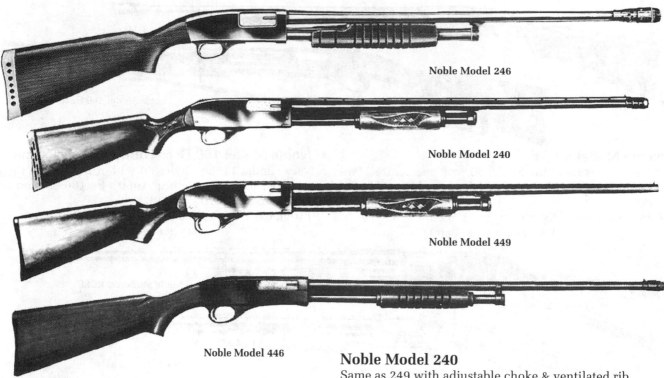

Noble Model 246

Noble Model 240

Noble Model 449

Noble Model 446

Noble Model 249

Gauge: 20
Action: Slide action; hammerless
Magazine: 5-shot tubular
Barrel: 28" modified or full choke
Finish: Blued; checkered walnut pistol grip stock & slide
   handle; recoil pad
Approximate wt.: 6½ lbs.
Comments: Produced in the early 1970's.
Estimated Value: Excellent: $170.00
                    Very good: $140.00

Noble Model 246

Same as 249 with adjustable choke.
Estimated Value: Excellent: $180.00
                    Very good: $145.00

Noble Model 243

Same as 249 with ventilated rib.
Estimated Value: Excellent: $185.00
                    Very good: $150.00

Noble Model 240

Same as 249 with adjustable choke & ventilated rib.
Estimated Value: Excellent: $200.00
                    Very good: $160.00

Noble Model 449

Similar to Model 249 without recoil pad & in 410 bore.
Estimated Value: Excellent: $180.00
                    Very good: $150.00

Noble Model 446

Similar to Model 246 without recoil pad & in 410 bore.
Estimated Value: Excellent: $185.00
                    Very good: $150.00

Noble Model 443

Similar to Model 243 without recoil pad & in 410 bore.
Estimated Value: Excellent: $190.00
                    Very good: $160.00

Noble Model 440

Similar to Model 240 without recoil pad & in 410 bore.
Estimated Value: Excellent: $195.00
                    Very good: $160.00

Noble Model 390 Deer Gun

Noble Model 390 Deer Gun

Similar to Model 339 with a 24" slug barrel; sights;
swivels.
Estimated Value: Excellent: $190.00
                    Very good: $150.00

Noble Model 339

Gauge: 12, 16
Action: Slide action; hammerless
Magazine: 6-shot tubular
Barrel: 28" modified or full choke
Finish: Blued; checkered walnut pistol grip stock & slide
   handle
Approximate wt.: 7½ lbs.
Comments: Made in the early 1970's.
Estimated Value: Excellent: $180.00
                    Very good: $140.00

Noble Model 330

Noble Model 330

Same as Model 339 with recoil pad, ventilated rib & adjustable choke.

Estimated Value: Excellent: $200.00
Very good: $160.00

Noble Model 336

Same as Model 339 with recoil pad & adjustable choke.

Estimated Value: Excellent: $190.00
Very good: $150.00

Noble Model 333

Same as Model 339 with recoil pad & ventilated rib.

Estimated Value: Excellent: $195.00
Very good: $155.00

Noble Model 80

Noble Model 757

Gauge: 20
Action: Slide action; hammerless
Magazine: 5-shot tubular
Barrel: 28" aluminum; adjustable choke
Finish: Black anodized aluminum; decorated receiver; checkered walnut pistol grip stock & slide handle; recoil pad
Approximate wt.: 4½ lbs.
Comments: A very light gun made in the early 1970's.
Estimated Value: Excellent: $195.00
Very good: $160.00

Noble Model 80

Gauge: 410
Action: Semi-automatic; hammerless
Magazine: 5-shot tubular
Barrel: 26" full choke
Finish: Blued; plain walnut pistol grip stock & forearm
Approximate wt.: 6 lbs.
Comments: Made in the mid 1960's.
Estimated Value: Excellent: $240.00
Very good: $200.00

Parker

Parker Single Barrel Trap

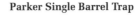

Parker Trojan

Parker Single Barrel Trap

Gauge: 12
Action: Slide action; hammerless; top lever break-open; box lock
Magazine: None
Barrel: 30", 32", 34", any choke; ventilated rib
Finish: Blued; checkered walnut straight, full or semi-pistol grip stock
Approximate wt.: 6½ to 7½ lbs.
Comments: Grades differ according to workmanship, checkering & engraving. Made from about 1917 to 1941. Manufacture of Parker guns was taken over by Remington in 1934 & this gun was called Remington Parker Model 930. There is a wide range of values for this gun. Prices for pre-1934 models.
Estimated Value: Excellent: $3,200.00 - $12,500.00
Very good: $2,150.00 - $10,750.00

Parker Trojan

Gauge: 12, 16, 20
Action: Top lever break-open; hammerless; box lock
Magazine: None
Barrel: Double barrel; 26", 28", 30", full & full or modified & full chokes
Finish: Blued; checkered walnut pistol grip stock & forearm
Approximate wt.: 6½ to 8 lbs.
Comments: Made from about 1915 to 1939.
Estimated Value: Excellent: $1,295.00
Very good: $1,050.00

Parker Hammerless Double

Gauge: 10, 12, 16, 20, 28, 410
Action: Box lock; top lever, break-open; hammerless; selective trigger & automatic ejectors after 1934
Magazine: None
Barrel: Double barrel; 26", 28", 30", 32"; any choke combination
Finish: Blued; checkered walnut straight, full or semi-pistol grip stock & forearm
Approximate wt.: 6½ to 8½ lbs.
Comments: Grades vary according to workmanship, checkering & engraving. Manufacture of Parker guns was taken over by Remington in 1934 & this gun was called Remington Parker Model 920 until it was discontinued in 1941. Prices for pre-1934 models.
Estimated Value: Excellent: $2,250.00 - $54,000.00
                        Very good: $1,295.00 - $21,000.00

Parker Hammerless Double G.H.E.

Parker Hammerless Double A.H.E.

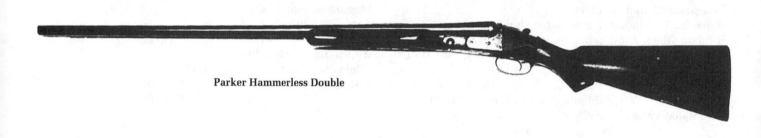

Parker Hammerless Double

Pedersen

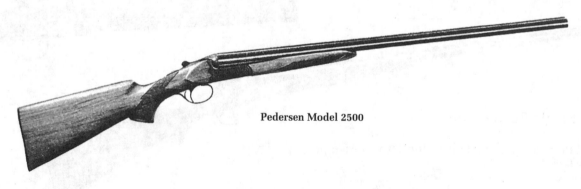

Pedersen Model 2500

Pedersen Model 2000 Grade II

Gauge: 12, 20
Action: Box lock; top lever, break-open; hammerless; automatic ejectors; single selective trigger
Magazine: None
Barrel: Double barrel; length to customer's specifications
Finish: Blued; checkered walnut pistol grip stock & tapered forearm; engraved
Approximate wt.: 7½ lbs.
Comments: Made in the mid 1970's.
Estimated Value: Excellent: $1,620.00
                        Very good: $1,295.00

Pedersen Model 2000 Grade I

Similar to Grade II with fancier engraving, gold filling on receiver, select walnut.
Estimated Value: Excellent: $1,950.00
                        Very good: $1,550.00

Pedersen Model 2500

A field version of the 2000; no engraving.
Estimated Value: Excellent: $485.00
                        Very good: $390.00

Pedersen Model 1000 Grade II

Pedersen Model 1000 Grade I

Pedersen Model 1500

Pedersen Model 4000 Deluxe

Pedersen Model 1000 Grade III

Gauge: 12, 20
Action: Box lock; top lever, break-open; hammerless; automatic ejectors; single selective trigger
Magazine: None
Barrel: Over & under double barrel; length made to customers specifications; ventilated rib
Finish: Blued; checkered walnut pistol grip stock & forearm; recoil pad
Approximate wt.: 7½ lbs.
Comments: Produced in the mid 1970's.
Estimated Value: Excellent: $875.00
  Very good: $690.00

Pedersen Model 1000 Grade II

Similar to Grade III with engraving & fancier wood; made to customers specs. Add $15.00 for magnum.
Estimated Value: Excellent: $1,870.00
  Very good: $1,490.00

Pedersen Model 1000 Grade I

Similar to Grade II with extensive engraving, select wood, gold filling on receiver; made to customers specs; in hunting, skeet or trap models.
Estimated Value: Excellent: $2,250.00
  Very good: $1,815.00

Pedersen Model 1500

A field version of the 1000 with standard barrel lengths only (26", 28", 30" or 32").
Estimated Value: Excellent: $550.00
  Very good: $435.00

Pedersen Model 4000 Deluxe

Gauge: 10, 12, 410
Action: Slide action; hammerless; side ejection
Magazine: Tubular
Barrel: 26", 28", 30", variety of chokes; ventilated rib
Finish: Blued; checkered walnut pistol grip stock & slide handle; recoil pad; floral engraving on receiver
Approximate wt.: 6¾ lbs.
Comments: Made in the mid 1970's.
Estimated Value: Excellent: $435.00
  Very good: $345.00

Premier

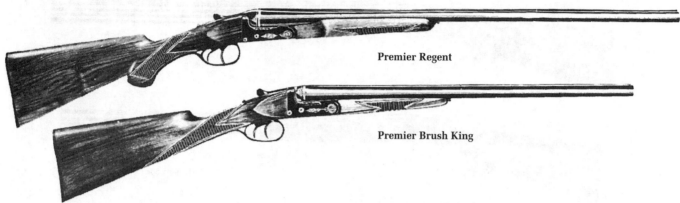

Premier Regent

Premier Brush King

Premier Regent

Gauge: 12, 16, 20, 28, 410
Action: Box lock; top lever, break-open; hammerless; double triggers
Magazine: None
Barrel: Side by side double barrel; 26", 28" modified & full chokes; matte rib
Finish: Blued; checkered walnut pistol grip stock & tapered forearm
Approximate wt.: 7 lbs.
Comments: Produced from the 1950's to the 1970's.
Estimated Value: Excellent: $295.00
                       Very good: $240.00

Premier Brush King

Similar to Regent except: 12 & 20 gauge only; 22" improved cyl. & modified choke barrels; straight stock.
Estimated Value: Excellent: $310.00
                       Very good: $245.00

Premier Magnum

Similar to Regent except: 10 gauge magnum with 32" barrels or 12 gauge magnum with 30" barrels; both gauges in full & full choke; recoil pad; beavertail forearm. Add $25.00 for 10 gauge magnum.
Estimated Value: Excellent: $325.00
                       Very good: $260.00

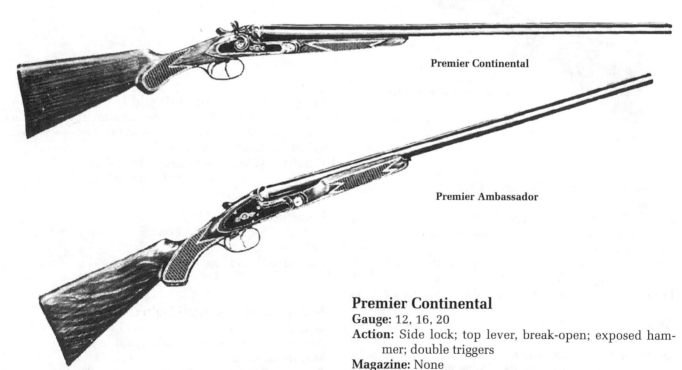

Premier Continental

Premier Ambassador

Premier Ambassador

A hammerless version of the Continental. Also available in 410 gauge.
Estimated Value: Excellent: $380.00
                       Very good: $300.00

Premier Continental

Gauge: 12, 16, 20
Action: Side lock; top lever, break-open; exposed hammer; double triggers
Magazine: None
Barrel: Side by side double barrel; 26" mod. & full choke
Finish: Blued; checkered walnut pistol grip stock & tapered forearm
Approximate wt.: 7 lbs.
Comments: Produced from the 1950's to the 1970's.
Estimated Value: Excellent: $400.00
                       Very good: $320.00

Remington

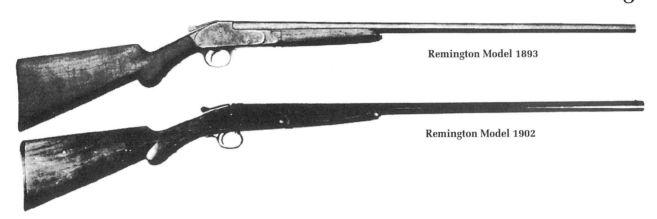

Remington Model 1893

Remington Model 1902

Remington Model 1893

Gauge: 10, 12, 16, 20
Action: Top lever break-open; semi-hammer (cocking lever on left), takedown; single shot
Magazine: None
Barrel: 28", 30", 32" or 34"; plain barrel with bead sight
Finish: Blued; case hardened receiver; smooth walnut, pistol grip stock & forearm
Approximate wt.: 5½ to 6½ lbs.
Comments: Made from about 1893 to 1906. Approximately 25,000 were produced. Also known as the Model No. 3 & the '93.
Estimated Value: Excellent: $200.00
Very good: $160.00

Remington Model 1902 or No. 9

Similar to the Model 1893 except improved with automatic ejector. Made from about 1902 to 1912. Also called Model No. 9.
Estimated Value: Excellent: $210.00
Very good: $165.00

Remington Parker 930

Remington took over production of the Parker shotguns from 1934 to 1941; single shot hammerless.
Estimated Value: Excellent: $1,650.00 - $2,700.00
Very good: $1,100.00 - $2,150.00

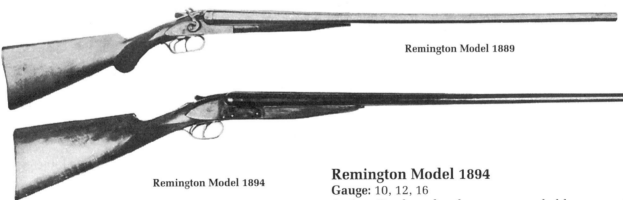

Remington Model 1889

Remington Model 1894

Remington Model 1889

Gauge: 10, 12, 16
Action: Top lever break-open; side lock; breech loading black powder; exposed hammers; double trigger
Magazine: None
Barrel: Side by side double barrel; 28"-32" full, modified or cylinder bore; Damascus or steel
Finish: Blued; checkered walnut semi-pistol grip stock & short forearm
Approximate wt.: 7½ to 9 lbs.
Comments: Made from about 1889 to 1909 in seven grades. Approximately 30,000 produced. Prices are for Standard Grade.
Estimated Value: Excellent: $600.00
Very good: $490.00

Remington Model 1894

Gauge: 10, 12, 16
Action: Top lever break-open; concealed hammers; triple lock; double triggers; some models have automatic ejectors
Magazine: None
Barrel: Side by side double barrel; 26"-32" tapered barrels; full, modified or cylinder bore; ordnance steel or Damascus barrels with concave matted rib
Finish: Blued; checkered walnut, straight or semi-pistol grip stock & short tapered forearm; special engraving & inlays on higher grades
Approximate wt.: 7½ to 8½ lbs.
Comments: Made from about 1894 to 1910 in seven grades. Receivers marked Remington Arms Co. on left side. Prices for Standard Grade. Deduct $125.00 for Damascus barrels.
Estimated Value: Excellent: $750.00
Very good: $600.00

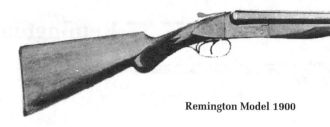

Remington Model 1900

Remington Model 1900

Gauge: 12, 16
Action: Top lever break-open; concealed hammer; double triggers; automatic ejectors optional
Magazine: None
Barrel: Side by side double barrel; 28" or 32" steel or Damascus in standard chokes; matted rib
Finish: Checkered walnut pistol grip stock & short tapered forearm with gap at front for disassembly
Approximate wt.: 8 to 9 lbs.
Comments: Similar to Model 1894 except: lower grade; takedown model; internal forearm release. Made from about 1900 to 1910. Deduct $100.00 for Damascus barrels.
Estimated Value: Excellent: $540.00
                            Very good: $430.00

Remington Parker 920

Remington took over production of Parker shotguns from 1934 to 1941; double barrel hammerless; double triggers; 12 gauge.
Estimated Value: Excellent: $1,075.00
                            Very good: $ 825.00

Remington Model 32

Remington Model 3200 Field Grade

Remington Model 3200 Magnum

Remington Model 3200 Field Grade

Gauge: 12
Action: Top lever break-open; concealed hammer; selective single trigger; automatic ejectors
Magazine: None
Barrel: 26"-30" over & under double barrel; ventilated rib; modified & full or improved cylinder & modified chokes
Finish: Blued; pointing dogs engraved on receiver; checkered walnut pistol grip stock & matching forearm
Approximate wt.: 7¾ to 8¾ lbs.
Comments: A modern version of the Model 32 started back in production in the early 1970's. Still available in Trap & Skeet models. Other models valued higher than Field Grade.
Estimated Value: Excellent: $940.00
                            Very good: $750.00

Remington Model 32

Gauge: 12
Action: Top lever break-open; concealed hammers; single selective trigger; automatic ejectors
Magazine: None
Barrel: Over & under double barrel; 26-32" plain, solid or ventilated rib; full & modified choke standard but any combination available
Finish: Blued; engraved receiver; checkered walnut pistol grip stock & forearm
Approximate wt.: 7¾ to 8½ lbs.
Comments: One of the first modern American over & under double barrel shotguns produced. Made from about 1932 to 1942. Made in about six grades, high grades with fancier wood & engravings. Add $35.00 for solid rib; $50.00 for ventilated rib.
Estimated Value: Excellent: $825.00
                            Very good: $660.00

Remington Model 3200 Magnum

Similar to the Model 3200 Field Grade except: chambered for 12 gauge magnum; 30" barrels in full & full or modified & full chokes; receiver decorated with engraved scrollwork.
Estimated Value: Excellent: $1,070.00
                            Very good: $ 855.00

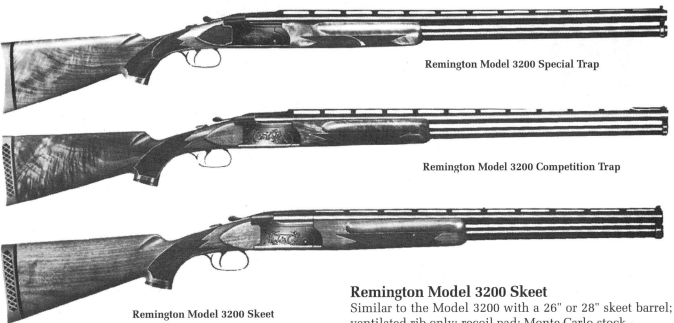

Remington Model 3200 Special Trap

Remington Model 3200 Competition Trap

Remington Model 3200 Skeet

Remington Model 3200 Skeet
Similar to the Model 3200 with a 26" or 28" skeet barrel; ventilated rib only; recoil pad; Monte Carlo stock.
Estimated Value: Excellent: $1,100.00
                   Very good: $ 825.00

Remington Model 3200 Special Trap
Similar to the Model 3200 with a 32" barrel; ventilated rib only; Monte Carlo stock available; recoil pad.
Estimated Value: Excellent: $1,200.00
                   Very good: $ 950.00

Remington Model 3200 Competition Trap
Similar to the Model 3200 Special Trap with a higher quality finish. Monte Carlo stock available. Discontinued in 1983.
Estimated Value: Excellent: $1,300.00
                   Very good: $ 975.00

Remington Model 3200 Competition Skeet
Similar to the Model 3200 Skeet with a higher quality finish. Discontinued in 1983.
Estimated Value: Excellent: $1,300.00
                   Very good: $ 975.00

Remington Model 3200 Pigeon
Similar to the Model 3200 Competition Skeet with 28" improved modified & full choke barrels for live birds. Discontinued in 1983.
Estimated Value: Excellent: $1,320.00
                   Very good: $1,000.00

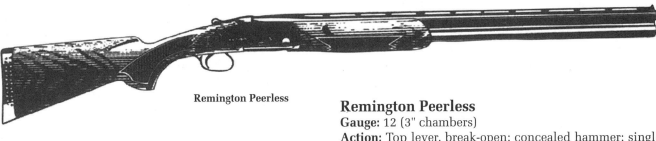

Remington Peerless

Remington Peerless
Gauge: 12 (3" chambers)
Action: Top lever, break-open; concealed hammer; single selective trigger; automatic ejectors; top tang automatic safety
Magazine: None
Barrel: 26", 28", or 30" over & under double barrel; ventilated rib; improved cylinder, modified, and full choke Remchoke tubes
Finish: Blued; removable engraved (bird hunting scenes) side plates on action; checkered American Walnut pistol grip stock and forearm
Approximate wt.: 7½ lbs.
Comments: Introduced in 1993.
Estimated Value: New (Retail): $1,225.00
                       Excellent: $ 920.00
                       Very good: $ 735.00

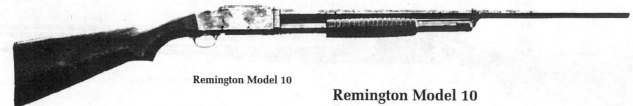

Remington Model 10

Remington Model 1908

Gauge: 12

Action: Slide action; hammerless; bottom ejection; repeating

Magazine: 5-shot tubular

Barrel: 26"-32" steel barrel in full, modified or cylinder bore

Finish: Blued; plain or checkered walnut straight or pistol grip stock & forearm

Approximate wt.: 7½ to 8 lbs.

Comments: Made from about 1908 to 1910 in six grades with fancy checkering & engraving on higher grades. Marking on top of barrel "Remington Arms Co." & patent date. About 10,000 made.

Estimated Value: Excellent: $325.00
                      Very good: $250.00

Remington Model 10

Gauge: 12

Action: Slide action; hammerless; bottom ejection; repeating

Magazine: 5-shot tubular

Barrel: 26"-32" steel barrel in full, modified or cylinder bore

Finish: Blued; plain or checkered walnut straight or pistol grip stock & forearm

Approximate wt.: 7½ to 8 lbs.

Comments: Made from about 1910 to 1929, an improved version of the Model 1908. Made in seven grades with fancy checkering & engraving on higher grades. Also produced in 20" barrel riot gun. Solid rib optional from 1910 to 1922; ventilated rib optional from 1922 to 1928. Prices are for Standard Grade.

Estimated Value: Excellent: $350.00
                      Very good: $275.00

Remington Model 29

Remington Model 17

Gauge: 20

Action: Slide action; hammerless; bottom ejection; repeating

Magazine: 3-shot tubular

Barrel: 26"-32" steel in full, modified or cylinder bore; matted sighting groove on receiver or optional solid rib; 20" barrel on riot gun

Finish: Blued; plain or checkered walnut pistol grip stock & forearm

Approximate wt.: 7½ to 8 lbs.

Comments: Made from about 1917 to 1933 in seven grades. Higher grades have higher quality finish.

Estimated Value: Excellent: $310.00
                      Very good: $250.00

Remington Model 29

Gauge: 12

Action: Slide action; hammerless; bottom ejection; repeating

Magazine: 5-shot tubular

Barrel: 26"-32" steel in full, modified or cylinder bore; optional solid or ventilated rib; 20" barrel on riot gun

Finish: Blued; plain or checkered walnut pistol grip stock & forearm

Approximate wt.: 7½ to 8 lbs.

Comments: Made from about 1929 to 1933 in nine grades. Higher grades have higher quality finish. Prices are for Standard Grade.

Estimated Value: Excellent: $300.00
                      Very good: $240.00

Remington Model 31

Gauge: 12, 16, 20

Action: Slide action; hammerless; side ejection; repeating

Magazine: 3-shot tubular or 5-shot tubular

Barrel: 26", 32" steel; full, modified, cylinder or skeet chokes; optional solid or ventilated rib

Finish: Blued; slightly groove on receiver; plain or checkered pistol grip stock & forearm; forearm checkered or grooved

Approximate wt.: 6½ to 8 lbs.

Comments: Made from about 1931 to 1949 in eight grades. Higher grades differ in quality of finish. Prices for Standard Grades. Add $20.00 for solid rib; $25.00 for ventilated rib.

Estimated Value: Excellent: $320.00
                      Very good: $260.00

Remington Model 31 Skeet

Similar to the Model 31 except: 12 gauge only; 26" barrel; solid or ventilated rib; skeet choke. Add $20.00 for ventilated rib.

Estimated Value: Excellent: $485.00
                      Very good: $390.00

Remington Model 31 R Riot Gun

Similar to the Model 31 in 12 gauge only with 20" plain barrel.

Estimated Value: Excellent: $245.00
                      Very good: $195.00

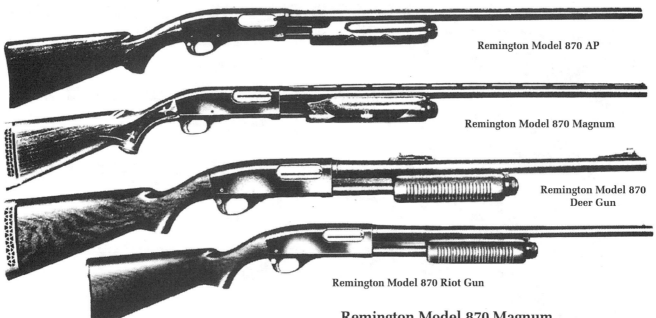

Remington Model 870 AP

Remington Model 870 Magnum

Remington Model 870 Deer Gun

Remington Model 870 Riot Gun

Remington Model 870 AP

Gauge: 12, 16, 20
Action: Slide action; hammerless; side ejection; repeating
Magazine: 4-shot tubular
Barrel: 26", 28", 30" in 12 gauge; 26" or 28" in 16 & 20 gauge; full, modified or improved cylinder bore; plain or ventilated rib
Finish: Blued; plain or fancy; fluted comb, pistol grip stock & grooved slide handle
Approximate wt.: 6½ to 8 lbs.
Comments: Made in many styles, grades & variations from about 1950 to 1964. Higher grades have higher quality finish. Prices for Standard Grade. Add $25.00 for ventilated rib.
Estimated Value: Excellent: $290.00
                        Very good: $230.00

Remington Model 870 Magnum

Similar to the Model 870 AP except: 12 gauge magnum; 30" full choke barrel; recoil pad. Made from about 1955 to 1964. Add $25.00 for ventilated rib.
Estimated Value: Excellent: $300.00
                        Very good: $240.00

Remington Model 870 Riot Gun

Same as the Model 870 AP except: 12 gauge only; 20" plain barrel; improved cylinder bore.
Estimated Value: Excellent: $275.00
                        Very good: $220.00

Remington Model 870 Deer Gun

Similar to the Model 870 AP except: 12 gauge only; 26" barrel for slugs; rifle type adjustable sights. Made from about 1959 to 1964.
Estimated Value: Excellent: $270.00
                        Very good: $215.00

Remington Model 870 Wingmaster

Remington Model 870 Special Purpose

Similar to the Model 870 with oil-finish wood & Parkerized metal; recoil pad & nylon camo strap; 12 gauge; ventilated rib, 26" or 30" barrel. Introduced in 1985. "Rem Choke." Deduct 20% for synthetic stock.
Estimated Value: New (retail): $483.00
                        Excellent: $360.00
                        Very good: $290.00

Remington Model 870 SP Deer Gun

Similar to the 870 Special Purpose with 20" improved cylinder or rifled barrel & rifle sights. Introduced in 1986.
Estimated Value: New (retail): $423.00
                        Excellent: $315.00
                        Very good: $250.00

Remington Model 870 Wingmaster Field Gun

Gauge: 12, 16, 20; 28; 410 added in 1969; 16 gauge discontinued in the late 1980's.
Action: Slide action; hammerless; side ejection; repeating
Magazine: 4-shot tubular
Barrel: 26"-30" in 12 gauge; 26" or 28" in 16 & 20 gauge; 25" in 28 & 410 bore; full, modified or improved cylinder bore; plain barrel or ventilated rib; "Rem Choke"
Finish: Blued; checkered walnut pistol grip stock with matching slide handle; recoil pad
Approximate wt.: 6½ to 7¼ lbs.
Comments: Improved version of the Model 870AP. Made in many grades & styles from about 1964 to present. Left hand models available & also lightweight models. Prices for standard grades. Add 10% for left hand model. Add 8% for gauges 28 or 410.
Estimated Value: New (retail): $492.00
                        Excellent: $370.00
                        Very good: $295.00

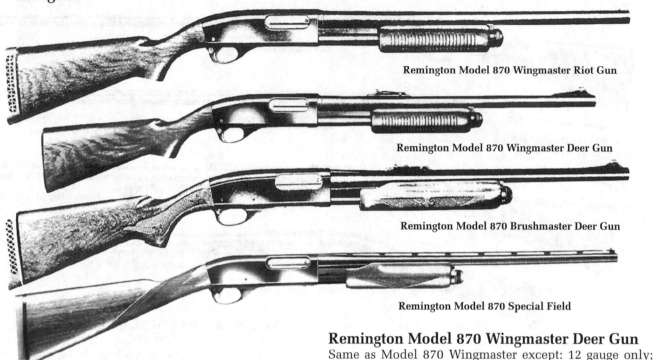

Remington Model 870 Wingmaster Riot Gun

Remington Model 870 Wingmaster Deer Gun

Remington Model 870 Brushmaster Deer Gun

Remington Model 870 Special Field

Remington Model 870 Wingmaster Riot Gun, Police

Similar to the Model 870 Wingmaster except: 12 gauge only; 18" or 20" improved cylinder barrel; plain stock & grooved slide handle; designed for law enforcement use. Add 8% for rifle sights. Blued or parkerized finish.

Estimated Value: Excellent: $280.00
                    Very good: $225.00

Remington Model 870 Wingmaster Magnum

Same as the Model 870 Field Grade except: 12 or 20 magnum gauge only; full or modified choke. Add $30.00 for left hand model; add 10% for "Rem Choke."

Estimated Value: Excellent: $350.00
                    Very good: $280.00

Remington Model 870 Wingmaster Deer Gun

Same as Model 870 Wingmaster except: 12 gauge only; 20" barrel; rifle sights. Produced from 1964 to mid 1980's.

Estimated Value: Excellent: $340.00
                    Very good: $275.00

Remington Model 870 Brushmaster Deer Gun

Same as the Model 870 Wingmaster Deer Gun except: 12 & 20 gauge; checkered stock & slide; recoil pad. Left hand version introduced in 1983; discontinued in mid 1990's. Add 8% for 12 gauge.

Estimated Value: Excellent: $340.00
                    Very good: $275.00

Remington Model 870 Special Field

Similar to the Model 870 with a straight grip stock, 21" or 23" ventilated rib barrel; 12 or 20 gauge; 3" chamber. Introduced in 1984; discontinued in mid 1990's. Some models have "Rem Choke."

Estimated Value: Excellent: $355.00
                    Very good: $285.00

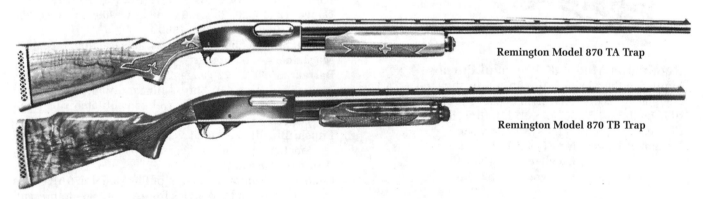

Remington Model 870 TA Trap

Remington Model 870 TB Trap

Remington Model 870 SA Skeet

Similar to the Model 870 except: skeet choke; ventilated rib only; recoil pad. Made from the late 1970's to early 1980's; 25" or 26" barrel.

Estimated Value: Excellent: $325.00
                    Very good: $260.00

Remington Model 870 TB Trap, TA Trap, TC Trap

Similar to the Model 870 with a 30" full choke barrel; ventilated rib; recoil pad; choice of Monte Carlo stock.

Estimated Value: Excellent: $400.00
                    Very good: $320.00

Remington Model 870 Competition Trap

Similar to the Model 870; single shot; 30" full choke; ventilated rib barrel; recoil pad; non-glare matte finish receiver. Introduced in 1982.

Estimated Value: Excellent: $615.00
                    Very good: $490.00

Remington Model 870 Ltd. 20

Same as the Model 870 Wingmaster Field except: 20 gauge only; 23" barrel with ventilated rib; lightweight. Made from 1980 to 1984.

Estimated Value: Excellent: $335.00
                    Very good: $265.00

Remington Model 870SP Cantilever

Same as the Model 870SP Deer Gun except: no sights; equipped with cantilever scope mount, rings & changeable choke tubes (rifled choke tube for slugs & improved cylinder choke tube). Introduced in 1989.

Estimated Value: New (retail): $483.00
                    Excellent: $360.00
                    Very good: $290.00

Remington Model 870 Youth Gun

Same as the Model 870 Wingmaster Field except: 20 gauge only; 21" barrel with ventilated rib; lightweight; short stock (12½" length of pull). Made from 1984 to present; changeable choke tubes after 1985; Add 10% for Rifled deer barrel with sights

Estimated Value: New (retail): $292.00
                    Excellent: $220.00
                    Very good: $180.00

Remington Model 870 Express

Gauge: 12, 20, 28, or .410 (magnums)
Action: Slide action; hammerless; side ejection repeating
Magazine: 4-shot tubular
Barrel: **20", 21", 25",** 26" or 28" ventilated rib; "Rem Choke" or rifled deer barrel with sights
Finish: Blued; checkered hardwood or synthetic pistol grip stock & forearm
Approximate wt.: **6 to** 7¼ lbs.
Comments: Introduced in 1987. Add 10% for rifled barrel.

Estimated Value: New (retail): $292.00
                    Excellent: $220.00
                    Very good: $180.00

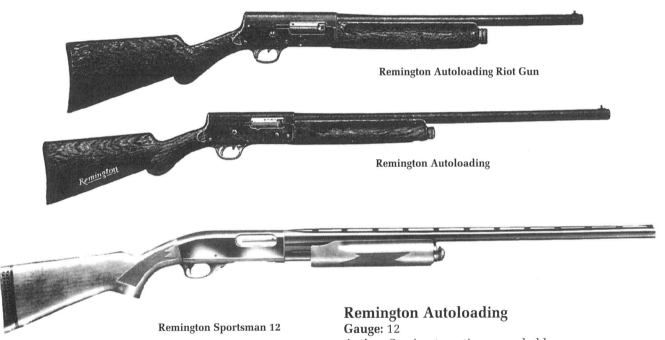

Remington Autoloading Riot Gun

Remington Autoloading

Remington Sportsman 12

Remington Sportsman 12 Pump

Gauge: 12, regular or magnum
Action: Slide action; hammerless; side ejection; repeating
Magazine: 4-shot tubular
Barrel: 28" modified, 30" full; ventilated rib
Finish: Blued; checkered walnut semi-pistol grip stock & slide handle; steel receiver; recoil pad
Approximate wt.: 6½ to 7½ lbs.
Comments: Introduced in 1984; discontinued in late 1980's. Add $25.00 for "Rem Choke."

Estimated Value: Excellent: $270.00
                    Very good: $215.00

Remington Autoloading

Gauge: 12
Action: Semi-automatic; concealed hammer
Magazine: 5-shot tubular
Barrel: 26", 28" steel; full, modified or cylinder bore
Finish: Blued; matted sight groove; plain or checkered straight or pistol grip stock & forearm
Approximate wt.: 7¾ lbs.
Comments: Made from about 1905 to 1910 in six grades. Prices for Standard Grade.

Estimated Value: Excellent: $275.00
                    Very good: $220.00

Remington Autoloading Riot Gun

Similar to Autoloading except: 20" barrel; weighs 6¾ lbs.
Estimated Value: Excellent: $280.00
                    Very good: $225.00

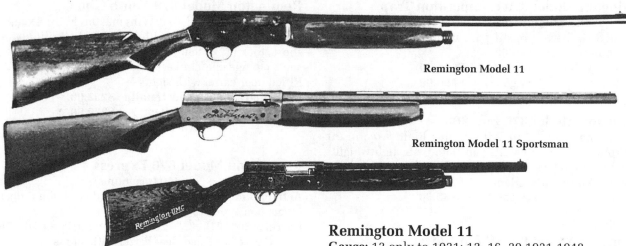

Remington Model 11

Remington Model 11 Sportsman

Remington Model 11 Riot Gun

Remington Model 11 Sportsman

Same as the Model 11 with a 2-shot magazine. Made from about 1931 to 1948 in six grades. Prices for the Standard Grade. Add $15.00 for solid rib; $25.00 for ventilated rib.

Estimated Value: Excellent: $350.00
                    Very good: $280.00

Remington Model 11 Riot Gun

Same as the Model 11 except with a 20" plain barrel.

Estimated Value: Excellent: $260.00
                    Very good: $210.00

Remington Model 11

Gauge: 12 only to 1931; 12, 16, 20 1931-1948
Action: Semi-automatic; concealed hammer; side ejection; repeating
Magazine: 4-shot, bottom load
Barrel: 26" or 28" to 1931; 26", 28", 30", 32" 1931-1948; full, modified or cylinder
Finish: Blued; wood semi-pistol grip stock; straight grip on Trap grades; checkering & fancy wood on higher grades
Approximate wt.: 7½ to 8½ lbs.
Comments: Made from about 1911 to 1948 in six grades. Optional solid or ventilated rib available; rounded grip ends on stock from 1911 to 1916. Prices are for Standard Grade. Add $15.00 for ribbed barrel.

Estimated Value: Excellent: $280.00
                    Very good: $225.00

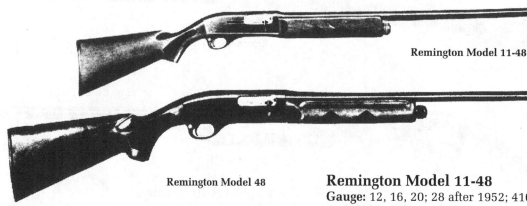

Remington Model 11-48

Remington Model 48

Remington Model 11-48 Riot Gun

Same general specifications as the Model 11-48 except: 12 gauge only; 20" plain barrel. Made from about 1954 to 1968.

Estimated Value: Excellent: $260.00
                    Very good: $210.00

Remington Model 48

Similar to the Model 11-48 except: 2-shot magazine; 12, 16, 20 gauge. Made from about 1948 to 1959 in several grades to replace the Model 11 Sportsman. Prices for Standard Model. Add $30.00 for ventilated rib.

Estimated Value: Excellent: $240.00
                    Very good: $195.00

Remington Model 11-48

Gauge: 12, 16, 20; 28 after 1952; 410 after 1954
Action: Semi-automatic; hammerless; side ejection; take down; cross bolt safety
Magazine: 4-shot tubular; 3-shot in 28 & 410 gauge
Barrel: 26", 28", 30" in 12, 16, & 20 gauge; 25" in 28 & 410 bore; full, modified or improved cylinder
Finish: Checkered walnut pistol grip stock with fluted comb, matching semi-beavertail forearm; higher grades are fancier
Approximate wt.: 6½ to 7½ lbs.
Comments: Made from about 1949 to 1968 in about seven grades. Replacing the Model 11, it had an improved action & the rear of the receiver was rounded off flush with the stock. Prices are for Standard Model. Add $30.00 for ventilated rib.

Estimated Value: Excellent: $285.00
                    Very good: $225.00

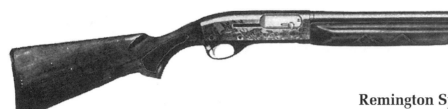

Remington Sportsman 58

Remington Sportsman 58 Magnum

Similar to the Sportsman 58 except: 12 gauge magnum; 30" barrel; recoil pad. Made from the late 1950's to early 1960's. Add $30.00 for ventilated rib.

Estimated Value: Excellent: $320.00
                Very good: $260.00

Remington Sportsman 58 Rifled Slug Special

Same as the Sportsman 58 except: 12 gauge only; 26" barrel for slugs; equipped with rifle sights.

Estimated Value: Excellent: $295.00
                Very good: $240.00

Remington Sportsman 58

Gauge: 12, 16, 20
Action: Semi-automatic; hammerless; side ejection; solid breech; gas operated sliding bolt; fixed barrel
Magazine: 2-shot tubular
Barrel: 26", 28", 30"; plain or ventilated rib; full, modified, improved cylinder or skeet chokes
Finish: Blued; checkered walnut pistol grip stock with fluted comb & matching semi-beavertail forearm
Approximate wt.: 6½ to 7½ lbs.
Comments: Made from about 1956 to 1963. Prices for Standard Model. Add $30.00 for ventilated rib.

Estimated Value: Excellent: $300.00
                Very good: $240.00

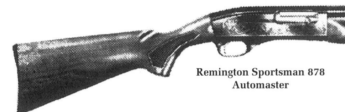

Remington Sportsman 878
Automaster

Remington Sportsman 12 Auto

Gauge: 12
Action: Gas operated semi-automatic
Magazine: 4-shot tubular
Barrel: 28" modified, 30" full; ventilated rib; "Rem Choke" available
Finish: Checkered hardwood semi-pistol grip stock & forearm
Approximate wt.: 7¾ lbs.
Comments: Produced in the mid 1980's. Add $30.00 for "Rem Choke."

Estimated Value: Excellent: $370.00
                Very good: $290.00

Remington Model 878 Automaster

Gauge: 12
Action: Semi-automatic; gas operated; hammerless
Magazine: 2-shot tubular
Barrel: 26"-30"; full, modified, improved cylinder or skeet chokes
Finish: Blued; plain or checkered walnut pistol grip stock & forearm
Approximate wt.: 7 lbs.
Comments: Made similar to the Sportsman 58 to fill in the sales line with a lower priced, plain, standard grade shotgun. Made from about 1959 to 1962 in two grades. Prices for Standard Model. Add $30.00 for ventilated rib.

Estimated Value: Excellent: $280.00
                Very good: $225.00

Remington Model 1100 Field Grade

Remington Model 1100 Ltd. 20

Same as the Model 1100 Field except: 20 gauge only; 23" ventilated rib barrel; lightweight; made from 1980 to 1984.

Estimated Value: Excellent: $425.00
                Very good: $335.00

Remington Model 1100 Youth Gun

Same as the Model 1100 Field except: 20 gauge only; 21" ventilated rib barrel; lightweight; short stock (12½" length of pull). Made from 1984 to present. Changeable choke tubes after 1985; Add $13.00 for Rem-choke.

Estimated Value: New (retail): $625.00
                Excellent: $470.00
                Very good: $375.00

Remington Model 1100 Field Grade

Gauge: 12, 16, 20; 28 & 410 after 1970; 16 discontinued
Action: Semi-automatic; gas operated sliding bolt; fixed barrel; solid breech; hammerless; takedown
Magazine: 4-shot tubular
Barrel: 26", 28" in 16 & 20 gauge; 26", 28", 30" in 12 gauge; 25" in 28 & 410; full, modified, improved cylinder & skeet chokes; ventilated rib available
Finish: Blued; checkered wood pistol grip stock with fluted comb & matching forearm; engraved receiver
Approximate wt.: 6½ to 7½ lbs.
Comments: An improved, low-recoil shotgun to replace the 58, 11-48 & 878. Made from about 1963 to present in several grades. Add $13.00 for "Rem Choke." Add 8% for gauges 28 or 410.

Estimated Value: New (retail): $625.00
                Excellent: $470.00
                Very good: $375.00

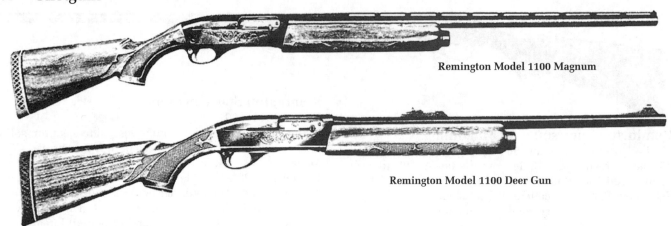

Remington Model 1100 Magnum

Remington Model 1100 Deer Gun

Remington Model 1100 Magnum

Similar to the Model 1100 except: 12 or 20 gauge magnum; 28" or 30" barrel; full or modified chokes; recoil pad. Add $30.00 for left hand model.

Estimated Value: Excellent: $425.00
                    Very good: $340.00

Remington Model 1100 Deer Gun

Similar to the Model 1100 with a 22" plain barrel & adjustable rifle sights; bored for rifle slugs; 12 or 20 gauge lightweight. Left hand version introduced in 1983.

Estimated Value: New (retail): $584.00
                    Excellent: $440.00
                    Very good: $350.00

Remington Model 1100 Special Purpose

Similar to the Model 1100 with oil-finished wood & Parkerized metal; recoil pad & nylon camo strap; 12 gauge only; ventilated rib barrel. Introduced in 1985. Discontinued 1987.

Estimated Value: Excellent: $490.00
                    Very good: $395.00

Remington Model 1100 SP Deer Gun

Similar to the Model 1100 Special Purpose with a 21" improved cylinder barrel & rifle sights. Produced in mid 1980's.

Estimated Value: Excellent: $410.00
                    Very good: $325.00

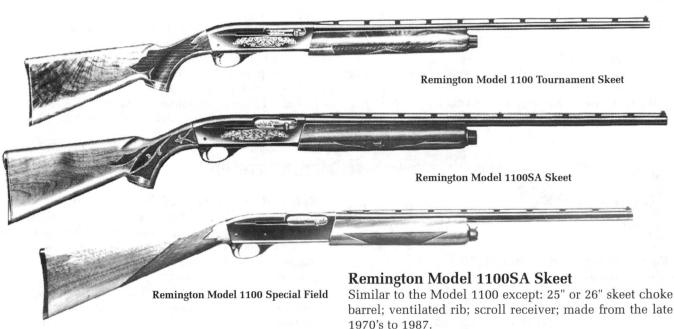

Remington Model 1100 Tournament Skeet

Remington Model 1100SA Skeet

Remington Model 1100 Special Field

Remington Model 1100 Special Field

Similar to the Model 1100 except: straight grip stock & 21" or 23" ventilated rib barrel; 12 gauge or LT 20 Model, 2¾" chamber. Introduced in 1983.

Estimated Value: New (retail): $625.00
                    Excellent: $470.00
                    Very good: $375.00

Remington Model 1100SA Skeet

Similar to the Model 1100 except: 25" or 26" skeet choke barrel; ventilated rib; scroll receiver; made from the late 1970's to 1987.

Estimated Value: Excellent: $460.00
                    Very good: $365.00

Remington Model 1100 Tournament Skeet

Similar to the Model 1100SA Skeet with higher quality finish.

Estimated Value: Excellent: $485.00
                    Very good: $390.00

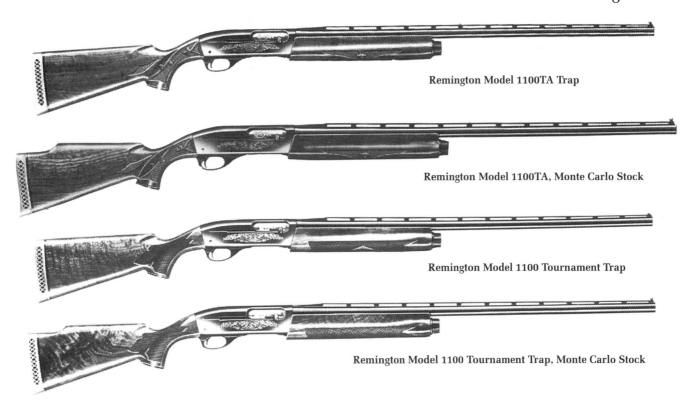

Remington Model 1100TA Trap

Remington Model 1100TA, Monte Carlo Stock

Remington Model 1100 Tournament Trap

Remington Model 1100 Tournament Trap, Monte Carlo Stock

Remington Model 1100TA Trap

Similar to the Model 1100 with a 30" full or modified trap barrel; ventilated rib only; recoil pad; choice of Monte Carlo stock (add $10.00). Add $30.00 for left hand model. Discontinued in 1987.

Estimated Value: Excellent: $510.00
Very good: $410.00

Remington Model 1100 Tournament Trap

Similar to the Model 1100 TA Trap with higher quality finish. Add $10.00 for Monte Carlo stock. Discontinued in 1987.

Estimated Value: Excellent: $610.00
Very good: $485.00

Remington Model 11-87 Premiere

Remington Model SP-10

Gauge: 10

Action: Gas operated (non-corrosive stainless steel gas system) semi-automatic; safety in rear of trigger guard

Magazine: 3-shot tubular

Barrel: 26" or 30" matte, non-reflective blued finish with ventilated rib; full & modified choke tubes

Finish: Checkered walnut pistol grip stock & forearm with low gloss satin finish to reduce glare or camo.

Approximate wt.: 11 lbs. (26" barrel); 11¼ lbs. (30" barrel)

Comments: Introduced in 1989. Some critical components of the Model SP-10 & other Remington 10 gauge shotguns are not interchangeable. Add 9% for camo finish.

Estimated Value: New (retail): $1,033.00
Excellent: $775.00
Very good: $620.00

Remington Model 11-87 Premiere

Gauge: 12, regular or magnum, interchangeably

Action: Gas operated, semi-automatic

Magazine: 3-shot tubular

Barrel: 26", 28" or 30" with "Rem Choke"

Finish: Blued; checkered walnut pistol grip stock & forearm

Approximate wt.: 8¼ lbs.

Comments: Right & left hand models available. Introduced in 1987. Add 10% for left hand model.

Estimated Value: New (retail): $670.00
Excellent: $500.00
Very good: $400.00

Remington Model 11-87 Premiere Trap

Similar to the Model 11-87 Premiere except: 30" barrel; Full choke or with "Rem Choke." Monte Carlo or regular stock. Add $13.00 for "Rem Choke" or Monte Carlo stock. Add 4% for sporting clay

Estimated Value: Excellent: $525.00
Very good: $420.00

Remington Model 11-87 Premiere Skeet

Similar to the Model 11-87 Premiere except: 26" skeet or "Rem Choke" barrel. Weight 7¾ lbs. Add $13.00 for "Rem Choke."

| Estimated Value: | Excellent: | $515.00 |
| | Very good: | $410.00 |

Remington Model 11-87 Special Purpose

Similar to the Model 11-87 Premier except: 26" or 30" "Rem Choke" barrel, non-glare finish, recoil pad, ventilated rib & camo strap. Introduced in 1987.

Estimated Value:	New (retail):	$644.00
	Excellent:	$480.00
	Very good:	$385.00

Remington Model 11-87 Cantilever

Same as the Model 11-87 Special Purpose Deer Gun except: no sights; equipped with cantilever scope mount, rings & changeable choke tubes (rifled choke tube for slugs & improved cylinder tube). Introduced in 1989.

Estimated Value:	New (retail):	$725.00
	Excellent:	$540.00
	Very good:	$435.00

Remington Model 11-87 Special Purpose Deer Gun

Similar to the Model 11-87 Special Purpose except: 21" improved cylinder barrel & rifle sights.

Estimated Value:	New (retail):	$624.00
	Excellent:	$470.00
	Very good:	$375.00

Richland

Richland Model 200

Gauge: 12, 16, 20, 28, 410
Action: Box lock; top lever, break-open; hammerless; double trigger
Magazine: None
Barrel: Side by side double barrel; 22" improved cylinder & modified in 20 gauge; 26", 28" improved & modified or modified & full chokes
Finish: Blued; checkered walnut pistol grip stock & tapered forearm; cheekpiece; recoil pad
Approximate wt.: 6 to 7 lbs.
Comments: Manufactured from the early 1960's to mid 1980's. Imported from Spain.

| Estimated Value: | Excellent: | $300.00 |
| | Very good: | $240.00 |

Richland Model 202

Same as the Model 200 with an extra set of barrels. Produced until the mid 1970's.

| Estimated Value: | Excellent: | $400.00 |
| | Very good: | $320.00 |

Richland Model 200

Richland Model 707 Deluxe

Gauge: 12, 20
Action: Box lock; top lever, break-open; hammerless; double trigger
Magazine: None
Barrel: **Side by side** double barrel; 26", 28", 30" variety of chokes
Finish: Blued; checkered walnut pistol grip stock & tapered forearm; recoil pad
Approximate wt.: 7 lbs.
Comments: Made from the mid 1960's to the mid 1970's.

| Estimated Value: | Excellent: | $335.00 |
| | Very good: | $270.00 |

Richland Model 707 Deluxe

Richland Model 711 Long Range Waterfowl

Richland Model 711 Long Range Waterfowl

Gauge: 10, 12, and 20; magnum
Action: Box lock; top lever, break-open; hammerless; double trigger
Magazine: None
Barrel: Side by side double barrel; 30", 32" full choke
Finish: Blued; checkered walnut pistol grip stock & tapered forearm
Approximate wt.: 8 to 10 lbs.
Comments: Made from the early 1960's. Made in 10 gauge magnum only from 1981 to 1985.

| Estimated Value: | Excellent: | $320.00 |
| | Very good: | $250.00 |

Richland Model 747

Gauge: 12 or 20, magnum
Action: Box lock; top lever, break-open; hammerless; single selective trigger
Magazine: None
Barrel: Over & under double barrel; 22" or 26" improved cylinder & modified, 28" modified & full
Finish: Blued; grey receiver; checkered walnut pistol grip stock & forearm; ventilated rib
Approximate wt.: 7 lbs.
Comments: Introduced in the mid 1980's.

| Estimated Value: | Excellent: | $365.00 |
| | Very good: | $295.00 |

Richland Model 808
Gauge: 12
Action: Box lock; top lever, break-open; hammerless; non-selective single trigger
Magazine: None
Barrel: Over & under double barrel; 26" improved cylinder & modified; 28" modified & full; 30" full & full
Finish: Blued; checkered walnut pistol grip stock & forearm; ribbed barrel
Approximate wt.: 7 lbs.
Comments: Made from the early to late 1960's.
Estimated Value: Excellent: $400.00
                         Very good: $320.00

Richland Model 844
Gauge: 12 magnum
Action: Box lock; top lever, break-open; hammerless; non-selective single trigger
Magazine: None
Barrel: Over & under double barrel; 26" improved cylinder & modified; 28" modified & full; 30" full & full
Finish: Blued; checkered walnut pistol grip stock & forearm; ribbed barrel
Approximate wt.: 7 lbs.
Comments: Made in the early 1970's.
Estimated Value: Excellent: $315.00
                         Very good: $250.00

Richland Model 828

Richland Model 808

Richland Model 828
Gauge: 28
Action: Box lock; top lever, break-open; hammerless
Magazine: None
Barrel: Over & under double barrel; 26" improved & modified; 28" modified & full chokes
Finish: Blued; case hardened receiver; checkered walnut pistol grip stock & forearm; ribbed barrel
Approximate wt.: 7 lbs.
Comments: Made in the early 1970's.
Estimated Value: Excellent: $380.00
                         Very good: $300.00

Richland Model 41 Ultra
Gauge: 410
Action: Box lock; top lever, break-open; hammerless; over & under double barrel; single non-selective trigger
Magazine: None
Barrel: Over & under double barrel; 26" chrome lined, modified & full; ventilated rib
Finish: Blued; grey engraved receiver; checkered walnut pistol grip stock & forearm
Approximate wt.: 6 lbs.
Comments: A lightweight 410 shotgun introduced in 1985.
Estimated Value: Excellent: $260.00
                         Very good: $210.00

Ruger

Ruger Over & Under "Red Label"

Ruger Over & Under "Red Label"
Gauge: 28, 20, 12 (3" chambers)
Action: Box lock; top lever, break-open; hammerless; single selective trigger
Magazine: None
Barrel: Over & under double barrel; 26" or 28" with a variety of screw-in choke combinations; ventilated rib; stainless steel receiver on 12 gauge beginning in 1986; stainless steel receiver on 20 gauge beginning in 1990
Finish: Checkered walnut, English straight grip or pistol grip stock & semi-beavertail forearm; recoil pad
Approximate wt.: 7 lbs.
Comments: Introduced in the late 1970's; 12 gauge model added in 1982. English stock introduced in 1992.
Estimated Value: New (retail): $1,215.00
                         Excellent: $ 910.00
                         Very good: $ 730.00

Ruger "Red Label" Sporting Clay
Similar to Ruger Over & Under Red Label except: 12 & 20 gauge only (3" chambers); 30" barrels; checkered walnut pistol grip stock and forearm; four screw-in chokes with each gun (modified, improved cylinder, and two skeet chokes); two bead sighting system; introduced in 1992.
Estimated Value: New (retail): $1,349.00
                         Excellent: $1,012.00
                         Very good: $ 800.00

Ruger Over & Under Woodside
Similar to Ruger "Red Label" except: improved cocking mechanism enhances opening ease; 12 and 20 gauge only; has unique stock design in which the buttstock extends forward as two side panels and is inletted into cutouts in the sides of the receiver; the stock material is select Circassian walnut in pistol grip or straight grip styles. Introduced in 1995.
Estimated Value: New (retail): $1,675.00
                         Excellent: $1,260.00
                         Very good: $1,020.00

SKB

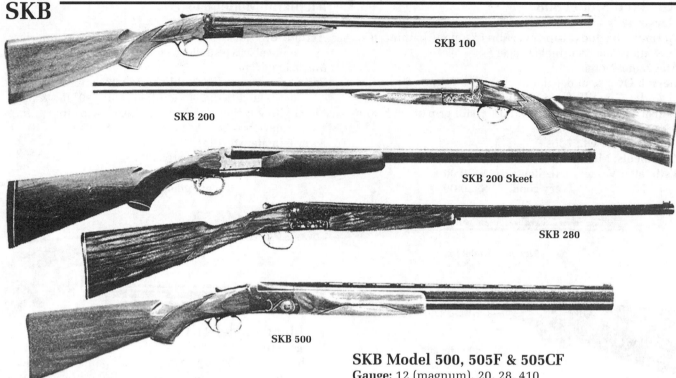

SKB 100

SKB 200

SKB 200 Skeet

SKB 280

SKB 500

SKB Model 100
Gauge: 12, 12, magnum, 20
Action: Box lock; top lever, break-open; hammerless; single selective trigger
Magazine: None
Barrel: Side by side double barrel; 26", 28" improved cylinder & modified or 30" full & full in 12 gauge
Finish: Blued; checkered hardwood pistol grip stock & short tapered forearm
Approximate wt.: 6 to 7 lbs.
Comments: Made from the mid 1960's to mid 1970's.

| Estimated Value: | Excellent: | $340.00 |
| | Very good: | $265.00 |

SKB Model 200 & 200E
Similar to the SKB 100 with engraved silverplate frame; wide forearm; select walnut; automatic selective ejectors; 200E has straight grip stock.

| Estimated Value: | Excellent: | $670.00 |
| | Very good: | $530.00 |

SKB Model 200 Skeet
Similar to the 200 with 25" skeet choke barrels & recoil pad.

| Estimated Value: | Excellent: | $560.00 |
| | Very good: | $450.00 |

SKB Model 280
Similar to the 200 without silver frame. Has straight grip stock.

| Estimated Value: | Excellent: | $500.00 |
| | Very good: | $375.00 |

SKB Model 400
Similar to the Model 200 with sideplate receiver; straight stock available.

| Estimated Value: | Excellent: | $895.00 |
| | Very good: | $715.00 |

SKB Model 500, 505F & 505CF
Gauge: 12 (magnum), 20, 28, 410
Action: Box lock; top lever, break-open; hammerless
Magazine: None
Barrel: Over & under double barrel; 26" improved cylinder & modified; 28", 30" modified & full; ventilated rib; chrome lined. 505CF has "inter" choke system
Finish: Blued; checkered walnut pistol grip stock & forearm; recoil pad on magnum; front sight; engraved receiver on Model 500
Approximate wt.: 6½ to 8 lbs.
Comments: Made from the mid 1960's to mid 1980's as Model 500; As 505 to present. Add 4% for sporting clay.

Estimated Value:	New (retail):	$999.00
	Excellent:	$745.00
	Very good:	$600.00

SKB Model 500 Skeet & 505 CSK
Similar to the Model 500 with 26" or 28" skeet choke barrels. Model 500 discontinued in mid 1980's & replaced by Model 505CSK. Discontinued in early 1990's

| Estimated Value: | Excellent: | $620.00 |
| | Very good: | $500.00 |

SKB Model 600 & 605F
Similar to the 500 with select wood; trigger mounted barrel selector; silverplate receiver; middle sight.

| Estimated Value: | Excellent: | $ 730.00 |
| | Very good: | $ 585.00 |

SKB Model 600 Trap & 605 Trap
Similar to the 600 with regular or Monte Carlo stock; 12 gauge only; recoil pad, 30" or 32" full choke barrels on Model 600; "inter" choke system on Model 605 Trap (late 1980's). Discontinued in early 1990's

| Estimated Value: | Excellent: | $725.00 |
| | Very good: | $580.00 |

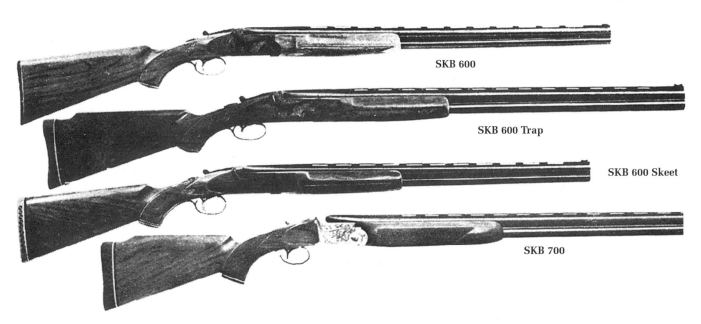

SKB 600

SKB 600 Trap

SKB 600 Skeet

SKB 700

SKB Model 600 Skeet & 605 CSK
Similar to the 600 with 26" or 28" skeet choke barrels (Model 600) & recoil pad; "inter" choke system on 605CSK (late 1980's). Discontinued in early 1990's

Estimated Value:	Excellent:	$720.00
	Very good:	$575.00

SKB Model 680
Similar to the 600 with a straight grip stock.

Estimated Value:	Excellent:	$800.00
	Very good:	$640.00

SKB Model 700
Similar to the 600 with higher quality finish & more extensive engraving.

Estimated Value:	Excellent:	$850.00
	Very good:	$680.00

SKB Model 885
Gauge: 12, 20, 28, 410; 3" chambers except 28 gauge
Action: Box lock; top lever break-open; hammerless, single selective trigger; automatic ejectors
Magazine: None
Barrel: Over & under double; 26" or 28" chrome bores with inter-choke system & ventilated rib
Finish: Blued; checkered semi-fancy American walnut pistol grip stock & forearm; engraved receiver with classic side plate styling; engraved trigger guard tang, safety, and top lever
Approximate wt.: 6 to 8 lbs.
Comments: Made from late 1980's to mid 1990's. Add 2% for 28 gauge or 410; 8% for Sporting Clays.

Estimated Value:	Excellent:	$1,200.00
	Very good:	$ 960.00

SKB Model 685
Similar to the Model 885 except: different engraving with gold plated scenes; regular box lock without classic side plates; add 3% for 28 gauge or 410; 8% for Sporting Clays.

Estimated Value:	Excellent:	$1,160.00
	Very good:	$ 930.00

SKB Model 585 Field
Similar to the Model 685 except: standard American walnut stock & forearm; less engraving; add 4% for 28 gauge or 410; 12% for Sporting Clays.

Estimated Value:	New (Retail):	$1,249.00
	Excellent:	$ 935.00
	Very good:	$ 750.00

SKB Model 785
Gauge: 12, 20, 28, 410
Action: Box lock with Greener style cross bolt
Magazine: None
Barrel: Over & under double barrel; choke tubes; chrome lined; ventilated rib; the 12 and 20 gauge are equipped with ventilated side ribs (between barrels) to improve heat dissipation
Finish: Blued, checkered American Black walnut pistol grip stock and forearm; scroll pattern engraved receiver.
Approximate wt.: 7½ to 9 lbs.
Comments: Introduced in 1996; priced for Field grade. Add 4% for 28 and 410 gauge; add 4% for Trap or Skeet grade; add 7% for Sporting Clays model.

Estimated Value:	New (retail):	$1,899.00
	Excellent:	$1,425.00
	Very good:	$1,150.00

SKB 785

SKB Model 1300

Gauge: 12, 20, regular or magnum
Action: Semi-automatic
Magazine: 5-shot; 3-shot with plug
Barrel: 26" or 28" "Inter Choke"; ventilated rib; slug barrel with rifle sights available
Finish: Blued, black receiver; checkered walnut pistol grip stock & forearm
Approximate wt.: 6½ to 7¼ lbs.
Comments: Add 1% for slug barrel with rifle sights.
Estimated Value: Excellent: $450.00
                        Very good: $360.00

SKB Model 1900

Similar to the Model 1300 with light receiver featuring engraved hunting scene, gold trigger. Add 5% for 30" barrel Trap Model
Estimated Value: Excellent: $500.00
                        Very good: $400.00

SKB Model 3000

A presentation deluxe version of the Model 1900. High-back receiver. A trap version is available (add 2%).
Estimated Value: Excellent: $550.00
                        Very good: $450.00

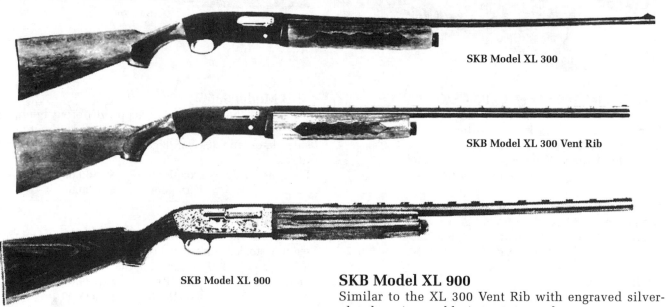

SKB Model XL 300

SKB Model XL 300 Vent Rib

SKB Model XL 900

SKB Model XL 300

Gauge: 12, 20
Action: Gas operated; semi-automatic; hammerless
Magazine: 5-shot tubular
Barrel: 26" improved cylinder or skeet; 28" modified or full; 30" modified or full chokes
Finish: Blued; decorated receiver; checkered walnut pistol grip stock & forearm
Approximate wt.: 6 to 7 lbs.
Comments: Made from the early to late 1970's.
Estimated Value: Excellent: $290.00
                        Very good: $235.00

SKB XL 300 Vent Rib

Similar to the XL 300 with front sights & ventilated rib.
Estimated Value: Excellent: $320.00
                        Very good: $255.00

SKB Model XL 100 Slug

A no-frills slug gun with 20" barrel; rifle sights; swivels; similar to the XL 300.
Estimated Value: Excellent: $255.00
                        Very good: $205.00

SKB Model XL 900

Similar to the XL 300 Vent Rib with engraved silver-plated receiver; gold trigger & name plate.
Estimated Value: Excellent: $350.00
                        Very good: $280.00

SKB Model XL 900 Slug

Similar to the XL 900 with a 24" barrel for slugs; rifle sights; swivels.
Estimated Value: Excellent: $360.00
                        Very good: $285.00

SKB Model XL 900 Trap

Similar to the XL 900 with middle sight; no silver receiver; recoil pad; choice of regular or Monte Carlo stock.
Estimated Value: Excellent: $375.00
                        Very good: $300.00

SKB Model XL 900 Skeet

Similar to the XL 900 Trap with skeet stock & skeet choke barrel.
Estimated Value: Excellent: $365.00
                        Very good: $290.00

SKB Model XL 900 MR

Similar to the XL 900 except: for 3" magnum; recoil pad
Estimated Value: Excellent: $380.00
                        Very good: $300.00

Sarasqueta

Sarasqueta Sidelock

Sarasqueta Sidelock Grades 4 to 12
Gauge: 12, 16, 20, 28
Action: Side lock; top lever, break-open; hammerless; double triggers
Magazine: None
Barrel: Side by side double barrel; standard barrel lengths & chokes available to customer specifications
Finish: Blued; checkered walnut straight or pistol grip stock & forearm
Approximate wt.: Varies
Comments: A Spanish shotgun. Grades differ as to quality & extent of engraving.
Estimated Value: Excellent: $650.00 - $2,500.00
Very good: $550.00 - $2,000.00

Sarasqueta Folding Shotgun
Gauge: 410
Action: Box lock; top lever, break-open; exposed hammer
Magazine: None
Barrel: Side by side double barrel; 26" choice of chokes
Finish: Blued; case-hardened frame; walnut pistol grip stock & forearm
Approximate wt.: Varies
Comments: A "folding" shotgun produced in the 1970's.
Estimated Value: Excellent: $250.00
Very good: $200.00

Sarasqueta Model 2 & 3
Gauge: 12, 16, 20, 28
Action: Box lock; top lever, break-open; hammerless; double triggers
Magazine: None
Barrel: Side by side double barrel; standard barrel lengths & chokes made to customer specifications
Finish: Blued; checkered walnut straight grip stock & forearm
Approximate wt.: Varies
Comments: Made from the mid 1930's. Grades differ only in engraving style.
Estimated Value: Excellent: $400.00 - $550.00
Very good: $325.00 - $450.00

Sarasqueta Over & Under Deluxe
Gauge: 12
Action: Side lock; top lever, break-open; hammerless; double triggers; automatic ejectors
Magazine: None
Barrel: Over & under double barrel; lengths & chokes made to customer's specifications
Finish: Blued; checkered walnut pistol grip stock & forearm
Approximate wt.: Varies
Comments: Made from the mid 1930's.
Estimated Value: Excellent: $1,200.00
Very good: $ 850.00

Sarasqueta Folding Shotgun

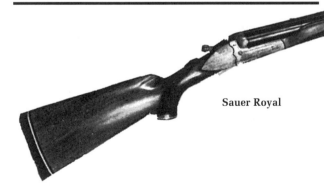

Sauer Royal

Sauer

Sauer Royal
Gauge: 12, 20
Action: Box lock; top lever, break-open; hammerless; automatic ejectors; single selective trigger
Magazine: None
Barrel: Side by side double barrel; 28" mod & full, 26" improved & mod in 20 gauge; 30" full in 12 gauge
Finish: Blued; engraved frame; checkered walnut pistol grip stock & tapered forearm; recoil pad
Approximate wt.: 7 to 8 lbs.
Comments: Produced from the mid 1950's to late 1970's.
Estimated Value: Excellent: $1,200.00
Very good: $ 960.00

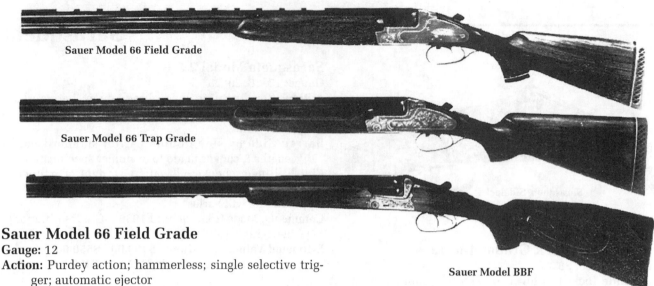

Sauer Model 66 Field Grade

Sauer Model 66 Trap Grade

Sauer Model BBF

Sauer Model 66 Field Grade

Gauge: 12

Action: Purdey action; hammerless; single selective trigger; automatic ejector

Magazine: None

Barrel: Over & under double barrel; 28" modified & full choke; ventilated rib

Finish: Blued; checkered walnut pistol grip stock & forearm; recoil pad; engraving

Approximate wt.: 7 lbs.

Comments: Made from the mid 1960's to mid 1970's. Prices are for Grade I. Fancier Grades II & III differ in quality & extent of engraving.

Estimated Value: Excellent: $1,520.00
                  Very good: $1,220.00

Sauer Model 66 Trap Grade

Basically the same as the Field Grade with 30" barrels & a trap stock. Also produced in three grades.

Estimated Value: Excellent: $1,600.00
                  Very good: $1,275.00

Sauer Model 66 Skeet

Basically the same as the Trap Model with 25" barrel in skeet choke. Prices are for Grade I. Made from mid 1960's to mid 1970's.

Estimated Value: Excellent: $1,575.00
                  Very good: $1,260.00

Sauer Model BBF

Gauge: 16

Caliber: 30-30, 30-06, 7 x 65

Action: Kersten lock; Blitz action; top lever, break-open; hammerless; double trigger

Magazine: None

Barrel: Over & under rifle-shotgun combination; 25" Krupp barrels; rifle barrel & full choke shotgun barrel

Finish: Blued; checkered walnut Monte Carlo pistol grip stock & forearm; engraved; sights; swivels

Approximate wt.: 6 lbs.

Comments: Made from the mid 1960's to 1970's; Available in deluxe model with extensive engraving.

Estimated Value: Excellent: $1,650.00
                  Very good: $1,320.00

Savage

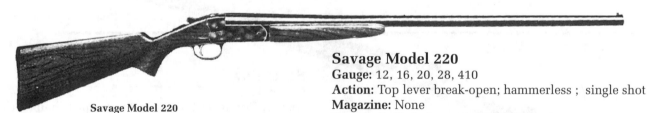

Savage Model 220

Savage Model 220

Gauge: 12, 16, 20, 28, 410

Action: Top lever break-open; hammerless ; single shot

Magazine: None

Barrel: Full choke; 28" 30", 32" in 12 & 16 gauge; 26", 28", 30", 32" in 20 gauge; 28" & 30" in 28 gauge; 26" & 28" in 410 bore

Finish: Blued; plain wood, pistol grip stock & forearm

Approximate wt.: 6 lbs.

Comments: Made from 1930's until late 1940's. Reintroduced in the mid 1950's with 36" barrel. Replaced by 220L in mid 1960's.

Estimated Value: Excellent: $110.00
                  Very good: $ 90.00

Savage Model 220L

Savage Model 220P

Basically the same as 220 except: no 410 gauge, has "Poly-Choke" & recoil pad.

Estimated Value: Excellent: $115.00
Very good: $ 95.00

Savage Model 220L

Similar to Model 220 except: has side lever break open. Made from mid 1960's to early 1970's.

Estimated Value: Excellent: $95.00
Very good: $75.00

Savage Model 311

Savage Model 311 Waterfowler

Similar to the Model 311 with Parkerized finish.

Estimated Value: Excellent: $260.00
Very good: $220.00

Savage Model 311

Gauge: 12, 20; regular or magnum
Action: Top lever, break open; hammerless, double trigger
Magazine: None
Barrel: Side by side double barrel; 28" matted rib barrels
Finish: Blued; hardwood, semi-pistol grip stock & tapered forearm
Approximate wt.: 7 lbs.
Comments: The Model 311 was originally a Stevens shotgun. In 1988 Savage dropped the Stevens designation; discontinued in late 1980's.
Estimated Value: Excellent: $245.00
Very good: $200.00

Savage Model 24D

Savage Model 24

Gauge: 20, 410
Caliber: 22 short, long, long rifle; 22 magnum
Action: Top lever, break open; exposed hammer; single trigger; bottom opening lever in mid 1980's
Magazine: None
Barrel: Over & under double barrel; 24" rifle barrel over shotgun barrel
Finish: Blued; checkered walnut finish hardwood pistol grip stock & forearm; sporting rear & ramp front sights; case hardened receiver
Approximate wt.: 6 lbs.
Comments: Made from the early 1950's to late 1980's.
Estimated Value: Excellent: $200.00
Very good: $160.00

Savage Model 24D

Deluxe version of the Model 24. Discontinued in mid 1980's.

Estimated Value: Excellent: $215.00
Very good: $175.00

Savage Model 24F Combination & "Predator"

Gauge: 20, 12 gauge with 3" chamber
Caliber: 222 Rem., 223 Rem., 30-30 Win.,22 Hornet, 22 LR
Action: Top lever, break open; exposed hammer with barrel selector; hammer block safety
Magazine: None
Barrel: 24" rifle barrel over 24" shotgun barrel; any combination of rifle caliber & shotgun gauge; shotgun barrel in modified choke; modified & full choke tubes available
Finish: DuPont Rynite® two-piece stock & forearm
Approximate wt.: 8 lbs.
Comments: Produced from the late 1980's to present; add 4% for choke tube; 4% for Camo Rynite® stock on 12 gauge with 222 Rem. or 223 Rem.
Estimated Value: New (retail): $400.00
Excellent: $300.00
Very good: $240.00

Savage Model 24V Combination

Same as the Model 24F Combination except: walnut finish hardwood stock & forearm; 20 gauge, 3" chamber under 222 Rem., 223 Rem. or 30-30 Win. rifle barrel. Made from the late 1980's to early 1990's.

Estimated Value: Excellent: $275.00
Very good: $215.00

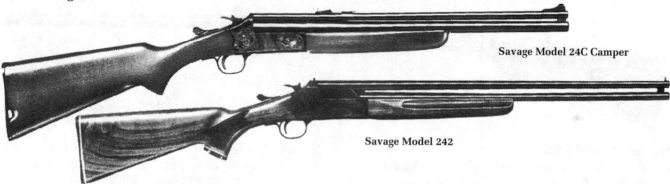

Savage Model 24C Camper

Savage Model 242

Savage Model 24C Camper, 24CS
A shorter version of the Model 24; 20" barrel; 5¾ lbs.; 22LR over 20 gauge barrel; buttplate opens for ammo storage area. Add $45.00 for satin nickel finish (24CS) & extra pistol grip stock; discontinued late 1980's.

Estimated Value: Excellent: $205.00
                   Very good: $165.00

Savage Model 242
Similar to the Model 24 with 410 gauge over & under shotgun barrels; full choke; bead sights; made only in late 1970's.

Estimated Value: Excellent: $190.00
                   Very good: $160.00

Savage Model 389
Gauge: 12, regular or magnum
Caliber: 222 or 308
Action: Top lever, break-open; hammerless; double trigger; shotgun barrel over rifle barrel; tang safety
Magazine: None
Barrel: 25¾" over & under double barrel; changeable choke tubes
Finish: Blued; checkered walnut pistol grip stock & matching forearm; sling studs
Approximate wt.: 8 lbs.
Comments: Produced from the late 1980's to the early 1990's.

Estimated Value: Excellent: $720.00
                   Very good: $575.00

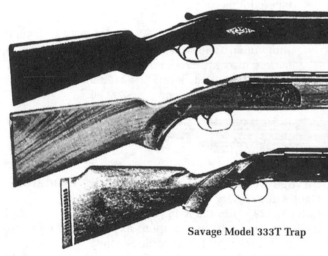

Savage Model 420

Savage Model 333

Savage Model 333T Trap

Savage Model 420
Gauge: 12, 16, 20
Action: Box lock; top lever, break-open; hammerless; double triggers or non-selective single trigger
Magazine: None
Barrel: Over & under double barrel; 26" to 30" modified & full or cylinder bore & modified chokes
Finish: Blued; plain walnut pistol grip stock & forearm
Approximate wt.: 6¾ to 7¾ lbs.
Comments: Made from the mid 1930's until World War II. Add $25.00 for single trigger.

Estimated Value: Excellent: $420.00
                   Very good: $335.00

Savage Model 430
Similar as Model 420 with special checkered walnut stock & forearm; matted upper barrel; recoil pad. Add $25.00 for single trigger.

Estimated Value: Excellent: $480.00
                   Very good: $385.00

Savage Model 333
Gauge: 12, 20
Action: Top lever, break-open; hammerless; single trigger
Magazine: None
Barrel: Over & under double barrel; 26" to 30"; variety of chokes; ventilated rib
Finish: Blued; checkered walnut pistol grip stock & forearm
Approximate wt.: 6¼ to 7¼ lbs.
Comments: Made from the early to late 1970's.

Estimated Value: Excellent: $540.00
                   Very good: $430.00

Savage Model 333T Trap
Similar to 333 with Monte Carlo stock & recoil pad in 12 gauge, 30" barrel.

Estimated Value: Excellent: $565.00
                   Very good: $450.00

Savage Model 330
Similar to 333 without ventilated rib.

Estimated Value: Excellent: $485.00
                   Very good: $385.00

Savage Model 312 Field

Gauge: 12, regular or magnum
Action: Top lever, break-open; concealed hammers; single trigger with safety acting as barrel selector
Magazine: None
Barrel: Over & under double barrel; 26" or 28"; ventilated rib; ivory bead front sight & bead middle sight; changeable choke tubes in full, modified & improved cylinder with wrench
Finish: Blued barrels; satin chrome receiver; cut-checkered walnut pistol grip stock & matching forearm; recoil pad
Approximate wt.: 7 lbs.
Comments: Produced from 1990 to 1993
Estimated Value: Excellent: $450.00
Very good: $360.00

Savage Model 312T

Same as Model 312 Field except: 30" barrels; 2 full & 1 modified choke tubes; Monte Carlo stock; approximate wt., 7¼ lbs. Produced in early 1990's
Estimated Value: Excellent: $475.00
Very good: $380.00

Savage Model 312 SC

Same as the Model 312 Field except: 28" barrels only; seven choke tubes included (1 full, 2 improved cylinder, 2 modified, 1 #1 skeet & 1 #2 skeet); "Sporting Clays" engraved on receiver. Produced in early 1990's
Estimated Value: Excellent: $460.00
Very good: $370.00

Savage Model 320 Field

Same as the Savage Model 312 Field except: 20 gauge (3" chambers) with 26" barrels. Produced in the early 1990's.
Estimated Value: Excellent: $440.00
Very good: $350.00

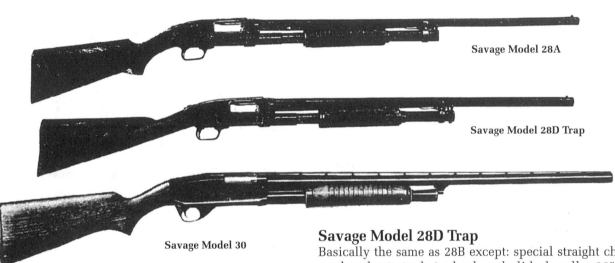

Savage Model 28A

Savage Model 28D Trap

Savage Model 30

Savage Model 28A & B Standard

Gauge: 12
Action: Slide action; hammerless; solid breech; side ejection
Magazine: 5-shot tubular
Barrel: 26", 28", 30" or 32" cylinder, modified or full choke; raised rib on 28B
Finish: Blued; checkered wood pistol grip stock & grooved slide handle
Approximate wt.: 7½ lbs.
Comments: Made from the late 1920's until mid 1930's. Add $10.00 for matted rib.
Estimated Value: Excellent: $235.00
Very good: $190.00

Savage Model 28C Riot

Basically the same as 28A except with a 20" cylinder bore barrel. This was for use by police, bank guards, etc., for protection.
Estimated Value: Excellent: $200.00
Very good: $160.00

Savage Model 28D Trap

Basically the same as 28B except: special straight checkered walnut stock & checkered slide handle; 30" full choke barrel.
Estimated Value: Excellent: $260.00
Very good: $200.00

Savage Model 28S Special

Basically the same as 28B except: ivory bead front sight; checkered pistol grip stock; checkered forearm.
Estimated Value: Excellent: $240.00
Very good: $195.00

Savage Model 30

Gauge: 12, 20, 410
Action: Slide action; hammerless
Magazine: 4-shot tubular
Barrel: 26", 28", 30"; cylinder bore, modified or full choke; ventilated rib
Finish: Blued; decorated receiver; walnut pistol grip stock & grooved slide handle
Approximate wt.: 6½ lbs.
Comments: Made from late 1950's to late 1960's.
Estimated Value: Excellent: $215.00
Very good: $170.00

Savage Model 30 FG

Savage Model 30D

Savage Model 30 AC

Savage Model 30 AC
Same as Model 30 FG with adjustable choke.

Estimated Value: Excellent: $185.00
                          Very good: $145.00

Savage Model 30 FG (Field Grade)
Similar to Model 30 with plain receiver, no ventilated rib & horizontal groove in slide handle.

Estimated Value: Excellent: $175.00
                          Very good: $140.00

Savage Model 30D (Deluxe)
1970's version of the Model 30 FG with recoil pad & horizontal groove in slide handle. Discontinued in the late 1970's.

Estimated Value: Excellent: $190.00
                          Very good: $150.00

Savage Model 30 FG Slug Gun
Same as Model 30 FG with 22" barrel & rifle sights, 12 gauge. Introduced in 1971, discontinued in the late 1970's.

Estimated Value: Excellent: $190.00
                          Very good: $150.00

Savage Model 30T Trap
Fancy version Model 30 in 12 gauge; 30" full choke barrel; Monte Carlo stock; grooved slide handle; recoil pad. Introduced in mid 1960's.

Estimated Value: Excellent: $225.00
                          Very good: $180.00

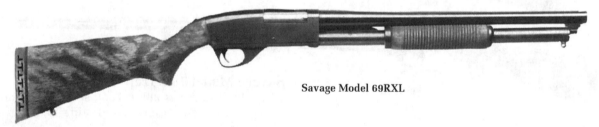

Savage Model 69RXL

Savage Model 67
Gauge: 12, 20, regular or magnum
Action: Slide action; hammerless; side ejecting; repeating
Magazine: 4-shot tubular, 3-shot in magnum
Barrel: 28" modified
Finish: Blued; hardwood, semi-pistol grip stock & grooved slide handle
Approximate wt.: 6¼ to 7½ lbs.
Comments: The Model 67 was originally a Stevens shotgun. In 1988 Savage dropped the Stevens designation; discontinued late 1980's.

Estimated Value: Excellent: $195.00
                          Very good: $155.00

Savage Model 67 VRT
Similar to the Model 67 with a ventilated rib barrel, interchangeable choke tubes & recoil pad. Discontinued late 1980's.

Estimated Value: Excellent: $225.00
                          Very good: $180.00

Savage Model 67 Slug
Similar to Model 67 with a 21" cylinder bore barrel, recoil pad, rifle sights & scope mount. Discontinued in late 1980's.

Estimated Value: Excellent: $210.00
                          Very good: $170.00

Savage Model 69R, 69N, 69RXL, 69RXG
Gauge: 12, regular or magnum
Action: Slide action; hammerless; top tang safety
Magazine: 6-shot tubular, 4-shot on 69R
Barrel: 18¼" cylinder bore, 20" on 69R
Finish: Blued; walnut stock & grooved slide handle; recoil pad, swivels; 69N has satin nickel finish; 69RXG has plastic pistol grip & sling
Approximate wt.: 6½ lbs.
Comments: A law enforcement shotgun introduced in 1982. Add 30% for model 69N. (69R & 69N discontinued in mid 1980's.) Discontinued late 1980's.

Estimated Value: Excellent: $205.00
                          Very good: $165.00

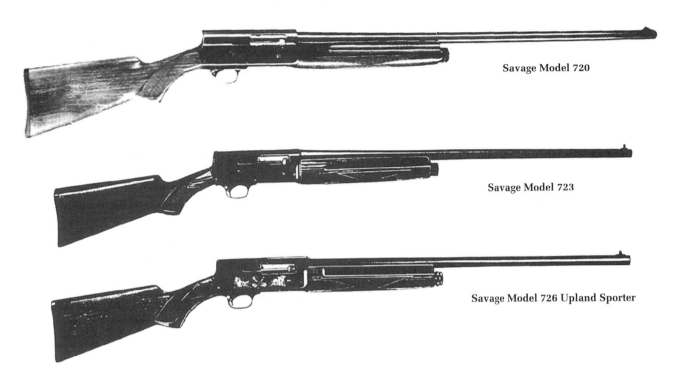

Savage Model 720

Savage Model 723

Savage Model 726 Upland Sporter

Savage Model 720

Gauge: 12
Action: Browning patent; semi-automatic; hammerless
Magazine: 4-shot tubular
Barrel: 28", 30" or 32" cylinder bore, modified or full choke
Finish: Blued; checkered walnut pistol grip stock & forearm; after 1940, engraved receiver
Approximate wt.: 8½ lbs.
Comments: Originally a Springfield shotgun, this takedown model was made from about 1930 until the late 1940's. In the early 1940's, Model 720R (Riot Gun) was introduced with a 20" barrel.
Estimated Value: Excellent: $285.00
Very good: $230.00

Savage Model 720-P

Basically the same as 720 with "Poly-Choke" produced from the late 1930's to 1940's; 3 or 5-shot; 12 gauge only.
Estimated Value: Excellent: $290.00
Very good: $235.00

Savage Model 721

Same as 720 with matted rib.
Estimated Value: Excellent: $295.00
Very good: $240.00

Savage Model 722

Same as 720 except with ventilated rib.
Estimated Value: Excellent: $300.00
Very good: $240.00

Savage Model 723

Same as 720 except no 32" barrel; available in 16 gauge. Weighs about 7½ lbs.
Estimated Value: Excellent: $280.00
Very good: $225.00

Savage Model 724

Same as 723 except with matted rib.
Estimated Value: Excellent: $295.00
Very good: $235.00

Savage Model 725

Same as 723 except with ventilated rib.
Estimated Value: Excellent: $310.00
Very good: $250.00

Savage Model 726 Upland Sporter

Basically the same as 720 except no 32" barrel; 2-shot tubular magazine; available in 16 gauge; decorated receiver.
Estimated Value: Excellent: $300.00
Very good: $240.00

Savage Model 727 Upland Sporter

Same as Model 726 except with matted rib.
Estimated Value: Excellent: $310.00
Very good: $245.00

Savage Model 728 Upland Sporter

Same as Model 726 except with ventilated rib.
Estimated Value: Excellent: $320.00
Very good: $255.00

Savage Model 740C Skeet Gun

Basically the same as Model 726 with a skeet stock & "Cutts Compensator." Discontinued in the late 1940's.
Estimated Value: Excellent: $300.00
Very good: $240.00

Savage Model 745 Lightweight

Similar to Model 720 with light alloy receiver. Made from late 1930's to 1940's; 3- or 5-shot; 12 gauge only.
Estimated Value: Excellent: $280.00
Very good: $225.00

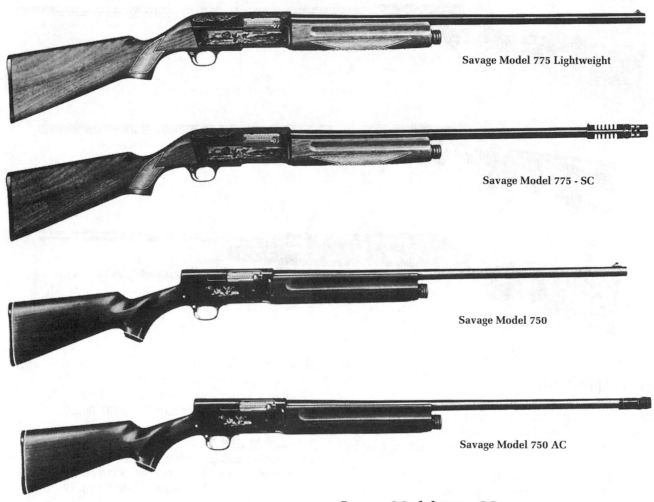

Savage Model 775 Lightweight

Savage Model 775 - SC

Savage Model 750

Savage Model 750 AC

Savage Model 755

Gauge: 12, 16
Action: Semi-automatic; hammerless
Magazine: 4-shot tubular; 3-shot tubular
Barrel: 26" cylinder bore; 28" full or modified; 30" full choke
Finish: Blued; checkered walnut pistol grip stock & forearm
Approximate wt.: 8 lbs.
Comments: Made from the late 1940's until late 1950's; top of receiver flush with stock.
Estimated Value: Excellent: $260.00
                       Very good: $210.00

Savage Model 755 - SC

Similar to 755 with Savage "Super Choke."
Estimated Value: Excellent: $270.00
                       Very good: $215.00

Savage Model 775 Lightweight

Similar to 755 with alloy receiver. Produced until mid 1960's.
Estimated Value: Excellent: $250.00
                       Very good: $200.00

Savage Model 775 - SC

Basically the same as Model 775 with Savage "Super Choke" & 26" barrel.
Estimated Value: Excellent: $265.00
                       Very good: $210.00

Savage Model 750

Gauge: 12
Action: Browning patent; semi-automatic; hammerless
Magazine: 4-shot tubular
Barrel: 26" cylinder bore; 28" full or modified
Finish: Blued; checkered walnut pistol grip stock & forearm; decorated receiver
Approximate wt.: 7¼ lbs.
Comments: Made from the early to late 1960's.
Estimated Value: Excellent: $325.00
                       Very good: $260.00

Savage Model 750 SC

Similar to Model 750 with Savage "Super Choke." Made from 1962 for two years.
Estimated Value: Excellent: $335.00
                       Very good: $265.00

Savage Model 750 AC

Same as Model 750 except: adjustable choke. Made during mid 1960's.
Estimated Value: Excellent: $300.00
                       Very good: $240.00

Sears

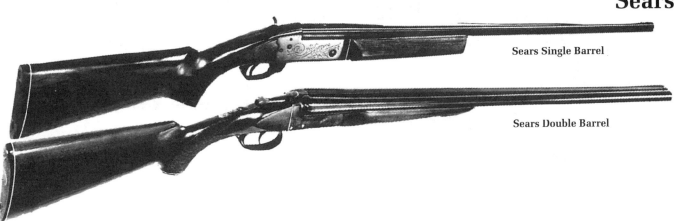

Sears Single Barrel

Sears Double Barrel

Sears Single Barrel
Gauge: 12, 20, 410
Action: Box lock; top lever, break-open; exposed hammer; automatic ejector
Magazine: None
Barrel: Full choke; 26" in 410; 28" in 20; 30" in 12
Finish: Blued; wood pistol grip stock & forearm
Approximate wt.: 7 lbs.
Comments: Manufactured in the 1970's & 1980's.
Estimated Value: Excellent: $100.00
                     Very good: $ 80.00

Sears Double Barrel
Gauge: 12, 20
Action: Box lock; top lever, break-open; hammerless; double triggers
Magazine: None
Barrel: 28" double barrel side by side; variety of chokes
Finish: Blued; epoxied black frame; walnut pistol grip stock & forearm
Approximate wt.: 7½ lbs.
Comments: Made to the early 1980's.
Estimated Value: Excellent: $215.00
                     Very good: $175.00

Sears Ted Williams Over & Under
Gauge: 12, 20
Action: Box lock; top lever, break-open; hammerless; automatic ejectors, selective trigger
Magazine: None
Barrel: Over & under double barrel; 26", 28" in standard chokes; ventilated rib; chrome lined
Finish: Blued; engraved steel receivers; checkered walnut pistol grip stock & forearm; recoil pad
Approximate wt.: 6¾ lbs.
Comments: Produced to the late 1970's.
Estimated Value: Excellent: $430.00
                     Very good: $345.00

Sears Ted Williams Over & Under

Sears Bolt Action
Gauge: 410
Action: Bolt action; repeating
Magazine: 3-shot detachable clip
Barrel: 24" full choke
Finish: Blued; wood pistol grip stock & forearm
Approximate wt.: 5½ lbs.
Comments: Made to the late 1970's.
Estimated Value: Excellent: $115.00
                     Very good: $ 95.00

Sears Model 140
Gauge: 12, 20
Action: Bolt action; repeating
Magazine: 2-shot detachable clip
Barrel: 25" adjustable choke
Finish: Blued; wood pistol grip stock & forearm
Approximate wt.: 7 lbs.
Comments: Made to the late 1970's.
Estimated Value: Excellent: $110.00
                     Very good: $ 90.00

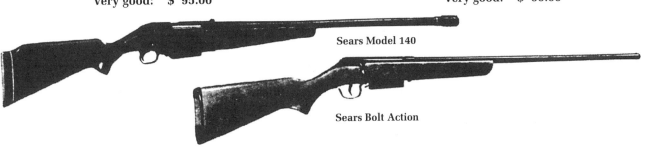

Sears Model 140

Sears Bolt Action

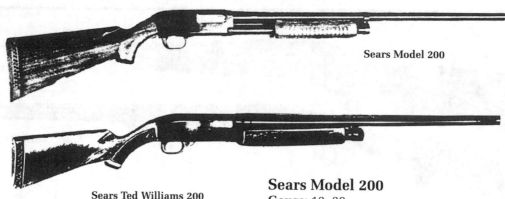

Sears Model 200

Sears Ted Williams 200

Sears Ted Williams 300
Gauge: 12, 20
Action: Semi-automatic, gas operated; hammerless
Magazine: 3-shot tubular
Barrel: 27" adjustable choke; 28" modified or full chokes; ventilated rib
Finish: Blued; checkered walnut pistol grip stock & forearm; recoil pad
Approximate wt.: 7 lbs.
Comments: Add $10.00 for variable choke.
Estimated Value: Excellent: $290.00
                       Very good: $230.00

Sears Model 200
Gauge: 12, 20
Action: Slide action; hammerless; repeating
Magazine: 4-shot tubular
Barrel: 28" full or modified chokes
Finish: Blued; alloy receiver; wood pistol grip stock & forearm; recoil pad
Approximate wt.: 6½ lbs.
Comments: Add $20.00 for variable choke.
Estimated Value: Excellent: $200.00
                       Very good: $160.00

Sears Ted Williams 200
A fancier version of the 200 with checkered wood.
Estimated Value: Excellent: $220.00
                       Very good: $175.00

Smith & Wesson

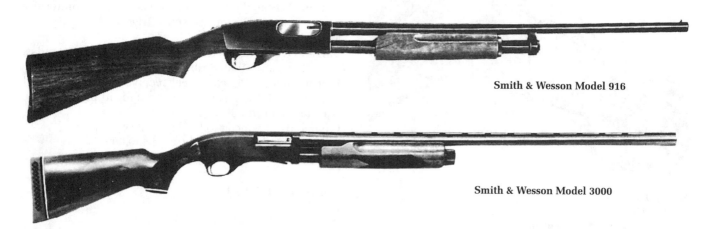

Smith & Wesson Model 916

Smith & Wesson Model 3000

Smith & Wesson Model 916
Gauge: 12
Action: Slide action; hammerless; side ejection
Magazine: 5-shot tubular
Barrel: 20" cylinder bore; 26" improved cylinder, 28" modified, full or cylinder bore; ventilated rib on some models
Finish: Blued; satin finish receiver; walnut semi-pistol grip stock & grooved slide handle; recoil pad available
Approximate wt.: 7 lbs.
Comments: Made from the early 1970's to about 1980. Add $20.00 for Deer Model or ventilated rib.
Estimated Value: Excellent: $185.00
                       Very good: $150.00

Smith & Wesson Model 3000
Gauge: 12, 20, regular or magnum
Action: Slide action; repeating; hammerless
Magazine: 3-shot tubular
Barrel: 26" improved cylinder; 28" modified or full, 30" full; ventilated rib
Finish: Blued; checkered walnut pistol grip stock & fluted slide handle; recoil pad
Approximate wt.: 7 lbs.
Comments: Made from 1982 to 1985. Add $25.00 for "Multi-Choke" system.
Estimated Value: Excellent: $300.00
                       Very good: $225.00

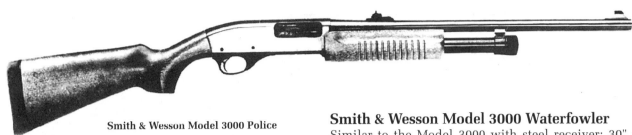

Smith & Wesson Model 3000 Police

Smith & Wesson Model 3000 Police

Similar to the Model 3000 with 18" or 20" slug or police cylinder barrel; blued or Parkerized finish; bead or rifle sights; walnut finish, hardwood stock & grooved slide handle or plastic pistol grip & slide handle or folding stock. Add $25.00 for rifle sights; $10.00 for plastic pistol grip; $70.00 for folding stock.

Estimated Value: Excellent: $250.00
                   Very good: $185.00

Smith & Wesson Model 3000 Waterfowler

Similar to the Model 3000 with steel receiver; 30" full choke barrel; Parkerized finish; dull, oil-finished wood; camouflaged sling & swivels. Made from 1982 to 1985. Add $25.00 for "Multi-Choke" system.

Estimated Value: Excellent: $320.00
                   Very good: $240.00

Smith & Wesson Model 3000 Slug

Similar to the Model 3000 with a 22" slug barrel; rifle sights; swivels.

Estimated Value: Excellent: $270.00
                   Very good: $200.00

Smith & Wesson Model 1000

Smith & Wesson Model 1000

Gauge: 12, 20, regular or magnum
Action: Semi-automatic, gas operated; hammerless; side ejection
Magazine: 3-shot tubular
Barrel: 26", 28", 30"; variety of chokes; ventilated rib
Finish: Blued; engraved alloy receiver; steel receiver on magnum; checkered walnut pistol grip stock & forearm; sights
Approximate wt.: 7½ lbs.
Comments: Manufactured from the early 1970's to mid 1980's. Add $46.00 for magnum; $30.00 for "Multi-Choke" system.

Estimated Value: Excellent: $380.00
                   Very good: $285.00

Smith & Wesson Model 1000 Super 12

Similar to the Model 1000 except: "Multi-Choke" system; designed to use magnum shells. Made in 1984 and 1985.

Estimated Value: Excellent: $450.00
                   Very good: $335.00

Smith & Wesson Model 1000 Trap

Similar to the Model 1000 with Monte Carlo stock; steel receiver; 30" multi-choke barrel; other trap features.

Estimated Value: Excellent: $450.00
                   Very good: $340.00

Smith & Wesson Model 1000S, Superskeet

Similar to the Model 100 with 25" skeet choke barrel; muzzle vents & other extras. Add $200.00 for Superskeet Model.

Estimated Value: Excellent: $400.00
                   Very good: $320.00

Smith & Wesson Model 1000 Slug

Similar to the Model 1000 with a 22" slug barrel, rifle sights & steel receiver.

Estimated Value: Excellent: $380.00
                   Very good: $285.00

Smith & Wesson Model 1000 Waterfowler

Similar to the Model 1000 with a steel receiver; dull oil-finish stock; 30" full choke barrel; Parkerized finish; swivels; recoil pad; camouflage sling. Introduced in 1982. Discontinued in 1985.

Estimated Value: Excellent: $435.00
                   Very good: $325.00

Smith & Wesson Model 1000 Super 12 Waterfowler

Similar to the Model 1000 Waterfowler with the "Multi-Choke" system. Introduced in 1984. Discontinued in 1985.

Estimated Value: Excellent: $470.00
                   Very good: $350.00

Stevens

Stevens Model No. 93

Stevens Models No. 93, 97 Nitro Special

Gauge: 12, 16
Action: Top lever, break-open; exposed hammer; single shot; Model 97 has automatic ejector
Magazine: None
Barrel: Special steel; 28", 30", 32"
Finish: Blued; nickel plated, case hardened frame; plain walnut pistol grip stock & lipped forearm
Approximate wt.: 7 to 7½ lbs.
Comments: Made from 1907 to 1918.

Estimated Value:	Excellent:	$95.00
	Very good:	$75.00

Stevens Model No. 97 Nitro Special

Stevens Models No. 100, 110, 120

Gauge: 12, 16, 20
Action: Top lever, break-open; automatic ejector; exposed hammer; single shot
Magazine: None
Barrel: 28", 30", 32"
Finish: Blued; case hardened frame; walnut pistol grip stock & forearm; No. 100 no checkering; 110 & 120 checkered walnut
Approximate wt.: 6 to 7 lbs.
Comments: Produced from 1902 to 1904.

Estimated Value:	Excellent:	$95.00
	Very good:	$75.00

Stevens Model No. 120

Stevens Model No. 140

Similar to the Model 120 except it is hammerless & has an automatic safety. Made from 1902 to 1904.

Estimated Value:	Excellent:	$115.00
	Very good:	$ 95.00

Stevens Model No. 140

Stevens Models No. 160, 165, 170

Gauge: 12, 16, 20
Action: Break-open; exposed hammer; single shot; automatic ejector except on 160
Magazine: None
Barrel: 26", 28", 30", 32"
Finish: Blued; case hardened frame; checkered walnut pistol grip stock & forearm except 160 which is plain
Approximate wt.: 6 to 7 lbs.
Comments: Made from the 1903 to 1908.

Estimated Value:	Excellent:	$90.00
	Very good:	$70.00

Stevens Model No. 170

Stevens Model No. 182 Trap Gun

Stevens Model No. 180
Gauge: 12, 16, 20
Action: Top lever, break-open; hammerless; automatic ejector; single shot
Magazine: None
Barrel: 26", 28", 30" modified; 32" or 36" full choke
Finish: Blued; case hardened frame; checkered walnut pistol grip stock & forearm
Approximate wt.: 6½ lbs.
Comments: Produced from 1903 to 1918.
Estimated Value: Excellent: $110.00
  Very good: $ 90.00

Stevens Model No. 180

Stevens Model No. 185, 190, 195
Gauge: 12
Action: Top lever, break-open; hammerless; automatic shell ejector; single shot
Magazine: None
Barrel: Round with octagon breech; 30" or 32"
Finish: Blued; case hardened frame; checkered walnut pistol grip stock & forearm; frame engraved on No. 190, 195
Approximate wt.: 7 to 8 lbs.
Comments: These guns differ in quality of finish & engraving. Produced from 1903 to 1906.
Estimated Value: Excellent: $160.00
  Very good: $130.00

Stevens Model No. 182 Trap Gun
Similar to Model No. 180 except: Trap Grade; 12 gauge only; matted top of barrel; scroll work on frame. Made from around 1912 to 1920.
Estimated Value: Excellent: $165.00
  Very good: $135.00

Stevens Model No. 195

Stevens Model No. 970
Similar to the 185, this 12 gauge was made from around 1912 to 1918.
Estimated Value: Excellent: $100.00
  Very good: $ 80.00

Stevens Model No. 970

Stevens Model No. 85 Dreadnaught

Stevens Model No. 85 Dreadnaught
Gauge: 12
Action: Top lever, break-open; exposed hammer
Magazine: None, single shot
Barrel: 28", 30", 32" full choke
Finish: Blued; case hardened frame; plain walnut pistol grip stock & lipped forearm
Approximate wt.: 7½ lbs.
Comments: Made from around 1910 to mid 1920's.
Estimated Value: Excellent: $85.00
  Very good: $70.00

Stevens Model No. 89 Dreadnaught

Stevens Model No. 89 Dreadnaught
Same as the No. 85 with automatic ejector. Made until 1938.
Estimated Value: Excellent: $90.00
  Very good: $75.00

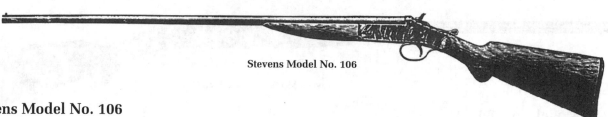

Stevens Model No. 106

Stevens Model No. 106

Gauge: 410
Action: Top lever, break-open; exposed hammer; single shot
Magazine: None
Barrel: 26" or 30"
Finish: Blued; case hardened frame; plain walnut pistol grip stock & forearm
Approximate wt.: 4½ lbs.
Comments: This lightweight, light-gauge gun was made from around 1912 to 1935.
Estimated Value: Excellent: $95.00
                        Very good: $75.00

Stevens Model No. 108

Same as the No. 106 with automatic ejector.
Estimated Value: Excellent: $100.00
                        Very good: $ 80.00

Stevens Springfield Model No. 958

Very similar to Model No. 108. Made from mid 1920's to early 1930's.
Estimated Value: Excellent: $90.00
                        Very good: $70.00

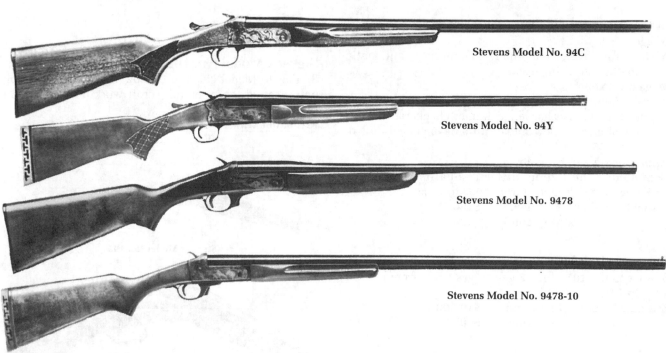

Stevens Model No. 94C

Stevens Model No. 94Y

Stevens Model No. 9478

Stevens Model No. 9478-10

Stevens Model No. 94 & 94C

Gauge: 12, 16, 20, 410
Action: Top lever, break-open; exposed hammer
Magazine: None
Barrel: 26", 28", 30", 32", 36" full choke
Finish: Blued; case hardened frame; checkered or plain walnut semi-pistol grip stock & grooved forearm
Approximate wt.: 6 to 8 lbs.
Comments: 94 made from 1939 to 1960. 94C made from 1960 to mid 1980's.
Estimated Value: Excellent: $100.00
                        Very good: $80.00

Stevens Model No. 94Y

Similar to 94C in youth version. Shorter stock; recoil pad, 26" barrel; 20 gauge modified or 410 full choke. Made from 1960 to 1963.
Estimated Value: Excellent: $90.00
                        Very good: $75.00

Stevens Model No. 9478

Similar to the Model 94C with lever release on the trigger guard; no checkering. Add $8.00 for 36" barrel.
Estimated Value: Excellent: $85.00
                        Very good: $70.00

Stevens Model No. 9478-10, Waterfowl

Similar to the Model 9478 with a 36" full choke barrel; 10 gauge only; recoil pad.
Estimated Value: Excellent: $110.00
                        Very good: $ 90.00

Stevens Model No. 9478-Y

Similar to the Model 9478 in 410 full or 20 modified gauges; 26" barrel; short stock with rubber buttplate.
Estimated Value: Excellent: $90.00
                        Very good: $75.00

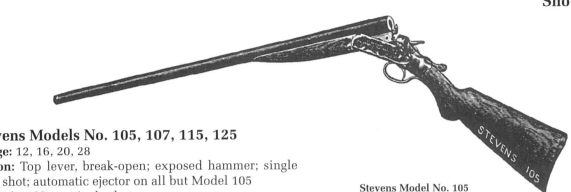

Stevens Model No. 105

Stevens Models No. 105, 107, 115, 125
Gauge: 12, 16, 20, 28
Action: Top lever, break-open; exposed hammer; single shot; automatic ejector on all but Model 105
Magazine: None, single shot
Barrel: 26" or 28"
Finish: Blued; case hardened frame; checkered walnut straight grip stock & forearm except No. 107 (plain)
Approximate wt.: 5½ lbs.
Comments: A lightweight series of shotguns produced until about World War II for Model 105; 1950's for Model 107 & 1920's for Models 115 & 125.
Estimated Value: Excellent: $95.00
Very good: $75.00

Stevens Springfield Model No. 95
Very similar to the Model 107. Made from the mid 1920's until the mid 1930's.
Estimated Value: Excellent: $90.00
Very good: $70.00

Stevens Model No. 107

Stevens Model No. 115

Stevens Model No. 125

Stevens Model No. 116

Stevens Model No. 116 & 117
Similar to the Model 115 with automatic ejector. Model No. 117 is equipped with Lyman sights. 116 made from 1932 to 1942; 117 made from 1932 to 1936.
Estimated Value: Excellent: $100.00
Very good: $ 80.00

Stevens Model No. 250

Gauge: 12
Action: Top lever, break-open; exposed hammers; double trigger
Magazine: None
Barrel: 28", 30", 32" Side by side double barrel
Finish: Blued; checkered walnut pistol grip stock & forearm
Approximate wt.: 8 lbs.
Comments: Made from 1903 to 1908.
Estimated Value: Excellent: $245.00
                            Very good: $195.00

Stevens Model No. 250

Stevens Model No. 350

Stevens Model No. 260 & 270

Similar to Model 250 with special Damascus or twist barrels; available in 16 gauge. Manufactured from 1903 to 1906.
Estimated Value: Excellent: $220.00
                            Very good: $175.00

Stevens Model No. 355

Stevens Model No. 350, 360, 370

Gauge: 12, 16
Action: Top lever, break-open; hammerless; double trigger
Magazine: None
Barrel: Side by side double barrel, matted rib, 28", 30", 32"
Finish: Blued; checkered walnut pistol grip stock & forearm
Approximate wt.: 7½ to 8½ lbs.
Comments: Produced from 1903 to 1908.
Estimated Value: Excellent: $195.00
                            Very good: $155.00

Stevens Model No. 385

Stevens Model No. 235

Stevens Model No. 255

Stevens Model No. 355, 365, 375, 385

Gauge: 12, 16
Action: Top lever, break-open; hammerless; double trigger
Magazine: None
Barrel: Side by side double barrel; Krupp steel; matted rib; 28", 30", 32"
Finish: Blued; checkered walnut straight or pistol grip stock & forearm; 355 & 365 plain; 375 some engraving; 385 engraved frame
Approximate wt.: 7 to 8½ lbs.
Comments: Made from 1907. 355 discontinued in World War I; all others in 1913.
Estimated Value: Excellent: $220.00
                            Very good: $175.00

Stevens Model No. 235, 255, 265

Gauge: 12, 16
Action: Top lever, break-open; exposed hammers; double triggers; box lock
Magazine: None
Barrel: Double barrel; matted rib; 28", 30, 32"
Finish: Blued; checkered walnut pistol grip stock & forearm; case hardened frame; No. 255 has checkered buttplate
Approximate wt.: 7 to 8½ lbs.
Comments: Made from around 1907 until 1928 (No. 235); 255 & 265 stopped around World War I.
Estimated Value: Excellent: $250.00
                            Very good: $200.00

Stevens Riverside Model No. 215

Gauge: 12, 16
Action: Top lever, break-open; exposed hammer; double trigger
Magazine: None
Barrel: Side by side double barrel; 26", 28", 30", 32"; matted rib; full and modified chokes
Finish: Blued; case hardened frame; checkered walnut pistol grip stock & forearm
Approximate wt.: 7½ to 8½ lbs.
Comments: Made from around 1912 to 1942.
Estimated Value: Excellent: $220.00
                       Very good: $175.00

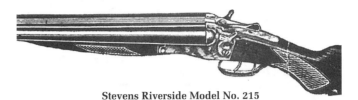

Stevens Riverside Model No. 215

Stevens Riverside Model No. 315

Gauge: 12, 16
Action: Top lever, break-open; hammerless; double trigger
Magazine: None
Barrel: Side by side double barrel; 26", 28", 30", 32"; matted rib; full and modified chokes
Finish: Blued; case hardened frame; checkered walnut semi-pistol grip stock & forearm
Approximate wt.: 7 to 7½ lbs.
Comments: Made from around 1912 until 1936.
Estimated Value: Excellent: $215.00
                       Very good: $170.00

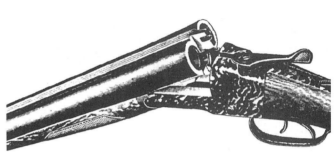

Stevens Riverside Model No. 315

Stevens Model No. 335

Similar to the 315. Produced from around 1912 to 1930.
Estimated Value: Excellent: $195.00
                       Very good: $155.00

Stevens Model No. 335

Stevens Model No. 345

Similar to the No. 335 in 20 gauge. Made from around 1912 to 1926.
Estimated Value: Excellent: $210.00
                       Very good: $165.00

Stevens Model No. 345

Stevens Model No. 330

Stevens Model No. 330

Gauge: 12, 16, 20, 410
Action: Top lever, break-open; hammerless; double trigger; takedown
Magazine: None
Barrel: Side by side double barrel; 26"-32"; right modified, left full choke; both full choke in 410
Finish: Blued; case hardened frame; checkered black walnut pistol grip stock & forearm
Approximate wt.: 5¾ to 7¾ lbs.
Comments: Made from the mid 1920's until the mid 1930's.
Estimated Value: Excellent: $215.00
                       Very good: $175.00

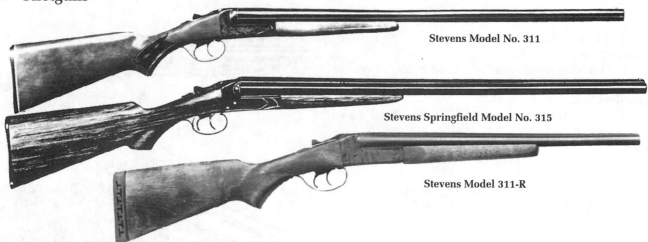

Stevens Model No. 311

Stevens Springfield Model No. 315

Stevens Model 311-R

Stevens Model 311,
Stevens Springfield Model No. 311
Springfield Hammerless

Gauge: 12, 16, 20, 410
Action: Top lever, break-open; hammerless; double trigger; takedown
Magazine: None
Barrel: Side by side double barrel; 24"-32"; modified and full chokes; both full choke in 32" 12 gauge; matted rib
Finish: Blued; case hardened frame; smooth walnut semi-pistol grip stock & forearm
Approximate wt.: 5½ to 7¾ lbs.
Comments: Made from about 1931 to late 1980's. Add $30.00 for selective single trigger. 16 gauge discontinued in late 1970's. See Savage Model 311.
Estimated Value: **Excellent:**   **$245.00**
                       Very good: **$195.00**

Stevens Springfield Model No. 315

A higher quality version of the Model 311; discontinued.
Estimated Value: **Excellent:**   **$260.00**
                       Very good: **$210.00**

Stevens Model 311-R

A law enforcement version of the Model 311 with 18¼" cylinder bore barrel; recoil pad; 12 gauge only. Produced from 1982 to 1988. See Savage Model 311-R.
Estimated Value: **Excellent:**   **$235.00**
                       Very good: **$190.00**

Stevens Model No. 530

Gauge: 12, 16, 20, 410
Action: Top lever, break-open; hammerless; box lock; double trigger
Magazine: None
Barrel: Side by side double barrel; 26"-32"; modified choke and full chokes; both full choke in 32" 12 gauge & 410.
Finish: Blued; case hardened frame; checkered walnut pistol grip stock & forearm;
Approximate wt.: 6 to 7½ lbs.
Comments: Made from about 1935 to 1952.
Estimated Value: **Excellent:**   **$220.00**
                       Very good: **$175.00**

Stevens Model No. 530 ST

Same as 530 with non-selective single trigger.
Estimated Value: **Excellent:**   **$225.00**
                       Very good: **$180.00**

Stevens Model No. 530M

Same as Model No 530 except: plastic stock. Discontinued in late 1940's.
Estimated Value: **Excellent:**   **$200.00**
                       Very good: **$160.00**

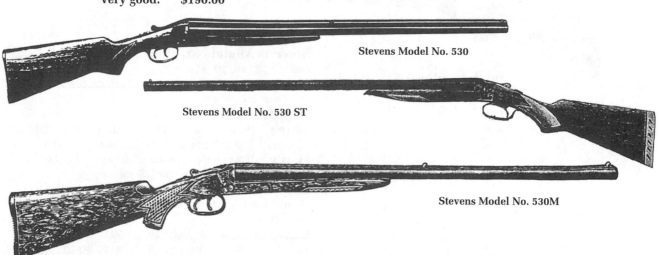

Stevens Model No. 530

Stevens Model No. 530 ST

Stevens Model No. 530M

Stevens Model 511

Stevens Model 511
Gauge: 12, 20, regular or magnum
Action: Box lock; top lever, break-open; double trigger
Magazine: None
Barrel: Double barrel; 28" modified & full choke
Finish: Blued; checkered hardwood semi-pistol grip stock & small forearm; case hardened frame
Approximate wt.: 7¾ lbs.
Comments: Produced in the late 1970's.
Estimated Value: Excellent: $230.00
                       Very good: $185.00

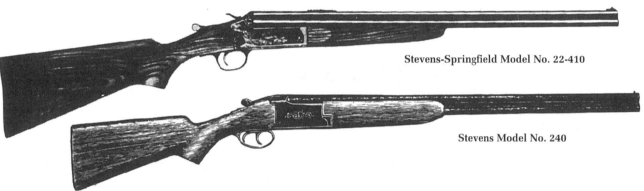

Stevens-Springfield Model No. 22-410

Stevens Model No. 240

Stevens Model No. 240
Gauge: 410
Action: Top lever, break-open; hammerless; double trigger; takedown
Magazine: None
Barrel: 26" Over & under double barrel; both barrels full choke
Finish: Blued; checkered plastic or wood pistol grip stock & forearm
Approximate wt.: 6½ lbs.
Comments: Made from about 1940 to 1948.
Estimated Value: Excellent: $345.00
                       Very good: $275.00

Stevens-Springfield Model No. 22-410
Gauge: 410 & 22 caliber rifle
Action: Top lever, break-open; exposed hammer; single trigger; separate extractors
Magazine: None
Barrel: 24" Over & under double barrel; 22 rifle over 410 shotgun
Finish: Blued; case hardened frame; plastic semi-pistol grip stock & forearm; open rear, ramp front sights
Approximate wt.: 6 lbs.
Comments: Made from about 1940 to 1948. Later produced as Savage.
Estimated Value: Excellent: $175.00
                       Very good: $140.00

Stevens Model 58

Stevens Model No. 59

Stevens Model No. 58
Gauge: 410
Action: Bolt-action
Magazine: 3-shot detachable box
Barrel: 24" full choke
Finish: Blued; plain walnut one-piece pistol grip stock & forearm
Approximate wt.: 5½ lbs.
Comments: Made from about 1935 to late 1970's. Later versions have checkering.
Estimated Value: Excellent: $100.00
                       Very good: $ 80.00

Stevens Model No. 59
Similar to Model No. 58 except: 5-shot tubular magazine. Made from about 1939 to early 1970's.
Estimated Value: Excellent: $115.00
                       Very good: $ 95.00

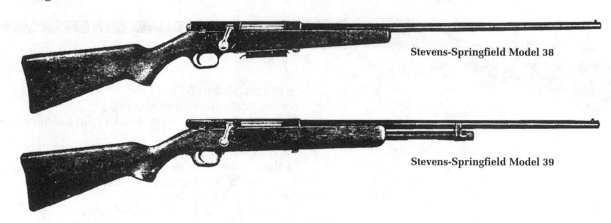

Stevens-Springfield Model 38

Stevens-Springfield Model 39

Stevens-Springfield Model 38
Similar to Stevens Model No. 58. Made 1939 to 1947.

Estimated Value:	Excellent:	$95.00
	Very good:	$80.00

Stevens-Springfield Model 39
Similar to Stevens Model No. 59. Made 1939 to 1947.

Estimated Value:	Excellent:	$110.00
	Very good:	$ 90.00

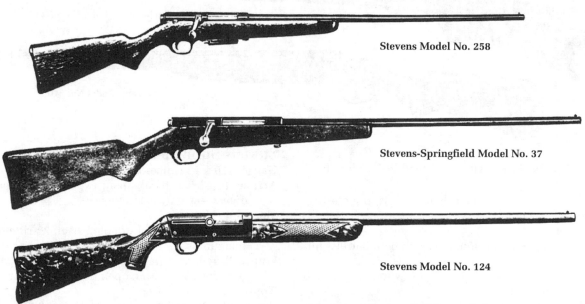

Stevens Model No. 258

Stevens-Springfield Model No. 37

Stevens Model No. 124

Stevens Model No. 258
Gauge: 20
Action: Bolt action; repeating
Magazine: 2-shot detachable box
Barrel: 26" full choke
Finish: Blued; plain walnut one-piece pistol grip stock & forearm
Approximate wt.: 6¼ lbs.
Comments: This takedown shotgun was produced from 1939 until 1942.

Estimated Value:	Excellent:	$100.00
	Very good:	$ 80.00

Stevens Model No. 254
A single shot version of the Model 258.

Estimated Value:	Excellent:	$85.00
	Very good:	$70.00

Stevens-Springfield Model 238
Similar to Stevens Model 258. Made 1939 to 1947.

Estimated Value:	Excellent:	$100.00
	Very good:	$80.00

Stevens-Springfield Model 237
Similar to Stevens Model No. 254. Single shot. Made from 1939 to 1942.

Estimated Value:	Excellent:	$90.00
	Very good:	$70.00

Stevens-Springfield Model No. 37
Similar to Stevens-Springfield Model 237 except 410 bore. Made from 1939 to 1942.

Estimated Value:	Excellent:	$95.00
	Very good:	$80.00

Stevens Model No. 124
Gauge: 12
Action: Semi-automatic; side ejection; hammerless
Magazine: 2-shot
Barrel: 28" improved cylinder, modified or full choke
Finish: Blued; checkered plastic pistol grip stock & forearm
Approximate wt.: 7 lbs.
Comments: Made from about 1950 to 1956.

Estimated Value:	Excellent:	$160.00
	Very good:	$125.00

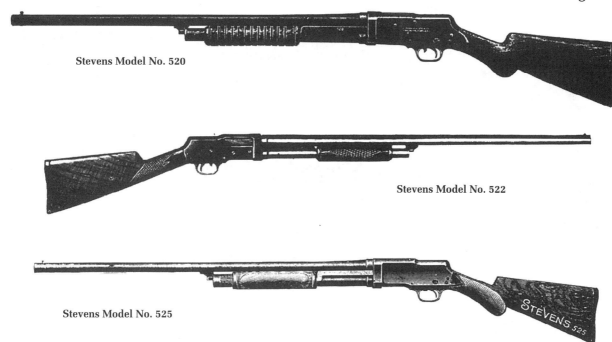

Stevens Model No. 520

Stevens Model No. 522

Stevens Model No. 525

Stevens Model No. 520, 521, 522

Gauge: 12

Action: Browning patent; slide action; takedown; side ejection; hammerless

Magazine: 5-shot tubular

Barrel: 26"-32"; full choke, modified or cylinder; matted rib on 521

Finish: Blued; walnut pistol grip stock & grooved slide handle; checkered straight grip & slide handle on 522

Approximate wt.: 8 lbs.

Comments: Made from about 1907 until World War II; 522 discontinued in 1928.

Estimated Value: Excellent: $195.00
                       Very good: $155.00

Stevens Models No. 525, 530, 535

Similar to 520 except fancier grades; 525 is custom built; 530 custom built with engraved receiver & rib; 535 custom built, heavily engraved. Made from 1912 to 1918. Add $75.00 for engraving.

Estimated Value: Excellent: $240.00
                       Very good: $195.00

Stevens Model No. 535

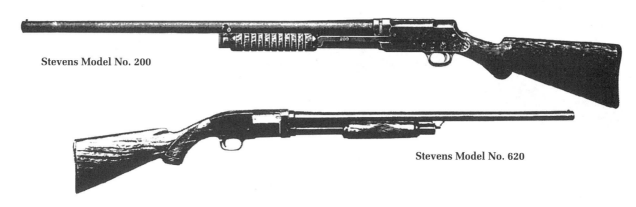

Stevens Model No. 200

Stevens Model No. 620

Stevens Model No. 200

Gauge: 20

Action: Pedersen patent slide action; hammerless; side ejection; takedown

Magazine: 5-shot tubular

Barrel: 26"-32"; full choke, modified or cylinder bore

Finish: Blued; walnut pistol grip stock & grooved slide handle

Approximate wt.: 6½ lbs.

Comments: Made from about 1912 to 1918.

Estimated Value: Excellent: $205.00
                       Very good: $165.00

Stevens Model No. 620

Gauge: 12, 16, 20

Action: Slide action; hammerless; side ejection

Magazine: 5-shot tubular

Barrel: 26"-32"; full choke, modified or cylinder bore

Finish: Blued; checkered walnut pistol grip stock & slide handle

Approximate wt.: 6 to 7¾ lbs.

Comments: A takedown shotgun made from about 1932 to 1958

Estimated Value: Excellent: $200.00
                       Very good: $160.00

Stevens Model No. 620-P

Stevens Model No. 77

Stevens Model No. 620-P
Same as Model No. 620 with "Poly-Choke."
Estimated Value: Excellent: $210.00
Very good: $165.00

Stevens Model No. 621
Same as Model No. 620 with matted rib. Made from 1932 to 1937.
Estimated Value: Excellent: $215.00
Very good: $170.00

Stevens Model No. 77
Gauge: 12, 16
Action: Slide action; hammerless; side ejection
Magazine: 5-shot tubular
Barrel: 26" or 28" improved cylinder, modified or full choke
Finish: Blued; plain walnut pistol grip stock & grooved slide handle
Approximate wt.: 7 lbs.
Comments: Made from the mid 1950's to early 1970's.
Estimated Value: Excellent: $195.00
Very good: $155.00

Stevens Model No. 77-SC
Same as 77 with Savage "Super Choke" & recoil pad.
Estimated Value: Excellent: $205.00
Very good: $160.00

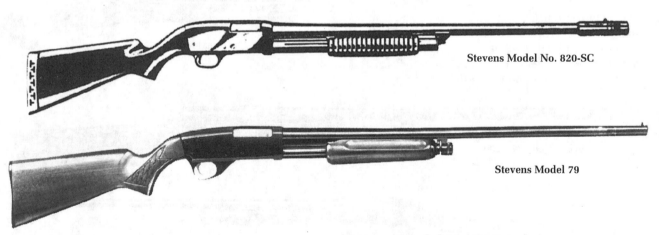

Stevens Model No. 820-SC

Stevens Model 79

Stevens Model No. 79
Gauge: 12, 20, 410, regular or magnum
Action: Slide action; hammerless; side ejection, repeating
Magazine: 4-shot tubular; 3-shot in magnum
Barrel: 28" modified or 30" full in 12 gauge; 28" modified or full in 20 gauge; 26" full in 410
Finish: Blued; checkered hardwood semi-pistol grip stock & fluted slide handle
Approximate wt.: 7 lbs.
Comments: Produced in the late 1970's.
Estimated Value: Excellent: $185.00
Very good: $145.00

Stevens Model No. 820
Gauge: 12
Action: Slide action; hammerless; side ejection
Magazine: 5-shot tubular
Barrel: 28" improved cylinder, modified or full choke
Finish: Blued; plain walnut semi-pistol grip stock & grooved slide handle
Approximate wt.: 7½ lbs.
Comments: Produced from about 1950 to 1956.
Estimated Value: Excellent: $190.00
Very good: $150.00

Stevens Model No. 820-SC
Same as No. 820 with Savage "Super Choke."
Estimated Value: Excellent: $215.00
Very good: $170.00

Stevens Model 79 VR

Stevens Model 79 Slug
Similar to the Model 79 with a 21" barrel for slugs; rifle sights.
Estimated Value: Excellent: $190.00
           Very good: $150.00

Stevens Model 79 VR
Similar to the Model 79 with a ventilated rib.
Estimated Value: Excellent: $205.00
           Very good: $165.00

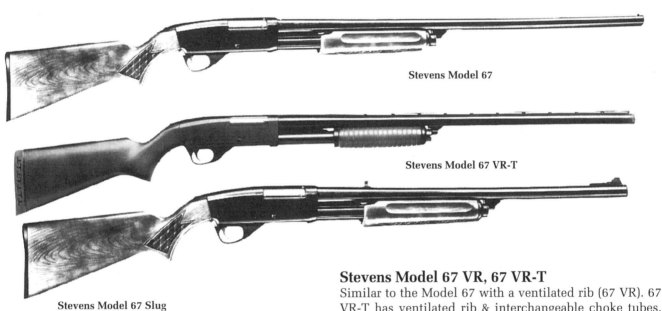

Stevens Model 67

Stevens Model 67 VR-T

Stevens Model 67 Slug

Stevens Model 67, 67T
Gauge: 12, 20 or 410, regular or magnum
Action: Slide action; hammerless; side ejecting; repeating
Magazine: 4-shot tubular; 3-shot in magnum
Barrel: 28" modified or full; 26" full in 410; 30" full in 12 gauge; 67T has interchangeable choke tubes in 12 & 20 gauge only
Finish: Blued; hardwood, semi-pistol grip stock & fluted or grooved slide handle; some with recoil pad
Approximate wt.: 6¾ lbs.
Comments: Produced from the late 1970's to late 1980's. Add $16.00 for 67T. See Savage Model 67.
Estimated Value: Excellent: $195.00
           Very good: $160.00

Stevens Model 67 Slug
Similar to the Model 67 with a 21" barrel for slugs & rifle sights; 12 gauge only. See Savage Model 67 Slug.
Estimated Value: Excellent: $210.00
           Very good: $170.00

Stevens Model 67 VR, 67 VR-T
Similar to the Model 67 with a ventilated rib (67 VR). 67 VR-T has ventilated rib & interchangeable choke tubes. Add 7% for interchangeable choke tubes in 12 or 20 gauge only. Discontinued 1988. See Savage Model 67 VR-T.
Estimated Value: Excellent: $200.00
           Very good: $160.00

Stevens Model 67VRT-K
Similar to the Model 67VRT-T except: laminated camo stock. Produced from 1986 to 1988.
Estimated Value: Excellent: $210.00
           Very good: $175.00

Stevens Model 67T-Y, 67VRT-Y
Gauge: 20
Action: Slide action; hammerless; repeating
Magazine: 4-shot
Barrel: 22" with three interchangeable choke tubes; ventilated rib on 67VRT-Y
Finish: Blued; hardwood, semi-pistol grip stock & grooved slide handle
Approximate wt.: 6 lbs.
Comments: Designed for the young shooter with a shorter 12" pull stock. Deduct $16.00 for plain barrel (67T-Y). Made from 1985 to 1988.
Estimated Value: Excellent: $200.00
           Very good: $160.00

Universal

Universal Model 101

Universal Model 101
Gauge: 12
Action: Box lock; top lever, break-open; exposed hammer; single shot
Magazine: None
Barrel: 28", 30" full choke
Finish: Blued; plain wood pistol grip stock & tapered forearm
Approximate wt.: 7½ lbs.
Comments: Manufactured in the late 1960's.
Estimated Value: Excellent: $95.00
                        Very good: $75.00

Universal Single Wing
Similar to the Model 101. Made from the early to mid 1970's.
Estimated Value: Excellent: $100.00
                        Very good: $ 80.00

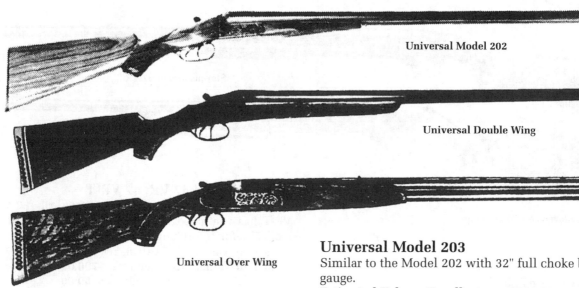

Universal Model 202

Universal Double Wing

Universal Over Wing

Universal Model 202
Gauge: 12, 20, 410
Action: Box lock; top lever, break-open; hammerless; double triggers
Magazine: None
Barrel: Side by side double barrel; 26" improved cylinder & modified; 28" modified & full chokes
Finish: Blued; checkered walnut pistol grip stock & forearm
Approximate wt.: 7 lbs.
Comments: Made in the late 1960's. Add 5% for 410.
Estimated Value: Excellent: $200.00
                        Very good: $160.00

Universal Double Wing
Similar to the Model 202 with recoil pad. Made from 1970 to 1975; 12 or 20 gauge magnum.
Estimated Value: Excellent: $225.00
                        Very good: $180.00

Universal Model 203
Similar to the Model 202 with 32" full choke barrels & 10 gauge.
Estimated Value: Excellent: $230.00
                        Very good: $185.00

Universal Model 2030
Similar to the Double Wing with 32" full choke barrels & 10 gauge.
Estimated Value: Excellent: $250.00
                        Very good: $200.00

Universal Over Wing
Gauge: 12, 20
Action: Box lock; top lever, break-open; hammerless
Magazine: None
Barrel: Over & under double barrel; 26", 28", 30"; ventilated rib
Finish: Blued; checkered walnut pistol grip stock & forearm; sights; recoil pad; engraving available
Approximate wt.: 8 lbs.
Comments: Made from about 1970 to 1975. Add 10 % for single trigger.
Estimated Value: Excellent: $400.00
                        Very good: $320.00

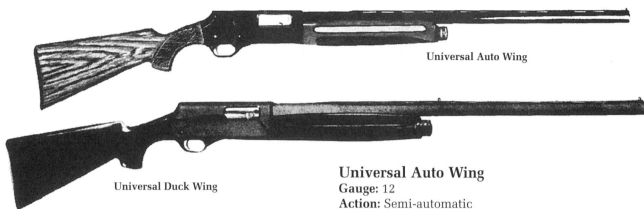

Universal Auto Wing

Universal Duck Wing

Universal Auto Wing
Gauge: 12
Action: Semi-automatic
Magazine: 5-shot tubular
Barrel: 26", 28", 30"; variety of chokes; ventilated rib
Finish: Blued; checkered walnut pistol grip stock & forearm; sights
Approximate wt.: 8 lbs.
Comments: Made from about 1970 to 1975.
Estimated Value: Excellent: $270.00
                        Very good: $210.00

Universal Duck Wing
Similar to the Auto Wing with 28" or 30" full choke barrel. Teflon coated. Discontinued in the early 1970's.
Estimated Value: Excellent: $295.00
                        Very good: $235.00

Valmet

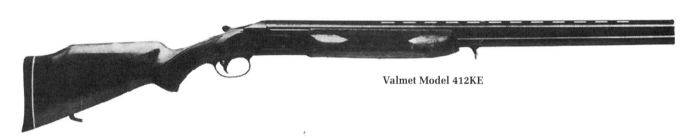

Valmet Model 412KE

Valmet Model 412KE
Gauge: 12
Action: Top lever, break-open; hammerless; automatic ejectors
Magazine: None
Barrel: Over & under double barrel; 26" improved cylinder & modified; 28" modified & full; 30" modified & full in 12 gauge; ventilated rib
Finish: Blued; checkered walnut pistol grip stock & forearm; Monte Carlo stock with recoil pad; swivels
Approximate wt.: 7 lbs.
Comments: Made in Finland with interchangeable barrels available that make the shotgun a combination shotgun/rifle or a double rifle. Produced from the early 1980's to mid 1980's.
Estimated Value: Excellent: $600.00
                        Very good: $480.00

Valmet Model 412K
Similar to the Model 412KE with 36" barrels. Introduced in 1982.
Estimated Value: Excellent: $610.00
                        Very good: $490.00

Valmet Model 412KE Trap
Similar to the Model 412KE except:30" full choke barrels.
Estimated Value: Excellent: $650.00
                        Very good: $520.00

Valmet Model 412KE Skeet
Similar to the Model 412KE with 26" or 28" cylinder bore & improved cylinder bore or skeet choke barrels.
Estimated Value: Excellent: $625.00
                        Very good: $500.00

Valmet Model 412K Combination
Similar to the Model 412K with a 12 gauge improved modified barrel over a rifle barrel in caliber 222, 223, 243, 30-06, 308; 24" barrels. Introduced in 1982.
Estimated Value: Excellent: $675.00
                        Very good: $540.00

Valmet 12 Gauge
Gauge: 12
Action: Box lock; top lever, break-open; single selective trigger
Magazine: None
Barrel: Over & under double barrel; 26" improved cylinder & modified; 28" modified & full; 30" modified & full or full & full chokes
Finish: Blued; checkered walnut pistol grip stock & wide forearm
Approximate wt.: 8 lbs.
Comments: Made from the late 1940's to the late 1960's in Finland.
Estimated Value: Excellent: $475.00
                        Very good: $380.00

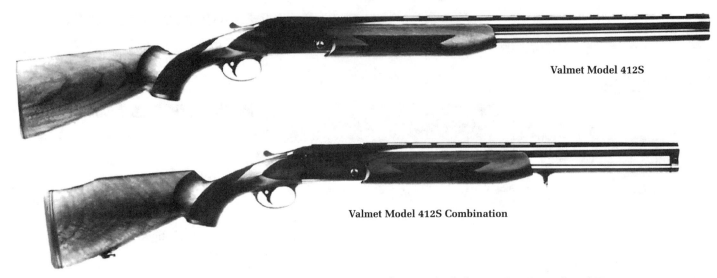

Valmet Model 412S

Valmet Model 412S Combination

Valmet Model 412S

Gauge: 12, 20; regular or magnum

Action: Top lever, break-open; hammerless; automatic ejectors

Magazine: None

Barrel: Over & under double barrel; 26" cylinder bore & improved cylinder, improved cylinder or modified; 28" cylinder bore & modified or modified & full; 30" improved modified & full, modified & full; 36" full; ventilated rib

Finish: Blued; checkered walnut pistol grip stock & forearm, adjustable for barrel differences; buttplate adjusts to fit shooter

Approximate wt.: 7 lbs.

Comments: A shooting system with interchangeable barrels & adjustable buttplate; produced in Finland. Introduced in 1984.

Estimated Value: Excellent: $775.00
                       Very good: $620.00

Valmet Model 412 ST Standard Trap

Similar to the Model 412S with Monte Carlo stock, 12 gauge only, 30" or 32" barrel. Introduced in 1987. Add 30% for Premium Grade Model.

Estimated Value: Excellent: $ 925.00
                       Very good: $ 745.00

Valmet Model 412ST Standard Skeet

Similar to the Model 412S with 28" skeet choke barrel. Introduced in 1987. Add 30% for Premium Grade Model.

Estimated Value: Excellent: $ 900.00
                       Very good: $ 720.00

Valmet Model 412S Combination

Similar to the Model 412S with 24" 12 gauge improved/modified barrel over a 222, 223, 243, 30-06 or 308 caliber rifle barrel.

Estimated Value: Excellent: $ 890.00
                       Very good: $ 710.00

Weatherby

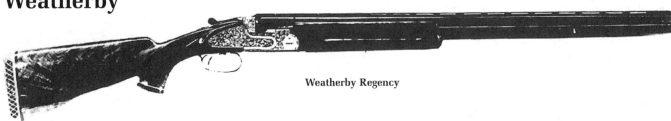

Weatherby Regency

Weatherby Regency Skeet

Similar to the Regency in skeet chokes with a 26" or 28" barrel.

Estimated Value: Excellent: $975.00
                       Very good: $780.00

Weatherby Regency Trap

Similar to the Regency with a wide ventilated rib barrel; 30" or 32" full & full, full & improved modified, or full & modified chokes; choice of regular or Monte Carlo stock; 12 gauge only.

Estimated Value: Excellent: $1,000.00
                       Very good: $ 800.00

Weatherby Regency

Gauge: 12, 20

Action: Box lock; top lever, break-open; hammerless; automatic ejectors; single selective trigger

Magazine: None

Barrel: Over & under double barrel; 26", 28", 30"; variety of chokes; ventilated rib

Finish: Blued; checkered walnut pistol grip stock & fluted forearm; recoil pad

Approximate wt.: 7 to 7½ lbs.

Comments: Made from the early 1970's to the early 1980's.

Estimated Value: Excellent: $950.00
                       Very good: $760.00

Weatherby Olympian

Weatherby Olympian Skeet
Similar to the Olympian with 26" or 28" skeet choke barrel.

Estimated Value: **Excellent:**   **$780.00**
                    Very good: **$625.00**

Weatherby Olympian Trap
Similar to the Olympian; ventilated rib between barrels; 30" or 32" full & modified or full & improved modified chokes; Monte Carlo or regular stock.

Estimated Value: **Excellent:**   **$800.00**
                    Very good: **$640.00**

Weatherby Olympian
Gauge: 12, 20
Action: Box lock; top lever, break-open; selective automatic ejectors
Magazine: None
Barrel: Over & under double barrel; 26" or 28" full & modified; 26" or 28" modified & improved cylinder; 30" full & modified; ventilated rib
Finish: Blued; checkered walnut pistol grip stock & fluted forearm; recoil pad
Approximate wt.: 7 to 8 lbs.
Comments: Made from the 1970's to early 1980's.
Estimated Value: **Excellent:**   **$750.00**
                    Very good: **$600.00**

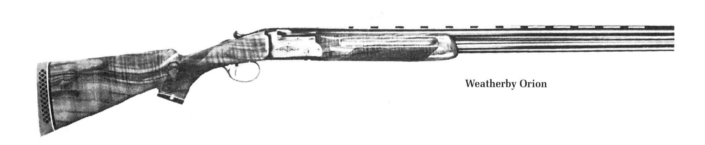

Weatherby Orion

Weatherby Orion Trap
Similar to the Orion Grade I except: 12 gauge only; 30" or 32" full & modified barrels; multi-choke after 1983; wide rib on top & ventilated rib between barrels; curved recoil pad; Monte Carlo or regular stock. Made in 1980's to early 1990's

Estimated Value: **Excellent:**   **$950.00**
                    Very good: **$760.00**

Weatherby Orion Skeet
Similar to the Orion Grade I except: 26" skeet choke barrels or multi-choke after 1983; 12 or 20 gauge.

Estimated Value: **Excellent:**   **$910.00**
                    Very good: **$730.00**

Weatherby Orion Grades I, II, & III
Gauge: 12, 20, 28, 410
Action: Box lock; top lever, break-open; selective automatic ejectors; single selective trigger
Magazine: None
Barrel: Over & under double barrel; 26" or 28" modified & improved cylinder; 28" or 30" full & modified; ventilated rib. Multi-choke after 1983
Finish: Blued; checkered walnut pistol grip stock & fluted forearm; recoil pad; engraved receiver
Approximate wt.: 6½ to 7½ lbs.
Comments: Introduced in 1982. 28 gauge & 410 added in 1988. Add 6% for grade II; Add 26% for Grade III. Add 13% for sporting clays
Estimated Value: **New (retail):**   **$1,289.00**
                    Excellent: **$ 965.00**
                    Very good: **$ 775.00**

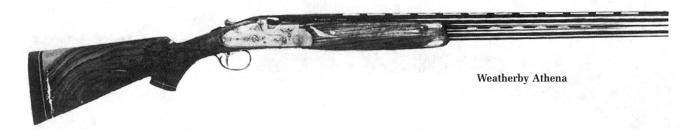

Weatherby Athena

Weatherby Athena Grade IV & Grade V
Gauge: 12, 20, 28, 410
Action: Box lock; top lever, break-open; selective automatic ejectors; single selective trigger
Magazine: None
Barrel: Over & under double barrel; 26" or 28" modified & improved cylinder; 28" modified & full choke; ventilated rib on top & between barrels. Multi-choke after 1983
Finish: Blued; special selected checkered walnut pistol grip stock & fluted forearm; high-lustre finish; rosewood grip cap; recoil pad; silver grey engraved receiver
Approximate wt.: 7 to 8 lbs.
Comments: A high-quality superposed shotgun introduced in 1982. 28 gauge & 410 added 1988. Add 18% for Grade V.
Estimated Value:

New (retail):	$ 2200.00
Excellent:	$1,650.00
Very good:	$1,320.00

Weatherby Athena Single Barrel Trap
Similar to the Athena Trap except: a single ventilated rib barrel configuration. Produced from the late 1980's to early 1990's
Estimated Value:

Excellent:	$1,600.00
Very good:	$1,275.00

Weatherby Athena Trap
Similar to the Athena in 12 gauge only in 30" or 32" full & improved modified or full & modified barrels; wide rib with center bead sight; curved recoil pad; Monte Carlo stock. Multi-choke after 1983.
Estimated Value:

Excellent:	$1,625.00
Very good:	$1,300.00

Weatherby Athena Skeet
Similar to the Athena with 26" skeet choke barrels.
Estimated Value:

Excellent:	$1,575.00
Very good:	$1,260.00

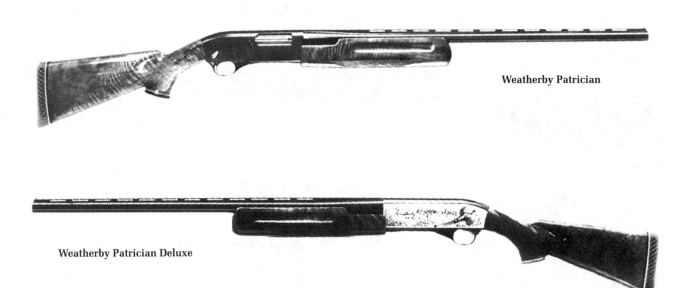

Weatherby Patrician

Weatherby Patrician Deluxe

Weatherby Patrician & Patrician II
Gauge: 12 reg. (Patrician); 12 magnum (Patrician II)
Action: Slide action; hammerless; side ejection
Magazine: Tubular
Barrel: 26", 28", 30"; variety of chokes; ventilated rib
Finish: Blued; checkered walnut pistol grip stock & grooved slide handle; recoil pad
Approximate wt.: 7½ lbs.
Comments: Made from the early 1970's to early 1980's. Add 7% for Trap.
Estimated Value:

Excellent:	$350.00
Very good:	$280.00

Weatherby Patrician Deluxe
Similar to the Patrician with decorated satin silver receiver & higher quality wood.
Estimated Value:

Excellent:	$450.00
Very good:	$350.00

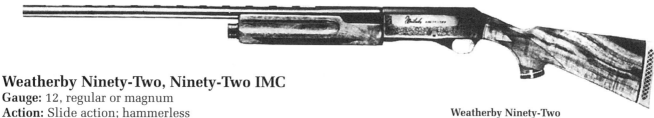

Weatherby Ninety-Two

Weatherby Ninety-Two, Ninety-Two IMC
Gauge: 12, regular or magnum
Action: Slide action; hammerless
Magazine: 2-shot tubular, with plug
Barrel: 26" improved cylinder or skeet, 28" modified or full, 30" full; ventilated rib. Multi-choke barrel on all after 1983
Finish: Blued; checkered walnut pistol grip stock & slide handle; high-gloss finish; rosewood grip cap; etched receiver; recoil pad
Approximate wt.: 7½ lbs.
Comments: Introduced in 1982. Trap Model discontinued in 1983; regular model discontinued in 1988.
Estimated Value: Excellent: $360.00
Very good: $290.00

Weatherby Ninety-Two Buckmaster
Similar to the Ninety-Two with a 22" slug barrel & rifle sights.
Estimated Value: Excellent: $365.00
Very good: $295.00

Weatherby Centurion

Weatherby Centurion Deluxe
Similar to the Centurion with a decorated satin silver receiver & higher quality wood.
Estimated Value: Excellent: $400.00
Very good: $320.00

Weatherby Centurion & Centurion II
Gauge: 12 reg.(Centurion); 12 mag.(Centurion II)
Action: Semi-automatic, gas operated; hammerless
Magazine: Tubular
Barrel: 26", 28", 30"; variety of chokes; ventilated rib
Finish: Blued; checkered walnut pistol grip stock & grooved forearm; recoil pad
Approximate wt.: 7½ lbs.
Comments: Made from the early 1970's to early 1980's. Add 7% for Trap.
Estimated Value: Excellent: $350.00
Very good: $280.00

Weatherby Eighty-Two

Weatherby Eighty-Two Buckmaster
Similar to the Eighty-Two except: 22" slug barrel & rifle sights.
Estimated Value: Excellent: $450.00
Very good: $365.00

Weatherby Eighty-Two, Eighty-Two IMC
Gauge: 12, regular or magnum
Action: Gas operated, semi-automatic; hammerless
Magazine: 2-shot tubular with plug
Barrel: 26" improved cylinder or skeet, 28" modified or full, 30" full; ventilated rib. "Multi-Choke" barrel after 1983
Finish: Blued; checkered walnut pistol grip stock & forearm; high gloss finish; rosewood grip cap; etched receiver; recoil pad
Approximate wt.: 7½ lbs.
Comments: Made from 1982 to 1991. Add 7% for Trap
Estimated Value: Excellent: $445.00
Very good: $360.00

Western

Western Long Range
Gauge: 12, 16, 20, 410
Action: Box lock; top lever, break-open; hammerless; double or single trigger
Magazine: None
Barrel: Side by side double barrel; 26"- 32"; modified & full choke
Finish: Blued; plain walnut pistol grip stock & forearm
Approximate wt.: 7 lbs.
Comments: Made from the mid 1920's until the early 1940's by Western Arms Corp. which was later bought by Ithaca Arms Company. Add $25.00 for single trigger.
Estimated Value: Excellent: $350.00
                              Very good: $280.00

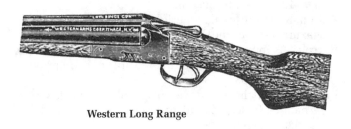

Western Long Range

Western Field

Western Field Model 100

Western Field Standard Double

Western Field Model 150C

Western Field Model 100
Gauge: 12, 16, 20, 410
Action: Box lock; thumb sliding, break-open; hammerless; single shot
Magazine: None
Barrel: 26"-30", full choke
Finish: Blued; wood semi-pistol grip stock & tapered forearm
Approximate wt.: 6¼ to 7 lbs.
Comments: Manufactured to the mid 1970's.
Estimated Value: Excellent: $100.00
                              Very good: $ 80.00

Western Field Standard Double
Gauge: 12, 16, 20, 410
Action: Box lock; top lever, break-open; hammerless
Magazine: None
Barrel: Side by side double barrel; 26"- 30"; modified & full or full & full chokes; ribbed barrels
Finish: Blued; wood semi-pistol grip stock & short tapered forearm
Approximate wt.: 6½ to 7 lbs.
Comments: Made to the mid 1970's.
Estimated Value: Excellent: $220.00
                              Very good: $175.00

Western Field Model 150C
Gauge: 410
Action: Bolt action; repeating
Magazine: 3-shot; top loading
Barrel: 25"; full choke; 3" chamber
Finish: Blued; wood Monte Carlo pistol grip one-piece stock & forearm
Approximate wt.: 5½ lbs.
Comments: Manufactured to the early 1980's.
Estimated Value: Excellent: $100.00
                              Very good: $ 80.00

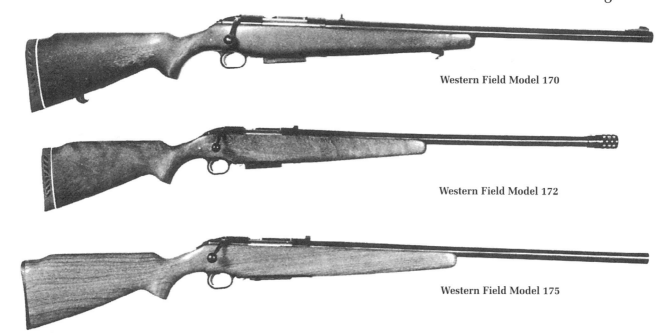

Western Field Model 170

Western Field Model 172

Western Field Model 175

Western Field Model 170
Gauge: 12
Action: Bolt action; repeating
Magazine: 3-shot detachable clip
Barrel: 28"
Finish: Blued; wood Monte Carlo semi-pistol grip one-
  piece stock & forearm; recoil pad; sights; swivels
Approximate wt.: 7 lbs.
Comments: Made to the late 1970's.
Estimated Value: Excellent: $110.00
                       Very good: $ 85.00

Western Field Model 172
Similar to the Model 170 without sights or swivels;
adjustable choke.
Estimated Value: Excellent: $100.00
                       Very good: $80.00

Western Field Model 175
Similar to the Model 172 in 20 gauge with a 26" barrel;
without adjustable choke.
Estimated Value: Excellent: $90.00
                       Very good: $70.00

Western Field Bolt Action
Gauge: 12, 20, regular or magnum, 410
Action: Bolt action; repeating
Magazine: 3-shot detachable box; 410 top loading
Barrel: 28" full choke; 25" in 410
Finish: Blued; smooth walnut finish hardwood one-piece
  pistol grip stock & forearm
Approximate wt.: 6½ lbs.
Comments: Add $10.00 for 12 gauge.
Estimated Value: Excellent: $95.00
                       Very good: $75.00

Western Field Model 550

Western Field Model 550
Gauge: 12, 20, 410, regular or magnum
Action: Slide action; hammerless; repeating
Magazine: 4-shot magnum, 5-shot regular, tubular
Barrel: 26" 410; 30" 12 gauge; full or modified choke
Finish: Blued; smooth hardwood pistol grip stock with
  fluted comb, grooved slide handle
Approximate wt.: 6½ lbs.
Comments: Add $20.00 for ventilated rib & variable
  choke.
Estimated Value: Excellent: $200.00
                       Very good: $160.00

Western Field Model 550 Deluxe
Gauge: 12, 20, regular or magnum
Action: Slide action; hammerless; repeating
Magazine: 5-shot tubular; 4-shot magnum
Barrel: 28" with 3 interchangeable "Accu-Choke" tubes;
  ventilated rib
Finish: Blued; checkered hardwood pistol grip stock &
  slide handle; recoil pad; engraved receiver
Approximate wt.: 7¼ lbs.
Comments: Produced in the 1980's.
Estimated Value: Excellent: $205.00
                       Very good: $165.00

Winchester

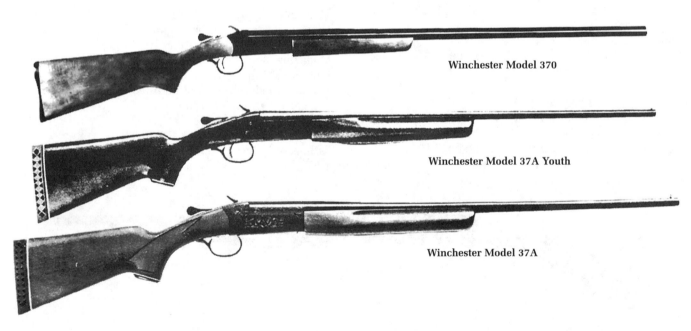

Winchester Model 20

Winchester Model 37

Winchester Model 20

Gauge: 410
Action: Top lever, break-open; box lock; exposed hammer; single shot
Magazine: None
Barrel: 26" full choke
Finish: Blued; plain or checkered wood pistol grip stock & lipped forearm
Approximate wt.: 6 lbs.
Comments: Made from about 1920 to 1925.
Estimated Value: Excellent: $270.00
                        Very good: $215.00

Winchester Model 37

Gauge: 12, 16, 20, 28, 410
Action: Top lever, break-open; partial visible hammer; automatic ejector
Magazine: None
Barrel: 26"-32"; full choke, modified or cylinder bore
Finish: Blued; plain walnut semi-pistol grip stock & forearm
Approximate wt.: 6 lbs.
Comments: Made from the late 1930's to mid 1960's. Add $300.00 for 28 gauge & $25.00 for 410 gauge.
Estimated Value: Excellent: $225.00
                        Very good: $180.00

Winchester Model 370

Winchester Model 37A Youth

Winchester Model 37A

Winchester Model 370

Gauge: 12, 16, 20, 28, 410
Action: Top lever, break-open; box lock; exposed hammer; single shot; automatic ejector
Magazine: None
Barrel: 26"-32" or 36" full choke; modified in 20 gauge
Finish: Blued; plain wood semi-pistol grip stock & forearm
Approximate wt.: 5¼ to 6¼ lbs.
Comments: Made from the late 1960's to mid 1970's.
Estimated Value: Excellent: $110.00
                        Very good: $ 90.00

Winchester Model 37A

Similar to the Model 370 but also available in 36" Waterfowl barrel; has checkered stock, fluted forearm; engraved receiver; gold plated trigger. Manufactured to the late 1970's. Add 6% for 36" barrel.
Estimated Value: Excellent: $115.00
                        Very good: $ 95.00

Winchester Model 37A Youth

Similar to the 37A with 26" barrel.
Estimated Value: Excellent: $100.00
                        Very good: $ 88.00

Winchester Model 21

Gauge: 12, 16, 20
Action: Box lock; top lever, break-open; hammerless, double or single trigger
Magazine: None
Barrel: 26-32" Side by side double barrel; matted or ventilated rib; full, modified or cylinder bore
Finish: Checkered walnut, pistol grip stock & forearm
Approximate wt.: 7 lbs.
Comments: Made in this grade from 1930 to late 1950's. Fancier grades were produced. Prices here for Field Grade.
Estimated Value: Excellent: $2,700.00
Very good: $2,150.00

Winchester Model 24

Gauge: 12, 16, 20
Action: Box lock; top lever, break-open; hammerless, automatic ejectors; double triggers
Magazine: None
Barrel: Side by side double barrel, 28" cylinder bore & modified in 12 gauge; other modified & full choke; raised matted rib
Finish: Blued; plain or checkered walnut pistol grip stock & forearm
Approximate wt.: 7½ lbs.
Comments: Made from the late 1930's to the late 1950's.
Estimated Value: Excellent: $375.00
Very good: $300.00

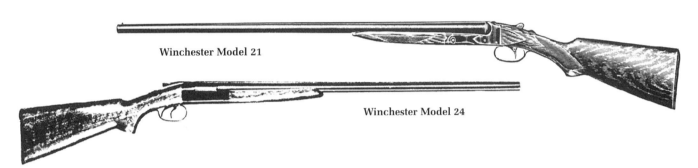

Winchester Model 21

Winchester Model 24

Winchester Model 23 Custom

Gauge: 12
Action: Box lock; top lever, break-open; hammerless, single selective trigger
Magazine: None
Barrel: Side by side double barrel, 25½" "Winchoke"
Finish: Blued; checkered walnut, pistol grip stock & forearm
Approximate wt.: 6¾ lbs.
Comments: Introduced in 1987.
Estimated Value: Excellent: $1,550.00
Very good: $1,250.00

Winchester Model 23 Classic

Similar to the Model 23 Custom with 26" barrels; 12, 20 or 28 gauge improved cylinder & modified; 410 modified & full choke; engraving on receiver. Add 5% for 28 gauge or 410 bore.
Estimated Value: Excellent: $1,600.00
Very good: $1,275.00

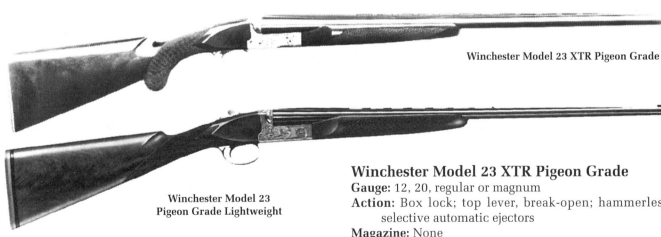

Winchester Model 23 XTR Pigeon Grade

Winchester Model 23
Pigeon Grade Lightweight

Winchester Model 23 XTR Pigeon Grade

Gauge: 12, 20, regular or magnum
Action: Box lock; top lever, break-open; hammerless; selective automatic ejectors
Magazine: None
Barrel: Side by side double barrel; 26" improved cylinder & modified; 28" modified & full choke; tapered ventilated rib; Winchoke after 1980
Finish: Blued; checkered walnut semi-pistol grip stock & forearm; silver grey engraved receiver
Approximate wt.: 6½ to 7 lbs.
Comments: Made from the late 1970's to late 1980's.
Estimated Value: Excellent: $1,125.00
Very good: $ 890.00

Winchester Model 23 Pigeon Grade Lightweight

Similar to the Model 23 XTR Pigeon Grade with a straight grip stock; rubber butt pad; 25½" ventilated rib barrels. Introduced in 1981. Discontinued in 1987. Add 3% for Winchoke.
Estimated Value: Excellent: $1,150.00
Very good: $ 900.00

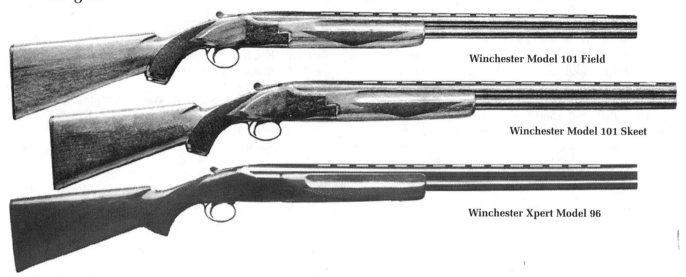

Winchester Model 101 Field

Winchester Model 101 Skeet

Winchester Xpert Model 96

Winchester Model 101 Field

Gauge: 12, 20, 28, 410, regular or magnum, 28, 410 discontinued in the late 1970's

Action: Box lock; top lever, break-open; hammerless; single trigger; automatic ejector

Magazine: None

Barrel: Over & under double barrel; 26"-30", various chokes; ventilated rib

Finish: Blued; checkered walnut pistol grip stock & wide forearm; recoil pad on magnum; engraved receiver

Approximate wt.: 6½ to 7½ lbs.

Comments: Made from the mid 1960's to about 1980. Add $30.00 for 410 or 28 gauge; $10.00 for magnum.

Estimated Value: **Excellent:**   **$950.00**
                                  Very good: **$710.00**

Winchester Model 101 Skeet

Similar to the Model 101 with skeet stock & choke. Add $30.00 for 410 or 28 gauge.

Estimated Value: **Excellent:**   **$1,000.00**
                                  Very good: **$ 750.00**

Winchester Model 101 Trap

Similar to the Model 101 with regular or Monte Carlo stock; recoil pad; 30"-32" barrels; 12 gauge only.

Estimated Value: **Excellent:**   **$1,000.00**
                                  Very good: **$ 750.00**

Winchester Xpert Model 96

A lower cost version of the Model 101, lacking engraving as well as some of the internal & external extras. Produced in the late 1970's.

Estimated Value: **Excellent:**   **$650.00**
                                  Very good: **$490.00**

Winchester Xpert Model 96 Trap

Similar to the Xpert Model 96 with Monte Carlo stock & 30" barrel.

Estimated Value: **Excellent:**   **$675.00**
                                  Very good: **$500.00**

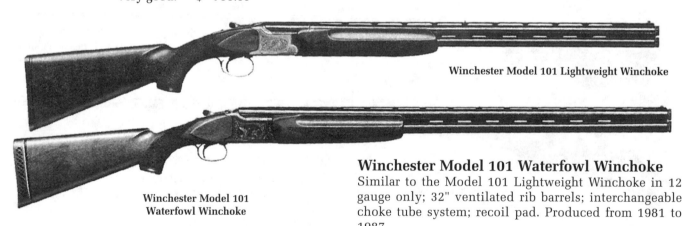

Winchester Model 101 Lightweight Winchoke

Winchester Model 101 Waterfowl Winchoke

Winchester Model 101 Lightweight Winchoke

Similar to the Model 101 Field with interchangeable choke tube system; lighter weight; ventilated rib between barrel. Introduced in 1981. 12 or 20 gauge.

Estimated Value: **Excellent:**   **$1,050.00**
                                  Very good: **$ 840.00**

Winchester Model 101 Waterfowl Winchoke

Similar to the Model 101 Lightweight Winchoke in 12 gauge only; 32" ventilated rib barrels; interchangeable choke tube system; recoil pad. Produced from 1981 to 1987.

Estimated Value: **Excellent:**   **$920.00**
                                  Very good: **$690.00**

Winchester Model 101 Waterfowler

Similar to the Model 101 Waterfowl Winchoke with sandblasted blued finish & low-lustre finish. Introduced in 1987.

Estimated Value: **Excellent:**   **$1,180.00**
                                  Very good: **$ 940.00**

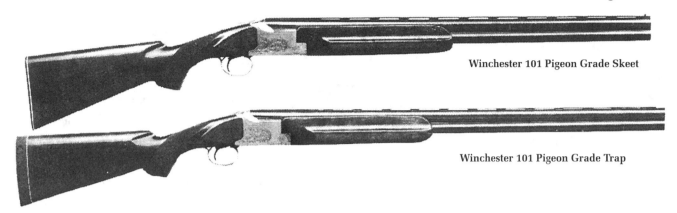

Winchester 101 Pigeon Grade Skeet

Winchester 101 Pigeon Grade Trap

Winchester 101 Pigeon Grade

Gauge: 12, 20, regular or magnum
Action: Box lock; top lever, break-open; selective automatic ejectors; single selective trigger
Magazine: None
Barrel: Over & under double barrel; 26" improved cylinder & modified; 28" modified & full; ventilated rib
Finish: Blued; checkered walnut pistol grip stock & fluted forearm; silver grey engraved receiver; recoil pad on magnum
Approximate wt.: 7¼ lbs.
Comments: Made from the late 1970's to early 1980's.
Estimated Value: Excellent: $900.00
Very good: $720.00

Winchester 101 Pigeon Grade Skeet

Similar to the Pigeon Grade with 27" or 28" skeet choke barrels; front & center sighting beads; 410 or 28 gauge available.
Estimated Value: Excellent: $1,000.00
Very good: $ 800.00

Winchester 101 Pigeon Grade Trap

Similar to the Pigeon Grade with a 30" or 32" barrel; recoil pad; regular or Monte Carlo stock.
Estimated Value: Excellent: $1,000.00
Very good: $ 825.00

Winchester Pigeon Grade Lightweight

Winchester Pigeon Grade Featherweight

Winchester Model 1001

Gauge: 12
Action: Top lever, break-open, hammerless; single selective trigger; automatic ejectors
Magazine: None
Barrel: Over & under double barrel; 28" or 30" chrome lined barrels with "WinPlus" choke system; ventilated rib
Finish: Dark blue; checkered walnut pistol grip stock and forearm; scroll engraving on frame sides; silver nitrate finish frame sides on Sporting Clays models.
Approximate wt.: 7 to 7½ lbs.
Comments: Introduced in 1993; Made in Brescia, Italy Add 14% for Sporting Clays model.
Estimated Value: New (Retail): $1,100.00
Excellent: $ 825.00
Very good: $ 670.00

Winchester Pigeon Grade Lightweight

Gauge: 12, 20, 3" chambers; 28 introduced in 1984
Action: Top lever, break-open
Magazine: None
Barrel: Over & under double barrel; 27" or 28" interchangeable choke tubes; ventilated rib on top & between barrels
Finish: Blued, silver grey stain finish receiver with etching of gamebirds & scroll work; checkered walnut rounded pistol grip stock & fluted forearm; recoil pad; straight stock available on 28 gauge
Approximate wt.: 6½ to 7½ lbs.
Comments: Introduced in 1981.
Estimated Value: Excellent: $1,435.00
Very good: $1,150.00

Winchester Pigeon Grade Featherweight

Similar to the Pigeon Grade Lightweight with 25½" barrels; improved cylinder & improved modified or improved cylinder & modified; straight grip English style stock; rubber butt pad. Introduced in 1981.
Estimated Value: Excellent: $1,185.00
Very good: $ 890.00

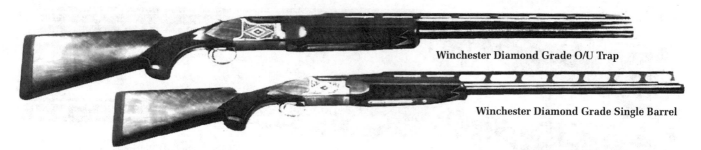

Winchester Diamond Grade O/U Trap

Winchester Diamond Grade Single Barrel

Winchester Diamond Grade O/U Trap
Gauge: 12
Action: Top lever, break-open
Magazine: None
Barrel: Over & under double barrel; 30" or 32" full choke top, interchangeable choke tube system bottom; ventilated rib on top & between barrels
Finish: Blued, silver grey stain finish on receiver with engraving; checkered walnut pistol grip stock & lipped forearm; ebony inlay in pistol grip; regular or Monte Carlo stock; recoil pad
Approximate wt.: 8¾ to 9 lbs.
Comments: Introduced in 1982.
Estimated Value: Excellent: $1,395.00
                       Very good: $1,115.00

Winchester Diamond Grade Single Barrel
Similar to the Diamond Grade O/U Trap but with only one 32" or 34" barrel; interchangeable choke tube system; high-ventilated rib. Introduced in 1982.
Estimated Value: Excellent: $1,610.00
                       Very good: $1,285.00

Winchester Diamond Grade O/U Skeet
Similar to the Diamond Grade O/U Trap in 12, 20, 28 gauges & 410 bore; 27" barrels. Introduced in 1982. Add $75.00 for Winchoke.
Estimated Value: Excellent: $1,435.00
                       Very good: $1,150.00

Winchester Diamond Grade Combination
Similar to the Diamond Grade O/U Trap with a set of 30" or 32" barrels & a 34" high-rib single barrel; lower barrel & single barrel use interchangeable choke tube system. Introduced in 1982.
Estimated Value: Excellent: $2,200.00
                       Very good: $1,765.00

Winchester Model 501
Grand European Skeet

Winchester Super Grade

Winchester Super Grade, Shotgun Rifle
Gauge: 12, 3" chamber
Caliber: 30-06, 300 Win. mag; 243 Win.
Action: Top lever, break-open
Magazine: None
Barrel: Over & under combination; 12 gauge shotgun barrel with interchangeable choke tube system over rifle barrel
Sights: Folding leaf rear, blade front
Finish: Blued; silver grey satin finish engraved receiver; checkered walnut Monte Carlo pistol grip stock & fluted forearm; recoil pad; swivels
Approximate wt.: 8½ lbs.
Comments: A limited production shotgun/rifle combination available in early 1980's.
Estimated Value: Excellent: $1,910.00
                       Very good: $1,435.00

Winchester Model 501 Grand European Trap
Gauge: 12
Action: Top lever, break-open
Magazine: None
Barrel: Over & under double barrel; 30" or 32" improved modified & full choke; ventilated rib on top & between barrels
Finish: Blued; silver grey satin finish engraved receiver; checkered walnut pistol grip stock & fluted lipped forearm; regular or Monte Carlo stock; recoil pad
Approximate wt.: 8¼ to 8½ lbs.
Comments: A trap shotgun produced from the early 1980's to late 1980's.
Estimated Value: Excellent: $1,300.00
                       Very good: $1,050.00

Winchester Model 501 Grand European Skeet
Similar to the Model 501 Grand European Trap with 27" skeet choke barrels; weighs 6½ to 7½ lbs. Produced from 1981 to 1987. 12 or 20 gauge.
Estimated Value: Excellent: $1,290.00
                       Very good: $ 975.00

Winchester Model 1901

Winchester Model 36

Winchester Model 1901
Gauge: 10
Action: Lever action; repeating
Magazine: 4-shot tubular
Barrel: 30", 32" full choke
Finish: Blued; walnut, pistol grip stock & forearm
Approximate wt.: 8 to 9 lbs.
Comments: Made from 1901 to about 1920, an improved
    version of the Model 1887.
Estimated Value: **Excellent:**   **$900.00**
                       Very good: **$750.00**

Winchester Model 36
Gauge: 9mm shot or ball cartridges
Action: Bolt action; single shot; rear cocking piece
Magazine: None
Barrel: 18"
Finish: Blued; straight grip one-piece stock & forearm
Approximate wt.: 3 lbs.
Comments: Made from the early to late 1920's.
Estimated Value: **Excellent:**   **$350.00**
                       Very good: **$300.00**

Winchester Model 41

Winchester Model 97

Winchester Model 41
Gauge: 410
Action: Bolt action; single shot, rear cocking piece
Magazine: None
Barrel: 24" full choke
Finish: Blued; plain or checkered straight or pistol grip
    one-piece stock & forearm
Approximate wt.: 5 lbs.
Comments: Made from about 1920 for 15 years.
Estimated Value: **Excellent:**   **$250.00**
                       Very good: **$200.00**

Winchester Model 97
Gauge: 12, 16
Action: Slide action; exposed hammer; repeating
Magazine: 5-shot tubular
Barrel: 26", 28", 30", 32" modified, full choke or cylinder
    bore
Finish: Blued; plain wood, semi-pistol grip stock &
    grooved slide handle
Approximate wt.: 7¾ lbs.
Comments: Made from 1897 to late 1950's. Made in Field
    Grade, Pigeon Grade & Tournament Grade. Prices
    for Field grade. Add $600.00 for Pigeon Grade &
    $250.00 for Tournament Grade.
Estimated Value: **Excellent:**   **$500.00**
                       Very good: **$400.00**

Winchester Model 97 Riot Gun

Winchester Model 97 Trench

Winchester Model 97 Riot
Similar to the Model 97 with a 20" cylinder bore barrel.
Estimated Value: **Excellent:**   **$400.00**
                       Very good: **$320.00**

Winchester Model 97 Trench
Similar to the 97 Riot Gun with handguard & bayonet.
Used in World War I.
Estimated Value: **Excellent:**   **$600.00**
                       Very good: **$480.00**

Winchester Model 12 Pre-'65

Winchester Model 12 Skeet Pre-'65

Winchester Model 12 Trap Pre-'65

Winchester Model 12 Duck Pre-'65

Winchester Model 12 Field After '72

Winchester Model 12 Super Pigeon After '72

Winchester Model 12 Trap After '72

Winchester Model 42

Winchester Model 12 Limited Edition

Gauge: 20

Action: Slide action; hammerless; repeating

Magazine: 5-shot tubular

Barrel: 26" improved cylinder choke, ventilated rib; metal or white bead front sight

Finish: Blued; checkered walnut pistol grip stock and slide handle; Grade I plain blued receiver, Grade IV has engraving and gold plate dog and bird scenes

Approximate wt.: 6½ lbs.

Comments: Introduced in 1993; Limited edition of 4,000 guns in Grade I and 1,000 guns in Grade IV; add 63% for Grade IV.

Estimated Value: **Excellent:** $660.00
                       Very good: $530.00

Winchester Model 12

Gauge: 12, 16, 20, 28

Action: Slide action; hammerless; repeating

Magazine: 5-shot tubular

Barrel: 26"-32", standard chokes available

Finish: Blued; plain or checkered walnut pistol grip stock & slide handle; some slide handles grooved

Approximate wt.: 6½ to 7½ lbs.

Comments: Made in various grades: Standard, Featherweight, Rib Barrel, Riot Gun, Duck, Skeet, Trap, Pigeon, Super Pigeon from 1912 to about 1964. In 1972 Field Gun, Skeet & Trap were reissued. Deduct 50% for guns made after 1971. In 1963, Model 12 was offered with Hydro-coil recoil reducing system. Price for Standard Grade made before 1964. Add $50.00 for ventilated rib; $40.00 for raised matted rib; approximately 50% for Pigeon & approximately 120% for Super Pigeon grades. Deduct approximately 25% for Riot Gun.

Estimated Value: **Excellent:** $700.00
                       Very good: $575.00

Winchester Model 42

Gauge: 410

Action: Slide action; hammerless; repeating

Magazine: 5-shot tubular & 6-shot tubular

Barrel: 26", 28" modified, full choke or cylinder bore

Finish: Blued; plain walnut pistol grip stock & grooved slide handle

Approximate wt.: 6 lbs.

Comments: Made from the mid 1930's to mid 1960's.

Estimated Value: **Excellent:** $775.00
                       Very good: $625.00

Winchester Model 42 Skeet

Winchester Model 42 Skeet
Similar to the Model 42 available in straight stock; has matted rib & skeet choke barrel.
Estimated Value: Excellent: $850.00
                   Very good: $680.00

Winchester Model 42 Deluxe
Similar to the Model 42 with higher quality finish; ventilated rib; select wood; checkering.
Estimated Value: Excellent: $1,000.00
                   Very good: $800.00

Winchester Model 25

Winchester Model 25 Riot Gun

Winchester Model 1200 Field
Gauge: 12, 16, 20, regular or magnum; 16 gauge dropped in mid 1970's
Action: Front lock; rotary bolt; slide action; repeating
Magazine: 4-shot tubular
Barrel: 26"-30"; various chokes or adjustable choke (Winchoke)
Finish: Blued; checkered walnut pistol grip stock & slide handle; recoil pad; alloy receiver
Approximate wt.: 6½ to 7½ lbs.
Comments: Made from the late 1960's to the late 1970's. Add $15.00 for magnum; $5.00 for adjustable choke; $25.00 for ventilated rib.
Estimated Value: Excellent: $220.00
                   Very good: $175.00

Winchester Model 25
Gauge: 12
Action: Slide action; hammerless; repeating
Magazine: 4-shot tubular
Barrel: 26", 28"; improved cylinder, modified or full chokes
Finish: Blued; plain walnut semi-pistol grip stock & grooved slide handle; sights
Approximate wt.: 7½ lbs.
Comments: Made from the late 1940's to mid 1950's.
Estimated Value: Excellent: $350.00
                   Very good: $290.00

Winchester Model 25 Riot Gun
Similar to the Model 25 with a 25" cylinder bore barrel.
Estimated Value: Excellent: $290.00
                   Very good: $230.00

Winchester Model 1200 Field

Winchester Model 1200 Skeet

Winchester Model 1200 Trap

Winchester Model 1200 Deer
Similar to the Model 1200 with 22" barrel, rifle sights. Made from the mid 1960's to mid 1970's.
Estimated Value: Excellent: $230.00
                   Very good: $185.00

Winchester Model 1200 Trap
Similar to the 1200 with a 30" full choke barrel; ventilated rib; regular or Monte Carlo stock. Made to the mid 1970's.
Estimated Value: Excellent: $260.00
                   Very good: $210.00

Winchester Model 1200 Skeet
Similar to 1200 except: 12 & 20 gauge only; 26" skeet choke; ventilated rib barrel. Made to the mid 1970's.
Estimated Value: Excellent: $250.00
                   Very good: $200.00

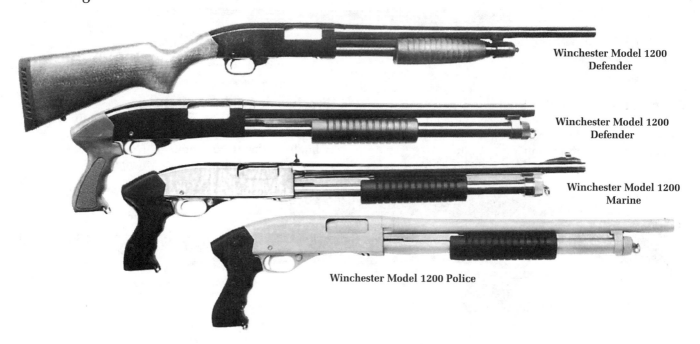

Winchester Model 1200
Defender

Winchester Model 1200
Defender

Winchester Model 1200
Marine

Winchester Model 1200 Police

Winchester Model 1200 & 1300 Defender

Gauge: 12, regular & magnum, 20
Action: Slide action front lock rotary bolt
Magazine: 6-shot tubular; 5-shot in magnum
Barrel: 18" blue steel cylinder bore
Finish: Blued; plain wood or synthetic semi-pistol grip stock & grooved slide handle; full one hand type pistol grip model made beginning in 1984
Approximate wt.: 6¾ lbs.; pistol grip model 5½ lbs.
Comments: Made from 1982 to present. Also available with rifle sights (add 7%).
Estimated Value: New (retail): $290.00
                      Excellent: $220.00
                      Very good: $175.00

Winchester Model 1200 Police

Same as the Model 1200 Defender except: stainless steel barrel & satin chrome finish on all other external metal parts. Also made with shoulder stock or pistol grip (1984) in 12 gauge only. Introduced in 1982.
Estimated Value: Excellent: $300.00
                      Very good: $240.00

Winchester Model 1200 & 1300 Marine

Same as the Model 1200 Police except: rifle sights standard. Made from 1982 to present.
Estimated Value: New (retail): $460.00
                      Excellent: $345.00
                      Very good: $275.00

Winchester Model 1300 XTR

Winchester Model 1300XTR Deer Gun

Winchester Model 1300XTR Deer Gun

Similar to the Model 1300XTR with a 22" barrel, rifle sights; sling; recoil pad. 12 gauge only. Made from about 1980 to mid 1980's.
Estimated Value: Excellent: $300.00
                      Very good: $240.00

Winchester Model 1300 XTR

Gauge: 12, 20, regular or magnum
Action: Slide action; hammerless; repeating
Magazine: 3-shot tubular
Barrel: 26", 28", 30"; improved cylinder, modified or full choke; ventilated rib available
Finish: Blued; checkered walnut pistol grip stock & slide handle
Approximate wt.: 6½ lbs.
Comments: Made from the late 1970's to early 1980's. Add $15.00 for ventilated rib.
Estimated Value: Excellent: $290.00
                      Very good: $230.00

Winchester Model 1300 Winchoke

Winchester Model 1300 Winchoke

Gauge: 12, 20 magnum
Action: Slide action; hammerless; repeating
Magazine: 4-shot tubular
Barrel: 26" or 28"; ventilated rib; Winchoke system (changeable choke tubes)
Finish: Blued; checkered walnut straight or pistol grip stock & slide handle; recoil pad on 12 gauge
Approximate wt.: 7¼ lbs.
Comments: Made from early 1980's to mid 1990's. Ladies and Youth Model added 1990.
Estimated Value: Excellent: $250.00
Very good: $200.00

Winchester Model 1300 Win-Tuff Deer Gun

Similar to the Model 1300XTR Deer Gun with rifled barrel. Black finish; Laminated or walnut stock and forearm.
Estimated Value: Excellent: $295.00
Very good: $235.00

Winchester Model 1300 Featherweight

Similar to the Model 1300 Winchoke with a 22" barrel; weighs 6½ lbs.
Estimated Value: Excellent: $270.00
Very good: $215.00

Winchester Model 1300 Waterfowl

Similar to the Model 1300 Featherweight with sling swivels, 30" barrel; 12 gauge only; weighs 7 lbs.; dull finish on later models. Discontinued in 1991.
Estimated Value: Excellent: $295.00
Very good: $235.00

Winchester Model 1300 Turkey

Similar to the Model 1300 Waterfowl with a 22" barrel. Camo or black finish. Add 5% for National Wild Turkey Federation Model or Ladies Model.
Estimated Value: New (retail): $370.00
Excellent: $280.00
Very good: $225.00

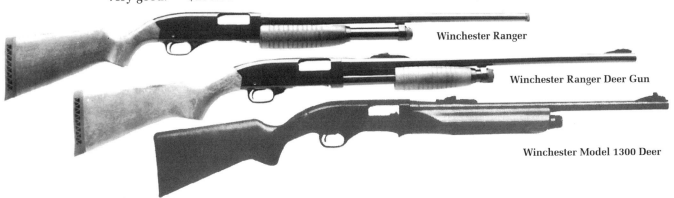

Winchester Ranger

Winchester Ranger Deer Gun

Winchester Model 1300 Deer

Winchester Ranger, 1300 Ranger

Gauge: 12, 20, regular or magnum interchangeably
Action: Slide action; hammerless; side ejecting
Magazine: 4-shot tubular; factory installed removable plug
Barrel: 26" or 28"; ventilated rib; interchangeable choke tubes
Finish: Blued; walnut-finished or synthetic, semi-pistol grip stock & grooved slide handle; recoil pad
Approximate wt.: 7¼ lbs.
Comments: Introduced in 1982. Add 10% for 1300 Field Model.
Estimated Value: New (retail): $309.00
Excellent: $235.00
Very good: $190.00

Winchester Ranger Youth, 1300 Ranger Youth

Similar to the Ranger in 20 gauge; stock & forearm are modified for young shooters. Stock can be replaced with regular size stock; 22" modified or Winchoke barrel. Introduced in 1983.
Estimated Value: New (retail): $309.00
Excellent: $230.00
Very good: $185.00

Winchester Ranger Deer Gun, 1300 Ranger Deer Gun

Similar to the Ranger with 22" or 24" cylinder bore deer barrel, rifle sights & recoil pad. Introduced in 1983.
Estimated Value: Excellent: $250.00
Very good: $200.00

Winchester Model 1300 Deer

Gauge: 12, 20, regular or magnum
Action: Slide action, hammerless, side ejecting
Magazine: 4-shot tubular
Barrel: 22" plain or ventilated rib; smooth bore or rifled with rifle sights
Finish: Matte black, camo, or black shadow; walnut or synthetic semi-pistol grip stock and checkered or grooved slide handle
Approximate wt.: 7 lbs.
Comments: Add 36% for walnut stock; add 45% for camo finish; add 8% for rifled barrel
Estimated Value: New (retail) $296.00
Excellent: $225.00
Very good: $175.00

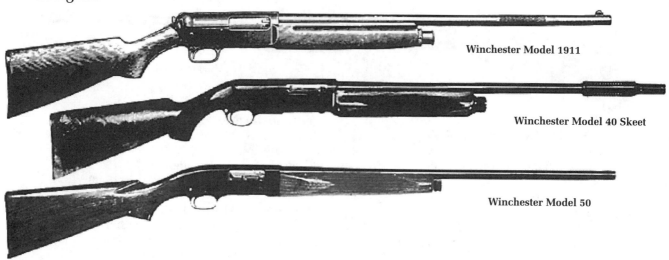

Winchester Model 1911

Winchester Model 40 Skeet

Winchester Model 50

Winchester Model 1911

Gauge: 12
Action: Semi-automatic; hammerless
Magazine: 4-shot tubular
Barrel: 26"-32"; various chokes
Finish: Blued; plain or checkered semi-pistol grip stock & forearm
Approximate wt.: 8 lbs.
Comments: Made from 1911 to the mid 1920's.
Estimated Value: Excellent: $525.00
                       Very good: $420.00

Winchester Model 40

Gauge: 12
Action: Semi-automatic; hammerless
Magazine: 4-shot tubular
Barrel: 28", 30"; modified or full choke
Finish: Blued; plain walnut pistol grip stock & forearm
Approximate wt.: 8 lbs.
Comments: Made in the early 1940's.
Estimated Value: Excellent: $400.00
                       Very good: $320.00

Winchester Model 40 Skeet

Similar to the Model 40 with a 24" skeet barrel; checkering; "Cutts Compensator."
Estimated Value: Excellent: $450.00
                       Very good: $360.00

Winchester Model 50

Gauge: 12, 20
Action: Semi-automatic; non-recoiling barrel; hammerless
Magazine: 2-shot tubular
Barrel: 26"-30"; variety of chokes
Finish: Blued; checkered walnut pistol grip stock & forearm
Approximate wt.: 7¾ lbs.
Comments: Made from the mid 1950's to early 1960's. Add $25.00 for ventilated rib.
Estimated Value: Excellent: $350.00
                       Very good: $280.00

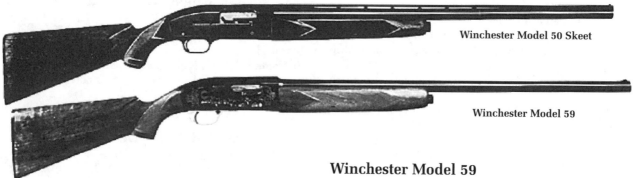

Winchester Model 50 Skeet

Winchester Model 59

Winchester Model 50 Trap

Similar to the Model 50 except 12 gauge only; Monte Carlo stock; 30" full choke; ventilated rib
Estimated Value: Excellent: $425.00
                       Very good: $340.00

Winchester Model 50 Skeet

Similar to the Model 50 with a skeet stock; 26" skeet choke barrel; ventilated rib
Estimated Value: Excellent: $420.00
                       Very good: $335.00

Winchester Model 59

Gauge: 12
Action: Semi-automatic; hammerless; non-recoiling barrel
Magazine: 2-shot tubular
Barrel: 26"-30"; variety of chokes; steel & glass fiber composition; interchangeable choke tubes available
Finish: Blued; checkered walnut pistol grip stock & forearm; alloy receiver
Approximate wt.: 6½ lbs.
Comments: Made from the late 1950's to mid 1960's.
Estimated Value: Excellent: $380.00
                       Very good: $300.00

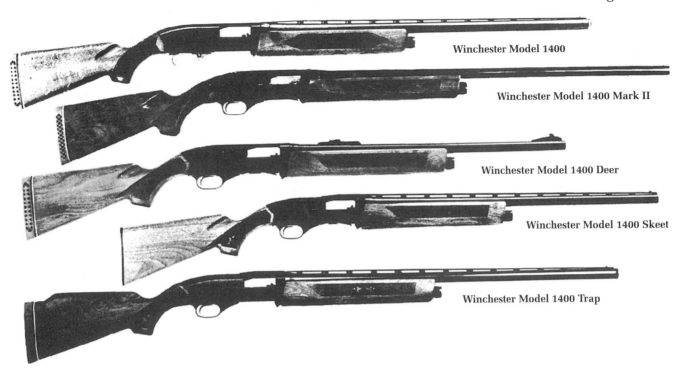

Winchester Model 1400

Winchester Model 1400 Mark II

Winchester Model 1400 Deer

Winchester Model 1400 Skeet

Winchester Model 1400 Trap

Winchester Model 1400 or 1400 Winchoke

Gauge: 12, 16, 20
Action: Semi-automatic, gas operated
Magazine: 2-shot tubular
Barrel: 26", 28", 30"; variety of chokes or adjustable choke; all 1979 models have adjustable choke
Finish: Blued; checkered walnut pistol grip stock & forearm; recoil pad available; Cycolak stock available with recoil reduction system until late 1970's
Approximate wt.: 7½ lbs.
Comments: Made from the mid 1960's to late 1970's. Add $25.00 for ventilated rib or Cycolak stock & recoil reduction system.

Estimated Value:	Excellent:	$270.00
	Very good:	$220.00

Winchester Model 1400 Mark II

Similar to the 1400 except: lighter weight & with minor improvements.Produced from the late 1960's to late 1970's.

Estimated Value:	Excellent:	$290.00
	Very good:	$230.00

Winchester Model 1400 Deer Gun

Similar to the 1400 with a 22" barrel for slugs & sights.

Estimated Value:	Excellent:	$275.00
	Very good:	$220.00

Winchester Model 1400 Skeet

Similar to the 1400 in 12 or 20 gauge; 26" barrel with ventilated rib. Add $25.00 for recoil reduction system.

Estimated Value:	Excellent:	$300.00
	Very good:	$240.00

Winchester Model 1400 Trap

Similar to the 1400 in 12 gauge with a 30" full choke, ventilated rib barrel. Available with Monte Carlo stock. Add $25.00 for recoil reduction system.

Estimated Value:	Excellent:	$305.00
	Very good:	$245.00

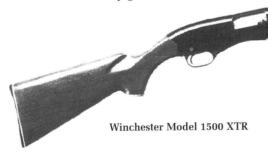

Winchester Model 1500 XTR

Winchester Model 1500 XTR Winchoke

Similar to the 1500XTR with removable choke tube system; 28" barrel only; add $35.00 for ventilated rib. Made in early 1980's.

Estimated Value:	Excellent:	$320.00
	Very good:	$240.00

Winchester Model 1500 XTR

Gauge: 12, 20, regular or magnum
Action: Semi-automatic, gas operated
Magazine: 3-shot tubular
Barrel: 26", 28", 30"; improved cylinder, modified or full choke; ventilated rib available
Finish: Blued; checkered walnut pistol grip stock & forearm; alloy receiver
Approximate wt.: 6½ to 7 lbs.
Comments: Made from late 1970's to early 1980's. Add $25.00 for ventilated rib.

Estimated Value:	Excellent:	$300.00
	Very good:	$225.00

Winchester Super X Model I

Winchester Super X Model 1, Super X Model 1 XTR

Gauge: 12
Action: Semi-automatic, gas operated
Magazine: 4-shot tubular
Barrel: 26"-30"; various chokes; ventilated rib
Finish: Blued; scroll engraved alloy receiver; checkered walnut pistol grip stock & forearm
Approximate wt.: 8¼ lbs.
Comments: Made from the mid 1970's to early 1980's.
Estimated Value: Excellent: $375.00
                        Very good: $285.00

Winchester Super X Model 1 Skeet

Similar to the Super X Model 1 with skeet stock; 26" skeet choke; ventilated rib barrel.
Estimated Value: Excellent: $400.00
                        Very good: $300.00

Winchester Super X Model 1 Trap

Similar to the Super X Model 1 with regular or Monte Carlo stock; 30" full choke barrel; recoil pad.
Estimated Value: Excellent: $425.00
                        Very good: $320.00

Winchester Ranger 1400 Ranger

Winchester Ranger, 1400 Ranger

Gauge: 12, 20 regular or magnum
Action: Gas operated semi-automatic
Magazine: 2-shot
Barrel: 26" or 28"; Winchoke interchangeable tubes & ventilated rib
Finish: Blued; hardwood semi-pistol grip stock & forearm
Approximate wt.: 7 lbs.
Comments: Introduced in 1983. Add 10% for walnut stock. Discontinued in mid 1990's.
Estimated Value: Excellent: $255.00
                        Very good: $200.00

Winchester Ranger Deer, 1400 Ranger Deer

Similar to the 1400 Ranger with 22" or 24" cylinder bore deer barrel, rifle sights. Introduced in 1984.
Estimated Value: Excellent: $285.00
                        Very good: $225.00

Winchester Ranger Deer Combo

Similar to the Ranger 1400 Deer with extra 28" ventilated rib Winchoke barrel, hardwood stock.
Estimated Value: Excellent: $325.00
                        Very good: $260.00

Winchester 1400 Slug Hunter

Similar to the Ranger 1400 except: walnut stock; 22" barrel, improved cylinder and rifled sabot Winchoke tubes; drilled and tapped with scope base and rings; rifle sights; Produced from the late 1980's to early 1990's
Estimated Value: Excellent: $315.00
                        Very good: $250.00

Zoli

Zoli Silver Snipe

Zoli Silver Snipe

Gauge: 12, 20
Action: Box lock; top lever, break open; hammerless; single trigger
Magazine: None
Barrel: Over & under double barrel; 26", 28", 30"; ventilated rib; chrome lined
Finish: Blued; checkered walnut pistol grip stock & forearm; engraved
Approximate wt.: 7 lbs.
Comments: Manufactured in Italy.
Estimated Value: Excellent: $575.00
                        Very good: $445.00

Zoli Golden Snipe

Similar to the Silver Snipe with automatic ejectors.
Estimated Value: Excellent: $620.00
                        Very good: $475.00

Zoli 300 Gray Eagle

Gauge: 12
Action: Box lock; top lever, break-open; hammerless
Magazine: None
Barrel: Over & under double barrel; 26", 28"; ventilated rib; chrome lined; 3" chambers
Finish: Blued; checkered walnut pistol grip stock & forearm
Approximate wt.: 7 lbs.
Comments: Manufactured in Italy.
Estimated Value: Excellent: $500.00
                        Very good: $400.00

Zoli 302 Gray Eagle

Similar to the 300 in 20 gauge. Weight about 6¼ lbs.
Estimated Value: Excellent: $490.00
                        Very good: $390.00

Rifles

Anschutz.....................................150
Armalite.....................................153
Browning 154
BSA 161
Carl Gustaf..............................164
Charles Daly 165
Charter Arms 165
Colt..165
FN 168
Harrington & Richardson 169
Heckler & Koch...........................176
High Standard 177
Husqvarna.................................178
Ithaca 181
Iver Johnson.............................183

Johnson 185
Kimber 186
Kleinguenther...........................187
Mannlicher 188
Mark X 193
Marlin 195
Mauser 214
Military, Argentine...................218
Military, British 219
Military, Chilean 220
Military, German 221
Military, Italian.........................222
Military, Japanese....................223
Military, Mexican......................225

Military, Russian 226
Military, Spanish.....................227
Military, U.S. 229
Mitchell Arms 231
Mossberg..................................232
Musketeer 245
New England 245
New Haven 246
Newton 247
Noble...247
Pedersen 249
Plainfield 250
Remington 251
Ruger..278
Sako 283
Savage 288
Sears...304
Sedgley 305
Smith & Wesson 306
Standard 307
Stevens......................................307
Thompson Center.....................320
Universal 321
Valmet......................................323
Walther 324
Weatherby 325
Western Field 329
Winchester................................332

Anschutz

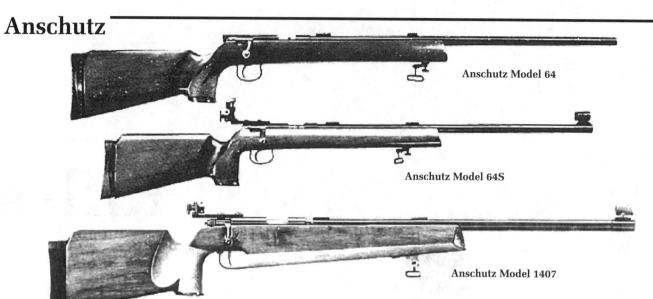

Anschutz Model 64

Anschutz Model 64S

Anschutz Model 1407

Anschutz Model 64 & 64L Match

Caliber: 22 long rifle
Action: Bolt action; single shot
Magazine: None
Barrel: Blued; 26"
Sights: None
Stock & Forearm: Match style; checkered walnut one-piece pistol grip stock & forearm; thumb rest; cheekpiece; adjustable butt plate; forward swivel
Approximate wt.: 7¾ lbs.
Comments: A match rifle made from about 1967 to the early 1980's. Add $10.00 for left hand action (64L).
Estimated Value: Excellent: $375.00
                       Very good: $300.00

Anschutz Model 64S & 64SL Match

Similar to the Model 64 & 64L with special match sights. Add $20.00 for left hand version (64SL).
Estimated Value: Excellent: $405.00
                       Very good: $325.00

Anschutz Mark 12 Target

Similar to the Model 64 with a heavy barrel; non-adjustable butt plate; handstop; tapered stock & forearm. Introduced in the late 1970's.
Estimated Value: Excellent: $350.00
                       Very good: $250.00

Anschutz Model 1407, 1807, 1407L, 1807L

Caliber: 22 long rifle
Action: Bolt action; single shot
Magazine: None
Barrel: Blued; 26"
Sights: None
Stock & Forearm: Walnut one-piece pistol grip stock & wide forearm; thumb rest; cheekpiece; adjustable butt plate; forward swivel
Approximate wt.: 10 lbs.
Comments: Match rifles made from about 1967 to 1980's. Add $50.00 for left hand action (1407L), (1807L).
Estimated Value: Excellent: $500.00
                       Very good: $400.00

Anschutz Model 184

Caliber: 22 long rifle
Action: Bolt action; repeating
Magazine: 5-shot detachable clip
Barrel: Blued; 21½"
Sights: Folding leaf rear, hooded ramp front
Stock & Forearm: Checkered walnut Monte Carlo one-piece pistol grip stock & lipped forearm; swivels
Approximate wt.: 6 lbs.
Comments: Made from the mid 1960's to mid 1970's.
Estimated Value: Excellent: $300.00
                       Very good: $240.00

Anschutz Model 54

Anschutz Model 54

Caliber: 22 long rifle
Action: Bolt action; repeating
Magazine: Detachable 5-shot clip or 10-shot clip
Barrel: Blued; 24"
Sights: Folding leaf rear, hooded ramp front
Stock & Forearm: Checkered walnut Monte Carlo one-piece pistol grip stock & lipped forearm
Approximate wt.: 6¾ lbs.
Comments: Made from the late 1960's to early 1980's.
Estimated Value: Excellent: $375.00
                       Very good: $300.00

Anschutz Model 54M

Similar to Model 54 in 22 Winchester magnum with a 4-shot clip.
Estimated Value: Excellent: $400.00
                       Very good: $325.00

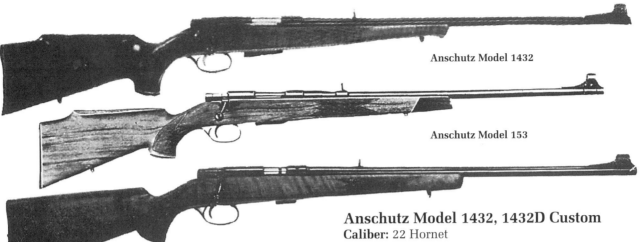

Anschutz Model 1432

Anschutz Model 153

Anschutz Model 1422D

Anschutz Model 141

Caliber: 22 long rifle, 22 magnum
Action: Bolt action; repeating
Magazine: Detachable 5-shot clip
Barrel: Blued; 24"
Sights: Folding leaf rear, hooded ramp front
Stock & Forearm: Checkered walnut Monte Carlo one-piece pistol grip stock & forearm
Approximate wt.: 6 lbs.
Comments: Made from the middle to late 1960's.
Estimated Value: Excellent: $280.00
Very good: $225.00

Anschutz Model 153

Similar to the Model 141 with abruptly ended forearm trimmed in different wood. Made from the middle to late 1960's.
Estimated Value: Excellent: $295.00
Very good: $235.00

Anschutz Achiever

Caliber: 22 long rifle
Action: Bolt action; repeating
Magazine: 5 or 10-shot clip; single shot adapter
Barrel: 18½" or 19½"; blued
Sights: Hooded ramp, adjustable folding leaf rear
Stock & Forearm: Strippled European hardwood one-piece pistol grip stock & forearm; Adjustable stock
Approximate wt.: 5 lbs.
Comments: Introduced in 1988.
Estimated Value: New (retail): $400.00
Excellent: $300.00
Very good: $240.00

Anschutz Model 1432, 1432D Custom

Caliber: 22 Hornet
Action: Bolt action; repeating
Magazine: 5-shot clip
Barrel: Blued; 24"
Sights: Folding leaf rear, hooded ramp front
Stock & Forearm: Checkered walnut Monte Carlo one-piece pistol grip stock & lipped forearm; swivels
Approximate wt.: 6¾ lbs.
Comments: Discontinued late 1980's.
Estimated Value: Excellent: $675.00
Very good: $540.00

Anschutz Model 1422D, 1522D, 1532D, Custom

Similar to the Model 1432D Custom except: different calibers: 1422D is 22 long rifle; 1522D is 22 magnum; 1532D is 222 Remington. Discontinued in late 1980's.
Estimated Value:

	1422D	1522D	1532D
Excellent:	$750.00	$780.00	$700.00
Very good:	$600.00	$620.00	$565.00

Anschutz Model 1422DCL, 1522DCL, 1532DCL, Classic

Similar to the Custom models of this series except without deluxe features. Checkered walnut, one-piece pistol grip stock & tapered forearm.
Estimated Value:

	1422DCL	1522DCL	1532DCL
Excellent:	$700.00	$725.00	$650.00
Very good:	$565.00	$575.00	$520.00

Anschutz Bavarian 1700, 1700D

Caliber: 22 long rifle, 22 Hornet, 222 Remington
Action: Bolt action; repeating; adjustable trigger
Magazine: 5-shot clip
Barrel: 24"; blued
Sights: Hooded ramp front; folding leaf rear
Stock & Forearm: Select checkered Monte Carlo walnut one-piece pistol grip stock & lipped forearm, cheekpiece; swivels; Classic has deep fluted comb; Custom has hand-carved cheekpiece and rosewook grip cap
Approximate wt.: 7¼ lbs.
Comments: Introduced in 1988. Add 10% for 22 Hornet or 222 Remington caliber.
Estimated Value: New (retail): $1,365.00
Excellent: $1,025.00
Very good: $ 820.00

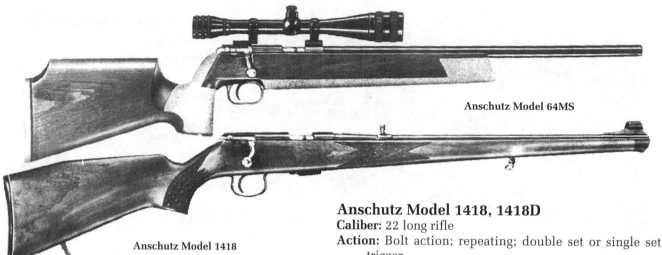

Anschutz Model 64MS

Anschutz Model 1418

Anschutz Model 64MS

Caliber: 22 long rifle
Action: Bolt action; single shot; adjustable two-stage trigger
Magazine: None
Barrel: 21¾" medium heavy
Sights: None; tapped for scope
Stock & Forearm: Silhouette-style one-piece stippled pistol grip stock & forearm
Approximate wt.: 8 lbs.
Comments: A silhouette-style rifle made from about 1982 to present; add 6% for left hand model.
Estimated Value: New (retail): $990.00
Excellent: $745.00
Very good: $600.00

Anschutz Model 54.18MS

Similar to the Model 64MS with a 22" barrel. Weighs 8½ lbs. Add 5% for left hand model. Add 25% for Repeating Model; 50% for Repeating Deluxe (introduced 1990).
Estimated Value: New (retail): $1,580.00
Excellent: $1,185.00
Very good: $ 950.00

Anschutz Model 164

Caliber: 22 long rifle
Action: Bolt action; repeating
Magazine: 5-shot clip or 10-shot clip
Barrel: Blued; 23"
Sights: Folding leaf rear, hooded ramp front
Stock & Forearm: Checkered walnut Monte Carlo one-piece pistol grip stock & lipped forearm
Approximate wt.: 6 lbs.
Comments: Made from the late 1960's to early 1980's.
Estimated Value: Excellent: $350.00
Very good: $280.00

Anschutz Model 164M

Similar to the Model 164 in 22 Winchester magnum with a 4-shot clip.
Estimated Value: Excellent: $375.00
Very good: $300.00

Anschutz Model 1418, 1418D

Caliber: 22 long rifle
Action: Bolt action; repeating; double set or single set trigger
Magazine: 5-shot clip or 10-shot clip
Barrel: Blued; 19¾"
Sights: Folding leaf rear, hooded ramp front
Stock & Forearm: Checkered European Monte Carlo stock & full-length forearm; cheekpiece; swivels
Approximate wt.: 5½ lbs.
Comments: Introduced in the late 1970's. Currently called 1418D.
Estimated Value: New (retail): $1,160.00
Excellent: $ 875.00
Very good: $ 695.00

Anschutz Model 1416D, 1516D, Classic

Similar to the Model 1418D, 1518D except regular length forearm, different stock with more defined pistol grip, 23" barrel. Add $20.00 for magnum (1516D).
Estimated Value: New (retail): $750.00
Excellent: $560.00
Very good: $450.00

Anschutz Model 1518, 1518D

Similar to the Model 1418 except; 22 WMR only; 4-shot clip magazine. Currently called 1518D.
Estimated Value: New (retail): $1,170.00
Excellent: $ 875.00
Very good: $ 700.00

Anschutz Model 1433D

Similar to the Model 1418D except in 22 Hornet caliber. Discontinued late 1980's.
Estimated Value: Excellent: $750.00
Very good: $600.00

Anschutz Model 1411, 1811

Caliber: 22 long rifle
Action: Bolt action; single shot
Magazine: None
Barrel: 27½" heavy
Sights: None; tapped for scope
Stock & Forearm: Select walnut one-piece Monte Carlo pistol grip stock & forearm; adjustable cheekpiece; hand rest swivel; adjustable butt plate
Approximate wt.: 12 lbs.
Comments: A match-style rifle.
Estimated Value: Excellent: $675.00
Very good: $550.00

Anschutz Model 520

Anschutz Mark 2000
Caliber: 22 long rifle
Action: Bolt action; hammerless; single shot
Magazine: None
Barrel: Blued; medium heavy; 26"
Sights: None; sights can be purchased separately to fit
Stock & Forearm: Smooth hardwood one-piece semi-pistol grip stock & forearm
Approximate wt.: 8½ lbs.
Comments: A match rifle designed for young shooters. Made from the early 1980's to mid 1980's.
Estimated Value: Excellent: $250.00
Very good: $200.00

Anschutz Model 520 Sporter & Mark 525 Sporter
Caliber: 22 long rifle
Action: Semi-automatic
Magazine: 10-shot clip
Barrel: Blued; 24"
Sights: Folding leaf rear, hooded ramp front
Stock & Forearm: Checkered walnut Monte Carlo semi-pistol stock & fluted forearm
Approximate wt.: 6½ lbs.
Comments: Introduced in the early 1980's; presently called Mark 525 Sporter.
Estimated Value: New (retail): $550.00
Excellent: $420.00
Very good: $330.00

Armalite

Armalite AR-7 Explorer

Armalite AR-7 Custom

Armalite AR-180 Sporter

Armalite AR-180 Sporter
Caliber: 223
Action: Semi-automatic, gas operated
Magazine: 5-shot detachable box
Barrel: Blued; 18"
Sights: Adjustable rear & front; scope available
Stock & Forearm: Pistol grip; nylon folding stock; fiberglass forearm
Approximate wt.: 6½ lbs.
Comments: Made from the early 1970's to 1980's.
Estimated Value: Excellent: $620.00
Very good: $495.00

Armalite AR-7 Explorer
Caliber: 22 long rifle
Action: Semi-automatic
Magazine: 8-shot clip
Barrel: 16" aluminum & steel lined
Sights: Peep rear, blade front
Stock & Forearm: Fiberglass pistol grip stock (no forearm); stock acts as case for gun when dismantled
Approximate wt.: 2¾ lbs.
Comments: A lightweight alloy rifle designed to float; breaks down to fit into stock. Made from the early 1960's until the 1970's by Armalite. After about 1973 marketed as Charter Arms AR-7 Explorer until 1990.
Estimated Value: Excellent: $125.00
Very good: $ 90.00

Armalite AR-7 Custom
A sport version of the Explorer with a walnut Monte Carlo one-piece pistol grip stock & forearm. Slightly heavier.
Estimated Value: Excellent: $120.00
Very good: $ 90.00

Browning

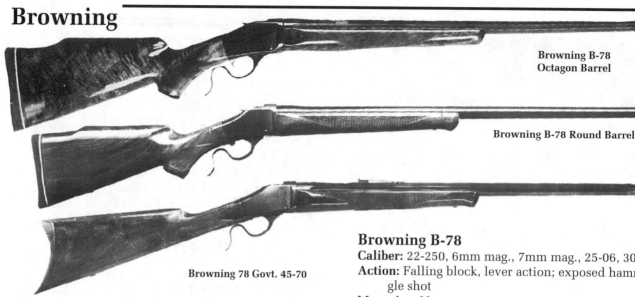

Browning B-78 Octagon Barrel

Browning B-78 Round Barrel

Browning 78 Govt. 45-70

Browning Model 1885 Single Shot

Caliber: 22 Hornet, 223 Rem., 243 Win., 22-250 Rem., 270 Win., 30-06 Springfield, 7mm Rem. magnum, 45-70 Gov't

Action: Falling block, lever action; single shot; exposed hammer; made in low wall and high wall models

Magazine: None, single shot

Barrel: 24" & 28"; octagon; blued

Sights: Drilled & tapped for scope; open sights on 45-70 model

Stock & Forearm: Checkered walnut straight grip stock & lipped forearm; recoil pad

Approximate wt.: 6½ lbs. low wall; 8¾ lbs. high wall

Comments: Introduced in 1985. Based on John Browning's Winchester 1885.

Estimated Value: New (retail): $940.00
                        Excellent: $700.00
                        Very good: $565.00

Browning B-78

Caliber: 22-250, 6mm mag., 7mm mag., 25-06, 30-06

Action: Falling block, lever action; exposed hammer; single shot

Magazine: None

Barrel: Blued; 26" round or octagon

Sights: None

Stock & Forearm: Checkered walnut Monte Carlo pistol grip stock & forearm

Approximate wt.: 7¾ to 8½ lbs.

Comments: A replica of John Browning's first patented rifle in 1878. Produced from the mid 1970's to early 1980's.

Estimated Value: Excellent: $500.00
                        Very good: $400.00

Browning 78 Govt. 45-70

Similar to 78 in Government 45-70 caliber with iron sights & straight grip stock, octagonal bull barrel. Made from the mid 1970's to the early 1980's.

Estimated Value: Excellent: $475.00
                        Very good: $380.00

Browning T Bolt T-1

Browning T Bolt T-2

Browning T Bolt, T-1 & T-2

Caliber: 22 short, long, long rifle

Action: Bolt action; hammerless; side ejection; repeating; single shot conversion

Magazine: Removable 5-shot box

Barrel: Blued; 22"

Sights: Peep rear, ramp front

Stock & Forearm: Walnut one-piece smooth (T-1) or checkered (T-2) pistol grip stock & forearm

Approximate wt.: 6 lbs.

Comments: Made from the mid 1960's to the mid 1970's in Belgium. Add 3% for T-2.

Estimated Value: Excellent: $340.00
                        Very good: $270.00

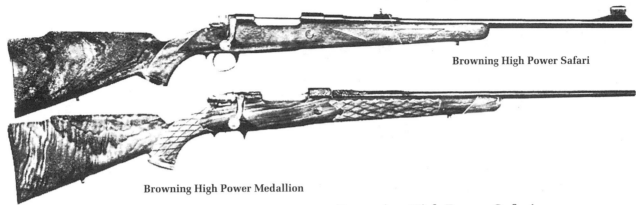

Browning High Power Safari

Browning High Power Medallion

Browning High Power Medallion

A higher grade version of the Safari with more engraving & higher quality wood. Made from the early 1960's to mid 1970's.

Estimated Value: Excellent: $1,200.00
Very good: $ 960.00

Browning High Power Olympian

Highest grade of High Power models with complete engraving & some gold inlay. Made from the early 1960's to mid 1970's.

Estimated Value: Excellent: $2,000.00
Very good: $1,600.00

Browning High Power Safari

Caliber: 243, 270, 30-06, 308, 300 mag., 375 mag. in 1960; later in 264, 338, 222, 22-250, 243, 7mm mag.
Action: Mauser-type bolt action; repeating
Magazine: 3- or 5-shot clip, depending on caliber
Barrel: Blued; 22" or 24"
Sights: Adjustable sporting rear, hooded ramp front
Stock & Forearm: Checkered walnut Monte Carlo one-piece pistol grip stock & forearm; magnum calibers have recoil pad; swivels
Approximate wt.: 6 to 8 lbs.
Comments: Made from about 1960 through the mid 1970's. Add 10% for Long action.
Estimated Value: Excellent: $800.00
Very good: $640.00

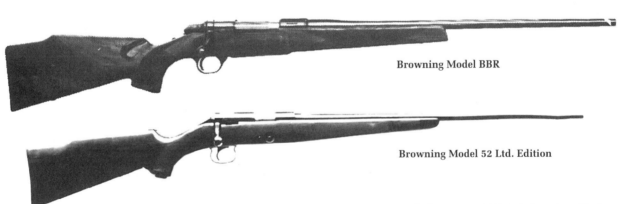

Browning Model BBR

Browning Model 52 Ltd. Edition

Browning Model 52 Ltd. Edition

Caliber: 22 long rifle
Action: Bolt action; repeating; adjustable trigger
Magazine: 5-shot, detachable box
Barrel: 24"
Sights: None; tapped for scope
Stock & Forearm: Checkered high-grade walnut, pistol grip one-piece stock and forearm; rosewood fore-end
Approximate wt.: 7 lbs.
Comments: A limited edition reproduction of the Model 52 introduced in 1991. Only 5,000 of this model was to be produced.
Estimated Value: Excellent: $375.00
Very good: $300.00

Browning Model BBR, BBR Lightning Bolt

Caliber: 30-06 Sprg., 270 Win., 25-06 Rem., 7mm Rem. mag., 300 Win. mag.
Action: Bolt action; short throw; repeating
Magazine: 4-shot; 3-shot in magnum; hinged floorplate,
Barrel: 24" floating barrel; recessed muzzle
Sights: None; tapped for scope
Stock & Forearm: Checkered walnut Monte Carlo one-piece pistol grip stock & forearm; sling studs; recoil pad on mag.; stock & forearm changed slightly in 1982
Approximate wt.: 8 lbs.
Comments: A high-powered hunting rifle made from late 1970's to 1985. A limited edition (1,000) with engraved elk scenes was introduced in 1984. Add 25% for Limited Edition.
Estimated Value: Excellent: $400.00
Very good: $320.00

Browning A-Bolt

Browning A-Bolt Stalker

Browning A-Bolt 22

Browning A-Bolt II Eclipse

Browning A-Bolt II Eclipse Varmit

Browning A-Bolt, & A-Bolt II Hunter

Caliber: 22-250 Rem., 223, 257 Roberts, 7mm-08 Rem., 25-06 Rem., 243 Win., 270 Win., 280, 7mm Rem. magnum, 300 Win. magnum, 30-06 Springfield, 308 Win., 338 Win. magnum, 375 H&H

Action: Bolt action; hammerless; repeating; short or long action

Magazine: 4-shot; 3-shot mag. hinged floorplate

Barrel: 22" or 24" blued

Sights: None, drilled & tapped for scope mounts. Hunter model available with open sights

Stock & Forearm: Checkered walnut, one-piece pistol grip stock & forearm; swivels; recoil pad on mag.

Approximate wt.: 6½ to 7¼ lbs.

Comments: Introduced in 1985; add 12% for sights. Add 14% for Boss shooting system.

Estimated Value: New (retail): $606.00
Excellent: $455.00
Very good: $365.00

Browning A-Bolt & A-Bolt II Stalker

Similar to the A-Bolt & A-Bolt II Hunter except: calibers 375 H&H, 338 win. mag., 300 win. mag., 7mm rem. mag., 25-06 rem., 270 rem., 280 rem., 30-06 sprg., 284 win., & 257 Roberts. In three special finishes; Stainless Stalker has matte stainless steel with graphite fiberglass composite stock; Camo Stalker has multi-laminated wood stock with various shades of black & green, matte blue finish (discontinued 1991); Composite Stalker has graphite/fiberglass composite stock. Add 28% for stainless steel. Add 14% for Boss shooting system.

Estimated Value: New (retail): $625.00
Excellent: $470.00
Very good: $375.00

Browning A-Bolt 22

Similar to the A-Bolt & A-Bolt II Hunter except: 22 long rifle or 22 mag.caliber; 5 or 15-shot clip; 22" barrel; wt. 5½ lbs.; Add 3% for open sights; Add 16% for mag.; Add 32% for Gold Medallion model. Priced for Grade I.

Estimated Value: New (retail): $425.00
Excellent: $320.00
Very good: $255.00

Browning Euro-Bolt II

Similar to the A-Bolt & A-Bolt II Hunter except: calibers 7mm Rem. magnum, 270 Win., 30-06 Sprg., 243 Win., and 308 Win.; European mannlicher-style bolt handle and lipped forearm; Monte Carlo stock. Add 11% for Boss System (Ballistic Optimizing Shooting System).

Estimated Value: New (retail): $824.00
Excellent: $620.00
Very good: $500.00

Browning A-Bolt II Varmint

Similar to the A-Bolt II Hunter except: calibers 22-250, 308 Win., and 223 Rem.; heavier target barrel equipped with the Boss shooting system; black laminated wood stock; gloss or satin matte finish. Introduced in 1994.

Estimated Value: New (retail): $940.00
Excellent: $705.00
Very good: $565.00

Browning A-Bolt II Eclipse

Caliber: 270 Win., 30-06 Sprg., 7mm Rem. magnum, 22/250 Rem., 243 Win., 308 Win.

Action: Bolt action; repeating; short or long action

Magazine: 4-shot; 3-shot in magnum caliber

Barrel: 22"; 26" in magnum caliber; equipped with the Browning Boss shooting system located at the muzzle of the barrel; it reduces recoil by about 30% to 50% and has an adjustment which affects the barrels vibration for best accuracy.

Sights: None

Stock & Forearm: Gray/black multi-laminated hardwood stock and forearm; custom thumb hole style stock for maximum control

Approximate wt.: 7½ to 8 lbs.

Comments: Introduced in 1996.

Estimated Value: New (retail): $1,025.00
Excellent: $ 770.00
Very good: $ 615.00

Browning A-Bolt II Eclipse Varmint

Similar to the A-Bolt II Eclipse except: calibers 22/250 Rem., 223 Rem., and 308 Win.; 26" heavy barrel.

Estimated Value: New (retail): $1,055.00
Excellent: $790.00
Very good: $635.00

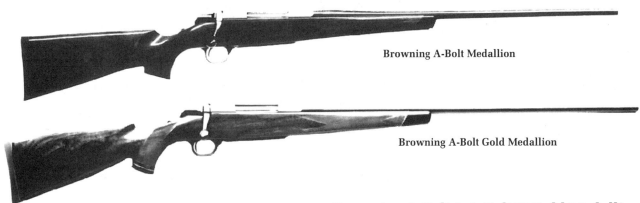

Browning A-Bolt Medallion

Browning A-Bolt Gold Medallion

Browning A-Bolt & A-Bolt II Medallion

Caliber: 22-250 Rem., 223 Rem., 257 Roberts, 7mm-08 Rem., 25-06 Rem., 243 Win., 270 Win., 280 Rem., 284 Win., 7mm Rem. magnum, 300 Win. magnum, 30-06 Springfield, 308 Win., 338 Win. magnum, 375 H&H

Action: Bolt action; hammerless; repeating; short or long action

Magazine: 4-shot; 3-shot magnum; hinged floorplate

Barrel: 22" or 26"; blued, free-floating; optional Boss shooting system

Sights: None, drilled & tapped for scope mounts.

Stock & Forearm: Checkered select high-gloss walnut, one-piece pistol grip stock & forearm; rosewood fore-end; swivels; recoil pad on mag.

Approximate wt.: 6½ to 7¼ lbs.

Comments: Add 12% for sights. Add 14% for Boss shooting system.

Estimated Value:	New (retail):	$707.00
	Excellent:	$530.00
	Very good:	$425.00

Browning A-Bolt & A-Bolt II Gold Medallion

Similar to the A-Bolt & A-Bolt II Medallion except: calibers 300 Win. mag., 7mm Rem.mag., 270 Win., & 30-06 Sprg.; Higher grade of select walnut, grip palm swell, high cheekpiece and fluted comb. Brass spacers between stock and recoil pad, pistol grip & cap, and fore-end & tip; engraving covers flat sides of receiver and "Gold Medallion" is gold-filled. Add 10% for Boss shooting system.

Estimated Value:	New (retail):	$950.00
	Excellent:	$715.00
	Very good:	$570.00

Browning A-Bolt & A-Bolt II Micro Medallion

A scaled down version of the A-Bolt & A-Bolt II Medallion series. Shorter length of pull; shorter barrel (20" barrel); Slimmer overall proportions. 4-shot magazine in calibers 22 Hornet, 243, 308, 7mm-08 Rem., 284 Win., 223 Rem., & 22-250.

Estimated Value:	New (retail):	$707.00
	Excellent:	$530.00
	Very good:	$425.00

Browning BL-22 Grade I

Browning BL-22 Grade II

Browning BL-22 Grade I

Caliber: 22 short, long, long rifle (any combination)

Action: Lever action; short throw lever; exposed hammer

Magazine: Tubular; 15 long rifles; 17 longs; 22 shorts

Barrel: Blued; 20"

Sights: Folding adjustable rear, bead front

Stock & Forearm: Plain walnut straight grip stock & forearm; barrel band

Approximate wt.: 5 lbs.

Comments: A small, lightweight 22 caliber rifle produced from about 1959 to present.

Estimated Value:	New (retail):	$345.00
	Excellent:	$260.00
	Very good:	$200.00

Browning BL-22 Grade II

Similar to BL-22 with engraving; gold plated trigger; checkered stock & forearm.

Estimated Value:	New (retail):	$395.00
	Excellent:	$295.00
	Very good:	$235.00

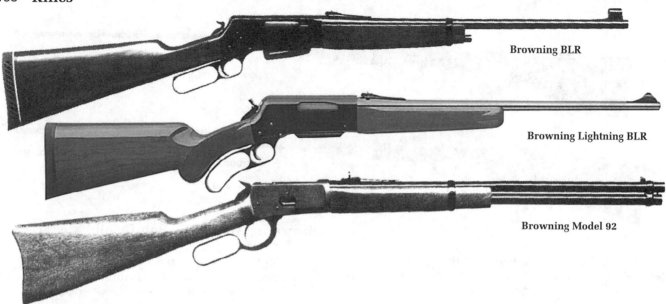

Browning BLR

Browning Lightning BLR

Browning Model 92

Browning BLR, '81 BLR
Caliber: 243, 270 win., 30-06, 308, 358. 22-250 Rem. (added in 1982); Calibers 222, 223 Rem., 257 Roberts, 284, & 7mm-08 Rem. added later.
Action: Lever action; exposed hammer; repeating
Magazine: 4-shot removable box
Barrel: Blued; 20"
Sights: Adjustable rear, hooded ramp front
Stock & Forearm: Checkered walnut straight grip stock & forearm; recoil pad; barrel band
Approximate wt.: 6½ to 8½
Comments: Produced from early 1970's to mid 1990's. Add 6% for long action.
Estimated Value: Excellent: $420.00
                  Very good: $340.00

Browning Lightning BLR
Caliber: 223 Rem., 22/250 Rem., 243 Win., 7mm-08 Rem., 308 Win., in short action; 270 Win., 30-06 Sprg., 7mm Rem. magnum, in long action
Action: Lever action; repeating; exposed hammer; short and long action
Magazine: 4-shot, 3-shot in magnum caliber; removable box magazine
Barrel: Blued; 20", 22", 24" round barrel
Sights: Adjustable rear with ramp front sight; drilled and tapped for scope mounts
Stock & Forearm: Checkered hardwood pistol grip stock and forearm
Approximate wt.: 7 to 9 lbs.
Comments: Introduced in 1996. Add 6% for long action model.
Estimated Value: New (retail): $577.00
                  Excellent: $435.00
                  Very good: $345.00

Browning Model 1895

Browning Model 92, B-92
Caliber: 44 magnum, 357 magnum (added 1982)
Action: Lever action; exposed three position hammer; repeating
Magazine: 11-shot tubular
Barrel: 20"; round; Blued
Sights: Adjustable cloverleaf rear, blade front
Stock & Forearm: Plain walnut straight grip stock & forearm; barrel band
Approximate wt.: 5½ lbs.
Comments: An authentic remake of the 1892 Winchester designed by John Browning. Introduced in the late 1970's. Discontinued in late 1980's.
Estimated Value: Excellent: $350.00
                  Very good: $280.00

Browning Model 1895
Caliber: 30-06 Springfield
Action: Lever action; exposed hammer; repeating
Magazine: 5-shot non-detachable box
Barrel: 24"; Blued
Sights: Buckhorn rear, beaded ramp front
Stock & Forearm: Walnut straight grip stock & lipped forearm; High Grade has checkered stock with engraved steel grey receiver
Approximate wt.: 8 lbs.
Comments: Produced in mid 1980's, this is a newer version of John Browning's Model 1895 first produced by Winchester in 1896. Add 30% for High Grade.
Estimated Value: Excellent: $450.00
                  Very good: $360.00

Browning Model 1886

Caliber: 45-70 Gov't
Action: Lever action; exposed hammer; repeating
Magazine: 8-shot tubular, side-port load
Barrel: 26" octagon
Sights: Open buckhorn
Stock & Forearm: Smooth walnut straight-grip stock & forearm; metal, crescent butt plate
Approximate wt.: 9¼ lbs.
Comments: Based on the Winchester Model 1886 designed by John Browning. Produced in late 1980's. Add 35% for High Grade.
Estimated Value: **Excellent:** $475.00
                       Very good: $380.00

Browning Model 53 Limited Edition

Caliber: 32-20 Win., round nose or hollow point only
Action: Lever action; exposed hammer; repeating
Magazine: 7-shot tubular, side-port load
Barrel: 22"; round; Blued
Sights: Post bead front, adjustable rear
Stock & Forearm: Checkered, high-gloss walnut straight-grip stock & forearm
Approximate wt.: 6½ lbs.
Comments: A limited edition version of the Winchester Model 53 designed by Browning. Only 5,000 produced in 1991.
Estimated Value: **Excellent:** $475.00
                       Very good: $380.00

Browning Model 1886 Limited Edition

Browning Model 1886
Limited Edition High Grade

Browning Model BPR

Browning Model 1886 Ltd. Edition

Caliber: 45-70 Gov't
Action: Lever action; exposed hammer; repeating
Magazine: 8-shot tubular, side-port load
Barrel: 22"; Blued; round
Sights: Open buckhorn
Stock & Forearm: Select walnut straight-grip stock & forearm; metal, crescent butt plate
Approximate wt.: 8 lbs.
Comments: A limited edition carbine based on the Winchester Model 1886 designed by John Browning. Produced in 1992. Add 35% for High Grade.
Estimated Value: **Excellent:** $560.00
                       Very good: $450.00

Browning Model BPR

Caliber: 22 long rifle; 22 Win. mag.
Action: Slide action; hammerless; repeating; slide release on trigger guard
Magazine: 15-shot tubular; 11-shot on magnum
Barrel: Blued; 20¼"
Sights: Adjustable folding leaf rear, gold bead front
Stock & Forearm: Checkered walnut pistol grip stock & slide handle
Approximate wt.: 6¼ lbs.
Comments: Made from the late 1970's to early 1980's.
Estimated Value: **Excellent:** $200.00
                       Very good: $160.00

Browning Model BPR Grade II

Similar to the BPR in magnum only; engraved squirrels & rabbits on receiver.
Estimated Value: **Excellent:** $300.00
                       Very good: $230.00

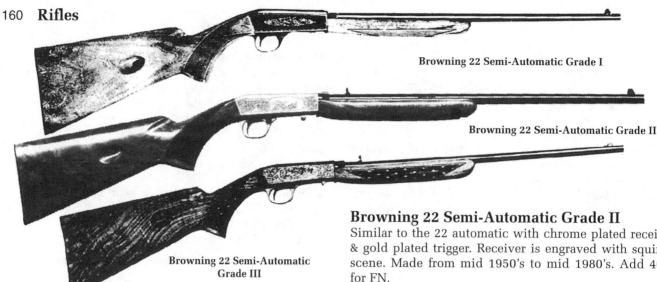

Browning 22 Semi-Automatic Grade I

Browning 22 Semi-Automatic Grade II

Browning 22 Semi-Automatic
Grade III

Browning 22 Semi-Automatic Grade I
Caliber: 22 short or long rifle
Action: Browning semi-automatic; hammerless; bottom ejection
Magazine: Tubular in stock; 11 long rifles; 16 shorts
Barrel: Blued; 22¼" or 19¼"
Sights: Adjustable rear, dovetail bead front
Stock & Forearm: Hand checkered walnut pistol grip stock & forearm
Approximate wt.: 4¾ lbs.
Comments: This takedown model has been in production since the mid 1950's. Add 40% for FN.
Estimated Value: New (retail): $399.00
                         Excellent: $299.00
                         Very good: $240.00

Browning 22 Semi-Automatic Grade II
Similar to the 22 automatic with chrome plated receiver & gold plated trigger. Receiver is engraved with squirrel scene. Made from mid 1950's to mid 1980's. Add 40% for FN.
Estimated Value: Excellent: $350.00
                         Very good: $280.00

Browning 22 Semi-Automatic Grade III
This is the same rifle as the Grade II except engraving is of bird dog & birds, high-quality finish. Made from mid 1950's to mid 1980's. Add 40% for FN.
Estimated Value: Excellent: $675.00
                         Very good: $540.00

Browning 22 Semi-Automatic Grade VI
Same as the 22 Semi-Automatic Grade I except: higher grade wood and finish; 24 Karat gold plated engraved blued or greyed receiver.
Estimated Value: New (Retail): $819.00
                         Excellent: $615.00
                         Very good: $490.00

Browning BAR Grade I

Browning BAR Grade I
Caliber: 243 Win., 270 Win., 280 Rem., 308 Win., 30-06, 7mm Rem. mag., 300 Win. mag., 338 Win. mag.
Action: Semi-automatic gas operated; side ejection; hammerless
Magazine: 4-shot; 3-shot in mag.
Barrel: Blued; 22" or 24"
Sights: Optional Folding rear & hooded ramp front, or
Stock & Forearm: Checkered walnut pistol grip stock & forearm; swivels; recoil pad on mag.
Approximate wt.: 7 to 8¼ lbs.
Comments: Made from the late 1960's to early 1990's. Add 7% for magnum calibers. Add 3% for sights.
Estimated Value: Excellent: $500.00
                         Very good: $400.00

Browning BAR Grade II
Engraved version of BAR. Discontinued in the early 1970's. Add $50.00 for magnum.
Estimated Value: Excellent: $550.00
                         Very good: $440.00

Browning BAR Grade III
Similar to Grade I except: elaborate engraving featuring antelope head. Discontinued early 1970's. Reintroduced in 1979 with rams & elk engravings. Add 6% for mag calibers. Discontinued in mid 1980's.
Estimated Value: Excellent: $900.00
                         Very good: $720.00

Browning Model BAR Grade IV
Similar to Grade I with elaborate engraving featuring two running antelope & running deer. Magnum has moose & elk engravings. Add 5% for magnum caliber. Produced from 1971 until mid 1980's.
Estimated Value: Excellent: $1,375.00
                         Very good: $1,100.00

Browning BAR Grade V
Similar to other grades of BAR. This is the fanciest model. Produced from 1971 to 1974.
Estimated Value: Excellent: $2,750.00
                         Very good: $2,200.00

Browning BAR Grade IV

Browning Model BAR-22 Grade II

Browning BAR Mark II

Caliber: 338 Win. magnum, 300 Win. magnum, 270 Win., 7mm Rem. magnum, 30-06 Sprg., 270 Win., 308 Win., 243 Win.

Action: Gas operated semi-automatic; side ejection; hammerless

Magazine: 4-shot; 3-shot magnum; hinged floor plate

Barrel: Blued; 22" or 24" with or without the Boss shooting system

Sights: Optional adjustable rear, hooded ramp front

Stock & Forearm: Checkered walnut pistol grip stock & forearm; swivels

Approximate wt.: 7½ to 8½ lbs.

Comments: Introduced in the early 1990's. Add 8% for magnum calibers; 12% for Boss shooting system; 3% for open sights.

Estimated Value: New (retail): $714.00
                Excellent: $535.00
                Very good: $430.00

Browning Model BAR-22

Caliber: 22 long rifle

Action: Semi-automatic; blow back; hammerless; repeating

Magazine: 15-shot tubular

Barrel: 20"; Blued; recessed bore at muzzle

Sights: Adjustable folding leaf rear, gold bead front

Stock & Forearm: Checkered walnut pistol grip stock & forearm; fluted comb

Approximate wt.: 5¾ lbs.

Comments: Produced in the late 1970's to mid 1980's.

Estimated Value: Excellent: $225.00
                Very good: $180.00

Browning Model BAR-22 Grade II

Similar to the BAR-22 with engraved receiver, squirrels & rabbits.

Estimated Value: Excellent: $275.00
                Very good: $225.00

BSA

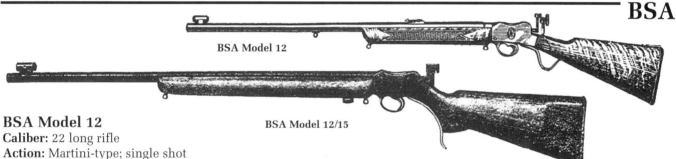

BSA Model 12

BSA Model 12/15

BSA Model 12

Caliber: 22 long rifle

Action: Martini-type; single shot

Magazine: None

Barrel: 29"; blued

Sights: Matched sights; some with open sights

Stock & Forearm: Checkered walnut straight grip stock & forearm; swivels

Approximate wt.: 9 lbs.

Comments: Made in England from about 1910 to 1930.

Estimated Value: Excellent: $300.00
                Very good: $235.00

BSA Model 13

Similar to Model 12 with a 25" barrel. Weighs about 6 lbs.

Estimated Value: Excellent: $270.00
                Very good: $215.00

BSA Model 13 Sporting

Similar to Model 13 in 22 Hornet caliber.

Estimated Value: Excellent: $325.00
                Very good: $260.00

BSA Centurion

Similar to Model 15 with a special barrel guaranteed to produce accurate groups.

Estimated Value: Excellent: $390.00
                Very good: $310.00

BSA Model 12/15

Similar to Model 12 & 15 in pre-war & post-war models. Made to about 1950.

Estimated Value: Excellent: $325.00
                Very good: $260.00

BSA Model 12/15 Heavy Barrel

Similar to Model 12/15 with heavy barrel. Weighs about 11 lbs.

Estimated Value: Excellent: $350.00
                Very good: $280.00

BSA Model 15

Caliber: 22 long rifle

Action: Martini-type; single shot

Magazine: None

Barrel: Blued; 29"

Sights: Special BSA match sights

Stock & Forearm: Walnut stock & forearm; cheekpiece; swivels

Approximate wt.: 9½ lbs.

Comments: A match rifle made in England from about 1915 to the early 1930's.

Estimated Value: Excellent: $405.00
                Very good: $325.00

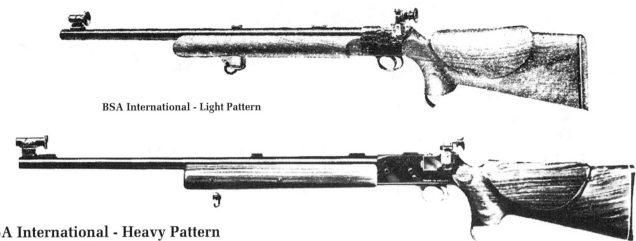

BSA International - Light Pattern

BSA International Mark III

BSA International - Heavy Pattern
Caliber: 22 long rifle
Action: Martini-type; single shot
Magazine: None
Barrel: Blued; 29"; heavy
Sights: Special Parker-Hale match sights
Stock & Forearm: Match style pistol grip stock with cheekpiece, wide forearm; hand stop; swivels
Approximate wt.: 13¾ lbs.
Comments: A target rifle made in England in the 1950's.
Estimated Value: Excellent: $540.00
                       Very good: $435.00

BSA International - Light Pattern
Similar to Heavy Pattern but lighter weight with a 26" barrel.
Estimated Value: Excellent: $430.00
                       Very good: $345.00

BSA International Mark II
Similar to Heavy & Light Patterns (choice of barrel). Stock & forearm changed slightly. Made from early to late 1950's.
Estimated Value: Excellent: $445.00
                       Very good: $360.00

BSA International Mark III
Similar to Heavy Pattern with different stock & forearm; alloy frame; floating barrel. Made from the late 1950's to late 1960's.
Estimated Value: Excellent: $510.00
                       Very good: $410.00

BSA Martini ISU

BSA Majestic Deluxe

BSA Majestic Deluxe
Caliber: 22 Hornet, 222, 243, 30-06, 308 Win., 7x57 mm
Action: Mauser-type bolt action; repeating
Magazine: 4-shot box
Barrel: Blued; 22"
Sights: Folding leaf rear, hooded ramp front
Stock & Forearm: Checkered walnut Monte Carlo one-piece pistol grip stock & lipped forearm; swivels; cheekpiece; recoil pad
Approximate wt.: 7½ lbs.
Comments: Made in England in the early to mid 1960's.
Estimated Value: Excellent: $345.00
                       Very good: $275.00

BSA Martini ISU
Caliber: 22 long rifle
Action: Martini-type; single shot
Magazine: None
Barrel: Blued; 28"
Sights: Special Parker-Hale match sights
Stock & Forearm: Match-style walnut pistol grip; adjustable butt plate
Approximate wt.: 10½ lbs.
Comments: A match rifle, made in England.
Estimated Value: Excellent: $585.00
                       Very good: $465.00

BSA Mark V
Similar to ISU except; heavier barrel; Wt. abt. 12½ lbs.
Estimated Value: Excellent: $600.00
                       Very good: $485.00

BSA Majestic Deluxe Featherweight

BSA Monarch Deluxe

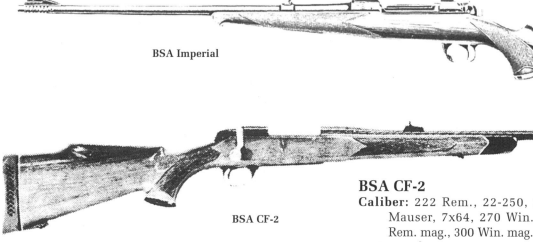

BSA Deluxe Varmint

BSA Majestic Deluxe Featherweight
Similar to Deluxe with recoil reducer in barrel. Available in some magnum calibers. Add 20% for 458 Win. magnum caliber.

Estimated Value: Excellent: $345.00
　　　　　　　　　Very good: $275.00

BSA Monarch Deluxe
Similar to Majestic Deluxe with slight changes in stock & forearm & with a recoil pad. Made from mid 1960's to late 1970's.

Estimated Value: Excellent: $325.00
　　　　　　　　　Very good: $260.00

BSA Deluxe Varmint
Similar to Monarch Deluxe with a heavier 24" barrel.

Estimated Value: Excellent: $335.00
　　　　　　　　　Very good: $265.00

BSA Imperial

BSA CF-2

BSA Imperial
Caliber: 22 Hornet, 222, 243, 257 Roberts, 270 Win., 7x57mm, 300 Savage, 30-06, 308 Win.
Action: Bolt action; repeating
Magazine: 4-shot box
Barrel: Blued; 22"; recoil reducer
Sights: Open rear, ramp front
Stock & Forearm: Checkered walnut Monte Carlo one-piece pistol grip stock & lipped forearm; cheekpiece
Approximate wt.: 7 lbs.
Comments: Made in the early 1960's.
Estimated Value: Excellent: $360.00
　　　　　　　　　Very good: $290.00

BSA CF-2
Caliber: 222 Rem., 22-250, 243 Win., 6.5x55, 7mm Mauser, 7x64, 270 Win., 308 Win., 30-06, 7mm Rem. mag., 300 Win. mag.
Action: Bolt action; repeating
Magazine: 4- or 5-shot box, 3-shot in magnum
Barrel: Blued; 23½"; 24" heavy barrel available in some calibers
Sights: Hooded ramp front, adjustable rear
Stock & Forearm: Checkered walnut Monte Carlo one-piece pistol grip stock & forearm; cheekpiece; contrasting fore-end tip & grip cap; swivels; recoil pad; European style has oil finish, American style has polyeurethane finish with white spacers.
Approximate wt.: 7½ to 8½ lbs.
Comments: Add 14% for European style; 8% for magnum calibers with heavy barrel.
Estimated Value: Excellent: $400.00
　　　　　　　　　Very good: $320.00

Carl Gustaf

Carl Gustaf Grade II

Carl Gustaf Grade II Magnum

Carl Gustaf Grade III

Carl Gustaf Swede

Carl Gustaf Grade II
Caliber: 22-250, 243, 25-06, 270, 6.5x55, 30-06, 308
Action: Bolt action; repeating
Magazine: 5-shot staggered column
Barrel: Blued; 23½"
Sights: Leaf rear, hooded ramp front
Stock & Forearm: Checkered walnut Monte Carlo one-piece pistol grip stock & forearm; swivels
Approximate wt.: 7 lbs.
Comments: Manufactured in Sweden.
Estimated Value: Excellent: $515.00
                         Very good: $410.00

Carl Gustaf Grade II Magnum
Similar to Grade II except magnum calibers; recoil pad; 3-shot magazine.
Estimated Value: Excellent: $540.00
                         Very good: $430.00

Carl Gustaf Grade III
Similar to Grade II with select wood; more checkering; high-quality finish; no sights.
Estimated Value: Excellent: $620.00
                         Very good: $500.00

Carl Gustaf Grade III Magnum
Similar to Grade II Magnum with select wood; more checkering; high-quality finish; no sights.
Estimated Value: Excellent: $650.00
                         Very good: $520.00

Carl Gustaf Swede
Similar to Grade II with lipped forearm but lacking the Monte Carlo comb.
Estimated Value: Excellent: $540.00
                         Very good: $430.00

Carl Gustaf Swede Deluxe
Similar to Grade III with lipped forearm.
Estimated Value: Excellent: $650.00
                         Very good: $520.00

Carl Gustaf Varmint Target

Carl Gustaf Varmint Target
Caliber: 22-250, 222, 243, 6.5x55
Action: Bolt action; repeating; large bolt knob
Magazine: 5-shot staggered column
Barrel: Blued; 27"
Sights: None
Stock & Forearm: Plain walnut Monte Carlo one-piece pistol grip stock & forearm
Approximate wt.: 9½ lbs.
Comments: Manufactured in Sweden.
Estimated Value: Excellent: $540.00
                         Very good: $430.00

Charles Daly

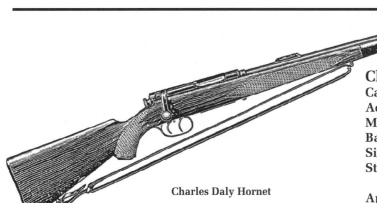

Charles Daly Hornet

Charles Daly Hornet
Caliber: 22 Hornet
Action: Bolt action; double triggers
Magazine: 5-shot box
Barrel: 24"
Sights: Leaf rear, hooded ramp front
Stock & Forearm: Checkered walnut one-piece stock & forearm
Approximate wt.: 7¾ lbs.
Comments: Made during the 1930's. Also marked under the name Herold Rifle.
Estimated Value: Excellent: $970.00
Very good: $775.00

Charter Arms

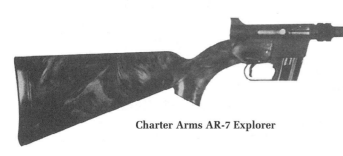

Charter Arms AR-7 Explorer

Charter Arms AR-7 Explorer
Caliber: 22 long rifle
Action: Semi-automatic
Magazine: 8-shot clip
Barrel: 16" aluminum & steel lined, black or silvertone

Sights: Peep rear, blade front
Stock & Forearm: Fiberglass, pistol grip stock (no forearm); stock acts as case for gun when dismantled. Also available in silvertone or camouflage.
Approximate wt.: 2¾ lbs.
Comments: A lightweight alloy rifle designed to float. Also dismantles to fit into stock. Made from about 1973 to 1990 by Charter Arms. Made by Armalite from about 1960 to 1973. Made by Survival Arms Inc. from 1990 to mid 1990's.
Estimated Value: Excellent: $130.00
Very good: $100.00

Colt

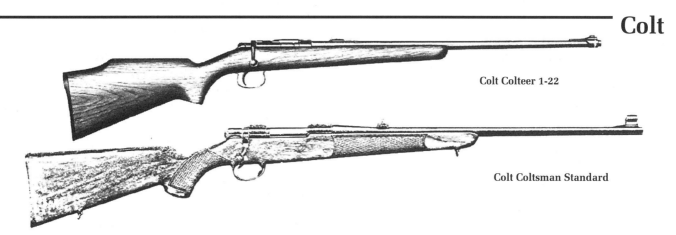

Colt Colteer 1-22

Colt Coltsman Standard

Colt Colteer 1-22
Caliber: 22 short, long, long rifle
Action: Bolt action; hammerless; single shot
Magazine: None
Barrel: Blued; 20", 22"
Sights: Open rear, ramp front
Stock & Forearm: Plain walnut Monte Carlo pistol grip stock & forearm
Approximate wt.: 5 lbs.
Comments: Made for 10 years from about 1957.
Estimated Value: Excellent: $125.00
Very good: $100.00

Colt Coltsman Standard
Caliber: 300 H & H magnum, 30-06
Action: Mauser-type, bolt action; repeating
Magazine: 5-shot box
Barrel: Blued; 22"
Sights: No rear, ramp front
Stock & Forearm: Checkered walnut one-piece pistol grip stock & tapered forearm; swivels
Approximate wt.: 7 lbs.
Comments: Made from about 1957 to the early 1960's.
Estimated Value: Excellent: $385.00
Very good: $310.00

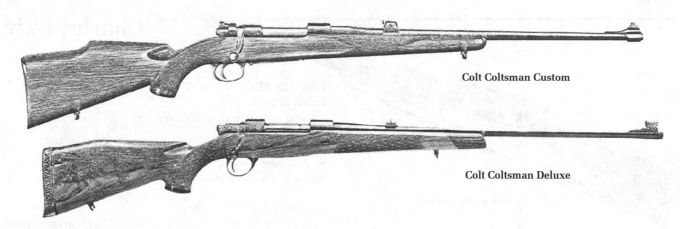

Colt Coltsman Custom

Colt Coltsman Deluxe

Colt Coltsman Custom

Similar to the deluxe with select wood; cheekpiece; engraving.

Estimated Value: Excellent: $520.00
                       Very good: $410.00

Colt Coltsman Deluxe

Similar to standard with higher quality wood & finish; adjustable rear sight; Monte Carlo stock.

Estimated Value: Excellent: $430.00
                       Very good: $325.00

Colt Coltsman Sako Custom

Colt Coltsman Sako-Medium

Caliber: 243, 308 Win.
Action: Medium stroke, Sako-type bolt action; repeating
Magazine: 5-shot box
Barrel: Blued; 24"
Sights: Folding leaf rear, hooded ramp front
Stock & Forearm: Checkered walnut Monte Carlo one-piece pistol grip stock & tapered forearm
Approximate wt.: 7 lbs.
Comments: Made from the early to mid 1960's.
Estimated Value: Excellent: $390.00
                       Very good: $310.00

Colt Coltsman Sako-Short

Caliber: 222, 222 magnum, 243, 308
Action: Short Sako-type bolt action; repeating
Magazine: 5-shot box
Barrel: Blued; 22"
Sights: Open rear, hooded ramp front
Stock & Forearm: Checkered walnut Monte Carlo pistol grip stock & tapered forearm; swivels
Approximate wt.: 7 lbs.
Comments: Made from the late 1950's to mid 1960's.
Estimated Value: Excellent: $375.00
                       Very good: $300.00

Colt Coltsman Deluxe Sako-Short

Similar to Sako-Short with adjustable rear sight; higher quality finish; in calibers 243, 308. Discontinued in the early 1960's.

Estimated Value: Excellent: $430.00
                       Very good: $325.00

Colt Colstman Custom Sako-Short

Similar to Deluxe Sako-Short with select wood; cheekpiece; engraving. Made until mid 1960's.

Estimated Value: Excellent: $485.00
                       Very good: $395.00

Colt Coltsman Custom Sako-Medium

Similar to standard Sako-Medium with higher quality finish & recoil pad.

Estimated Value: Excellent: $460.00
                       Very good: $365.00

Colt Coltsman Sako-Long

Caliber: 264, 270 Win., 300 H&H, 30-06, 375 H&H
Action: Long stroke, Sako-type bolt action; repeating
Magazine: 5-shot box
Barrel: Blued; 24"
Sights: Folding leaf rear, hooded ramp front
Stock & Forearm: Checkered walnut one-piece pistol grip stock & tapered forearm; swivels
Approximate wt.: 7 lbs.
Comments: Made from the early to mid 1960's.
Estimated Value: Excellent: $400.00
                       Very good: $325.00

Colt Coltsman Custom Sako-Long

Similar to Sako-Long with higher quality finish; recoil pad; Monte Carlo stock.

Estimated Value: Excellent: $450.00
                       Very good: $360.00

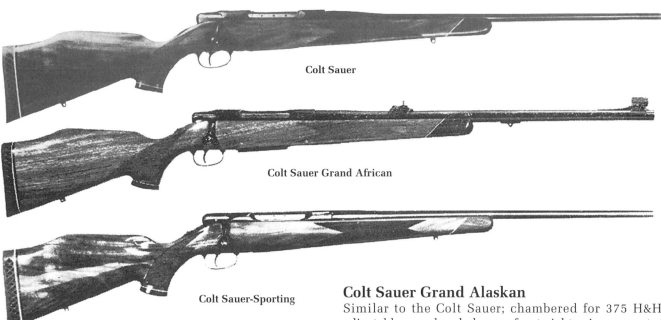

Colt Sauer

Colt Sauer Grand African

Colt Sauer-Sporting

Colt Sauer

Caliber: 25-06, 270, 30-06, 300 Win. mag., 7mm Rem. mag., 300 Weath. mag., 375 H&H mag., 458 Win. mag.

Action: Long stroke, Sauer-type bolt action; repeating

Magazine: 5-shot detachable box

Barrel: Blued; 24"

Sights: None; tapped for scope

Stock & Forearm: Checkered walnut Monte Carlo one-piece pistol grip stock & tapered forearm; swivels; recoil pad

Approximate wt.: 7½ to 8 lbs.

Comments: Made from early 1970's to mid 1980's. Add $50.00 for magnum.

Estimated Value: Excellent: $1025.00
                     Very good: $ 820.00

Colt Sauer Grand Alaskan

Similar to the Colt Sauer; chambered for 375 H&H; adjustable rear, hooded ramp front sights. Approx. wt. 9 lbs. Mid 1970's to mid 1980's.

Estimated Value: Excellent: $1,075.00
                     Very good: $ 865.00

Colt Sauer Grand African

Similar to Sauer with higher quality finish; adjustable sights; 458 Win. caliber only; 10 lbs. Mid 1970's to mid 1980's.

Estimated Value: Excellent: $1,160.00
                     Very good: $ 860.00

Colt Sauer-Sporting

Similar to Sauer with short stroke action; chambered for 22-250, 243, 308 calibers. Made from mid 1970's to mid 1980's. Approx. wt. 7½ to 8½ lbs.

Estimated Value: Excellent: $1020.00
                     Very good: $ 815.00

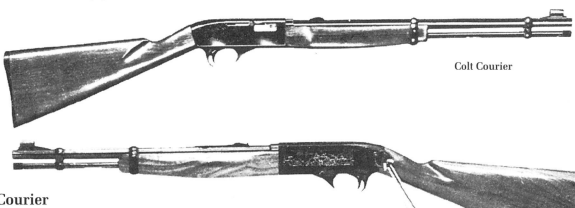

Colt Courier

Colt Stagecoach

Colt Courier

Caliber: 22 long rifle

Action: Semi-automatic

Magazine: 15-shot tubular

Barrel: Blued; 19½"

Sights: Open rear, hooded ramp front

Stock & Forearm: Plain walnut straight grip stock & forearm; barrel band

Approximate wt.: 5 lbs.

Comments: Made from the mid 1960's to late 1970's.

Estimated Value: Excellent: $130.00
                     Very good: $105.00

Colt Stagecoach

Similar to the Courier except: engraving, 16½" barrel; saddle ring with leather string. Made from mid 1960's to 1976.

Estimated Value: Excellent: $140.00
                     Very good: $125.00

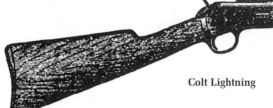

Colt Lightning

Colt Lightning

Caliber: 22 long rifle
Action: Slide action; exposed hammer; repeating
Magazine: Tubular: 15 longs, 16 shorts
Barrel: Blued; 24" round or octagon
Sights: Open rear, bead front
Stock & Forearm: Plain walnut straight pistol grip stock & checkered slide handle
Approximate wt.: 5¾ lbs.
Comments: Made from the 1880's to about 1905.
Estimated Value: Excellent: $850.00
 Very good: $680.00

Colt AR-15

Colt AR-15, AR-15A2, AR-15A2 Carbine

Caliber: 223; 9mm (1986 only)
Action: Gas operated semi-automatic
Magazine: 5-shot clip (223 cal.); 20-shot clip (9mm cal.)
Barrel: 20" with flash supressor; 16" with collapsible stock. Also heavy barrel available
Sights: Adjustable rear, post front adjustable for elevation; 3X & 4X scopes available
Stock & Forearm: Pistol grip; fiberglass shoulder stock & handguard; swivels; carrying handle; collapsible stock available in both calibers
Approximate wt.: 6 to 8 lbs.
Comments: Made from the mid 1960's to early 1990's. Add 10% for collapsible stock (AR-15A2 Government model carbine); add 14% for target sight & heavy barrel (AR-15 A2H Bar).
Estimated Value: Excellent: $650.00
 Very good: $525.00

Colt AR-15 A2 Delta H-Bar

Similar to the AR-15 A2 with 20" heavy barrel, 3x9 rubber armored variable power scope, removable cheekpiece, leather military style sling & aluminum carrying case.
Estimated Value: Excellent: $1,020.00
 Very good: $ 815.00

Colt Target Lightweight

Similar to the AR-15 in 223 Rem., 9mm, or 7.62x39mm calibers, 16" barrel, introduced in the early 1990's.
Estimated Value: New (Retail): $987.00
 Excellent: $740.00
 Very good: $595.00

Colt Match Target

Similar to the AR-15 in 223 Rem. only with a 20" barrel. Introduced in the early 1990's. Add 5% for H-Bar.
Estimated Value: New (Retail): $1,019.00
 Excellent: $ 765.00
 Very good: $ 610.00

Colt Target Competition H-Bar

Similar to the AR-15 in 223 Rem. only with a 20" or 16" heavy barrel. Introduced in the early 1990's, 8-shot clip in mid 1990's.
Estimated Value: New (Retail): $1,044.00
 Excellent: $ 785.00
 Very good: $ 625.00

FN

FN Mauser Deluxe

FN Mauser Deluxe

Caliber: 220, 243, 244, 250-3000, 270, 7mm, 300, 308, 30-06
Action: Mauser-type bolt action; repeating
Magazine: 5-shot box
Barrel: Blued; 24"
Sights: Adjustable rear, hooded ramp front
Stock & Forearm: Checkered one-piece pistol grip stock & forearm; swivels
Approximate wt.: 7½ to 8 lbs.
Comments: Made from World War II to the early 1960's.
Estimated Value: Excellent: $540.00
 Very good: $430.00

FN Mauser Deluxe Presentation

Similar to the Deluxe with Monte Carlo stock; engraving; select wood.
Estimated Value: Excellent: $865.00
 Very good: $690.00

FN Supreme

FN Supreme
Caliber: 243, 270, 7mm, 30-06, 308
Action: Mauser-type bolt action; repeating
Magazine: 5-shot box, 4-shot box in 308 or 243 calibers
Barrel: Blued; 22", 24"
Sights: Adjustable rear, hooded ramp front
Stock & Forearm: Checkered wood Monte Carlo one-piece pistol grip stock & tapered forearm; cheek-piece; swivels
Approximate wt.: 8 lbs.
Comments: Made from the late 1950's to the mid 1970's.
Estimated Value: **Excellent:** $620.00
Very good: $495.00

FN Supreme Magnum
Similar to the Supreme in 264 magnum, 7mm magnum, and 300 Win. magnum calibers & 3-shot box magazine.
Estimated Value: **Excellent:** $675.00
Very good: $540.00

Harrington & Richardson

Harrington & Richardson 1873 Springfield Commemorative

Harrington & Richardson Little Big Horn Commemorative 174

Harrington & Richardson Cavalry 171 Deluxe Carbine

Harrington & Richardson 1873 Springfield Commemorative
Caliber: 45-70 Gov't
Action: Trap door; single shot
Magazine: None
Barrel: Blued; 32"
Sights: Adjustable rear, blade front
Stock & Forearm: One-piece straight grip stock & full-length forearm; barrel band; swivels
Approximate wt.: 8¾ lbs.
Comments: Manufactured in the early 1970's to mid 1980's; replica of the 1873 U.S. Springfield Rifle.
Estimated Value: **Excellent:** $345.00
Very good: $275.00

Harrington & Richardson Little Big Horn Commemorative 174
Carbine version of the trap door Springfield, 22" barrel; 7¼ lbs. Discontinued in 1984.
Estimated Value: **Excellent:** $350.00
Very good: $275.00

Harrington & Richardson Cavalry Carbine 171
Similar to the Little Big Horn with saddle ring.
Estimated Value: **Excellent:** $300.00
Very good: $240.00

Harrington & Richardson Cavalry 171 Deluxe
Similar to the Cavalry Carbine 171 with engraving.
Estimated Value: **Excellent:** $320.00
Very good: $255.00

Harrington & Richardson 158 Topper

Harrington & Richardson Mustang

Harrington & Richardson Model 157

Harrington & Richardson Shikari 155

Harrington & Richardson 158 Topper

Caliber: 22 Hornet, 30-30, 357 magnum, 44 magnum
Action: Box lock; top lever, break-open; exposed hammer; single shot
Magazine: None
Barrel: Blued; 22"
Sights: Adjustable rear, ramp front
Stock & Forearm: Hardwood straight or semi-pistol grip stock & forearm; recoil pad
Approximate wt.: 5 lbs.
Comments: Made from the early 1960's to mid 1980's, magnum calibers added 1982.
Estimated Value: Excellent: $115.00
                        Very good: $ 90.00

Harrington & Richardson 158 C, 58 Topper, 258

Similar to the 158 with extra interchangeable 26" 410 or 20 gauge shotgun barrel. Add 18% for nickel finish.
Estimated Value: Excellent: $160.00
                        Very good: $130.00

Harrington & Richardson Mustang

Similar to the 158 with gold plated trigger & hammer; straight stock. Made in the mid to late 1960's.
Estimated Value: Excellent: $125.00
                        Very good: $100.00

Harrington & Richardson Model 157

Similar to the 158 with semi-pistol grip stock, full-length forearm & swivels. Discontinued in 1984.
Estimated Value: Excellent: $110.00
                        Very good: $ 85.00

Harrington & Richardson Shikari 155

Caliber: 44 magnum, 45-70 Gov't
Action: Single shot; exposed hammer
Magazine: None
Barrel: Blued; 24", 28"
Sights: Folding leaf rear, blade front
Stock & Forearm: Wood straight grip stock & forearm; barrel band
Approximate wt.: 7 to 7¼ lbs.
Comments: Manufactured from early 1970's to early 1980's.
Estimated Value: Excellent: $110.00
                        Very good: $ 85.00

Harrington & Richardson Pioneer 765

Harrington & Richardson Plainsman 865

Harrington & Richardson Plainsman 865

Similar to the 765 with 5-shot clip; 22" barrel. Made from about 1950 to 1986.
Estimated Value: Excellent: $95.00
                        Very good: $75.00

Harrington & Richardson Pioneer 765

Caliber: 22 short, long, long rifle
Action: Bolt action; single shot
Magazine: None
Barrel: Blued; 24"
Sights: Open rear, hooded bead front
Stock & Forearm: Wood Monte Carlo one-piece semi-pistol grip stock & forearm
Approximate wt.: 5 lbs.
Comments: Made from the late 1940's to mid 1950's.
Estimated Value: Excellent: $70.00
                        Very good: $60.00

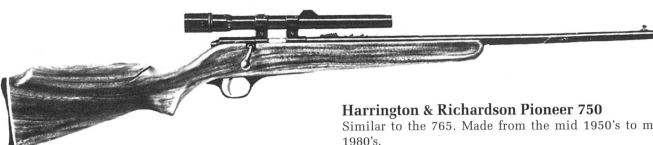

Harrington & Richardson Pioneer 750

Harrington & Richardson Pioneer 750

Similar to the 765. Made from the mid 1950's to mid 1980's.

Estimated Value: Excellent: $75.00
Very good: $60.00

Harrington & Richardson 866

Similar to the 865 with full-length forearm. Made in early 1970's.

Estimated Value: Excellent: $95.00
Very good: $75.00

Harrington & Richardson Model 751

Similar to the 750 with full-length forearm. Made from the early to mid 1970's.

Estimated Value: Excellent: $80.00
Very good: $65.00

Harrington & Richardson Sahara 755

Harrington & Richardson Model 760

Harrington & Richardson Model 760

Similar to the 755 with short forearm. Discontinued in 1970.

Estimated Value: Excellent: $75.00
Very good: $60.00

Harrington & Richardson Medalist 450

Caliber: 22 long rifle
Action: Bolt action; repeating
Magazine: 5-shot detachable box
Barrel: Blued; 26"
Sights: None
Stock & Forearm: Target style with pistol grip; swivels
Approximate wt.: 10½ lbs.
Comments: A target rifle made from the late 1940's to early 1960's.
Estimated Value: Excellent: $150.00
Very good: $120.00

Harrington & Richardson Medalist 451

Similar to the 450 with extension rear sight & Lyman front sight.

Estimated Value: Excellent: $165.00
Very good: $135.00

Harrington & Richardson Sahara 755

Caliber: 22 short, long, long rifle
Action: Blow back; hammerless; single shot; automatic ejector
Magazine: None
Barrel: Blued; 22"
Sights: Open rear, military front
Stock & Forearm: Monte Carlo one-piece semi-pistol grip stock & full-length forearm
Approximate wt.: 4 lbs.
Comments: Made from the early 1960's to early 1970's.
Estimated Value: Excellent: $85.00
Very good: $70.00

Harrington & Richardson Sportster 250

Caliber: 22 long rifle
Action: Bolt action; repeating
Magazine: 5-shot detachable box
Barrel: Blued; 23"
Sights: Open rear, ramp front
Stock & Forearm: Wood one-piece semi-pistol grip stock & forearm
Approximate wt.: 6 lbs.
Comments: Made from the late 1940's to the early 1960's.
Estimated Value: Excellent: $75.00
Very good: $60.00

Harrington & Richardson 251

Similar to the 250 with a special Lyman rear sight.

Estimated Value: Excellent: $75.00
Very good: $60.00

Harrington & Richardson Fieldsman 852

Harrington & Richardson Fieldsman 852
Caliber: 22 short, long, long rifle
Action: Bolt action; repeating
Magazine: Tubular: 15 long rifles, 17 longs, 21 shorts
Barrel: Blued; 24"
Sights: Open rear, bead front
Stock & Forearm: Plain wood one-piece semi-pistol grip stock & forearm
Approximate wt.: 5½ lbs.
Comments: Made only in the early 1950's.
Estimated Value: Excellent: $100.00
Very good: $80.00

Harrington & Richardson Model 300

Harrington & Richardson Ultra 301

Harrington & Richardson Model 330

Harrington & Richardson Model 300
Caliber: 22-250 Rem., 243 Win., 270, 308, 30-06, 300 mag., 7mm mag.
Action: Mauser-type bolt action; repeating
Magazine: 5-shot box, 3-shot in magnum
Barrel: Blued; 22" or 24"
Sights: Open rear, ramp front
Stock & Forearm: Checkered walnut Monte Carlo one-piece pistol grip stock & forearm; cheekpiece; recoil pad; swivels
Approximate wt.: 7¾ lbs.
Comments: Made from the mid 1960's to early 1980's.
Estimated Value: Excellent: $430.00
Very good: $345.00

Harrington & Richardson Ultra 301
Similar to the 300 with full-length forearm & 18" barrel; no swivels.
Estimated Value: Excellent: $450.00
Very good: $360.00

Harrington & Richardson Model 330
Similar to the Model 300 with less fancy finish. Discontinued in the early 1970's.
Estimated Value: Excellent: $345.00
Very good: $275.00

Harrington & Richardson Model 333
Similar to the Model 330 with no checkering or sights.
Estimated Value: Excellent: $260.00
Very good: $200.00

Harrington & Richardson
Ultra Wildcat 317

Harrington & Richardson 317 Presentation
Similar to the 317 with select wood, special basketweave checkering.
Estimated Value: Excellent: $600.00
Very good: $475.00

Harrington & Richardson Ultra Wildcat 317
Caliber: 17 Rem., 222, 223 or 17/223 (Handload)
Action: Bolt action, Sako-type; repeating
Magazine: 6-shot box
Barrel: Blued; 24"
Sights: None
Stock & Forearm: Wood Monte Carlo one-piece pistol grip stock & forearm; cheekpiece; recoil pad; swivels
Approximate wt.: 7¾ lbs.
Comments: Made from the late 1960's to mid 1970's.
Estimated Value: Excellent: $540.00
Very good: $430.00

Harrington & Richardson Ultra Medalist 370

Harrington & Richardson Model 340

Harrington & Richardson Ultra Medalist 370

Caliber: 22-250, 243, 6mm
Action: Sako bolt action; repeating
Magazine: 4-shot box
Barrel: 24" heavy
Sights: Open
Stock & Forearm: Monte Carlo one-piece grip stock & forearm; cheekpiece; recoil pad; swivels
Approximate wt.: 9 lbs.
Comments: Made from the late 1960's to mid 1970's.
Estimated Value: Excellent: $470.00
Very good: $375.00

Harrington & Richardson Model 340

Caliber: 243 Win., 270 Win., 30-06, 308 Win., 7mm Mauser (7x57)
Action: Bolt action; repeating; hinged floorplate; adjustable trigger
Magazine: 5-shot
Barrel: Blued; 22"
Sights: None; drilled & tapped for sights or scope
Stock & Forearm: Checkered walnut one-piece pistol grip stock & forearm; cheekpiece; recoil pad
Approximate wt.: 7¼ lbs.
Comments: Introduced in 1981 in 30-06; other calibers added later. Discontinued in 1984.
Estimated Value: Excellent: $345.00
Very good: $275.00

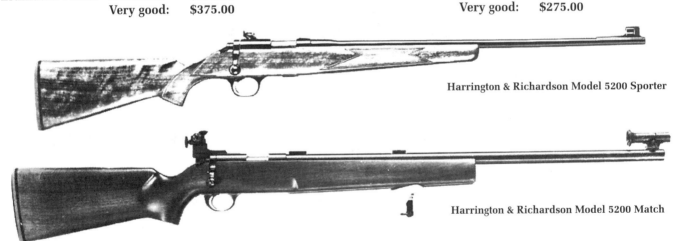

Harrington & Richardson Model 5200 Sporter

Harrington & Richardson Model 5200 Match

Harrington & Richardson Model 5200 Match

Caliber: 22 long rifle
Action: Bolt action, single shot; adjustable trigger
Magazine: None
Barrel: 28" heavy target weight, recessed muzzle
Sights: None; tapped for sights; scope bases included
Stock & Forearm: Smooth walnut one-piece match-style stock & forearm; swivels & hand stop; rubber recoil pad
Approximate wt.: 11 lbs.
Comments: A moderately priced match rifle produced from 1981 to 1986.
Estimated Value: Excellent: $375.00
Very good: $300.00

Harrington & Richardson Model 5200 Sporter

Caliber: 22 long rifle
Action: Bolt action; repeating
Magazine: 5-shot clip
Barrel: 24" recessed muzzle
Sights: Adjustable receiver sight; hooded ramp front
Stock & Forearm: Checkered walnut one-piece semi-pistol grip stock & forearm; rubber recoil pad
Approximate wt.: 6½ lbs.
Comments: A sporting version of the Model 5200 introduced in 1982. Discontinued 1983.
Estimated Value: Excellent: $350.00
Very good: $280.00

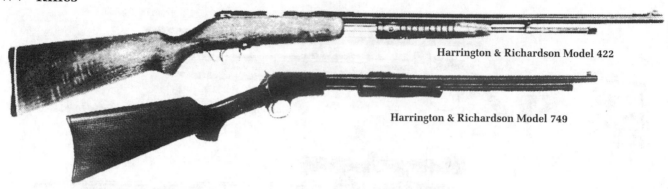

Harrington & Richardson Model 422

Harrington & Richardson Model 749

Harrington & Richardson Model 422
Caliber: 22 short, long, long rifle
Action: Slide action; hammerless; repeating
Magazine: Tubular: 15 long rifles, 17 longs, 21 shorts
Barrel: Blued; 24"
Sights: Open rear, ramp front
Stock & Forearm: Plain walnut semi-pistol grip stock & grooved slide handle
Approximate wt.: 6 lbs.
Comments: Made from the mid to late 1950's.
Estimated Value: Excellent: $130.00
                       Very good: $100.00

Harrington & Richardson Model 749
Caliber: 22 short, long, long rifle
Action: Slide action; hammerless; repeating
Magazine: Tubular: 18 shorts, 15 longs, 13 long rifles
Barrel: 19"; round, tapered
Sights: Open rear, blade front
Stock & Forearm: Plain hardwood pistol grip stock & tapered slide handle
Approximate wt.: 5 lbs.
Comments: Made in the early 1970's.
Estimated Value: Excellent: $120.00
                       Very good: $ 95.00

Harrington & Richardson Reising 60

Harrington & Richardson General 65

Harrington & Richardson Leatherneck 165

Harrington & Richardson General 65
Caliber: 22 long rifle
Action: Semi-automatic
Magazine: 10-shot detachable box
Barrel: Blued; 23"
Sights: Peep rear, covered blade front
Stock & Forearm: Wood one-piece semi-pistol grip stock & forearm
Approximate wt.: 9 lbs.
Comments: Used as a Marine training rifle during World War II.
Estimated Value: Excellent: $325.00
                       Very good: $260.00

Harrington & Richardson Reising 60
Caliber: 45
Action: Semi-automatic
Magazine: 12 or 20-shot detachable box
Barrel: Blued; 18¼"
Sights: Open rear, blade front
Stock & Forearm: Plain wood one-piece semi-pistol grip stock & forearm
Approximate wt.: 7¼ lbs.
Comments: Manufactured during World War II.
Estimated Value: Excellent: $460.00
                       Very good: $365.00

Harrington & Richardson Leatherneck 165
Lighter version of the 65 with ramp front sights. Made from World War II until the early 1960's.
Estimated Value: Excellent: $150.00
                       Very good: $125.00

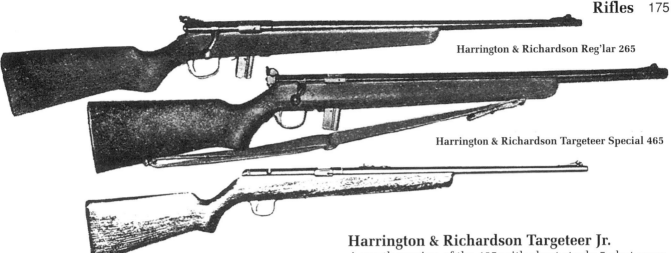

Harrington & Richardson Reg'lar 265

Harrington & Richardson Targeteer Special 465

Harrington & Richardson Leatherneck 150

Harrington & Richardson Reg'lar 265
Similar to the 165 in bolt action with a 22" barrel. Made from World War II until about 1950.

Estimated Value:	Excellent:	$95.00
	Very good:	$70.00

Harrington & Richardson Ace 365
Similar to the Model 265 except single shot. Made in the mid 1940's.

Estimated Value:	Excellent:	$75.00
	Very good:	$60.00

Harrington & Richardson Targeteer Special 465
Similar to the 265 with 25" barrel; swivels; slightly heavier. Made in the mid 1940's.

Estimated Value:	Excellent:	$115.00
	Very good:	$ 95.00

Harrington & Richardson Targeteer Jr.
A youth version of the 465 with short stock; 5-shot magazine; 20" barrel. Made from the late 1940's to early 1950's.

Estimated Value:	Excellent:	$100.00
	Very good:	$ 80.00

Harrington & Richardson Leatherneck 150
Caliber: 22 long rifle
Action: Semi-automatic; hammerless
Magazine: 5-shot detachable box
Barrel: Blued; 22"
Sights: Open rear, ramp front
Stock & Forearm: Wood one-piece semi-pistol grip stock & forearm
Approximate wt.: 7 lbs.
Comments: Made from the late 1940's to early 1950's.

Estimated Value:	Excellent:	$140.00
	Very good:	$110.00

Harrington & Richardson Model 151
Similar to the 150 with a special peep rear sight.

Estimated Value:	Excellent:	$145.00
	Very good:	$115.00

Harrington & Richardson Model 308

Harrington & Richardson Lynx 800
Caliber: 22 long rifle
Action: Semi-automatic; hammerless
Magazine: 10-shot clip
Barrel: Blued 22"
Sights: Open rear, ramp front
Stock & Forearm: Walnut one-piece semi-pistol grip stock & forearm
Approximate wt.: 6 lbs.
Comments: Made from the late 1950's to about 1960.

Estimated Value:	Excellent:	$95.00
	Very good:	$75.00

Harrington & Richardson Model 308
Caliber: 243, 264, 308
Action: Semi-automatic; gas operated
Magazine: 3-shot detachable box
Barrel: Blued; 22"
Sights: Adjustable rear, bead front
Stock & Forearm: Checkered walnut Monte Carlo one-piece pistol grip stock & forearm; cheekpiece; swivels
Approximate wt.: 7 lbs.
Comments: Made in the mid 1960's only; changed to the model 360 in 1967.

Estimated Value:	Excellent:	$315.00
	Very good:	$250.00

Harrington & Richardson Model 360
Same as the Model 308. Made from 1967 to the early 1970's.

Estimated Value:	Excellent:	$325.00
	Very good:	$260.00

Harrington & Richardson Model 700 Deluxe

Harrington & Richardson Model 700 Deluxe

Similar to the Model 700 with select custom finish; checkering; cheekpiece; recoil pad; 4X scope.
Estimated Value: Excellent: $280.00
Very good: $225.00

Harrington & Richardson Model 700

Caliber: 22 WMR
Action: Semi-automatic; hammerless
Magazine: 5- or 10-shot detachable box
Barrel: 22"
Sights: Adjustable folding rear; ramp blade front
Stock & Forearm: Plain walnut Monte Carlo one-piece pistol grip stock & forearm
Approximate wt.: 6½ lbs.
Comments: Produced in the late 1970's to mid 1980's.
Estimated Value: Excellent: $190.00
Very good: $150.00

Heckler & Koch

Heckler & Koch Model 300

Heckler & Koch Model 270

Heckler & Koch Model 270

Caliber: 22 long rifle
Action: Semi-automatic; blow back design
Magazine: 5- or 20-shot detachable box
Barrel: Blued; 20"
Sights: Diopter sights, adjustable for windage & elevation
Stock & Forearm: Plain walnut, one-piece semi-pistol grip stock & lipped forearm
Approximate wt.: 5½ lbs.
Comments: Discontinued in mid 1980's.
Estimated Value: Excellent: $250.00
Very good: $200.00

Heckler & Koch Model 300

Caliber: 22 Win. mag.
Action: Semi-automatic; blow back design
Magazine: 5- or 15-shot detachable box
Barrel: Blued; 20"
Sights: Adjustable post front, adjustable V-notch rear
Stock & Forearm: Checkered walnut Monte Carlo one-piece pistol grip stock & lipped forearm; cheekpiece; swivels
Approximate wt.: 5¾ lbs.
Comments: Discontinued 1992.
Estimated Value: Excellent: $375.00
Very good: $300.00

Heckler & Koch Model SL-6 & SL-7

Caliber: 223 (SL-6), 308 (SL-7)
Action: Semi-automatic
Magazine: 4-shot clip (SL-6); 3-shot clip (SL-7); 10-shot clip available for both rifles
Barrel: 17¾" round black matte finish
Sights: Ring & post front; diopter adjustable rear
Stock & Forearm: Smooth European one-piece stock & forearm with ventilated wood handguard over barrel
Approximate wt.: 8½ lbs.
Comments: Produced in the mid 1980's.
Estimated Value: Excellent: $550.00
Very good: $450.00

Heckler & Koch Model 91 & 93

Caliber: 223 (Model 93); 308 (Model 91)
Action: Semi-automatic
Magazine: 25-shot clip (Model 93); 20-shot clip (Model 91); 5-shot clip available for both rifles
Barrel: 16¼" matte black (Model 93); 17¾" matte black (Model 91)
Sights: Ring & post front; diopter adjustable rear
Stock & Forearm: Matte black, fixed, high-impact plastic three-piece stock, forearm & pistol grip; a retractable metal stock is available
Approximate wt.: 8 lbs. (Model 93); 10 lbs. (Model 91)
Comments: Made from the 1970's to 1992. Add 12% for retractable metal stock.
Estimated Value: Excellent: $800.00
Very good: $650.00

Heckler & Koch Model 94 Carbine

Similar to the Model 91 & Model 93 in 9mm caliber; 30-shot clip; 16½" barrel; weighs 6½ lbs.; Add 12% for retractable metal stock.
Estimated Value: Excellent: $820.00
Very good: $660.00

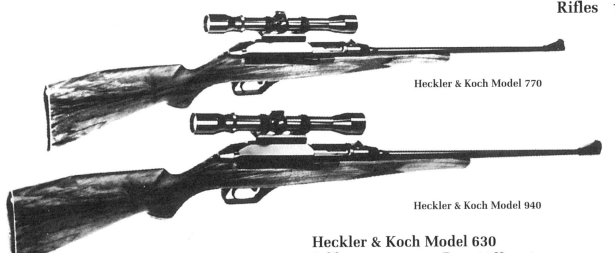

Heckler & Koch Model 770

Heckler & Koch Model 940

Heckler & Koch Model 770
Similar to the Model 630 in 243 or 308 Win. calibers; 20" barrel; weighs 8 lbs. 3-shot magazine.
Estimated Value: Excellent: $560.00
Very good: $450.00

Heckler & Koch Model 940
Similar to the Model 630 in 30-06 Springfield caliber; 22" barrel; weighs 8¾ lbs. 3-shot magazine.
Estimated Value: Excellent: $575.00
Very good: $435.00

Heckler & Koch Model 630
Caliber: 221, 222, 223, Rem., 22 Hornet
Action: Semi-automatic
Magazine: 4-shot box; 10-shot available
Barrel: Blued; 18"
Sights: Adjustable post front, adjustable V-notch rear
Stock & Forearm: Checkered walnut Monte Carlo pistol grip, one-piece stock & lipped forearm; cheekpiece; swivels
Approximate wt.: 7 lbs.
Comments: Available in 223 Remington caliber only after mid 1980's. Made from about 1982 to late 1980's.
Estimated Value: Excellent: $520.00
Very good: $400.00

High Standard

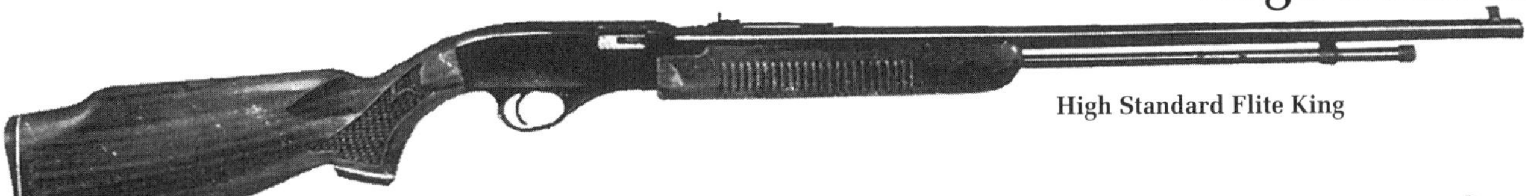

High Standard Flite King

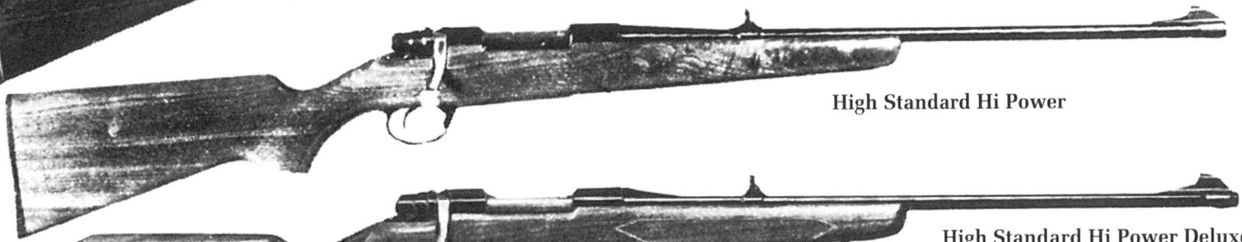

High Standard Hi Power

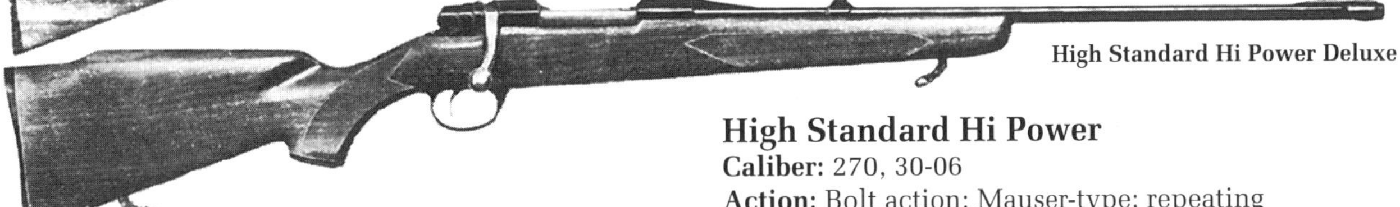

High Standard Hi Power Deluxe

High Standard Flite King
Caliber: 22 short, long, long rifle
Action: Slide action; hammerless; repeating
Magazine: Tubular: 17 long rifle, 19 long, 24 short
Barrel: Blued; 24"
Sights: Adjustable rear, post front
Stock & Forearm: Checkered walnut Monte Carlo pistol grip stock & grooved slide handle; early models have no checkering
Approximate wt.: 5½ lbs.
Comments: Made from about 1962 to late 1970's.
Estimated Value: Excellent: $125.00
Very good: $100.00

High Standard Hi Power
Caliber: 270, 30-06
Action: Bolt action; Mauser-type; repeating
Magazine: 4-shot box
Barrel: Blued; 22"
Sights: Folding leaf rear, ramp front
Stock & Forearm: Walnut one-piece semi-pistol grip stock & tapered forearm
Approximate wt.: 7 lbs.
Comments: Made from the early to mid 1960's.
Estimated Value: Excellent: $270.00
Very good: $215.00

High Standard Hi Power Deluxe
Similar to Hi Power with a checkered Monte Carlo stock & swivels.
Estimated Value: Excellent: $300.00
Very good: $240.00

High Standard Sport King

High Standard Sport King Special

High Standard Sport King Carbine

High Standard Sport King Deluxe

High Standard Sport King
Caliber: 22 short, long, long rifle
Action: Semi-automatic
Magazine: Tubular: 15 long rifles, 17 longs, 21 shorts
Barrel: Blued; 22¼"
Sights: Open rear, post front
Stock & Forearm: Checkered wood Monte Carlo one-piece pistol grip stock & forearm
Approximate wt.: 5½ lbs.
Comments: Sport King had no Monte Carlo stock before the mid 1970's; field model was made from about 1960 to the late 1970's.
Estimated Value: Excellent: $110.00
Very good: $ 90.00

High Standard Sport King Special
Similar to Sport King without checkering. Made from the early 1950's to mid 1960's.
Estimated Value: Excellent: $120.00
Very good: $ 95.00

High Standard Sport King Deluxe
Same specifications as Sport King. Made as Deluxe until mid 1970's.
Estimated Value: Excellent: $135.00
Very good: $100.00

High Standard Sport King Carbine
Carbine version of the Sport King. Straight stock; 18¼" barrel; smaller magazine; swivels. Made from the early 1960's to early 1970's.
Estimated Value: Excellent: $135.00
Very good: $110.00

Husqvarna

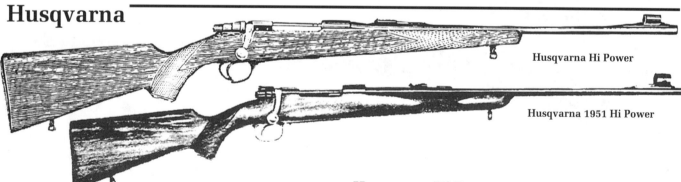

Husqvarna Hi Power

Husqvarna 1951 Hi Power

Husqvarna 1950 Hi Power
Similar to the Hi Power in 220, 270 & 30-06 calibers only. Made only in the early 1950's.
Estimated Value: Excellent: $365.00
Very good: $290.00

Husqvarna 1951 Hi Power
Similar to the Hi Power with a slightly higher comb stock. Made only in 1951.
Estimated Value: Excellent: $375.00
Very good: $300.00

Husqvarna Hi Power
Caliber: 220 Swift, 270, 30-06, 6.5x55, 8x57, 9.3x57
Action: Mauser-type bolt action; repeating
Magazine: 5-shot box
Barrel: Blued; 23¾"
Sights: Open rear, hooded ramp front
Stock & Forearm: Checkered beech one-piece pistol grip stock & tapered forearm; swivels
Approximate wt.: 7¾ lbs.
Comments: Made from World War II to early 1950's.
Estimated Value: Excellent: $360.00
Very good: $285.00

Husqvarna 1100 Hi Power Deluxe

Husqvarna 1000 Super Grade
Similar to the 1100 with a Monte Carlo stock.
Estimated Value: Excellent: **$450.00**
Very good: **$365.00**

Husqvarna 1100 Hi Power Deluxe
Similar to the 1951 Hi Power with walnut stock & forearm; made from the early to mid 1950's.
Estimated Value: Excellent: **$435.00**
Very good: **$345.00**

Husqvarna 3100 Crown Grade

Husqvarna 3000 Crown Grade

Husqvarna P-3000 Presentation

Husqvarna 6000 Imperial Custom

Husqvarna 3100 Crown Grade
Caliber: 243, 270, 7mm Rem., 30-06, 308 Win.
Action: Mauser-type bolt action; repeating
Magazine: 5-shot box
Barrel: Blued; 23¾"
Sights: Open rear, hooded ramp front
Stock & Forearm: Checkered walnut one-piece pistol grip stock & tapered forearm; swivels
Approximate wt.: 7 lbs.
Comments: Made from the mid 1950's to mid 1970's.
Estimated Value: Excellent: **$475.00**
Very good: **$380.00**

Husqvarna 3000 Crown Grade
Similar to 3100 with Monte Carlo stock.
Estimated Value: Excellent: **$500.00**
Very good: **$400.00**

Husqvarna P-3000 Presentation
A fancy version of the 3000 with engraving; select wood; adjustable trigger. Made in the late 1960's.
Estimated Value: Excellent: **$780.00**
Very good: **$625.00**

Husqvarna 6000 Imperial Custom
Similar to the 3100 Crown Grade with higher quality finish; folding sight; adjustable trigger. Made in the late 1960's.
Estimated Value: Excellent: **$565.00**
Very good: **$450.00**

Husqvarna 4100 Lightweight

Husqvarna 4000 Lightweight

Husqvarna 456 Lightweight

Husqvarna 7000 Imperial Monte Carlo

Husqvarna 4100 Lightweight
Caliber: 243, 270, 7mm, 306, 308 Win.
Action: Mauser-type bolt action; repeating
Magazine: 5-shot box
Barrel: Blued; 20½"
Sights: Open rear, hooded ramp front
Stock & Forearm: Checkered walnut one-piece pistol grip stock & tapered forearm
Approximate wt.: 6 lbs.
Comments: Made from the mid 1950's to mid 1970's.
Estimated Value: Excellent: $500.00
                        Very good: $400.00

Husqvarna 4000 Lightweight
Similar to 4100 with Monte Carlo stock & no rear sight.
Estimated Value: Excellent: $520.00
                        Very good: $415.00

Husqvarna 456 Lightweight
Similar to 4100 with full-length stock & forearm. Made from about 1960 to 1970.
Estimated Value: Excellent: $530.00
                        Very good: $425.00

Husqvarna 7000 Imperial Monte Carlo
Similar to 4000 with higher quality wood; lipped forearm; folding sight; adjustable trigger. Made in the late 1960's.
Estimated Value: Excellent: $595.00
                        Very good: $475.00

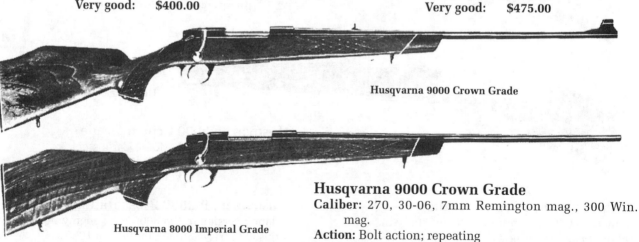

Husqvarna 9000 Crown Grade

Husqvarna 8000 Imperial Grade

Husqvarna 9000 Crown Grade
Caliber: 270, 30-06, 7mm Remington mag., 300 Win. mag.
Action: Bolt action; repeating
Magazine: 5-shot box
Barrel: Blued; 23¾"
Sights: Leaf rear, hooded ramp front
Stock & Forearm: Checkered walnut Monte Carlo one-piece pistol grip stock & forearm; swivels
Approximate wt.: 7¼ lbs.
Comments: Made in the early 1970's.
Estimated Value: Excellent: $525.00
                        Very good: $420.00

Husqvarna 8000 Imperial Grade
Similar to 9000 with select wood; engraving; no sights.
Estimated Value: Excellent: $650.00
                        Very good: $520.00

Husqvarna 610 Varmint

Husqvarna 610 Varmint
Caliber: 222
Action: Short stroke bolt action; repeating
Magazine: 4-shot detachable box
Barrel: Blued; 23¾"
Sights: None; tapped for scope
Stock & Forearm: Checkered walnut Monte Carlo one-piece pistol grip stock & forearm; cheekpiece
Approximate wt.: 6½ lbs.
Comments: Made in the late 1960's.
Estimated Value: Excellent: $460.00
 Very good: $365.00

Husqvarna 358 Magnum
Caliber: 358 Norma mag.
Action: Bolt action; repeating
Magazine: 3-shot box
Barrel: Blued; 25½"
Sights: Folding leaf rear, hooded ramp front
Stock & Forearm: Checkered walnut Monte Carlo one-piece pistol grip stock & forearm; cheekpiece
Approximate wt.: 7¾ lbs.
Comments: Made in the late 1960's.
Estimated Value: Excellent: $510.00
 Very good: $410.00

Ithaca

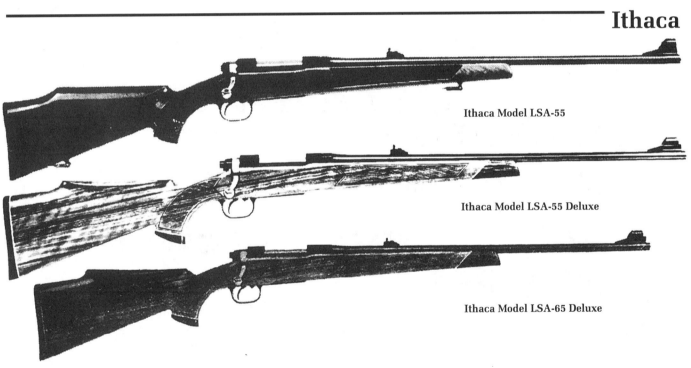

Ithaca Model LSA-55

Ithaca Model LSA-55 Deluxe

Ithaca Model LSA-65 Deluxe

Ithaca Model LSA-55
Caliber: 222, 22-250, 6mm, 243, 308
Action: Bolt action; repeating
Magazine: 3-shot detachable box
Barrel: Blued; 22"
Sights: Iron; adjustable rear, hooded ramp front
Stock & Forearm: Monte Carlo one-piece pistol grip stock & tapered forearm
Approximate wt.: 6½ lbs.
Comments: Made from the early 1970's to late 1970's.
Estimated Value: Excellent: $375.00
 Very good: $300.00

Ithaca Model LSA-55 Heavy Barrel
Similar to the LSA-55 except: cheekpiece; recoil pad; heavy barrel; weighs 8½ lbs.
Estimated Value: Excellent: $430.00
 Very good: $345.00

Ithaca Model LSA-55 Deluxe
Similar to the LSA-55 except: checkering; recoil pad.
Estimated Value: Excellent: $420.00
 Very good: $335.00

Ithaca Model LSA-65
Similar to Model LSA-55 in 25-06, 270, 30-06, with a 4-shot magazine; weighs 7 lbs.
Estimated Value: Excellent: $400.00
 Very good: $320.00

Ithaca Model LSA-65 Deluxe
Similar to Model LSA-55 Deluxe in same calibers & weight as LSA-65.
Estimated Value: Excellent: $435.00
 Very good: $345.00

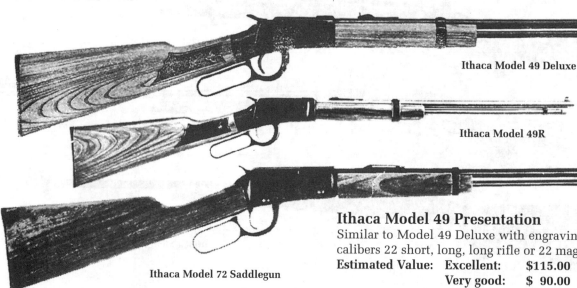

Ithaca Model LSA-55 Turkey Gun

Ithaca Model 49 Saddlegun

Ithaca Model 49 Deluxe

Ithaca Model 49R

Ithaca Model 72 Saddlegun

Ithaca Model 49 Saddlegun

Caliber: 22 short, long, long rifle
Action: Lever action; exposed hammer; single shot
Magazine: None
Barrel: Blued; 18"
Sights: Adjustable rear, bead front
Stock & Forearm: Plain wood straight grip stock & forearm; barrel band; recent model has checkering
Approximate wt.: 5½ lbs.
Comments: Made from about 1960 to late 1970's.
Estimated Value:　Excellent:　$90.00
　　　　　　　　　Very good:　$75.00

Ithaca Model LSA-55 Turkey Gun

Caliber: 222 under 12 gauge full choke
Action: Top lever, break open; exposed hammer
Magazine: None
Barrel: 24½" rifle under full choke shotgun with matted rib
Sights: Folding rear, dovetail front
Stock & Forearm: Checkered walnut Monte Carlo pistol grip stock & forearm; cheekpiece; recoil pad; swivels
Approximate wt.: 7 lbs.
Comments: An over & under combination manufactured to the late 1970's.
Estimated Value:　Excellent:　$475.00
　　　　　　　　　Very good:　$385.00

Ithaca Model 49 Youth

Similar to Model 49 with an abbreviated stock for young shooters.
Estimated Value:　Excellent:　$90.00
　　　　　　　　　Very good:　$75.00

Ithaca Model 49 Magnum

Similar to Model 49 in 22 magnum rim fire.
Estimated Value:　Excellent:　$95.00
　　　　　　　　　Very good:　$80.00

Ithaca Model 49 Deluxe

Similar to Model 49 with checkered stock, gold hammer & trigger & swivels. Discontinued in the mid 1970's.
Estimated Value:　Excellent:　$100.00
　　　　　　　　　Very good:　$ 80.00

Ithaca Model 49 Presentation

Similar to Model 49 Deluxe with engraving & nameplate; calibers 22 short, long, long rifle or 22 magnum.
Estimated Value:　Excellent:　$115.00
　　　　　　　　　Very good:　$ 90.00

Ithaca Model 49R (Repeater)

Similar to Model 49 with 20" barrel & 15-shot tubular magazine. Sold only in the late 1960's to early 1970's.
Estimated Value:　Excellent:　$135.00
　　　　　　　　　Very good:　$110.00

Ithaca Model 72 Saddlegun

Caliber: 22 long rifle
Action: Lever action; exposed hammer; repeating
Magazine: 15-shot tubular
Barrel: Blued; 18½"
Sights: Adjustable rear, hooded ramp front
Stock & Forearm: Plain walnut straight grip stock & forearm; barrel band
Approximate wt.: 5½ lbs.
Comments: Made from the early to late 1970's.
Estimated Value:　Excellent:　$160.00
　　　　　　　　　Very good:　$130.00

Ithaca Model 72 Deluxe

Ithaca Model 72 Magnum

Similar to Model 72 in 22 magnum. Magazine holds 11 shots.

Estimated Value: Excellent: $175.00
                       Very good: $140.00

Ithaca Model 72 Deluxe

Similar to Model 72 except: brushed silver receiver; engraving; octagon barrel; blade front sight.

Estimated Value: Excellent: $190.00
                       Very good: $150.00

Ithaca Model X5-T

Ithaca Model X5-C

Caliber: 22 long rifle
Action: Semi-automatic; hammerless
Magazine: 7-shot clip
Barrel: Blued; 22"
Sights: Open rear, Raybar front
Stock & Forearm: Wood one-piece semi-pistol grip stock & forearm
Approximate wt.: 6¼ lbs.
Comments: Made from the late 1950's to about 1965.

Estimated Value: Excellent: $140.00
                       Very good: $115.00

Ithaca Model X5-T

Similar to X5-C with a 16-shot tubular magazine.

Estimated Value: Excellent: $150.00
                       Very good: $120.00

Iver Johnson

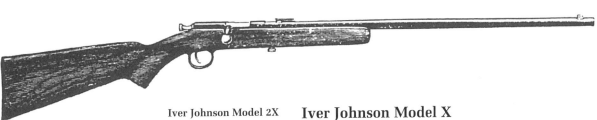

Iver Johnson Model 2X

Iver Johnson Model X

Caliber: 22 short, long, long rifle
Action: Bolt action; single shot
Magazine: None
Barrel: Blued; 22"
Sights: Open rear, blade front
Stock & Forearm: Wood one-piece pistol grip stock & forearm
Approximate wt.: 4 lbs.
Comments: Made from the late 1920's to the early 1930's.

Estimated Value: Excellent: $110.00
                       Very good: $ 85.00

Iver Johnson Lever Action

Caliber: 22 short, long, long rifle; 22 Win. magnum
Action: Lever action, side ejection; exposed hammer
Magazine: 21 shorts, 17 longs, 15 long rifles (mixed simultaneously); 12 magnum, tubular under barrel
Barrel: 18½"; round, blued
Sights: Hooded ramp front, adjustable rear
Stock & Forearm: Smooth hardwood stock & forearm, barrel band
Approximate wt.: 5¾ lbs.
Comments: Produced in the mid 1980's. Add 7% for magnum.

Estimated Value: Excellent: $175.00
                       Very good: $140.00

Iver Johnson Model 2X

Similar to the Model X with a 24" barrel & improved stock. Made from about 1932 to the mid 1950's.

Estimated Value: Excellent: $120.00
                       Very good: $ 90.00

Iver Johnson Li'l Champ

Caliber: 22 short, long or long rifle
Action: Bolt action; single shot
Magazine: None, single shot
Barrel: Blued; 16¼"
Sights: Blade front, adjustable rear
Stock & Forearm: Molded one-piece stock & forearm; nickel plated bolt
Approximate wt.: 2¾ lbs.
Comments: A lightweight gun designed for young beginners.
Estimated Value: Excellent: $70.00
                      Very good: $55.00

Iver Johnson Wagonmaster

Caliber: 22 short, long or long rifle; 22 magnum
Action: Lever action; repeating
Magazine: 15 long rifles, 17 longs, 21 shorts, can be mixed & loaded simultaneously; tubular
Barrel: Blued; 18¼"
Sights: Hooded ramp front, adjustable leaf rear
Stock & Forearm: Smooth wood straight grip stock & forearm; barrel band
Approximate wt.: 5¾ lbs.
Comments: Currently available. Add 12% for magnum.
Estimated Value: Excellent: $145.00
                      Very good: $115.00

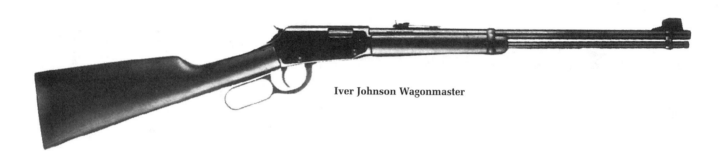

Iver Johnson Wagonmaster

Iver Johnson Li'l Champ

Iver Johnson Targetmaster

Caliber: 22 short, long or long rifle
Action: Slide action, repeating
Magazine: 12 long rifles, 15 longs, 19 shorts, can be mixed & loaded simultaneously; tubular
Barrel: Blued; 18½"
Sights: Hooded ramp front, adjustable rear
Stock & Forearm: Smooth hardwood straight grip stock & grooved slide handle
Approximate wt.: 5¾ lbs.
Comments: Produced in the 1980's.
Estimated Value: Excellent: $140.00
                      Very good: $115.00

Iver Johnson Survival Carbine

Caliber: 30 carbine, 223 (5.7mm)
Action: Gas operated semi-automatic
Magazine: 5-, 15- or 30-shot detachable clip
Barrel: 18"; blued or stainless steel
Sights: Aperture rear, blade front with protective ears
Stock & Forearm: Hard plastic, one-piece pistol grip stock & forearm; metal handguard; folding stock available
Approximate wt.: 5 lbs.
Comments: Produced from 1983 to 1986. Add 20% for folding stock; 25% for stainless steel finish.
Estimated Value: Excellent: $200.00
                      Very good: $160.00

Iver Johnson Trailblazer

Caliber: 22 long rifle
Action: Semi-automatic, hammerless
Magazine: Clip
Barrel: Blued; 18½"
Sights: Open rear, blade front
Stock & Forearm: Checkered walnut, one-piece Monte Carlo semi-pistol grip stock & forearm
Approximate wt.: 5 lbs.
Comments: Produced from 1984 to 1986.
Estimated Value: Excellent: $115.00
                      Very good: $ 95.00

Iver Johnson PM 30G

Iver Johnson PM 30G, Model M1, PM30

Caliber: 30 M1, 223 (discontinued 1985)
Action: Gas operated, semi-automatic
Magazine: 15-shot detachable clip; 5- or 30-shot available
Barrel: 18"; blued or stainless steel
Sights: Aperture rear, blade front with protective ears
Stock & Forearm: Wood, semi-pistol grip one-piece stock & forearm; slot in stock; metal ventilated or wood handguard
Approximate wt.: 6 lbs.
Comments: Made from about 1960 to late 1970's by Plainfield. Reintroduced in the late 1970's to early 1990's by Iver Johnson. Add 20% for stainless steel (discontinued 1985); add 7% for walnut stock.
Estimated Value: Excellent: $225.00
Very good: $180.00

Iver Johnson PM30S, Model M1 Sporter

Similar to the M1 Carbine with a wood hand guard & no slot in the stock. Discontinued in the early 1980's.
Estimated Value: Excellent: $200.00
Very good: $160.00

Iver Johnson PM30P, Commando or Paratrooper

Similar to the M1 Carbine with pistol grip at rear & at forearm; telescoping wire shoulder stock. Add 20% for stainless steel.
Estimated Value: Excellent: $235.00
Very good: $190.00

Iver Johnson Model EW22 HBA, MHBA

Similar to the Model PM30 except: 22 long rifle or 22WRM; Add 75% for magnum; made to early 1990's.
Estimated Value: Excellent: $135.00
Very good: $110.00

Iver Johnson Model 9MM

Similar to the Model PM30 in 9MM Parabellum with 16" barrel & 20-shot magazine; weighs 5½ lbs.
Estimated Value: Excellent: $210.00
Very good: $165.00

Johnson

Johnson MMJ Spitfire

Johnson Custom Deluxe Sporter

Similar to the MMJ with a Monte Carlo pistol grip stock & rear peep sight.
Estimated Value: Excellent: $275.00
Very good: $220.00

Johnson Folding Stock

Similar to the MMJ with a special metal folding shoulder stock.
Estimated Value: Excellent: $290.00
Very good: $225.00

Johnson MMJ Spitfire

Caliber: 223
Action: Semi-automatic
Magazine: 5-, 15-, 30-shot clip
Barrel: Blued; 18"
Sights: Adjustable rear, ramp front
Stock & Forearm: Wood one-piece semi-pistol grip stock & forearm; wood hand guard
Approximate wt.: 5 lbs.
Comments: A conversion of the M1 carbine. Made in the mid 1960's.
Estimated Value: Excellent: $260.00
Very good: $220.00

Kimber

Kimber Model 82, 82A
Caliber: 22 long rifle, 22 Win. mag., 22 Hornet (after 1982)
Action: Bolt action; repeating; rear locking bolt lugs
Magazine: 5-shot detachable box (10-shot available) in 22 long rifle; 3-shot in 22 Hornet; 4-shot in 22 Win. mag.
Barrel: 22½" blued; light sporter; sporter; target
Sights: None, drilled for scope; beaded ramp front & folding leaf rear available
Stock & Forearm: Checkered walnut, one-piece pistol grip stock & forearm (Classic); available with optional Monte Carlo stock & cheekpiece; swivels
Approximate wt.: 6½ lbs.
Comments: Produced as Model 82 from 1980 to 1986 & as Model 82A after 1986. Add 6% for .22 WMR or .22 Hornet; add 10% for Cascade stock (discontinued in 1987); add 33% for Custom Classic stock; add 52% for Super America stock (discontinued 1986). Discontinued 1992.

Estimated Value:	Excellent:	$895.00
	Very good:	$715.00

Kimber Model 82

Kimber 82A Government
A single shot 22 bolt action target rifle designed for the Army; heavy target barrel & stock; built on the Kimber 82A action.

Estimated Value:	Excellent:	$475.00
	Very good:	$380.00

Kimber Model 84C Single Shot

Kimber Model 82 M/S
Similar to the Model 82 except single shot; 20½" heavy barrel, adjustable target trigger; competition stock; 22 long rifle caliber only; this gun is designed for metallic silhouette shooting. Produced from 1982 to 1992.

Estimated Value:	Excellent:	$550.00
	Very good:	$445.00

Kimber Mini-Classic
An adult 22 bolt action with an 18" barrel, lipped forearm; built on the 82A action. Introduced in 1988.

Estimated Value:	Excellent:	$500.00
	Very good:	$400.00

Kimber Model 82B
Similar to the Model 82A with internal improvements. Introduced in 1986. Available with sporter or varmint barrel. Classic stock standard. Add 12% for Cascade stock (discontinued 1987); add 33% for Custom Classic stock; add 100% for Brownell stock (discontinued 1987); add 50% for Super America stock; 14% for Continental stock; add 95% for Super Continental stock. Discontinued 1992.

Estimated Value:	Excellent:	$625.00
	Very good:	$500.00

Kimber Model 84, 84A
Similar to the Model 82 except Mini-Mauser-type action. Introduced in 1984 in 223 Rem. caliber; 221 Fireball, 222 Rem. mag., 17 Rem. 17 Match IV, 6x47 & 6x45 calibers added in 1986. Known as Model 84A in 1987. Add 12% for Cascade stock (discontinued in 1987)); add 28% for Custom Classic stock.

Estimated Value:	Excellent:	$750.00
	Very good:	$600.00

Kimber Model 84B
Similar to the Model 84 with internal improvements. Produced from 1987 to 1992. Add 12% for Continental stock; 90% for Super Continental; 50% for Super America.

Estimated Value:	Excellent:	$800.00
	Very good:	$650.00

Kimber Model 84C Single Shot
Caliber: 17 Rem., 223 Rem.
Action: Mauser-type bolt action single shot; adjustable trigger
Magazine: None, single shot
Barrel: 25"; fluted stainless steel
Sights: None
Stock & Forearm: Checkered walnut, one-piece pistol grip stock & wide forearm; matte blue receiver
Approximate wt.: 7½ lbs.
Comments: Introduced in the mid 1990's.

Estimated Value:	New (retail):	$999.00
	Excellent:	$750.00
	Very good:	$600.00

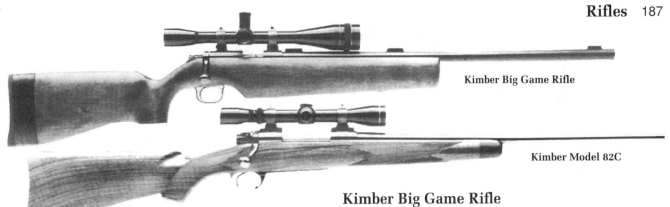

Kimber Big Game Rifle

Kimber Model 82C

Kimber Model 84C Centerfire

Caliber: 17 Rem., 222 Rem., 223 Rem.
Action: Mauser-type bolt action, repeating; adjustable trigger
Magazine: 4-shot; hinged floor plate
Barrel: 22"; blued or stainless steel
Sights: None
Stock & Forearm: Checkered walnut, one-piece pistol grip stock & wide forearm; polished blued action
Approximate wt.: 6¾ lbs.
Comments: Introduced in the mid 1990's. Add 39% for Super America Model.
Estimated Value: New (retail): $1,145.00
Excellent: $ 860.00
Very good: $ 690.00

Kimber Model 82C

Caliber: 22 long rifle
Action: Bolt action, repeating; rear bolt locking lugs, rocker style safety
Magazine: 4-shot detachable box; optional 10-shot magazine available
Barrel: Blued; 22½"; 20", 18"; also stainless steel
Sights: None; drilled for scope mount
Stock & Forearm: Walnut or synthetic one-piece pistol grip stock & forearm; Monte Carlo on Super America Model; swivel studs
Approximate wt.: 6½ lbs.
Comments: Introduced in 1993; add 69% for Super America Model. Add 15% for stainless steel barrel; add 14% for Varmint.
Estimated Value: New (Retail): $785.00
Excellent: $590.00
Very good: $470.00

Kimber Big Game Rifle

Caliber: 270 Win., 280 Rem., 7mm Rem. magnum, 30-06, 300 Win. magnum, 338 Win. magnum, 375 H&H, 416 Rigby (African model) introduced in 1989
Action: Bolt action, repeating, combining features of the pre-'64 Winchester Model 70 & the Mauser 98
Magazine: 5-shot in calibers .270, 280 & 30-06, 3-shot in calibers 7mm mag., 300 mag., 338 mag. 375 H&H, or 416 Rigby
Barrel: 22½" featherweight barrel in 270, 280, 30-06; 24" medium barrel in 7mm, 300, 338; 24" heavy barrel in 375 H&H or 416 Rigby
Sights: None
Stock & Forearm: Checkered walnut one-piece pistol grip stock & forearm; black forearm tip; swivels
Approximate wt.: 7¾ to 8½ lbs.
Comments: Produced from 1988 to 1992; add 11% for 375 H&H; add 30% for Custom Classic; add 11% for Super America; add 100% for African.
Estimated Value: Excellent: $1,350.00
Very good: $1,075.00

Kimber K770

Caliber: 270 Win., 30-06 Sprg.
Action: Bolt action, repeating
Magazine: 4-shot box with hinged floor plate
Barrel: Blued; 22½"
Sights: None
Stock & Forearm: Checkered hardwood pistol grip stock & forearm
Approximate wt.: 7 lbs.
Comments: Introduced in the mid 1990's; add 65% for Super America Model.
Estimated Value: New (Retail): $745.00
Excellent: $560.00
Very good: $450.00

Kleinguenther

Kleinguenther MV 2130

Caliber: 243, 270, 30-06, 300 mag., 308, 7mm Rem.
Action: Mauser-type bolt action, repeating
Magazine: 2-shot box
Barrel: Blued; 25"
Sights: None; drilled for scope
Stock & Forearm: Checkered walnut Monte Carlo one-piece pistol grip stock & tapered forearm; recoil pad
Approximate wt.: 7 lbs.
Comments: Made in the 1970's.
Estimated Value: Excellent: $590.00
Very good: $470.00

Kleinguenther K-14

Caliber: Same as MV 2130, also 25-06, 7x57, 375 H&H
Action: Bolt action
Magazine: Hidden clip, 3-shot
Barrel: Blued; 24", 26"
Sights: Open rear, ramp front
Stock & Forearm: Checkered walnut one-piece pistol grip stock & tapered forearm; recoil pad
Approximate wt.: 7¼ lbs.
Comments: Made in the 1970's.
Estimated Value: Excellent: $640.00
Very good: $515.00

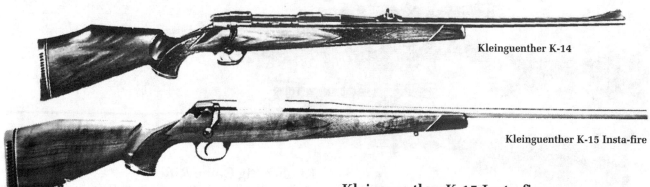

Kleinguenther K-14

Kleinguenther K-15 Insta-fire

Kleinguenther Model K-22

Caliber: 22 long rifle, 22 WMR
Action: Bolt action; repeating; adjustable trigger
Magazine: 5-shot hidden clip
Barrel: 21½" chrome-poly steel
Sights: None; tapped for scope
Stock & Forearm: Checkered beechwood, Monte Carlo pistol grip one-piece stock & forearm; swivels; cheekpiece
Approximate wt.: 6½ lbs.
Comments: A rimfire rifle designed to be as accurate as the K-15. Made from mid 1980's to early 1990's. Add 16% for magnum, 30% for deluxe, 110% for deluxe custom.
Estimated Value: Excellent: $300.00
  Very good: $240.00

Kleinguenther K-15 Insta-fire

Caliber: 243, 25-06, 270, 30-06, 308 Win., 308 Norma mag., 300 Win. mag., 7mm Rem. mag., 375 H&H, 7x57, 270 mag., 300 Weath. mag., 257 Weath. mag.
Action: Bolt action; repeating; adjustable trigger
Magazine: 5-shot hidden clip; 3-shot in magnum
Barrel: 24"; 26" in magnum
Sights: None; tapped for scope
Stock & Forearm: Checkered walnut Monte Carlo one-piece pistol grip stock & forearm; rosewood fore-end & cap; swivels; left or right hand model
Approximate wt.: 7½ lbs.
Comments: A high-powered rifle advertised as "the world's most accurate hunting rifle." Engraving & select wood at additional cost. Add 5% for magnum or left hand model. Made from late 1970's to early 1990's.
Estimated Value: Excellent: $1,000.00
  Very good: $ 800.00

Mannlicher

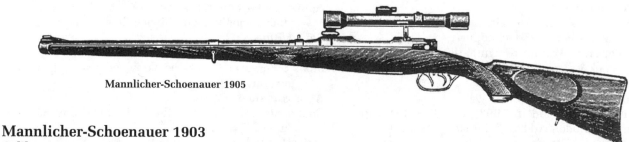

Mannlicher-Schoenauer 1905

Mannlicher-Schoenauer 1903

Caliber: 6.5 x 53mm
Action: Bolt action; repeating; double set trigger; "butter knife" style bolt handle
Magazine: 5-shot rotary
Barrel: Blued; 17¾"
Sights: Two leaf rear, ramp front
Stock & Forearm: Walnut semi-pistol grip stock & tapered, full-length forearm; swivels; cheekpiece
Approximate wt.: 6½ lbs.
Comments: Made from 1903 to World War II.
Estimated Value: Excellent: $1,025.00
  Very good: $ 820.00

Mannlicher-Schoenauer 1905

Similar to 1903 with a 19¾" barrel & in 9x56mm caliber.
Estimated Value: Excellent: $975.00
  Very good: $775.00

Mannlicher-Schoenauer 1908

Similar to the 1903 with a 19¾" barrel & in 7x57 & 8x56mm calibers.
Estimated Value: Excellent: $950.00
  Very good: $755.00

Mannlicher-Schoenauer 1910

Similar to 1903 with a 19¾" barrel & in 9.5x56mm caliber.
Estimated Value: Excellent: $960.00
  Very good: $765.00

Mannlicher-Schoenauer 1924

Similar to 1903 with a 19¾" barrel & in 30-06. Made from 1924 to World War II.
Estimated Value: Excellent: $1,100.00
  Very good: $ 875.00

Mannlicher-Schoenauer High Velocity

Mannlicher-Schoenauer 1950 Sporter

Mannlicher-Schoenauer 1950 Carbine

Mannlicher-Schoenauer 1952 Sporter

Mannlicher-Schoenauer 1952 Carbine

Mannlicher-Schoenauer High Velocity
Caliber: 7x64, 30-06, 8x60, 9.3x62, 10.75x68
Action: Bolt action; repeating; "butter knife" bolt handle
Magazine: 5-shot rotary
Barrel: Blued; 23¾"
Sights: Three leaf rear, ramp front
Stock & Forearm: Checkered walnut one-piece pistol grip stock & tapered forearm; cheekpiece; swivels
Approximate wt.: 7½ lbs.
Comments: Made from the early 1920's to World War II.
Estimated Value: Excellent: $1,050.00
                Very good: $ 845.00

Mannlicher-Schoenauer 1950 Sporter
Caliber: 257, 270 Win., 30-06
Action: Bolt action; repeating; "butter knife" bolt handle
Magazine: 5-shot rotary
Barrel: Blued; 24"
Sights: Folding leaf rear, hooded ramp front
Stock & Forearm: Checkered walnut one-piece pistol grip stock & tapered forearm; cheekpiece; swivels
Approximate wt.: 7¼ lbs.
Comments: Made in the early 1950's.
Estimated Value: Excellent: $1,025.00
                Very good: $ 820.00

Mannlicher-Schoenauer 1950 Carbine
Similar to the Sporter with a 20" barrel & full-length forearm.
Estimated Value: Excellent: $900.00
                Very good: $730.00

Mannlicher-Schoenauer 1950-6.5
Similar to the 1950 Carbine with 18" barrel & in 6.5x53mm caliber.
Estimated Value: Excellent: $920.00
                Very good: $740.00

Mannlicher-Schoenauer 1952 Sporter
Similar to the 1950 Sporter with slight changes in stock & with slanted bolt handle. Made from about 1952 to 1956.
Estimated Value: Excellent: $1,045.00
                Very good: $ 840.00

Mannlicher-Schoenauer 1952 Carbine
Similar to 1952 Sporter with a 20" barrel & full-length forearm.
Estimated Value: Excellent: $1,050.00
                Very good: $ 845.00

Mannlicher-Schoenauer 1952-6.5
Similar to 1952 Carbine with 18" barrel & in 6.5x53mm caliber.
Estimated Value: Excellent: $1,000.00
                Very good: $ 800.00

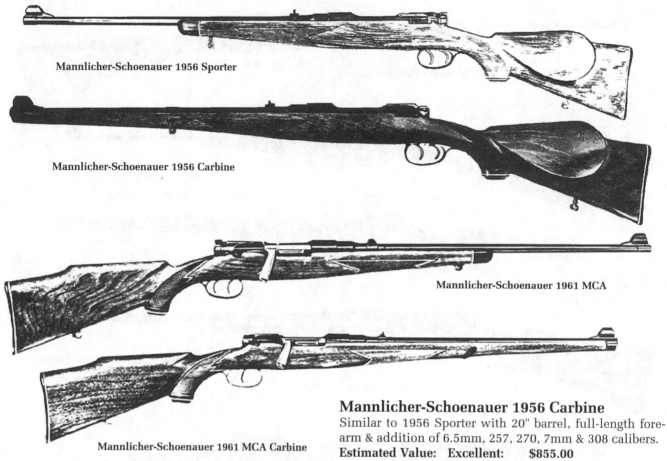

Mannlicher-Schoenauer 1956 Sporter

Mannlicher-Schoenauer 1956 Carbine

Mannlicher-Schoenauer 1961 MCA

Mannlicher-Schoenauer 1961 MCA Carbine

Mannlicher-Schoenauer 1956 Sporter

Caliber: 243, 30-06
Action: Bolt action; repeating; "butter knife" slanted bolt handle
Magazine: 5-shot rotary
Barrel: Blued; 22"
Sights: Folding leaf rear, hooded ramp front
Stock & Forearm: Checkered walnut pistol grip stock & forearm; high comb; cheekpiece; swivels
Approximate wt.: 7 lbs.
Comments: Made from the mid 1950's to about 1960.
Estimated Value: Excellent: $840.00
　　　　　　　　　　 Very good: $675.00

Mannlicher-Schoenauer 1956 Carbine

Similar to 1956 Sporter with 20" barrel, full-length fore-arm & addition of 6.5mm, 257, 270, 7mm & 308 calibers.
Estimated Value: Excellent: $855.00
　　　　　　　　　　 Very good: $685.00

Mannlicher-Schoenauer 1961 MCA

Similar to 1956 Sporter with Monte Carlo stock. Made from the early 1960's to early 1970's.
Estimated Value: Excellent: $865.00
　　　　　　　　　　 Very good: $695.00

Mannlicher-Schoenauer 1961 MCA Carbine

Similar to 1956 Carbine with Monte Carlo stock. Made from early 1960's to early 1970's.
Estimated Value: Excellent: $920.00
　　　　　　　　　　 Very good: $735.00

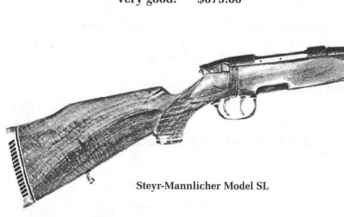

Steyr-Mannlicher Model SL

Steyr-Mannlicher Model SL

Caliber: 222 Rem., 222 Rem. magnum, 223 Rem., 5.6x50 magnum
Action: Bolt action; repeating
Magazine: 5-shot rotary
Barrel: Blued; 23½"
Sights: Open rear, ramp front
Stock & Forearm: Checkered walnut Monte Carlo pistol grip, one-piece stock & tapered forearm; recoil pad; cheekpiece; swivels
Approximate wt.: 5½ lbs.
Comments: Made from the mid 1960's to present.
Estimated Value: Excellent: $1,515.00
　　　　　　　　　　 Very good: $1,215.00

Steyr-Mannlicher SL Carbine

Similar to the SL with a 20" barrel & full-length forearm.
Estimated Value: Excellent: $1,450.00
　　　　　　　　　　 Very good: $1,160.00

Steyr-Mannlicher Model SL Varmint

Steyr-Mannlicher Model L

Steyr-Mannlicher Model L Carbine

Steyr-Mannlicher Model SL Varmint
Similar to the Model SL with a fiberglass or walnut half stock & 26" heavy barrel. 222 Rem. or 223 Rem. calibers.
Estimated Value: New (retail): $2,450.00
                 Excellent: $1,840.00
                 Very good: $1,470.00

Steyr-Mannlicher Model L Varmint
Similar to the Model L with a varmint stock & 26" heavy barrel. 22-250 Rem., 243 Win. or 308 Win.
Estimated Value: New (retail): $2,450.00
                 Excellent: $1,840.00
                 Very good: $1,470.00

Steyr-Mannlicher Model L
Similar to the SL in 22-250 Rem., 5.6x57, 6mm Rem., 7mm, 243 Win., 308 Win.
Estimated Value: New (retail): $2,250.00
                 Excellent: $1,690.00
                 Very good: $ 1,350.00

Steyr-Mannlicher Model L Carbine
Similar to the Model L with a 20" barrel & full-length forearms.
Estimated Value: New (retail): $2,450.00
                 Excellent: $1,840.00
                 Very good: $1,470.00

Steyr-Mannlicher Model M

Steyr-Mannlicher Model M Professional

Steyr-Mannlicher Model M Professional
Similar to the Model M with a parkerized metal finish & ABS Cycolac stock; 23½" barrel only.
Estimated Value: New (retail): $995.00
                 Excellent: $750.00
                 Very good: $600.00

Steyr-Mannlicher Model M
Caliber: 6.5x55, 7x64, 270 Win., 30-06, 25-06 Rem.; 7x57, 9.3x62
Action: Bolt action; repeating
Magazine: 5-shot rotary
Barrel: Blued; 20" on full stock; 23½" on half stock
Sights: Open rear, ramp front
Stock & Forearm: Checkered walnut Monte Carlo pistol grip stock; standard or full-length forearm; cheekpiece; swivels; left hand model available
Approximate wt.: 6½ lbs.
Comments: Made from the mid 1970's to present. Add 8% for left hand model; 8% for full stock.
Estimated Value: New (retail): $2,226.00
                 Excellent: $1,670.00
                 Very good: $1,340.00

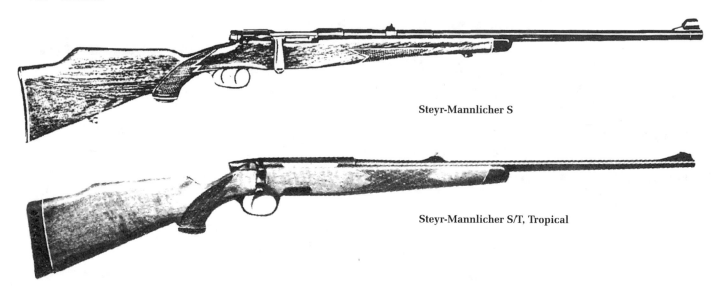

Steyr-Mannlicher S

Steyr-Mannlicher S/T, Tropical

Steyr-Mannlicher S

Similar to Model M with 26" barrel in magnum caliber, 7mm Rem., 257 Weath., 264 Win. 6.5x68, 300 H&H, 300 Win., 338 Win., 375 H&H & 458 Win. Half stock only; butt magazine optional. Add $50.00 for buttstock 4-shot magazine.

Estimated Value:	New (retail):	$3,150.00
	Excellent:	$2,360.00
	Very good:	$1,890.00

Steyr-Mannlicher S/T, Tropical

Similar to the Model S with a heavy barrel; 375 H&H mag. 9.3x64 & 458 Win. mag. calibers. Add $50.00 for buttstock magazine.

Estimated Value:	New (retail):	$2,850.00
	Excellent:	$2,140.00
	Very good:	$1,720.00

Mannlicher-Schoenauer M-72 LM Carbine

Steyr-Mannlicher ML 79, Luxus

Caliber: 7x57, 7x64, 270 Win., 30-06 Springfield; others available on request
Action: Bolt action; short stroke; repeating
Magazine: 3-shot detachable, 6-shot available
Barrel: 23½"; 20" on full stock model
Sights: Adjustable V-notch open rear, adjustable hooded ramp front
Stock & Forearm: Checkered European walnut Monte Carlo one-piece pistol grip stock & forearm; cheekpiece; swivels; full-length stock available
Approximate wt.: 7 lbs.
Comments: Currently produced. Add 7% for full-length stock or 6-shot magazine.

Estimated Value:	New (retail):	$2,478.00
	Excellent:	$1,860.00
	Very good:	$1,490.00

Mannlicher-Schoenauer M-72, M-72S

Caliber: 22-250, 5.6x57, 243, 6.5x57, 6mm, 7x57, 270
Action: Bolt action; repeating
Magazine: 5-shot rotary
Barrel: Blued; 23½"
Sights: Open rear, ramp front
Stock & Forearm: Checkered walnut one-piece pistol grip stock & tapered forearm; cheekpiece; recoil pad; swivels
Approximate wt.: 7½ lbs.
Comments: Made from mid to late 1970's.

| Estimated Value: | Excellent: | $900.00 |
| | Very good: | $720.00 |

Mannlicher-Schoenauer M-72 LM Carbine

Similar to M-72 with a 20" barrel & full-length forearm.

| Estimated Value: | Excellent: | $925.00 |
| | Very good: | $750.00 |

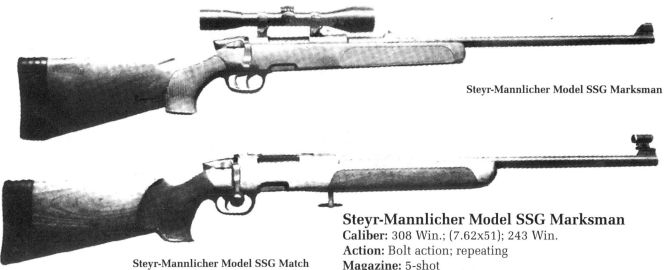

Steyr-Mannlicher Model SSG Marksman

Steyr-Mannlicher Model SSG Match

Steyr-Mannlicher Model SSG Marksman
Caliber: 308 Win.; (7.62x51); 243 Win.
Action: Bolt action; repeating
Magazine: 5-shot
Barrel: 26"; heavy barrel available
Sights: Folding leaf rear, hooded ramp front; match sights available
Stock & Forearm: Checkered European walnut or ABs cycolac synthetic one-piece stock & forearm
Approximate wt.: 8½ lbs.
Comments: Currently produced. Deduct 20% for ABS Cycolac stock.

Estimated Value:	New (retail):	$2,195.00
	Excellent:	$1,650.00
	Very good:	$1,315.00

Steyr-Mannlicher Model SSG Match
A match rifle similar to the SSG Marksman with a heavy barrel; peep sight; stippled checkering; hand stop; weight: 11 lbs.; deduct 12% for ABS Cycolac stock.

Estimated Value:	New (retail):	$2,660.00
	Excellent:	$1,995.00
	Very good:	$1,600.00

Mark X

Mark X Classic

Mark X Alaskan

Mark X Alaskan
Caliber: 375 H & H, 458 Win. magnum
Action: Mauser-type bolt action; repeating; adjustable trigger
Magazine: 3-shot box with hinged floor plate
Barrel: Blued; 24"
Sights: Adjustable rear, hooded ramp front
Stock & Forearm: Checkered, select walnut, Monte Carlo pistol grip, one-piece stock & forearm; recoil pad; swivels
Approximate wt.: 6 lbs.
Comments: Distributed by Interarms.

Estimated Value:	Excellent:	$450.00
	Very good:	$360.00

Mark X Classic
Caliber: 22-250, 25-06, 243, 270, 308, 30-06, 7mm mag., 7x57, 300 Win. mag.
Action: Bolt action; Mauser-type; repeating; adjustable trigger
Magazine: 3-shot box with hinged floor plate
Barrel: 24"
Sights: None on some models; others adjustable rear, hooded ramp front
Stock & Forearm: Checkered walnut Monte Carlo one-piece pistol grip stock & forearm; swivels
Approximate wt.: 7½ lbs.
Comments: Add $15.00 for sights.

Estimated Value:	Excellent:	$350.00
	Very good:	$280.00

Mark X Viscount

Mark X Mini Mark X

Mark X Cavalier

Mark X Cavalier

Similar to the Mark X Classic with fancier stock; cheek-piece; recoil pad. Add $15.00 for sights.

Estimated Value: **Excellent:** $400.00
                       Very good: $320.00

Mark X Viscount

Similar to the Mark X Classic except: special hammer-forged, chrome vanadium steel barrel; add 5% for mag.

Estimated Value: **Excellent:** $370.00
                       Very good: $295.00

Mark X LTW

Similar to the Viscount with lightweight Carbolite stock in 270, 30-06 or 7mm Rem. magnum. Introduced in 1988. Add 5% for mag. Discontinued early 1990's.

Estimated Value: **Excellent:** $390.00
                       Very good: $315.00

Mark X Mini Mark X

Caliber: 223, 7.62x39
Action: Bolt action; repeating; Mauser action scaled down for 223 caliber
Magazine: 5-shot
Barrel: Blued; 20"
Sights: Adjustable rear, hooded ramp front
Stock & Forearm: Checkered walnut, Monte Carlo one-piece pistol grip stock & forearm
Approximate wt.: 6¼ lbs.
Comments: Produced in the late 1980's to mid 1990's.

Estimated Value: **Excellent:** $365.00
                       Very good: $290.00

Mark X Whitworth Express

Mark X Marquis

Caliber: 243, 270, 7x57mm, 308, 30-06
Action: Bolt action; Mauser-type; repeating
Magazine: 5-shot box with hinged floor plate
Barrel: 20"
Sights: Adjustable rear, hooded ramp front
Stock & Forearm: Checkered walnut Monte Carlo one-piece full-length pistol grip stock & forearm; swivels; cheekpiece
Approximate wt.: 7½ lbs.
Comments: Distributed by Interarms.

Estimated Value: **Excellent:** $375.00
                       Very good: $300.00

Mark X Continental

Similar to the Marquis with a "butter knife" bolt handle & double set triggers.

Estimated Value: **Excellent:** $400.00
                       Very good: $320.00

Mark X Whitworth Express, Safari

Caliber: 375 H&H mag., 458 Win. mag.
Action: Bolt action; Mauser style; repeating; adjustable trigger
Magazine: 3-shot box with hinged floor plate
Barrel: 24"
Sights: 3 leaf express rear sight; hooded ramp front
Stock & Forearm: Checkered European walnut, Monte Carlo one-piece stock & forearm; cheekpiece; swivels; recoil pad
Approximate wt.: 7½ lbs.
Comments: Produced in the late 1980's to mid 1990's.

Estimated Value: **Excellent:** $580.00
                       Very good: $465.00

Marlin

Marlin Model 65

Marlin Model 100

Marlin Model 65 & 65E
Caliber: 22 short, long, long rifle
Action: Bolt action; single shot
Magazine: None
Barrel: 24" round
Sights: Open rear, bead front; peep rear, hooded front on 65E
Stock & Forearm: Pistol grip stock & grooved forearm
Approximate wt.: 5 lbs.
Comments: This was a takedown rifle that was made between 1932 & 1935.
Estimated Value: Excellent: $85.00
Very good: $70.00

Marlin Model 100
Caliber: 22 short, long, long rifle
Action: Bolt action; single shot
Magazine: None
Barrel: 24" round
Sights: Open rear, bead front
Stock & Forearm: Plain pistol grip stock & forearm
Approximate wt.: 4¾ lbs.
Comments: Takedown model was manufactured from 1936 to 1960. In 1960 it became the Model 100G or Glenfield & was replaced in the mid 1960's by the Glenfield 10.
Estimated Value: Excellent: $90.00
Very good: $75.00

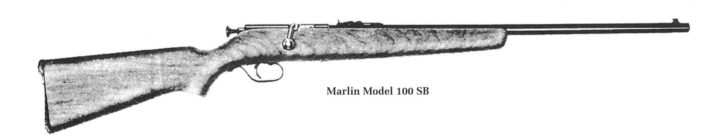

Marlin Model 100 SB

Marlin Model 100S Tom Mix Special
Same as Model 100 except hooded front sight, peep rear sight. Made from 1937 to 1942.
Estimated Value: Excellent: $200.00
Very good: $165.00

Marlin Model 100 SB
Same as Model 100 except it is smooth bore to use with shot cartridges. Discontinued in 1941.
Estimated Value: Excellent: $110.00
Very good: $ 90.00

Marlin Model 100G; Glenfield 10
Basically same as Marlin Model 100.
Estimated Value: Excellent: $90.00
Very good: $75.00

Marlin Model 101 & 101-DL
Basically same as Model 100 except beavertail forearm. Peep rear, hooded front sights on 101-DL. Made from 1951 to late 1970's.
Estimated Value: Excellent: $95.00
Very good: $80.00

Marlin Model 122 Target Rifle
Caliber: 22 short, long, long rifle
Action: Bolt action; single shot
Magazine: None
Barrel: 22" round
Sights: Open rear, hooded ramp front
Stock & Forearm: Wood Monte Carlo pistol grip stock & forearm; swivels
Approximate wt.: 5 lbs.
Comments: Made from about 1961 to 1965.
Estimated Value: Excellent: $100.00
Very good: $ 80.00

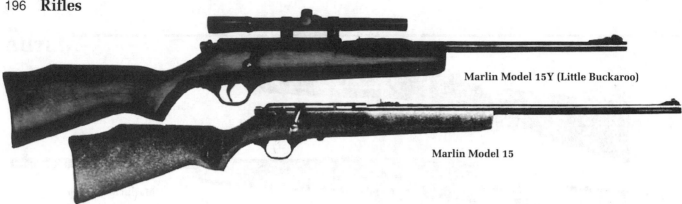

Marlin Model 15Y (Little Buckaroo)

Marlin Model 15

Marlin Model 15, 15Y (Little Buckaroo), 15YN

Caliber: 22 short, long or long rifle
Action: Bolt action; single shot
Magazine: None
Barrel: 22" round, 16¼" on 15Y & 15YN
Sights: Adjustable open rear, ramp front
Stock & Forearm: Checkered hardwood, Monte Carlo pistol grip one-piece stock & forearm
Approximate wt.: 5½ lbs., 4½ lbs. (15Y)
Comments: Model 15 made from late 1970's to the mid 1980's. 15Y & 15YN are for young shooters; produced from the late 1980's to date.
Estimated Value: New (retail): $172.00
                              Excellent: $130.00
                              Very good: $100.00

Marlin Model 2000 & 2000 A Target

Caliber: 22 long rifle
Action: Bolt action; thumb safety; red cocking indicator
Magazine: None; single shot
Barrel: Heavy, 22" selected Micro-groove with match chamber and recessed muzzle
Sights: Adjustable target peep rear, hooded front with seven aperture inserts
Stock & Forearm: High-comb fiberglass/Kevlar stock with stipple-finish forearm; stock butt plate adj. for length of pull, height, & angle on 2000 A
Approximate wt.: 8 lbs.
Comments: A target rifle produced from 1992 to date.
Estimated Value: New (retail): $603.00
                              Excellent: $450.00
                              Very good: $360.00

Marlin Model 80

Marlin Model 80DL

Marlin Model 80G

Marlin Model 80 & 80E

Caliber: 22 short, long, long rifle
Action: Bolt action; takedown type; repeating
Magazine: 8-shot detachable box
Barrel: 24"
Sights: Open rear, bead front; peep rear, hooded front on 80E
Stock & Forearm: Plain pistol grip stock & forearm
Approximate wt.: 6¼ lbs.
Comments: Production began about 1934, continued until the mid 1940's.
Estimated Value: Excellent: $110.00
                              Very good: $ 90.00

Marlin Model 80C

Basically the same gun as the Model 80 with slight improvements. Forearm is semi-beavertail. Production began in 1946, it was replaced by the 80G in 1960.
Estimated Value: Excellent: $115.00
                              Very good: $ 95.00

Marlin Model 80DL

Same rifle as Model 80C except; swivels; hooded front sight; peep rear sight. Discontinued in 1965.
Estimated Value: Excellent: $115.00
                              Very good: $ 95.00

Marlin Model 80G

The same rifle as Marlin Model 80C. Made from about 1960 to 1966.
Estimated Value: Excellent: $110.00
                              Very good: $ 85.00

Marlin Model 81

Marlin Model 81E

Marlin Model 81-DL

Marlin Glenfield Model 81G

Marlin Model 81 & 81E

Caliber: 22 short, long, long rifle
Action: Bolt action; repeating
Magazine: Tubular under barrel: 24 shorts, 20 longs, 18 long rifles
Barrel: 24"
Sights: Open rear, bead front; peep rear, hooded front on 81E
Stock & Forearm: Plain pistol grip stock & forearm
Approximate wt.: 6¼ lbs.
Comments: This takedown model was produced from about 1937 to mid 1940's.
Estimated Value: Excellent: $105.00
                      Very good: $ 85.00

Marlin Model 81C

An improved Model 81; semi-beavertail forearm. It was produced from 1946 to 1970.
Estimated Value: Excellent: $115.00
                      Very good: $ 90.00

Marlin Model 81-DL

Same as Model 81C exept it has swivels; hooded front sight, peep rear sight. Made from about 1946 to 1965.
Estimated Value: Excellent: $110.00
                      Very good: $ 90.00

Marlin Glenfield Model 81G

Basically the same as the Marlin Model 81C. It was produced as the 81G from about 1960 to 1965.
Estimated Value: Excellent: $100.00
                      Very good: $ 80.00

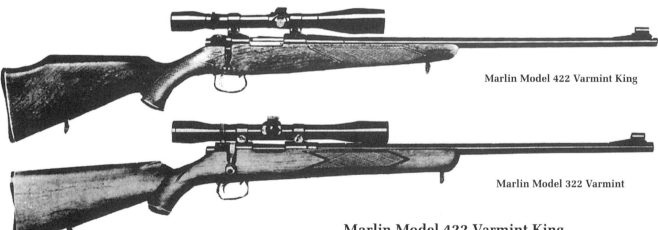

Marlin Model 422 Varmint King

Marlin Model 322 Varmint

Marlin Model 322 Varmint

Caliber: 222 Rem.
Action: Bolt action (Sako Short, Mauser); repeating
Magazine: 3-shot clip
Barrel: 24"
Sights: Peep sight rear, hooded ramp front
Stock & Forearm: Checkered hardwood stock & forearm
Approximate wt.: 7½ lbs.
Comments: Made for only 3 years beginning about 1954.
Estimated Value: Excellent: $400.00
                      Very good: $320.00

Marlin Model 422 Varmint King

Caliber: 222 Rem.
Action: Bolt action; repeating
Magazine: 3-shot detachable clip
Barrel: 24" round
Sights: Peep sight rear, hooded ramp front
Stock & Forearm: Checkered Monte Carlo pistol grip stock & forearm
Approximate wt.: 7 lbs.
Comments: Replaced Model 322 about 1958 but was discontinued after one year.
Estimated Value: Excellent: $410.00
                      Very good: $325.00

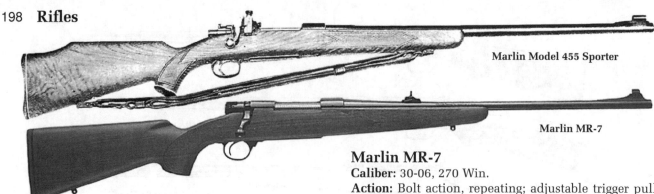

Marlin Model 455 Sporter

Marlin MR-7

Marlin Model 455 Sporter

Caliber: 270, 30-06, 308
Action: Bolt action; FN Mauser action with Sako trigger
Magazine: 5-shot box
Barrel: 24" round, stainless steel
Sights: Receiver sight - Lyman 48, hooded ramp front
Stock & Forearm: Checkered wood Monte Carlo stock & forearm; cheekpiece
Approximate wt.: 8½ lbs.
Comments: Made from about 1957 to 1959.
**Estimated Value: Excellent: $400.00
                     Very good: $320.00**

Marlin MR-7

Caliber: 30-06, 270 Win.
Action: Bolt action, repeating; adjustable trigger pull; 3-position safety
Magazine: 4-shot detachable box with hinged floor plate
Barrel: 22" round, blued; 6-groove rifling and recessed muzzle
Sights: Brass bead ramp front, adjustable rear
Stock & Forearm: Cut checkered black walnut one-piece, pistol grip stock and forearm; swivel studs and rubber rifle butt pad
Approximate wt.: 7½ lbs.
Comments: Introduced in 1996. Add 8% for sights.
**Estimated Value: New (retail): $572.00
                     Excellent: $430.00
                     Very good: $345.00**

Marlin Model 980

Marlin Model 781

Marlin Glenfield 20

Marlin Model 980

Caliber: 22 Win. mag.
Action: Bolt action; repeating
Magazine: 8-shot clip
Barrel: Blued; 24" round
Sights: Open rear, hooded ramp front
Stock & Forearm: Monte Carlo one-piece stock & forearm; swivels
Approximate wt.: 6 lbs.
Comments: Made from about 1962 until 1970.
**Estimated Value: Excellent: $105.00
                     Very good: $ 85.00**

Marlin Model 780

Caliber: 22 short, long, long rifle
Action: Bolt action; repeating
Magazine: 7-shot clip
Barrel: Blued; 22"
Sights: Adjustable rear, ramp front
Stock & Forearm: Checkered walnut Monte Carlo one-piece semi-pistol grip stock & forearm
Approximate wt.: 6 lbs.
Comments: Produced from about 1971 to the late 1980's.
**Estimated Value: Excellent: $120.00
                     Very good: $ 95.00**

Marlin Model 781

Same as Model 780 except tubular magazine; 25 shorts, 19 longs, 17 long rifles. Weighs 5½ lbs.
**Estimated Value: Excellent: $125.00
                     Very good: $100.00**

Marlin Glenfield 20, 25, 25N, 25M, 25MN

Caliber: 22 long rifle; 22 mag. (25M) (25MN)
Action: Bolt action; thumb safety
Magazine: 7-shot clip
Barrel: 22" round, blued; micro-groove barrel
Sights: Open rear, ramp front;
Stock & Forearm: Checkered walnut finish, semi-pistol grip stock & plain forearm; Model 25N has no checkering
Approximate wt.: 5½ lbs.
Comments: Produced from about 1966 to the early 1980's as Model 20; currently sold as Model 25N. Add 15% for magnum (25M, 25MN).
**Estimated Value: New (retail): $174.00
                     Excellent: $130.00
                     Very good: $105.00**

Marlin Model 782

Marlin Model 783

Marlin Model 880

Marlin Model 881

Marlin Model 880 SQ Squirrel

Marlin Model 782

Caliber: 22 Win. magnum
Action: Bolt action; repeating
Magazine: 7-shot clip
Barrel: 22"
Sights: Adjustable rear, ramp front
Stock & Forearm: Monte Carlo one-piece semi-pistol grip stock & forearm
Approximate wt.: 6 lbs.
Comments: Produced from 1971 to the late 1980's.
Estimated Value: Excellent: $175.00
  Very good: $140.00

Marlin Model 783

Same as Model 782 except 12-shot tubular magazine.
Estimated Value: Excellent: $180.00
  Very good: $145.00

Marlin Model 880 SQ Squirrel Rifle

Caliber: 22 long rifle
Action: Bolt action; repeating
Magazine: 7-shot clip
Barrel: 22" heavy micro-groove with double bedding screws; drilled and tapped for sights
Sights: None; receiver is grooved for scope mount
Stock & Forearm: Black fiberglass-filled synthetic one-piece pistol grip stock and forearm
Approximate wt.: 6½ lbs.
Comments: Introduced in 1996.
Estimated Value: New (retail): $264.00
  Excellent: $200.00
  Very good: $160.00

Marlin Model 880 & 880 SS

Caliber: 22 long rifle
Action: Bolt action; thumb safety, red cocking indicator
Magazine: 7-shot clip
Barrel: 22"; blued or stainless steel (880 SS)
Sights: Ramp front, brass bead with wide scan hood; adjustable folding semi-buckhorn rear
Stock & Forearm: Monte Carlo pistol grip checkered walnut one-piece stock & forearm; swivel studs & rubber rifle butt pad
Approximate wt.: 5½ lbs.
Comments: Made from 1989 to date; add 7% for 880 SS.
Estimated Value: New (retail): $241.00
  Excellent: $180.00
  Very good: $145.00

Marlin Model 881

Same as the Model 880 except: tubular magazine; which holds 17 long rifles; Produced from 1989 to date.
Estimated Value: New (retail): $251.00
  Excellent: $185.00
  Very good: $150.00

Marlin Model 882, 882L & 882SS

Same as the Model 880 except: 22 Win. mag. rim fire only. Produced from 1989 to date; walnut or laminated (882 L) stock; add 6% for laminated stock. Add 7% for stainless steel (882SS).
Estimated Value: New (retail): $265.00
  Excellent: $200.00
  Very good: $160.00

Marlin Model 883, 883N, & 883 SS

Same as the Model 882 except: 12-shot tubular magazine. Produced from 1989 to date. Add 10% for nickel plate (883N); add 6% for stainless steel (883 SS).
Estimated Value: New (retail): $275.00
  Excellent: $205.00
  Very good: $165.00

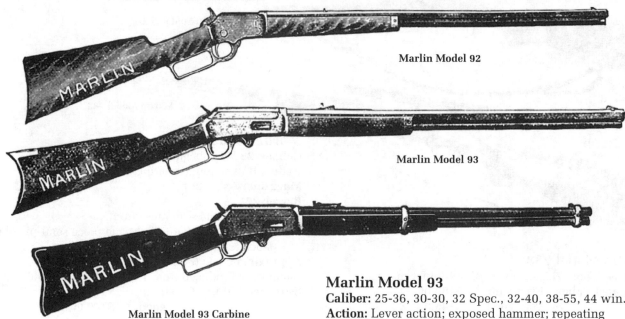

Marlin Model 92

Marlin Model 93

Marlin Model 93 Carbine

Marlin Model 92

Caliber: 22 short, long, long rifle; 32 short or long, rim fire or center fire

Action: Lever action; exposed hammer

Magazine: 22 caliber: 25 shorts, 20 longs, 28 long rifles; 32 caliber: 17 shorts, 14 longs; tubular under barrel; 16" barrel: 15 shorts, 12 longs, 10 long rifles

Barrel: 16", 24", 26", 28" round or octagon, blued

Sights: Open rear, blade front

Stock & Forearm: Plain walnut straight grip stock & forearm

Approximate wt.: 5 to 6 lbs.

Comments: Made from about 1892 to 1916. Also known as Model 1892.

Estimated Value: Excellent: $600.00
                       Very good: $480.00

Marlin Model 93

Caliber: 25-36, 30-30, 32 Spec., 32-40, 38-55, 44 win.

Action: Lever action; exposed hammer; repeating

Magazine: 10-shot tubular; under barrel

Barrel: 26"-32" round or octagon

Sights: Open rear, bead front

Stock & Forearm: Plain walnut straight grip stock & forearm

Approximate wt.: 7 to 8 lbs.

Comments: Manufactured from about 1893 to 1915 & 1920 to 1933. Produced in both takedown & solid frame models. Also known as Model 1893.

Estimated Value: Excellent: $750.00
                       Very good: $600.00

Marlin Model 93 Carbine

Basically same as the Model 93 except: produced in 30-30 & 32 special caliber only; standard carbine sights; 20" round barrel; 7-shot magazine. Weighs between 6 & 7 lbs.

Estimated Value: Excellent: $725.00
                       Very good: $580.00

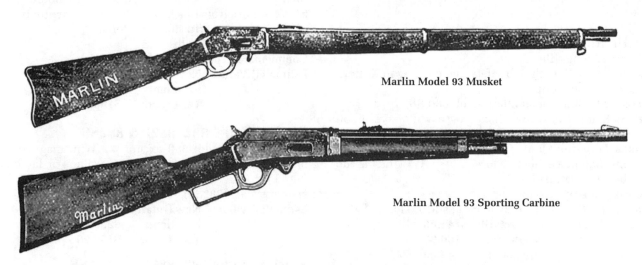

Marlin Model 93 Musket

Marlin Model 93 Sporting Carbine

Marlin Model 93 Sporting Carbine

Basically the same as Model 93 Carbine except the smaller magazine carries 5 shots.

Estimated Value: Excellent: $720.00
                       Very good: $575.00

Marlin Model 93 Musket

Same as the Model 93 except: 30" standard barrel; equipped with a musket stock; military forearm; ramrod; angular bayonet. Production stopped about 1915.

Estimated Value: Excellent: $975.00
                       Very good: $775.00

Marlin Model 1894 (Current)

Marlin Model 1894C

Marlin Model 1895

Marlin Model 1895S

Marlin Model 1897

Marlin Model 1894, 1894S

Caliber: 25-20, 32-30, 38-40; (early models made from 1894 to 1935); Current model is 44 mag. (1970's to present); 41 mag. added 1984; 45 long Colt added 1988: 41 mag. & 45 long Colt dropped in 1990

Action: Lever action; exposed hammer; repeating

Magazine: 10-shot tubular

Barrel: Round or octagon, 20", 24"-32"; 20" currently

Sights: Open rear, bead front

Stock & Forearm: Plain or checkered walnut straight or pistol grip stock & forearm

Approximate wt.: 7 lbs.

Comments: Made from about 1894 to 1935 in both take-down & solid frame models. Reintroduced in the late 1970's in 44 magnum with 20" barrel. Hammer block safety added 1986 (1894 S).

		Current	Early
Estimated Value:	New (retail):	$460.00	
	Excellent:	$345.00	$800.00
	Very good:	$275.00	$675.00

Marlin Model 1894CL

Similar to the late model 1894S except: 25-20 or 32-30 caliber; 218 Bee added in 1990. 6-shot magazine; 22" barrel; weighs 6¼ lbs. Produced from 1988 to mid 1990's.

Estimated Value:	Excellent:	$375.00
	Very good:	$300.00

Marlin Model 1894C, 1894CS, 1894M

Similar to the current model 1894 except: 357 Mag. caliber; 18½" barrel; 9-shot magazine. Produced from 1979 to date. Hammer block safety added in 1986.

Estimated Value:	New (retail):	$460.00
	Excellent:	$345.00
	Very good:	$275.00

Marlin Model 1895

Caliber: 33 WCF, 38-56, 40-65, 40-70, 40-82, 45-70

Action: Lever action; exposed hammer; repeating

Magazine: 9-shot tubular, under barrel

Barrel: 24" octagon or round, blued

Sights: Open rear, bead front

Stock & Forearm: Walnut straight or pistol grip stock & forearm

Approximate wt.: 8 lbs.

Comments: Made in solid frame & takedown models from about 1895 to 1920.

Estimated Value:	Excellent:	$825.00
	Very good:	$665.00

Marlin Model 1895S, 1895SS

Similar to the Model 1895; introduced in the late 1970's; 45-70 gov't caliber; 22" barrel; 4-shot magazine; swivels.

Estimated Value:	New (retail):	$523.00
	Excellent:	$390.00
	Very good:	$315.00

Marlin Model 1897

Caliber: 22 short, long, long rifle

Action: Lever action; exposed hammer; repeating

Magazine: 25 shorts, 20 longs, 18 long rifles in full-length; 16 shorts, 12 longs, 10 long rifles in half length; tubular under barrel

Barrel: Blued; 16", 24", 26", 28"

Sights: Open rear, bead front

Stock & Forearm: Plain walnut straight or pistol grip stock & forearm

Approximate wt.: 6 lbs.

Comments: Made from abt. 1897 to 1914 & 1919 to 1921.

Estimated Value:	Excellent:	$500.00
	Very good:	$400.00

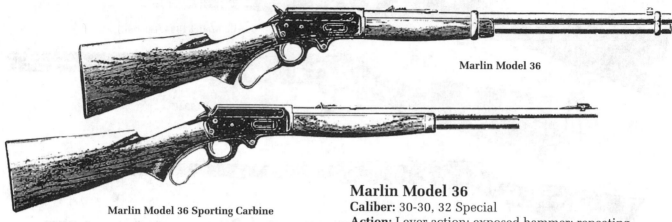

Marlin Model 36

Marlin Model 36 Sporting Carbine

Marlin Model 36 Sporting Carbine

Same as Model 36A except: lighter; 20" barrel

Estimated Value: Excellent: $325.00
Very good: $260.00

Marlin Model 36

Caliber: 30-30, 32 Special
Action: Lever action; exposed hammer; repeating
Magazine: 6-shot tubular
Barrel: 20" round, blued
Sights: Open rear, bead front
Stock & Forearm: Pistol grip stock & semi-beavertail forearm; carbine barrel band
Approximate wt.: 6½ lbs.
Comments: Made from about 1936 to 1942 & 1946 to 1948.

Estimated Value: Excellent: $320.00
Very good: $260.00

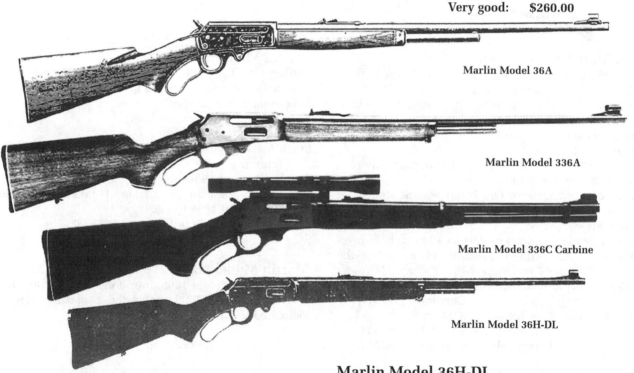

Marlin Model 36A

Marlin Model 336A

Marlin Model 336C Carbine

Marlin Model 36H-DL

Marlin Model 36A

Same as Model 36 except: barrel is 24", ⅔ magazine; weighs slightly more; hooded front sight.

Estimated Value: Excellent: $300.00
Very good: $240.00

Marlin Model 336A & 336A-DL

Basically the same as Model 36A with a rounded breech bolt & improved action. Produced from about 1950 to 1963. Reintroduced in the 1970's; discontinued in early 1980's. Checkered stock & forearm & swivels on 336A-DL.

Estimated Value: Excellent: $250.00
Very good: $200.00

Marlin Model 36H-DL

Same as Model 36A except stock & forearm are checkered & have swivels.

Estimated Value: Excellent: $325.00
Very good: $260.00

Marlin Model 336C Carbine, 336CS

Basically the same as the Model 36 except: checkered walnut stock; round breech bolt & improved action. 35 Rem. caliber was introduced & the 32 Special dropped in 1963; 375 Win. added in 1984. Produced from abt. 1948 to date. Hammer block safety added in 1986.

Estimated Value: New (retail): $444.00
Excellent: $330.00
Very good: $270.00

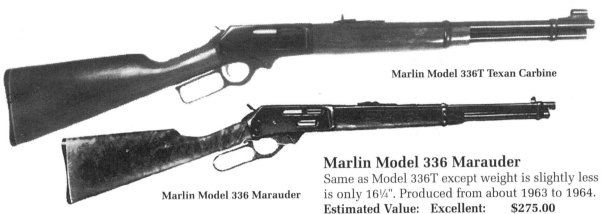

Marlin Model 336T Texan Carbine

Marlin Model 336 Marauder

Marlin Model 336 Marauder

Same as Model 336T except weight is slightly less & barrel is only 16¼". Produced from about 1963 to 1964.
Estimated Value: Excellent: $275.00
                  Very good: $220.00

Marlin Model 336T Texan Carbine, 336TS

Same as Model 336C except stock is straight, 18½" barrel. It was never produced in 32 caliber, but was available from 1963 to 1967 in 44 magnum. Produced from 1953 to 1987 in 30-30 caliber.
Estimated Value: Excellent: $275.00
                  Very good: $220.00

Marlin Model 336 ER

Similar to the Model 336 C in 356 Winchester or 308 Winchester calibers; recoil pad, swivels & strap. Produced 1983 to 1988.
Estimated Value: Excellent: $300.00
                  Very good: $240.00

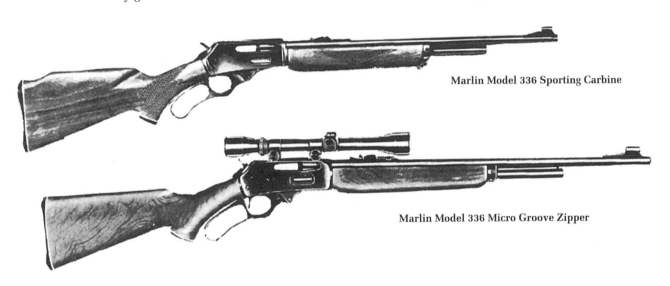

Marlin Model 336 Sporting Carbine

Marlin Model 336 Micro Groove Zipper

Marlin Model 336 LTS

Similar to the Model 336TS except: 30-30 Win. caliber, 16¼" barrel, rubber butt pad; weighs 6½ lbs. Produced from 1988 to early 1990's.
Estimated Value: Excellent: $280.00
                  Very good: $225.00

Marlin Model 336 Micro Groove Zipper

Caliber 219 Zipper; otherwise same rifle as Model 336A.
Estimated Value: Excellent: $350.00
                  Very good: $280.00

Marlin Model 336 Zane Grey Century

Same basic rifle as Model 336A except: 22" octagon barrel; brass fore-end cap; brass butt plate & medallion on receiver. Only 10,000 were produced in 1972.
Estimated Value: Excellent: $350.00
                  Very good: $280.00

Marlin Model 336 Sporting Carbine

Same as Model 336A except weight is slightly less & barrel is 20".
Estimated Value: Excellent: $230.00
                  Very good: $185.00

Marlin Model 336 Zane Grey Century

Marlin Model 39

Marlin Model 39A

Marlin Model 39A Mountie

Marlin Model 39M

Marlin Model 39M Golden Mountie

Marlin Model 39

Caliber: 22 short, long, long rifle
Action: Lever action; exposed hammer; repeating; take-down-type
Magazine: 25 shorts, 20 longs, 18 long rifles; tubular under barrel
Barrel: 24" octagon
Sights: Bead font, open adjustable rear
Stock & Forearm: Plain pistol grip stock & forearm
Approximate wt.: 6½ lbs.
Comments: Made from about 1921 to 1937.
Estimated Value: **Excellent:**   **$350.00**
                       Very good: **$280.00**

Marlin Model 39A

Same as Model 39 except: round barrel; heavier stock; semi-beavertail forearm; weighs 6½ lbs. Began production about 1938 & was discontinued in 1957. Replaced by Golden 39A.
Estimated Value: **Excellent:**   **$260.00**
                       Very good: **$200.00**

Marlin Model 39M

Similar to 39A except: 20" barrel; less capacity magazine; straight grip stock.
Estimated Value: **Excellent:**   **$220.00**
                       Very good: **$175.00**

Marlin Model 39A Mountie

Same as Model 39 except: straight grip, lighter stock with trim forearm; weight is 6 to 6½ lbs.; 20" barrel; produced from 1950's to 1960.
Estimated Value: **Excellent:**   **$210.00**
                       Very good: **$170.00**

Marlin Model 39M Golden Mountie

Same as Model 39A except: gold plated trigger; 20" barrel; weighs 6 lbs.; magazine capacity 21 shorts, 16 longs, or 15 long rifles. Produced from 1950's to 1988.
Estimated Value: **Excellent:**   **$260.00**
                       Very good: **$210.00**

Marlin Model Golden 39A

Marlin Model Golden 39A, 39AS

Caliber: 22 short, long, long rifle
Action: Lever-action; exposed hammer; takedown-type; gold plated trigger; 39AS has hammer block safety & rebounding hammer
Magazine: 26 shorts, 21 longs, 19 long rifle; tubular
Barrel: 24"; micro-groove round barrel
Sights: Bead front with removable hood; adjustable folding semi-buckhorn rear
Stock & Forearm: Walnut plain or checkered pistol grip stock & forearm; steel nose cap on forearm tip
Approximate wt.: 6¾ lbs.
Comments: Made from about 1958 to date; sling swivels; hammer block safety added in 1988.
Estimated Value: New (retail): $445.00
                        Excellent: $335.00
                        Very good: $270.00

Marlin Model 39TDS

Similar to the Model 39AS except: smaller; tubular magazine holds 16 shorts, 12 longs, 11 long rifles; 16½" barrel; weighs 5¼ lbs. Produced from 1988 to mid 1990's. Comes with floatable zippered case; gun can be disassembled and assembled without tools.
Estimated Value: Excellent: $335.00
                        Very good: $270.00

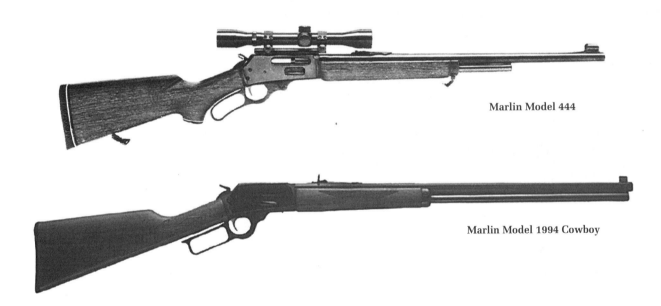

Marlin Model 444

Marlin Model 1994 Cowboy

Marlin Model 444, 444S, 444SS

Caliber: 444 Marlin
Action: Action-lever; repeating
Magazine: 5-shot tubular under barrel
Barrel: Blued; 24" or 22" micro-groove
Sights: Folding open rear, hooded ramp front
Stock & Forearm: Monte Carlo or plain straight or pistol grip stock; barrel band; swivels
Approximate wt.: 7½ lbs.
Comments: Made from about 1965 to present. Currently called 444SS. Hammer block safety added 1986.
Estimated Value: New (retail): $523.00
                        Excellent: $390.00
                        Very good: $315.00

Marlin Model 1994 Cowboy

Caliber: 45 long Colt
Action: Lever action, repeating; squared finger lever
Magazine: 10-shot tubular
Barrel: 24" tapered, octagon, blued
Sights: Adjustable marble, semi-buckhorn rear, carbine type hooded front; receiver is tapped for scope mount
Stock & Forearm: Cut checkered black walnut, straight grip stock and forearm, with metal end
Approximate wt.: 7½ lbs.
Comments: Introduced in 1996.
Estimated Value: New (retail): $668.00
                        Excellent: $500.00
                        Very good: $400.00

Marlin Glenfield Model 30

Caliber: 30-30 Win.
Action: Lever action; repeating
Magazine: 6-shot tubular
Barrel: Blued; 20" round
Sights: Adjustable rear, bead front
Stock & Forearm: Walnut, plain or checkered; semi-pistol grip stock & forearm
Approximate wt.: 7 lbs.
Comments: Made from about 1966 to the late 1970's.
Estimated Value: Excellent: $220.00
Very good: $175.00

Marlin Glenfield Model 30GT

Similar to the Glenfield 30 with a straight grip stock & 18½" barrel. Made from the late 1970's to early 1980's.
Estimated Value: Excellent: $210.00
Very good: $170.00

Marlin Glenfield Model 30A & Marlin 30AS

Similar to the Glenfield 30. Made from the late 1970's to present.
Estimated Value: New (retail): $378.00
Excellent: $285.00
Very good: $225.00

Marlin Model 375

Caliber: 375 Win.
Action: Lever-action; side ejection; repeating
Magazine: 5-shot tubular
Barrel: 20" round
Sights: Adjustable semi-buckhorn rear, ramp front with brass bead
Stock & Forearm: Plain walnut pistol grip stock & forearm with fluted comb; swivels
Approximate wt.: 6¾" lbs.
Comments: Produced from 1980 to mid 1980's.
Estimated Value: Excellent: $320.00
Very good: $255.00

Marlin Glenfield Model 30

Marlin Model 375

Marlin Model 57

Marlin Model 57

Caliber: 22 short, long, long rifle
Action: Lever action; repeating
Magazine: Tubular under barrel; 19 long rifles, 21 longs, 27 shorts
Barrel: Blued; 22" round
Sights: Open rear, hooded ramp front
Stock & Forearm: Plain Monte Carlo pistol grip stock & forearm
Approximate wt.: 6¼ lbs.
Comments: Made from about 1959 to 1965.
Estimated Value: Excellent: $175.00
Very good: $145.00

Marlin Model 56 Levermatic

Caliber: 22 short, long, long rifle
Action: Lever-action; repeating
Magazine: 8-shot clip
Barrel: Blued; 22" round
Sights: Open rear, hooded ramp front
Stock & Forearm: Monte Carlo pistol grip stock & forearm
Approximate wt.: 5¾ lbs.
Comments: Similar to Model 57, produced from about 1955 to 1965.
Estimated Value: Excellent: $165.00
Very good: $135.00

Marlin Model 57M Levermatic

Caliber: 22 Win. mag.
Action: Lever action; repeating
Magazine: 15-shot tubular; under barrel
Barrel: 24" round
Sights: Open rear, hooded ramp front
Stock & Forearm: Monte Carlo pistol grip stock & forearm
Approximate wt.: 6¼ lbs.
Comments: Similar to Model 57; produced from about 1960 to 1969.
Estimated Value: Excellent: $180.00
Very good: $145.00

Marlin Model 62 Levermatic

Caliber: 256 mag. (1963 to 1966); 30 carbine (1966 to 1969)
Action: Lever action; repeating
Magazine: 4-shot clip
Barrel: Blued; 23" round
Sights: Open rear, hooded ramp front
Stock & Forearm: Monte Carlo pistol grip stock & forearm
Approximate wt.: 7 lbs.
Comments: Made from about 1963 to 1969.
Estimated Value: Excellent: $225.00
Very good: $180.00

Marlin Model 56 Levermatic

Marlin Model 62 Levermatic

Marlin Model 18 Baby Slide Action

Marlin Model 18 Baby Slide Action

Caliber: 22 short, long, long rifle
Action: Slide action; exposed hammer; repeating
Magazine: Tubular under barrel; 15 shorts, 12 longs, 10 long rifles
Barrel: Blued; 20" round or octagon
Sights: Open rear, bead front
Stock & Forearm: Plain walnut straight grip stock & slide handle
Approximate wt.: 3½ to 4 lbs.
Comments: Produced from about 1906 to about 1910
Estimated Value: Excellent: $360.00
Very good: $285.00

Marlin Model 20

Marlin Model 29

Marlin Model 20 or 20 S

Caliber: 22 short, long, long rifle
Action: Slide action; exposed hammer; repeating
Magazine: 25 shorts, 20 longs, 18 long rifles in full-length; 15 shorts, 12 longs, 10 long rifles in half-length; tubular, under barrel
Barrel: Blued; 24" octagon
Sights: Open rear, bead front
Stock & Forearm: Plain walnut straight grip stock & grooved slide handle
Approximate wt.: 5 lbs.
Comments: Produced from abt. 1907 to 1920 as Model 20 and as model 20S until discontinued about 1922.
Estimated Value: Excellent: $340.00
Very good: $270.00

Marlin Model 29

Similar to Model 20 except: 23" round barrel and smooth slide handle. Made from about 1913 to 1916.
Estimated Value: Excellent: $315.00
Very good: $250.00

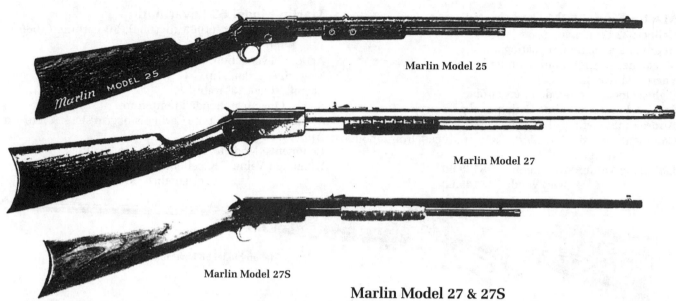

Marlin Model 25

Marlin Model 27

Marlin Model 27S

Marlin Model 25

Caliber: 22 short & 22 CB caps only
Action: Slide action; exposed hammer; repeating
Magazine: 15-shot tubular, under barrel
Barrel: Blued; 23" octagon
Sights: Open rear, bead front
Stock & Forearm: Plain walnut straight grip stock & slide handle
Approximate wt.: 4 lbs.
Comments: Produced for about one year in 1909
Estimated Value: Excellent: $350.00
              Very good: $275.00

Marlin Model 27 & 27S

Caliber: 25-20, 32-30, & 25 Stevens RF
Action: Slide action; exposed hammer; repeating
Magazine: 6-shot, ⅔ tubular
Barrel: Blued; 24" octagon
Sights: Open rear, bead front
Stock & Forearm: Plain walnut straight grip stock & grooved slide handle
Approximate wt.: 5¾ lbs.
Comments: Takedown model produced from about 1910 to 1915 as model 27 and as model 27S from 1920 to 1932
Estimated Value: Excellent: $335.00
              Very good: $270.00

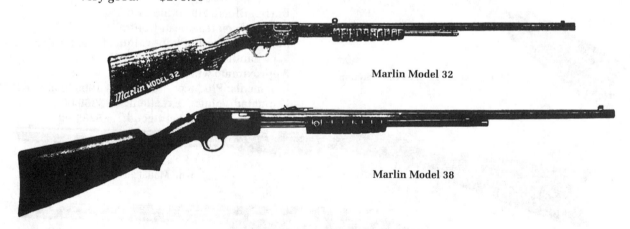

Marlin Model 32

Marlin Model 38

Marlin Model 32

Caliber: 22 short, long, long rifle
Action: Slide action; concealed hammer; repeating
Magazine: 25 shorts, 20 longs, 18 long rifles in full-length; 15 shorts, 12 longs, 10 long rifles in ⅔ length; tubular, under barrel
Barrel: Blued; 24" octagon
Sights: Open rear, bead front
Stock & Forearm: Walnut pistol grip stock & grooved slide handle
Approximate wt.: 5½ lbs.
Comments: Takedown model produced for about one year about 1914 .
Estimated Value: Excellent: $360.00
              Very good: $290.00

Marlin Model 38

Caliber: 22 short, long, long rifle
Action: Slide action; exposed hammer; repeating
Magazine: 15 shorts, 12 longs, 10 long rifles, ⅔ tubular, under barrel
Barrel: Blued; 24" octagon or round
Sights: Open rear, bead front
Stock & Forearm: Plain pistol grip stock & grooved slide handle
Approximate wt.: 5½ lbs.
Comments: Takedown model; Produced from about 1921 to about 1930.
Estimated Value: Excellent: $325.00
              Very good: $260.00

Marlin Model 37

Marlin Model 47

Marlin Model 37

Caliber: 22 short, long, long rifle
Action: Slide action; exposed hammer; repeating
Magazine: 25 shorts, 20 longs, 18 long rifles; tubular,
Barrel: 24" round
Sights: Open rear, bead front
Stock & Forearm: Walnut pistol grip stock & forearm
Approximate wt.: 5 lbs.
Comments: Takedown model; Made from about 1923 to 1933
Estimated Value: Excellent: $310.00
Very good: $250.00

Marlin Model 47

Basically same as Model 37, used as a bonus giveaway with purchase of Marlin Stocks. Discontinued in 1931 after six years production.
Estimated Value: Excellent: $500.00
Very good: $400.00

Marlin Model 50

Marlin Model A-1

Marlin Model A-1E

Marlin Model 50 & 50E

Caliber: 22 long rifle
Action: Semi-automatic; takedown model; side ejection
Magazine: 6-shot detachable box
Barrel: Blued; 24"; round
Sights: Open rear, bead front; peep sights on 50E
Stock & Forearm: Plain one piece pistol grip stock & finger grooved forearm
Approximate wt.: 6 lbs.
Comments: Production started about 1931 & stopped about three years later.
Estimated Value: Excellent: $120.00
Very good: $ 95.00

Marlin Model A-1 & A-1E

Caliber: 22 long rifle
Action: Semi-automatic; side ejection
Magazine: 6-shot detachable box
Barrel: Blued; 24"
Sights: Open rear, bead front; peep sights on A-1E
Stock & Forearm: Plain pistol grip stock & forearm
Approximate wt.: 6 lbs.
Comments: Takedown model made from abt. 1935 to 1946.
Estimated Value: Excellent: $140.00
Very good: $115.00

Model A-1C & A-1DL

An improved Model A-1; semi-beavertail forearm. Produced from about 1940 for six years. Peep sights & swivels on A-1DL.
Estimated Value: Excellent: $170.00
Very good: $135.00

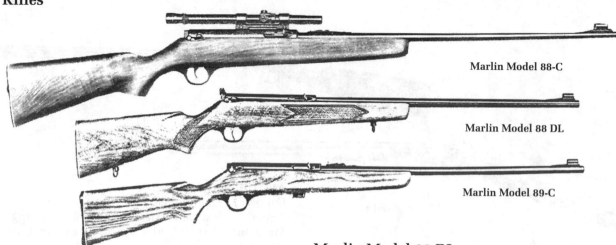

Marlin Model 88-C

Marlin Model 88 DL

Marlin Model 89-C

Marlin Model 88-C

Caliber: 22 long rifle
Action: Semi-automatic; side ejection
Magazine: 14-shot tubular, in stock
Barrel: Blued; 24" round
Sights: Open rear, hooded front
Stock & Forearm: Pistol grip stock & forearm
Approximate wt.: 6¾ lbs.
Comments: A takedown model produced from about 1947 to 1956.

Estimated Value: Excellent: $120.00
                       Very good: $ 95.00

Marlin Model 88 DL

Same as Model 88-C except checkered stock, swivels & peep sight on receiver. Produced for three years beginning about 1953.

Estimated Value: Excellent: $125.00
                       Very good: $100.00

Marlin Model 89-C & 89-DL

Same as Model 88-C except magazine is 7- or 12-shot clip & it has a tapered forearm. Produced from about 1950 to 1961. Model 89-DL has swivels & peep sights.

Estimated Value: Excellent: $110.00
                       Very good: $ 90.00

Marlin Model 98

Marlin Model 99C

Marlin Model 98

Caliber: 22 long rifle
Action: Semi-automatic; side ejection
Magazine: 15-shot tubular
Barrel: Blued; 22" round
Sights: Open rear, hooded ramp front
Stock & Forearm: Walnut Monte Carlo with cheekpiece
Approximate wt.: 6¾ lbs.
Comments: Produced from about 1957 to 1959. Replaced by Model 99.

Estimated Value: Excellent: $120.00
                       Very good: $ 95.00

Marlin Model 99

Caliber: 22 long rifle
Action: Semi-automatic; side ejection
Magazine: 18-shot tubular
Barrel: Blued; 22" round
Sights: Open rear, hooded ramp front
Stock & Forearm: Plain pistol grip stock & forearm
Approximate wt.: 5½ lbs.
Comments: Made from about 1959 until 1961.

Estimated Value: Excellent: $115.00
                       Very good: $ 90.00

Marlin Model 99 C

Same as Model 99 except Monte Carlo stock (some are checkered); gold plated trigger; grooved receiver. Produced from 1962 to late 1970's.

Estimated Value: Excellent: $110.00
                       Very good: $ 90.00

Marlin Model 99DL

Marlin Glenfield Model 99G

Marlin Model 99DL
Same as Model 99C except: Swivels & jeweled breech bolt. Made for five years beginning about 1960.
Estimated Value: Excellent: $120.00
Very good: $100.00

Marlin Glenfield Model 99G
Basically the same as Model 99 with a plain stock. Produced from about 1963 to 1965.
Estimated Value: Excellent: $95.00
Very good: $80.00

Marlin Model 989

Marlin Glenfield Model 989G

Marlin Model 922M
Caliber: 22 Win. magnum rimfire
Action: Semi-automatic; "last shot" bolt hold open; aluminium alloy receiver
Magazine: 7-shot clip
Barrel: Blued; 20½"; micro-groove rifling
Sights: Adjustable folding rear; ramp front with removable hood
Stock & Forearm: Checkered walnut Monte Carlo pistol grip stock & forearm; butt pad and swivel studs
Approximate wt.: 6½ lbs.
Comments: Introduced in 1993.
Estimated Value: New (Retail): $411.00
Excellent: $310.00
Very good: $245.00

Marlin Model 989
Caliber: 22 long rifle only
Action: Semi-automatic; side ejection
Magazine: 7-shot clip
Barrel: Blued; 22" round
Sights: Open rear, hooded ramp front
Stock & Forearm: Monte Carlo pistol grip stock & forearm
Approximate wt.: 5½ lbs.
Comments: Produced for four years beginning in 1962.
Estimated Value: Excellent: $130.00
Very good: $105.00

Marlin Glenfield Model 989G
Basically same as Marlin Model 989 except plain stock & bead front sight. Produced from about 1962 to 1964.
Estimated Value: Excellent: $120.00
Very good: $ 85.00

Marlin Model 99 M1

Marlin Model 989 M2

Marlin Model 99 M1
Caliber: 22 long rifle
Action: Semi-automatic; side ejection
Magazine: 9-shot tubular
Barrel: Blued; 18" micro-groove
Sights: Open rear, ramp front (military)
Stock & Forearm: Carbine stock, hand guard & barrel band; swivels
Approximate wt.: 4½ lbs.
Comments: Styled after the U.S. 30 M1 Carbine; in production from about 1966 to the late 1970's.

Estimated Value:	Excellent:	$120.00
	Very good:	$ 95.00

Marlin Model 989 M2
Same as the Model 99 M1 except: 7-shot clip magazine.

Estimated Value:	Excellent:	$115.00
	Very good:	$ 95.00

Marlin Model 60

Marlin Model 70P Papoose

Marlin Model 70P & 70PSS Papoose
Caliber: 22 long rifle
Action: Semi-automatic; side ejection
Magazine: 7-shot clip
Barrel: 16¼" quick takedown; 70PSS stainless steel
Sights: Adjustable rear, ramp front; 4X scope included
Stock & Forearm: Smooth walnut-finish hardwood, semi-pistol grip stock with abbreviated forearm; black fiberglass-filled synthetic stock on 70PSS
Approximate wt.: 3¼ lbs.
Comments: Produced from 1986 to mid 1990's as 70P, then changed to 70PSS with stainless steel barrel & bolt. A quick takedown rifle with built-in flotation case included. Priced for 70PSS.

Estimated Value:	New (retail):	$255.00
	Excellent:	$190.00
	Very good:	$155.00

Marlin Model 60 & 60 SS
Caliber: 22 long rifle
Action: Semi-automatic; side ejection
Magazine: 17-shot tubular; reduced to 14-shot in 1992
Barrel: Blued or stainless steel(60 ss); 22"; round
Sights: Open rear, ramp front
Stock & Forearm: Checkered or smooth hardwood semi-pistol grip stock & forearm; or Monte Carlo stock
Approximate wt.: 5½ lbs.
Comments: Producd from about 1960 to date. Add 50% for stainless steel (60 SS) barrel, bolt & outer magazine tube.

Estimated Value:	New (retail):	$159.00
	Excellent:	$120.00
	Very good:	$100.00

Marlin Model 75 C
Same as the Model 60 except: 13-shot magazine, 18" barrel. Discontinued in 1990.

Estimated Value:	Excellent:	$110.00
	Very good:	$ 90.00

Marlin Model 49

Marlin Model 49 DL

Marlin Glenfield Model 70

Marlin Model 70 Carbine, 70HC

Caliber: 22 long rifle
Action: Semi-automatic; hammerless; side ejection
Magazine: 7-shot clip; 70HC has 5, 15, or 25-shot clip
Barrel: Blued; 18"; round; micro-groove
Sights: Open rear, ramp front
Stock & Forearm: Walnut Monte Carlo one-piece stock & forearm; barrel band; swivels
Approximate wt.: 5½ lbs.
Comments: Model 70 1966 to 1990; 70HC 1988 to mid 1990's
Estimated Value: Excellent: $125.00
                       Very good: $100.00

Marlin Model 49

Caliber: 22 long rifle
Action: Semi-automatic; hammerless; side ejection
Magazine: 18-shot tubular
Barrel: Blued; 22"; round
Sights: Adjustable open rear, ramp front
Stock & Forearm: Monte Carlo plain two-piece pistol grip stock & forearm
Approximate wt.: 5½ lbs.
Comments: Made from the late 1960's to mid 1970's.
Estimated Value: Excellent: $115.00
                       Very good: $90.00

Marlin Model 49 DL

Same as the Model 49 except: checkered stock & forearm; gold plated trigger. Made from about 1971 to late 1970's.
Estimated Value: Excellent: $120.00
                       Very good: $100.00

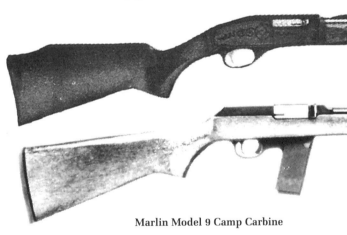

Marlin Glenfield Model 40

Marlin Model 9 Camp Carbine

Marlin Glenfield Model 40

Caliber: 22 long rifle
Action: Semi-automatic; hammerless; side ejection
Magazine: 18-shot tubular
Barrel: 22"
Sights: Adjustable open rear, ramp front
Stock & Forearm: Checkered hardwood Monte Carlo semi-pistol grip stock & forearm
Approximate wt.: 5½ lbs.
Comments: Produced in the late 1970's.
Estimated Value: Excellent: $120.00
                       Very good: $ 95.00

Marlin Model 9 & 9N Camp Carbine

Caliber: 9mm
Action: Semi-automatic; last-shot bolt hold-open
Magazine: 10-shot, 12-shot clip; 20-shot clip available
Barrel: 16½"; round; blued or nickel plate
Sights: Adjustable rear, ramp front with brass bead
Stock & Forearm: Walnut finished hardwood pistol grip stock & forearm; rubber butt pad
Approximate wt.: 6¾ lbs.
Comments: Produced from 1985 to present. Add 10% for nickel plate (9N).
Estimated Value: New (retail): $425.00
                       Excellent: $320.00
                       Very good: $255.00

Marlin Model 45

Similar to the Model 9 except: 45ACP caliber; 7-shot clip. Produced from 1986 to present.
Estimated Value: New (retail): $425.00
                       Excellent: $320.00
                       Very good: $255.00

Marlin Model 990

Marlin Model 995 Carbine

Marlin Model 995& 995SS

Caliber: 22 long rifle
Action: Semi-automatic; last shot bolt hold-open
Magazine: 7-shot clip; nickel plated on 995SS
Barrel: 18" blued; stainless steel on 995SS
Sights: Ramp front sight with orange post and cut-away wide-scan hood; adjustable open rear
Stock & Forearm: Checkered walnut finish Monte Carlo, one-piece pistol grip stock and forearm (995); black fiberglass filled synthetic Monte Carlo, one-piece pistol grip stock and forearm on 995SS with molded checkering
Approximate wt.: 5 lbs.
Comments: Model 995 discontinued in mid 1990's and Model 995SS introduced. Price is for 995SS; deduct 10% for blued model (995).
Estimated Value: New (retail): $238.00
                       Excellent: $180.00
                       Very good: $145.00

Marlin Model 990L

Caliber: 22 long rifle
Action: Semi-automatic; last-shot bolt hold-open
Magazine: 14-shot tubular
Barrel: 22" round with Miocro-groove rifling
Sights: Adjustable semi-buckhorn rear, ramp front with brass bead and wide-scan hood; grooved for scope
Stock & Forearm: Laminated hardwood Monte Carlo one-piece pistol grip stock & forearm
Approximate wt.: 5½ lbs.
Comments: Produced from 1992 to mid 1990's.
Estimated Value: Excellent: $170.00
                       Very good: $135.00

Marlin Model 990

Caliber: 22 long rifle
Action: Semi-automatic; side ejection
Magazine: 18-shot tubular
Barrel: 22" round
Sights: Adjustable folding semi-buckhorn rear, ramp front with brass bead
Stock & Forearm: Checkered walnut Monte Carlo one-piece pistol grip stock & forearm
Approximate wt.: 5½ lbs.
Comments: Produced from the late 1970's to 1988.
Estimated Value: Excellent: $150.00
                       Very good: $120.00

Mauser

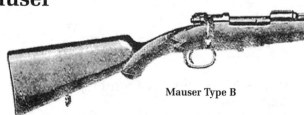

Mauser Type B

Mauser Type A Special British

Caliber: 30-06, 7x57, 8x60, 9x57, 9.3x62mm
Action: Bolt action; repeating
Magazine: 5-shot box
Barrel: Blued; 23½", octagon or round
Sights: Express rear, hooded ramp front
Stock & Forearm: Checkered walnut one-piece pistol grip stock & tapered forearm; swivels
Approximate wt.: 7¼ lbs.
Comments: Made from about 1910 to 1938.
Estimated Value: Excellent: $625.00
                       Very good: $500.00

Mauser Type A Short Model

Similar to Type A Special British with 21½" barrel & a short action.
Estimated Value: Excellent: $600.00
                       Very good: $480.00

Mauser Type A Magnum

Similar to Type A Special British with magnum action for 280 Ross, 318 Express, 10.75x68mm, 404 Express.
Estimated Value: Excellent: $700.00
                       Very good: $560.00

Mauser Type B

Caliber: 30-06, 7x57, 8x57, 8x60, 9.3x62, 10.75x68
Action: Bolt action; repeating
Magazine: 5-shot box
Barrel: Blued; 23½"
Sights: Leaf rear, ramp front
Stock & Forearm: Checkered walnut one-piece pistol grip stock & lipped forearm; swivels
Approximate wt.: 7½ lbs.
Comments: Made from about 1910 to 1940.
Estimated Value: Excellent: $675.00
                       Very good: $540.00

Mauser Type K

Similar to Type B with 21½" barrel & short action.
Estimated Value: Excellent: $600.00
                       Very good: $475.00

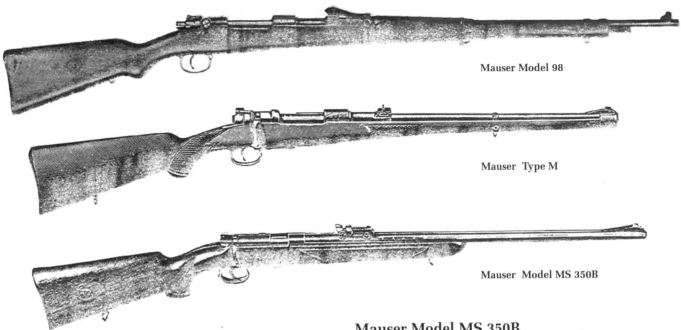

Mauser Model 98

Mauser Type M

Mauser Model MS 350B

Mauser Model 98
Caliber: 7mm, 7.9mm
Action: Bolt action; repeating
Magazine: 5-shot box
Barrel: Blued; 23½"
Sights: Adjustable rear, blade front
Stock & Forearm: Walnut one-piece semi-pistol grip stock & fluted forearm; barrel band
Approximate wt.: 7½ lbs.
Comments: Made from about 1920 to 1938.
Estimated Value: Excellent: $575.00
                        Very good: $460.00

Mauser Type M
Caliber: 30-06, 6.5x54, 7x57, 8x52, 8x60, 9x57
Action: Bolt action; repeating
Magazine: 5-shot box
Barrel: Blued; 19¾"
Sights: 3 leaf rear, ramp front
Stock & Forearm: Checkered walnut one-piece pistol grip stock & full-length forearm; swivels
Approximate wt.: 6½ lbs.
Comments: Made from about 1910 to 1940.
Estimated Value: Excellent: $650.00
                        Very good: $520.00

Mauser Type S
Caliber: 6.5x54, 7x57, 8x51, 8x60, 9x57
Action: Bolt action; repeating
Magazine: 5-shot box
Barrel: Blued; 19¾"
Sights: 3 leaf rear, ramp front
Stock & Forearm: Checkered walnut one-piece pistol grip stock & lipped full-length forearm; swivels
Approximate wt.: 6½ lbs.
Comments: Made from about 1910 to 1940.
Estimated Value: Excellent: $650.00
                        Very good: $520.00

Mauser Model MS 350B
Caliber: 22 long rifle
Action: Bolt action; repeating
Magazine: 5-shot box
Barrel: Blued; 27½"
Sights: Micrometer rear, ramp front
Stock & Forearm: Match-type; checkered pistol grip; swivels
Approximate wt.: 8 lbs.
Comments: Made from the mid 1920's to mid 1930's.
Estimated Value: Excellent: $500.00
                        Very good: $400.00

Mauser Model ES 350
Similar to MS 350B with different sights & 26¾" barrel. Made from the mid to late 1930's. Single shot.
Estimated Value: Excellent: $450.00
                        Very good: $360.00

Mauser Model ES 350B
Similar to MS 350B in single shot. Target sights.
Estimated Value: Excellent: $400.00
                        Very good: $320.00

Mauser Model ES 340
Caliber: 22 long rifle
Action: Bolt action; single shot
Magazine: None
Barrel: Blued; 25½"
Sights: Tangent curve rear, ramp front
Stock & Forearm: Checkered walnut one-piece pistol grip stock & forearm; swivels
Approximate wt.: 6½ lbs.
Comments: Made from the early 1920's to mid 1930's.
Estimated Value: Excellent: $300.00
                        Very good: $240.00

Mauser Model ES 340B
Similar to the ES 340 with a 26¾" barrel. Made from the mid to late 1930's.
Estimated Value: Excellent: $320.00
                        Very good: $250.00

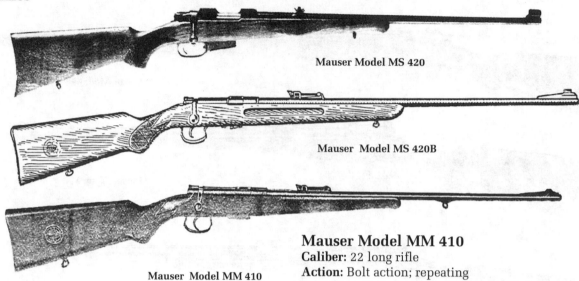

Mauser Model MS 420

Mauser Model MS 420B

Mauser Model MM 410

Mauser Model EL 320

Similar to ES 340 with a 23½" barrel, adjustable rear sight & bead front sight. Made from the late 1920's to mid 1930's.

Estimated Value: Excellent: $330.00
                       Very good: $265.00

Mauser Model MS 420

Caliber: 22 long rifle
Action: Bolt action; repeating
Magazine: 5-shot detachable box
Barrel: Blued; 25½"
Sights: Tangent curve rear, ramp front
Stock & Forearm: Checkered walnut one-piece pistol grip stock & forearm; swivels
Approximate wt.: 6½ lbs.
Comments: Made from the mid 1920's to mid 1930's.
Estimated Value: Excellent: $380.00
                       Very good: $300.00

Mauser Model MS 420B

Similar to MS 420 with better wood. Made from the mid to late 1930's.

Estimated Value: Excellent: $450.00
                       Very good: $360.00

Mauser Model MM 410

Caliber: 22 long rifle
Action: Bolt action; repeating
Magazine: 5-shot detachable box
Barrel: Blued; 23½"
Sights: Tangent curve rear, ramp front
Stock & Forearm: Checkered one-piece pistol grip stock & forearm; swivels
Approximate wt.: 6½ lbs.
Comments: Made from the mid 1920's to mid 1930's.
Estimated Value: Excellent: $360.00
                       Very good: $285.00

Mauser Model MM 410 B

Similar to MM 410 except lighter weight model. Made from mid to late 1930's.
Estimated Value: Excellent: $400.00
                       Very good: $320.00

Mauser Model DSM 34

Similar to the 98 in appearance, in 22 long rifle with a 26" barrel. Made from the mid 1930's to late 1930's. Single shot.
Estimated Value: Excellent: $425.00
                       Very good: $340.00

Mauser Model KKW

Similar to DSM 34. Made from the mid to late 1930's.
Estimated Value: Excellent: $400.00
                       Very good: $320.00

Mauser Model 2000

Mauser Model 2000

Caliber: 270 Win., 308 Win., 30-06
Action: Bolt action; repeating; adjustable trigger
Magazine: 5-shot box; hinged floor plate
Barrel: 24" Krupp steel
Sights: Folding leaf rear, hooded ramp front
Stock & Forearm: Checkered walnut Monte Carlo one-piece pistol grip stock & forearm; swivels; cheekpiece
Approximate wt.: 7½ lbs.
Comments: Made from the late 1960's to early 1970's.
Estimated Value: Excellent: $375.00
                       Very good: $300.00

Mauser 660 Safari

Mauser 3000

Mauser Model 3000
Caliber: 243, 270, 30-06, 308, 375 H&H mag., 7mm mag., 300 Win. mag.
Action: Bolt action; repeating
Magazine: 5-shot box
Barrel: 22", 26" magnum
Sights: None
Stock & Forearm: Checkered walnut Monte Carlo one-piece pistol grip stock & forearm; recoil pad
Approximate wt.: 7 lbs.
Comments: Made in the 1970's. Add $50.00 for mag.
Estimated Value: Excellent: $500.00
Very good: $400.00

Mauser Model 660
Caliber: 243, 25-06, 270, 308, 30-06, 7x57, 7mm
Action: Short bolt action; repeating
Magazine: 5-shot box
Barrel: Blued; 24"
Sights: None
Stock & Forearm: Checkered walnut Monte Carlo one-piece pistol grip stock & forearm; recoil pad
Approximate wt.: 7 lbs.
Comments: Made in the early 1970's.
Estimated Value: Excellent: $650.00
Very good: $490.00

Mauser Model 660 Safari
Similar to 660 except: 28" barrel; express rear sight & ramp front sight; calibers 458 Win., 375 H&H, 338 Win., & 7mm Rem.; approximate weight 9 lbs.
Estimated Value: Excellent: $700.00
Very good: $525.00

Mauser Varminter 10

Mauser Model 66S
Caliber: 243, 6.5x57, 270, 7x64, 30-06, 308, 5.6x61 V.H. mag., 6.5x68 mag., 7mm Rem. mag., 7mm V.H. mag., 8x68S mag., 300 Win. mag., 300 Weath. mag., 9.3x62 mag., 9.3x64 mag.
Action: Mauser telescopic short bolt action; repeating
Magazine: 5-shot box
Barrel: Blued; 21", 24", 26"; interchangeable barrels available
Sights: Adjustable rear, hooded ramp front
Stock & Forearm: European walnut, checkered Monte Carlo one-piece pistol grip stock & forearm; rosewood tip; recoil pad; full-length forearm available
Approximate wt.: 7 lbs.
Comments: Add 10% for full-length forearm.
Estimated Value: Excellent: $1,000.00
Very good: $ 800.00

Mauser Model 66SM
Similar to the Model 66S with lipped forearm (no rosewood tip) & internal alterations. Add 10% for full-length forearm.
Estimated Value: Excellent: $1,160.00
Very good: $ 870.00

Mauser Model 66SL
Similar to the Model 66SM with select walnut stock & forearm. Add 75% for Diplomat Model with custom engraving.
Estimated Value: Excellent: $1,370.00
Very good: $1,025.00

Mauser Model 66S Big Game
Similar to Model 66S in 375 H&H or 458 Win. magnum caliber; 26" barrel; fold down rear sight; weighs about 10 lbs.
Estimated Value: Excellent: $1,320.00
Very good: $1,050.00

Mauser Varminter 10
Caliber: 22-250
Action: Bolt action; repeating
Magazine: 5-shot box
Barrel: Blued; 24", heavy
Sights: None
Stock & Forearm: Checkered walnut Monte Carlo one-piece pistol grip stock & forearm
Approximate wt.: 8 lbs.
Comments: Made in the 1970's.
Estimated Value: Excellent: $440.00
Very good: $350.00

Mauser Model 77 DJV Sportsman
Similar to the Model 77 with stippled stock & forearm; no sights.

Estimated Value: Excellent: $1,150.00
                   Very good: $ 860.00

Mauser Model 77 Big Game
Similar to the Model 77 in 375 H&H magnum caliber; 26" barrel.

Estimated Value: Excellent: $1,070.00
                   Very good: $ 800.00

Mauser Model 77
Caliber: 243 Win., 270 Win., 308 Win., 30-06, 6.5x57, 7x64, 7mm Rem. mag., 6.5x68 mag., 300 Win. mag., 9.3x62 mag., 8x68S mag.
Action: Mauser short bolt action; repeating
Magazine: 3-shot clip
Barrel: Blued; 20", 24", 26"
Sights: Adjustable rear, hooded ramp front
Stock & Forearm: Checkered walnut one-piece pistol grip stock & lipped forearm; recoil pad; swivels
Approximate wt.: 7½ lbs.
Comments: Produced in the early 1980's. Add 10% for 20" or 26" barrel or full-length forearm.

Estimated Value: Excellent: $915.00
                   Very good: $685.00

Military, Argentine

Argentine Model 1891 Mauser

Argentine Model 1891 Carbine

Argentine Model 1909 Mauser

Argentine Model 1909 Carbine

Argentine Model 1891 Mauser
Caliber: 7x65mm rimless
Action: Manually-operated bolt action; straight bolt handle
Magazine: 5-shot single column box
Barrel: 29" round barrel; cleaning rod in forearm
Sights: Barley corn front; rear adjustable for elevation
Stock & Forearm: Military-type one-piece straight grip stock & full forearm; bayonet lug; two barrel bands
Approximate wt.: 8½ lbs.
Comments: Similar to 7.65mm M1890 Turkish Mauser; obsolete.

Estimated Value: Very good: $125.00
                   Good: $ 90.00

Argentine Model 1909 Carbine
Similar to Model 1909 Rifle except: 17½" barrel; approximate wt. 6½ lbs.; with & without bayonet lugs.

Estimated Value: Very good: $145.00
                   Good: $110.00

Argentine Model 1891 Carbine
Similar to Model 1891 Rifle except: 17½" barrel; approximate wt. 6½ lbs.; two versions, one with & one without bayonet lug; some still used as police weapons.

Estimated Value: Very good: $120.00
                   Good: $ 90.00

Argentine Model 1909 Mauser
Caliber: 7.65mm rimless
Action: Manually-operated bolt with straight handle
Magazine: 5-shot staggered row box magazine
Barrel: 29" round barrel
Sights: Barley corn, tangent leaf rear
Stock & Forearm: Military-type one-piece semi-pistol grip stock & full forearm; two barrel bands; cleaning rod in forearm
Approximate wt.: 9 lbs.
Comments: A slight modification of the German Gewehr 98; obsolete.

Estimated Value: Very good: $150.00
                   Good: $115.00

Military, British

British Lee-Enfield Mark I Rifle

British Lee-Enfield Mark I Carbine

British Lee-Enfield Mark I Carbine
Similar to Lee Enfield Mark I Rifle except 21" barrel.
Estimated Value: Very good: $135.00
                       Good: $105.00

British Lee-Enfield Mark I
Caliber: 303
Action: Bolt action; repeating; curved bolt handle
Magazine: 10-shot detachable box with cut-off
Barrel: 30"
Sights: Barley corn front, vertical leaf rear
Stock & Forearm: Plain military-type stock & forearm
Approximate wt.: 9¼ lbs.
Comments: Adopted by British Army about 1899.
Estimated Value: Very good: $140.00
                       Good: $110.00

British Lee-Enfield No. 1 SMLE MK1

British Lee-Enfield No. 1 SMLE MK III

British (Pattern 14)
No. 3 MK 1

British (Pattern 14) No. 3 MK 1
Caliber: 303
Action: Bolt action; modified Mauser-type action; cocked as bolt is moved foreward
Magazine: 5-shot non-removable box
Barrel: 26"
Sights: Blade front with protective ears, vertical leaf with aperture rear
Stock & Forearm: Plain military stock with wood hand guard over barrel
Approximate wt.: 9 lbs.
Comments: Made in U.S.A. during World War I for the British Army.
Estimated Value: Very good: $150.00
                       Good: $115.00

British Lee-Enfield No. 1 SMLE MK1
Caliber: 303
Action: Bolt action; curved bolt handle
Magazine: 10-shot detachable box with cut-off
Barrel: 25¼"
Sights: Barley corn front with protective ears; tangent leaf rear
Stock & Forearm: Plain wood military stock to the muzzle with full-length wood hand guard over barrel
Approximate wt.: 8 lbs.
Comments: Adopted about 1902 by British Army.
Estimated Value: Very good: $160.00
                       Good: $120.00

British Lee-Enfield No. 1 SMLE MK III
Similar to No. 1 SMLE MK I except: modified & simplified for mass production; adopted in 1907 & modified again in 1918.
Estimated Value: Very good: $165.00
                       Good: $120.00

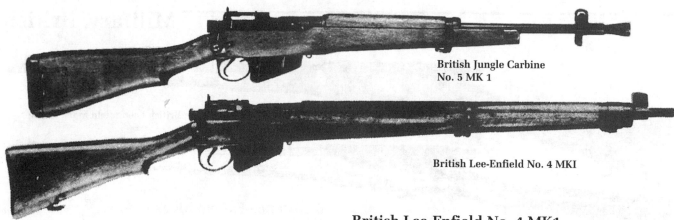

British Jungle Carbine
No. 5 MK 1

British Lee-Enfield No. 4 MKI

British Jungle Carbine No. 5 MK1
Caliber: 303
Action: Bolt action
Magazine: 10-shot detachable box
Barrel: 18¾"
Sights: Blade front with protective ears; vertical leaf rear with aperture
Stock & Forearm: Military-type one-piece stock & forearm; wood hand guard over barrel; one barrel band
Approximate wt.: 7 lbs.
Comments: Made during World War II for jungle fighting.
Estimated Value: Very good: $180.00
                        Good: $145.00

British Lee-Enfield No. 4 MK1
Caliber: 303
Action: Bolt action
Magazine: 10-shot detachable box
Barrel: 25"
Sights: Blade front with protective ears; vertical leaf with aperture rear
Stock & Forearm: Plain military stock with wood hand guard over barrel
Approximate wt.: 8¾ lbs.
Comments: First produced about 1931 & was redesigned for mass production in 1939 by utilizing stamped parts & other short cuts.
Estimated Value: Very good: $135.00
                        Good: $100.00

Military, Chilean

Chilean Model 1895

Chilean Model 1895 Short

Chilean Model 1895 Carbine

Chilean Model 1895 Short
Similar to Model 1895 Rifle except: 22" barrel; approximate wt. 8½ lbs.
Estimated Value: Very good: $110.00
                        Good: $ 90.00

Chilean Model 1895 Carbine
Similar to Model 1895 Rifle except: 18¼" barrel; approximate wt. 7½ lbs.
Estimated Value: Very good: $100.00
                        Good: $ 80.00

Chilean Model 1895
Caliber: 7mm
Action: Bolt action; straight or turned bolt handle; similar to the Spanish Model 1893 Mauser
Magazine: 5-shot staggered non-detachable box
Barrel: 29"
Sights: Barley corn front; leaf rear
Stock & Forearm: Plain military-type stock with wood hand guard over barrel
Approximate wt.: 9 lbs.
Comments: Since Chile's adoption of the FN rifle, quantities of the Chilean Mausers have been purchased by U.S.A. arms dealers.
Estimated Value: Very good: $120.00
                        Good: $100.00

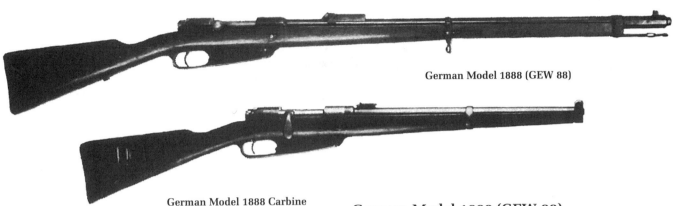

German Model 1888 (GEW 88)

German Model 1888 Carbine

German Model 1888 (GEW 88)
Caliber: 7.92mm
Action: Bolt action; straight bolt handle
Magazine: 5-shot in line non-detachable box
Barrel: 29"
Sights: Barley corn front; leaves with "v" notches rear
Stock & Forearm: Plain straight grip military stock; no hand guard but uses a metal barrel jacket that covers barrel to muzzle
Approximate wt.: 8¾ lbs.
Comments: This arm is sometimes called a Mauser or Mannlicher but actually it is neither; it combines the magazine of the Mannlicher with the bolt features of the Mauser 1871/84; it is unsafe to use with the modern 7.92mm cartridge.

Estimated Value: Very good: $110.00
Good: $ 90.00

German Model 1888 Carbine
Similar to the Model 1888 Rifle except: 18" barrel; approximate wt. 6¾ lbs.; full-length stock to muzzle; curved flattened top bolt handle.

Estimated Value: Very good: $115.00
Good: $ 95.00

German Model 1891
Similar to Model 1888 Carbine except: stacking hook under forearm & although it is called a rifle, it has an 18" barrel like the carbines.

Estimated Value: Very good: $120.00
Good: $100.00

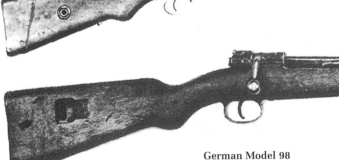

German Gewehr
98 (GEW 98)

German Model 98
(Kar 98) Carbine

German Gewehr 98 (GEW 98)
Caliber: 7.92mm
Action: Bolt action; straight or curved bolt handle
Magazine: 5-shot staggered non-detachable box; also during World War II, 20- & 25-shot magazines
Barrel: 29"
Sights: Barley corn front; tangent bridge-type or tangent leaf "v" rear
Stock & Forearm: Plain military semi-pistol grip stock & forearm; wood hand guard
Approximate wt.: 9 lbs.
Comments: This was one of the principle rifles of the German Army in World War I; it also appeared in a caliber 22 training rifle in World War I by fitting a liner in the barrel.

Estimated Value: Very good: $175.00
Good: $130.00

German Model 98 (Kar 98) Carbine
Similar to Model Gewehr 98 Rifle except: 17" barrel; approximate wt. 7½ lbs.; full stock to muzzle; section of forearm from barrel band to muzzle tapered to much smaller size than rest of forearm; curved bolt handle.

Estimated Value: Very good: $150.00
Good: $125.00

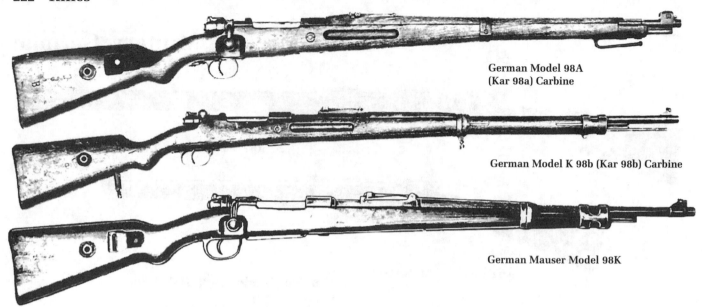

German Model 98A
(Kar 98a) Carbine

German Model K 98b (Kar 98b) Carbine

German Mauser Model 98K

German Model 98A (Kar 98a) Carbine

Similar to Model Gewehr 98 Rifle except: 24" barrel; appeared in 1904 & made in tremendous quantities until 1918; used in World War I & had limited use in World War II; cut out in stock below bolt handle; curved bolt handle; grip grooves on forearm; stacking hook.

Estimated Value: Very good: $165.00
                Good: $125.00

German Model K 98b (Kar 98b) Carbine

Although designed as a carbine, it is same length & is similar to Gewehr 98 Rifle except: turned down bolt; grip grooved forearm; these were used in the 1920's & early in World War II.

Estimated Value: Very good: $175.00
                Good: $130.00

German Mauser Model 98K

Caliber: 7.92mm

Action: Bolt action; turned down bolt handle

Magazine: 5-shot staggered row non-detachable box

Barrel: 24"

Sights: Barley corn open or hooded front, tangent rear with "v" notch

Stock & Forearm: Plain military semi-pistol grip stock & forearm; wood hand guard; cut out in stock under bolt handle

Approximate wt.: 8¾ lbs.

Comments: The standard infantry rifle during World War II; widely fluctuating prices on these rifles because some have special unit markings which affect their values.

Estimated Value: Very good: $150.00 - $500.00
                Good: $120.00 - $400.00

Military, Italian

Italian Mannlicher Carcano M 1891

Mannlicher Carcano M 1891 Carbine

Italian Mannlicher Carcano M 1891

Caliber: 6.5mm

Action: Bolt action; straight bolt handle; a modified Mauser-type action

Magazine: 6-shot in line non-detachable box

Barrel: 30½"

Sights: Barley corn front, tangent rear with "v" notch graduated from 500 to 2000 meters

Stock & Forearm: Plain straight grip military stock with wood hand guard over barrel

Approximate wt.: 8¾ lbs.

Comments: Uses knife-type bayonet.

Estimated Value: Very good: $90.00
                Good: $60.00

Italian Mannlicher Carcano M 1891 Carbine

Generally the same specifications as M 1891 Military rifle except: 18" barrel; bent bolt handle; folding bayonet permanently attached; approximate wt. 7 lbs.

Estimated Value: Very good: $100.00
                Good: $ 70.00

Italian Mannlicher Carcano M 1891 TS Carbine

Italian Mannlicher Carcano M 1891 TS Carbine

Similar to M 1891 Carbine except: uses knife-type removable bayonet.

Estimated Value: Very good: $95.00
Good: $60.00

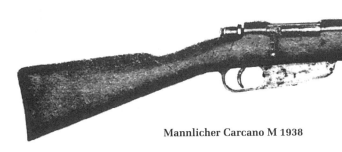

Mannlicher Carcano M 1938

Italian Mannlicher Carcano M 1938 Carbine

Similar to M 1938 Military Rifle except: 18" barrel; folding bayonet permanently attached.

Estimated Value: Very good: $110.00
Good: $ 90.00

Italian Mannlicher Carcano M 1938 TS Carbine

Same as M 1938 Carbine except: detachable knife-type bayonet.

Estimated Value: Very good: $120.00
Good: $100.00

Italian Mannlicher Carcano M 1938

Caliber: 7.35mm, 6.5mm
Action: Bolt action; bent bolt handle
Magazine: 6-shot in line, non-detachable box
Barrel: 21"
Sights: Barley corn front, adjustable rear
Stock & Forearm: Plain straight grip military stock; wood handle guard over barrel
Approximate wt.: 7½ lbs.
Comments: First of the Italian rifles chambered for the 7.35mm cartridge; in 1940 the 7.35mm caliber was dropped; this is the type rifle allegedly used to assassinate President John F. Kennedy in 1963; it was a 6.5mm made in 1940 & sold in U.S.A. as Army surplus.

Estimated Value: Very good: $100.00
Good: $ 80.00

Military, Japanese

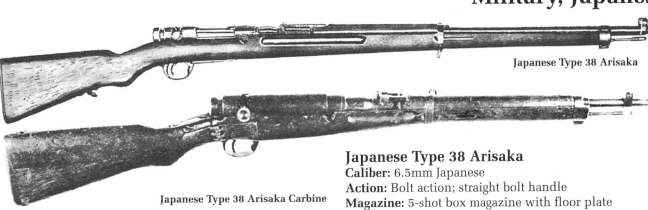

Japanese Type 38 Arisaka

Japanese Type 38 Arisaka Carbine

Japanese Type 38 Arisaka Carbine

Similar to Type 38 Arisaka Rifle except: 20" barrel; folding bayonet; approximate wt. 7¼ lbs.; some were converted for paratrooper use by fitting of a hinged butt stock.

Estimated Value:			Paratrooper
		Carbine	Carbine
	Very good:	$150.00	$180.00
	Good:	$110.00	$135.00

Japanese Type 38 Arisaka

Caliber: 6.5mm Japanese
Action: Bolt action; straight bolt handle
Magazine: 5-shot box magazine with floor plate
Barrel: 31½" round
Sights: Barley corn front with protecting ears, rear sight adjustable for elevation
Stock & Forearm: Military finish; plain wood one-piece full stock; semi-pistol grip; steel buttplate; cleaning rod under barrel; wood hand guard on top of barrel; two steel barrel bands with bayonet lug on front band
Approximate wt.: 9¼ lbs.
Comments: Adopted by Japanese Military in 1905, the 38th year of the Meiji reign.

Estimated Value: Very good: $170.00
Good: $130.00

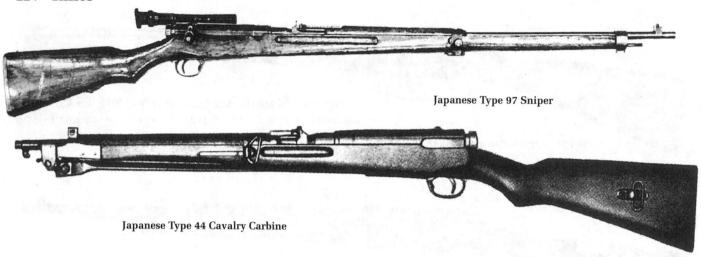

Japanese Type 97 Sniper

Japanese Type 44 Cavalry Carbine

Japanese Type 97 Sniper
Similar to Type 38 Arisaka Rifle except: a snipers version adopted in 1937 with a 2.5 power scope; approximate wt. with scope: 11 lbs. Priced for rifle with scope.

Estimated Value:	Very good:	$275.00
	Good:	$220.00

Japanese Type 44 Cavalry Carbine
Similar to Type 38 Arisaka carbine except: heavier weight, about 9 lbs.; adopted by Japanese Military in 1911, the 44th year of the Meiji reign; permanently attached folding bayonet.

Estimated Value:	Very good:	$150.00
	Good:	$110.00

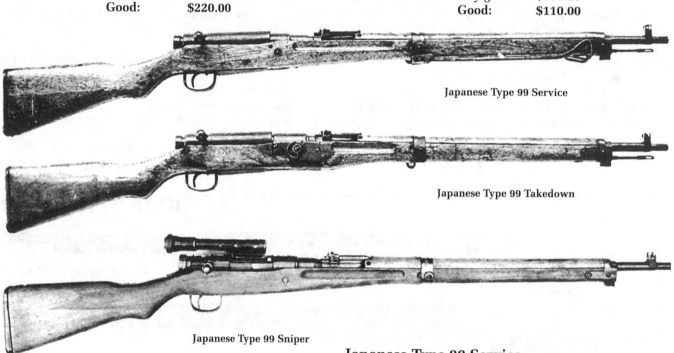

Japanese Type 99 Service

Japanese Type 99 Takedown

Japanese Type 99 Sniper

Japanese Type 99 Takedown
Similar to Type 99 Service Rifle except it has a 25" barrel only. A takedown model, it has a screw-in key that serves as a locking pin. When key is removed, the barrel can be unscrewed from the receiver; however, the takedown arrangement was unsatisfactory because it weakened the receiver & affected the accuracy.

Estimated Value:	Very good:	$175.00
	Good:	$130.00

Japanese Type 99 Sniper
Similar to Type 99 Service Rifle except: adopted in 1942 & equipped with a 4X scope; 25½" barrel only. Prices include matching number & scope mounted.

Estimated Value:	Very good:	$300.00
	Good:	$250.00

Japanese Type 99 Service
Caliber: 7.7mm Japanese
Action: Bolt action
Magazine: 5-shot magazine, non-detachable
Barrel: 25½" or 31½" round
Sights: Fixed front, adjustable or fixed rear
Stock & Forearm: Military finish; plain wood, one-piece full stock; semi-pistol grip; steel buttplate; cleaning rod under barrel; some had bipod attached under forearm; wood hand guard on top of barrel; two steel barrel bands with bayonet lug on front band
Approximate wt.: 8½ to 9 lbs.
Comments: Some of the last rifles made were of poor quality & unsafe to shoot with heavy load cartridges. Adopted by Japanese Military in 1939, which was Japanese year of 2599.

Estimated Value:	Very good:	$150.00
	Good:	$115.00

Military, Mexican

Mexican Model 1895 Mauser

Mexican Model 1902

Mexican Arisaka (Japanese Type 38 Rifle)

Mexican Model 1936

Mexican Model 1954

Mexican Model 1895 Mauser

Almost identical to the Spanish 1893 Military Rifle in caliber 7mm. See Spanish Model 1893 for description.
Estimated Value: Very good: $100.00
Good: $ 80.00

Mexican Models 1902 & 1912 Mauser

Almost identical to the Model 1895 Mauser Military Rifle except that the actions were almost the same as Model 98 7.92 German rifle except in 7mm caliber.
Estimated Value: Very good: $110.00
Good: $ 90.00

Mexican Arisaka (Japanese Type 38 Rifle)

Between 1910 & 1920, Mexico procured arms from many companies. The Arisaka Rifle was purchased from Japan in caliber 7mm & had the Mexican escutcheon stamped on the receiver.
Estimated Value: Very good: $150.00
Good: $110.00

Mexican Model 1936

Caliber: 7mm
Action: Bolt action; curved bolt handle; Mauser short-type action
Magazine: 5-shot staggered row, non-detachable box
Barrel: 20"
Sights: Hooded barley corn front; tangent rear with "V" notch
Stock & Forearm: Plain semi-pistol grip stock with grip grooves in forearm; wood hand guard
Approximate wt.: 8½ lbs.
Comments: A very well made arm of Mexican manufacture; resembles the U.S. Springfield M 1903 - A-1 in appearance.
Estimated Value: Very good: $160.00
Good: $120.00

Mexican Model 1954

Caliber: 30-06
Action: Bolt action; curved bolt handle
Magazine: 5-shot staggered row, non-detachable box
Barrel: 24"
Sights: Hooded barley corn front; ramp-type aperture rear
Stock & Forearm: Plain semi-pistol grip military stock & wood hand guard; stock is made of laminated plywood
Approximate wt.: 9 lbs.
Comments: This rifle is patterned after the U.S. Springfield M 1903 - A3 Military Rifle.
Estimated Value: Very good: $200.00
Good: $160.00

Military, Russian

Russian Moisin-Nagant M 1891

Caliber: 7.62 mm
Action: Bolt action; straight bolt; hexagonal receiver
Magazine: 5-shot box with hinged floor plate
Barrel: 31½"
Sights: Blade front, leaf rear
Stock & Forearm: Plain straight grip, military stock & gripped grooved forearm; early models had no hand guard & used swivels for attaching sling; later models (beginning about 1908) used sling slots & had wood hand guard
Approximate wt.: 9¾ lbs.
Comments: Adopted in 1891 by Imperial Russia.
Estimated Value: Very good: $100.00
                                      Good: $ 80.00

Russian M 1910 Carbine

Caliber: 7.62 mm
Action: Bolt action; straight bolt handle; hexagonal receiver
Magazine: 5-shot box with floor plate
Barrel: 20"
Sights: Blade front, leaf-type rear adjustable for elevation
Stock & Forearm: Plain straight grip military stock; sling slots in stock & forearm; wood hand guard & grip grooved forearm
Approximate wt.: 7½ lbs.
Comments: This carbine does not accept a bayonet.
Estimated Value: Very good: $110.00
                                      Good: $ 90.00

Russian Moisin-Nagant M 1891

Russian M 1910 Carbine

Russian M 1938 Carbine

Russian Tokarev M 1938

Russian Tokarev M 1938

Caliber: 7.62 mm
Action: Semi-automatic; gas operated
Magazine: 10-shot removable box
Barrel: 25"
Sights: Hooded post front, tangent rear
Stock & Forearm: Plain semi-pistol grip two-piece stock & forearm; cleaning rod on right side of forearm; sling swivels
Approximate wt.: 8¾ lbs.
Comments: The first of the Tokarev series; wasn't very successful & was replaced by the Tokarev M 1940.
Estimated Value: Very good: $250.00
                                      Good: $200.00

Russian M 1938 Carbine

This carbine replaced by M1910 & is very similar except: it has a round receiver; hooded front sight & tangent-type rear graduated from 100 to 1000 meters; no bayonet attachment.
Estimated Value: Very good: $95.00
                                      Good: $70.00

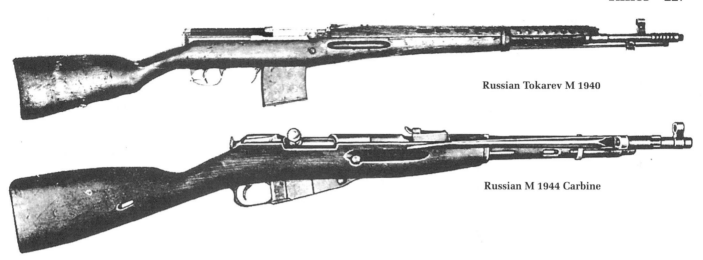

Russian Tokarev M 1940

Russian M 1944 Carbine

Russian Tokarev M 1940
Similar to Tokarev M 1938 except: improved version; cleaning rod in forearm under barrel; 24½" barrel.

Estimated Value: Very good: $300.00
Good: $240.00

Russian M 1944 Military Carbine
Similar to the M 1938 except: introduced during World War II; permanently fixed bayonet which folds along the right side of the stock; barrel length 20½".

Estimated Value: Very good: $235.00
Good: $190.00

Military, Spanish

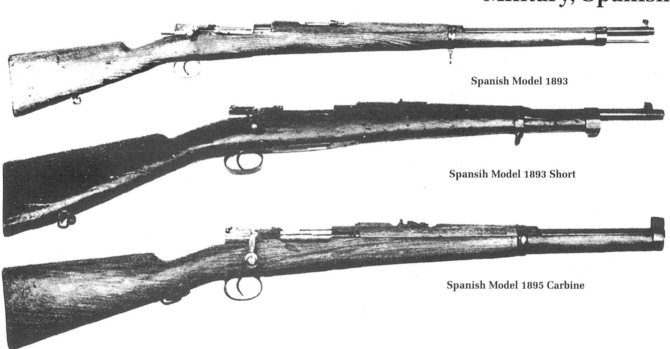

Spanish Model 1893

Spansih Model 1893 Short

Spanish Model 1895 Carbine

Spanish Model 1893
Caliber: 7mm
Action: Bolt action; straight bolt handle
Magazine: 5-shot staggered row non-detachable
Barrel: 30"
Sights: Barley corn front, leaf rear
Stock & Forearm: Plain straight grip military stock with wood hand guard over barrel
Approximate wt.: 9 lbs.
Comments: A number of variations in the Model 1893 were made; it was the principal rifle used in the Spanish-American War.

Estimated Value: Very good: $95.00
Good: $75.00

Spanish Model 1893 Short
Similar to the M 1893 Rifle except: 22" barrel; approximate wt. 8½ lbs.; curved bolt handle.

Estimated Value: Very good: $90.00
Good: $65.00

Spanish Model 1895 Carbine
Similar to the M 1893 Rifle except: 18" barrel; full stock to muzzle; barley corn front sight with protective ears; approximate wt. 7½ lbs.

Estimated Value: Very good: $100.00
Good: $ 80.00

Spanish Model 1916 Short

Caliber: 7mm
Action: Bolt action; bolt handle curved down
Magazine: 5-shot staggered row, non-detachable box
Barrel: 24"
Sights: Barley corn front with ears, tangent rear
Stock & Forearm: Plain military stock & wood hand guard
Approximate wt.: 8½ lbs.
Comments: Made in large quantities during Spanish Civil War; later many were converted to caliber 7.62mm NATO.
Estimated Value: Very good: $100.00
Good: $ 80.00

Spanish Standard Model Mauser

Caliber: 7.92mm
Action: Bolt action; straight bolt handle
Magazine: 5-shot staggered row, non-detachable box
Barrel: 24"
Sights: Barley corn front, tangent rear
Stock & Forearm: Plain military semi-pistol grip stock & forearm grooved for finger grip; wood hand guard
Approximate wt.: 9 lbs.
Comments: Procured in large quantities from other countries during the Spanish Civil War.
Estimated Value: Very good: $110.00
Good: $ 90.00

Spanish Model 1943

Caliber: 7.92mm
Action: Bolt action; curved bolt handle
Magazine: 5-shot staggered row, non-detachable box
Barrel: 24"
Sights: Barley corn front, tangent rear
Stock & Forearm: Plain military semi-pistol grip stock & forearm grooved for finger grip; wood hand guard
Approximate wt.: 9 lbs.
Comments: Adopted in 1943 & continued to mid 1950's; this is a modified copy of the German 7.92mm Kar 98K.
Estimated Value: Very good: $150.00
Good: $110.00

Spanish Model
1916 Short

Spanish Standard
Model Mauser

Spanish Model 1943

Military, U.S.

U.S. M 1903 Springfield

U.S. M 1903 Springfield

Caliber: 30-06

Action: Bolt action; repeating; cocked as bolt handle is rotated clockwise to close & lock; knob at rear protrudes when piece is cocked; manual thumb safety at rear of bolt; turned down bolt handle; action is basically a modification of the Mauser Model 98

Magazine: 5-shot staggered row, non-detachable box magazine

Barrel: 24"

Sights: Blade front, leaf with aperture & notched battle rear

Stock & Forearm: Plain straight one-piece stock & forearm; wood hand guard over barrel; a cleaning rod-type bayonet contained in the forearm under barrel

Approximate wt.: 8¾ lbs.

Comments: Adopted by U.S. 1903; made by Springfield & Rock Island.

Estimated Value: Very good: $300.00
Good: $225.00

U.S. M 1903 - A1 Springfield

Basically the same as M 1903 Military rifle except: pistol grip stock; checkered buttplate & serrated trigger; adopted in 1929; & made until 1939 by Springfield Armory — last serial number was about 1,532,878; in 1942 Remington Arms Co. made about 348,000 with a few minor modifications before the M 1903 A3 was adopted; serial numbers from 3,000,001 to 3,348,085.

Estimated Value: Very good: $320.00
Good: $240.00

U.S. M 1903 - A3 Springfield

Generally the same as the U.S. M 1903 - A1 except: many parts are stamped sheet metal & other modifications to lower cost & increase production; straight or pistol grip stock; made during World War II under emergency conditions.

Estimated Value: Very good: $225.00
Good: $170.00

U.S. M 1917 Enfield

Caliber: 30-06

Action: Bolt action; repeating; cocked as bolt is moved forward; bolt handle is crooked rear-ward; modified Mauser-type action

Magazine: 5-shot staggered row, non-detachable box-type

Barrel: 26"

Sights: Blade front with protecting ears, leaf with aperture rear

Stock & Forearm: Plain one-piece semi-pistol grip stock & forearm; wood hand guard over barrel

Approximate wt.: 8¼ lbs.

Comments: This gun was developed from the British P-13 & P-14 system as an emergency arm for U.S. in World War I. Made from about 1917 to 1918. Also manufactured in the U.S. for Great Britain in caliber 303 in 1917.

Estimated Value: Very good: $220.00
Good: $165.00

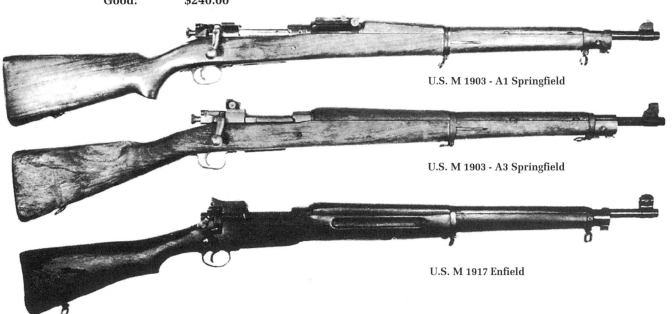

U.S. M 1903 - A1 Springfield

U.S. M 1903 - A3 Springfield

U.S. M 1917 Enfield

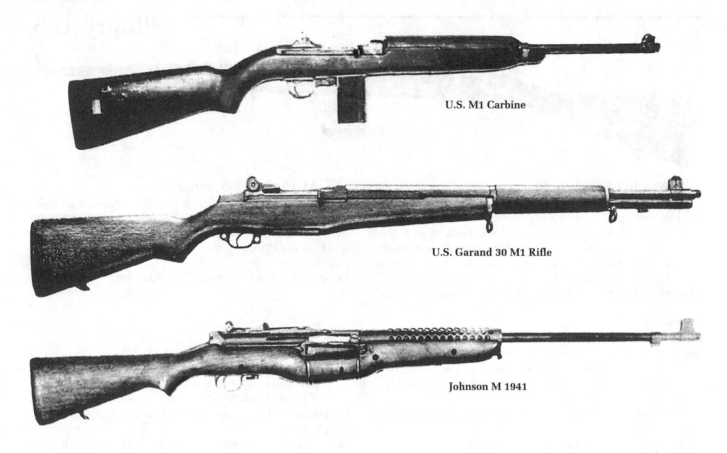

U.S. M1 Carbine

U.S. Garand 30 M1 Rifle

Johnson M 1941

U.S. Garand M1 Rifle
Caliber: 30-06, 308 Win. (7.62 NATO)
Action: Semi-automatic; gas operated
Magazine: 8-shot staggered row, non-detachable box
Barrel: 24"
Sights: Blade front with protective ears, aperture rear or flip-over type rear
Stock & Forearm: One-piece stock & forearm; wood hand guard over top of barrel
Approximate wt.: 9½ lbs.
Comments: Produced by Winchester & Springfield during World War II. Additional M1's produced after World War II by International Harvester & Harrington & Richardson. Add $150.00 for Winchester.
Estimated Value: Very good: $700.00
Good: $525.00

U.S. M1 Carbine
Caliber: 30 M1 Carbine
Action: Semi-automatic; gas operated
Magazine: 15- or 30-shot staggered row, detachable box
Barrel: 18"
Sights: Blade front with protective ears, aperture rear or flip-down rear
Stock & Forearm: One-piece wood stock & forearm; wood hand guard on top of barrel
Approximate wt.: 5½ lbs.
Comments: Developed during World War II to replace the sidearms used by non-commissioned officers, special troops & company grade officers.
Estimated Value: Very good: $375.00
Good: $280.00

U.S. M1 A1 Carbine
Same general specifications as U.S. M1 Carbine except: folding metal stock; 25" overall length when folded; approximate wt. 6¼ lbs.
Estimated Value: Very good: $550.00
Good: $410.00

Johnson M 1941
Caliber: 30-06
Action: Semi-automatic; recoil action; hesitation-locked breech; barrel partially recoils to begin unlocking phase; manual safety in front of trigger guard
Magazine: 10-shot rotary-type; a vertical feed magazine was also made
Barrel: 22"
Sights: Post front with protective ears, aperture rear
Stock & Forearm: Plain wood semi-pistol grip stock & forearm; metal hand guard over barrel above forearm
Approximate wt.: 9½ lbs.
Comments: The Johnson was thought to be superior to the M1 but a series of tests & demonstrations in 1939 & 1940 indicated otherwise; used by U.S. Marines for a limited period in World War II & by the Dutch in the East Indies; many rebarreled in other calibers after World War II.
Estimated Value: Very good: $600.00
Good: $450.00

Mitchell Arms

Mitchell Deluxe Model 9301

Mitchell Deluxe Model 9302

Mitchell Deluxe Model 9301 & 9302
Caliber: 22 long rifle (9301); 22 WRM (9302)
Action: Bolt action; repeating;
Magazine: 10-shot clip (9301); 5-shot clip (9302)
Barrel: Blued; 22" or 24"
Sights: Adjustable rear, ramp front
Stock & Forearm: Checkered walnut one-piece Monte Carlo pistol grip stock and forearm
Approximate wt.: 6 lbs.
Comments: Introduced in the early 1990's. Add 2% for 22WRM (9302)
Estimated Value: New (retail): $312.00
　　　　　　　　 Excellent: $235.00
　　　　　　　　 Very good: $190.00

Mitchell Standard Model 9303 & 9304
Same as Deluxe Model 9301 & 9302 except: plain, smooth, one-piece walnut stock & forearm; add 2% for WRM. Introduced in the early 1990's.
Estimated Value: New (retail): $275.00
　　　　　　　　 Excellent: $205.00
　　　　　　　　 Very good: $165.00

Mitchell Model 15/22

Mitchell Model 15/22 & 15/22D Carbine
Caliber: 22 long rifle
Action: Semi-automatic
Magazine: 15-shot clip
Barrel: Blued; 20" or 22"
Sights: Open adjustable rear, ramp front
Stock & Forearm: Checkered walnut and rosewood one-piece semi-pistol grip stock and forearm on 1522D. Plain, smooth walnut one-piece semi-pistol grip stock and forearm on 15/22
Approximate wt.: 5½ lbs.
Comments: Produced from the early 1990's to the mid 1990's's. Model 15/22D is deluxe model, add 25%.
Estimated Value: Excellent: $120.00
　　　　　　　　 Very good: $100.00

Mossberg

Mossberg Model 35

Mossberg Model B
Caliber: 22 short, long, long rifle
Action: Bolt action; single shot
Magazine: None
Barrel: Blued; 22"
Sights: Open rear, bead front
Stock & Forearm: Plain wood semi-pistol grip stock & forearm
Approximate wt.: 5 lbs.
Comments: Made in the early 1930's.
Estimated Value: Excellent: $90.00
Very good: $75.00

Mossberg Model R
Caliber: 22 short, long, long rifle
Action: Bolt action; repeating
Magazine: Tubular; 14 long rifles, 16 longs, 20 shorts
Barrel: Blued; 24"
Sights: Open rear, bead front
Stock & Forearm: Walnut semi-pistol grip stock & forearm
Approximate wt.: 5 lbs.
Comments: Made in the early 1930's.
Estimated Value: Excellent: $120.00
Very good: $ 95.00

Mossberg Model 10
Caliber: 22 short, long, long rifle
Action: Bolt action; single shot
Magazine: None
Barrel: Blued; 22"
Sights: Open rear, bead front
Stock & Forearm: Walnut semi-pistol grip stock & forearm; swivels
Approximate wt.: 4 lbs.
Comments: Made from the early to mid 1930's. Takedown-type.
Estimated Value: Excellent: $90.00
Very good: $75.00

Mossberg Model 20
Similar to the Model 10 with a 24" barrel & grooved forearm. Made in the mid 1930's.
Estimated Value: Excellent: $95.00
Very good: $80.00

Mossberg Model 30
Similar to the Model 20 with peep rear sight & hooded ramp front sight. Made in mid 1930's.
Estimated Value: Excellent: $105.00
Very good: $ 85.00

Mossberg Model 40
Similar to the Model 30 with tubular magazine that holds 16 long rifles, 18 longs, 22 shorts; bolt action; repeating. Made in the mid 1930's.
Estimated Value: Excellent: $115.00
Very good: $ 95.00

Mossberg Model M
Caliber: 22 short, long, long rifle
Action: Bolt action; single shot; cocking piece
Magazine: None
Barrel: 20" round
Sights: Open rear, blade front
Stock & Forearm: Plain one-piece semi-pistol grip stock & tapered forearm
Approximate wt.: 4¼ lbs.
Comments: A boys' rifle made in the early 1930's.
Estimated Value: Excellent: $90.00
Very good: $75.00

Mossberg Model 14
Caliber: 22 short, long, long rifle
Action: Bolt action; single shot
Magazine: None
Barrel: Blued; 24"
Sights: Peep rear, hooded ramp front
Stock & Forearm: Plain one-piece semi-pistol grip stock & forearm; swivels
Approximate wt.: 5½ lbs.
Comments: Made in the mid 1930's.
Estimated Value: Excellent: $85.00
Very good: $70.00

Mossberg Model 34
Similar to the Model 14, made in the mid 1930's.
Estimated Value: Excellent: $90.00
Very good: $70.00

Mossberg Model 35
Caliber: 22 long rifle
Action: Bolt action; single shot
Magazine: None
Barrel: Blued; 26" heavy
Sights: Micrometer rear, hooded ramp front
Stock & Forearm: Plain walnut one-piece semi-pistol grip stock & forearm; cheekpiece; swivels
Approximate wt.: 8¼ lbs.
Comments: Made in the mid 1930's.
Estimated Value: Excellent: $130.00
Very good: $110.00

Mossberg Model 35A
Similar to the Model 35; target stock & sights. Made in the late 1930's.
Estimated Value: Excellent: $135.00
Very good: $115.00

Mossberg Model 35A-LS
Similar to the Model 35A with special Lyman sights.
Estimated Value: Excellent: $140.00
Very good: $120.00

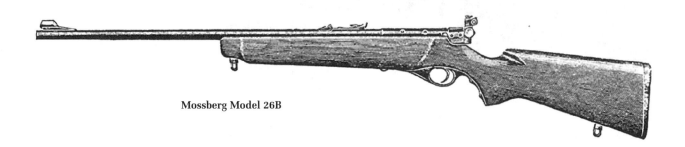

Mossberg Model 26B

Mossberg Model 25

Caliber: 22 short, long, long rifle
Action: Bolt action; single shot
Magazine: None
Barrel: Blued; 24"
Sights: Peep rear, hooded ramp front
Stock & Forearm: Plain walnut one-piece pistol grip stock & forearm; swivels
Approximate wt.: 5 lbs.
Comments: Made in the mid 1930's.
Estimated Value: Excellent: $80.00
 Very good: $65.00

Mossberg Model 25A

Similar to the Model 25 with higher quality finish & better wood. Made in the late 1930's.
Estimated Value: Excellent: $95.00
 Very good: $75.00

Mossberg Model 26B

Caliber: 22 short, long, long rifle
Action: Bolt action; single shot
Magazine: None
Barrel: Blued; 26"
Sights: Micrometer rear, hooded ramp front
Stock & Forearm: Plain one-piece semi-pistol grip stock & forearm; swivels
Approximate wt.: 5½ lbs.
Comments: Made in the late 1930's.
Estimated Value: Excellent: $90.00
 Very good: $70.00

Mossberg Model 26C

Similar to the 26 B without swivels or peep sight.
Estimated Value: Excellent: $80.00
 Very good: $65.00

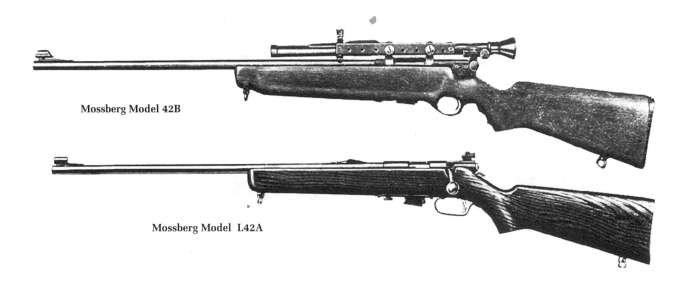

Mossberg Model 42B

Mossberg Model L42A

Mossberg Model 42

Caliber: 22 short, long, long rifle
Action: Bolt action; repeating
Magazine: 7-shot detachable
Barrel: Blued; 24"
Sights: Open rear, receiver peep, hooded ramp front
Stock & Forearm: Plain walnut one-piece semi-pistol grip stock & forearm; swivels
Approximate wt.: 5 lbs.
Comments: Made in the mid 1930's; takedown model.
Estimated Value: Excellent: $100.00
 Very good: $ 80.00

Mossberg Model 42A & L42A

Similar to the Model 42 but higher quality. L42A is left hand action. Made in the late 1930's.
Estimated Value: Excellent: $115.00
 Very good: $95.00

Mossberg Model 42B

An improved version of the Model 42 A with micrometer peep sight & 5-shot magazine. Made from the late 1930's to early 1940's.
Estimated Value: Excellent: $120.00
 Very good: $100.00

Mossberg Model 42 C

Mossberg Model 42 M

More modern version of the Model 42 with a 23" barrel; full-length; two-piece stock & forearm; cheekpiece; 7-shot magazine. Made from the early 1940's to early 1950's.

Estimated Value: Excellent: $110.00
               Very good: $ 90.00

Mossberg Model 42 C

Similar to the Model 42B without the peep sight.
Estimated Value: Excellent: $95.00
               Very good: $75.00

Mossberg Model 42 MB

Similar to the Model 42. Used as military training rifle in Great Britain in World War II; full stock.
Estimated Value: Excellent: $175.00
               Very good: $140.00

Mossberg Model L43

Mossberg Model 43, L43

Caliber: 22 long rifle
Action: Bolt action; repeating
Magazine: 7-shot detachable box
Barrel: Blued; 26"
Sights: Special Lyman sights
Stock & Forearm: Walnut one-piece semi-pistol grip stock & forearm; cheekpiece; swivels
Approximate wt.: 8¼ lbs.
Comments: Made in the late 1930's. L43 is left handed.
Estimated Value: Excellent: $120.00
               Very good: $100.00

Mossberg Model 44

Caliber: 22 short, long, long rifle
Action: Bolt action; repeating
Magazine: Tubular; 16 long rifles, 18 longs, 22 shorts
Barrel: Blued; 24"
Sights: Peep rear, hooded ramp front
Stock & Forearm: Plain walnut one-piece semi-pistol grip stock & forearm; swivels
Approximate wt.: 6 lbs.
Comments: Made in the mid 1930's.
Estimated Value: Excellent: $110.00
               Very good: $ 90.00

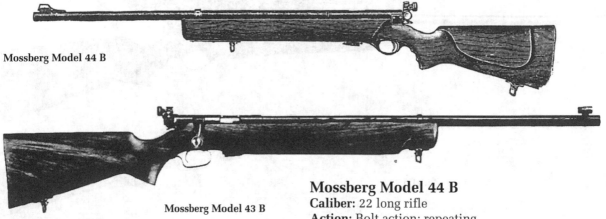

Mossberg Model 44 B

Mossberg Model 43 B

Mossberg Model 43 B

Similar to the Model 44 B with special Lyman sights.
Estimated Value: Excellent: $140.00
               Very good: $120.00

Mossberg Model 44 U.S.

Improved version of the Model 44 B. Made in the early 1930's to late 1940's; used as a training rifle for U.S. armed forces in World War II.
Estimated Value: Excellent: $160.00
               Very good: $130.00

Mossberg Model 44 B

Caliber: 22 long rifle
Action: Bolt action; repeating
Magazine: 7-shot detachable box
Barrel: 26" heavy barrel
Sights: Micrometer receiver, hooded front
Stock & Forearm: Plain one-piece semi-pistol grip stock & forearm; swivels; cheekpiece
Approximate wt.: 8 lbs.
Comments: Made in the late 1930's to early 1940's.
Estimated Value: Excellent: $130.00
               Very good: $110.00

Mossberg Model 35 B

Single shot version of the 44 B. Made in the 1930's.
Estimated Value: Excellent: $120.00
               Very good: $ 95.00

Mossberg Model 45

Mossberg Model L45 A

Mossberg Model 45 B

Mossberg Model 46

Mossberg Model 45
Caliber: 22 short, long, long rifle
Action: Bolt action; repeating
Magazine: Tubular; 15 long rifles, 18 longs, 22 shorts
Barrel: Blued; 24"
Sights: Peep rear, hooded ramp front
Stock & Forearm: Plain one-piece semi-pistol grip stock & forearm; swivels
Approximate wt.: 6¾ lbs.
Comments: Made in the mid 1930's.
Estimated Value: Excellent: $105.00
Very good: $85.00

Mossberg Model 45 C
Similar to the Model 45 without sights.
Estimated Value: Excellent: $90.00
Very good: $75.00

Mossberg Model 45 A & L45 A
Improved version of the Model 45, made in the late 1930's. L45A is left hand action.
Estimated Value: Excellent: $110.00
Very good: $ 90.00

Mossberg Model 45 AC
Similar to the Model 45 A without sights.
Estimated Value: Excellent: $100.00
Very good: $80.00

Mossberg Model 45 B
Similar to the Model 45 A with open rear sight. Made in the late 1930's.
Estimated Value: Excellent: $110.00
Very good: $85.00

Mossberg Model 46
Caliber: 22 short, long, long rifle
Action: Bolt action; repeating
Magazine: Tubular; 15 long rifles, 18 longs, 22 shorts
Barrel: Blued; 26"
Sights: Micrometer rear, hooded ramp front
Stock & Forearm: Plain one-piece semi-piece grip stock & forearm; cheekpiece; swivels
Approximate wt.: 7½ lbs.
Comments: Made in the mid 1930's.
Estimated Value: Excellent: $115.00
Very good: $ 95.00

Mossberg Model 46 C

A heavy barrel version of the Model 46.

| Estimated Value: | Excellent: | $120.00 |
| | Very good: | $100.00 |

Mossberg Model 46 A

An improved version of the Model 46; made in the late 1930's.

| Estimated Value: | Excellent: | $115.00 |
| | Very good: | $ 95.00 |

Mossberg Model 46 AC

Similar to the 46A with open rear sight.

| Estimated Value: | Excellent: | $100.00 |
| | Very good: | $80.00 |

Mossberg Model 46 A-LS & L46 A-LS

Similar to the Model 46 A with special Lyman sights. L46A-LS is left hand action.

| Estimated Value: | Excellent: | $120.00 |
| | Very good: | $ 100.00 |

Mossberg Model 46 B

Similar to the Model 46 A with open rear sight and receiver peep sight. Made in the late 1930's.

| Estimated Value: | Excellent: | $115.00 |
| | Very good: | $ 95.00 |

Mossberg Model 46 BT

A heavy barrel version of the Model 46 B. Made in the late 1930's.

| Estimated Value: | Excellent: | $120.00 |
| | Very good: | $ 100.00 |

Mossberg Model 46 M

Similar to the Model 46 with full-length two-piece forearm. Made about 1940 to the early 1950's.

| Estimated Value: | Excellent: | $115.00 |
| | Very good: | $ 95.00 |

Mossberg Model 346 K & 346 B

Caliber: 22 short, long, long rifle
Action: Bolt action; repeating
Magazine: Tubular; 20 long rifles, 23 longs, 30 shorts
Barrel: Blued; 26"
Sights: Micrometer rear, hooded front; peep sights (346B)
Stock & Forearm: Plain Monte Carlo one-piece pistol grip stock & lipped forearm; cheekpiece; swivels
Approximate wt.: 7 lbs.
Comments: Made from the late 1940's to mid 1950's.

| Estimated Value: | Excellent: | $120.00 |
| | Very good: | $ 100.00 |

Mossberg Model L46 A-LS

Mossberg Model 46 B

Mossberg Model 46 BT

Mossberg Model 46 M

Mossberg Model 346 K

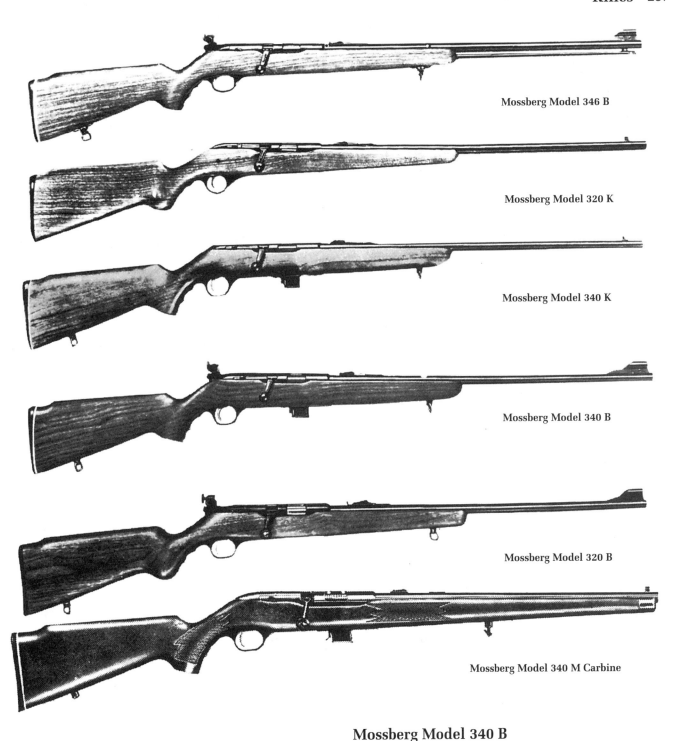

Mossberg Model 346 B

Mossberg Model 320 K

Mossberg Model 340 K

Mossberg Model 340 B

Mossberg Model 320 B

Mossberg Model 340 M Carbine

Mossberg Model 320 K
Single shot version of the Model 346 K. Weighs about 5¾ lbs. Discontinued about 1960.

| Estimated Value: | Excellent: | $100.00 |
| | Very good: | $ 80.00 |

Mossberg Model 340 K
Similar to the Model 346 K with 7-shot clip magazine.

| Estimated Value: | Excellent: | $95.00 |
| | Very good: | $75.00 |

Mossberg Model 340 B
Similar to the 346B with 7-shot clip magazine.

| Estimated Value: | Excellent: | $100.00 |
| | Very good: | $ 80.00 |

Mossberg Model 320 B
Similar to the 340K in single shot; auto safety. Made from about 1960 for 11 years.

| Estimated Value: | Excellent: | $95.00 |
| | Very good: | $75.00 |

Mossberg Model 340 M Carbine
Similar to the Model 340K with full-length forearm & 18" barrel. Made in the early 1970's.

| Estimated Value: | Excellent: | $120.00 |
| | Very good: | $100.00 |

Mossberg Model 342 K

Mossberg Model 342 K

Similar to the 340K with 18" barrel; hinged forearm for forward grip; side mounted swivels. Made from late 1950's to mid 1970's.

Estimated Value: Excellent: $110.00
                   Very good: $ 85.00

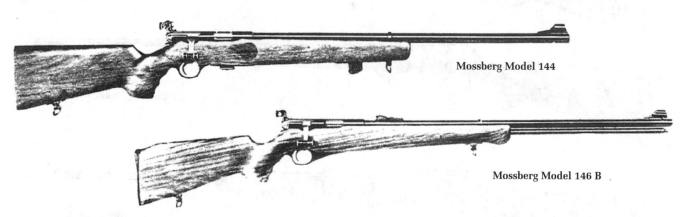

Mossberg Model 144

Mossberg Model 146 B

Mossberg Model 144

Caliber: 22 long rifle
Action: Bolt action; repeating
Magazine: 7-shot clip
Barrel: Blued; 26", heavy
Sights: Micrometer receiver, hooded front
Stock & Forearm: Walnut one-piece semi-pistol grip stock & forearm; hand rest; swivels
Approximate wt.: 8 lbs.
Comments: Made from the late 1940's to mid 1980's.
Estimated Value: Excellent: $180.00
                       Very good: $135.00

Mossberg Model 146 B

Caliber: 22 short, long, long rifle
Action: Bolt action; repeating
Magazine: Tubular; 20 long rifles, 23 longs, 30 shorts
Barrel: Blued; 26"
Sights: Micrometer receiver, hooded front
Stock & Forearm: Plain Monte Carlo one-piece pistol grip stock & lipped forearm; cheekpiece; swivels
Approximate wt.: 7 lbs.
Comments: Made from the late 1940's to mid 1950's.
Estimated Value: Excellent: $120.00
                       Very good: $100.00

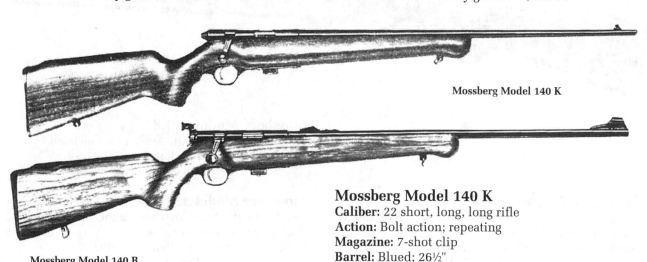

Mossberg Model 140 K

Mossberg Model 140 B

Mossberg Model 140 B

Similar to the 140 K with hooded ramp front sight, peep rear sight. Made in the late 1950's.

Estimated Value: Excellent: $110.00
                       Very good: $ 90.00

Mossberg Model 140 K

Caliber: 22 short, long, long rifle
Action: Bolt action; repeating
Magazine: 7-shot clip
Barrel: Blued; 26½"
Sights: Open rear, bead front
Stock & Forearm: Walnut Monte Carlo one-piece pistol grip stock & forearm; cheekpiece; swivels
Approximate wt.: 5¾ lbs.
Comments: Made in the mid 1950's.
Estimated Value: Excellent: $100.00
                       Very good: $ 80.00

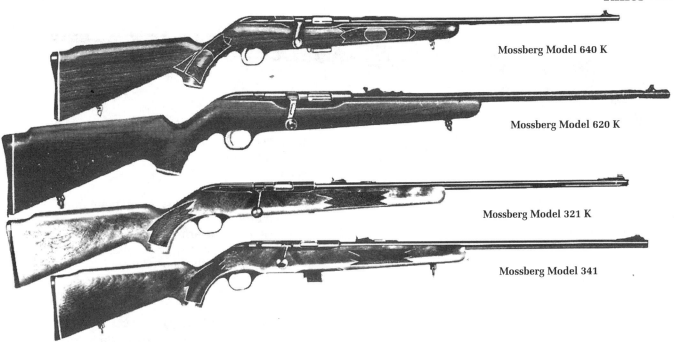

Mossberg Model 640 K

Mossberg Model 620 K

Mossberg Model 321 K

Mossberg Model 341

Mossberg Model 640 K
Caliber: 22 magnum
Action: Bolt action; repeating
Magazine: 5-shot box
Barrel: Blued; 24"
Sights: Open rear, bead front; adjustable
Stock & Forearm: Checkered walnut Monte Carlo one-piece pistol grip stock & forearm; swivels
Approximate wt.: 6 lbs.
Comments: Made from about 1960 to mid 1980's.
Estimated Value: Excellent: $125.00
Very good: $105.00

Mossberg Model 620 K
Similar to the 640 K in single shot. Discontinued in mid 1960's.
Estimated Value: Excellent: $100.00
Very good: $80.00

Mossberg Model 321 K
Caliber: 22 short, long, long rifle
Action: Bolt action; single shot
Magazine: None
Barrel: Blued; 24"
Sights: Open rear, ramp front
Stock & Forearm: Checkered Monte Carlo one-piece pistol grip stock & forearm
Approximate wt.: 6½ lbs.
Comments: Made from the early 1970's to early 1980's.
Estimated Value: Excellent: $85.00
Very good: $70.00

Mossberg Model 341
Similar to the 321 K with 7-shot clip magazine; swivels; bolt action; repeating; adjustable sights.
Estimated Value: Excellent: $100.00
Very good: $ 80.00

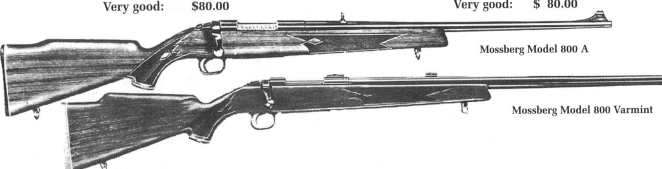

Mossberg Model 800 A

Mossberg Model 800 Varmint

Mossberg Model 800 A
Caliber: 308, 243, 22-250, 222 Rem.
Action: Bolt action; repeating
Magazine: 4-shot box
Barrel: Blued; 22"
Sights: Leaf rear, ramp front
Stock & Forearm: Checkered wood Monte Carlo one-piece pistol grip stock & forearm; swivels
Approximate wt.: 6½ lbs.
Comments: Made from late 1960's to the late 1970's.
Estimated Value: Excellent: $220.00
Very good: $175.00

Mossberg Model 800 Varmint
Similar to the 800 A with a 24" barrel and scope mounts. In 243 and 22-250 calibers.
Estimated Value: Excellent: $230.00
Very good: $185.00

Mossberg Model 800 Target
Similar to the 800 A with scope mounts and scope in 308, 243, 22-250 calibers. Made from late 1960's to early 1970's.
Estimated Value: Excellent: $250.00
Very good: $190.00

Mossberg Model 810

Mossberg Model 810

Caliber: 30-06, 7mm Rem. mag., 270 Win.
Action: Bolt action; repeating
Magazine: 4-shot detachable box
Barrel: Blued; 22"
Sights: Leaf rear, ramp front
Stock & Forearm: Checkered Monte Carlo one-piece pistol grip stock & forearm; swivels; recoil pad
Approximate wt.: 7½ to 8 lbs.
Comments: Add 7% for 7mm Rem. mag. Made from early to late 1970's.
Estimated Value: **Excellent:**   **$235.00**
                                  Very good: **$190.00**

Mossberg Model RM-7A

Caliber: 30-06
Action: Bolt action; repeating
Magazine: 4-shot rotary
Barrel: 22" round
Sights: Adjustable folding leaf rear, ramp front
Stock & Forearm: Checkered walnut one-piece pistol grip stock & forearm; fluted comb; recoil pad
Approximate wt.: 7½ lbs.
Comments: Made in the late 1970's.
Estimated Value: **Excellent:**   **$220.00**
                                  Very good: **$175.00**

Mossberg Model RM-7B

Similar to the Model RM-7A except: 7mm Rem. magnum caliber, 3-shot magazine, 24" barrel.
Estimated Value: **Excellent:**   **$235.00**
                                  Very good: **$190.00**

Mossberg Model 1500 Mountaineer

Mossberg Model 1700 Classic Hunter L/S

Mossberg Model 1500 Varmint

Mossberg Model 1500 Mountaineer

Caliber: 223, 22-250, 243, 270, 308, 30-06, 7mm magnum, 300 Win. magnum, 338 Win. magnum
Action: Bolt action, hammerless; repeating
Magazine: 5- or 6-shot box
Barrel: 22" or 24"
Sights: Available without or with adjustable rear, hooded ramp front
Stock & Forearm: Checkered walnut one-piece pistol grip stock & forearm; recoil pad on magnum
Approximate wt.: 7¾ lbs.
Comments: Produced from 1985 to 1988. Add 6% for magnum; Add 8% for sights.
Estimated Value: **Excellent:**   **$255.00**
                                  Very good: **$200.00**

Mossberg Model 1500 Varmint

Similar to the Model 1500 with a 24" heavy barrel in 223, 22-250 or 308 caliber; Monte Carlo stock; available in blued or parkerized finish. Discontinued late 1980's.
Estimated Value: **Excellent:**   **$320.00**
                                  Very good: **$250.00**

Mossberg Model 1550 Mountaineer

Similar to the Model 1500 with removable magazine, 22" barrel, in 243, 270, and 30-06 calibers; add 8% for sights. Discontinued late 1980's.
Estimated Value: **Excellent:**   **$275.00**
                                  Very good: **$215.00**

Mossberg Model 1700 Classic Hunter L/S

Similar to the Model 1500 with 22" barrel, removable magazine, lipped forearm, pistol grip cap & recoil pad, in calibers: 243, 270 and 30-06. Discontinued late 1980's.
Estimated Value: **Excellent:**   **$340.00**
                                  Very good: **$270.00**

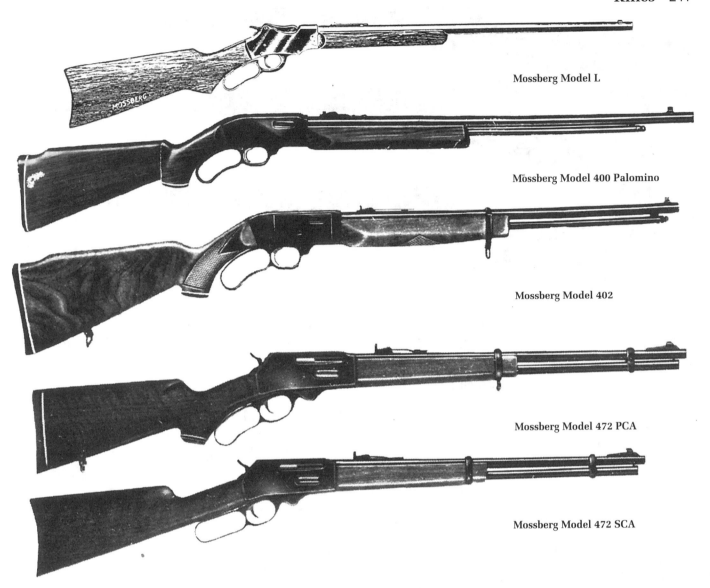

Mossberg Model L

Mossberg Model 400 Palomino

Mossberg Model 402

Mossberg Model 472 PCA

Mossberg Model 472 SCA

Mossberg Model L
Caliber: 22 short, long, long rifle
Action: Lever-action, falling block; single shot
Magazine: None
Barrel: Blued; 24"
Sights: Open rear, bead front
Stock & Forearm: Plain walnut semi-pistol grip stock &
    small forearm
Approximate wt.: 5 lbs.
Comments: Made from the late 1920's to early 1930's.
Estimated Value: **Excellent:**   **$285.00**
                  Very good: **$225.00**

Mossberg Model 400 Palomino
Caliber: 22 short, long, long rifle
Action: Lever-action, hammerless; repeating
Magazine: Tubular; 15 long rifles, 17 longs, 20 shorts
Barrel: Blued; 24"
Sights: Adjustable open rear, bead front
Stock & Forearm: Checkered walnut Monte Carlo pistol
    grip stock & forearm; barrel bands; swivels
Approximate wt.: 4¾ lbs.
Comments: Made in the early 1960's.
Estimated Value: **Excellent:**   **$120.00**
                  Very good: **$100.00**

Mossberg Model 402
Similar to the Model 400 with smaller capacity maga-
zine. Discontinued in the early 1970's.
Estimated Value: **Excellent:**   **$110.00**
                  Very good: **$ 90.00**

Mossberg Model 472 PCA, SCA; 479 PCA, SCA
Caliber: 30-30, 35 Rem.
Action: Lever-action; exposed hammer; repeating
Magazine: 6-shot tubular
Barrel: Blued; 20"
Sights: Adjustable rear, ramp front
Stock & Forearm: Plain pistol grip stock & forearm; bar-
    rel band; swivels; or straight grip stock (SCA)
Approximate wt.: 7½ lbs.
Comments: Sold first as the 472 Series, then 479 Series.
Estimated Value: **Excellent:**   **$175.00**
                  Very good: **$140.00**

Mossberg Model 472 PRA

Mossberg Model 472 Brush Gun

Mossberg Model 479

Mossberg Model 472 Brush Gun
Similar to the Model 472 PCA with 18" barrel; straight stock; 5-shot magazine.
Estimated Value: **Excellent:** $180.00
                    Very good: $145.00

Mossberg Model 479
Caliber: 30-30 Win.
Action: Lever action, exposed hammer, repeating
Magazine: 5-shot tubular
Barrel: 20"
Sights: Adjustable open rear, beaded ramp front; drilled and tapped for scope
Stock & Forearm: Hardwood semi-pistol grip stock and forearm; barrel band
Approximate wt.: 6¾ lbs.
Comments: Produced from the early to mid 1980's.
Estimated Value: **Excellent:** $200.00
                    Very good: $150.00

Mossberg Model 472 PRA, SBA
Similar to the 472 PCA with 24" barrel; hooded front sight. Discontinued in the late 1970's.
Estimated Value: **Excellent:** $180.00
                    Very good: $145.00

Mossberg Model K
Caliber: 22 short, long, long rifle
Action: Slide action; hammerless; repeating
Magazine: Tubular; 14 long rifles, 16 longs, 20 shorts
Barrel: Blued; 22"
Sights: Open rear, bead front
Stock & Forearm: Plain walnut straight grip stock & grooved slide handle
Approximate wt.: 5 lbs.
Comments: Made from the early 1920's to early 1930's; takedown model.
Estimated Value: **Excellent:** $175.00
                    Very good: $140.00

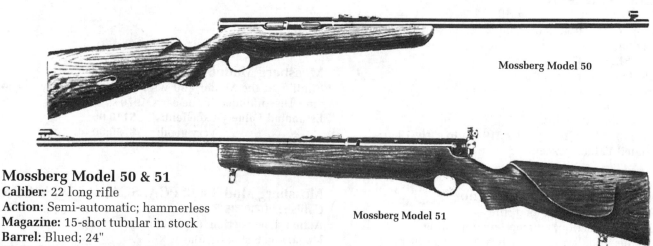

Mossberg Model 50

Mossberg Model 51

Mossberg Model 50 & 51
Caliber: 22 long rifle
Action: Semi-automatic; hammerless
Magazine: 15-shot tubular in stock
Barrel: Blued; 24"
Sights: Open rear, hooded ramp front; peep sights, swivels (Model 51)
Stock & Forearm: Walnut one-piece semi-pistol grip stock & forearm
Approximate wt.: 7 lbs.
Comments: Made from the late 1930's to early 1940's.
Estimated Value: **Excellent:** $120.00
                   Very good: $100.00

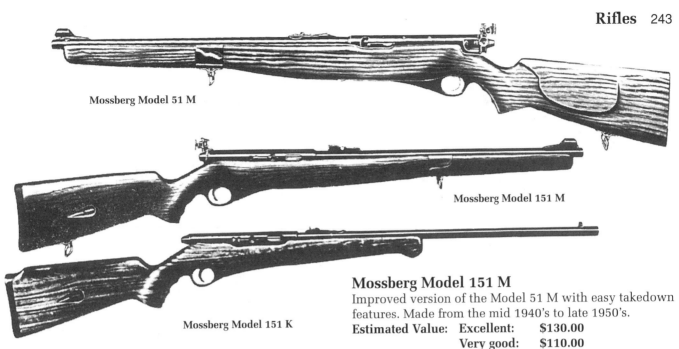

Mossberg Model 51 M

Mossberg Model 151 M

Mossberg Model 151 K

Mossberg Model 151 M
Improved version of the Model 51 M with easy takedown features. Made from the mid 1940's to late 1950's.
Estimated Value: **Excellent:**   **$130.00**
Very good: **$110.00**

Mossberg Model 51 M
Similar to the Model 51 with full-length, two-piece forearm & 20" barrel. Made from the late 1930's to mid 1940's.
Estimated Value: **Excellent:**   **$125.00**
Very good: **$100.00**

Mossberg Model 151 K
Similar to the 151 M with Monte Carlo stock; standard length lipped forearm; 24" barrel; no peep sight or swivels. Made in early 1950's.
Estimated Value: **Excellent:**   **$135.00**
Very good: **$110.00**

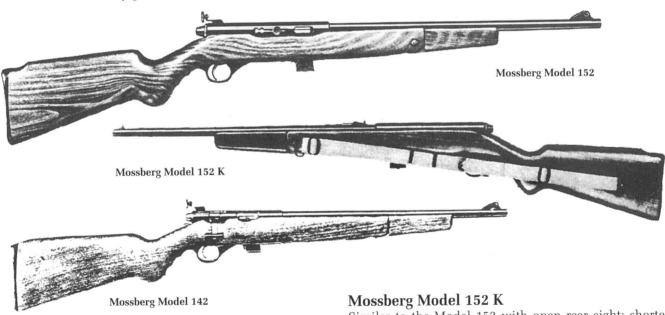

Mossberg Model 152

Mossberg Model 152 K

Mossberg Model 142

Mossberg Model 152
Caliber: 22 long rifle
Action: Semi-automatic
Magazine: 7-shot detachable box
Barrel: Blued; 18"
Sights: Peep rear, military front
Stock & Forearm: Plain one-piece semi-pistol grip stock & hinged forearm for forward grip; side mounted swivels
Approximate wt.: 5 lbs.
Comments: Made from the late 1940's to late 1950's.
Estimated Value: **Excellent:**   **$120.00**
Very good: **$ 95.00**

Mossberg Model 152 K
Similar to the Model 152 with open rear sight; shorter barrel. Made in the 1950's.
Estimated Value: **Excellent:**   **$115.00**
Very good: **$ 95.00**

Mossberg Model 142
Similar to the Model 152 in bolt action; available in short, long or long rifle; with peep sight.
Estimated Value: **Excellent:**   **$100.00**
Very good: **$ 80.00**

Mossberg Model 142 K
Similar to the Model 142 with open rear sight.
Estimated Value: **Excellent:**   **$90.00**
Very good: **$75.00**

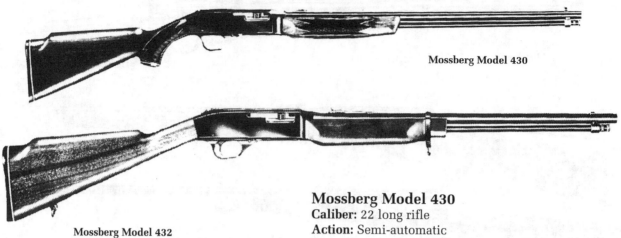

Mossberg Model 430

Mossberg Model 432

Mossberg Model 351 C (Carbine)

Mossberg Model 351 K

Mossberg Model 350 K

Mossberg Model 430
Caliber: 22 long rifle
Action: Semi-automatic
Magazine: 18-shot tubular
Barrel: Blued; 24"
Sights: Open rear, bead front
Stock & Forearm: Checkered walnut Monte Carlo pistol grip stock & forearm
Approximate wt.: 6¼ lbs.
Comments: Made in the early 1970's.
Estimated Value:　Excellent:　$100.00
　　　　　　　　　　Very good:　$ 80.00

Mossberg Model 432
Similar to the Model 430 with straight grip stock; barrel band; smaller capacity magazine.
Estimated Value:　Excellent:　$110.00
　　　　　　　　　　Very good:　$ 90.00

Mossberg Model 351 C (Carbine)
Similar to the 351K with 18½" barrel; barrel bands; swivels. Made from the mid 1960's to early 1970's.
Estimated Value:　Excellent:　$100.00
　　　　　　　　　　Very good:　$ 80.00

Mossberg Model 351 K
Caliber: 22 long rifle
Action: Semi-automatic
Magazine: 15-shot tubular, in stock
Barrel: Blued; 24"
Sights: Open rear, bead front
Stock & Forearm: Walnut Monte Carlo one-piece semi-pistol grip stock and forearm
Approximate wt.: 6 lbs.
Comments: Made from about 1960 to 1970.
Estimated Value:　Excellent:　$95.00
　　　　　　　　　　Very good:　$75.00

Mossberg Model 350 K
Caliber: 22 long rifle
Action: Semi-automatic
Magazine: 7-shot clip
Barrel: Blued; 23½"
Sights: Open rear, bead front
Stock & Forearm: Walnut Monte Carlo one-piece semi-pistol grip stock & forearm
Approximate wt.: 6 lbs.
Comments: Made from the late 1950's to early 1970's.
Estimated Value:　Excellent:　$110.00
　　　　　　　　　　Very good:　$ 90.00

Mossberg Model 377 Plinkster

Mossberg Model 352 K Carbine

Mossberg Model 377 Plinkster
Caliber: 22 long rifle
Action: Semi-automatic; hammerless
Magazine: 15-shot tubular; stock load
Barrel: 20" round
Sights: None; 4X scope standard
Stock & Forearm: Structural foam; one-piece Monte Carlo pistol grip stock & forearm; thumb hole
Approximate wt.: 6¼ lbs.
Comments: Produced from the late 1970's to mid 1980's.
Estimated Value: Excellent: $110.00
Very good: $ 95.00

Mossberg Model 352 K Carbine
Caliber: 22 long rifle
Action: Semi-automatic
Magazine: 7-shot clip
Barrel: Blued; 18½"
Sights: Open rear, bead front
Stock & Forearm: Walnut Monte Carlo one-piece pistol grip stock & forearm; swivels; hinged forearm
Approximate wt.: 5 lbs.
Comments: Made from the late 1950's to early 1970's.
Estimated Value: Excellent: $100.00
Very good: $ 80.00

Mossberg Model 353
Similar to the 352 K except: 18" barrel, adjustable sight. Made from the early 1970's to mid 1980's.
Estimated Value: Excellent: $115.00
Very good: $ 90.00

Musketeer

Musketeer Mauser

Musketeer Mauser
Caliber: 243, 25-06, 270, 264 mag., 308, 30-06, 7mm mag., 300 mag.
Action: FN Mauser bolt action
Magazine: 5-shot, 3-shot magnum
Barrel: Blued; 24"
Sights: Leaf rear, hooded ramp front
Stock & Forearm: Checkered walnut Monte Carlo one-piece pistol grip stock & forearm
Approximate wt.: 7¼ lbs.
Comments: Made from the 1960's to the early 1970's.
Estimated Value: Excellent: $320.00
Very good: $250.00

Musketeer Carbine
Same as Musketeer Mauser except shorter barrel.
Estimated Value: Excellent: $300.00
Very good: $240.00

New England

New England Handi-Rifle
Caliber: 223 Rem., 22 Hornet, 22-250, 30-30 Win., 243 Win., 270 Win., 30-06, 45-70 Gov't
Action: Break open top release lever; exposed hammer
Magazine: None; single shot
Barrel: Blued; 22"
Sights: Ramp front; adjustable folding rear, tapped for scope mounts; calibers 223 Rem., 243 Win., & 30-06 have no sights, they are equipped with scope mounts
Stock & Forearm: Hardwood, walnut finish, pistol grip, Monte Carlo or plain smooth stock & lipped forearm
Approximate wt.: 7 lbs.
Comments: Introduced in 1989. Add 10% for Monte Carlo stock.
Estimated Value: New (retail): $205.00
Excellent: $155.00
Very good: $120.00

New England Handi-Gun Combination
Same as the Handi-Rifle except any combination of rifle or shotgun barrels are available to be used interchangeably. Shotgun barrels have brass bead front sight with blued or nickel finish (add 10%); 22" barrel in 12 or 20 gauge. Prices are for rifle & shotgun barrel combinations. Introduced in 1989.
Estimated Value: New (retail): $285.00
Excellent: $215.00
Very good: $170.00

New Haven

New Haven Model 453 T
Caliber: 22 short, long, long rifle
Action: Semi-automatic; hammerless
Magazine: 7-shot clip
Barrel: Blued; 18"
Sights: Open rear, bead front
Stock & Forearm: Plain one-piece Monte Carlo pistol grip stock & forearm
Approximate wt.: 5½ lbs.
Comments: Introduced in the late 1970's.
Estimated Value: Excellent: **$100.00**
　　　　　　　　Very good: **$ 80.00**

New Haven Model 453 TS
Similar to the Model 453 T with a 4X scope.
Estimated Value: Excellent: **$120.00**
　　　　　　　　Very good: **$100.00**

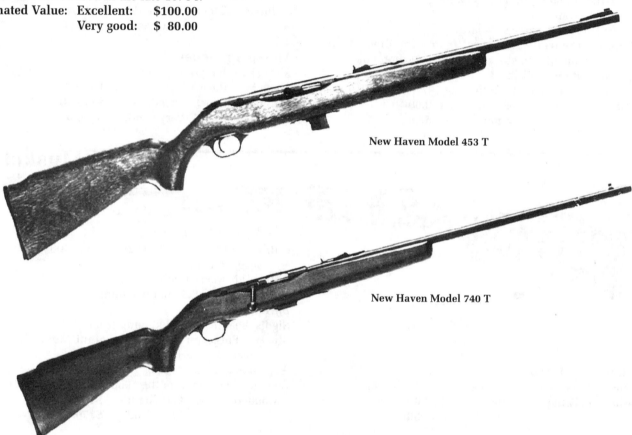

New Haven Model 453 T

New Haven Model 740 T

New Haven Model 679
Caliber: 30-30 Win.
Action: Lever-action; exposed hammer; repeating
Magazine: 5-shot tubular
Barrel: Blued; 20"
Sights: Open rear, ramp front
Stock & Forearm: Plain birch semi-pistol grip stock & forearm; barrel band
Approximate wt.: 6¾ lbs.
Comments: Made from the late 1970's to early 1980's.
Estimated Value: Excellent: **$180.00**
　　　　　　　　Very good: **$145.00**

New Haven Model 740 T
Caliber: 22 Win. mag.
Action: Bolt action; hammerless; repeating
Magazine: 5-shot clip
Barrel: Blued; 26"
Sights: Open rear, blade front
Stock & Forearm: Plain birch one-piece Monte Carlo pistol grip stock & forearm
Approximate wt.: 6½ lbs.
Comments: Introduced in the late 1970's.
Estimated Value: Excellent: **$95.00**
　　　　　　　　Very good: **$75.00**

New Haven Model 740 TS
Similar to the Model 740 T with 4X scope.
Estimated Value: Excellent: **$110.00**
　　　　　　　　Very good: **$ 90.00**

Newton

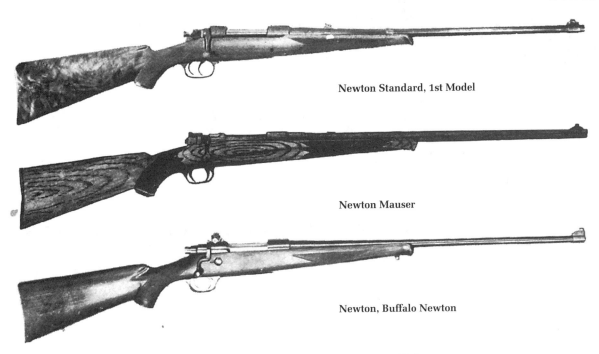

Newton Standard, 1st Model

Newton Mauser

Newton, Buffalo Newton

Newton Standard, 1st Model
Caliber: 22, 256, 280, 30-06, 30 Newton, 35 Newton
Action: Bolt action; double set trigger
Magazine: 5-shot box
Barrel: Blued; 24"
Sights: Open rear, ramp front
Stock & Forearm: Checkered wood pistol grip stock & forearm
Approximate wt.: 7½ lbs.
Comments: Made for a short time before World War I.
Estimated Value: Excellent: $750.00
                        Very good: $600.00

Newton Standard, 2nd Model
Very similar to 1st Model with improved action. Made to about 1920's.
Estimated Value: Excellent: $725.00
                        Very good: $625.00

Newton, Buffalo Newton
Similar to the 2nd Model made from the early 1920's to early 1930's.
Estimated Value: Excellent: $675.00
                        Very good: $540.00

Newton Mauser
Caliber: 256
Action: Mauser-type bolt action; reversed double set trigger
Magazine: 5-shot box
Barrel: Blued; 24"
Sights: Open rear, ramp front
Stock & Forearm: Checkered wood pistol grip stock & forearm
Approximate wt.: 7 lbs.
Comments: Made in the early 1920's.
Estimated Value: Excellent: $650.00
                        Very good: $520.00

Noble

Noble Model 33

Noble Model 33A
Similar to the Model 33 with a wood stock and grooved slide handle. Made until the mid 1950's.
Estimated Value: Excellent: $120.00
                        Very good: $100.00

Noble Model 33
Caliber: 22 short, long, long rifle
Action: Slide action; hammerless; repeating
Magazine: Tubular; 15 long rifles, 17 longs, 21 shorts
Barrel: Blued; 24"
Sights: Open rear, blade front
Stock & Forearm: Semi-pistol grip tenite stock & slide handle
Approximate wt.: 6 lbs.
Comments: Made from the late 1940's to early 1950's.
Estimated Value: Excellent: $110.00
                        Very good: $ 90.00

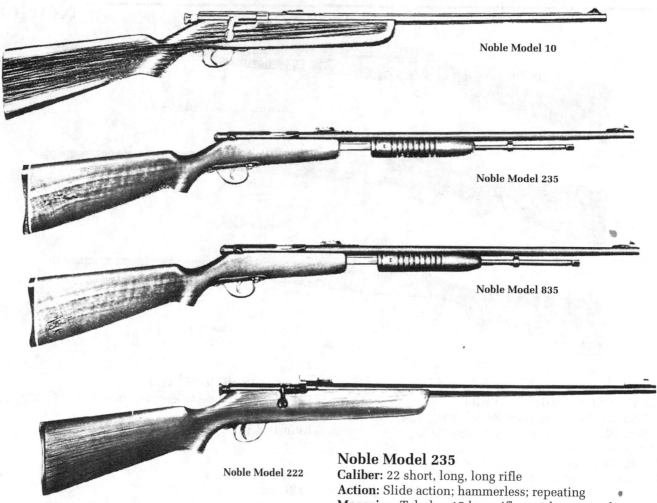

Noble Model 10

Noble Model 235

Noble Model 835

Noble Model 222

Noble Model 10

Caliber: 22 short, long, long rifle
Action: Bolt action; single shot
Magazine: None
Barrel: Blued; 24"
Sights: Open rear, bead front
Stock & Forearm: Walnut one-piece semi-pistol grip stock & forearm
Approximate wt.: 4 lbs.
Comments: Made from the middle to late 1950's.
Estimated Value: **Excellent:** $75.00
                    Very good: $65.00

Noble Model 20

Similar to the Model 10 with 22" barrel; slightly curved buttplate; manual cocking device. Made from the late 1950's to early 1960's.
Estimated Value: **Excellent:** $85.00
                    Very good: $70.00

Noble Model 235

Caliber: 22 short, long, long rifle
Action: Slide action; hammerless; repeating
Magazine: Tubular; 15 long rifles, 17 longs, 21 shorts
Barrel: Blued; 24"
Sights: Open rear, ramp front
Stock & Forearm: Wood semi-pistol grip stock & grooved slide handle
Approximate wt.: 5½ lbs.
Comments: Made from the early 1950's to the early 1970's.
Estimated Value: **Excellent:** $100.00
                    Very good: $ 80.00

Noble Model 835

Similar to the Model 235. Made in the early 1970's.
Estimated Value: **Excellent:** $110.00
                    Very good: $ 90.00

Nobel Model 222

Caliber: 22 short, long, long rifle
Action: Bolt action; single shot; manual cocking
Magazine: None
Barrel: Blued; 22"
Sights: Peep or "V" notch rear, ramp front
Stock & Forearm: Wood one-piece semi-pistol grip stock & forearm
Approximate wt.: 5 lbs.
Comments: Made from the late 1950's to early 1970's.
Estimated Value: **Excellent:** $80.00
                    Very good: $65.00

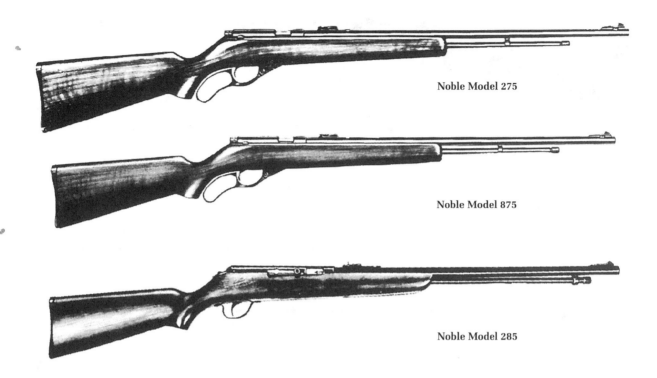

Noble Model 275

Noble Model 875

Noble Model 285

Noble Model 275 & 875

Caliber: 22 short, long, long rifle
Action: Lever-action; hammerless; repeating
Magazine: Tubular; 15 long rifles, 17 longs, 21 shorts
Barrel: Blued; 24"
Sights: Open rear, ramp front
Stock & Forearm: Wood one-piece semi-pistol grip stock & forearm
Approximate wt.: 5½ lbs.
Comments: Made from the late 1950's to early 1970's (Model 275); early to mid 1970's (Model 875).
Estimated Value: Excellent: $125.00
Very good: $100.00

Noble Model 285 & 885

Caliber: 22 long rifle
Action: Semi-automatic
Magazine: 15-shot tubular
Barrel: Blued; 22"
Sights: Open adjustable rear, blade front
Stock & Forearm: Wood one-piece semi-pistol grip stock & forearm
Approximate wt.: 5½ lbs.
Comments: Made from the early to mid 1970's.
Estimated Value: Excellent: $120.00
Very good: $100.00

Pedersen

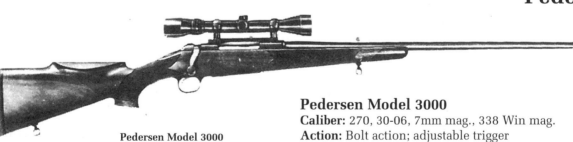

Pedersen Model 3000

Pedersen Model 3000

Caliber: 270, 30-06, 7mm mag., 338 Win mag.
Action: Bolt action; adjustable trigger
Magazine: 3-shot box
Barrel: Blued; 22", 24"
Sights: None
Stock & Forearm: Checkered walnut one-piece pistol grip stock & forearm; cheekpiece; swivels
Approximate wt.: 6¾ lbs.
Comments: Made in three grades during the 1970's.
Estimated Value:

	Grade I	Grade II	Grade III
Excellent:	$865.00	$670.00	$540.00
Very good:	$675.00	$535.00	$430.00

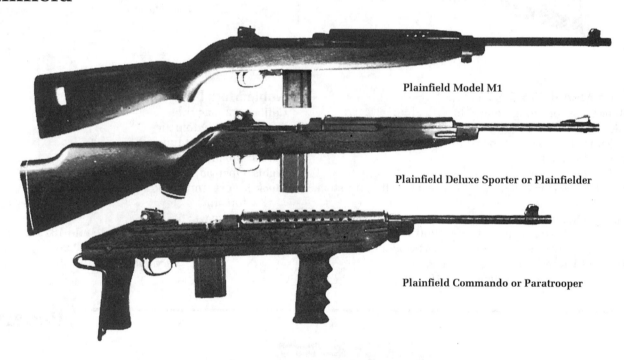

Pedersen Model 4700

Pedersen Model 4700
Caliber: 30-30, 35 Rem.
Action: Lever-action; exposed hammer; repeating
Magazine: 5-shot tubular
Barrel: Blued; 24"
Sights: Open rear, hooded ramp front
Stock & Forearm: Walnut pistol grip stock & short forearm; barrel band; swivels
Approximate wt.: 7½ lbs.
Comments: Made during the 1970's.
Estimated Value: Excellent: $270.00
                       Very good: $215.00

Plainfield

Plainfield Model M1

Plainfield Deluxe Sporter or Plainfielder

Plainfield Commando or Paratrooper

Plainfield Model M1
Caliber: 30 M1, 223 (5.7mm)
Action: Semi-automatic, gas operated
Magazine: 15-shot detachable clip
Barrel: Blued or stainless steel; 18"
Sights: Open adjustable rear, gold beaded ramp front
Stock & Forearm: Wood one-piece semi-pistol grip stock & forearm; slot in stock; metal ventilated hand guard
Approximate wt.: 6 lbs.
Comments: Made from about 1960 to late 1970's. Reintroduced in the late 1970's by Iver Johnson. See Iver Johnson; add 30% for stainless steel.
Estimated Value: Excellent: $200.00
                       Very good: $160.00

Plainfield Model M1 Sporter
Similar to the M1 Carbine with a wood hand guard & no slot in the stock. See Iver Johnson.
Estimated Value: Excellent: $210.00
                       Very good: $170.00

Plainfield Deluxe Sporter or Plainfielder
Similar to the Sporter with a checkered walnut Monte Carlo pistol grip stock & forearm.
Estimated Value: Excellent: $220.00
                       Very good: $175.00

Plainfield Commando or Paratrooper
Similar to the M1 Carbine with pistol grip at rear & at forearm; telescoping wire shoulder stock. Add 30% for stainless steel. See Iver Johnson.
Estimated Value: Excellent: $235.00
                       Very good: $190.00

Remington

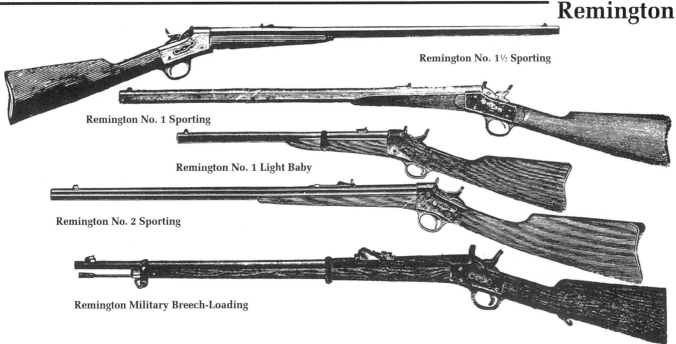

Remington No. 1½ Sporting

Remington No. 1 Sporting

Remington No. 1 Light Baby

Remington No. 2 Sporting

Remington Military Breech-Loading

Remington Military Breech-Loading
Caliber: C.F. 43 Spanish, 43 Egyptian, 50-70 Government, 58 Berdan. Early models used rim fire cartridges. Models for center fire cartridges produced after 1872.
Action: Single shot; rolling block with single trigger; visible hammer
Magazine: None
Barrel: 30" to 36" round
Sights: Military (post front and folding leaf rear)
Stock & Forearm: Plain walnut straight stock & forearm; long forearm with ram rod; steel buttplate on stock
Approximate wt.: 8 to 11 lbs.
Comments: Made from about 1867 to 1902 (large number sold to Egypt, France & Spain) & sold commercially in U.S.A. Some are unmarked; some have Arabic marked barrels & some marked Remington's.
Estimated Value: Excellent: $200.00
  Very good: $175.00

Remington No. 1 Sporting
Caliber: Early guns for rim fire 50-70, 44 long & extra long or 46 long & extra long. After 1872 made for centerfire 40-50, 40-70, 44-77, 45-70, or 45 sporting cartridge.
Action: Single shot; rolling block with single trigger; visible hammer
Magazine: None
Barrel: 28" or 30" tapered octagon
Sights: Sporting front, folding leaf rear
Stock & Forearm: Plain walnut straight grip stock with flanged-top steel buttplate & short plain walnut forearm with thin round front
Approximate wt.: 8½ to 12 lbs.
Comments: Made from about 1868 to 1902.
Estimated Value: Excellent: $400.00
  Very good: $320.00

Remington No. 1 Light Baby Carbine
Caliber: 44-40
Action: Single-shot; rolling block with single trigger; visible hammer
Magazine: None
Barrel: 20", light round
Sights: Pointed post front, military folding leaf rear
Stock & Forearm: Plain oiled walnut straight stock with metal buttplate & short forearm; barrel band
Approximate wt.: 5¾ lbs.
Comments: Made from about 1892 to 1902.
Estimated Value: Excellent: $420.00
  Very good: $330.00

Remington No. 1½ Sporting
Similar to No. 1 Sporting Rifle except: lighter action, stocks & smaller caliber barrels; approximate wt. 5½ to 7 lbs.; made in following pistol calibers: rim fire 22 short, long & extra long; 25 Stevens & 25 longs; 32 or 38 long & extra long; center fire Winchester 32-20; 38-40; or 44-40; barrel lengths 24", 26", 28", or 30". Made from about 1869 to 1902.
Estimated Value: Excellent: $375.00
  Very good: $300.00

Remington No. 2 Sporting
Caliber: Early models were for rim fire 22, 25, 32 or 38. Later models for center fire 22, 25-21, 25-25, 25-20, 32 long, 38 long or 38-40
Action: Single-shot; rolling block
Magazine: None
Barrel: 24" to 30" lightweight; octagon
Sights: Bead front sight; sporting adjustable rear
Stock & Forearm: Plain, oil-finish, walnut, straight grip stock & lipped forearm
Approximate wt.: 5 to 6 lbs.
Comments: Made from about 1873 to 1902
Estimated Value: Excellent: $350.00
  Very good: $290.00

Remington No. 5 1897 Model Military

Remington No. 5 1897 Carbine
Caliber: 7mm
Action: Single shot; rolling block; ornance steel; smokeless powder action with case hardened steel frame; visible hammer
Magazine: None
Barrel: 20" round, smokeless steel barrel
Sights: Post front, military rear
Stock & Forearm: Plain straight grip, oiled walnut, two-piece stock & forearm; steel buttplate; short forearm; barrel band; hand guard on top of barrel
Approximate wt.: 5 lbs.
Comments: Made from about 1897 to 1906.
Estimated Value: Excellent: $340.00
 Very good: $270.00

Remington No. 5 1897 Model Military
Caliber: 7mm, 30 Government
Action: Single-shot; rolling block; smokeless powder action with case hardened frame; visible hammer
Magazine: None
Barrel: 30" light round tapered barrel
Sights: Post front, folding leaf rear
Stock & Forearm: Plain straight grip oiled walnut, two-piece, full stock with steel buttplate & capped forearm; two barrel bands; hand guard on top of barrel
Approximate wt.: 8½ lbs.
Comments: Made from about 1897 to 1906.
Estimated Value: Excellent: $300.00
 Very good: $225.00

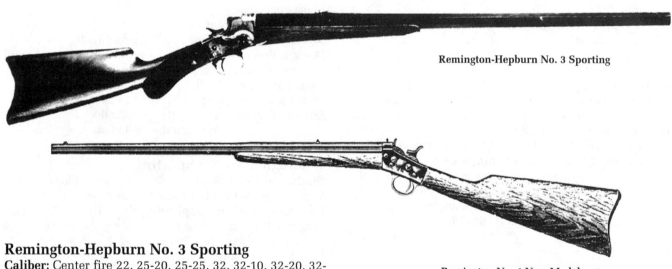

Remington-Hepburn No. 3 Sporting

Remington No. 4 New Model

Remington-Hepburn No. 3 Sporting
Caliber: Center fire 22, 25-20, 25-25, 32, 32-10, 32-20, 32-40, 38, 38-40, 38-50, 38-55, 40-60, 40-65, 40-82, 45-70 Government or 45-90. Also made by order for 40-50, 40-70, 40-90 or 44-77 bottle neck Remington, 45-90, 45-105 or 50-90 Sharps & 50-70 Government.
Action: Hepburn drop block; side-lever opens & closes action; single-shot with low visible hammer; early models with single trigger; later models with single or double set triggers
Magazine: None
Barrel: 28" to 32" round, octagon or half octagon
Sights: Blade front; sporting rear adjustable for elevation
Stock & Forearm: Plain straight grip or checkered pistol grip, oiled wood stock with steel buttplate & matching short forearm
Approximate wt.: 8 to 12 lbs.
Comments: Made from about 1880 to 1906.
Estimated Value: Excellent: $750.00
 Very good: $600.00

Remington No. 4 New Model
Caliber: Rim fire only in 22 short, long and long rifle, 25 Stevens or 32 long
Action: Single-shot; rolling block; light short action with automatic shell ejector; visible hammer
Magazine: None
Barrel: 22½" light octagon in 22 & 25 caliber; 24" in 32 caliber; round barrel after about 1931
Sights: Bead front, plain "V" notch rear
Stock & Forearm: Plain varnished, two-piece straight grip stock & forearm; short round front forearm
Approximate wt.: 4¼ lbs.
Comments: Made from about 1891 to 1934.
Estimated Value: Excellent: $250.00
 Very good: $200.00

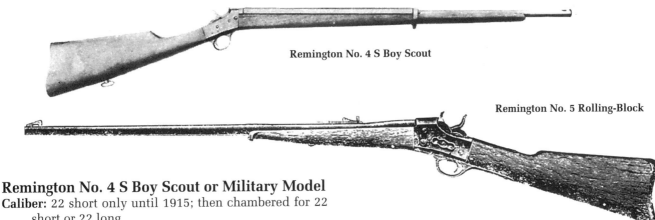

Remington No. 4 S Boy Scout

Remington No. 5 Rolling-Block

Remington No. 4 S Boy Scout or Military Model

Caliber: 22 short only until 1915; then chambered for 22 short or 22 long

Action: Single-shot; case hardened No. 4 rolling-block action; visible hammer

Magazine: None

Barrel: 28" medium, round barrel

Sights: Blade front; open "v" notch rear adjustable for elevation

Stock & Forearm: Musket-style, oiled walnut, one-piece, full-length stock & forearm with steel buttplate & one barrel band; bayonet lug; hand guard on barrel

Approximate wt.: 5 lbs.

Comments: Called Boy Scout model from 1913 to 1915; Renamed Military Model about 1916. Made from about 1913 to 1932.

Estimated Value: Excellent: $500.00
Very good: $420.00

Remington No. 5 Rolling-Block

Caliber: 7mm Mauser, 30-30 or 30-40 Krag

Action: New Ordnance steel, single-shot; rolling block; smokeless powder action with case hardened frame

Magazine: None

Barrel: 28"-30"; light steel round barrel

Sights: Blade front, Rocky Mountain rear

Stock & Forearm: Plain walnut, two-piece straight grip stock & forearm; steel buttplate; lipped forearm

Approximate wt.: 7¼ lbs.

Comments: Made from about 1896 to 1906.

Estimated Value: Excellent: $350.00
Very good: $280.00

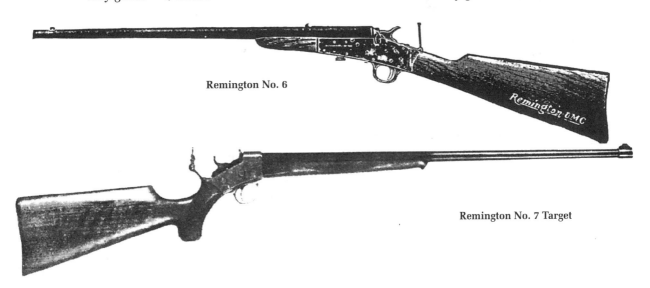

Remington No. 6

Remington No. 7 Target

Remington No. 6

Caliber: 22 short, long, long rifle, 32 short & long RF

Action: Single-shot; rolling-block; visible hammer **Magazine:** None

Barrel: 20" round tapered barrel

Sights: Bead front; open rear; also tang peep sight available

Stock & Forearm: Plain walnut straight grip stock & forearm; steel buttplate

Approximate wt.: 4 lbs.

Comments: Made from about 1902 to 1934.

Estimated Value: Excellent: $225.00
Very good: $180.00

Remington No. 7 Target

Caliber: 22 long rifle, 32 MRF or 25 Stevens RF

Action: Single shot; rolling block; visible hammer

Magazine: None

Barrel: 24", 26" 28"; half-octagon barrel

Sights: Bead front, adjustable dovetail rear

Stock & Forearm: Checkered walnut pistol grip stock & forearm; rubber buttplate; lipped forearm

Approximate wt.: 7 lbs.

Comments: Made from about 1904 to 1906.

Estimated Value: Excellent: $700.00
Very good: $520.00

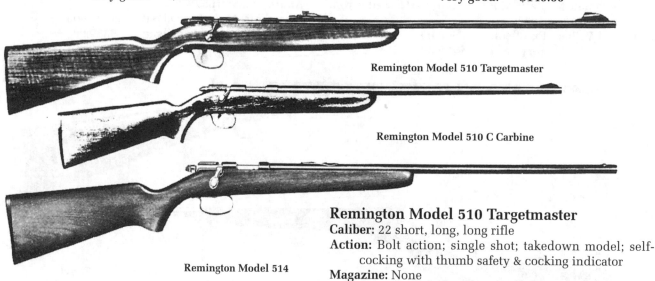

Remington Model 33

Remington Model 41

Remington Model 41

Caliber: 22 short, long, long rifle 22 WRF
Action: Bolt action; single-shot; exposed knurled cocking-piece
Magazine: None
Barrel: 27" round
Sights: Bead or hooded ramp front sight, open rear adjustable for elevation or peep rear sight
Stock & Forearm: Plain one-piece pistol grip stock & forearm; hard rubber buttplate
Approximate wt.: 5 lbs.
Comments: Made from about 1936 to 1940.
Estimated Value: **Excellent:** $135.00
Very good: $110.00

Remington Model 33

Caliber: 22 short, long, long rifle
Action: Single-shot; bolt action; takedown model; exposed knurled cocking-piece
Magazine: None
Barrel: 24" round
Sights: Bead front, open rear, adjustable for elevation
Stock & Forearm: Plain varnished walnut one-piece pistol grip stock & forearm
Approximate wt.: 4 lbs.
Comments: Made from about 1931 to 1936; finger grooves added to forearm in 1934.
Estimated Value: **Excellent:** $130.00
Very good: $105.00

Remington Model 33 NRA Junior Target

Same as Model 33 except: post front sight; reep rear sight; equipped with 1" leather sling; swivels; approximate wt. 4½ lbs.
Estimated Value: **Excellent:** $170.00
Very good: $140.00

Remington Model 510 Targetmaster

Remington Model 510 C Carbine

Remington Model 514

Remington Model 514 & 514 BR

Caliber: 22 short, long, long rifle
Action: Bolt action; single-shot; self-cocking
Magazine: None
Barrel: 21" (514 BR) or 24" light round
Sights: Sporting or target sights
Stock & Forearm: Plain walnut one-piece pistol grip stock & forearm
Approximate wt.: 4¼ lbs.
Comments: Made from about 1948 to 1972 in three models; 514 Standard Model; 514 P had target sights (peep rear sight); 514 BR Boys Rifle had 1" shorter stock & 21" barrel.
Estimated Value: **Excellent:** $100.00
Very good: $80.00

Remington Model 510 Targetmaster

Caliber: 22 short, long, long rifle
Action: Bolt action; single shot; takedown model; self-cocking with thumb safety & cocking indicator
Magazine: None
Barrel: 25" light round
Sights: Sporting or target sights
Stock & Forearm: Plain walnut one-piece pistol grip stock & forearm
Approximate wt.: 5 lbs.
Comments: Made from about 1939 to 1962 in three models: 510 A Standard model; 510 P with peep sights; & 510 SB, a smooth-bore chambered for 22 shot shells.
Estimated Value: **Excellent:** $125.00
Very good: $100.00

Remington Model 510 C Carbine

Same as Model 510 single-shot rifle except: 21" barrel & approximate wt. of 5½ lbs. Made from about 1961 to 1962.
Estimated Value: **Excellent:** $110.00
Very good: $ 90.00

Remington Model 10 Nylon

Remington Model 10 Nylon
Caliber: 22 short, long, long rifle
Action: Bolt action; self-cocking; single-shot
Magazine: None
Barrel: 19½" round
Sights: Ramp front; adjustable open rear
Stock & Forearm: Nylon checkered one-piece pistol grip stock & forearm; shotgun buttplate
Approximate wt.: 4 lbs.
Comments: Made from about 1963 to 1964.
Estimated Value: Excellent: $90.00
                        Very good: $75.00

Remington Model 10 SB
Same as Model 10 except: smooth bore; chambered for 22 shot shells.
Estimated Value: Excellent: $95.00
                        Very good: $80.00

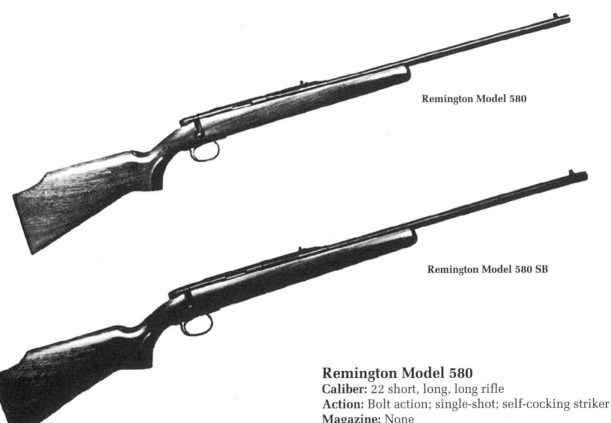

Remington Model 580

Remington Model 580 SB

Remington Model 580
Caliber: 22 short, long, long rifle
Action: Bolt action; single-shot; self-cocking striker
Magazine: None
Barrel: 24" round
Sights: Bead front; adjustable open rear
Stock & Forearm: Plain wood Monte Carlo one-piece pistol grip stock & forearm; plastic shotgun buttplate
Approximate wt.: 5 lbs.
Comments: Made from about 1967 to late 1970's also available in boys' model with shorter stock for young shooters.
Estimated Value: Excellent: $95.00
                        Very good: $80.00

Remington Model 580 SB
Same as Model 580 except: smooth bore for 22 long rifle shot shell only.
Estimated Value: Excellent: $100.00
                        Very good: $ 80.00

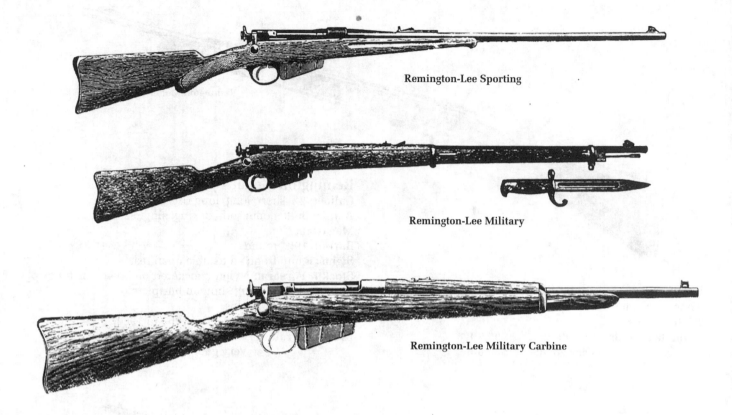

Remington-Lee Sporting

Remington-Lee Military

Remington-Lee Military Carbine

Remington-Lee Sporting

Caliber: 6mm U.S. Navy, 30-30 Sporting, 30-40 U.S. Government, 7mm Mauser, or 7.65mm Mauser

Action: Smokeless powder, bolt action; repeating

Magazine: 5-shot removable box

Barrel: 24" to 28" round smokeless steel barrel

Sights: Bead or blade front, open rear adjustable for elevation

Stock & Forearm: Checkered walnut one-piece semi-pistol grip stock & grooved forearm;

Approximate wt.: 6¾ lbs.

Comments: Some were produced with deluxe grand walnut stock, half-octagon barrel & Lyman sights. Made from about 1897 to 1906.

Estimated Value: Excellent: $500.00
                         Very good: $400.00

Remington-Lee Military

Caliber: 30-40 Krag, 303 British, 6mm Lee Navy, 7mm Mauser or 7.65 mm Mauser

Action: Smokeless powder, bolt action; repeating, rimless cartridges

Magazine: 5-shot removable box

Barrel: 29" round smokeless steel barrel

Sights: Post front; folding leaf rear

Stock & Forearm: Plain walnut one-piece straight grip stock & long forearm; cleaning rod; barrel bands; wood hand guard on top of barrel

Approximate wt.: 8½ lbs.

Comments: Made from about 1897 to 1902.

Estimated Value: Excellent: $425.00
                         Very good: $340.00

Remington-Lee Military Carbine

Similar to Remington-Lee rifle except: 20" barrel; one barrel band; approximate wt. 6½ lbs.

Estimated Value: Excellent: $400.00
                         Very good: $320.00

Remington Model 1907-15

Caliber: 8mm Lebel

Action: Smokeless powder bolt action; repeating; self-cocking striker with knurled top for uncocking & manual cocking

Magazine: 5-shot box

Barrel: 26" to 31" round with 4 groove rifling

Sights: Ivory bead dovetail front, folding leaf rear

Stock & Forearm: Plain walnut one-piece stock & long forearm; barrel bands; cleaning rod

Approximate wt.: 8 to 9 lbs.

Comments: Made from about 1907 to 1915; left side of action marked "Remington MLE 1907-15"; right side of barrel near action marked "RAC 1907-15."

Estimated Value: Excellent: $300.00
                         Very good: $240.00

Remington Model 1907-15 Carbine

Same as Remington Model 1907-15 except: 22" barrel; no barrel bands; short forearm; approximate wt. 6½ lbs.

Estimated Value: Excellent: $275.00
                         Very good: $220.00

Remington, Enfield Pattern, 1914 Military

Caliber: 303 British (rimmed)

Action: British smokeless powder bolt action; repeating; self-cocking on down stroke of bolt handle

Magazine: 5-shot box

Barrel: 26" round tapered barrel

Sights: Protected post front; protected folding leaf rear

Stock & Forearm: Oil finished walnut, one-piece stock & forearm; wood hand guard on top of barrel; modified pistol grip stock; full-length forearm with two barrel bands

Approximate wt.: 10 lbs.

Comments: Made from about 1915 to 1916 for the British Army; Serial No. on action & bolt, "R" preceeding action serial no.; approximately 600,000 produced.

Estimated Value: Excellent: $325.00
                   Very good: $260.00

Remington, Enfield U.S. Model 1917 Military

Caliber: 30-06 Government, rimless

Action: Smokeless powder bolt action; repeating; self-cocking on down stroke of bolt handle; actions made with interchangeable parts

Magazine: 5-shot box

Barrel: 26" round tapered

Sights: Protected post front, protected folding leaf rear

Stock & Forearm: Plain one-piece walnut stock & forearm; wood hand guard over barrel; modified pistol grip stock; full-length forearm with finger grooves and two barrel beads; sling loops & bayonet lug

Approximate wt.: 10 lbs.

Comments: Made from abt. 1917 to 1918. Marked "Model of 1917," Remington & serial no. on bridge.

Estimated Value: Excellent: $350.00
                   Very good: $280.00

Remington, Enfield Pattern, 1914 Military

Remington, Enfield U. S. Model 1917 Military

Remington Model 30 (Early Variety)

Remington Model 30 (Intermediate Variety)

Remington Model 30 (Early Variety)

Caliber: 30-06 Government

Action: Improved 1917 Enfield bolt action; repeating; self-cocking when bolt is closed; hinged floor plate

Magazine: 5-shot box

Barrel: 24" light round

Sights: Slip-on band front sight, adjustable rear sight

Stock & Forearm: Plain walnut, one-piece pistol grip stock & grooved lipped forearm; steel buttplate

Approximate wt.: 8 lbs.

Comments: Made from about 1921 to 1926; approximately 8,500 produced; marked "Remington Arms Co. Inc., Remington Ilion Works, Ilion, N.Y. Made in U.S.A."

Estimated Value: Excellent: $490.00
                   Very good: $390.00

Remington Model 30 (Intermediate Variety)

Same as Model 30 (Early Variety) rifle except: calibers 30-06 Government, 25, 30, 32 and 35 Remington & 7mm Mauser; 22" barrel length; also made in 20" barrel carbine. Made from about 1926 to 1930. Approximate wt. 7 lbs.

Estimated Value: Excellent: $475.00
                   Very good: $380.00

Remington Model 30 Express

Remington Model 34

Remington Model 341 Sportsmaster

Remington Model 30 Express

Caliber: 25, 30, 32 or 35 Remington, 30-06 Government, 7mm Mauser until 1936. After 1936 caliber 257 Roberts & 30-06 government only

Action: Bolt action; repeating; self-cocking; thumb safety

Magazine: 5-shot box

Barrel: 22" or 24" round barrel

Sights: Bead front, adjustable open rear

Stock & Forearm: Plain or checkered walnut pistol grip one-piece stock & forearm; early models have grooved forearm with lipped tip

Approximate wt.: 7½ lbs.

Comments: Made from about 1921 to 1940.

Estimated Value: **Excellent:**   **$500.00**
                    Very good: **$400.00**

Remington Model 30R Carbine

Same as Model 30 Express except: 20" barrel; plain walnut one-piece stock and forearm; approximate wt. 7 lbs.

Estimated Value: **Excellent:**   **$475.00**
                    Very good: **$380.00**

Remington Model 30S Sporting

Similar to Model 30 Express except: caliber 257 Roberts, 7mm Mauser or 30-06; approximate wt. 8 lbs.; rear peep sight; special grade high-comb stock; produced from about 1930 to 1940; 24" barrel.

Estimated Value: **Excellent:**   **$520.00**
                    Very good: **$415.00**

Remington Model 34

Caliber: 22 short, long, long rifle

Action: Bolt action; repeating; takedown model; self-cocking; thumb safety

Magazine: Tubular under barrel; 22 shorts, 17 longs, 15 long rifles

Barrel: 24" round

Sights: Bead front, adjustable open rear

Stock & Forearm: Plain wood, one-piece pistol grip stock & grooved forearm

Approximate wt.: 5½ lbs.

Comments: Made from about 1933 to 1935; also produced in Model 34 NRA target model with peep rear sight & sling swivels.

Estimated Value: **Excellent:**   **$175.00**
                    Very good: **$145.00**

Remington Model 341 Sportsmaster

Caliber: 22 short, long, long rifle

Action: Bolt action; repeating; takedown model; self-cocking; thumb safety

Magazine: Tubular under barrel; 22 shorts, 17 longs, 15 long rifles

Barrel: 27" round

Sights: Bead front, open rear adjustable for elevation

Stock & Forearm: Plain wood one-piece pistol grip stock & forearm

Approximate wt.: 6 lbs.

Comments: Made from about 1935 to 1940.

Estimated Value: **Excellent:**   **$150.00**
                    Very good: **$120.00**

Remington Model 341 S Sportsmaster

Same as Model 341 except: smooth bore for 22 shot cartridges.

Estimated Value: **Excellent:**   **$145.00**
                    Very good: **$115.00**

Remington Model 37 Rangemaster

Remington Model 37 (1940 Model)

Remington Model 37 Rangemaster

Caliber: 22 long rifle
Action: Bolt action; repeating; self-cocking; thumb safety: adjustable trigger
Magazine: 5-shot clip & single-shot adapter
Barrel: 28" heavy, semi-floating target barrel
Sights: Target sights; drilled for scope mount
Stock & Forearm: Heavy target, one-piece walnut stock & forearm; high flute comb stock with plain pistol grip & steel buttplate; early models had rounded beavertail forearm with one barrel band; barrel band dropped in 1938 & forearm modified
Approximate wt.: 12 lbs.
Comments: Made from about 1937 to 1940.
Estimated Value: Excellent: $400.00
                       Very good: $320.00

Remington Model 37 (1940 Model)

Similar to Model 37 rifle except: improved trigger mechanism; re-designed stock; wide beavertail forearm; produced from about 1940 to 1955.
Estimated Value: Excellent: $435.00
                       Very good: $350.00

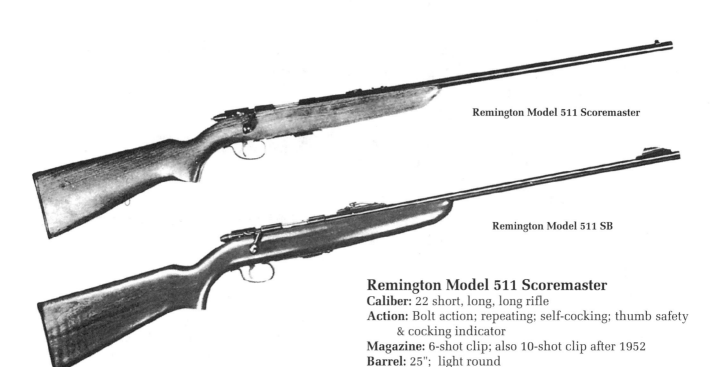

Remington Model 511 Scoremaster

Remington Model 511 SB

Remington Model 511 Scoremaster

Caliber: 22 short, long, long rifle
Action: Bolt action; repeating; self-cocking; thumb safety & cocking indicator
Magazine: 6-shot clip; also 10-shot clip after 1952
Barrel: 25"; light round
Sights: Open sporting sights
Stock & Forearm: Plain walnut one-piece pistol grip stock & forearm
Approximate wt.: 5¾ lbs.
Comments: Made from about 1939 to 1962 with production stopped during World War II
Estimated Value: Excellent: $135.00
                       Very good: $105.00

Remington Model 511 SB

Same as Model 511 Scoremaster Rifle except: smooth bore for using 22 shot cartridges.
Estimated Value: Excellent: $130.00
                       Very good: $100.00

Remington Model 512 Sportmaster

Caliber: 22 short, long, long rifle
Action: Bolt action; repeating; self cocking; thumb safety; cocking indicator
Magazine: Tubular ; 22 shorts, 17 longs, 15 long rifles
Barrel: 25" light round
Sights: Bead front, open rear adjustable for elevation
Stock & Forearm: Plain walnut one-piece pistol grip stock & forearm; composition buttplate
Approximate wt.: 5½ lbs.
Comments: Made from about 1940 to 1942 & from 1946 to 1962; the pre-war & post-war models may have minor differences in markings & stocks.
Estimated Value: **Excellent:** **$130.00**
Very good: **$105.00**

Remington Model 512 SB

Same as Model 512 Sportmaster except: smooth bore for 22 shot cartridges.
Estimated Value: **Excellent:** **$125.00**
Very good: **$100.00**

Remington Model 513 T Matchmaster

Caliber: 22 long rifle
Action: Bolt action; repeating; self-cocking; cocking indicator; adjustable trigger
Magazine: 6-shot clip
Barrel: 27" medium round barrel; semi-floating type
Sights: Target sights; top of receiver grooved for scope mount after 1954
Stock & Forearm: Plain, heavy, high fluted comb; walnut one-piece pistol grip stock & beavertail forearm
Approximate wt.: 9 lbs.
Comments: Made from abt. 1940 to 1942 & 1945 to 1968.
Estimated Value: **Excellent:** **$225.00**
Very good: **$180.00**

Remington Model 513 S Sporter Rifle

Similar to Model 513 T Matchmaster except: lighter sporting checkered walnut one-piece stock & forearm; approximate wt. 6¾ lbs.; ramp front sight & adjustable open rear sight; produced from about 1940 to 1958.
Estimated Value: **Excellent:** **$250.00**
Very good: **$200.00**

Remington Model 512 Sportmaster

Remington Model 512 SB

Remington Model 513 T Matchmaster

Remington Model 720

Remington Model 721

Remington Model 720

Caliber: 257 Roberts, 270 Win., 30-06 Government
Action: Bolt action; repeating; self-cocking; side safety
Magazine: 5-shot box; removable floor plate
Barrel: 20", 22" or 24" round
Sights: Ramp front, adjustable open rear sights
Stock & Forearm: Checkered walnut one-piece pistol grip stock & forearm
Approximate wt.: 8 lbs.
Comments: Made from about 1941 to 1946.
Estimated Value: **Excellent:** **$400.00**
Very good: **$325.00**

Remington Model 721

Caliber: 270, 30-06 or 300 mag.; 280 Rem. (after 1959)
Action: Bolt action; repeating; self-cocking; adj. trigger
Magazine: **3 or** 4-shot box with fixed floor plate
Barrel: 24" or 26" round
Sights: Ramp front, sporting rear with step elevator
Stock & Forearm: Checkered or plain walnut one-piece pistol grip stock & forearm
Approximate wt.: 8 lbs.
Comments: Made from about 1948 to 1958 in six grades: standard grade made from 1948 to 1961. Priced for standard grade.
Estimated Value: **Excellent:** **$270.00**
Very good: **$215.00**

Remington Model 722

Remington Model 521 TL Target

Remington Model 521 TL Target

Caliber: 22 long rifle

Action: Bolt action; repeating; self-cocking; thumb safety; cocking indicator

Magazine: 5- or 10-shot clip

Barrel: 25" medium weight round barrel

Sights: Post front, Lyman #57 receiver sight (peep sight)

Stock & Forearm: Heavy target one-piece pistol grip stock & beavertail forearm; varnished or oil finished; rubber buttplate

Approximate wt.: 6½ lbs.

Comments: Made from about 1948 to 1968; a low cost rifle intended for junior target shooters.

Estimated Value: **Excellent:**   **$150.00**
                 Very good: **$120.00**

Remington Model 722

Caliber: 257 Roberts or 300 Savage; in 1950 222 Rem.; in 1956 308 Win. & 244 Rem.; in 1958 222 Rem. mag.; in 1960 243 Win.

Action: Bolt action; repeating; adjustable trigger

Magazine: 4 or 5-shot box; fixed floor plate

Barrel: 22" or 24" round

Sights: Ramp bead front, open adjustable rear

Stock & Forearm: Checkered or plain varnished walnut one-piece pistol grip stock & forearm; after 1950 option of high-comb stock & tapered forearm

Approximate wt.: 7 to 8½ lbs.

Comments: Made from about 1948 to 1958 in seven grades; standard grade made from about 1948 to 1961. Priced for standard grade.

Estimated Value: **Excellent:**   **$300.00**
                 Very good: **$240.00**

Remington Model 725 (Early)

Remington Model 725 (Late)

Remington Model 725 Magnum

Remington Model 725 Magnum

Caliber: 375 or 458 Win. magnum

Action: Bolt action; repeating; self-cocking; thumb safety

Magazine: 3-shot box

Barrel: 26" heavy round barrel with muzzle brake

Sights: Ramp front, deluxe adjustable rear

Stock & Forearm: Fancy reinforced, checkered walnut Monte Carlo one-piece pistol grip stock & forearm; stock with cap & rubber recoil pad; black forearm tip; quick detachable leather sling

Approximate wt.: 9 lbs.

Comments: Made from about 1960 to 1961 in three grades. Priced for ADL grade.

Estimated Value: **Excellent:**   **$700.00**
                 Very good: **$575.00**

Remington Model 725 (Early)

Caliber: 270, 280, 30-06

Action: Bolt action; repeating; self-cocking; thumb safety

Magazine: 4-shot box

Barrel: 22" round

Sights: Adjustable open rear, hooded ramp front

Stock & Forearm: Checkered walnut Monte Carlo one-piece pistol grip stock & forearm; capped grip stock with shotgun buttplate & sling loops

Approximate wt.: 7½ lbs.

Comments: Made from about 1958 to 1959.

Estimated Value: **Excellent:**   **$375.00**
                 Very good: **$300.00**

Remington Model 725 (Late)

Same as Model 725 (Early) except: in additional calibers 243 Win.; 244 Rem.; 222 Rem.; 24" barrel in 222 Rem. and aluminum buttplate on all calibers. Made from about 1960 to 1961 in three grades. Priced for standard grade.

Estimated Value: **Excellent:**   **$400.00**
                 Very good: **$320.00**

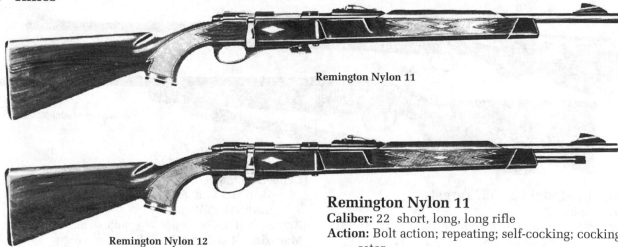

Remington Nylon 11

Remington Nylon 12

Remington Nylon 11
Caliber: 22 short, long, long rifle
Action: Bolt action; repeating; self-cocking; cocking indicator
Magazine: 6- or 10-shot clip
Barrel: 19½" round
Sights: Ramp front, adjustable open rear
Stock & Forearm: Polished brown nylon one-piece stock, forearm & hand guard over barrel; checkered, capped, pistol grip stock with shotgun buttplate; checkered forearm with blunt reversed cap; white liners & two white diamond inlays on each side
Approximate wt.: 4½ lbs.
Comments: Made from about 1962 to 1964.
Estimated Value: Excellent: $100.00
Very good: $ 80.00

Remington Nylon 12
Similar to Remington Nylon 11 Rifle except: tubular magazine under barrel holds 14 to 21 shots.
Estimated Value: Excellent: $110.00
Very good: $ 90.00

Remington Model 600

Remington Model 600 Magnum

Remington Model 660

Remington Model 600
Caliber: 6mm Rem., 222 Rem., 243 Win., 308 Win., 35 Rem.
Action: Bolt action; repeating
Magazine: 5-shot box
Barrel: 18½"; ventilated rib
Sights: Open rear, bead front
Stock & Forearm: Checkered walnut Monte Carlo one-piece pistol grip stock & forearm
Approximate wt.: 6 lbs.
Comments: A carbine-style rifle made in the mid 1960's.
Estimated Value: Excellent: $300.00
Very good: $240.00

Remington Model 600 Magnum
Similar to the Model 600 except: magnum calibers; 4-shot magazine; walnut & beechwood stock; recoil pad.
Estimated Value: Excellent: $400.00
Very good: $325.00

Remington Model 660
Similar to the Model 600 except: 20" barrel without ventilated rib; beaded front sight; made in the late 1960's & early 1970's.
Estimated Value: Excellent: $290.00
Very good: $235.00

Remington Model 660 Magnum
Similar to the Model 600 Magnum except: 20" barrel without ventilated rib; beaded front sight; made in the late 1960's to early 1970's.
Estimated Value: Excellent: $375.00
Very good: $300.00

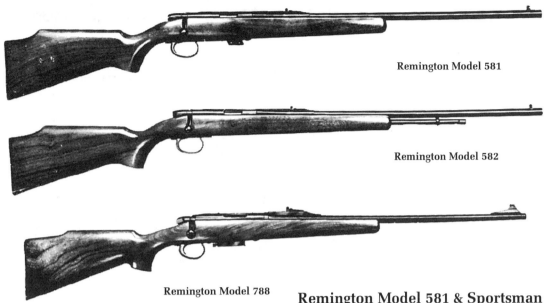

Remington Model 581

Remington Model 582

Remington Model 788

Remington Model 788
Caliber: 222, 22-250, 223 Rem., 6mm Rem., 243 Win., 308 Win.; 7mm-08 Rem. added 1980
Action: Bolt action; repeating; self-cocking; thumb safety
Magazine: 5-shot clip in 222; 4-shot clip in other calibers
Barrel: 24" round tapered barrel in calibers 222, 22-250 & 223 Rem.; 22" barrel in other calibers; 18½" barrel available 1980
Sights: Blade front, adjustable rear
Stock & Forearm: Monte Carlo one-piece pistol grip stock & forearm
Approximate wt.: 7½ lbs.
Comments: Made from about 1967 to 1983. Add $5.00 for left hand action, $50.00 for scope.
Estimated Value: Excellent: $275.00
                       Very good: $225.00

Remington Model 581 & Sportsman 581 S
Caliber: 22 short, long, long rifle
Action: Bolt action; repeating; self-cocking; thumb safety
Magazine: 5-shot clip; single shot adapter
Barrel: 24"; round
Sights: Bead front, adjustable open rear sight
Stock & Forearm: Plain hard wood Monte Carlo one-piece pistol grip stock & forearm
Approximate wt.: 5¼ lbs.
Comments: Made from about 1967 to 1983; reintroduced in 1986 to present as "Sportsman" 581-S.
Estimated Value: New (retail): $239.00
                       Excellent: $180.00
                       Very good: $145.00

Remington Model 582
Same as Model 581 except: 15 to 20-shot tubular magazine . Add 8% for swivels & sling.
Estimated Value: Excellent: $175.00
                       Very good: $140.00

Remington Model 591

Remington Model 592

Remington Model 592
Same as Model 591 except 10-shot tubular magazine under barrel.
Estimated Value: Excellent: $200.00
                       Very good: $160.00

Remington Model 591
Caliber: 5mm Rem. rim fire
Action: Bolt action; repeating; self-cocking; thumb safety
Magazine: 4-shot removable clip
Barrel: 24"; round
Sights: Bead post front; adjustable open rear
Stock & Forearm: Monte Carlo plain one-piece hardwood pistol grip stock & forearm
Approximate wt.: 5 lbs.
Comments: Made from about 1970 to 1974.
Estimated Value: Excellent: $190.00
                       Very good: $150.00

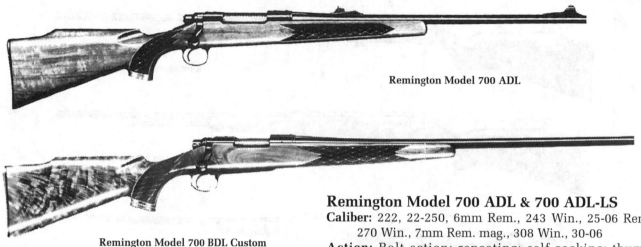

Remington Model 700 ADL

Remington Model 700 BDL Custom

Remington Model 700 ADL & 700 ADL-LS

Caliber: 222, 22-250, 6mm Rem., 243 Win., 25-06 Rem. 270 Win., 7mm Rem. mag., 308 Win., 30-06

Action: Bolt action; repeating; self-cocking; thumb safety; checkered bolt handle

Magazine: 3 or 5-shot box magazine

Barrel: 22" or 24" round tapered barrel

Sights: Ramp front; adjustable, notched, removable rear

Stock & Forearm: Checkered walnut Monte Carlo pistol grip, one-piece stock & forearm; synthetic stock; 700 ADL-LS has laminated stock

Approximate wt.: 7½ lbs.

Comments: Produced from abt. 1962 to present. Add 5% for mag. Deduct 12% for synthetic stock; add 10% for laminated stock (LS). Models produced in late 1987 were recalled by Remington. These rifles may contain an improperly manufactured part in the trigger mechanism.

Estimated Value: New (retail): $472.00
Excellent: $355.00
Very good: $285.00

Remington Model 700 BDL Custom

Similar to Model 700 ADL except: custom deluxe grade with black forearm end; sling strap; additional calibers: 17 Rem., 223 Rem., 264 Win. mag., 280 Rem., 7mm-08 Rem., 300 Win. mag., 35 Whelen, 338 Win. mag.; Add 5% for mag.; Models produced in late 1987 were recalled by Remington. These rifles may contain an improperly manufactured part in the trigger mechanism.

Estimated Value: New (retail): $576.00
Excellent: $430.00
Very good: $345.00

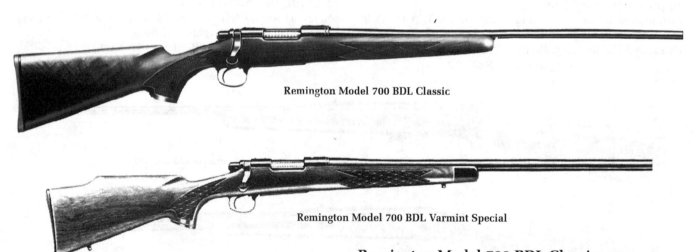

Remington Model 700 BDL Classic

Remington Model 700 BDL Varmint Special

Remington Model 700 BDL Varmint Special

Similar to 700 BDL except: heavy barrel without sights in 222 Rem., 22-250 Rem., 223 Rem., 6mm Rem., 243 Win., 25-06 Rem., 7mm-08, 308 Win. Models produced in late 1987 were recalled by Remington. These rifles, may contain an improperly manufactured part in the trigger mechanism.

Estimated Value: Excellent: $425.00
Very good: $350.00

Remington Model 700 BDL Classic

Similar to 700 BDL except: stock styling changes; calibers 22-250 Rem., 6mm Rem., 243 Win., 270 Win., 30-06. Add 5% for mag.. A limited number were available in 7mm mag. (in 1981); 257 Roberts (in 1982); 300 H & H magnum (in 1983); 250 Savage (in 1984); 350 Rem. magnum (in 1985); 264 Win. magnum (in 1986). Models produced in late 1987 were recalled by Remington. These rifles may contain an improperly manufactured part in the trigger mechanism. Produced in 220 Swift in 1992.

Estimated Value: Excellent: $390.00
Very good: $310.00

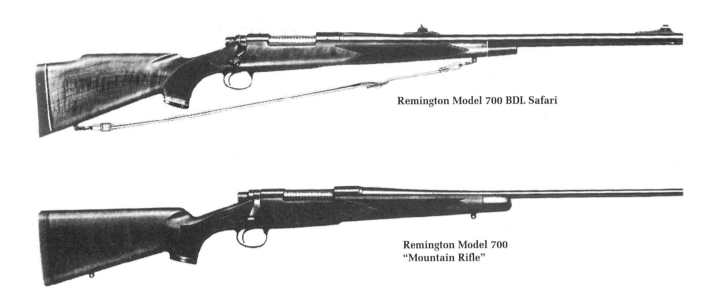

Remington Model 700 BDL Safari

Remington Model 700
"Mountain Rifle"

Remington Model 700 "Mountain Rifle" DM
Similar to 700 BDL except: 270 Win., 280 Rem. & 30-06 caliber, 25-06 Rem. added 1992.; approx. wt. 7 lbs.; 4-shot detachable magazine; no sights; introduced in 1986. Models produced in late 1987 were recalled by Remington. These rifles may contain an improperly manufactured part in the trigger mechanism.
Estimated Value: New (retail): $629.00
                   Excellent: $470.00
                   Very good: $375.00

Remington Model 700 BDL Safari
Similar to Model 700 BDL except: 375 H & H mag. & 458 Win. mag.; recoil pad. 8mm Rem. mag. caliber added in 1986. Models produced in late 1987 were recalled by Remington. These rifles may contain an improperly manufactured part in the trigger mechanism. Available after 1989 as a special order model from the custom shop.
Estimated Value: Excellent: $650.00
                   Very good: $520.00

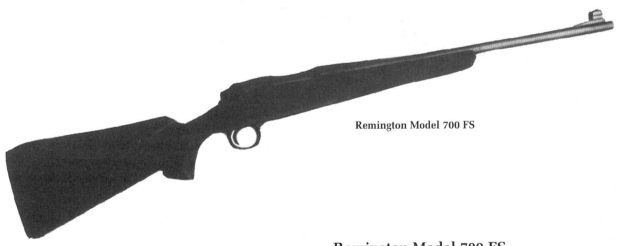

Remington Model 700 FS

Remington Model 700 RS
Similar to the Model 700 BDL except: DuPont Rynite® stock; textured finish; calibers: 270 Win., 280 Rem., 30-06. Introduced in 1987. Models produced in late 1987 were recalled by Remington. These rifles may contain an improperly manufactured part in the trigger mechanism.
Estimated Value: Excellent: $410.00
                   Very good: $325.00

Remington Model 700 FS
Similar to Model 700 ADL except it has a Kelvar® reinforced fiberglass stock (grey or grey camo); in calibers: 243 Win., 270 Win., 30-06, 308 Win., 7mm Rem. magnum. Produced from 1987 to 1990. Models produced in late 1987 were recalled by Remington. These rifles may contain an improperly manufactured part in the trigger mechanism.
Estimated Value: Excellent: $465.00
                   Very good: $375.00

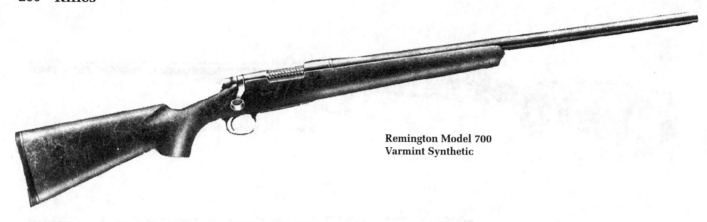

Remington Model 700
Varmint Synthetic

Remington Model 700 Varmint Synthetic

Caliber: 22-250 Rem., 220 swift, 223 Rem., 308 Win.

Action: Bolt action; repeating; thumb safety

Magazine: 4 or 5-shot box

Barrel: 24" black matte finish; 26" heavy or stainless steel fluted

Sights: None, drilled and tapped for scope mount

Stock & Forearm: Composite Kevlar, fiberglass, and graphite; textured black and grey non-reflective finish; swivel studs

Approximate wt.: 8¾ lbs.

Comments: Introduced 1992. Add 20% for stainless steel fluted barrel.

Estimated Value:

New (retail):	$686.00
Excellent:	$515.00
Very good:	$410.00

Remington Model 700 Sendero

Caliber: 25-06 Rem., 270 Win., 7mm Rem. magnum, 300 Win. magnum

Action: Bolt action; repeating

Magazine: 3 or 4-shot box

Barrel: 26" heavy, black matte finish or stainless steel fluted

Sights: None, drilled and tapped for scope mount

Stock & Forearm: Smooth black Kevlar fiberglass and graphite one piece pistol grip stock and forearm

Approximate wt.: 7¼ lbs.

Comments: Introduced 1994. Add 4% for magnum; add 20% for stainless steel fluted barrel.

Estimated Value:

New (retail):	$686.00
Excellent:	$515.00
Very good:	$410.00

Remington Model 700 AS

Remington Model 700 Camo Synthetic

Caliber: 22-250 Rem., 243 Win., 270 Win., 280 Rem., 7mm-08 Rem., 7mm Rem. magnum, 30-06, 308 Win., 300 Wby. magnum

Action: Bolt action; repeating; thumb safety

Magazine: 3 or 5-shot box

Barrel: 22" or 24" camouflaged

Sights: Hooded ramp front, adjustable rear

Stock & Forearm: Camouflaged synthetic one-piece pistol grip stock and forearm; recoil pad; swivel studs

Approximate wt.: 7¾ lbs.

Comments: Produced from 1992 to mid 1990's. Add 5% for mag.

Estimated Value:

Excellent:	$435.00
Very good:	$345.00

Remington Model 700 AS

Caliber: 22-250, 243 Win., 270 Win., 280 Rem., 30-06 Win., 7mm Rem. magnum, 300 Weatherby magnum

Action: Bolt action; repeating; thumb safety

Magazine: 3 or 4-shot box

Barrel: 22"; blued in all calibers except 22-250, 7mm Rem. mag. & 300 Weatherby mag. which have 24" blued barrel

Sights: Hooded ramp front; adjustable rear

Stock & Forearm: Synthetic resin, one-piece pistol grip stock & forearm; solid recoil pad

Approximate wt.: 6¾ lbs.

Comments: Made from 1990 to 1992. Add 4% for 7mm Remington mag. & 300 Weatherby mag.

Estimated Value:

Excellent:	$420.00
Very good:	$340.00

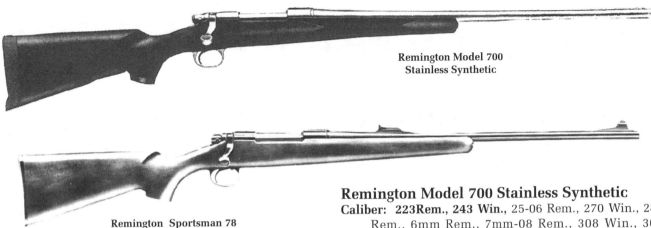

Remington Model 700
Stainless Synthetic

Remington Sportsman 78

Remington Sportsman 78

Similar to the Model 700 except: lesser quality finish; hardwood with no checkering; 22" barrel; 270 Win. & 30-06 calibers in 1984; 243 & 308 calibers added in 1985; 223 caliber added in 1986. Models produced in late 1987 were recalled by Remington. These rifles may contain an improperly manufactured part in the trigger mechanism; Discontinued 1990.

Estimated Value: **Excellent:**   **$300.00**
                    Very good: **$240.00**

Remington Model 700 Stainless Synthetic

Caliber: **223Rem., 243 Win.,** 25-06 Rem., 270 Win., 280 Rem., 6mm Rem., 7mm-08 Rem., 308 Win., 300 Wby. mag., 30-06 Sprg., 7mm Rem. mag., 7mm Wby. mag., 300 Win. mag., 338 Win. mag.

Action: Bolt action; repeating; thumb safety

Magazine: 4-shot box

Barrel: 24" stainless steel, matte finish

Sights: None, drilled and tapped for scope mount

Stock & Forearm: Black textured checkered synthetic one piece pistol grip stock & forearm; swivel studs

Approximate wt.: 8¾ lbs.

Comments: Introduced 1992. Add 5% for mag.

Estimated Value: **New (retail):**   **$623.00**
                    Excellent: **$465.00**
                    Very good: **$375.00**

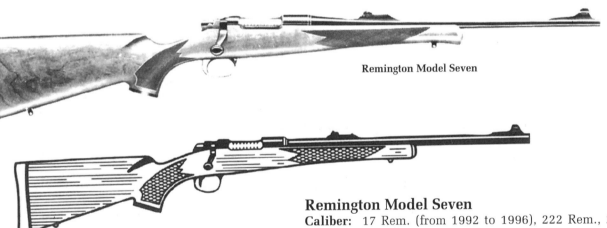

Remington Model Seven

Remington Model Seven Youth

Remington Model Seven Youth

Same as Model Seven except: shorter stock; calibers 243 Win., 7mm-08 Rem.; approximate wt. 6 lbs. Introduced in 1993.

Estimated Value: **New (retail):**   **$465.00**
                    Excellent: **$350.00**
                    Very good: **$280.00**

Remington Model Seven

Caliber: 17 Rem. (from 1992 to 1996), 222 Rem., 223 Rem., 243 Win., 6mm Rem., 7mm-08 Rem., 308 Win.

Action: Bolt action; repeating

Magazine: 4 or 5-shot box with steel floor plate

Barrel: 18½"or 20" ; Blued; stainless steel(in 1994)

Sights: Adj. rear on inclined ramp; ramp front

Stock & Forearm: Checkered walnut one-piece pistol grip stock & slightly lipped forearm; recoil pad

Approximate wt.: 6¼ lbs.

Comments: Introduced in 1983. 222 caliber discontinued in 1985. Models produced in late 1987 were recalled by Remington. These rifles may contain an improperly manufactured part in the trigger mechanism; Add 5% for 17 Rem.; Add 10% for stainless steel.

Estimated Value: **New (retail):**   **$569.00**
                    Excellent: **$425.00**
                    Very good: **$340.00**

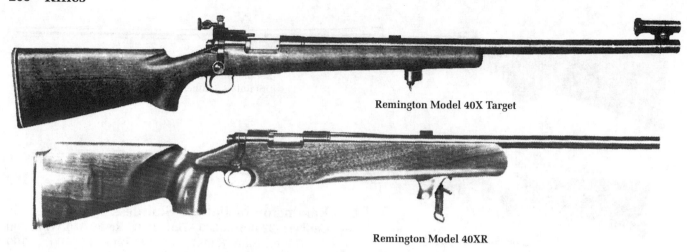

Remington Model 40X Target

Remington Model 40XR

Remington Model 40XB Rangemaster

Remington Model 40X Target

Caliber: 22 long rifle in 1960; 222 Rem. in 1961; 308, 30-06; others on special order

Action: Bolt action; single-shot; self-cocking; thumb safety; adjustable trigger

Magazine: None

Barrel: 28" standard or heavy round barrel with bedding device in forearm

Sights: Removable target sights, scope block on barrel

Stock & Forearm: Oiled, plain, heavy target one-piece pistol grip stock & blade front; rubber shotgun buttplate; high fluted comb stock

Approximate wt.: 11 to 12 lbs.

Comments: Made from about 1956 to 1963. Replaced by Model 40XB match rifle in 1964 to 1975.

Estimated Value: Excellent: $450.00
                       Very good: $360.00

Remington Model 40XR

A target rifle similar to the Model 40X Target with widened stock & forearm; adjustable buttplate; hand stop; introduced in the late 1970's. 22 long rifle only; Add 15% for Kelvar® stock. Models produced in late 1987 were recalled by Remington. These rifles may contain an improperly manufactured part in the trigger mechanism.

Estimated Value: Excellent: $700.00
                       Very good: $560.00

Remington Model 40XB Rangemaster

Similar to the Model 40X target except: stainless steel barrel. Available in calibers 222 Rem., 22-250 Rem., 243 Win., 6mm Rem., 25-06 Rem., 7mm Rem. mag.7.62mm NATO, 30-06, 30-338, 300 Win. mag.; add 7% for repeating model. Models produced in late 1987 were recalled by Remington. These rifles may contain an improperly manufactured part in the trigger mechanism; Discontinued 1989.

Estimated Value: Excellent: $750.00
                       Very good: $625.00

Remington Model 40XBBR

Remington Model 40XB KS

Similar to the Model 40XB Rangemaster except: DuPont Kevlar reinforced stock, free-floating barrel and match-grade trigger. Available in left or right hand models, single shot or repeating models. Available as a special order item.

Estimated Value: Excellent: $800.00
                       Very good: $660.00

Remington Model 40XBBR

Similar to the Model 40XB Rangemaster with a 20" or 24" barrel. Models produced in late 1987 were recalled by Remington. These rifles may contain an improperly manufactured part in the trigger mechanism.

Estimated Value: Excellent: $750.00
                       Very good: $660.00

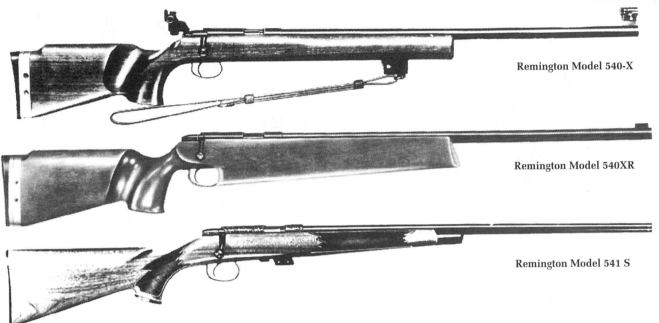

Remington Model 540-X

Remington Model 540XR

Remington Model 541 S

Remington Model 540-X, 540XR

Caliber: 22 long rifle
Action: Bolt action; single shot; self-cocking striker; slide safety; adjustable match trigger
Magazine: None
Barrel: 26" heavy target barrel
Sights: Receiver drilled & tapped for scope mount; sights optional equipment
Stock & Forearm: Full pistol grip, heavy wood one-piece stock & forearm; thumb-grooved stock with 4-way adjustable buttplate rail
Approximate wt.: 8¾ lbs.
Comments: Made from about 1970 to 1983. A heavy rifle designed for bench shooting.
Estimated Value: Excellent: $320.00
Very good: $250.00

Remington Model 541 S Custom & 541-T

Caliber: 22 short, long, long rifle
Action: Bolt action; repeating; self-cocking; thumb safety
Magazine: 5-shot clip
Barrel: 24"; standard or heavy barrel (541-T HB)
Sights: None; drilled and tapped for scope
Stock & Forearm: One-piece checkered pistol grip stock & forearm
Approximate wt.: 5½ lbs.
Comments: Designed after the Remington Model 540 X Target Rifle; made from abt. 1972 to 1983 as Model 541 S. Reintroduced in 1986 as Model 541-T. Add 7% for heavy barrel.
Estimated Value: New (retail): $455.00
Excellent: $340.00
Very good: $275.00

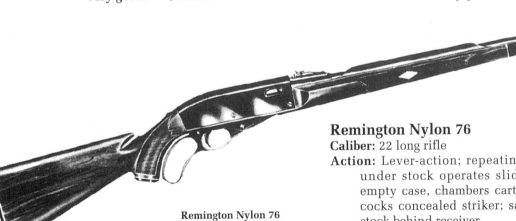

Remington Nylon 76

Remington Nylon 76

Caliber: 22 long rifle
Action: Lever-action; repeating; side ejection; lever under stock operates sliding bolt which ejects empty case, chambers cartridge from magazine & cocks concealed striker; safety located on top of stock behind receiver
Magazine: 14-shot tubular magazine in stock
Barrel: 19½" round
Sights: Blade front, open rear sight
Stock & Forearm: Checkered nylon two-piece stock & forearm; pistol grip stock; forearm lipped at tip with nylon hand guard over barrel
Approximate wt.: 4½ lbs.
Comments: Made from about 1962 to 1964; the only lever action repeater made by Remington Arms Co.
Estimated Value: Excellent: $175.00
Very good: $140.00

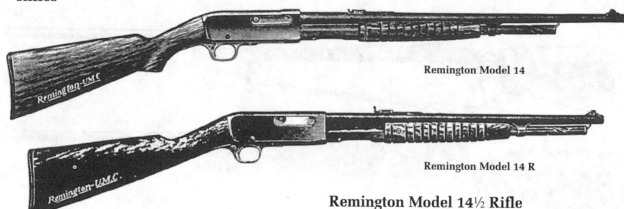

Remington Model 14

Remington Model 14 R

Remington Model 14 Rifle

Caliber: 25, 30, 32, 35 Rem.
Action: Slide action; hammerless; takedown model
Magazine: 5-shot tubular, under barrel
Barrel: 22" round
Sights: Bead front, adjustable rear
Stock & Forearm: Plain or checkered walnut pistol grip
   stock & grooved or checkered forearm
Approximate wt.: 7 lbs.
Comments: Made from about 1912 to 1935 in four
   grades; higher grades had checkering & engraving.
   Priced for standard grade.
Estimated Value: **Excellent:**   **$345.00**
                       Very good: **$275.00**

Remington Model 14½ Rifle

Similar to Model 14 rifle except: caliber 38-40 & 44-40
only; 22½" barrel; 11-shot magazine; discontinued about
1925; standard grade only.
Estimated Value: **Excellent:**   **$400.00**
                       Very good: **$320.00**

Remington Model 14½ Carbine

Same as Model 14½ rifle except: 18½" barrel & 9-shot
magazine.
Estimated Value: **Excellent:**   **$425.00**
                       Very good: **$340.00**

Remington Model 14 R Carbine

Same as Model 14 rifle except: 18½" barrel; straight grip
stock; approximate wt. 6 lbs.; standard grade only.
Estimated Value: **Excellent:**   **$300.00**
                       Very good: **$240.00**

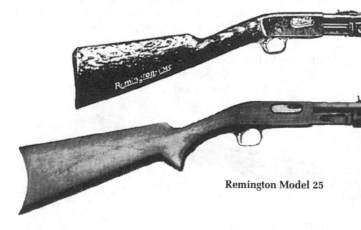

Remington Model No. 12

Remington Model 25

Remington Model No. 12 Rifle

Caliber: 22 short, long, long rifle
Action: Slide action; hammerless; takedown model
Magazine: 10- to 15-shot tubular, under barrel
Barrel: 22" or 24" round or octagon
Sights: Bead front, rear adjustable for elevation
Stock & Forearm: Plain or engraved; varnished plain or
   checkered, straight or pistol grip, walnut stock with
   rubber or steel buttplate; forearm grooved or check-
   ered walnut
Approximate wt.: 5½ lbs.
Comments: Made from about 1909 to 1936 in four
   grades; higher grades had checkering & engraving.
   Prices are for (plain) standard grade.
Estimated Value: **Excellent:**   **$225.00**
                       Very good: **$180.00**

Remington Model 25 Rifle

Caliber: 25-20, 32-20
Action: Slide action; hammerless; takedown model
Magazine: 10-shot tubular, under barrel
Barrel: 24"
Sights: Bead front, open rear
Stock & Forearm: Checkered or plain walnut pistol grip
   stock and grooved or checkered slide handle
Approximate wt.: 6 lbs.
Comments: Made from about 1923 to 1936 in four
   grades; higher grades had checkering & engraving.
   Prices are for (plain) standard grade.
Estimated Value: **Excellent:**   **$360.00**
                       Very good: **$290.00**

Remington Model 25 R Carbine

Same as Model 25 Rifle except: 18½" barrel; straight grip
stock; 6-shot magazine; approximate wt. 4½ lbs.; standard grade only.
Estimated Value: **Excellent:**   **$350.00**
                       Very good: **$280.00**

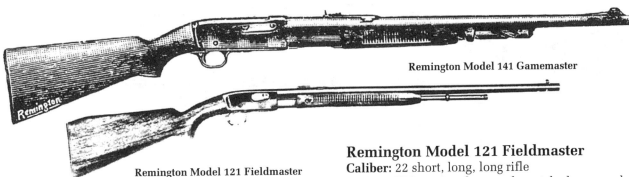

Remington Model 141 Gamemaster

Remington Model 121 Fieldmaster

Remington Model 141 Gamemaster

Caliber: 30, 32 & 35 Rem.
Action: Slide action; hammerless; takedown model
Magazine: 5-shot tubular, under barrel
Barrel: 24" round
Sights: Ramp front, adjustable rear
Stock & Forearm: Checkered or plain walnut pistol grip stock & grooved or checkered semi-beavertail slide handle
Approximate wt.: 7 lbs.
Comments: Made from about 1936 to 1942 & from 1946 to 1950 in four grades; higher grades had checkered pistol grip stock & forearm & engraving. Prices are for (plain) standard grade.
Estimated Value: Excellent: $330.00
Very good: $265.00

Remington 141 R Carbine

Same as Model 141 Gamemaster except: 18½" barrel; approximate wt. 5½ lbs.; standard grade only.
Estimated Value: Excellent: $325.00
Very good: $260.00

Remington Model 121 Fieldmaster

Caliber: 22 short, long, long rifle
Action: Slide action; hammerless; takedown model
Magazine: Tubular, under barrel; 20 shorts, 15 longs, 14 long rifles
Barrel: 24" round
Sights: Bead front, adjustable rear
Stock & Forearm: Checkered or plain walnut pistol grip stock & grooved or checkered semi-beavertail slide handle
Approximate wt.: 6 lbs.
Comments: Made from about 1936 to 1942 & from 1946 to 1950 in four grades; higher grades checkered & engraved. Priced for standard grade.
Estimated Value: Excellent: $260.00
Very good: $210.00

Remington Model 121 SB

Same as Model 121 except smooth bore barrel for 22 shot cartridges.
Estimated Value: Excellent: $275.00
Very good: $220.00

Remington Model 121 S

Similar to Model 121 except: caliber 22 Rem. special only; 12-shot magazine; standard grade.
Estimated Value: Excellent: $290.00
Very good: $240.00

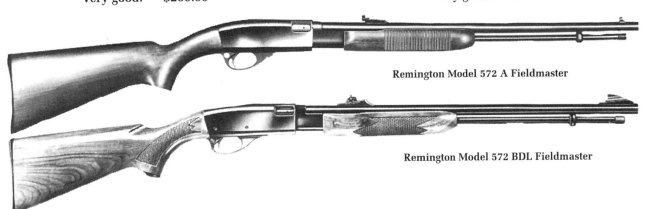

Remington Model 572 A Fieldmaster

Remington Model 572 BDL Fieldmaster

Remington Model 572 SB

Same as Model 572 A Gamemaster except: smooth bore for 22 shot cartridges; standard grade only.
Estimated Value: Excellent: $165.00
Very good: $125.00

Remington 572 BDL Fieldmaster

Deluxe version of the 572A Fieldmaster with Monte Carlo stock. Currently produced.
Estimated Value: New (retail): $353.00
Excellent: $265.00
Very good: $210.00

Remington Model 572 A Fieldmaster

Caliber: 22 short, long, long rifle
Action: Slide action; hammerless; solid frame; side ejection
Magazine: 14- to 20-shot tubular, under barrel
Barrel: 21" & 24" round tapered
Sights: Bead front, adjustable open rear
Stock & Forearm: Checkered or plain walnut pistol grip stock & grooved or checkered slide handle
Approximate wt.: 5½ lbs.
Comments: Made from about 1955 to 1987.
Estimated Value: Excellent: $175.00
Very good: $135.00

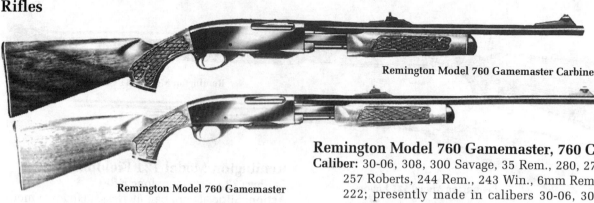

Remington Model 760 Gamemaster Carbine

Remington Model 760 Gamemaster

Remington Model 760 Gamemaster, 760 Carbine
Caliber: 30-06, 308, 300 Savage, 35 Rem., 280, 270 Win., 257 Roberts, 244 Rem., 243 Win., 6mm Rem., 223 & 222; presently made in calibers 30-06, 308 Win., 270 Rem., 243 Win. & 6mm Rem.

Action: Slide action; hammerless; side ejection; solid frame; cross-bolt safety

Magazine: 4-shot box

Barrel: 22" round tapered; 18½" on carbine

Sights: Ramp bead front, adjustable open rear

Stock & Forearm: Checkered or plain walnut pistol grip stock & semi-beavertail slide handle

Approximate wt.: 7½ lbs.

Comments: Made from about 1952 to about 1980; carbine from 1960 to 1969 in 270 or 280 caliber; 1962 to about 1980 in 30-06 & 308 Win.

Estimated Value:	Excellent:	$340.00
	Very good:	$275.00

Remington Model 760 BDL Gamemaster
Similar to Model 760 with basketweave checkering, Monte Carlo stock; available in 30-06, 270, 308 calibers.

Estimated Value:	Excellent:	$350.00
	Very good:	$280.00

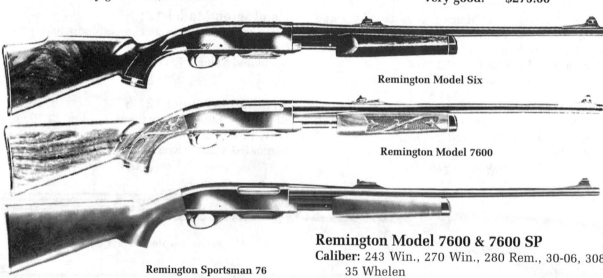

Remington Model Six

Remington Model 7600

Remington Sportsman 76

Remington Model Six
Caliber: 6mm Rem., 243 Win., 270 Win., 30-06, 308 Win.

Action: Slide action; hammerless; repeating

Magazine: 4-shot clip

Barrel: Blued; 22"

Sights: Blade ramp front, adjustable sliding ramp rear

Stock & Forearm: Checkered walnut Monte Carlo pistol grip stock & slide handle; black grip cap & fore-end tip; recessed finger groove in slide handle; cheekpiece; high-gloss finish

Approximate wt.: 7½ lbs.

Comments: Introduced in 1981 to replace the Model 760. Discontinued 1987. Custom grades are available at increased prices. 6mm Rem. dropped in 1985.

Estimated Value:	Excellent:	$400.00
	Very good:	$300.00

Remington Model 7600 & 7600 SP
Caliber: 243 Win., 270 Win., 280 Rem., 30-06, 308 Win., 35 Whelen

Action: Slide action; hammerless; repeating

Magazine: 4-shot clip

Barrel: Blued; 18½" or 22"

Sights: Blade ramp front, adjustable sliding ramp rear

Stock & Forearm: Satin or gloss finish; plain or Monte Carlo checkered walnut stock and slide handle

Approximate wt.: 7½ lbs.

Comments: Produced from mid 1980's to present. 7600 SP is Special Purpose model with non-reflective finish on wood and metal.

Estimated Value:	New (Retail):	$540.00
	Excellent:	$405.00
	Very good:	$325.00

Remington Sportsman 76
Similar to the Model 7600 with lesser quality finish; hardwood with no checkering; 22" barrel; 30-06 caliber only. Produced 1984 to 1987.

Estimated Value:	Excellent:	$300.00
	Very good:	$240.00

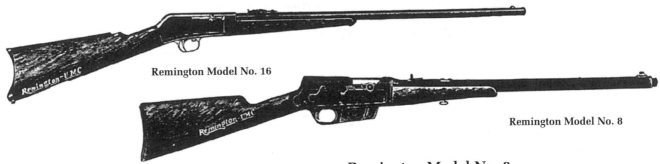

Remington Model No. 16

Remington Model No. 8

Remington Model No. 16

Caliber: 22 Rem. automatic
Action: Semi-automatic; hammerless; solid breech; sliding bolt; side ejection; takedown model
Magazine: 15-shot tubular, in stock
Barrel: 22" round
Sights: Bead front, adjustable notch sporting rear
Stock & Forearm: Plain or engraved; varnished, plain or checkered, straight grip, two-piece walnut stock & forearm; steel buttplate & blunt lip on forearm
Approximate wt.: 5¾ lbs.
Comments: Made from about 1914 to 1928 in four grades, A, C, D & F. Priced for standard grade.
Estimated Value: Excellent: $320.00
Very good: $255.00

Remington Model No. 8

Caliber: 25, 30, 32 or 35 Rem.
Action: Semi-automatic; top ejection; for smokless powder; takedown model; solid breech & sliding barrel type
Magazine: 5-shot detachable box
Barrel: 22" round
Sights: Bead front, open rear
Stock & Forearm: Plain or engraved; varnished, plain or checkered, two-piece walnut straight grip stock & forearm; rubber or steel buttplate & lipped forearm
Approximate wt.: 7¾ lbs.
Comments: Made from about 1906 to 1936 in five grades, A, C, D, E & F; jacket marked "Manufactured by the Remington Arms Co. Ilion, N.Y., U.S.A." "Browning's Patent's Oct. 8, 1900. Oct. 15, 1900. July 2, 1902." Priced for standard grade.
Estimated Value: Excellent: $400.00
Very good: $325.00

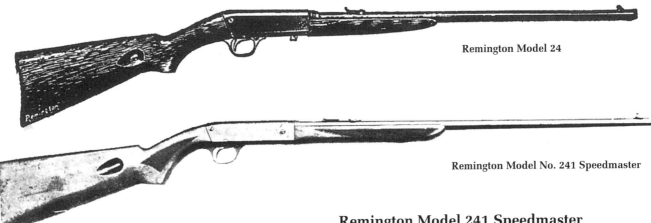

Remington Model 24

Remington Model No. 241 Speedmaster

Remington Model 24

Caliber: 22 long rifle only or 22 short only
Action: Semi-automatic; hammerless; solid breech; sliding bolt; bottom ejection
Magazine: 15-shot stock tube in 22 short & 10-shot in 22 long rifle
Barrel: 19" round
Sights: Bead front, adjustable rear
Stock & Forearm: Plain or engraved; varnished, plain or checkered, two-piece walnut semi-pistol grip stock & forearm; steel buttplate with lipped forearm
Approximate wt.: 4¾ lbs.
Comments: Made from about 1922 to 1935 in five grades, A, C, D, E & F. Priced for standard grade.
Estimated Value: Excellent: $250.00
Very good: $200.00

Remington Model 241 Speedmaster

Caliber: 22 long rifle only or 22 short only
Action: Semi-automatic; hammerless; solid breech; bottom ejection; takedown type; sliding bolt action; thumb safety
Magazine: 15-shot in 22 short; 10-shot in 22 long rifle; tubular in stock
Barrel: 24" round
Sights: Bead front, notched rear adjustable for elevation
Stock & Forearm: Plain or engraved; varnished walnut, plain or checkered, two-piece pistol grip stock & forearm; semi-beavertail
Approximate wt.: 6 lbs.
Comments: Improved version of Model 24; produced from about 1935 to 1951 in five grades, A, B, D, E & F. Priced for standard grade
Estimated Value: Excellent: $275.00
Very good: $225.00

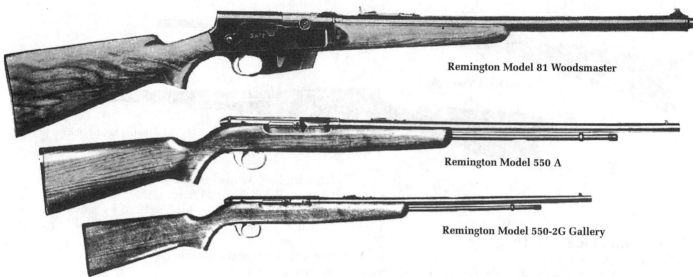

Remington Model 81 Woodsmaster

Remington Model 550 A

Remington Model 550-2G Gallery

Remington Model 550 A

Caliber: 22 short, long, long rifle

Action: Semi-automatic; hammerless; side ejection; solid breech; sliding bolt; floating power piston which permits using 22 short, long or long rifle interchangeable & still function as semi-automatic; takedown-type with thumb safety

Magazine: 20-shot in 22 short; 15-shot in 22 long rifle

Barrel: 24" round

Sights: Dovetail bead front, notched rear adjustable for elevation

Stock & Forearm: One-piece plain varnished pistol grip stock & forearm; hard rubber buttplate

Approximate wt.: 6½ lbs.

Comments: Replaced the Model 241 because it was less expensive to produce. Made from about 1941 to 1942 & from 1946 to 1970. Receiver top grooved for telescope sight mounts.

Estimated Value: Excellent: $135.00
Very good: $100.00

Remington Model 550-2G Gallery

Similar to Model 550 A except chambered for 22 short caliber only.

Estimated Value: Excellent: $160.00
Very good: $125.00

Remington Model 81 Woodsmaster

Caliber: From 1936 to 1942, 25, 30, 32, 35 Rem.; from 1946 to 1950, 30, 32, 35, 300 Savage

Action: Semi-automatic; top ejection; takedown model; solid breech; sliding barrel type

Magazine: 5-shot detachable box

Barrel: 22" round

Sights: Bead front, sporting rear with notched elevator

Stock & Forearm: Plain or engraved; varnished walnut, plain or checkered two-piece pistol grip stock & forearm; rubber buttplate & semi-beavertail forearm

Approximate wt.: 7¾ lbs.

Comments: Made from about 1936 to 1942 & from 1946 to 1950 in five grades, A, B, D, E & F. An improved version of the Model No. 8. Priced for standard grade.

Estimated Value: Excellent: $350.00
Very good: $285.00

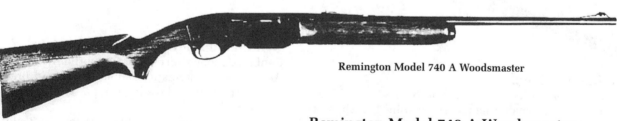

Remington Model 740 A Woodsmaster

Remington Model 740 ADL Deluxe Grade

Same as Model 740 A except: deluxe checkered stock & forearm; also grip cap & sling swivels.

Estimated Value: Excellent: $325.00
Very good: $260.00

Remington Model 740 BDL Special Grade

Similar to Model 740 ADL Deluxe Grade except stock & forearm have deluxe finish on select wood.

Estimated Value: Excellent: $350.00
Very good: $280.00

Remington Model 740 A Woodsmaster

Caliber: 30-06 or 308

Action: Semi-automatic; gas operated; side ejection; hammerless

Magazine: 4-shot detachable box

Barrel: 22" round

Sights: Ramp front, open rear adjustable for elevation

Stock & Forearm: Plain pistol two piece pistol grip stock & semi-beavertail forearm with finger grooves

Approximate wt.: 7½ lbs.

Comments: Made from about 1950 to 1960.

Estimated Value: Excellent: $300.00
Very good: $240.00

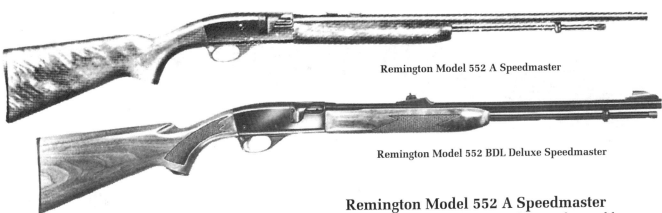

Remington Model 552 A Speedmaster

Remington Model 552 BDL Deluxe Speedmaster

Remington Model 552 BDL Deluxe Speedmaster

Same as Model 552 Speedmaster except: higher quality finish, Monte Carlo or regular, checkered stock & forearm; ramp front sight; adjustable rear; made from about 1961 to present.

Estimated Value: New (retail): $340.00
Excellent: $250.00
Very good: $200.00

Remington Model 552 GS Gallery Special

Same as Model 552 Speedmaster except: 22 short only.
Estimated Value: Excellent: $200.00
Very good: $160.00

Remington Model 552 A Speedmaster

Caliber: 22 short, long, long rifle interchangeably
Action: Semi-automatic; hammerless; side ejection; solid breech; sliding bolt; floating power piston which permits using 22 short, long, long rifle cartridges interchangeably
Magazine: 20-shot tubular in 22 short, 15-shot in long rifle; under barrel
Barrel: 21" & 23" round tapered
Sights: Bead front; notched adjustable rear
Stock & Forearm: Plain smooth two piece pistol grip stock & semi-beavertail forearm; buttplate
Approximate wt.: 5¾ lbs.
Comments: Made from about 1958 to 1987.
Estimated Value: Excellent: $175.00
Very good: $145.00

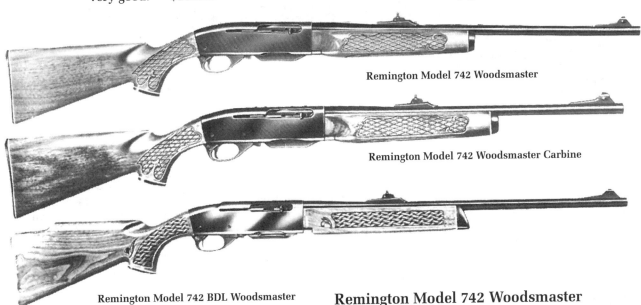

Remington Model 742 Woodsmaster

Remington Model 742 Woodsmaster Carbine

Remington Model 742 BDL Woodsmaster

Remington Model 742 Woodsmaster Carbine

Same as Model 742 Woodsmaster Rifle except: 18½" barrel; approx. wt. 6½ lbs.; calibers 280, 30-06 or 308.
Estimated Value: Excellent: $345.00
Very good: $275.00

Remington Model 742 BDL Woodsmaster

Same as Model 742 Woodsmaster Rifle except: 30-06 or 308 caliber.; checkered Monte Carlo stock; black tipped forearm.
Estimated Value: Excellent: $365.00
Very good: $290.00

Remington Model 742 Woodsmaster

Caliber: 280 Rem., 308 or 30-06; in 1963 6mm Rem.; in 1968, 243 Win.
Action: Semi-automatic; hammerless; gas operated
Magazine: 4-shot detachable box
Barrel: 22"; round tapered
Sights: Gold bead front, adjustable rear
Stock & Forearm: Plain or checkered & standard or deluxe finish two-piece walnut stock & semi-beavertail forearm; aluminum buttplate
Approximate wt.: 7½ lbs.
Comments: Manufactured from about 1960 to about 1980; in 1969 Remington advertised many fancy grades. Priced for standard grade.
Estimated Value: Excellent: $350.00
Very good: $280.00

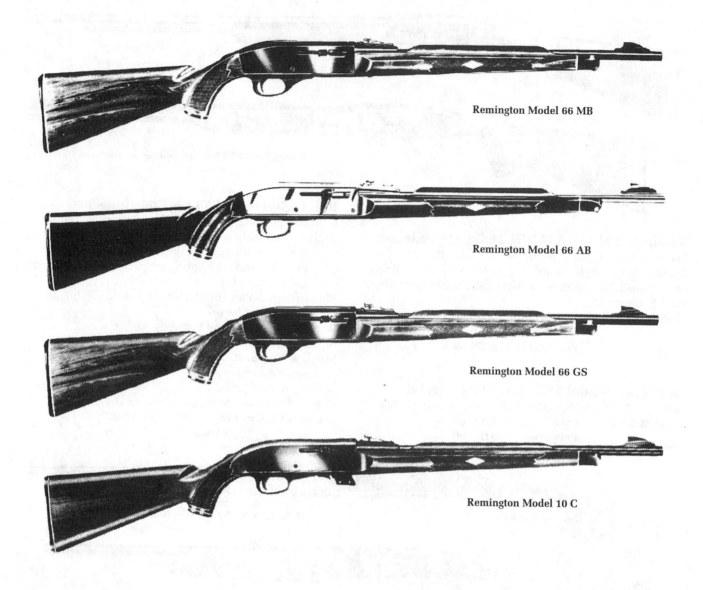

Remington Model 66 MB

Remington Model 66 AB

Remington Model 66 GS

Remington Model 10 C

Remington Model 66 MB & 66 SG

Caliber: 22 long rifle

Action: Semi-automatic; side ejection; solid breech; sliding bolt

Magazine: 14-shot tubular in stock

Barrel: 20" round

Sights: Blade front; rear sight adjustable for windage & elevation

Stock & Forearm: Du-Pont Zytel® nylon, brown or seneca green one-piece receiver, stock & forearm; checkered pistol grip stock & lipped forearm which covers top of barrel

Approximate wt.: 4 lbs.

Comments: Made from abt. 1959 to 1987; a design concept in which the stock, receiver & forearm are made in one piece; Model 66 SG is Seneca Green.

Estimated Value: **Excellent:**   **$120.00**
                      Very good: **$ 95.00**

Remington Model 66 AB, 66 BD

Same as Remington Model 66 MB except: black stock & forearm with chrome plated barrel & receiver covers; made from about 1962. AB discontinued in 1984. BD has black receiver, discontinued 1987.

Estimated Value: **Excellent:**   **$115.00**
                      Very good: **$ 90.00**

Remington Model 66 GS

Similar to the Model 66 MB except chambered for 22 short only (Gallery Special). Made from about 1963 to about 1980.

Estimated Value: **Excellent:**   **$110.00**
                      Very good: **$ 85.00**

Remington Model 10 C

Same as Remington Model 66 MB except 10-shot removable box magazine. Made from about 1970 to late 1970's.

Estimated Value: **Excellent:**   **$100.00**
                      Very good: **$ 75.00**

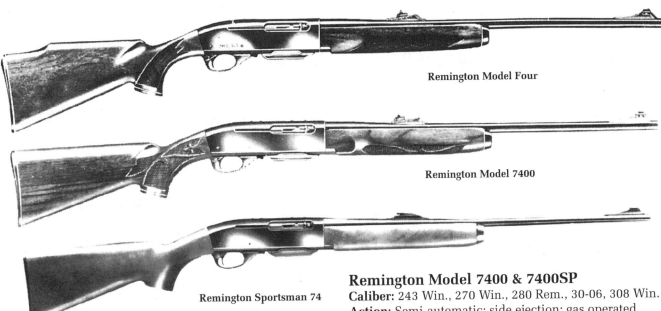

Remington Model Four

Remington Model 7400

Remington Sportsman 74

Remington Model Four

Caliber: 6mm Rem., 243 Win., 270 Win., 280 Rem. (7mm Express Rem); 30-06, 308 Win.

Action: Semi-automatic; side ejection; gas operated

Magazine: 4-shot clip

Barrel: Blued; 22"

Sights: Blade front ramp, adjustable sliding ramp rear

Stock & Forearm: Checkered walnut Monte Carlo pistol grip stock & forearm; black grip cap & fore-end tip; recessed finger groove in forearm; cheekpiece; high-gloss finish

Approximate wt.: 7½ lbs.

Comments: Produced from 1981 to 1987. Replaced the Model 742. Custom grades are available at increased prices. 6mm dropped in 1985

Estimated Value: Excellent: $430.00
Very good: $320.00

Remington Model 7400 & 7400SP

Caliber: 243 Win., 270 Win., 280 Rem., 30-06, 308 Win.

Action: Semi-automatic; side ejection; gas operated

Magazine: 4-shot clip

Barrel: Blued; 18½" or 22"

Sights: Adjustable, inclined ramp rear, ramp front

Stock & Forearm: Satin or gloss finish; checkered plain or Monte Carlo walnut stock and forearm

Approximate wt.: 7½ lbs.

Comments: Produced from the mid 1980's to present 7600SP is Special Purpose model with non-reflective finish on wood and metal.

Estimated Value: New (Retail) $573.00
Excellent: $430.00
Very good: $345.00

Remington Sportsman 74

Similar to the Model 7400 with lesser quality finish; hardwood with no checkering: 22" barrel; 30-06 caliber only. Produced 1984 to 1987.

Estimated Value: Excellent: $320.00
Very good: $240.00

Remington Model 522 Viper

Remington Model 522 Viper

Caliber: 22 long rifle

Action: Semi-automatic; last shot open bolt

Magazine: 10-shot clip

Barrel: Blued; 20"

Sights: Adjustable rear, ramp front; grooved scope mounting rail

Stock & Forearm: Black, checkered synthetic pistol grip stock and semi-beavertail forearm

Approximate wt.: 4½ lbs.

Comments: Introduced in 1993.

Estimated Value: New (Retail) $165.00
Excellent: $125.00
Very good: $100.00

Ruger

Ruger No. 1 Standard 1 B

Ruger No. 1 Light Sporter 1 A

Ruger No. 1 Medium Sporter 1 S

Ruger No. 1 Tropical 1 H

Ruger No. 1 International RSI

Ruger No. 1 Special Varminter 1 V

Ruger No. 1 Medium Sporter 1 S
Similar to No. 1 Light Sporter in heavier calibers, 7mm, 338, 300 & 45-70 with a 22" or 26" barrel, weighs 8 lbs.
Estimated Value: New (retail):   **$665.00**
                      Excellent: **$500.00**
                      Very good: **$400.00**

Ruger No. 1 Tropical 1 H
A 24" barrel version of No. 1 in 375 H&H mag., 404 jeffery, 416 Rigby, 416 Rem. mag., 458 mag. only. Approx. wt. 9 lbs.; open sights.
Estimated Value: New (retail):   **$665.00**
                      Excellent: **$500.00**
                      Very good: **$400.00**

Ruger No. 1 International RSI
Similar to the No. 1 with a 20" barrel with full-length forearm; available in calibers 243 Win., 30-06, 270 Win., & 7x57mm; weighs 7¼ lbs.
Estimated Value: New (retail):   **$688.00**
                      Excellent: **$520.00**
                      Very good: **$415.00**

Ruger No. 1 Special Varminter 1 V
Similar to No. 1 in 22 PPC, 22-250, 220 Swift, 223, 25-06, 6mm calibers; heavy 24" barrel. Approx. wt. 9 lbs.
Estimated Value: New (retail):   **$665.00**
                      Excellent: **$500.00**
                      Very good: **$400.00**

Ruger No. 1 Standard 1 B
Caliber: 218 Bee, 22 Hornet, 22-250, 220 Swift, 223, 243, 25-06, 6mm Rem., 257 Roberts, 280, 270, 30-06, 7mm Rem. mag., 300 Win. Mag.; 338 Win. mag.
Action: Falling block; under lever; single shot; hammerless
Magazine: None
Barrel: 26" tapered
Sights: None
Stock & Forearm: Checkered walnut pistol grip stock & forearm; swivels
Approximate wt.: 8 lbs.
Comments: Made from the late 1960's to present.
Estimated Value: New (retail):   **$665.00**
                      Excellent: **$500.00**
                      Very good: **$400.00**

Ruger No. 1 Light Sporter 1 A
Similar to No. 1 Standard 1 B in 243, 270, 30-06 or 7x57mm ; 22" barrel; Approx. weight 8 lbs., open sights.
Estimated Value: New (retail):   **$665.00**
                      Excellent: **$500.00**
                      Very good: **$400.00**

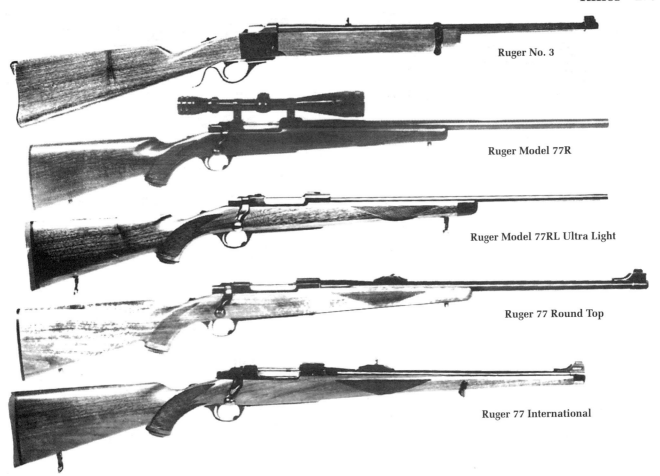

Ruger No. 3

Ruger Model 77R

Ruger Model 77RL Ultra Light

Ruger 77 Round Top

Ruger 77 International

Ruger No. 3
Caliber: 22 Hornet, 30-40 Krag, 45-70, 223, 375 Win., 44 mag.
Action: Falling block, under lever; hammerless; single shot
Magazine: None
Barrel: Blued; 22"
Sights: Folding leaf rear, bead front
Stock & Forearm: Plain walnut straight grip stock & forearm; barrel band
Approximate wt.: 6 lbs.
Comments: Made from the late 1960's to mid 1980's.
Estimated Value: Excellent: $375.00
Very good: $300.00

Ruger Model 77R, 77RS, & 77RS Tropical
Caliber: 220 Swift, 22-250, 25-06, 243 Win., 257, 270 Win., 280 Rem., 7mm Rem. mag., 7x57mm, 300 mag., 30-06, 35 Whelen, 338 mag., 458 Win. mag. (Tropical)
Action: Bolt action; repeating; either short or magnum action
Magazine: 5-shot box with hinged floor plate; 4-shot in magnum calibers
Barrel: Blued; 22" or 24"
Sights: Adjustable leaf rear, beaded ramp front; or no sights, integral scope mounts
Stock & Forearm: Checkered walnut, pistol grip, one-piece stock & tapered forearm; recoil pad
Approximate wt.: 6¾ lbs., 7 lbs., 8¾ lbs.
Comments: Made from the late 1960's to early 1990's. Add 16% for 458 mag. (Tropical); add 10% for sights.
Estimated Value: Excellent: $420.00
Very good: $335.00

Ruger 77 Round Top, M-77 ST
Similar to Model 77 with round top receiver & open sights. Made from early 1970's to early 1980's.
Estimated Value: Excellent: $350.00
Very good: $280.00

Ruger Model 77 International, M-77RSI
Similar to the Model 77 RS with 18½" barrel & full-length Mannlicher-type forearm; 22-250, 250-3000, 243, 308, 270 & 30-06 calibers; no sights, integral scope mounts. Produced from 1982 to present.
Estimated Value: New (retail): $642.00
Excellent: $480.00
Very good: $385.00

Ruger Model 77RL Ultra Light
Similar to the Model 77R with 20" barrel; weighs 6 lbs. Produced from 1984 to 1991. Calibers 22-250, 243, 270, 250-3000, 257, 30-06 & 308
Estimated Value: Excellent: $425.00
Very good: $340.00

Ruger 77 V Varmint & M-77 Varmint
Similar to Model 77 RS in 22-250, 220 Swift, 243, 6mm, 308 or 25-06 calibers; 24" heavy barrel or 26" tapered barrel; no sights. Made from early 1970's to early 1990's. Approx. wt. 9 lbs.
Estimated Value: Excellent: $430.00
Very good: $340.00

Ruger Model 77/22

Ruger Model 77 RLS

Caliber: 270, 30-06,
Action: Bolt action; repeating; long action
Magazine: 5-shot box; hinged floor plates; 4-shot mag.
Barrel: 18½"
Sights: Beaded ramp front; adjustable leaf rear
Stock & Forearm: Checkered pistol grip, one-piece stock & tapered forearm; rubber recoil pad; swivel studs
Approximate wt.: 6 lbs.
Comments: Made from the late 1960's to early 1990's
Estimated Value: Excellent: $440.00
                       Very good: $350.00

Ruger Model 77/22

Caliber: 22 long rifle; 22 mag. (after 1989); 22 Hornet (in early 1990's)
Action: Bolt action; repeating; three position safety
Magazine: Detachable rotary magazine; 10-shot (22 LR); 9-shot (22 mag.)
Barrel: 20" blued or 20" all stainless steel
Sights: Ramp front, folding leaf rear; or 1" scope rings
Stock & Forearm: Checkered walnut, one piece, pistol grip stock and forearm; stainless steel models have laminated wood or all-weather stocks (Zytel®)
Approximate wt.: 6¼ lbs.
Comments: Introduced in 1984. Add 6% for laminated stock & SS barrel; add 4½% for all-weather stock & SS barrel; add 5% for sights; add 5% for 22 Hornet.
Estimated Value: New (retail): $473.00
                       Excellent: $350.00
                       Very good: $285.00

Ruger Model 77 Mark II RL & VRL

Similar to the Model 77 Mark IIR except: calibers 223, 243, 257 Roberts, 270 Win. & 308, 30-06; 20" barrel; approx. wt. 6 lbs.; black fore-end tip; introduced in 1990.
Estimated Value: New (retail): $610.00
                       Excellent: $455.00
                       Very good: $365.00

Ruger Model 77 Mark II RS & VRS

Same as the Model 77 Mark II R except: calibers 6mm, 243, 25-06, 7mm Rem. mag., 270 Win., 30-06, 300 Win. mag., 308, 338 Win. mag., 458 Win. mag.; open sights (ramp front & express rear). Introduced in 1990.
Estimated Value: New (retail): $635.00
                       Excellent: $475.00
                       Very good: $380.00

Ruger Model 77 Mark II RP , VRP, & RSP

Same as the Model 77 Mark II R except: all stainless steel; all-weather fiberglass stock (DuPont Zytel®); calibers 223, 243, 270 Win., 280 Rem., 7mm Rem. mag., 30-06, 300 Win. mag., 308, 338 Win. mag.
Estimated Value: New (retail): $574.00
                       Excellent: $430.00
                       Very good: $345.00

Ruger Model 96/22

Caliber: 22 long rifle, 22 WMR
Action: Lever action, repeating; hammerless
Magazine: 10-shot (22 long rifle); 9-shot (22WMR); detachable rotary
Barrel: 18½"; blued
Sights: Gold bead front; adjustable for elevation, folding leaf rear
Stock & Forearm: Smooth hardwood, one-piece, pistol grip stock and forearm; metal barrel band at end of forearm
Approximate wt.: 5¼ lbs.
Comments: Introduced in 1996. Add 5% for 22 WMR
Estimated Value: New (retail): $328.00
                       Excellent: $245.00
                       Very good: $200.00

Ruger Model 96/44

Caliber: 44 magnum
Action: Lever action, repeating; hammerless
Magazine: 4-shot detachable rotary
Barrel: 18½"; blued
Sights: Gold bead front; adjustable folding leaf rear
Stock & Forearm: Smooth hardwood, one-piece, pistol grip stock and forearm; metal barrel band at end of forearm
Approximate wt.: 6 lbs.
Comments: Introduced in 1996.
Estimated Value: New (retail): $366.00
                       Excellent: $275.00
                       Very good: $220.00

Ruger Model 77 Mark II R & VR

Caliber: 223, 6mm, 243, 270, 30-06, 7mm, 308
Action: Bolt action; repeating; stainless steel bolt; three position swing back safety (in rear position bolt is locked & gun won't fire; center position the bolt will operate but gun won't fire; forward position bolt will operate & gun will fire); short action bolt
Magazine: 4-shot box with hinged floor plate
Barrel: Blued; 22"
Sights: None; 1" scope rings
Stock & Forearm: Checkered walnut, one-piece pistol grip stock & tapered forearm
Approximate wt.: 7 lbs.
Comments: Introduced in 1989 in 223 caliber, other calibers in 1990.
Estimated Value: New (retail): $574.00
                       Excellent: $430.00
                       Very good: $345.00

Ruger Model 77 Mark II V (Varmint)

Similar to the Model Mark II R except: calibers: 22PPC, 22-250, 220 Swift, 25-06, 223, 243, 6mm, and 308; laminated wood stock; 26" stainless steel heavy barrel; weighs 10 lbs. Introduced in 1992.
Estimated Value: New (retail): $684.00
                       Excellent: $515.00
                       Very good: $410.00

Ruger Model 77 Mark II Express

Caliber: 270, 7mm, 30-06, 300 Win., 338 Win. magnum

Action: Bolt action; repeating; 3 position safety

Magazine: 3 or 4-shot box; hinged floor plate

Barrel: 22" blued

Sights: Open express rear, on sighting rib; ramp front

Stock & Forearm: Checkered French walnut, one-piece pistol grip stock and forearm; rubber recoil pad; swivel studs

Approximate wt.: 7½ lbs.

Comments: Introduced in 1992.

Estimated Value: New (retail): $1,550.00
Excellent: $1,160.00
Very good: $ 930.00

Ruger Model 77 Mark II RSM & VRSM

Caliber: 375 H&H, 404 Jeffery, 416 Rigby, 458 Win. mag.

Action: Bolt action; repeating; stainless steel bolt; three position swing-back safety

Magazine: 3 or 4-shot box; removable floor plate

Barrel: 24" blued with sighting plane of cross serrations to reduce glare

Sights: Ramp front, open express rear

Stock & Forearm: Checkered walnut, one-piece pistol grip stock & forearm; swivel studs

Approximate wt.: 9¼ to 10 lbs.

Comments: Introduced in 1990.

Estimated Value: New (retail): $1,550.00
Excellent: $1,160.00
Very good: $ 930.00

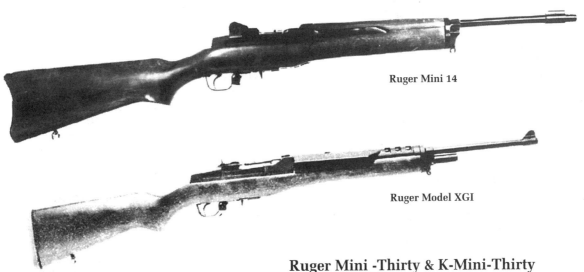

Ruger Mini 14

Ruger Model XGI

Ruger Mini 14 & K-Mini 14

Caliber: 223 Commercial or Military

Action: Semi-automatic, gas operated

Magazine: 5-shot detachable box; 10- & 20-shot available

Barrel: Blued; 18½"; also stainless steel after 1979

Sights: Adjustable rear, blade front

Stock & Forearm: Plain walnut, semi-pistol grip, one-piece stock & forearm; hand guard over barrel; folding stock & pistol grip available after mid 1980's

Approximate wt.: 6½ lbs.

Comments: Made from 1974 to present. Add 10% for stainless steel.

Estimated Value: New (retail): $516.00
Excellent: $385.00
Very good: $310.00

Ruger Mini 14/5-R & K-Mini 14/5 R Rifle

Similar to the Mini 14 with internal improvements & integral scope mounts. Introduced in 1982; add 9½% for stainles steel (K-Mini 14/R).

Estimated Value: New (retail): $556.00
Excellent: $420.00
Very good: $330.00

Ruger Mini -Thirty & K-Mini-Thirty

Caliber: 7.62x39mm

Action: Semi-automatic, gas operated

Magazine: 5-shot detachable staggered box

Barrel: 18½"; blued or stainless steel

Sights: Blade front; adjustable rear

Stock & Forearm: Plain walnut, pistol grip one-piece stock & forearm with hand guard over barrel

Approximate wt.: 7 lbs.

Comments: Introduced in 1988. A modified version of the Mini-14 Ranch Rifle. Add 9½% for stainless steel.

Estimated Value: New (retail): $556.00
Excellent: $420.00
Very good: $330.00

Ruger Model XGI

Caliber: 243 or 308

Action: Gas operated, semi-automatic, based on the Garand system used in the U.S. M1 & M14 military rifles

Magazine: 5-shot staggered column, detachable box

Barrel: 20" blued with hanguard cover

Sights: Ramp front & adjustable folding peep rear

Stock & Forearm: Plain one-piece American hardwood, reinforced with steel liners

Approximate wt.: 8 lbs.

Comments: Produced from 1986 to 1988.

Estimated Value: Excellent: $375.00
Very good: $300.00

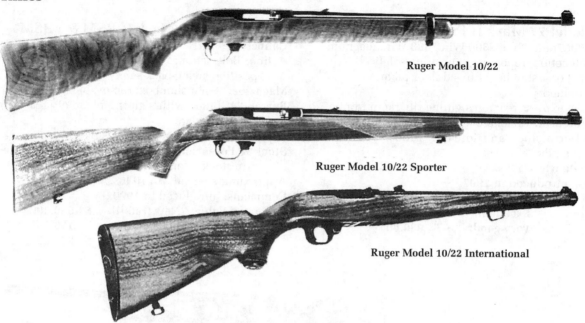

Ruger Model 10/22

Ruger Model 10/22 Sporter

Ruger Model 10/22 International

Ruger Model 10/22

Caliber: 22 long rifle
Action: Semi-automatic
Magazine: 10-shot detachable rotary
Barrel: Blued; 18½"
Sights: Adjustable leaf rear, bed front
Stock & Forearm: Plain hardwood one-piece semi-pistol grip stock & forearm; barrel band
Approximate wt.: 5 lbs.
Comments: Made from about 1964 to present. Add 20% for stainless steel.
Estimated Value: New (retail): **$213.00**
Excellent: **$160.00**
Very good: **$125.00**

Ruger Model 10/22, Deluxe Sporter

Similar to the Model 10/22 with Monte Carlo or regular checkered walnut stock; fluted bandless forearm.
Estimated Value: New (retail): **$274.00**
Excellent: **$200.00**
Very good: **$160.00**

Ruger Model 10/22, International

Similar to Model 10/22 with full-length stock and swivels. Add 8% for stainless steel barrel
Estimated Value: New(retail): **$262.00**
Excellent: **$195.00**
Very good: **$155.00**

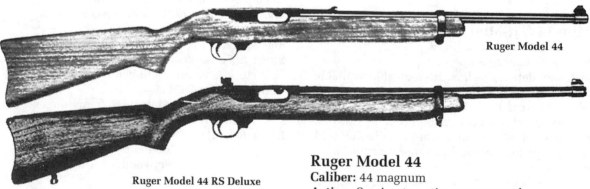

Ruger Model 44

Ruger Model 44 RS Deluxe

Ruger Model 10/22T

Caliber: 22 long rifle
Action: Semi-automatic
Magazine: 10-shot rotary
Barrel: 20" blued, hammer-forged spiral finish
Sights: None
Stock & Forearm: Laminated hardwood, one-piece pistol grip stock and forearm
Approximate wt.: 7¼ lbs.
Comments: Introduced in 1996.
Estimated Value: New (retail): **$392.00**
Excellent: **$295.00**
Very good: **$235.00**

Ruger Model 44

Caliber: 44 magnum
Action: Semi-automatic, gas operated
Magazine: 4-shot tubular
Barrel: Blued; 18½"
Sights: Leaf rear, bead front
Stock & Forearm: Plain walnut one-piece semi-pistol grip stock & forearm; barrel band
Approximate wt.: 5¾ lbs.
Comments: Made from about 1960 to mid 1980's.
Estimated Value: Excellent: **$340.00**
Very good: **$275.00**

Ruger Model 44 RS Deluxe

Similar to Model 44 with peep sight & swivels.
Estimated Value: Excellent: **$350.00**
Very good: **$285.00**

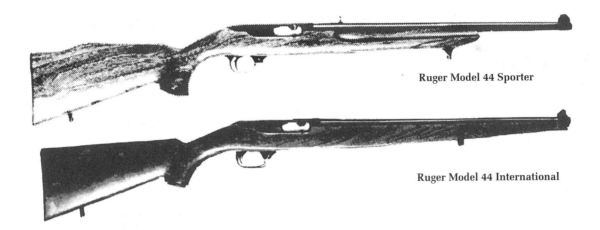

Ruger Model 44 Sporter

Ruger Model 44 International

Ruger Model 44 Sporter
Similar to Model 44 with Monte Carlo stock, fluted fore-arm & swivels. Made to early 1970's.
Estimated Value: Excellent: $370.00
Very good: $300.00

Ruger Model 44 International
Similar to Model 44 with a full-length stock & swivels. Made to early 1970's.
Estimated Value: Excellent: $400.00
Very good: $320.00

Sako

Sako Finsport 2700

Sako Vixen Sporter

Sako Vixen Mannlicher

Sako Finsport 2700
Caliber: 270 Win., 30-06, 7mm Rem. mag., 338 Win. mag.
Action: Long throw bolt action; adjustable trigger
Magazine: 5-shot
Barrel: Blued; 23½"
Sights: None
Stock & Forearm: Checkered walnut, Monte Carlo pistol grip, one-piece stock & forearm; recoil pad; swivels
Approximate wt.: 6½ lbs.
Comments: Produced 1983 to late 1980's.
Estimated Value: Excellent: $725.00
Very good: $580.00

Sako Vixen Sporter
Caliber: 218 Bee, 22 Hornet, 222, 222 mag., 223
Action: Bolt action, short stroke, Mauser-type
Magazine: 5-shot
Barrel: Blued; 23½"
Sights: Open rear, hooded ramp front
Stock & Forearm: Checkered walnut, Monte Carlo pistol grip, one-piece stock & forearm; swivels
Approximate wt.: 6½ lbs.
Comments: Made from World War II to the early 1970's.
Estimated Value: Excellent: $630.00
Very good: $500.00

Sako Vixen Mannlicher
Similar to Sporter with a full-length stock; 20" barrel; barrel band.
Estimated Value: Excellent: $645.00
Very good: $515.00

Sako Vixen Heavy Barrel

Sako Forester Sporter

Sako Forester Mannlicher

Sako Forester Heavy Barrel

Sako Finnbear

Sako Finnbear Mannlicher

Sako Vixen Heavy Barrel
Similar to Vixen Sporter with heavy barrel & in larger calibers only.
Estimated Value: Excellent: $650.00
                       Very good: $520.00

Sako Forester Sporter
Similar to Vixen Sporter with medium action & in 22-250, 243 & 308 calibers. Made from the late 1950's to early 1970's.
Estimated Value: Excellent: $645.00
                       Very good: $515.00

Sako Forester Mannlicher
Similar to Forester Sporter with full-length stock; 20" barrel; barrel band.
Estimated Value: Excellent: $670.00
                       Very good: $535.00

Sako Forester Heavy Barrel
Similar to Forester Sporter with a heavy 24" barrel.
Estimated Value: Excellent: $675.00
                       Very good: $540.00

Sako Finnbear
Similar to Vixen Sporter with long action; recoil pad; 25-06, 264 magnum, 270, 30-06, 300 magnum, 7mm magnum; 375 H&H. Made from the early 1960's to the early 1970's.
Estimated Value: Excellent: $680.00
                       Very good: $550.00

Sako Finnbear Mannlicher
Similar to Finnbear with: full-length stock; 20" barrel; barrel band.
Estimated Value: Excellent: $695.00
                       Very good: $555.00

Sako Model 74 Super Sporter

Sako Model 74 Super Sporter Heavy Barrel

Sako Model 74 Deluxe Sporter

Sako Model 74 Super Sporter

Similar to Vixen, Forester & Finnbear in short action, medium action & long action; 23" or 24" barrel. Made in 1970's.

Estimated Value: Excellent: $640.00
Very good: $520.00

Sako Model 74 Super Sporter Heavy Barrel

Similar to Model 74 Super Sporter in short, medium or long action & heavy barrel.

Estimated Value: Excellent: $650.00
Very good: $525.00

Sako Model 74 Deluxe Sporter

Similar to Model 74 Super Sporter with recoil pad, select wood & high-quality finish. Add $25.00 for magnum.

Estimated Value: Excellent: $675.00
Very good: $540.00

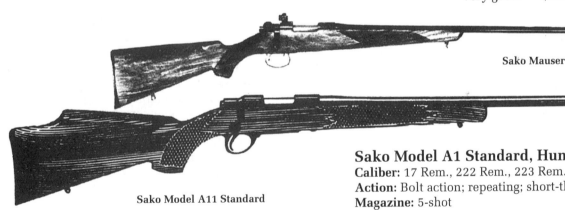

Sako Mauser

Sako Model A11 Standard

Sako Mauser

Caliber: 270, 30-06
Action: FN Mauser bolt action; repeating
Magazine: 5-shot box
Barrel: Blued; 24"
Sights: Leaf rear, hooded ramp front
Stock & Forearm: Checkered walnut Monte Carlo one-piece pistol grip stock & tapered forearm; swivels
Approximate wt.: 7½ lbs.
Comments: Made from World War II to about 1960.
Estimated Value: Excellent: $610.00
Very good: $490.00

Sako Mauser Magnum

Similar to Sako Mauser in magnum calibers 300 H&H & 375 H&H; recoil pad.

Estimated Value: Excellent: $675.00
Very good: $550.00

Sako Model A1 Standard, Hunter

Caliber: 17 Rem., 222 Rem., 223 Rem.
Action: Bolt action; repeating; short-throw
Magazine: 5-shot
Barrel: 23½"
Sights: None
Stock & Forearm: Checkered walnut Monte Carlo one-piece pistol grip stock & forearm; lacquer or oil finish; laminated grain & fiberglass available in 1989; swivels
Approximate wt.: 6½ lbs.
Comments: Add 4% for 17 Rem. caliber; add 20% for laminated stock & 30% for fiberglass stock.
Estimated Value: New (retail): $1,050.00
Excellent: $785.00
Very good: $630.00

Sako Model A11 Standard, Hunter

Similar to the A1 Standard Hunter except: medium throw action in 220 Swift, 22-250 Rem., 243 Win., 7mm-08, 308 Win. calibers. Add 12% for laminated stock and 30% for fiberglass stock.

Estimated Value: New (retail): $1,050.00
Excellent: $785.00
Very good: $630.00

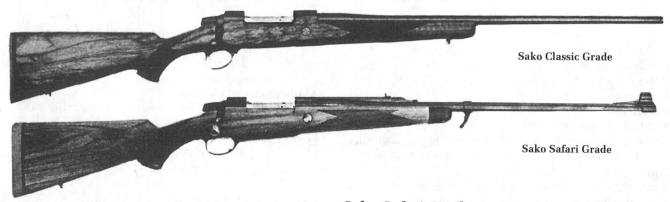

Sako Model A1 Deluxe

Sako Varmint

Sako Carbine

Sako Model A111 Standard, Hunter

Similar to the Model A1 Standard Hunter: long throw action; 25-06 Rem., 6.5x55, 270 Win., 280 Rem., 7x64, 30-06, 7mm Rem. magnum, 300 Win. magnum, 338 Win. magnum, 9.3x62, 375 H&H mag, 416 Rigby; recoil pad. Add 4% for mag. Add 12% for laminated stock; Add 30% for fiberglass stock.

Estimated Value:	New (retail):	$1,085.00
	Excellent:	$ 815.00
	Very good:	$ 650.00

Sako Model A1 Deluxe

A deluxe version of the A1 Standard Hunter; recoil pad.

Estimated Value:	New (retail):	$1,475.00
	Excellent:	$1,110.00
	Very good:	$ 885.00

Sako Model A11 Deluxe

Similar to the Model A11 Stanard Hunter with deluxe features; recoil pad.

Estimated Value:	New (retail):	$1,475.00
	Excellent:	$1,110.00
	Very good:	$ 885.00

Sako Model A111 Deluxe

Similar to the Model A111 Stanard Hunter with deluxe features. Add 3% for magnum.

Estimated Value:	New (retail):	$1,510.00
	Excellent:	$1,135.00
	Very good:	$ 900.00

Sako Varmint

Similar to Models A1, A11 & A111 Standard Hunter except: heavy varmint barrel; calibers 17 Rem., 222 Rem., 223 Rem., 22-250 Rem., 243 Win., 308 Win., 7mm-08

Estimated Value:	New (retail):	$1,240.00
	Excellent:	$ 930.00
	Very good:	$ 745.00

Sako Carbine, Mannlicher

Similar to Models A1, A11 & A111 Standard Hunter except: 20" barrel & full-length forearm; calibers 243 Win., 270 Win., 308 Win., 30-06, 338 Win. mag. Add 6% for 375 H&H & 3% for other magnums.

Estimated Value:	New (retail):	$1,275.00
	Excellent:	$ 960.00
	Very good:	$ 775.00

Sako Classic Grade

Sako Safari Grade

Sako Classic Grade

Similar to the A11 & A111 Standard Hunter except: styling changes; 243 Win., 270 Win., 30-06, 7mm Rem. mag.; select walnut stock. Add 5% for 7mm Rem. mag.

Estimated Value:	New (retail):	$1,050.00
	Excellent:	$ 790.00
	Very good:	$ 630.00

Sako Safari Grade

Similar to the A111 Deluxe with extended magazine, barrel band swivels, select French walnut stock; choice of satin or matte blue finish; calibers 300 Win. mag., 338 Win. mag., 375 H&H mag., 416 Rigby.

Estimated Value:	New (retail):	$2,765.00
	Excellent:	$2,075.00
	Very good:	$1,260.00

Sako Finnwolf Sporter

Sako Model 78

Caliber: 22 long rifle, 22 Win. magnum, 22 Hornet
Action: Bolt action; repeating
Magazine: 5-shot; 4-shot in magnum
Barrel: 22½"; heavy barrel available
Sights: Folding leaf rear, hooded ramp front
Stock & Forearm: One-piece checkered walnut Monte Carlo pistol grip stock & forearm; swivels
Approximate wt.: 6¾ lbs.
Comments: Made from the late 1970's to late 1980's. Add 5% for 22 Hornet.
Estimated Value: **Excellent:** $520.00
                                Very good: $415.00

Sako Finnwolf Sporter

Caliber: 243, 308
Action: Lever-action; hammerless; repeating
Magazine: 4-shot clip
Barrel: Blued; 23"
Sights: No rear, hooded ramp front
Stock & Forearm: Checkered walnut Monte Carlo one-piece pistol grip stock and tapered forearm; swivels
Approximate wt.: 7 lbs.
Comments: Made from the mid 1960's to early 1970's.
Estimated Value: **Excellent:** $620.00
                                Very good: $500.00

Sako Finnwolf Deluxe Sporter

Same as Finnwolf Sporter with select wood.
Estimated Value: **Excellent:** $675.00
                                Very good: $540.00

Sako Model 78

Sako Finnfire

Caliber: 22 long rifle
Action: Lever-action; repeating
Magazine: 5-shot clip
Barrel: 22½" standard or heavyweight; blued
Sights: Adjustable rear, hooded ramp front
Stock & Forearm: Checkered walnut one-piece pistol grip stock and tapered forearm; swivel studs
Approximate wt.: 5½ lbs.
Comments: Introduced in 1994. Add 11% for heavy barrel.
Estimated Value: **New (Retail):** $732.00
                                Excellent: $550.00
                                Very good: $440.00

Sako Model TRG-S

Caliber: 25-06 Rem., 270 Win., 6.5 x 55SS 30-06, 7mm Rem. magnum, 300 Win. magnum, 338 Win. magnum, 300 Whby magnum, 338 Lapua magnum, 375 H&H; 270 Whby mag., 7mm Whby mag., 340 Whby mag. (added in 1996)
Action: Bolt action, repeating; three bolt locking lugs
Magazine: 5-shot; 4-shot in 375 H&H; detachable box
Barrel: Blued; 22", 24", 26" in magnum calibers; matte blue finish
Sights: None; scope mount rails
Stock & Forearm: Fiberglass, plain one-piece pistol grip stock and forearm; swivel studs
Approximate wt.: 7¾ lbs.
Comments: Introduced in 1994. Add 5% for magnum.
Estimated Value: **New (Retail):** $790.00
                                Excellent: $590.00
                                Very good: $445.00

Savage

Savage Model 1904

Savage Model 1905

Savage Model 1911 Target

Savage Model 3

Savage Model 1904 & Model 04

Caliber: 22 short, long, long rifle
Action: Bolt action; single shot
Magazine: None
Barrel: 18"
Sights: Open rear, bead front
Stock & Forearm: Straight wood one-piece stock & forearm
Approximate wt.: 3 lbs.
Comments: This is a boy's lightweight takedown rifle produced from 1904 to 1917 as Model 1904 & from 1924 to 1930 as Model 04.
Estimated Value: Excellent: $150.00
  Very good: $130.00

Savage Model 3, 3S, 3ST

Caliber: 22 short, long, long rifle
Action: Bolt action; single shot
Magazine: None
Barrel: 26" before World War II, 24" after
Sights: Open rear, bead front; 3S & 3ST have peep rear & hooded front
Stock & Forearm: One-piece walnut semi-pistol grip stock & forearm; 3ST has swivels
Approximate wt.: 4 to 5 lbs.
Comments: A takedown model produced from 1933 until the early 1950's. The 3ST was discontinued before World War II.
Estimated Value: Excellent: $110.00
  Very good: $ 90.00

Savage Model 1905

Caliber: 22 short, long, long rifle
Action: Bolt action; single shot
Magazine: None
Barrel: 22
Sights: Open rear, bead front
Stock & Forearm: Plain one-piece straight grip stock & forearm
Approximate wt.: 5 lbs.
Comments: A lightweight takedown boy's rifle produced until about 1917.
Estimated Value: Excellent: $140.00
  Very good: $110.00

Savage Model 1911 Target

Caliber: 22 short
Action: Bolt action; single shot
Magazine: None
Barrel: 20"
Sights: Adjustable rear, bead front
Stock & Forearm: Walnut one-piece straight grip stock & forearm
Approximate wt.: 4 lbs.
Comments: Made from 1911 to 1916.
Estimated Value: Excellent: $160.00
  Very good: $135.00

Savage Mark IG and GY

Caliber: 22 short, long, long rifle
Action: Bolt action; self cocking, single shot
Magazine: None; single shot
Barrel: Blued; 20¾"; 19" (Mark I GY) youth model
Sights: Bead front, adjustable open rear; receiver is dove-tailed for scope mounting
Stock & Forearm: Walnut finished, checkered one-piece, Monte Carlo stock and forearm
Approximate wt.: 5½ lbs.
Comments: Introduced in the mid 1990's; also made in youth model (Mark I GY) and "smooth bore" shot shell model (Mark I SB)
Estimated Value: New (retail): $119.00
  Excellent: $ 90.00
  Very good: $ 75.00

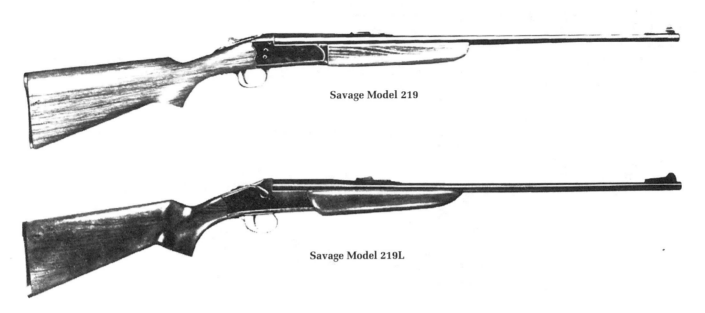

Savage Model 219

Savage Model 219L

Savage Model 219, 219L

Caliber: 22 Hornet, 25-20, 32-20, 30-30
Action: Hammerless; single shot; automatic ejector; shot-
gun style, top break lever; 219L has side lever
Magazine: Single shot
Barrel: 26"
Sights: Open rear, bead front
Stock & Forearm: Plain walnut pistol grip stock & fore-
arm
Approximate wt.: 6 lbs.
Comments: A takedown model made from 1938 to 1965
as Model 219; 1965 for two years as 219L.
Estimated Value: Excellent: $110.00
Very good: $ 85.00

Savage Model 221 Utility Gun

Same rifle as the Model 219 except it was offered in 30-
30 only with an interchangeable 12 gauge 30" shotgun
barrel. Prices include the 12 gauge interchangeable shotgun barrel.
Estimated Value: Excellent: $130.00
Very good: $105.00

Savage Model 221 Utility Gun

Savage Model 222

Same as Model 221 except shotgun barrel is 16 gauge; 28".
Estimated Value: Excellent: $130.00
Very good: $105.00

Savage Model 223

Same as Model 221 except shotgun barrel is 20 gauge, 28".
Estimated Value: Excellent: $130.00
Very good: $105.00

Savage Model 227

Same as Model 221 except it is 22 Hornet & the shotgun
barrel is 12 gauge, 30".
Estimated Value: Excellent: $135.00
Very good: $110.00

Savage Model 228

Same as Model 227 except shotgun barrel is 16 gauge, 28".
Estimated Value: Excellent: $135.00
Very good: $110.00

Savage Model 229

Same as Model 227 except shotgun barrel is 20 gauge, 28".
Estimated Value: Excellent: $135.00
Very good: $110.00

Savage Model 19

Savage Model 19 NRA

Savage Model 20

Savage Model 40

Savage Model 45

Savage Model 19, 19L Target
Caliber: 22 long rifle
Action: Bolt action; repeating; speed lock
Magazine: 5-shot detachable box
Barrel: 25"
Sights: Extension rear, hooded front
Stock & Forearm: Walnut pistol grip stock & beavertail forearm; swivels
Approximate wt.: 7½ lbs.
Comments: Made from 1933 to the mid 1940's. The model 19L has special Lyman receiver & front sights; add $10.00 to $15.00.
Estimated Value: Excellent: $210.00
Very good: $160.00

Savage Model 19 NRA Match Rifle
Caliber: 22 long rifle
Action: Bolt action; repeating
Magazine: 5-shot detachable box
Barrel: 25"
Sights: Adjustable peep rear, blade front
Stock & Forearm: Wood full military pistol grip stock & forearm
Approximate wt.: 7 lbs.
Comments: Made from 1919 until 1932.
Estimated Value: Excellent: $275.00
Very good: $220.00

Savage Mark IIG & GY
Caliber: 22 long rifle
Action: Bolt action; repeating
Magazine: 10-shot detachable clip
Barrel: Blued; 20¾"; 19" (Mark II GY) youth model
Sights: Bead front, adjustable open rear
Stock & Forearm: Walnut finished, checkered one-piece, hardwood stock and forearm
Approximate wt.: 5½ lbs.
Comments: Introduced in the mid 1990's; also made in youth model (Mark II GY).
Estimated Value: New (retail): $126.00
Excellent: $ 95.00
Very good: $ 75.00

Savage Model 19M
Same as the Model 19 except: heavier 28" barrel. Approximate wt. is 9¼ lbs.
Estimated Value: Excellent: $230.00
Very good: $185.00

Savage Model 19H Hornet
Same as Model 19 except loading port, bolt mechanism & magazine are like Model 23-D; 22 Hornet caliber only.
Estimated Value: Excellent: $310.00
Very good: $250.00

Savage Model 20
Caliber: 300 Savage, 250-3000
Action: Bolt action; repeating
Magazine: 5-shot
Barrel: 22" in 250 caliber; 24" in 300 caliber
Sights: Open rear, bead front; in 1926, rear peep sight
Stock & Forearm: Checkered walnut pistol grip stock & forearm; in 1926 cut to semi-pistol grip
Approximate wt.: 5¾ to 7 lbs.
Comments: Made from 1920 through 1929.
Estimated Value: Excellent: $330.00
Very good: $260.00

Savage Model 40
Caliber: 250-3000, 300 Savage, 30-30, 30-06
Action: Bolt action; repeating
Magazine: 4-shot detachable box
Barrel: 22" for caliber 250-3000 & 30-30; 24" for other models
Sights: Open rear, ramp front
Stock & Forearm: Plain walnut pistol grip stock & lipped forearm after 1936; checkered stock after 1940
Approximate wt.: 7½ lbs.
Comments: Made from 1928 until World War II.
Estimated Value: Excellent: $300.00
Very good: $240.00

Savage Model 45
This is a special grade version of the Model 40. It has a checkered stock & forearm & a special receiver sight. Discontinued in 1940.
Estimated Value: Excellent: $320.00
Very good: $255.00

Savage Model 23A
Sporter

Savage Model 23AA

Savage Model 23B

Savage Model 4

Savage Model 4S

Savage Model 4M

Savage Model 5

Savage Model 5S

Savage Model 4, 4S, 4M

Caliber: 22 short, long, long rifle; 4M chambered for 22 mag.

Action: Bolt action; repeating

Magazine: 5-shot detachable box

Barrel: 24"

Sights: Open rear, bead front; 4S has peep rear & hooded front

Stock & Forearm: Checkered walnut pistol grip stock & grooved forearm on pre-World War II models; plain on post-World War II models

Approximate wt.: 5½ lbs.

Comments: The Model 4 & 4S were produced from 1933 until the mid 1960's. 4M was made during the early to mid 1960's. Add $10.00 for model 4M.

Estimated Value: Excellent: $115.00
                     Very good: $ 90.00

Savage Model 5, 5S

Similar to the Model 4 except the magazine is tubular & the gun weighs about 6 lbs. The Model 5S has peep rear & hooded front sight. They were produced from the mid 1930's until 1961; caliber 22 short, long & long rifle. Add $10.00 for Model 5S.

Estimated Value: Excellent: $120.00
                     Very good: $ 95.00

Savage Model 23A Sporter, 23AA, 23B, 23C, 23D

Caliber: 22 long rifle (Model 23A, 23AA); from 1933 to 1947 in 22 Hornet (Model 23 D); 25-20 (Model 23B); 32-20 (Model 23C)

Action: Bolt action; from 1933 to 1942 (Model 23AA) speed lock

Magazine: 5-shot detachable box

Barrel: 23"; 25" from 1933 until 1942 on Model 23B

Sights: Open rear, bead or blade front

Stock & Forearm: Plain walnut semi-pistol grip stock & forearm

Approximate wt.: 6 to 6½ lbs.

Comments: Produced: 23A from 1923 to 1933; Model 23AA with improved lock, 1933 to 1942; Model 23B, 1933 to 1942; Model 23C, 23D, 1933 to 1947.

Estimated Value: Excellent: $225.00
                     Very good: $180.00

Savage Model 93G Magnum

Caliber: 22 WMR

Action: Bolt action; repeating

Magazine: 5-shot clip

Barrel: Blued; 20¾"

Sights: Bead front, sporting rear with height adjustment

Stock & Forearm: Walnut stained, cut checkered, hardwood one-piece Monte Carlo stock and forearm

Approximate wt.: 5¾ lbs.

Comments: Introduced in the mid 1990's.

Estimated Value: New (retail): $145.00
                     Excellent: $110.00
                     Very good: $ 90.00

Savage Model 110E

Savage Model 110 Sporter

Savage Model 110E (Early)
Caliber: 243 Win., 7mm Rem. mag., 30-06
Action: Bolt action; repeating
Magazine: 4-shot staggered box; 3-shot in magnum
Barrel: Blued; 20"; stainless steel in magnum
Sights: Open rear, ramp front
Stock & Forearm: One-piece checkered or plain walnut Monte Carlo stock & forearm; mag. has recoil pad
Approximate wt.: 6¾ to 7¾ lbs.
Comments: Made from 1963 to late 1970's. A later model was also designated 110E.
Estimated Value: Excellent: $225.00
                Very good: $170.00

Savage Model 110 Sporter
Caliber: 243, 270, 308, 30-06
Action: Bolt action; repeating
Magazine: 4-shot staggered box
Barrel: 22"
Sights: Open rear, ramp front
Stock & Forearm: Checkered walnut pistol grip stock & forearm
Approximate wt.: 6¾ lbs.
Comments: Made from 1958 until the early 1960's when it was replaced by 110E.
Estimated Value: Excellent: $220.00
                Very good: $175.00

Savage Model 110 MC
Same as 110 Sporter except: 22-250 caliber added; 24" barrel; Monte Carlo stock. Made from the late 1950's to about 1969.
Estimated Value: Excellent: $240.00
                Very good: $195.00

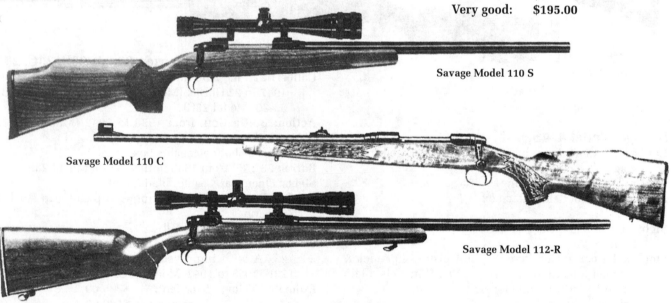

Savage Model 110 S

Savage Model 110 C

Savage Model 112-R

Savage Model 110 C
Caliber: 22-250, 243, 25-06, 270, 308, 30-06, 7mm Rem. mag., 300 Win. mag.
Action: Bolt action; repeating
Magazine: 4-shot clip, 3-shot clip in mag. calibers
Barrel: 22" & 24"; 24" in mag. calibers
Sights: Open rear, ramp front
Stock & Forearm: Checkered walnut Monte Carlo stock & forearm; mag.has recoil pad
Approximate wt.: 6¾ to 8 lbs.
Comments: This rifle was produced from 1966. to 1986. Add 10% for mag. calibers.
Estimated Value: Excellent: $300.00
                Very good: $225.00

Savage Model 110 S
Similar to the Model 110 C except: heavy barrel; no sights; stippled checkering; recoil pad; 7mm/08 & 308 calibers; Produced from late 1970's to mid 1980's.
Estimated Value: Excellent: $325.00
                Very good: $260.00

Savage Model 112-R
A varmint rifle similar to the Model 110 C except: plain walnut one-piece semi-pistol grip stock & forearm; swivels; recoil pad; no sights; 22-250 & 25-06 calibers; made from about 1979 to early 1980's.
Estimated Value: Excellent: $275.00
                Very good: $220.00

Savage Model 110 M

Savage Model 110 M

Caliber: 7mm Rem. mag., 264, 300, 338 Win.
Action: Bolt action; repeating
Magazine: 4-shot box, staggered
Barrel: 24"
Sights: Open rear, ramp front
Stock & Forearm: Walnut Monte Carlo pistol grip stock & forearm; recoil pad
Approximate wt.: 7½ to 8 lbs.
Comments: Made from 1963 to 1969.
Estimated Value: Excellent: $250.00
Very good: $190.00

Savage Model 110 D

Caliber: 223, 243, 270, 30-06, 7mm Rem. magnum, 338 Win. magnum
Action: Bolt action; repeating
Magazine: 4-shot internal box; 3-shot for magnums
Barrel: 22" blue; 24" for magnums
Sights: Hooded ramp front, adjustable rear
Stock & Forearm: Select walnut, checkered semi-pistol grip, Monte Carlo, one-piece stock & forearm
Approximate wt.: 6¾ lbs; 7 lbs. in magnum
Comments: Produced from 1986 to 1988. Add 18% for mag. calibers.
Estimated Value: Excellent: $295.00
Very good: $235.00

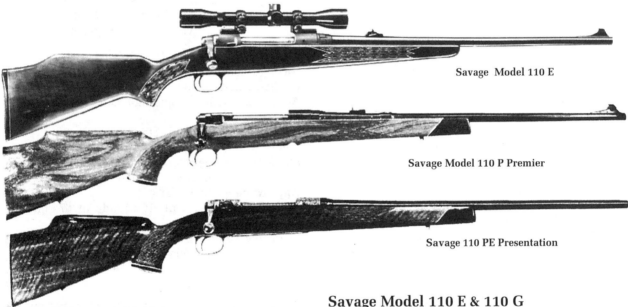

Savage Model 110 E

Savage Model 110 P Premier

Savage 110 PE Presentation

Savage Model 110 P Premier

Caliber: 243 Win., 7mm Rem. mag., 30-06
Action: Bolt action; repeating
Magazine: 4-shot box, staggered; 3-shot in mag.
Barrel: Blued 22"; 24" stainless steel in mag.
Sights: Open rear folding leaf, ramp front
Stock & Forearm: Walnut & rosewood Monte Carlo stock & forearm; swivels; mag. has recoil pad
Approximate wt.: 7 to 8 lbs.
Comments: Made from mid 1960's until 1970's; Add 10% for mag.
Estimated Value: Excellent: $390.00
Very good: $310.00

Savage 110 PE Presentation

Same as Models 110 P Premier except: receiver, floor plate & trigger guard are engraved. Produced for two years beginning in 1968. Add 10% for mag.
Estimated Value: Excellent: $550.00
Very good: $440.00

Savage Model 110 E & 110 G

Caliber: 22-250, 223, 243, 308 Win., 270, 30-06, 7mm Rem. mag., 300 Win. mag.
Action: Bolt action; repeating
Magazine: 4-shot box, internal box
Barrel: Blued 22"; 24" in 7mm mag. & 300 Win. mag.
Sights: None; Removable ramp front & removable adj. rear optional
Stock & Forearm: Checkered hardwood, Monte Carlo walnut finish, one-piece pistol grip stock & forearm
Approximate wt.: 7 lbs.
Comments: Sold from late 1970's to 1981 as Stevens, & 1982 to present as Savage. Add 5% for sights.
Estimated Value: Excellent: $300.00
Very good: $240.00

Savage Model 110 V & 110 GV

Similar to Model 110E & 110G except: 22-250 or 223 caliber. No sights; a heavy 26" barrel. Recoil pad. Produced from mid 1980's to early 1990's. Approx. wt is 9 lbs.
Estimated Value: Excellent: $315.00
Very good: $250.00

Savage Model 111

Savage Model 110 FP Police Rifle

Similar to the Model 110 G except: 223 Remington, 25-06 Rem., 30-06 Spfld., 308 Winchester, 7mm Rem., and 300 Win. caliber; heavy 24" barrel; non-reflective black finish on metal parts; black all-weather DuPont Rynite® one-piece stock & forearm; sling studs & bi-pod mount; no sights; drilled & tapped for scope mounts. Pillar bedded stock. Introduced in 1990.

Estimated Value:　New (retail):　$429.00
　　　　　　　　　Excellent:　$320.00
　　　　　　　　　Very good:　$260.00

Savage Model 110 F

Same as the Model 110G except: black DuPont Rynite® stock & forearm; add 4% for sights. Made from the late 1980's to early 1990's

Estimated Value:　Excellent:　$305.00
　　　　　　　　　Very good:　$245.00

Savage Model 110B

Same as the Model 110G except: brown laminate hardwood stock; ramp front sight & adjustable rear sight. Made from the 1980's to early 1990's.

Estimated Value:　Excellent:　$325.00
　　　　　　　　　Very good:　$260.00

Savage Model 111

Caliber: 7mm (7x57), 243, 270, 30-06, 7mm magnum
Action: Bolt action; repeating
Magazine: 4-shot box; 3-shot box in magnum
Barrel: 24"
Sights: Adjustable removable rear, removable hooded ramp front
Stock & Forearm: Checkered walnut Monte Carlo one-piece pistol grip stock & forearm; swivels
Approximate wt.: 6¾ lbs.
Comments: A deluxe high-powered rifle made from the mid to late 1970's. Add $10.00 for magnum.
Estimated Value:　Excellent:　$275.00
　　　　　　　　　　Very good:　$220.00

Savage Model 112 V

Caliber: 222, 223, 22-250, 220 Swift, 25-06, 243
Action: Bolt action; single shot; hammerless
Magazine: None
Barrel: 26" chrome-moly steel; tapered
Sights: None
Stock & Forearm: Checkered walnut one-piece pistol grip stock & forearm; fluted comb; swivels
Approximate wt.: 9¼ lbs.
Comments: A varmint rifle made in the mid to late 1970's.
Estimated Value:　Excellent:　$300.00
　　　　　　　　　　Very good:　$250.00

Savage Model 112 V

Savage Model 111FC & 111GC

Same as Model 111F and 111G except: detachable box magazine; 270 Win., 30-06 Sprng., 7mm Rem. magnum, and 300 Win. magnum calibers. Add 2% for 111FC.

Estimated Value:　New (retail):　$407.00
　　　　　　　　　Excellent:　$305.00
　　　　　　　　　Very good:　$245.00

Savage Model 111F & 111G

Caliber: 223 Rem., 22-250 Rem., 243 Win., 250 Sav., 25-06 Rem., 270 Win., 300 Sav., 30-06 Sprng., 308 Win., 7mm Rem. magnum, 7mm-08 Rem., 300 Win. magnum, 338 Win. magnum
Action: Bolt action; repeating; top loading
Magazine: 4-shot top loading; 3-shot in magnum
Barrel: 22" or 24"; blued
Sights: Open adjustable rear, ramp front; each receiver drilled and tapped for scope mounts
Stock & Forearm: Graphite/fiberglass filled (111F) or walnut finish hardwood one-piece checkered pistol grip stock and forearm with rubber recoil pad; swivel studs
Approximate wt.: 6¼ to 7 lbs.
Comments: Introduced in 1994. Add 5% for 111F.
Estimated Value:　New (Retail):　$358.00
　　　　　　　　　　Excellent:　$270.00
　　　　　　　　　　Very good:　$215.00

Savage Model 112FV

Savage Model 112FV & 112FVSS

Caliber: 22-250 or 223
Action: Bolt action; repeating; top loading
Magazine: 5-shot top loading
Barrel: 26" blued (112FV); 26" stainless steel (112FVSS); recessed target style muzzle
Sights: None; drilled and tapped for scope mounts
Stock & Forearm: Graphite/fiberglass filled, checkered one-piece stock and forearm; swivel studs
Approximate wt.: 9 lbs.
Comments: Introduced in 1994. Add 28% for stainless steel barrel (112FVSS)
Estimated Value: New (Retail): $400.00
                       Excellent: $300.00
                       Very good: $250.00

Savage Model 114C & 114CE

Caliber: 270 Win., 30-06 Sprng., 7mm Rem. magnum, 300 Win. magnum
Action: Bolt action; repeating
Magazine: 4-shot or 5-shot removable box
Barrel: 22" blued; 24" in magnum calibers
Sights: Open adjustable rear, ramp front; drilled and tapped for scope mount
Stock & Forearm: Select grade checkered walnut one-piece pistol grip stock and forearm; lipped forearm on 114CE; swivel studs
Approximate wt.: 7¼ lbs.
Comments: Introduced in 1994. Add 15% for 114CE.
Estimated Value: New (Retail): $525.00
                       Excellent: $395.00
                       Very good: $315.00

Savage Model 112FVSS-S

Similar to the Model FVSS except: single shot; 22-250 Rem., 223 Rem., 220 Swift, and 300 Win. mag. calibers. Introduced in 1994.
Estimated Value: New (retail): $510.00
                       Excellent: $385.00
                       Very good: $300.00

Savage Model 112BVSS

Same as the Model 112FVSS except: calibers 223, 22-250 Rem., 25-06 Rem., 30-06, 308 Win., 7mm, and 300 Win.; heavy-prone laminated wood stock and forearm.
Estimated Value: New (retail): $535.00
                       Excellent: $400.00
                       Very good: $320.00

Savage Model 112BVSS-S

Same as the Model 112FVSS-S except: heavy-prone laminated wood stock and forearm.
Estimated Value: New (retail): $535.00
                       Excellent: $400.00
                       Very good: $320.00

Savage Model 116SE

Caliber: 458 Win. magnum, 300 Win. magnum, 338 Win. magnum
Action: Bolt action; repeating
Magazine: 3-shot top loading
Barrel: 24" stainless steel with adjustable muzzle brake (AMB); sling stud
Sights: Special 3-leaf classic express rear; ramp front
Stock & Forearm: Select grade figured walnut, one-piece checkered pistol grip stock and forearm with ebony tip and rubber butt plate
Approximate wt.: 8½ lbs.
Comments: Introduced in 1994.
Estimated Value: New (Retail): $900.00
                       Excellent: $675.00
                       Very good: $540.00

Savage Model 116FSS

Savage Model 116FSS
Caliber: 223, 243 Win., 270 Win., 30-06 Sprng., 308 Win., 7mm Rem. magnum, 300 Win. magnum, 338 Win. magnum
Action: Bolt action; repeating
Magazine: 4-shot top loading; 3-shot in magnum
Barrel: 22" stainless steel; 24" in magnum
Sights: None; drilled and tapped for scope mounts
Stock & Forearm: Graphite/fiberglass filled, composite, one-piece, checkered pistol grip stock and forearm; swivel studs
Approximate wt.: 6¾ lbs.
Comments: Produced from early 1990's to present.
Estimated Value: New (Retail): $491.00
            Excellent: $370.00
            Very good: $300.00

Savage Model 116FCS
Similar to the Model 116FSS except: 270 Win., 30-06 Sprng., 7mm Rem. magnum, and 300 Win. magnum only; stainless steel removable box type magazine. Introduced in the early 1990's.
Estimated Value: New (retail): $554.00
            Excellent: $415.00
            Very good: $335.00

Savage Model 116FSK
Caliber: 270 Win., 30-06 Sprng., 7mm Rem. magnum, 300 Win., 338 Win. magnum
Action: Bolt action; repeating
Magazine: 4-shot top loading; 3-shot in magnum calibers
Barrel: 22" stainless steel; shock supressor muzzle
Sights: None, drilled and tapped for scope mounts
Stock & Forearm: Graphite/fiberglass filled one-piece stock and forearm
Approximate wt.: 6½ lbs.
Comments: Produced from the early 1990's to present.
Estimated Value: New (Retail): $554.00
            Excellent: $415.00
            Very good: $335.00

Savage Model 116FSAK
Same as the Model 116FSK except: it has an adjustable muzzle brake system with fluted barrel; on-off choice in recoil reduction.
Estimated Value: New (retail): $581.00
            Excellent: $435.00
            Very good: $350.00

Savage Model 116FCSAK
Same as the Model 116FSAK except: no 338 Win. magnum caliber, stainless steel removable box magazine. Introduced in 1994.
Estimated Value: New (retail): $644.00
            Excellent: $485.00
            Very good: $390.00

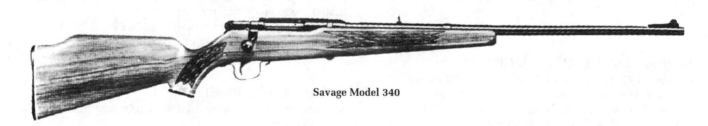

Savage Model 340

Savage Model 340 S
Same as Model 340 except: sights are peep rear, hooded front. Produced from about 1955 to 1960.
Estimated Value: Excellent: $200.00
            Very good: $160.00

Savage Model 340 C Carbine
Same as Model 340 except: caliber 30-30. 18" barrel; Produced in the 1960's. Peep sight, checkered stock & sling swivels.
Estimated Value: Excellent: $180.00
            Very good: $135.00

Savage Model 340
Caliber: 22 Hornet, 222 Rem., 223 Rem., 30-30
Action: Bolt action; repeating
Magazine: 4-shot clip in 22 Hornet & 222 Rem,; 3-shot clip in 30-30
Barrel: 20", 22", 24"
Sights: Open rear, ramp front; hooded ramp after 1980
Stock & Forearm: Plain walnut pistol grip stock & sorearm; checkered after 1965
Approximate wt.: 6 to 7 lbs.
Comments: Made from 1950 to 1986; before 1950 this model was manufactured as a Stevens.
Estimated Value: Excellent: $190.00
            Very good: $150.00

Savage Model 65 M

Savage Fox Model FB-1

Savage Model 65 M

Caliber: 22 magnum
Action: Bolt action; repeating
Magazine: 5-shot clip
Barrel: Blued; 22"
Sights: Open rear, ramp front
Stock & Forearm: Checkered walnut one-piece semi-pistol grip stock & forearm
Approximate wt.: 5¾ lbs.
Comments: Made in the late 1970's.
Estimated Value: Excellent: $100.00
Very good: $ 80.00

Savage Fox Model FB-1

Caliber: 22 short, long, long rifle
Action: Bolt action; repeating
Magazine: 5-shot detachable clip
Barrel: Blued; 24"
Sights: Adjustable leaf rear, hooded ramp front; drilled & tapped for scope
Stock & Forearm: Checkered walnut Monte Carlo one-piece semi-pistol grip stock & forearm; cheekpiece swivels; rosewood fore-end tip & grip cap
Approximate wt.: 6½ lbs.
Comments: Introduced in 1981, discontinued in 1982.
Estimated Value: Excellent: $210.00
Very good: $160.00

Savage Model 900B

Caliber: 22 long rifle
Action: Bolt action; repeating
Magazine: 5-shot clip and clip holder
Barrel: Blued; 21", free floated heavy target barrel with a snow cover to prevent obstructions from entering the barrel
Sights: Receiver peep sights, target front with 7 aperture inserts
Stock & Forearm: Natural finish hardwood target stock and forearm with butt hook and hand stop
Approximate wt.: 8¼ lbs.
Comments: Made in the mid 1990's.
Estimated Value: New (retail): $498.00
Excellent: $375.00
Very good: $300.00

Savage 900TR

Similar to the Model 900B except: no clip holders; no snow cover; walnut finish hardwood stock and forearm; 25" barrel; approximate wt.: 8 lbs.
Estimated Value: New (retail): $415.00
Excellent: $310.00
Very good: $250.00

Savage 900S (Silhouette Rifle)

Similar to the Model 900TR except: 21" heavy contour barrel; no sight; silhouette style high comb; satin walnut finish; scope bases installed.
Estimated Value: New (retail): $346.00
Excellent: $260.00
Very good: $210.00

Savage Model 982 DL

Savage Model 982 MDL

Savage Model 982 DL

Caliber: 22 short, long, long rifle
Action: Bolt action; repeating
Magazine: 5-shot clip, push button release
Barrel: Blued; 22"
Sights: Ramp front, folding leaf rear
Stock & Forearm: Checkered walnut one-piece Monte Carlo semi-pistol grip stock & forearm
Approximate wt.: 6 lbs.
Comments: Introduced in 1981, discontinued in 1982.
Estimated Value: Excellent: $115.00
Very good: $ 90.00

Savage Model 982 MDL

Caliber: 22 mag.
Action: Bolt action; repeating
Magazine: 5-shot detachable clip
Barrel: Blued; 22"
Sights: Ramp front, folding leaf rear; grooved for scope
Stock & Forearm: Checkered walnut Monte Carlo one-piece semi-pistol grip stock & forearm
Approximate wt.: 6 lbs.
Comments: Produced from 1981 to 1982.
Estimated Value: Excellent: $120.00
Very good: $ 95.00

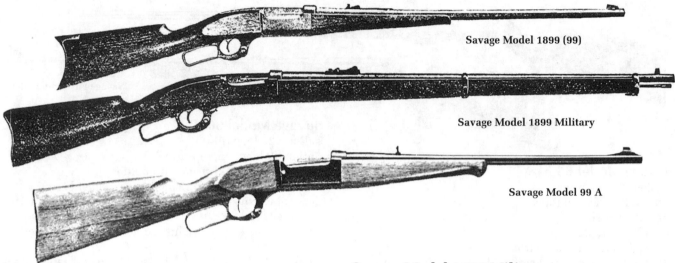

Savage Model 1899 (99)

Savage Model 1899 Military

Savage Model 99 A

Savage Model 1899 (99)

Caliber: 303 Savage, 25-35, 32-40, 38-55, 30-30
Action: Lever-action; hammerless
Magazine: 5-shot rotary
Barrel: 20", 22", or 26"; round, half octagon or octagon
Sights: Adj. rear dovetail; open sporting front
Stock & Forearm: Walnut straight grip stock & tapered forearm
Approximate wt.: 7½ lbs.
Comments: The backbone of the Savage line which has been manufactured in many variations over the years. Produced from 1899 to 1922.

Estimated Value:	Excellent:	$550.00
	Very good:	$440.00

Savage Model 1899 Military

Same as the Model 99 except: barrel is 28"; bayonet; stock is musket style; sights are military. Produced from about 1899 to 1907; caliber 30-30 Win.

Estimated Value:	Excellent:	$600.00
	Very good:	$480.00

Savage Model 99 A

Basically the same as Model 1899 in solid frame & in calibers 300 Savage, 303 Savage & 30-30. It was produced from 1922 to 1937. Later models in calibers 243, 308, 250 Savage, & 300 Savage from about 1970 to 1984. Add 30% for early models.

Estimated Value:	Excellent:	$325.00
	Very good:	$265.00

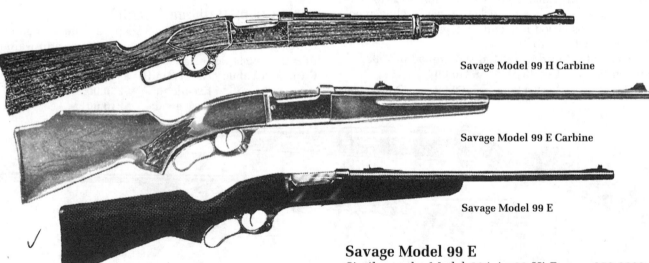

Savage Model 99 H Carbine

Savage Model 99 E Carbine

Savage Model 99 E

Savage Model 99 B

Takedown version of Model 99 A; produced from about 1922 to 1937.

Estimated Value:	Excellent:	$450.00
	Very good:	$360.00

Savage Model 99 H Carbine

Basically the same as 99 A with addition of 250-3000 caliber; short barrel; carbine stock & forearm; barrel bands. Produced from 1932 to 1941.

Estimated Value:	Excellent:	$410.00
	Very good:	$330.00

Savage Model 99 E

Similar to the Model 99A in 22 Hi Power, 250-3000, 30-30, 300 savage, 303 Savage; 22" or 24" barrel. Unlipped tapered forearm. Made from about 1922 to 1937.

Estimated Value:	Excellent:	$400.00
	Very good:	$320.00

Savage Model 99 E Carbine

Similar to the Model 99H in 243 Win., 250 Savage, 300 Savage, 308 Win., calibers only. Checkered walnut stock & tapered forearm without barrel band. Production began in 1961. Monte Carlo stock after 1982. Discontinued in 1985.

Estimated Value:	Excellent:	$300.00
	Very good:	$240.00

Savage Model 99 F

Savage Model 99 CD

Savage Model 99 K

Savage Model 99 EG II

Savage Model 99 R II

Savage Model 99 RS I

Savage Model 99 EG II
This is the Model G produced after World War II, from 1946 to 1961.

Estimated Value: **Excellent:**   **$300.00**
                  Very good: **$240.00**

Savage Model 99 CD
A solid frame version of Model 99F with a checkered pistol grip stock & forearm. In production from 1955 to about 1980; 4-shot detachable box magazine.

Estimated Value: **Excellent:**   **$315.00**
                  Very good: **$250.00**

Savage Model 99 G
A takedown version of the Model 99 E with a checkered walnut pistol grip stock & forearm. Made from about 1921 to 1941.

Estimated Value: **Excellent:**   **$425.00**
                  Very good: **$340.00**

Savage Model 99 K
A fancy Model 99 G with deluxe stock & light engraving. Rear peep sight; folding middle sight. Made from the early 1930's to the early 1940's.

Estimated Value: **Excellent:**   **$1,000.00**
                  Very good: **$ 800.00**

Savage Model 99 F
This is a lightweight takedown version of the Model 99E, produced until about 1940. Production resumed about 1955 to 1972 in caliber 243, 300 & 308. Add $160.00 for pre-1940.

Estimated Value: **Excellent:**   **$285.00**
                  Very good: **$225.00**

Savage Model 99 R II
Similar to other Model 99's. Production stopped in 1940 and resumed from 1946 to 1961 in 24" barrel with swivel attachments in a variety of calibers. Add 50% for pre-World War II models.

Estimated Value: **Excellent:**   **$300.00**
                  Very good: **$240.00**

Savage Model 99 RS I & 99 RS II
Same as Model 99 except: those before World War II have rear peep sight & folding middle sight. Those made after the war have a special receiver sight. Discontinued in 1961; solid frame. Add 50% for pre-World War II models. 99 RS I pre-WWII model; 99RS II after WWII.

Estimated Value: **Excellent:**   **$300.00**
                  Very good: **$240.00**

Savage Model 99 DL

Savage Model 99 C

Savage Model 99 PE Presentation

Savage Model 99 DE Citation

Savage Model 99 T

Savage Model 99 PE Presentation

Much like the Model 99 DL except engraved receiver, hand checkered Monte Carlo stock & forearm. Produced from 1968 to 1970.

Estimated Value:	Excellent:	$750.00
	Very good:	$600.00

Savage Model 99 DE Citation

A less elaborate example of the Model 99 PE. Produced from 1968 to 1970.

Estimated Value:	Excellent:	$550.00
	Very good:	$440.00

Savage Model 99 T

Basically the same as the other Model 99's. It is a solid frame with a checkered walnut pistol grip stock & forearm. Produced until 1940.

Estimated Value:	Excellent:	$380.00
	Very good:	$300.00

Savage Model 99 C

Caliber: 22-250, 243, 308, 7mm/08, (22-250 & 7mm/08 dropped in the 1980's)
Action: Hammerless lever action; cocking indicator
Magazine: 3- or 4-shot detachable clip
Barrel: 22" chrome-moly steel
Sights: Detachable hooded ramp front; adjustable rear
Stock & Forearm: Checkered walnut semi-pistol grip, two-piece stock & tapered forearm; Monte Carlo stock after 1982
Approximate wt.: 7½ lbs.
Comments: Made from 1965 to present.

Estimated Value:	New (retail):	$650.00
	Excellent:	$490.00
	Very good:	$390.00

Savage Model 99 DL

This is a late Model 99, in production from about 1960 to mid 1970's. Basically the same as Model 99 F with a Monte Carlo stock & swivels.

Estimated Value:	Excellent:	$290.00
	Very good:	$230.00

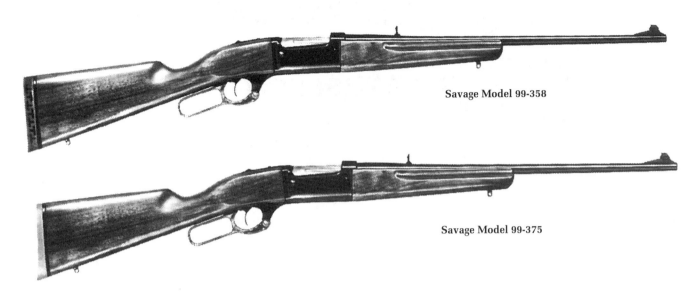

Savage Model 99-358

Savage Model 99-375

Savage Model 99-358

Similar to the Model 99 A in 358 caliber; forearm rounded; swivels; recoil pad. Made from late 1970's to early 1980's.

Estimated Value: Excellent: $300.00
Very good: $250.00

Savage Model 99-375

Similar to the Model 99-358 in 375 Win. caliber.

Estimated Value: Excellent: $325.00
Very good: $275.00

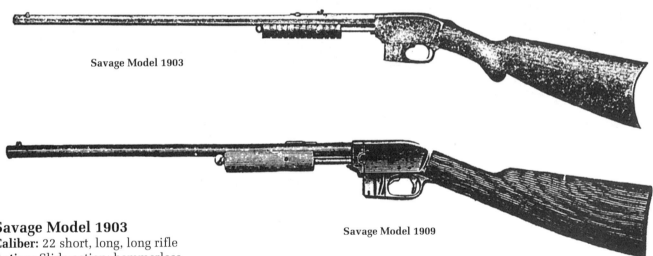

Savage Model 1903

Savage Model 1909

Savage Model 1903

Caliber: 22 short, long, long rifle
Action: Slide action; hammerless
Magazine: 5-shot detachable box
Barrel: 24" octagon
Sights: Open rear, bead front
Stock & Forearm: Checkered walnut pistol grip stock & grooved slide handle
Approximate wt.: 5 lbs.
Comments: This takedown model was produced from 1903 to 1922.

Estimated Value: Excellent: $225.00
Very good: $180.00

Savage Model 1909

A lighter version of the Model 1903 with a straight stock & forearm & a round 20" barrel. Discontinued about 1915.

Estimated Value: Excellent: $200.00
Very good: $160.00

Savage Model 1914

Caliber: 22 short, long, long rifle
Action: Slide action; hammerless
Magazine: Tubular; 20 shorts, 17 longs, 15 long rifles
Barrel: 24" octagon or half octagon
Sights: Open rear, bead front
Stock & Forearm: Plain wood pistol grip stock & grooved slide handle
Approximate wt.: 5¾ lbs.
Comments: A takedown rifle produced from about 1915 until 1924.

Estimated Value: Excellent: $195.00
Very good: $155.00

Savage Model 25

Savage Model 29

Savage Model 170 C

Savage Model 6

Savage Model 6 S

Savage Model 29

Similar to the Model 25 except prewar models were checkered; barrel is round on postwar models. Made from 1929 until the late 1960's. Add $50.00 for pre-World War II models with octagon barrel.

Estimated Value: Excellent: $200.00
Very good: $160.00

Savage Model 25

Caliber: 22 short, long, long rifle
Action: Slide action; hammerless
Magazine: Tubular; 20 shorts, 17 longs, 15 long rifles
Barrel: 24" octagon
Sights: Open rear, blade front
Stock & Forearm: Walnut pistol grip stock & grooved slide handle
Approximate wt.: 5¾ lbs.
Comments: A takedown model produced from the mid 1920's until 1929.

Estimated Value: Excellent: $225.00
Very good: $175.00

Savage Model 170

Caliber: 30-30, 35
Action: Slide action; hammerless; repeating
Magazine: 3-shot tubular
Barrel: Blued; 22"
Sights: Ramp front, folding leaf rear, hooded ramp after 1980
Stock & Forearm: Checkered walnut Monte Carlo semi-pistol grip stock & fluted slide handle; swivels
Approximate wt.: 6¾ lbs.
Comments: Made from the late 1970's to early 1980's

Estimated Value: Excellent: $175.00
Very good: $140.00

Savage Model 170 C

A carbine version of the Model 170; not available with a Monte Carlo stock; 18½" barrel; not available in 35 caliber.

Estimated Value: Excellent: $165.00
Very good: $130.00

Savage Model 1912

Caliber: 22 long rifle
Action: Semi-automatic; hammerless
Magazine: 7-shot detachable box
Barrel: 20" half octagon
Sights: Open rear, bead front
Stock & Forearm: Plain wood straight grip stock & fore-arm
Approximate wt.: 4½ lbs.
Comments: This takedown was Savage's first semi-automatic; discontinued in 1916.

Estimated Value: Excellent: $275.00
Very good: $210.00

Savage Model 6 & 6 S

Caliber: 22 short, long, long rifle
Action: Semi-automatic
Magazine: Tubular; 21 shorts, 17 longs, 15 long rifles
Barrel: 24"
Sights: Open rear, bead front; 6S has peep rear, hooded front
Stock & Forearm: Checkered walnut pistol grip before World War II; plain walnut pistol grip after the war
Approximate wt.: 6 lbs.
Comments: A takedown model manufactured from 1938 until late 1960's.

Estimated Value: Excellent: $125.00
Very good: $100.00

Savage Model 7

Savage Model 7 S

Savage Model 7 & 7 S

Basically the same as Model 6 & 6 S except they are equipped with a 5-shot detachable box magazine. Produced from the late 1930's until the early 1950's.

Estimated Value: Excellent: $115.00
                  Very good: $ 90.00

Savage Model 80

Savage Model 980 DL

Savage Model 980 DL

Caliber: 22 long rifle
Action: Semi-automatic
Magazine: 15-shot tubular
Barrel: Blued; 20"
Sights: Hooded ramp front, folding leaf adjustable rear
Stock & Forearm: Checkered walnut one-piece Monte Carlo semi-pistol grip stock and forearm
Approximate wt.: 6 lbs.
Comments: Produced from 1981 to 1984.
Estimated Value: Excellent: $130.00
                     Very good: $100.00

Savage Model 80

Caliber: 22 long rifle
Action: Semi-automatic
Magazine: 15-shot tubular
Barrel: Blued; 20"
Sights: Open rear, blade front
Stock & Forearm: Checkered walnut one-piece Monte Carlo pistol grip stock & forearm
Approximate wt.: 6 lbs.
Comments: Made from the mid to late 1970's. Due to a possible safety malfunction, certain models were recalled in 1982 and inspected by Stevens at no cost to the owner. Serial numbers that were recalled were B256621 or higher; C000001 or higher; D000001 or higher.
Estimated Value: Excellent: $110.00
                     Very good: $ 85.00

Savage Model 24F Predator

Gauge: 12, 20
Caliber: 22 Hornet, 223 Rem., 30-30 Win., rifle barrel over 12 gauge, 3" chamber shotgun barrel with changeable choke tubes; 22 long rifle, 22 Hornet, 223 Rem., 30-30 Win., rifle barrel over 20 gauge shotgun barrel with modified choke
Action: Break down rifle over shotgun barrel with a two-way opening lever; built-in two position barrel selector on the exposed hammer and a cross-bolt safety
Magazine: None
Barrel: 24" rifle over shotgun barrel
Sights: Rifle sight; drilled and tapped for scope mounts
Stock & Forearm: Black graphite fiberglass-filled composite material; pistol girp and recoil pad standard
Approximate wt.: 8 lbs.
Comments: A combination gun for predator and wild turkey hunting. Introduced in mid 1990's.
Estimated Value: New (retail): $400.00
                     Excellent: $300.00
                     Very good: $240.00

Savage Model 64G

Caliber: 22 long rifle
Action: Semi-automatic, hammerless
Magazine: 10-shot detachable clip
Barrel: Blued; 20¼"
Sights: Bead front, adjustable rear
Stock & Forearm: Checkered wood, one-piece Monte Carlo stock and forearm
Approximate wt.: 5½ lbs.
Comments: Produced in the 1990's.
Estimated Value: New (retail): $123.00
                     Excellent: $ 95.00
                     Very good: $ 75.00

Sears

Sears Model 53
Caliber: 243, 30-06
Action: Bolt action; repeating; hammerless
Magazine: 5-shot tubular
Barrel: Blued; 24"
Sights: Folding rear, ramp front
Stock & Forearm: Checkered walnut Monte Carlo one-piece grip stock & tapered forearm; swivels
Approximate wt.: 6¾ lbs.
Comments: Made until mid 1970's.
Estimated Value: Excellent: $165.00
                       Very good: $125.00

Sears Ted Williams Model 53 A
Same as Model 53 in 30-06 caliber only; 22" barrel.
Estimated Value: Excellent: $160.00
                       Very good: $120.00

Sears Ted Williams Model 73
Same as Ted Williams 53 A except: select wood & fancy finish.
Estimated Value: Excellent: $185.00
                       Very good: $150.00

Sears Model 2
Caliber: 22 short, long, long rifle
Action: Bolt action; repeating; hammerless
Magazine: 6-shot clip
Barrel: Blued; 20"
Sights: Open rear, bead front
Stock & Forearm: Wood Monte Carlo one-piece semi-pistol grip stock & tapered forearm
Approximate wt.: 5 lbs.
Comments: Manufactured in the 1970's.
Estimated Value: Excellent: $100.00
                       Very good: $ 80.00

Sears Model 1
Similar to Model 2 but single shot version, no Monte Carlo stock.
Estimated Value: Excellent: $80.00
                       Very good: $65.00

Sears Model 1

Sears Model 2

Sears Model 2200 Semi-Automatic
Caliber: 22 long rifle
Action: Semi-automatic; hammerless; side ejection
Magazine: 15-shot tubular
Barrel: Blued; 20", round
Sights: Sporting front, rear adjustable for elevation; receiver grooved for scope
Stock & Forearm: Checkered walnut-finish hardwood one-piece pistol grip stock & forearm
Approximate wt.: 5½ lbs.
Comments: Add $10.00 for scope. Due to a possible safety malfunction, certain models were recalled in 1982 & inspected by Stevens at no cost to the owner.
Estimated Value: Excellent: $110.00
                       Very good: $ 90.00

Sears Model 2200 Lever Action
Caliber: 22 short, long, long rifle
Action: Lever-action; single shot; exposed hammer
Magazine: None
Barrel: Blued; 18½", round
Sights: Sporting front, rear adjustable for elevation
Stock & Forearm: Smooth two-piece hardwood straight grip stock & forearm
Approximate wt.: 5½ lbs.
Comments: Manufactured to the mid 1980's.
Estimated Value: Excellent: $90.00
                       Very good: $72.00

Sears Model 2200, Bolt Action
Same as the Model 2200 Semi-Automatic except: bolt action repeater; 5-shot box magazine; 22 short, long, or long rifle caliber.
Estimated Value: Excellent: $100.00
                       Very good: $85.00

Sears Ted Williams Model 100

Sears Ted Williams Autoloading

Sears Ted Williams Deluxe Autoloading

Sears Ted Williams Deluxe Autoloading
Caliber: 22 short, long, long rifle
Action: Semi-automatic; hammerless; side ejection
Magazine: 5-shot clip
Barrel: Blued; 20"
Sights: Rear tangent, hooded ramp front
Stock & Forearm: Checkered walnut Monte Carlo one-piece pistol grip stock & tapered forearm; swivels
Approximate wt.: 6 lbs.
Comments: Manufactured in the 1970's.
Estimated Value: Excellent: $110.00
Very good: $ 90.00

Sears Ted Williams Model 100
Caliber: 30-30 Win.
Action: Lever-action; exposed hammer; repeating
Magazine: 6-shot tubular
Barrel: Blued; 20"
Sights: Open rear, blade front
Stock & Forearm: Walnut straight grip stock & forearm
Approximate wt.: 6½ lbs.
Comments: Made for Sears by Winchester.
Estimated Value: Excellent: $175.00
Very good: $140.00

Sears Ted Williams Autoloading
Caliber: 22 short, long, long rifle
Action: Semi-automatic; hammerless; side ejection
Magazine: Tubular; 15 long rifles, 17 longs, 21 shorts
Barrel: Blued; 20½"
Sights: None, scope
Stock & Forearm: Wood semi-pistol grip stock & forearm
Approximate wt.: 5 lbs.
Comments: Manufactured in the 1970's.
Estimated Value: Excellent: $115.00
Very good: $ 95.00

Sedgley

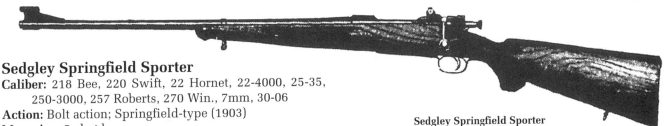

Sedgley Springfield Sporter

Sedgley Springfield Sporter
Caliber: 218 Bee, 220 Swift, 22 Hornet, 22-4000, 25-35, 250-3000, 257 Roberts, 270 Win., 7mm, 30-06
Action: Bolt action; Springfield-type (1903)
Magazine: 5-shot box
Barrel: 24"
Sights: Lyman rear, hooded ramp front
Stock & Forearm: Checkered walnut one-piece pistol grip stock & lipped forearm; swivels
Approximate wt.: 7½ lbs.
Comments: Manufactured in left & right hand action from the late 1920's to World War II.
Estimated Value: Excellent: $600.00
Very good: $480.00

Sedgley Mannlicher
Similar to the Sporter with a full-length forearm; 20" barrel.
Estimated Value: Excellent: $625.00
Very good: $500.00

Smith & Wesson

Smith & Wesson Model A

Smith & Wesson Model B

Smith & Wesson Model E

Smith & Wesson Model A

Caliber: 22-250, 243, 270, 308, 30-06, 7mm mag., 300 mag.

Action: Bolt action; repeating; adjustable trigger

Magazine: 5-shot box

Barrel: Blued; 23¾" tapered

Sights: Folding rear, hooded ramp front with silver bead

Stock & Forearm: Checkered walnut Monte Carlo one-piece pistol grip stock & tapered forearm

Approximate wt.: 7 lbs.

Comments: Made only in the early 1970's.

Estimated Value: Excellent: $360.00
Very good: $285.00

Smith & Wesson Model B

A 20" barrel version of the Model A; not available in 22-250 or magnum; Monte Carlo stock.

Estimated Value: Excellent: $320.00
Very good: $250.00

Smith & Wesson Model C

Same as Model B except straight grip stock.

Estimated Value: Excellent: $325.00
Very good: $255.00

Smith & Wesson Model D

Same as Model C with full-length forearm.

Estimated Value: Excellent: $350.00
Very good: $290.00

Smith & Wesson Model E

Same as Model B with full-length forearm.

Estimated Value: Excellent: $345.00
Very good: $275.00

Smith & Wesson Model 1500

Smith & Wesson Model 1700LS Classic Hunter

Similar to the Model 1500 except: lightweight with lipped forearm; 5-shot magazine with removable floor plate; calibers 243 Win., 270 Win., & 30-06. Made in the mid 1980's.

Estimated Value: Excellent: $400.00
Very good: $320.00

Smith & Wesson Model 1500 Deluxe Varmint

Similar to the Model 1500 with a 22" heavy barrel, adjustable trigger; 222 Rem., 22-250 Rem., & 223 Rem. calibers. Produced from 1982 to 1985. Add 3% for parkerized finish.

Estimated Value: Excellent: $360.00
Very good: $285.00

Smith & Wesson Model 1500, 1500 Mountaineer

Caliber: 30-06, 270 Win., 243 Win., 25-06 Rem., 7mm Rem. mag., 300 Win. mag.; 222 Rem.; 223 Rem. & 308 Win. added in 1982

Action: Bolt action; hammerless; repeating

Magazine: 5-shot box

Barrel: 23½"

Sights: None; Optional folding rear, hooded ramp front

Stock & Forearm: Checkered walnut pistol grip, one-piece stock & forearm; swivels; recoil pad on mag.

Approximate wt.: 7 lbs.

Comments: Discontinued 1985. Add 4% for magnum; 19% for Deluxe Model; 7% for sights.

Estimated Value: Excellent: $325.00
Very good: $260.00

Standard

Standard Model M
A slide action version of the Standard G.
Estimated Value: **Excellent:** $300.00
                       Very good: $250.00

Standard Model G
Caliber: 25-35, 30-30, 25 Rem., 30 Rem., 35 Rem.
Action: Semi-automatic; gas operated; hammerless; can also be operated as slide action by closing gas port
Magazine: 4- or 5-shot tubular
Barrel: Blued; 22"
Sights: Bead front, open rear
Stock & Forearm: Wood straight grip stock & slide handle
Approximate wt.: 7¾ lbs.
Comments: Made in the early 1900's, the Standard G was one of the first gas operated autoloaders available.
Estimated Value: **Excellent:** $375.00
                       Very good: $300.00

Stevens

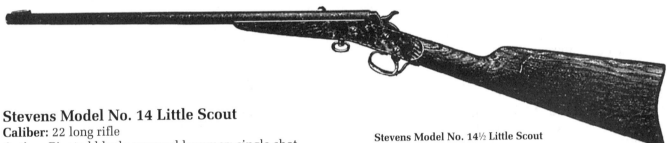

Stevens Model No. 14½ Little Scout

Stevens Model No. 14 Little Scout
Caliber: 22 long rifle
Action: Pivoted block; exposed hammer; single shot
Magazine: None
Barrel: 18" round
Sights: Blade front; open rear
Stock & Forearm: Plain walnut one-piece straight grip stock & forearm
Approximate wt.: 2½ lbs.
Comments: Made from 1904 to about 1912; then it was replaced by Model 14½.
Estimated Value: **Excellent:** $175.00
                       Very good: $140.00

Stevens Model No. 14½ Little Scout
Similar to Model No. 14 Little Scout except: rolling block action; two piece stock and short forearm. Produced from 1912 to World War II.
Estimated Value: **Excellent:** $165.00
                       Very good: $135.00

Stevens Model No. 16 Crack Shot
Caliber: 22 long rifle; 32 short
Action: Falling block; single shot; exposed hammer; lever action
Magazine: None
Barrel: 20" round
Sights: Open rear, blade front
Stock & Forearm: Plain walnut straight grip stock with slightly lipped forearm
Approximate wt.: 3¾ lbs.
Comments: Produced until 1912 when it was replaced by the Model No. 26.
Estimated Value: **Excellent:** $250.00
                       Very good: $200.00

Stevens Model No. 16½ Crack Shot

Stevens Model No. 16½ Crack Shot
Same as No. 16 except it is smooth bore for shot cartridges. Produced from 1907 to 1912.
Estimated Value: **Excellent:** $240.00
                       Very good: $190.00

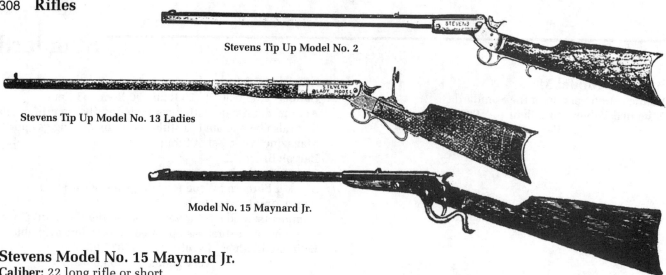

Stevens Tip Up Model No. 2

Stevens Tip Up Model No. 13 Ladies

Model No. 15 Maynard Jr.

Stevens Model No. 15 Maynard Jr.
Caliber: 22 long rifle or short
Action: Lever tip up; exposed hammer
Magazine: None
Barrel: 18"; part octagon
Sights: Open rear, blade front
Stock & Forearm: Plain walnut, straight stock & short forearm
Approximate wt.: 2¾ lbs.
Comments: Made to compete with cheap imports. Produced from 1901 to 1910.

Estimated Value:	Excellent:	$150.00
	Very good:	$120.00

Stevens Model No. 15½ Maynard Jr.
Same as the No. 15 except: smooth bore for 22 long rifle shot cartridges.

Estimated Value:	Excellent:	$145.00
	Very good:	$115.00

Stevens Tip Up Model No. 2, 5, 6, 7, 8, 9, 11 Ladies & 13 Ladies
Caliber: RF 22 long rifles, 25 Stevens, 32 long (in #11)
Action: Single shot, tip up; exposed hammer
Magazine: None
Barrel: 24" octagon for #2; 28" half octagon optional on #7, all others 24" half octagon
Sights: Beach combination front, open rear; peep on #5, #7 & #13; blade front, open rear on #2; open on #11
Stock & Forearm: Walnut straight stock & forearm; no forearm on #2 & #5
Approximate wt.: 5½ to 6½ lbs.
Comments: Produced until they were replaced in 1902 by a line of falling block rifles.

Estimated Value:	Excellent:	$270.00
	Very good:	$215.00

Stevens Model No. 17 Favorite

Stevens Model No. 27 Favorite

Stevens Model No. 18 Favorite

Stevens Tip Up Model No. 17 & 27 Favorite
Caliber: 22 long rifle, 25 RF, 32 RF
Action: Lever action; single shot; exposed hammer
Magazine: None
Barrel: 24" round (octagon barrel on Model 27); other lengths available as option
Sights: Open rear, Rocky Mountain front
Stock & Forearm: Plain walnut straight grip stock, short tapered forearm
Approximate wt.: 4 to 5 lbs.
Comments: Takedown model produced from the 1890's until the mid 1930's.

Estimated Value:	Excellent:	$175.00
	Very good:	$140.00

Stevens Model No. 18 & 28 Favorite
Same as Model No. 17 except it has a Beach combination front sight, Vernier peep rear sight & leaf middle sight. Model 28 has octagon barrel.

Estimated Value:	Excellent:	$200.00
	Very good:	$160.00

Stevens Model No. 20 Favorite

Stevens Model No. 20 Favorite

Same as the Model No. 17 except the barrel is smooth bore for 22 RF & 32 RF shot cartridges.

Estimated Value: Excellent: $195.00
                   Very good: $155.00

Stevens Model No. 19 & 29 Favorite

Same as the Model No. 17 except it has Lyman front sight, leaf middle sight & Lyman combination rear sight. Model 29 has octagon barrel.

Estimated Value: Excellent: $215.00
                   Very good: $170.00

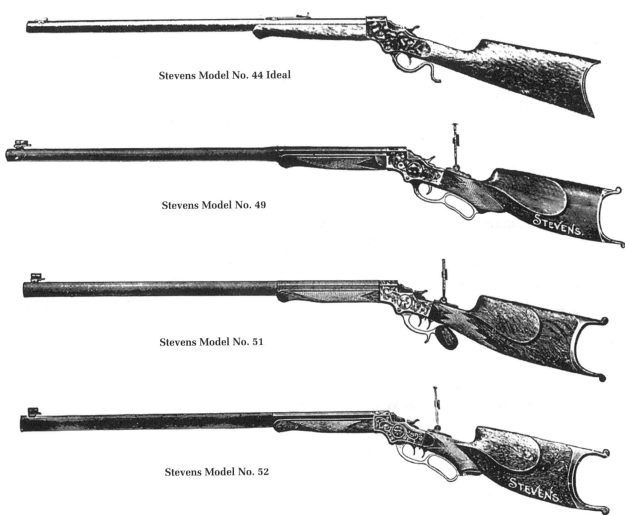

Stevens Model No. 44 Ideal

Stevens Model No. 49

Stevens Model No. 51

Stevens Model No. 52

Stevens Model No. 44 Ideal

Caliber: 22 long rifle; 25 RF, 25-20 SS, 32-20, 32-40, 38-55, 44-40

Action: Lever action rolling block; exposed hammer; single shot

Magazine: None

Barrel: 24" or 26"; round, octagon, or half-octagon

Sights: Open rear, Rocky Mountain front

Stock & Forearm: Plain walnut, straight grip

Approximate wt.: 7 lbs.

Comments: Produced from the late 1890's until the early 1930's; a takedown model.

Estimated Value: Excellent: $400.00
                       Very good: $320.00

Stevens Model No. 44½ Ideal

Same as the Model 44 except it has a falling block action. Discontinued in 1916.

Estimated Value: Excellent: $450.00
                   Very good: $360.00

Stevens Model No. 45 to 54

Structurally the same as the Model 44. They differ in engraving & finishes & are generally fancy models that bring high prices. Produced until World War I; target sights & stocks.

Estimated Value: Excellent: $550.00 - $1,000.00
                   Very good: $415.00 - $ 750.00

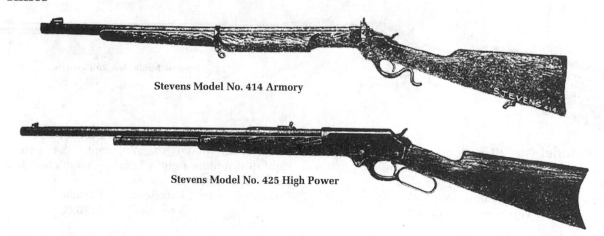

Stevens Model No. 414 Armory

Stevens Model No. 425 High Power

Stevens Model No. 414 Armory

Caliber: 22 long rifle or 22 short only
Action: Lever action rolling block; exposed hammer
Magazine: None; Single shot
Barrel: 26"; heavy round
Sights: Rocky Mountain front, adjustable receiver rear
Stock & Forearm: Plain walnut straight grip, military stock & forearms; bands; swivels
Approximate wt.: 8 lbs.
Comments: Made from 1912 until the early 1930's.
Estimated Value: Excellent: $360.00
Very good: $270.00

Stevens Model No. 425 High Power

Caliber: Rimless Rem. 25, 30, 32, 35; smokeless flatnose
Action: Lever action; exposed hammer; single extractor
Magazine: 5-shot tubular, under barrel
Barrel: 22" round
Sights: Post front, adjustable sporting rear
Stock & Forearm: Plain walnut straight grip stock & forearm
Approximate wt.: 7 lbs.
Comments: Made for about five years beginning in 1911.
Estimated Value: Excellent: $300.00
Very good: $240.00

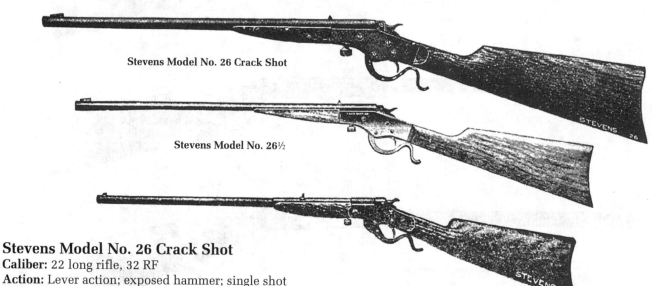

Stevens Model No. 26 Crack Shot

Stevens Model No. 26½

Stevens Model No. 12 Marksman

Stevens Model No. 26 Crack Shot

Caliber: 22 long rifle, 32 RF
Action: Lever action; exposed hammer; single shot
Magazine: None
Barrel: 18", 22"
Sights: Open rear, blade front
Stock & Forearm: Plain walnut straight grip stock & tapered forearm
Approximate wt.: 3¼ to 3½ lbs.
Comments: Produced from 1913 until just prior to World War II.
Estimated Value: Excellent: $175.00
Very good: $140.00

Stevens Model No. 26½

Same as the No. 26 except: smooth bore for shot cartridges.
Estimated Value: Excellent: $180.00
Very good: $145.00

Stevens Model No. 12 Marksman

Caliber: 22 long rifle, 25 RF, 32 RF
Action: Lever action tip up; exposed hammer
Magazine: None, single shot
Barrel: 20", round
Sights: Bead front, open rear
Stock & Forearm: Plain walnut straight grip stock & short tapered forearm
Approximate wt.: 4 lbs.
Comments: Replaced the Maynard Jr. Made from 1912 to 1916.
Estimated Value: Excellent: $160.00
Very good: $130.00

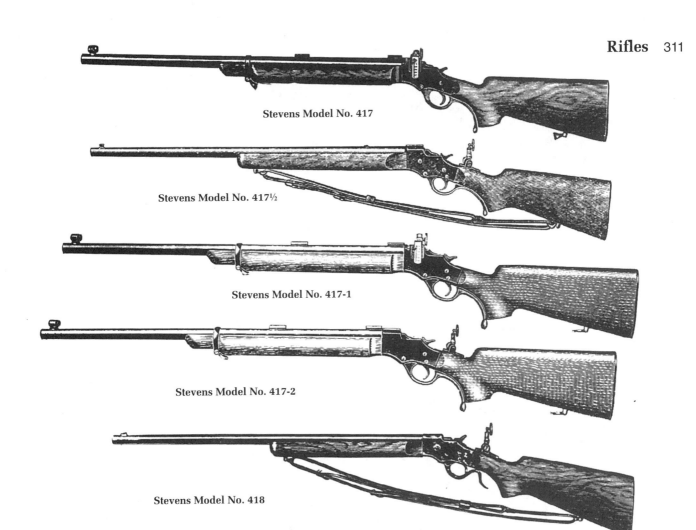

Stevens Model No. 417

Stevens Model No. 417½

Stevens Model No. 417-1

Stevens Model No. 417-2

Stevens Model No. 418

Stevens Model No. 417, 417½, 417-1, 417-2, 417-3 Walnut Hill

Caliber: 22 long rifle; 22 WRF, 25 Stevens

Action: Lever action; exposed hammer; single shot

Magazine: None

Barrel: 28" or 29" heavy

Sights: 417: Lyman 52L extension rear; 417½: Lyman 144 tang peep & folding center; 417-1: Lyman 48L rear; 417-2: 144 rear; 417-3: no sights

Stock & Forearm: Plain walnut pistol grip stock & forearm; bands, swivels

Approximate wt.: 8¼ to 10½ lbs.

Comments: Made from the early 1930's until the late 1940's. Models differ in sights.

Estimated Value: Excellent: $500.00

                    Very good: $400.00

Stevens Model No. 418, 418½ Walnut Hill

Caliber: No. 418: 22 long rifle, 22 short; No. 418½: 22 WRF or 25 Stevens RF

Action: Lever action; exposed hammer; single shot

Magazine: None

Barrel: 26"

Sights: Lyman 144 tang peep, blade front; 418½: Lyman 2A tang peep, bead front

Stock & Forearm: Plain walnut pistol grip stock & forearm; swivels

Approximate wt.: 6½ lbs.

Comments: Made from the early 1930's to just before World War II.

Estimated Value: Excellent: $425.00

                    Very good: $340.00

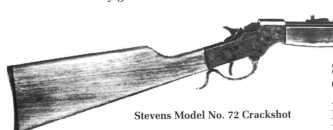

Stevens Model No. 72 Crackshot

Stevens Model No. 72 Crackshot

Caliber: 22 short, long, long rifle

Action: Lever action falling block; single shot

Magazine: None

Barrel: 22" octagon

Sights: Sporting front, open rear

Stock & Forearm: Plain walnut straight grip stock & tapered forearm; case hardened receiver

Approximate wt.: 4½ lbs.

Comments: Made from the early 1970's to 1988.

Estimated Value: Excellent: $110.00

                    Very good: $ 80.00

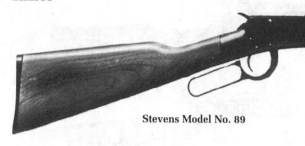

Stevens Model No. 89

Stevens Model No. 89

Caliber: 22 short, long, long rifle
Action: Lever action; exposed hammer; single shot
Magazine: None
Barrel: 18½"; round
Sights: Sporting front, open rear
Stock & Forearm: Straight walnut stock & forearm with carbine band
Approximate wt.: 5 lbs.
Comments: Produced from mid 1970's to mid 1980's.
Estimated Value: Excellent: $100.00
                       Very good: $ 80.00

Stevens Model No. 65
Little Krag

Stevens - Springfield Model No. 51 Reliance

Stevens - Springfield Model No. 52 Challenge

Stevens - Springfield Model No. 53 Springfield Jr.

Stevens Model No. 65 Little Krag

Caliber: 22 short, long, long rifle
Action: Bolt action; single shot
Magazine: None
Barrel: 20" round
Sights: Bead front, fixed peep or open rear
Stock & Forearm: Plain walnut one-piece straight grip stock & forearm
Approximate wt.: 3¼ lbs.
Comments: Produced from 1903 to about 1910.
Estimated Value: Excellent: $150.00
                       Very good: $120.00

Stevens - Springfield Model No. 51 Reliance

Caliber: 22 short, long, long rifle
Action: Bolt action; single shot
Magazine: None
Barrel: 20" round
Sights: Open rear, blade front
Stock & Forearm: Plain walnut one-piece straight grip stock & forearm
Approximate wt.: 3 lbs.
Comments: Takedown, made from 1930 for about five years.
Estimated Value: Excellent: $100.00
                       Very good: $ 80.00

Stevens - Springfield Model No. 52 Challenge

Caliber: 22 short, long, long rifle
Action: Bolt action; single shot
Magazine: None
Barrel: 22" round
Sights: Bead front, adjustable sporting rear
Stock & Forearm: Plain walnut one-piece pistol grip stock & forearm
Approximate wt.: 3½ lbs.
Comments: Takedown, produced from early 1930's to just before World War II.
Estimated Value: Excellent: $95.00
                       Very good: $75.00

Stevens - Springfield Model No. 53 Springfield Jr.

Caliber: 22 short, long, long rifle
Action: Bolt action; single shot
Magazine: None
Barrel: 24"
Sights: Bead front, adjustable sporting rear
Stock & Forearm: Plain walnut semi-pistol grip stock & forearm
Approximate wt.: 4½ lbs.
Comments: Produced from 1930 to late 1940's
Estimated Value: Excellent: $90.00
                       Very good: $75.00

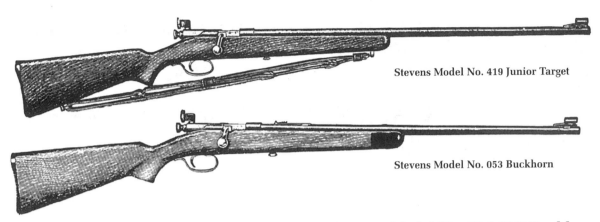

Stevens Model No. 419 Junior Target

Stevens Model No. 053 Buckhorn

Stevens Model No. 419 Junior Target
Caliber: 22 short, long, long rifle
Action: Bolt action; single shot
Magazine: None
Barrel: 26"
Sights: Blade front, peep rear
Stock & Forearm: Plain walnut pistol grip stock with grooved forearm; swivels
Approximate wt.: 5½ lbs.
Comments: Made from 1932 until 1936.
Estimated Value: Excellent: $95.00
Very good: $75.00

Stevens Model No. 53 & 053 Buckhorn
Caliber: 22 short, long, long rifle; 22WRF; 25 Stevens RF
Action: Bolt action; single shot
Magazine: None
Barrel: 24"; blued; round
Sights: 053 hooded ramp front, open middle, peep receiver; 53 open rear, bead front
Stock & Forearm: Plain walnut pistol grip stock & forearm
Approximate wt.: 5½ lbs.
Comments: Made from the mid 1930's to late 1940's.
Estimated Value: Excellent: $100.00
Very good: $ 80.00

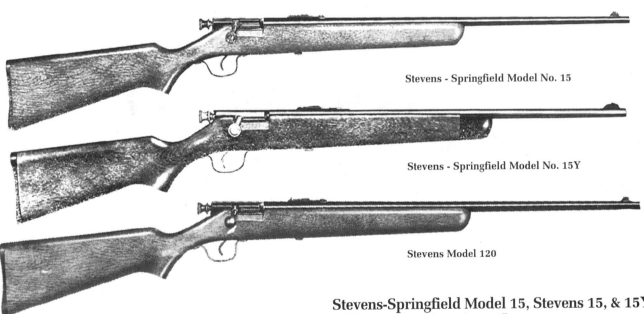

Stevens - Springfield Model No. 15

Stevens - Springfield Model No. 15Y

Stevens Model 120

Stevens Model 120
Caliber: 22 short, long, long rifle
Action: Bolt action; single shot; pull hammer
Magazine: None
Barrel: Blued; 24"; round
Sights: Blade front, adjustable rear
Stock & Forearm: Plain hardwood one-piece semi-pistol grip stock & forearm
Approximate wt.: 5 lbs.
Comments: Produced in the late 1970's.
Estimated Value: Excellent: $85.00
Very good: $70.00

Stevens-Springfield Model 15, Stevens 15, & 15Y
Caliber: 22 short, long, long rifle
Action: Bolt action; single shot
Magazine: None
Barrel: Stevens-Springfield Model 15 22"; Stevens 15 24"; Stevens 15Y 21"
Sights: Open rear; bead front
Stock & Forearm: Plain walnut pistol grip, 15Y; short butt stock, black tipped forearm
Approximate wt.: 4 to 5 lbs.
Comments: Stevens-Springfield model 15 late 1930's to late 1940's; Stevens 15, late 1940's to mid 1960's; Stevens 15Y, late 1950's to mid 1960's.
Estimated Value: Excellent: $90.00
Very good: $75.00

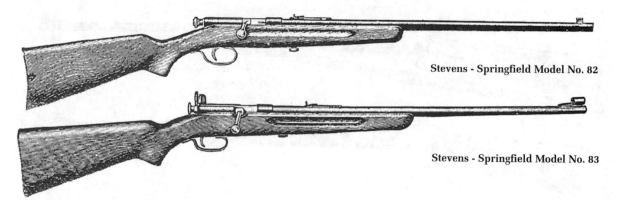

Stevens - Springfield Model No. 82

Stevens - Springfield Model No. 83

Stevens - Springfield Model No. 82

Caliber: 22 short, long, long rifle
Action: Bolt action; single shot
Magazine: None
Barrel: 22"; round
Sights: Open rear, bead front
Stock & Forearm: Plain walnut pistol grip stock, groove in forearm
Approximate wt.: 4 lbs.
Comments: Made from middle 1930's until 1940.
Estimated Value: Excellent: $95.00
                        Very good: $75.00

Stevens - Springfield Model No. 83

Caliber: 22 short, long, long rifle, 22 WRF, 25 Stevens RF
Action: Bolt action; single shot
Magazine: None
Barrel: 24"; round
Sights: Peep rear, open middle, hooded ramp front
Stock & Forearm: Plain walnut pistol grip stock with groove in forearm
Approximate wt.: 4½ lbs.
Comments: Made from middle 1930's until 1940.
Estimated Value: Excellent: $100.00
                        Very good: $ 80.00

Stevens Model No. 73

Stevens Model 125

Stevens Model 125

Caliber: 22 short, long, long rifle
Action: Bolt action; single shot
Magazine: None
Barrel: Blued; 22"; round
Sights: Sporting front, open rear with elevator
Stock & Forearm: Checkered hardwood one-piece semi-pistol grip stock & forearm
Approximate wt.: 5 lbs.
Comments: Discontinued in mid 1980's.
Estimated Value: Excellent: $80.00
                        Very good: $65.00

Stevens Model 125Y

A youth version of the Model 125 with shorter stock. Discontinued in the early 1980's.
Estimated Value: Excellent: $75.00
                        Very good: $60.00

Stevens Model 36

Caliber: 22 short, long, long rifle
Action: Bolt action; hammerless, single shot
Magazine: None, single shot
Barrel: 22"; round
Sights: Open rear, blade front
Stock & Forearm: Hardwood, one-piece semi-pistol grip stock & forearm
Approximate wt.: 5 lbs.
Comments: Produced from 1984 to 1985.
Estimated Value: Excellent: $80.00
                        Very good: $65.00

Stevens Model No. 73, 73Y

Caliber: 22 short, long, long rifle
Action: Bolt action; single shot
Magazine: None
Barrel: 20" on 73; 18" on 73Y
Sights: Sporting front, open rear
Stock & Forearm: Plain walnut pistol grip; short stock on 73Y
Approximate wt.: 73 - 4¾ lbs.; 73Y - 4½ lbs.
Comments: Made from 1965 to early 1980's.
Estimated Value: Excellent: $75.00
                        Very good: $60.00

Stevens Model No. 66 Buckhorn

Stevens Model No. 066 Buckhorn

Stevens Model No. 056 Buckhorn

Stevens Model No. 56 & 056 Buckhorn
Caliber: 22 short, long, long rifle
Action: Bolt action; repeating
Magazine: 5-shot clip
Barrel: 24"
Sights: 56: bead front, open rear; 056: hooded ramp front, open middle receiver peep
Stock & Forearm: Plain walnut pistol grip stock & black tipped forearm
Approximate wt.: 6 lbs.
Comments: Made from mid 1930's to late 1940's.
Estimated Value: Excellent: $100.00
Very good: $ 80.00

Stevens Model No. 66 Buckhorn
Caliber: 22 short, long, long rifle
Action: Bolt action; repeating
Magazine: Tubular, 19 shorts, 15 longs, 13 long rifles
Barrel: 24"
Sights: Open rear, bead front
Stock & Forearm: Plain walnut semi-pistol grip stock & forearm
Approximate wt.: 5 lbs.
Comments: Made from the 1920's to late 1940's
Estimated Value: Excellent: $110.00
Very good: $ 85.00

Stevens Model No. 066 Buckhorn
Same as the Model No. 66 except: hooded ramp front sight; open middle sight; receiver peep sight. Made from mid 1930's until late 1940's.
Estimated Value: Excellent: $115.00
Very good: $ 95.00

Stevens Model No. 322

Stevens Model No. 322, 322S
Caliber: 22 Hornet
Action: Bolt action; repeating
Magazine: 5-shot clip
Barrel: 21"; round
Sights: Ramp front, open rear; 322S has peep rear
Stock & Forearm: Plain walnut pistol grip stock & forearm
Approximate wt.: 6¾ lbs.
Comments: Made from the late 1940's to early 1950's.
Estimated Value: Excellent: $175.00
Very good: $140.00

Stevens Model No. 416

Stevens Model No. 416
Caliber: 22 long rifle
Action: Bolt action; repeating
Magazine: 5-shot clip
Barrel: 26" heavy
Sights: Receiver peep, hooded ramp front
Stock & Forearm: Plain walnut pistol grip stock & forearm
Approximate wt.: 9½ lbs.
Comments: Made from the late 1930's to late 1940's.
Estimated Value: Excellent: $160.00
Very good: $120.00

Stevens Model No. 325 & 325 S
Caliber: 30-30
Action: Bolt action; repeating
Magazine: 3-shot clip
Barrel: 21"; round
Sights: Open rear, bead front; 325S peep rear
Stock & Forearm: Walnut pistol grip stock & forearm
Approximate wt.: 6¾ lbs.
Comments: Made from the late 1940's to early 1950's.
Estimated Value: Excellent: $150.00
Very good: $120.00

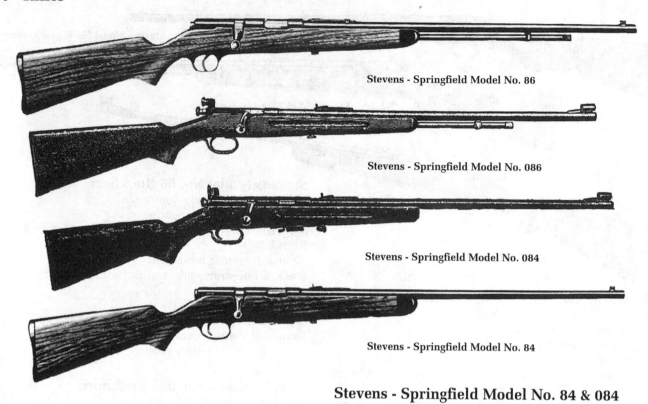

Stevens - Springfield Model No. 86

Stevens - Springfield Model No. 086

Stevens - Springfield Model No. 084

Stevens - Springfield Model No. 84

Stevens - Springfield Model No. 86, 086
(Stevens Model No. 86 after 1948)

Model 86 is same as Model 84 except: a tubular magazine that holds 21 shorts, 17 longs, 15 long rifles. Made from mid 1930's until mid 1960's. Model 86 Stevens or 086 Stevens is same as 84 or 084 Stevens except tubular magazines

Estimated Value: Excellent: $120.00
                        Very good: $ 95.00

Stevens - Springfield Model No. 84 & 084
(Stevens Model No. 84 after 1948)

Caliber: 22 short, long, long rifle
Action: Bolt action; repeating
Magazine: 5-shot clip
Barrel: 24"; round
Sights: 84: bead front, open rear; 84 Stevens or 084 peep rear & hooded ramp front
Stock & Forearm: Plain walnut pistol grip stock & forearm; black tip on forearm of Model 84
Approximate wt.: 6 lbs.
Comments: Made from early 1940 until the mid 1960's.

Estimated Value: Excellent: $110.00
                        Very good: $ 90.00

Stevens Model No. 34

Stevens Model No. 46

Stevens Model No 46

Similar to Model 34 except tubular magazine. Discontinued in late 1960's.

Estimated Value: Excellent: $105.00
                        Very good: $ 85.00

Stevens Model No. 34

Caliber: 22 short, long, long rifle
Action: Bolt action; repeating
Magazine: 5-shot clip
Barrel: 20"; blued; round
Sights: Sporting front, adj. open rear
Stock & Forearm: Plain walnut pistol grip before 1969; checkered Monte Carlo after 1969
Approximate wt.: 5½ lbs.
Comments: Made from mid 1960's to early 1980's.

Estimated Value: Excellent: $95.00
                        Very good: $75.00

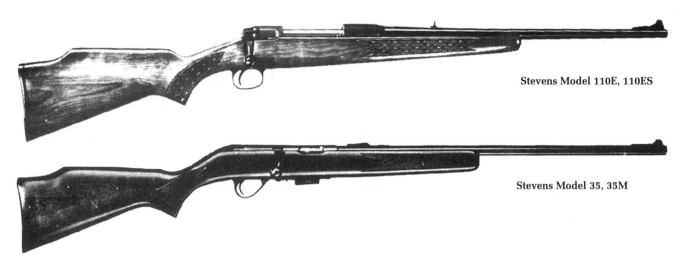

Stevens Model 110E, 110ES

Stevens Model 35, 35M

Stevens Model 110 E & 110 ES
Caliber: 243, 30-06, 308
Action: Bolt action; hammerless; repeating
Magazine: 4-shot box, internal
Barrel: Blued; 22"
Sights: Ramp front, open rear; 110 ES has 4X scope
Stock & Forearm: Checkered hardwood one-piece Monte Carlo semi-pistol grip stock & forearm
Approximate wt.: 7 lbs.
Comments: Made from the late 1970's to 1981 as Stevens. in 1982 as Savage. Add 10% for 110ES.
Estimated Value: Excellent: $250.00
Very good: $200.00

Stevens Model 35 & 35M
Caliber: 22 short, long, long rifle
Action: Bolt action; repeating
Magazine: 4-shot detachable clip
Barrel: Blued; 22"
Sights: Ramp front, sporting rear with step elevator; grooved for scope
Stock & Forearm: Checkered hardwood Monte Carlo one-piece semi-pistol grip stock & forearm
Approximate wt.: 4¾ lbs.
Comments: Produced from 1982 to 1985.
Estimated Value: Excellent: $85.00
Very good: $65.00

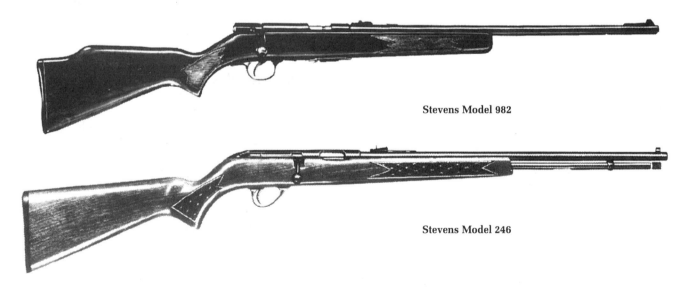

Stevens Model 982

Stevens Model 246

Stevens Model 246
Caliber: 22 short, long, long rifle
Action: Bolt action; repeating
Magazine: Tubular, 22 shorts, 17 longs, 15 long rifles
Barrel: Blued; 20"
Sights: Blade front, elevator open rear
Stock & Forearm: Checkered hardwood one-piece semi-pistol grip stock & forearm
Approximate wt.: 5 lbs.
Comments: Produced in the late 1970's.
Estimated Value: Excellent: $100.00
Very good: $ 80.00

Stevens Model 982
Caliber: 22 short, long, long rifle
Action: Bolt action; repeating
Magazine: 5-shot detachable clip; 10-shot available
Barrel: Blued; 22"
Sights: Ramp front, open rear with elevator
Stock & Forearm: Checkered hardwood one-piece Monte Carlo semi-pistol grip stock & forearm
Approximate wt.: 5¾ lbs.
Comments: Advertised in 1981 only.
Estimated Value: Excellent: $100.00
Very good: $ 80.00

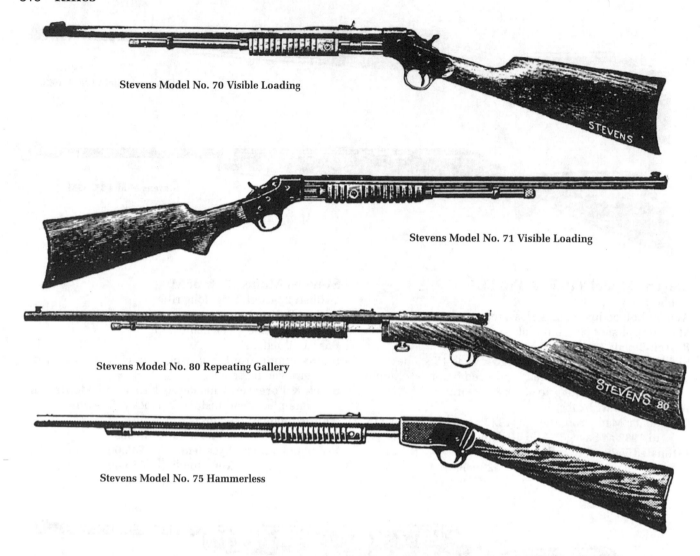

Stevens Model No. 70 Visible Loading

Stevens Model No. 71 Visible Loading

Stevens Model No. 80 Repeating Gallery

Stevens Model No. 75 Hammerless

Stevens Model No. 70 Visible Loading
Caliber: 22 short, long, long rifle
Action: Slide action; exposed hammer
Magazine: Tubular; 11 long rifles, 13 longs, 15 shorts
Barrel: 20"or 22"; round
Sights: Open rear, bead front
Stock & Forearm: Plain walnut straight grip stock & grooved slide handle
Approximate wt.: 4½ lbs.
Comments: Made from 1907 until the early 1930's.
Estimated Value: Excellent: $250.00
Very good: $200.00

Stevens Model No. 71 Visible Loading
Caliber: 22 short, long, long rifle
Action: Slide action; exposed hammer
Magazine: Tubular; 15 shorts, 13 longs, 11 long rifles
Barrel: 24"; octagon; blued
Sights: Bead front, adjustable flat-top sporting rear
Stock & Forearm: Plain walnut pistol grip stock & grooved slide handle
Approximate wt.: 5 lbs.
Comments: This replaced the No. 70; discontinued prior to World War II.
Estimated Value: Excellent: $225.00
Very good: $180.00

Stevens Model No. 75 Hammerless
Caliber: 22 short, long, long rifle
Action: Slide action; hammerless; side ejection
Magazine: Tubular, 20 shorts, 17 longs, 15 long rifles
Barrel: 24"; blued
Sights: Bead front, adjustable rear
Stock & Forearm: Plain walnut, straight grip stock & grooved slide handle
Approximate wt.: 5¼ lbs.
Comments: Made from the early 1930's until World War II.
Estimated Value: Excellent: $220.00
Very good: $175.00

Stevens Model No. 80 Repeating Gallery
Caliber: 22 short
Action: Slide action; hammerless
Magazine: 16-shot tubular
Barrel: 24" round
Sights: Open rear, bead front
Stock & Forearm: Plain walnut straight grip stock & grooved forearm
Approximate wt.: 5¼ lbs.
Comments: Takedown made for about five years beginning in 1906.
Estimated Value: Excellent: $260.00
Very good: $210.00

Stevens - Springfield Model No. 85

Stevens - Springfield Model No. 87

Stevens Model No. 57

Stevens Model No. 76

Stevens Model No. 987, 987 T

Stevens Springfield Model No. 85, 085 (Stevens Model No. 85 after 1948)

Caliber: 22 long rifle
Action: Semi-automatic; repeating
Magazine: 5-shot clip
Barrel: 24"; blued
Sights: Open rear, bead front on 85; hooded ramp front & peep rear on 085 & 85 Stevens
Stock & Forearm: Plain walnut pistol grip stock & forearm; 85 has black tipped forearm
Approximate wt.: 6 lbs.
Comments: Produced from the late 1930's until after World War II.
Estimated Value: Excellent: $120.00
Very good: $ 95.00

Stevens - Springfield Model No. 87, 087 (Stevens Model 87 after 1948)

Same as the No. 85, 085 except 15-shot tubular magazine.
Estimated Value: Excellent: $125.00
Very good: $100.00

Stevens Model No. 87 K Scout

Carbine version of Model No. 87; 20" barrel; produced until 1969.
Estimated Value: Excellent: $115.00
Very good: $ 90.00

Stevens Model 987 & 987 T

Caliber: 22 long rifle
Action: Semi-automatic
Magazine: 14-shot tubular
Barrel: Blued; 20"
Sights: Ramp front, open rear with elevator; 987T has 4X scope
Stock & Forearm: Checkered hardwood, one-piece semi-pistol grip Monte Carlo stock & forearm
Approximate wt.: 6 lbs.
Comments: Produced from 1981 to 1988. Add $10.00 for scope (987T).
Estimated Value: Excellent: $105.00
Very good: $ 80.00

Stevens Model No. 57 & 057

Caliber: 22 long rifle
Action: Semi-automatic; repeating
Magazine: 5-shot clip
Barrel: 24"
Sights: Open rear, bead front on 57; hooded ramp front, open middle, receiver peep on 057
Stock & Forearm: Plain walnut pistol grip stock & forearm; black tipped forearm on 57
Approximate wt.: 6 lbs.
Comments: Made from late 1930's to late 1940's.
Estimated Value: Excellent: $120.00
Very good: $ 95.00

Stevens Model No. 76 & 076

Same as Stevens Model 57 & 057 except: 15-shot tubular magazine.
Estimated Value: Excellent: $125.00
Very good: $100.00

Stevens Model No. 887-T

Stevens Model 887-T

Similar to the Model 887 with a 4X scope. Due to a possible safety malfunction certain models were recalled in 1982 & inspected by Stevens at no cost to the owner. Serial numbers recalled were B256621 or higher; C000001 or higher; D000001 or higher.

| Estimated Value: | Excellent: | $125.00 |
| | Very good: | $100.00 |

Stevens Model 887

Caliber: 22 long rifle
Action: Semi-automatic
Magazine: 15-shot tubular
Barrel: Blued 20"
Sights: Blade front, elevator open rear
Stock & Forearm: Checkered hardwood, one-piece semi-pistol grip stock & forearm
Approximate wt.: 6 lbs.
Comments: Produced in the late 1970's. Due to a possible safety malfunction, some models were recalled in 1982 & inspected by Stevens

| Estimated Value: | Excellent: | $115.00 |
| | Very good: | $ 95.00 |

Thompson Center

Thompson Center Contender Carbine

Thompson Center Youth Model Carbine

Caliber: 22 long rifle, 22 Win. mag., 22 hornet, 223 Rem., 7x30 Waters, 30-30 Win., 35 Rem., 44 magnum, 45 Colt/410 gauge. The 45 Colt rifled barrel is used for 410 gauge when a detachable internal choke is screwed into the muzzle.
Action: Single shot, frame accommodates any caliber interchangeable barrel, hammer adjusts for caliber.
Magazine: None, single shot
Barrel: Interchangeable to select caliber; 16¼" barrel; 45/410 barrel has ventilated rib
Sights: Adjustable; tapped for scope mounts; 45/410 barrel has fixed rear sight & bead front.
Stock & Forearm: 12" length of pull, walnut or allweather Rynite®, pistol grip stock & forearm; recoil pad
Approximate wt.: 4½ lbs.
Comments: Introduced in 1989. Add 7% for 45/410 Model.

Estimated Value:	New (retail):	$479.00
	Excellent:	$360.00
	Very good:	$285.00

Thompson Center Contender Carbine

Caliber: 17 Rem., 22 long rifle, 22 Hornet, 222 Rem., 223 Rem., 7mm , 7x30 Waters, 30-30 Win., 35 Rem., 357 Rem. maximum, 375 Win., 45 colt, 410 ga.
Action: Single shot, frame accommodates any caliber interchangeable barrel, hammer adjusts
Magazine: None; single shot
Barrel: Interchangeable; 21"; 410 ga. is smooth bore with screw-in choke and ventilated rib after early 1990's
Sights: Adj. rear; ramp front; tapped for scope mounts
Stock & Forearm: Walnut or all-weather Rynite, pistol grip stock & forearm; recoil pad.
Approximate wt.: 5¼ lbs.
Comments: Introduced in 1986. Based on the design of the popular Contender handgun. Add 48% for each additional barrel. Add 5% for ventilated rib. Add 6% for 17 Rem. Add 5% for 410 ga.

Estimated Value:	New (retail):	$515.00
	Excellent:	$385.00
	Very good:	$300.00

Thompson Center SST Contender Carbine

Same as the Contender Carbine except: all stainless steel; all weather Rynite®stock; no 17 Rem. or 45 Colt calibers; add 5% for C-410 smooth bore with choke; introduced in 1994.

Estimated Value:	New (retail):	$510.00
	Excellent:	$385.00
	Very good:	$300.00

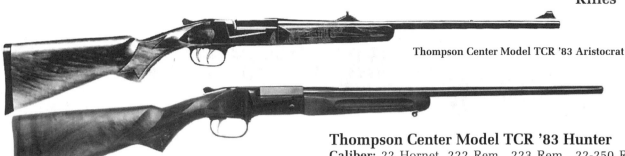

Thompson Center Model TCR '83 Aristocrat

Thompson Center Model TCR Hunter

Thompson Center Model TCR '83 Hunter
Caliber: 22 Hornet, 222 Rem., 223 Rem., 22-250 Rem., 243 Win., 270 Win., 7mm Rem. magnum, 308 Win., 30-06 Springfield; caliber can be selected by replacing different caliber barrel; also 12 gauge
Action: Top lever, break-open; single shot; hammerless
Magazine: None
Barrel: Interchangeable to select caliber; 23" or 25"
Sights: Ramp front, folding leaf rear.
Stock & Forearm: Checkered walnut semi-pistol grip stock & forearm; cheekpiece; recoil pad
Approximate wt.: 6¾ lbs.
Comments: Produced from 1983 to 1987. Add 30% for each extra barrel. Replaced by model TCR '87 Hunter
Estimated Value: Excellent: $375.00
Very good: $300.00

Thompson Center Model TCR Hunter
Caliber: 22 Hornet, 222 Rem., 223 Rem., 22-250 Rem., 243 Win., 270 Win., 7mm/08, 308 Win., 30-06 Springfield, 32-40 Win., also 12 gauge rifled slug barrel (1989), 12 gauge shotgun barrel (1988) & 10 gauge shotgun barrel (1988)
Action: Top lever, break-open; single shot hammerless; adjustable single trigger
Magazine: None, single shot
Barrel: Interchangeable to select caliber or gauge; 23" light sporter barrel; 25⅞" medium sporter barrel; 25" shotgun barrel; 22" rifled slug barrel
Sights: None; drilled & tapped for scope mounts; rifled slug barrel has adjustable iron sights; shotgun barrel has bead front sight
Stock & Forearm: Checkered walnut semi-pistol grip stock & grooved forearm; recoil pad
Approximate wt.: 6¾ lbs. (light sporter barrel); 7¼ lbs. (medium sporter barrel); 8 lbs. (shotgun barrel)
Comments: Produced from 1987 to early 1990's.
Estimated Value: Excellent: $475.00
Very good: $355.00

Thompson Center Model TCR '83 Aristocrat
Similar to the TCR '83 Hunter with checkered forearm & stainless steel barrel; adjustable double set triggers. Discontinued in 1987.
Estimated Value: Excellent: $400.00
Very good: $320.00

Thompson Center TCR Deluxe
Similar to the TCR '83 Aristocrat. Reintroduced in 1992 to 1994.
Estimated Value: Excellent: $505.00
Very good: $405.00

Universal

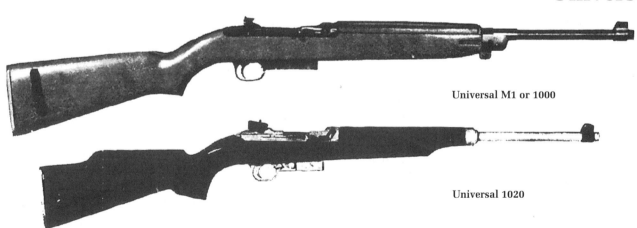

Universal M1 or 1000

Universal 1020

Universal M1 or 1000, 1003
Similar to the U.S. M1 Carbine with a 5-shot detachable clip. Made in 30 caliber from the mid 1960's to present. Add $50.00 for scope & detachable mount. See also Iver Johnson.
Estimated Value: Excellent: $225.00
Very good: $180.00

Universal 1020, 1020 TB, 1020 TCO, 1030
Similar to the 1000 with a Monte Carlo stock & a water resistant teflon finish in green, blue, tan, black or gray. Currently produced as 1020 TB (black) & 1020 TCO (green), 1030 (gray).
Estimated Value: Excellent: $250.00
Very good: $200.00

Universal 440 Vulcan

Universal M1 or 1000 Deluxe

Universal Ferret

Universal Model 2200 Leatherneck

Universal 440 Vulcan

Caliber: 44 magnum
Action: Slide action; hammerless; repeating
Magazine: 5-shot clip
Barrel: 18¼" carbine
Sights: Adjustable rear, ramp front with gold bead
Stock & Forearm: Walnut semi-pistol grip stock & slide handle
Approximate wt.: 6 lbs.
Comments: Made from the mid 1960's to early 1970's.
Estimated Value: Excellent: $220.00
                       Very good: $175.00

Universal M1 or 1000 Deluxe, 1005 SB, 1010N, 1015G, 1011

Same as the 1000 with a Monte Carlo stock; also available in nickel, gold plate or chrome.
Estimated Value:

	1005SB Blue	1010N Nickel	1015G Gold	1011 Chrome
Excellent:	$200.00	$210.00	$250.00	$215.00
Very good:	$160.00	$165.00	$200.00	$175.00

Universal Ferret

Similar to the M1 with a Monte Carlo stock, no sights, & in 256 caliber.
Estimated Value: Excellent: $225.00
                       Very good: $180.00

Universal Model 1035, 1040, 1045

Similar to the Model 1020 with a military stock.
Estimated Value: Excellent: $220.00
                       Very good: $175.00

Universal Model 1006

Similar to the Model 1005SB with stainless steel finish.
Estimated Value: Excellent: $250.00
                       Very good: $200.00

Universal Model 2200 Leatherneck

Similar to the Model 1003 in 22 caliber. Produced from the early 1980's to mid 1980's.
Estimated Value: Excellent: $200.00
                       Very good: $160.00

Valmet

Valmet Model 412 K Double

Valmet Finnish Lion

Valmet Model M-71 S

Valmet 412 KE Double & 412 SE Double
Similar to the Model 412 K Double with automatic ejectors. Introduced in early 1980's. Calibers 375 Win. & 9.3x74 only. Discontinued late 1980's.
Estimated Value: Excellent: $900.00
Very good: $720.00

Valmet Finnish Lion
Caliber: 22 long rifle
Action: Bolt action; single shot
Magazine: None
Barrel: Blued, 29", heavy
Sights: Extended peep rear, changeable front
Stock & Forearm: Free-rifle, pistol grip, with thumb hole, one-piece stock & forearm; palm rest; swivels; Swiss buttplate
Approximate wt.: 15 lbs.
Comments: International Match-type rifle; discontinued in the late 1970's.
Estimated Value: Excellent: $625.00
Very good: $500.00

Valmet Model M-72 S, M-715 S, M-71 S
Caliber: 223 (5.56mm)
Action: Semi- automatic, gas operated
Magazine: 15-or 30-shot, curved detachable box
Barrel: 16½"
Sights: Open tangent rear, hooded post front; both adjustable
Stock & Forearm: Wood or reinforced resin stock; pistol grip; swivels; wood stock & forearm & plastic pistol grip on Model M-71S
Approximate wt.: 8¾ lbs.
Comments: Similar to the M-62/S.
Estimated Value: Excellent: $650.00
Very good: $485.00

Valmet Model 412 K & 412 S Double
Caliber: 243, 308, 30-06
Action: Top lever, break-open, hammerless; extractors
Magazine: None
Barrel: Over & under double barrel; 24" with space between barrels
Sights: Open rear, blade front; drilled for scope
Stock & Forearm: Checkered walnut Monte Carlo pistol grip stock & forearm; recoil pad; swivels
Approximate wt.: 6½ lbs.
Comments: A double rifle produced in Finland as part of the 412 Shotgun Combination series.
Estimated Value: Excellent: $900.00
Very good: $720.00

Valmet Model M-62 S
Caliber: 7.62 x 39mm Russian
Action: Semi-automatic; gas piston, rotating bolt
Magazine: 15- or 30-shot, curved detachable box
Barrel: 16½"
Sights: Adjustable tangent peep rear, adjustable hooded post front
Stock & Forearm: Fixed metal tube or walnut stock; pistol grip; ventilated forearm
Approximate wt.: 8¾ lbs.
Comments: A powerful semi-automatic made in the mid 1970's. Add $15.00 for wood stock version.
Estimated Value: Excellent: $600.00
Very good: $450.00

Valmet Hunter
Similar to the Model 76 redesigned for hunting. Available in calibers: 223, 243, 30-06 or 308; 5-, 9-, 15- or 30-shot clip. Checkered wood pistol grip stock & forearm.

Estimated Value: Excellent: $595.00
                       Very good: $477.00

Valmet Model M-76 Military
Caliber: 223, 308, 7.62x39
Action: Gas operated, semi-automatic, rotating bolt
Magazine: 15- or 30-shot clip
Barrel: 16¾"or 20½"
Sights: Front adjustable in tunnel guard, folding leaf with peep rear; night sight
Stock & Forearm: Wood, synthetic or folding stock, checkered plastic pistol grip & forearm
Approximate wt.: 8 lbs.
Comments: Standard model has wood stock. Add 14% for synthetic stock; 16% for folding stock.

Estimated Value: Excellent: $525.00
                       Very good: $420.00

Walther

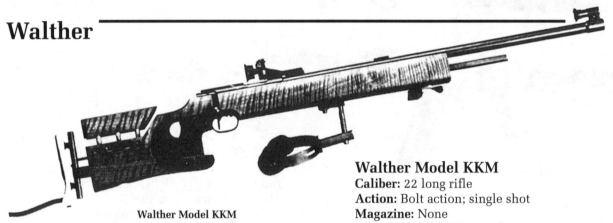

Walther Model KKM

Walther Model KKM
Caliber: 22 long rifle
Action: Bolt action; single shot
Magazine: None
Barrel: Blued; 28" tapered
Sights: Olympic front, changeable micro adjustable rear
Stock & Forearm: Walnut match-style with thumb hole; adjustable buttplate; heavy forearm with hand shelf; cheekpiece
Approximate wt.: 15 lbs.
Comments: A match rifle made from the 1950's to late 1970's.

Estimated Value: Excellent: $800.00
                       Very good: $650.00

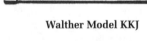

Walther Model KKJ

Walther Model KKJ
Caliber: 22 Hornet, 22 long rifle, 22 WRM
Action: Bolt action; repeating; double set trigger available
Magazine: 5-shot detachable clip
Barrel: Blued; 22½"
Sights: Adjustable rear, hooded ramp front
Stock & Forearm: Checkered walnut pistol grip stock & forearm; cheekpiece; swivels
Approximate wt.: 5½ lbs.
Comments: Made from about 1957 to late 1970's. Add $20.00 for double set trigger.

Estimated Value: Excellent: $500.00
                       Very good: $400.00

Walther Moving Target
Caliber: 22 long rifle
Action: Bolt action; single shot
Magazine: None
Barrel: Blued; 23½"
Sights: Micro adjustable rear, globe front
Stock & Forearm: Walnut, pistol grip, thumb hole, match-type with adjustable cheekpiece & buttplate
Approximate wt.: 8¼ lbs.
Comments: A match rifle made in 1970's.

Estimated Value: Excellent: $625.00
                       Very good: $500.00

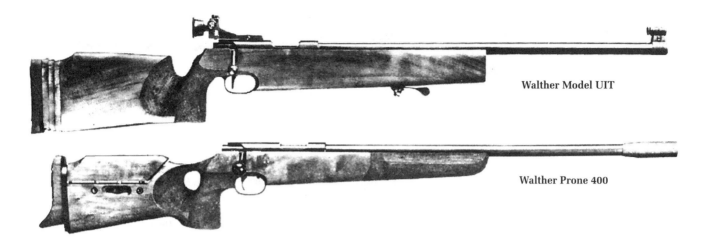

Walther Model UIT

Walther Prone 400

Walther Model UIT
Caliber: 22 long rifle
Action: Bolt action; single shot
Magazine: None
Barrel: 25½"
Sights: Changeable front, micro adjustable rear
Stock & Forearm: Match-style, walnut pistol grip stock & wide forearm
Approximate wt.: 10¼ lbs.
Comments: A match rifle made from the mid 1960's.
Estimated Value: Excellent: $1,050.00
                        Very good: $ 840.00

Walther Prone 400
Similar to the UIT with split stock & adjustable cheekpiece; thumb hole; no sights.
Estimated Value: Excellent: $650.00
                        Very good: $520.00

Weatherby

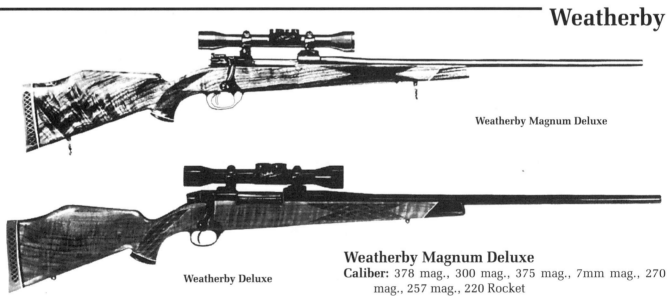

Weatherby Magnum Deluxe

Weatherby Deluxe

Weatherby Magnum Deluxe
Caliber: 378 mag., 300 mag., 375 mag., 7mm mag., 270 mag., 257 mag., 220 Rocket
Action: Bolt action; Mauser-type
Magazine: 3-shot
Barrel: Blued; 24"; 26" available on some calibers
Sights: None
Stock & Forearm: Checkered wood Monte Carlo one-piece pistol grip stock & tapered forearm; recoil pad; swivels; cheekpiece
Approximate wt.: 7 to 8 lbs.
Comments: Made from the late 1940's to the late 1950's.
Estimated Value: Excellent: $720.00
                        Very good: $575.00

Weatherby Deluxe
Similar to the Magnum Deluxe but in 270 Win. and 30-06 calibers only.
Estimated Value: Excellent: $625.00
                        Very good: $500.00

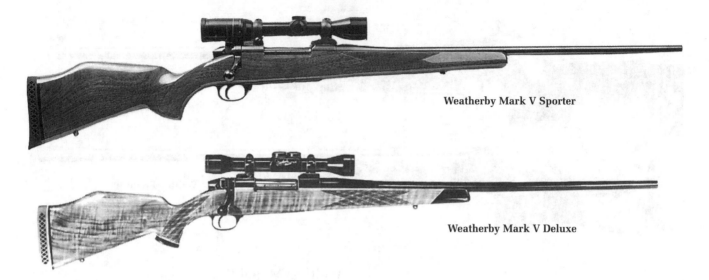

Weatherby Mark V Sporter

Weatherby Mark V Deluxe

Weatherby Mark V Sporter & Eurosport
Caliber: 22-250 Rem., .240 Wby. mag., 257 Wby. mag., 270 Wby mag., 7mm Wby. mag., 7mm Rem. mag., 300 Win., 338 Win., 375 H&H, 270 Win., 30-06 Sprng., 300 Wby mag., 340 Wby. mag.
Action: Bolt action; repeating
Magazine: 3 or 4-shot box
Barrel: 22", 24" or 26"; depending on caliber; low lustre blued
Sights: None
Stock & Forearm: Epoxy finish, checkered Monte Carlo, one-piece pistol grip stock and tapered forearm; recoil pad; swivel studs
Approximate wt.: 7½ to 9 lbs.
Comments: Introduced in the early 1990's.

Estimated Value:	New (retail):	$899.00
	Excellent:	$675.00
	Very good:	$540.00

Weatherby Mark V Deluxe
Caliber: 22-250 Rem., 240 Wby. mag., 257 Wby. mag., 270 Wby. mag., 7mm Wby. mag., 30-06, 300 Wby. mag., 340 Wby. mag., 378 Wby. mag., 416 Wby. mag. 460 Wby. mag.
Action: Bolt action; repeating
Magazine: 3- or 4-shot, depending on caliber
Barrel: Blued; 24" or 26"
Sights: None
Stock & Forearm: Checkered walnut Monte Carlo one-piece pistol grip stock & tapered forearm; recoil pad; swivels
Approximate wt.: 7¼ to 10½ lbs.
Comments: Made from the late 1950's to present. Also available in Euromark & Lazermark series. Add 4% for Euromark; add 8% for Lazermark; 10% for 416 mag. ; 6% for 378 Wby. mag.; 35% for 460 mag.

Estimated Value:	New (retail):	$1,399.00
	Excellent:	$1,050.00
	Very good:	$ 840.00

Weatherby Varmintmaster

Weatherby Fibermark

Weatherby Fibermark
Similar to the Mark V Deluxe except one-piece black fiberglass stock & forearm; weighs 7½ to 8 lbs. Produced from mid 1980's to early 1990's

Estimated Value:	Excellent:	$1,035.00
	Very good:	$ 825.00

Weatherby Varmintmaster
A scaled-down version of the Mark V Deluxe in 22-250 or 224 Weatherby mag.; 24" or 26" barrel. Add 5% for Lazermark Series.

Estimated Value:	Excellent:	$ 930.00
	Very good:	$ 750.00

Weatherby Classicmark I

Weatherby Weathermark Synthetic

Weatherby Alaskan

Weatherby Classicmark I

Caliber: 240 Wby. mag., 257 Wby. mag., 270 Wby. mag., 270 Win., 7mm Rem. mag., 7mm Wby. mag., 30-06, 300 Wby. mag., 340 Wby. mag., 375 H&H mag., 378 Wby. mag., 416 Wby. mag., 460 Wby. mag.

Action: Bolt action; repeating

Magazine: 4-shot (3-shot mag.), box with hinged floor plate

Barrel: 22", 24", or 26"; Blued;

Sights: None, drilled and tapped for scope mounts

Stock & Forearm: Oil-finished, checkered walnut, Monte Carlo pistol grip, one-piece stock & forearm; recoil pad, swivel studs

Approximate wt.: 8 to 10 lbs.

Comments: Produced in early 1990's. Add 5% to 15% for mag. calibers.

Estimated Value: Excellent: $ 900.00
Very good: $ 720.00

Weatherby Weathermark Synthetic

Caliber: 222 Rem., 240 Wby. mag., 257 Wby. mag.., 270 Wby. mag., 270 Win., 7mm Rem. mag., 7mm Wby. mag., 30-06 spfd., 300 Wby. mag., 340 Wby. mag., 375 H&H

Action: Bolt action; repeating

Magazine: 3- or 4-shot box; hinged floor plate

Barrel: 22", 24", or 26"; blued or stainless steel

Sights: None, drilled and tapped for scope mounts

Stock & Forearm: Checkered synthetic composite one-piece pistol grip stock and forearm; recoil pad

Approximate wt.: 7 to 8 lbs.

Comments: Introduced in 1992. Add 33% for stainless steel.

Estimated Value: New (retail): $ 749.00
Excellent: $ 560.00
Very good: $ 450.00

Weatherby Alaskan

Similar to the Weathermark except: non-glare electroless nickel plate finish. Introduced in 1992.

Estimated Value: Excellent: $ 660.00
Very good: $ 525.00

Weatherby Accumark

Weatherby Classicmark II

Similar to the Classicmark I except: deluxe American Walnut stock and forearm with satin-finish metalwork. Right hand version only

Estimated Value: Excellent: $1,350.00
Very good: $1,080.00

Weatherby Accumark

Caliber: 257 Wby. magnum, 270 Wby. magnum, 7mm Wby. magnum, 300 Wby. magnum, 340 Wby. magnum, 7mm Rem. magnum, 300 Win. magnum

Action: Bolt action; repeating

Magazine: 3- or 4-shot box; hinged floor plate

Barrel: 26" heavy fluted stainless steel with a specially designed bedding system using an aluminum platform

Sights: None, drilled for scope mounts

Stock & Forearm: Synthetic, one-piece Monte Carlo stock and forearm

Approximate wt.: 8½ lbs.

Comments: Introduced in 1996.

Estimated Value: New (retail): $ 1,199.00
Excellent: $ 900.00
Very good: $ 720.00

Weatherby Vanguard VGS

Weatherby Vanguard VGL

Weatherby Vanguard VGX

Weatherby Weatherguard

Weatherby Weatherguard
Caliber: 223 Rem., 243 Rem., 270 Win., 7mm-08 Rem., 7mm Rem. magnum, 30-06, 308 Win.
Action: Bolt action; repeating
Magazine: 4-shot (3-shot magnum), box with hinged floor plate
Barrel: 24"; blued;
Sights: None, drilled and tapped for scope mounts
Stock & Forearm: Checkered synthetic composite one-piece stock and forearm, pistol grip; recoil pad, swivel studs
Approximate wt.: 7 to 8 lbs.
Comments: An all-weather gun similar to the Vanguard series.
Estimated Value: Excellent: $ 450.00
                      Very good: $ 360.00

Weatherby Vanguard VGX, VGS, VGL
Caliber: 22-250, 25-06, 243, 264, 270, 30-06, 7mm Rem. mag., 300 Win. mag.
Action: Bolt action; repeating
Magazine: 5-shot (3-shot magnum), box with hinged floor plate
Barrel: Blued; 24"
Sights: None
Stock & Forearm: Checkered walnut, Monte Carlo pistol grip, one-piece stock & forearm; recoil pad, swivels; VGX has deluxe finish
Approximate wt.: 6½ to 8 lbs
Comments: Made from early 1970's to early 1990's. Add 30% for VGX.
Estimated Value: Excellent: $ 475.00
                      Very good: $ 380.00

Weatherby Classic II
Similar to the Vanguard with checkered stock and forearm; satin finish.
Estimated Value: Excellent: $ 560.00
                      Very good: $ 450.00

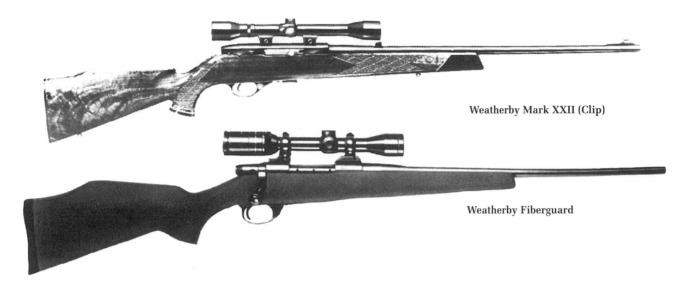

Weatherby Mark XXII (Clip)

Weatherby Fiberguard

Weatherby Mark XXII Deluxe

Caliber: 22 long rifle
Action: Semi-automatic; hammerless
Magazine: 5- or 10-shot clip or 15-shot tubular
Barrel: Blued; 24"
Sights: Open rear, ramp front
Stock & Forearm: Checkered walnut Monte Carlo one-piece pistol grip stock & tapered forearm; swivels
Approximate wt.: 6 lbs.
Comments: Made from the mid 1960's to early 1990's
Estimated Value: Excellent: $ 340.00
Very good: $ 270.00

Weatherby Vanguard Fiberguard

Caliber: 223, 243, 270, 7mm Rem. mag., 30-06, 308 Win.
Action: Bolt action; repeating; short action
Magazine: 6-shot in 223; 5-shot in 243, 270, 30-06 & 308; 3-shot in 7mm Rem. magnum
Barrel: Blued; 20"
Sights: None
Stock & Forearm: A rugged, all-weather fiberglass one-piece semi-pistol grip stock & forearm; forest green wrinkle finish with black butt pad
Approximate wt.: 6½ lbs.
Comments: Made from the mid 1980's to early 1990's.
Estimated Value: Excellent: $500.00
Very good: $400.00

Western Field

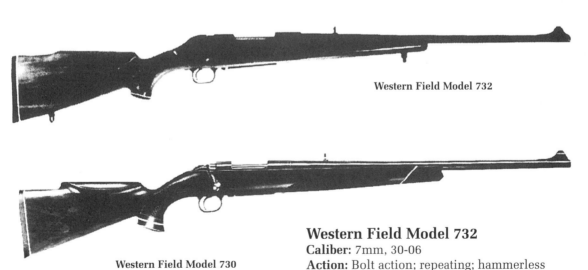

Western Field Model 732

Western Field Model 730

Western Field Model 732

Caliber: 7mm, 30-06
Action: Bolt action; repeating; hammerless
Magazine: 4- or 5-shot tubular, depending on caliber
Barrel: Blued; 22"
Sights: Leaf rear, bead front
Stock & Forearm: Checkered walnut Monte Carlo one-piece pistol grip stock & forearm; swivels
Approximate wt.: 8 lbs.
Comments: Manufactured into the late 1970's.
Estimated Value: Excellent: $220.00
Very good: $175.00

Western Field Model 730

Similar to 732. Produced until mid 1970's.
Estimated Value: Excellent: $200.00
Very good: $160.00

Western Field Model 780

Western Field Model 775

Western Field Bolt Action Repeater

Western Field Model 842

Western Field Bolt Action Repeater

Caliber: 22 short, long, long rifle; 22 WMR
Action: Bolt action; repeating
Magazine: 7-shot clip in 22; 5-shot in 22 WMR
Barrel: Blued; 24"
Sights: Adjustable rear, ramp front
Stock & Forearm: Walnut one-piece pistol grip stock & forearm
Approximate wt.: 6 lbs.
Comments: Discontinued in the early 1980's. Add $5.00 for 22 WMR.
Estimated Value: Excellent: $90.00
                       Very good: $75.00

Western Field Model 780

Caliber: 243, 308
Action: Bolt action; repeating
Magazine: 5-shot tubular
Barrel: Blued; 22"
Sights: Adjustable rear, bead front
Stock & Forearm: Checkered walnut Monte Carlo one-piece pistol grip stock & forearm
Approximate wt.: 6½ lbs.
Comments: Manufactured to the late 1970's.
Estimated Value: Excellent: $200.00
                       Very good: $160.00

Western Field Model 775, 776

Similar to the 780; produced until mid 1970's.
Estimated Value: Excellent: $180.00
                       Very good: $145.00

Western Field Bolt Action

Caliber: 30-06
Action: Bolt action; repeating
Magazine: 4-shot, hinged floorplate
Barrel: Blued; 22" round
Sights: Bead front, adjustable rear
Stock & Forearm: Smooth hardwood one-piece pistol grip stock & forearm with sling swivels
Approximate wt.: 7¾ lbs.
Comments: Made until the early 1980's.
Estimated Value: Excellent: $190.00
                       Very good: $155.00

Western Field Model 842

Caliber: 22 short, long, long rifle
Action: Bolt action; repeating
Magazine: Tubular; 18 long rifles, 20 longs, 22 shorts
Barrel: Blued; 24"
Sights: Adjustable rear, bead front
Stock & Forearm: Walnut Monte Carlo one-piece pistol grip stock & forearm
Approximate wt.: 6¼ lbs.
Comments: Manufactured until the mid 1970's.
Estimated Value: Excellent: $100.00
                       Very good: $ 80.00

Western Field Model 78 Deluxe
Caliber: 7mm mag., 30-06
Action: Bolt action
Magazine: 3-shot rotary magazine in 7mm, 4-shot in 30-06
Barrel: 24" in 7mm; 22" in 30-06
Sights: Bead front, adjustable rear
Stock & Forearm: Checkered walnut pistol grip stock & forearm; swivels
Approximate wt.: 7mm: 8¾ lbs.; 30-06: 7½ lbs.
Comments: Manufactured to the early 1980's.
Estimated Value: Excellent: $200.00
Very good: $160.00

Western Field Model 815
Caliber: 22 short, long, long rifle
Action: Bolt action; single shot; hammerless
Magazine: None
Barrel: Blued; 24"
Sights: Adjustable rear, bead front
Stock & Forearm: Wood Monte Carlo one-piece pistol grip stock & forearm
Approximate wt.: 8 lbs.
Comments: Made until the mid 1970's.
Estimated Value: Excellent: $70.00
Very good: $55.00

Western Field 72

Western Field Model 72
Caliber: 30-30
Action: Lever-action; exposed hammer; repeating; side ejection
Magazine: 6-shot tubular
Barrel: Blued; 18", 20"
Sights: Adjustable open rear, ramp front
Stock & Forearm: Walnut two-piece pistol grip stock & forearm; barrel band; fluted comb
Approximate wt.: 7½ lbs.
Comments: Made into the late 1970's.
Estimated Value: Excellent: $175.00
Very good: $140.00

Western Field Model 740
Similar to Model 72 with recoil pad & 20" barrel. Produced until mid 1970's.
Estimated Value: Excellent: $180.00
Very good: $145.00

Western Field Model 79
Caliber: 30-30
Action: Lever-action; exposed hammer; repeating; side ejection
Magazine: 6-shot tubular, side load
Barrel: Blued; 20" round
Sights: Bead front, rear adjustable for elevation
Stock & Forearm: Smooth hardwood pistol grip stock & forearm
Approximate wt.: 7 lbs.
Comments: Made to the early 1980's.
Estimated Value: Excellent: $170.00
Very good: $135.00

Western Field Model 865
Caliber: 22 short, long, long rifle
Action: Lever-action; hammerless; repeating
Magazine: Tubular; 13 long rifles, 15 longs, 20 shorts
Barrel: Blued; 20"
Sights: Adjustable rear, bead front
Stock & Forearm: Wood Monte Carlo pistol grip stock & forearm; barrel band; swivels
Approximate wt.: 7 lbs.
Comments: Made until the mid 1970's.
Estimated Value: Excellent: $120.00
Very good: $95.00

Western Field Model 895

Western Field Model 895
Caliber: 22 long rifle
Action: Semi-automatic; hammerless
Magazine: 18-shot tubular
Barrel: Blued; 24"
Sights: Open rear, bead front
Stock & Forearm: Checkered walnut Monte Carlo pistol grip stock & forearm
Approximate wt.: 7 lbs.
Comments: Made until mid 1970's.
Estimated Value: Excellent: $110.00
Very good: $90.00

Western Field Model 846

Western Field Model 850

Western Field Model 850

Caliber: 22 long rifle
Action: Semi-automatic; hammerless
Magazine: 7-shot clip
Barrel: Blued; 18"
Sights: Adjustable rear, bead front
Stock & Forearm: Wood one-piece semi-pistol grip stock & tapered forearm
Approximate wt.: 5½ lbs.
Comments: Made to the mid 1970's.
Estimated Value: Excellent: $100.00
                       Very good: $ 80.00

Western Field Semi-Automatic 895 Carbine

Caliber: 22 long rifle
Action: Semi-automatic; hammerless
Magazine: 15-shot tubular
Barrel: 21"
Sights: Blade front, rear adjustable for elevation
Stock & Forearm: Smooth hardwood one-piece pistol grip stock & forearm
Approximate wt.: 5½ lbs.
Comments: Made until the early 1960's.
Estimated Value: Excellent: $110.00
                       Very good: $ 90.00

Western Field Model 846

Caliber: 22 long rifle
Action: Semi-automatic; hammerless
Magazine: 15-shot tubular, stock load
Barrel: Blued; 18½"
Sights: Adjustable rear, bead front
Stock & Forearm: Checkered wood one-piece pistol grip stock & forearm; barrel band; swivels
Approximate wt.: 5¼ lbs.
Comments: Made until mid 1970's.
Estimated Value: Excellent: $105.00
                       Very good: $ 85.00

Winchester

Winchester Model 1900

Winchester Model 02

Winchester Model 02

Similar to the Model 1900 with extended trigger guard; addition of 22 long rifle & extra long. Made from about 1902 to the early 1930's.
Estimated Value: Excellent: $250.00
                       Very good: $200.00

Winchester Model 1900

Caliber: 22 short, long
Action: Bolt action; single shot; cocking piece
Magazine: None
Barrel: Blued; 18", round
Sights: Open rear, blade front
Stock & Forearm: Plain one-piece straight grip stock & forearm
Approximate wt.: 3 lbs.
Comments: Made from about 1900 to 1902.
Estimated Value: Excellent: $225.00
                       Very good: $180.00

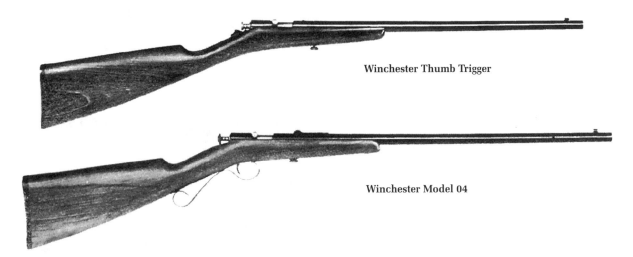

Winchester Thumb Trigger

Winchester Model 04

Winchester Thumb Trigger (Model 02)
Similar to the Model 02 with no trigger. The gun is discharged by pushing a button behind the cocking piece. Made until the early 1920's.

Estimated Value: Excellent: $350.00
                   Very good: $275.00

Winchester Model 04
Similar to the Model 02 with a 21" barrel & lipped forearm. Made from 1904 to the early 1930's.

Estimated Value: Excellent: $200.00
                   Very good: $160.00

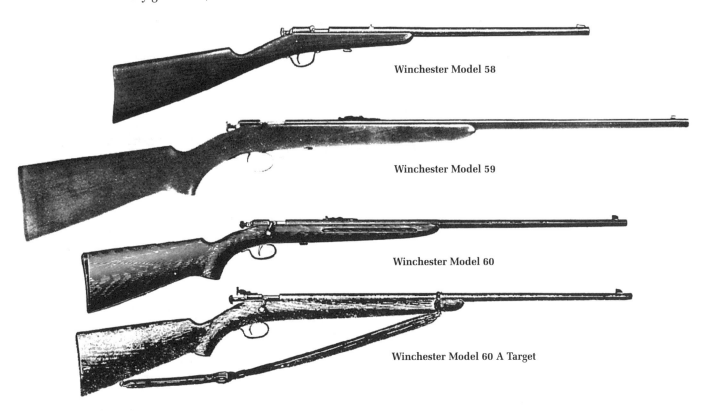

Winchester Model 58

Winchester Model 59

Winchester Model 60

Winchester Model 60 A Target

Winchester Model 58
Similar to the Model 1900 single shot. Made from the late 1920's to early 1930's.

Estimated Value: Excellent: $175.00
                   Very good: $140.00

Winchester Model 59
Similar to the Model 58 with a 23" barrel. Weighs about 4½ lbs. Made from about 1930 to 1931.

Estimated Value: Excellent: $185.00
                   Very good: $150.00

Winchester Model 60
Similar to the Model 59 with 23" or 27" barrel. Made from the early to mid 1930's.

Estimated Value: Excellent: $180.00
                   Very good: $150.00

Winchester Model 60 A Target
Similar to the Model 60 with special Lyman sights; swivels. Made to about 1940.

Estimated Value: Excellent: $190.00
                   Very good: $155.00

Winchester Model 67

Winchester Model 67 Boy's

Winchester Model 68

Winchester Model 677

Winchester Model 55

Winchester Model 67

Caliber: 22 short, long, long rifle
Action: Bolt action; single shot
Magazine: None
Barrel: Blued; 27"
Sights: Open rear, bead front
Stock & Forearm: Plain walnut one-piece semi-pistol grip stock & fluted forearm
Approximate wt.: 5 lbs.
Comments: Made from the mid 1930's to the early 1960's.

Estimated Value:	Excellent:	$110.00
	Very good:	$ 90.00

Winchester Model 67 Boy's

Similar to the Model 67 with a 20" barrel & youth stock.

Estimated Value:	Excellent:	$100.00
	Very good:	$ 80.00

Winchester Model 68

Similar to the Model 67 with peep rear sight. Made from the mid 1930's to mid 1940's.

Estimated Value:	Excellent:	$115.00
	Very good:	$ 90.00

Winchester Model 677

Similar to the Model 67 with no sights. Made only in the late 1930's for two years.

Estimated Value:	Excellent:	$175.00
	Very good:	$150.00

Winchester Model 55

Caliber: 22 short, long, long rifle
Action: Single shot
Magazine: None
Barrel: 22"
Sights: Open rear, bead front
Stock & Forearm: Plain wood one-piece semi-pistol grip stock & forearm
Approximate wt.: 5½ lbs.
Comments: Made from the late 1950's to the early 1960's.

Estimated Value:	Excellent:	$90.00
	Very good:	$75.00

Winchester Lee

Winchester Lee

Caliber: 6mm (236)
Action: Bolt action; repeating
Magazine: 5-shot detachable box
Barrel: 24", round, nickel steel
Sights: Open rear, bead front
Stock & Forearm: One-piece semi-pistol grip stock & fluted, lipped forearm
Approximate wt.: 7½ lbs.
Comments: Made from the late 1890's to early 1900's.
Estimated Value: Excellent: $850.00
                        Very good: $680.00

Winchester Lee Musket

Similar to the Winchester Lee with military sights, full-length musket forearm, 28" barrel, swivels.
Estimated Value: Excellent: $800.00
                        Very good: $650.00

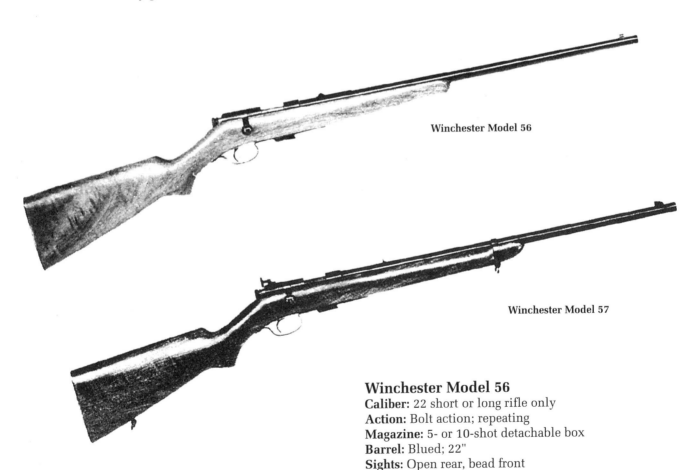

Winchester Model 56

Winchester Model 57

Winchester Model 56

Caliber: 22 short or long rifle only
Action: Bolt action; repeating
Magazine: 5- or 10-shot detachable box
Barrel: Blued; 22"
Sights: Open rear, bead front
Stock & Forearm: Plain walnut one-piece semi-pistol grip stock & lipped forearm
Approximate wt.: 5 lbs.
Comments: Made from the mid to late 1920's. A fancy version was available with checkered walnut stock & forearm.
Estimated Value: Excellent: $275.00
                        Very good: $225.00

Winchester Model 57

Similar to the Model 56 with longer, unlipped forearm; barrel band, swivels; special Lyman sights; target model. Made from the mid 1920's to mid 1930's.
Estimated Value: Excellent: $300.00
                        Very good: $240.00

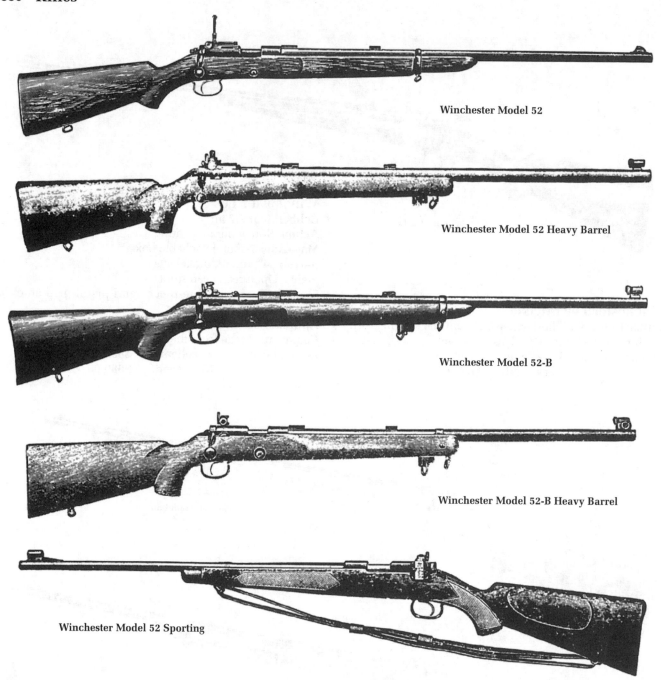

Winchester Model 52

Winchester Model 52 Heavy Barrel

Winchester Model 52-B

Winchester Model 52-B Heavy Barrel

Winchester Model 52 Sporting

Winchester Model 52

Caliber: 22 long rifle
Action: Bolt action; repeating
Magazine: 5-shot box
Barrel: Blued; 28"
Sights: Peep rear, blade front
Stock & Forearm: Plain walnut one-piece pistol grip stock & forearm
Approximate wt.: 8½ lbs.
Comments: Made from about 1920 to the late 1930's.
Estimated Value: Excellent: $450.00
Very good: $360.00

Winchester Model 52 Heavy Barrel

Similar to the Model 52 but with a heavy barrel & special Lyman sights.
Estimated Value: Excellent: $500.00
Very good: $400.00

Winchester Model 52 Sporting

Similar to the Model 52 except: 24" barrel; special Lyman sights; checkering; cheekpiece. Made to the late 1950's.
Estimated Value: Excellent: $520.00
Very good: $425.00

Winchester Model 52-B

Similar to the Model 52 with improved action; high comb stock available. Made from the mid 1930's to late 1940's.
Estimated Value: Excellent: $650.00
Very good: $520.00

Winchester Model 52-B Heavy Barrel

Similar to the Model 52-B with a heavy barrel.
Estimated Value: Excellent: $510.00
Very good: $410.00

Winchester Model 52-B Bull Gun

Winchester Model 52-B Sporting

Winchester Model 52-C Bull Gun

Winchester Model 52-C

Winchester Model 52-D Target

Winchester Model 52-B Bull Gun
Similar to the Model 52-B Heavy Barrel with still heavier barrel. Weighs about 12 lbs.
Estimated Value: Excellent: $510.00
Very good: $400.00

Winchester Model 52-B Sporting
Similar to the Model 52 Sporting with a 52-B action. Made to the early 1960's.
Estimated Value: Excellent: $500.00
Very good: $400.00

Winchester Model 52-C
Similar to the 52-B with more improvements on the action; high comb stock. Made from the late 1940's to early 1960's.
Estimated Value: Excellent: $695.00
Very good: $560.00

Winchester Model 52-C Heavy Barrel
Similar to the Model 52 Heavy Barrel with a 52-C action.
Estimated Value: Excellent: $500.00
Very good: $400.00

Winchester Model 52-C Bull Gun
Similar to the Model 52-B Bull Gun with a 52-C action.
Estimated Value: Excellent: $550.00
Very good: $440.00

Winchester Model 52-D Target
Similar to the 52-C except: single shot; hand stop on forearm. Made from the early 1960's to late 1970's; 22 long rifle caliber; approximate wt. 11 lbs.
Estimated Value: Excellent: $525.00
Very good: $420.00

Winchester Model 54 Sporting (Improved)

Winchester Model 54 Super

Winchester Model 54 Sniper

Winchester Model 54 National Match

Winchester Model 54
Caliber: 270, 7x57, 30-30, 30-06, 7.65x53mm, 9x57mm,
    7mm, 250-3000, 22 Hornet, 220 Swift, 257 Roberts
Action: Bolt action; repeating
Magazine: 5-shot box, non-detachable
Barrel: Blued; 24"
Sights: Open rear, bead front
Stock & Forearm: Checkered walnut one-piece pistol
    grip stock & forearm
Approximate wt.: 7½ lbs.
Comments: Made from the mid 1920's to about 1930.
Estimated Value: Excellent: $520.00
                    Very good: $390.00

Winchester Model 54 Carbine
Similar to the Model 54 with a 20" barrel; no checkering
on stock.
Estimated Value: Excellent: $525.00
                    Very good: $395.00

Winchester Model 54 Sporting (Improved)
Similar to the Model 54 with an improved action; 26"
barrel; additional calibers. Made from about 1930 for six
years.
Estimated Value: Excellent: $560.00
                    Very good: $450.00

Winchester Model 54 Carbine (Improved)
Similar to the Model 54 Carbine with improved action.
Made from 1930 to the mid 1930's.
Estimated Value: Excellent: $600.00
                    Very good: $480.00

Winchester Model 54 Super
Similar to the Model 54 with cheekpiece; select wood;
deluxe finish; swivels.
Estimated Value: Excellent: $750.00
                    Very good: $600.00

Winchester Model 54 Sniper
Similar to the Model 54 with a 26" heavy barrel; special
Lyman sights; 30-06 caliber only.
Estimated Value: Excellent: $620.00
                    Very good: $465.00

Winchester Model 54 Sniper Match
Deluxe version of the Model 54 Sniper with high-quality
finish.
Estimated Value: Excellent: $685.00
                    Very good: $550.00

Winchester Model 54 National Match
Similar to the Model 54 with special Lyman sights &
marksman stock.
Estimated Value: Excellent: $620.00
                    Very good: $500.00

Winchester Model 54 Target
Similar to the Model 54 with 24" barrel & special Lyman
sights.
Estimated Value: Excellent: $650.00
                    Very good: $520.00

Winchester Model 69

Winchester Model 69

Caliber: 22 short, long, long rifle
Action: Bolt action; repeating
Magazine: 5- or 10-shot detachable box
Barrel: Blued; 25"
Sights: Peep or open rear, ramp front
Stock & Forearm: Plain walnut one-piece semi-pistol grip stock & forearm
Approximate wt.: 5½ lbs.
Comments: Made from the mid 1930's to the early 1960's.
Estimated Value: Excellent: $150.00
                       Very good: $125.00

Winchester Model 69 Target

Similar to the Model 69 with peep sight only; swivels.
Estimated Value: Excellent: $160.00
                       Very good: $130.00

Winchester Model 69 Match

Similar to the Model 69 Target with special Lyman sights.
Estimated Value: Excellent: $175.00
                       Very good: $140.00

Winchester Model 697

Similar to the Model 69 with no sights. Made from the late 1930's to early 1940's.
Estimated Value: Excellent: $200.00
                       Very good: $160.00

Winchester Model 70 (1937)

Winchester Model 70 (1964)

Winchester Model 70 XTR

Winchester Model 70 (1937)

Caliber: 375 H&H mag., 300 H&H mag., 308 Win., 30-06, 7x57mm, 270 Win., 257 Roberts, 250-3000, 243, 220, 22 Hornet
Action: Bolt action; repeating
Magazine: 5-shot box; 4-shot box in magnum
Barrel: Blued; 24", 26"
Sights: Open rear, hooded ramp front
Stock & Forearm: Checkered walnut one-piece pistol grip stock & forearm
Approximate wt.: 7¾ lbs.
Comments: Made from about 1937 to 1963. Add $150.00 for mint, unfired condition.
Estimated Value: Excellent: $800.00
                       Very good: $650.00

Winchester Model 70 (1964)

Similar to the Model 70 (1937) except: improvements; Monte Carlo stock; swivels. Made from abt. 1964 to 1970; calibers 22-250, 22 Rem., 225, 243, 270, 308, 30-06.
Estimated Value: Excellent: $375.00
                       Very good: $300.00

Winchester Model 70 (1971), 70 XTR (1978), 70 XTR Sporter (1983)

Similar to the Model 70 (1964) with improvements. Made from 1971 to early 1990's. Calibers 270 Win., 30-06, 25-06 (1985), 308 Win. (1987), 243 (1988).
Estimated Value: Excellent: $350.00
                       Very good: $280.00

Winchester Model 70 XTR Featherwieght

Similar to the Model 70 XTR in calibers 22-250, 223 (introduced 1984); 243, 308 (short action); 270 Win., 257 Roberts, 7mm Mauser, 30-06 Springfield (standard action); recoil pad; lipped forearm; decorative checkering; 22" barrel. Produced from 1984 to early 1990's

Estimated Value: Excellent: $400.00
                    Very good: $320.00

Winchester Model 70 XTR European Featherweight

Similar to the Model 70XTR Featherweight in caliber 6.55x55 Swedish Mauser. Produced in 1986 & 1987.

Estimated Value: Excellent: $365.00
                    Very good: $275.00

Winchester Model 70 Lightweight Carbine

Similar to the Model 70XTR Featherweight with different outward appearance; 20" barrel; calibers 270 Win., 30-06 Springfield; 22-250 Rem., 223 Rem., 243 Win., 250 Savage; 308 Win.; weighs 6 to 6¼ lbs. Produced in 1986 & 1987.

Estimated Value: Excellent: $350.00
                    Very good: $280.00

Winchester Model 70 A, 70 A XTR

Similar to the Model 70 (1971) with a special steel barrel; adjustable sights. Made from the early 1970's to about 1981; 4-shot or 3-shot (magnum) box magazine. Add $20.00 for 264 Win. mag., 7mm Rem. mag., or 300 Win. mag.; Police Model $10.00 less.

Estimated Value: Excellent: $375.00
                    Very good: $300.00

Winchester Model 70 Super (1937)

Similar to the Model 70 (1937) with swivels; deluxe finish; cheekpiece. Made to early 1960's.

Estimated Value: Excellent: $1,000.00
                    Very good: $ 850.00

Winchester Model 70 Super

Similar to the Model 70 Super (1937) with recoil pad; select wood. Made from mid 1960's to mid 1970's.

Estimated Value: Excellent: $365.00
                    Very good: $290.00

Winchester Model 70 XTR Featherweight

Winchester Model 70 Lightweight Carbine

Winchester Model 70 A

Winchester Model 70 Super (1937)

Winchester Model 70 Super

Winchester Model 70 Target (1937)

Winchester Model 70 Target (1964)

Winchester Model 70 National Match

Winchester Model 70 Mannlicher

Winchester Model 70 Varmint (1956) (1964) (1971)

Winchester Model 70 Featherweight Sporter

Winchester Model 70 Target (1937)

Similar to the Model 70 (1937) with 24" barrel & improved stock. Made until about 1963.

Estimated Value: Excellent: $900.00
                   Very good: $675.00

Winchester Model 70 Target (1964) & 1971

Similar to the Model 70 Target (1937) with aluminum hand stop. Model (1971) has minor improvements; calibers 30-06, 308 Win., or 308 Int'l Army. Add $132.00 for Int'l Army.

Estimated Value: Excellent: $400.00
                   Very good: $320.00

Winchester Model 70 National Match

Similar to the Model 70 (1937) with marksman stock in 30-06 caliber. Made to the early 1960's.

Estimated Value: Excellent: $850.00
                   Very good: $680.00

Winchester Model 70 Mannlicher

Similar to the Model 70 (1964) with full-length forearm; 19" barrel; calibers 243, 270, 308, 30-06. Made to the early 1970's.

Estimated Value: Excellent: $375.00
                   Very good: $300.00

Winchester Model 70 Varmint (1956) (1964) (1971) 70 XTR Varmint

Similar to the Model 70 (1937) with heavy 24" or 26" barrel. Improvements made along with other Model 70's. Calibers 222 Rem., 22-250 or 243 Win. Add 90% for pre-1964 models. Discontinued 1988.

Estimated Value: Excellent: $500.00
                   Very good: $400.00

Winchester Model 70 Featherweight Sporter

A lightweight rifle similar to the Model 70 (1937) with improved stock. Made from the early 1950's to 1960's.

Estimated Value: Excellent: $825.00
                   Very good: $660.00

Winchester Model 70 Featherweight Super

Similar to the Featherweight Sporter with deluxe finish; cheekpiece; swivels. Made after 1964.

Estimated Value: Excellent: $350.00
                                  Very good: $280.00

Winchester Model 70 African (1956)

Similar to the Model 70 (1937) Super Grade with recoil pad; Monte Carlo stock; 3-shot magazine; 24" barrel. Available only in 458 caliber. Made to 1963.

Estimated Value: Excellent: $1,200.00
                                  Very good: $ 960.00

Winchester Model 70 African (1964)

Similar to the Model 70 African (1956) with improvements. Made to 1970.

Estimated Value: Excellent: $425.00
                                  Very good: $340.00

Winchester Model 70 African (1971)

Similar to the Model 70 African (1964) with floating barrel; caliber 458 Win. mag. Discontinued about 1981.

Estimated Value: Excellent: $525.00
                                  Very good: $420.00

Winchester Model 70 Westerner

Similar to the Model 70 Alaskan. Made in the early 1960's.

Estimated Value: Excellent: $800.00
                                  Very good: $640.00

Winchester Model 70 Westerner (1982)

Similar to the Model 70XTR with a 22" barrel & 4-shot magazine in calibers 243 Win., 270 Win., 308 win., & 30-06 Springfield; 24" barrel & 3-shot magazine in calibers 7mm Rem. mag., 300 Win. mag.; weighs about 7½ to 7¾ lbs.; recoil pad. Produced from 1982 to 1984.

Estimated Value: Excellent: $400.00
                                  Very good: $320.00

Winchester Model 70 Featherweight Super

Winchester Model 70 African (1956)

Winchester Model 70 African (1964)

Winchester Model 70 African (1971)

Winchester Model 70 Westerner (1982)

Winchester Model 70 Magnum

Winchester Model 70 Alaskan

Winchester Model 70 Deluxe

Winchester Model 70 Magnum (1964)

Similar to the Model 70 (1964) with Monte Carlo stock; recoil pad; swivels; 3-shot magazine. Made to the early 1970's.

Estimated Value: Excellent: $450.00
                  Very good: $360.00

Winchester Model 70 Alaskan

Similar to the Model 70 (1937) with 24" or 26" barrel. Made in the early 1960's.

Estimated Value: Excellent: $1,000.00
                  Very good: $ 800.00

Winchester Model 70 Deluxe (1964)

Similar to the Model 70 (1964) with Monte Carlo stock; recoil pad; deluxe features. Made to the early 1970's.

Estimated Value: Excellent: $460.00
                  Very good: $375.00

Winchester Model 70 XTR Sporter Magnum

Winchester Model 70 XTR Super Express Magnum

Winchester Model 70 Winlite

Winchester Model 70 XTR & 70 Classic Sporter or Mag.

Caliber: 22-250, 223, 243, 25-06 Rem., 264 Win. mag., 270 Win., 300 Win mag., 338 Win. mag.; 7mm Rem. mag., 300 Wby. mag., 30-06 Spfld.

Action: Bolt action; repeating; controlled round feeding after 1993

Magazine: 3-shot box

Barrel: Blued; 24" or 26"

Sights: None; drilled for scope mount

Stock & Forearm: Checkered walnut Monte Carlo one-piece pistol grip stock & forearm; recoil pad

Approximate wt.: 7¾ lbs.

Comments: Produced from 1982 to date. Add 7% for sights; add 18% for Boss shooting system.

Estimated Value: New (retail): $613.00
                  Excellent: $460.00
                  Very good: $365.00

Winchester Model 70 Winlite

Caliber: 270, 30-06, 7mm Rem. mag., 300 Win. mag., 300 Weatherby mag., 338 Win. mag.

Action: Bolt action; repeating

Magazine: 4-shot in 270 or 30-06; 3-shot in 7mm Rem. mag. or 338 Win. mag.

Barrel: 22" in 270 & 30-06; 24" in mag. calibers

Sights: None

Stock & Forearm: Fiberglass reinforced one-piece stock & forearm with thermoplastic bedding

Approximate wt.: 6¼ to 6¾ lbs.

Comments: Made from 1986 to 1991. Add 3% for 300 Weatherby mag.

Estimated Value: Excellent: $480.00
                  Very good: $385.00

Winchester Model 70 Classic Super Express Mag.

Same as the Model 70 Classic Sporter or Mag. with a 22" or 24" barrel in 458 Win. mag., 375 H & H mag., 416 Rem. mag. Controlled round feeding after 1993. Made from 1982 to present.

Estimated Value: New (retail): $865.00
                  Excellent: $650.00
                  Very good: $520.00

Winchester Model 70 Lightweight

Winchester Model 70 Win-Tuff Lightweight

Winchester Model 70 Win-Tuff Featherweight

Winchester Model 70 Win-Cam Featherweight

Winchester Model 70 Lightweight
Similar to the Model 70XTR with a 22" barrel; weighs
6¼ lbs.; calibers: 22-250 Rem., 223 Rem., 243 Win., 270
Win., 280 Win., 30-06 spring., 308 Win.; no sights.
Estimated Value: Excellent: **$375.00**
                         Very good: **$300.00**

Winchester Model 70 Win-Tuff Lightweight
Similar to the Model 70 Lightweight with laminated
stock of dye-shaded hardwoods. Available in calibers:
223 Rem., 243 Win., 270 Win., 308 Win., 30-06 Spring.;
short or long action; no sights.
Estimated Value: Excellent: **$350.00**
                         Very good: **$280.00**

Winchester Model 70 Win-Tuff Featherweight
Similar to the Model 70 Featherweight with laminated
stock of dye-shaded hardwood. Available in calibers: 243
Win., 270 Win., 30-06 Spring. Discontinued in 1991.
Estimated Value: Excellent: **$355.00**
                         Very good: **$285.00**

Winchester Model 70 Win-Cam Featherweight
Similar to the Model 70 Featherweight with laminated
stock of green & brown camouflage. Available in 270
Win. & 30-06 Spring. Discontinued in 1991.
Estimated Value: Excellent: **$360.00**
                         Very good: **$290.00**

Winchester Model 70 Stainless

Winchester Model 70 Super Grade

Winchester Model 70 Varmint

Winchester Model 70 Stainless

Caliber: 270, 30-06, 7mm Rem. mag., 300 Win. mag., 338 Win. mag.

Action: Bolt action; repeating; 3-position safety; controlled round feeding after 1993

Magazine: 5-shot; hinged floorplate

Barrel: Blued; 22", 24", or 26"

Sights: None

Stock & Forearm: Black synthetic composite impregnated with fiberglass and graphite one-piece checkered pistol grip stock and forearm; rubber recoil pad

Approximate wt.: 7¾ lbs.

Comments: Produced from 1992 to 1995; lightweight all weather rifle.

Estimated Value: Excellent: $505.00
Very good: $400.00

Winchester Model 70 Classic All-Terrain

Caliber: 270 Win., 30-06 Sprg., 7mm Rem. magnum, 300 Win. magnum

Action: Bolt action; repeating; 3-position safety

Magazine: 5-shot; 3-shot in magnum calibers

Barrel: 22", 24" stainless steel

Sights: None, drilled for scope mounts

Stock & Forearm: Checkered pistol grip, one-piece black fiberglass/graphite synthetic stock and forearm

Approximate wt.: 7¼ lbs.

Comments: Introduced in 1996; add 17% for BOSS (Ballistic Optimizing Shooting System) which is an adjustable device attached to the muzzle to control the shockwave vibrations of the barrel.

Estimated Value: New (retail): $672.00
Excellent: $500.00
Very good: $400.00

Winchester Model 70 SSM & Classic SM

Same as the Model 70 Stainless except: 24" or 26" barrel; black matte finish. Steel barrel and receiver; introduced in 1992. 375 H&H mag. added in 1994. Add 18% for BOSS shooting system.

Estimated Value: New (retail): $620.00
Excellent: $465.00
Very good: $375.00

Winchester Model 70 Super Grade & Classic Super Grade

Caliber: 270, 30-06, 7mm Rem. mag., 300 Win. mag., 338 Win. mag.

Action: Bolt action; repeating; 3-position safety; controlled feeding after 1993

Magazine: 5-shot; 3-shot in mag.; hinged floorplate

Barrel: Blued; 24" or 26"

Sights: None, scope base and rings

Stock & Forearm: Select checkered walnut, one-piece sculptured cheekpiece stock and forearm

Approximate wt.: 7¾ lbs.

Comments: Made from the late 1980's to present. Add 15% for BOSS Shooting System.

Estimated Value: New (retail): $840.00
Excellent: $630.00
Very good: $500.00

Winchester Model 70 Varmint & Heavy Varmint

Caliber: 22-250, 223, 243, 308. 220 swift (in 1994)

Action: Bolt action; repeating; 3-position safety

Magazine: 5-shot; hinged floorplate

Barrel: 26" counter-bored heavy barrel, blued, matte or stainless steel

Sights: None

Stock & Forearm: Checkered walnut one-piece pistol grip stock and forearm or black composite checkered matte finish stock and forearm

Approximate wt.: 9 lbs.

Comments: Introduced in the late 1980's. Priced for stainless steel.

Estimated Value: New (retail): $764.00
Excellent: $575.00
Very good: $460.00

Winchester Model 70 Sporter Win-Tuff

Winchester Model 70 Sporter DBM

Caliber: 25-06 Rem., 264 Win. mag., 270 Win., 270 Wby. mag. 30-06, 7mm Rem. mag., 300 Win. mag.,300 Wby. mag., 338 Win. mag.
Action: Bolt action; repeating
Magazine: 3-shot detachable box
Barrel: Blued; 24" or 26"
Sights: None, scope base and rings; sights optional
Stock & Forearm: Checkered walnut one-piece pistol grip stock and forearm
Approximate wt.: 7⅛ lbs.
Comments: Made from 1992 to mid 1990's. Add 6% for sights.
Estimated Value: Excellent: $420.00
Very good: $335.00

Winchester Model 70 Sporter Win-Tuff

Caliber: 270, 30-06, 7mm Rem. magnum, 300 Win. mag., 300 Wby. mag., 338 Win. mag.
Action: Bolt action; repeating; 3-position safety
Magazine: 5-shot in 270 and 30-06; 3-shot in magnum calibers; hinged floorplate
Barrel: 24" blued
Sights: None
Stock & Forearm: Brown laminated checkered, one-piece stock and forearm with cheekpiece
Approximate wt.: 7⅛ lbs.
Comments: Made in early 1990's.
Estimated Value: Excellent: $405.00
Very good: $325.00

Winchester Model 70 Classic Featherweight

Winchester Model 70 Featherweight Win-Tuff

Winchester Model 70 Featherweight Win-Tuff

Caliber: 22-250, 223 Rem., 243 Win., 308 Win., 30-06 Spgf. Calibers 65x55, 270 Win., 280 Rem., & 7mm-08 Rem. added in 1992
Action: Bolt action; repeating; 3-position safety; controlled round feeding after 1993
Magazine: 5 or 6-shot; hinged floorplate
Barrel: 22" blued
Sights: None
Stock & Forearm: Laminated brown hardwood or walnut one-piece checkered stock and forearm with a schnabel fore end (lipped)
Approximate wt.: 6 to 7 lbs.
Comments: Previously made in the 1980's in 243, 270, and 30-06 calibers; reintroduced in 1992 to mid 1990's in larger selection of calibers.
Estimated Value: Excellent: $420.00
Very good: $340.00

Winchester Model 70 Classic Featherweight

Same as the Model 70 Featherweight Win-Tuff except: no 6.5x55 caliber; weighs 7 to 8 lbs.; checkered walnut stock and forearm. Introduced in 1992. Controlled round feeding after 1993. Add 18% for BOSS shooting system.
Estimated Value: New (retail): $620.00
Excellent: $465.00
Very good: $375.00

Winchester Model 70 Classic Stainless

Caliber: 223 Rem., 22-250 Rem., 243 Win., 308 Win., 270 Win., 30-06 Sprng., 7mm Rem. mag., 300 Win. 300 Wby. mag., 338 Win. mag., 375 H&H
Action: Bolt action; repeating; controlled round feeding
Magazine: 3 to 5-shot box
Barrel: 22", 24" or 26"; stainless steel
Sights: None
Stock & Forearm: Black synthetic fiberglass/graphite checkered, one-piece pistol grip stock and tapered forearm; swivel studs
Approximate wt.: 7 to 7½ lbs.
Comments: Introduced in 1994; all stainless steel. Add 18% for BOSS shooting system.
Estimated Value: New (retail): $672.00
Excellent: $500.00
Very good: $400.00

Winchester Model 70 Classic Laredo

Caliber: 7mm Rem. magnum, 300 Win. magnum
Action: Bolt action, repeating; 3-position safety
Magazine: 3-shot
Barrel: Blued; 26" round
Sights: None, drilled for scope mounts
Stock & Forearm: Checkered one-piece, pistol grip stock and forearm
Approximate wt.: 7½ lbs.
Comments: Introduced in 1996; add 15% for the BOSS system. (This is used to control the shockwave pattern generated in the barrel. It consists of an attachment on the muzzle which can be adjusted.)
Estimated Value: New (retail): $764.00
Excellent: $575.00
Very good: $460.00

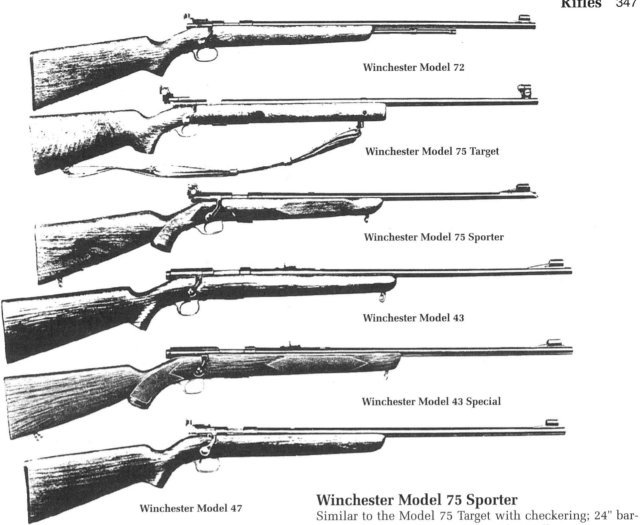

Winchester Model 72

Winchester Model 75 Target

Winchester Model 75 Sporter

Winchester Model 43

Winchester Model 43 Special

Winchester Model 47

Winchester Model 72

Caliber: 22 short, long, long rifle
Action: Bolt action; repeating
Magazine: Tubular; 15 long rifles, 16 longs, 20 shorts
Barrel: Blued; 25"
Sights: Peep or open rear, bead front
Stock & Forearm: Plain walnut one-piece semi-pistol grip stock & forearm
Approximate wt.: 5¾ lbs.
Comments: Made from the late 1930's to late 1950's.
Estimated Value: Excellent: $160.00
                       Very good: $130.00

Winchester Model 75 Target

Caliber: 22 long rifle
Action: Bolt action; repeating
Magazine: 5- or 10-shot detachable box
Barrel: Blued; 28"
Sights: Special target sights
Stock & Forearm: Plain walnut one-piece pistol grip stock & forearm
Approximate wt.: 8¾ lbs.
Comments: Made from the late 1930's to late 1950's.
Estimated Value: Excellent: $290.00
                       Very good: $230.00

Winchester Model 75 Sporter

Similar to the Model 75 Target with checkering; 24" barrel; hooded ramp front sight; weighs 5¾ lbs.
Estimated Value: Excellent: $300.00
                       Very good: $240.00

Winchester Model 43

Caliber: 218 Bee, 22 Hornet, 25-20, 32-30 (25-20 & 32-30 dropped in 1950)
Action: Bolt action; repeating
Magazine: 3-shot detachable
Barrel: Blued; 24"
Sights: Open rear, hooded ramp front
Stock & Forearm: Plain wood one-piece semi-pistol grip stock & forearm; swivels
Approximate wt.: 6 lbs.
Comments: Made from the late 1940's to late 1950's.
Estimated Value: Excellent: $400.00
                       Very good: $320.00

Winchester Model 43 Special

Similar to the Model 43 with checkering & choice of open rear sight or micrometer.
Estimated Value: Excellent: $425.00
                       Very good: $340.00

Winchester Model 47

Similar to the Model 43 in 22 short, long or long rifle single shot; 25" barrel. Made from the late 1940's to mid 1950's.
Estimated Value: Excellent: $150.00
                       Very good: $120.00

Winchester Model 670

Winchester Model 770

Winchester Model 770 Magnum

Winchester Model 670
Caliber: 243, 270, 30-06, 225, 243, 270, 308, 30-06 mag., 300 Win. mag., 264 Win. mag.,
Action: Bolt action; repeating
Magazine: 4-shot box; 3-shot box in magnum
Barrel: Blued; 19", 22", 24"
Sights: Open rear, ramp front
Stock & Forearm: Checkered hardwood Monte Carlo one-piece pistol grip stock & forearm
Approximate wt.: 7 lbs.
Comments: Made from the mid 1960's to the late 1970's.
Estimated Value: Excellent: $300.00
Very good: $240.00

Winchester Model 770
Caliber: 22-250, 222, 243, 270, 30-06
Action: Bolt action; repeating
Magazine: 4-shot box
Barrel: Blued; 22"
Sights: Open rear, hooded ramp front
Stock & Forearm: Checkered walnut Monte Carlo one-piece pistol grip stock & forearm; swivels
Approximate wt.: 7 lbs.
Comments: Made from the late 1960's to early 1970's.
Estimated Value: Excellent: $315.00
Very good: $250.00

Winchester Model 770 Magnum
Similar to the Model 770 in magnum with recoil pad & 24" barrel, 3-shot magazine.
Estimated Value: Excellent: $325.00
Very good: $260.00

Winchester Model 310

Winchester Model 320

Winchester Model 310
Caliber: 22 short, long, long rifle
Action: Bolt action; single shot
Magazine: None
Barrel: Blued; 22"
Sights: Adjustable rear, ramp front
Stock & Forearm: Checkered walnut Monte Carlo one-pistol grip stock & forearm; swivels
Approximate wt.: 6 lbs.
Comments: Made from the early to mid 1970's.
Estimated Value: Excellent: $95.00
Very good: $75.00

Winchester Model 320
Similar to the Model 310 in repeating bolt action with a 5-shot clip.
Estimated Value: Excellent: $125.00
Very good: $100.00

Winchester Model 121

Winchester Model 131

Winchester Model 121
Caliber: 22 short, long, long rifle
Action: Bolt action; single shot
Magazine: None
Barrel: Blued; 20½"
Sights: Open rear, bead post front
Stock & Forearm: Plain one-piece semi-pistol grip stock & forearm
Approximate wt.: 5 lbs.
Comments: Made from the late 1960's to early 1970's.
Estimated Value: Excellent: $75.00
                       Very good: $60.00

Winchester Model 121 Deluxe
Similar to the Model 121 with Monte Carlo stock; swivels; slightly different sights.
Estimated Value: Excellent: $85.00
                       Very good: $65.00

Winchester Model 121 Youth
Similar to the Model 121 with shorter barrel & youth stock.
Estimated Value: Excellent: $80.00
                       Very good: $65.00

Winchester Model 131
Similar to the Model 121 with semi-Monte Carlo stock; 7-shot clip magazine; bolt action repeater.
Estimated Value: Excellent: $100.00
                       Very good: $80.00

Winchester Model 141
Similar to the 131 with tubular magazine.
Estimated Value: Excellent: $110.00
                       Very good: $90.00

Winchester Model 70 Ranger Youth/Ladies

Winchester Ranger Youth/Ladies & 70 Ranger Youth/Ladies
A scaled down bolt action (short action) carbine for young or small shooters; calibers 243 Win.,or 308 Win., 20" or 22" barrel; weighs 5¾ lbs.; beaded ramp front sight, semi-buckhorn, folding-leaf rear; plain wood, one-piece stock & forearm with swivels. Introduced in the mid 1980's.
Estimated Value: New (retail): $482.00
                       Excellent: $360.00
                       Very good: $290.00

Winchester Ranger & Model 70 Ranger
Caliber: 223 (in 1992); 243 (in 1991) 270 Win., 30-06 Spfld.
Action: Bolt action; repeating
Magazine: 4-shot
Barrel: Blued; 22"
Sights: Beaded ramp front, adjustable rear
Stock & Forearm: Plain one-piece semi-pistol grip wood stock & forearm
Approximate wt.: 7⅛ lbs.
Comments: Introduced in the mid 1980's.
Estimated Value: New (retail): $482.00
                       Excellent: $360.00
                       Very good: $290.00

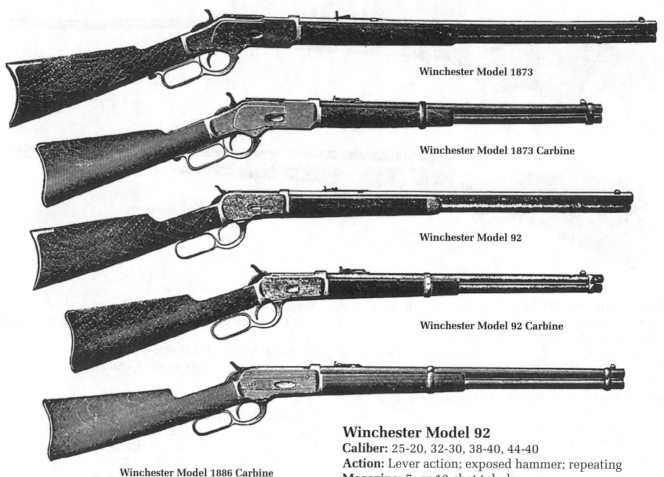

Winchester Model 1873

Winchester Model 1873 Carbine

Winchester Model 92

Winchester Model 92 Carbine

Winchester Model 1886 Carbine

Winchester Model 1873

Caliber: 32-20, 38-40, 44-40, 22
Action: Lever action; exposed hammer; repeating
Magazine: 6- or 15-shot tubular
Barrel: 24" or 26" round, octagon or half-octagon
Sights: Open rear, blade front
Stock & Forearm: Straight grip stock & forearm
Approximate wt.: 8 lbs.
Comments: Thousands of this model were sold by
 Winchester until 1920. Add $200.00 to $500.00 for
 Deluxe engraved models. Price range is for the dif-
 ferent models i.e., 1st, 2nd and 3rd models.
Estimated Value: **Excellent:**   **$1,500.00 - $2,800.00**
                  Very good: **$1,200.00 - $2,200.00**

Winchester Model 1873 Carbine

Similar to the Model 1873 with a 20" barrel & 12-shot
magazine. Three models made from 1873 to 1920.
Estimated Value: **Excellent:**   **$1,400.00 - $2,700.00**
                  Very good: **$1,150.00 - $2,150.00**

Winchester Model 1873 Musket

Similar to the Model 1873 with a 30" round barrel, full-
length forearm & 17-shot magazine. Three models made
from 1873 to 1920.
Estimated Value: **Excellent:**   **$1,800.00 - $3,000.00**
                  Very good: **$1,400.00 - $2,400.00**

Winchester Model 92

Caliber: 25-20, 32-30, 38-40, 44-40
Action: Lever action; exposed hammer; repeating
Magazine: 7- or 13-shot tubular
Barrel: 24" round, octagon or half-octagon
Sights: Open rear, bead front
Stock & Forearm: Plain walnut straight grip stock & fore-
 arm
Approximate wt.: 7 lbs.
Comments: Made from about 1892 to early 1930's.
Estimated Value: **Excellent:**   **$900.00**
                  Very good: **$750.00**

Winchester Model 92 Carbine

Similar to the Model 92 with a 20" barrel; barrel band; &
5- or 11-shot magazine. Discontinued in the early 1940's.
Estimated Value: **Excellent:**   **$950.00**
                  Very good: **$800.00**

Winchester Model 1886

Caliber: 45-70, 33 Win.; also others on early models
Action: Lever action; exposed hammer; repeating
Magazine: 4- or 8-shot tubular
Barrel: 26" round, octagon or half-octagon
Sights: Open rear, blade front
Stock & Forearm: Plain wood straight grip stock & forearm
Approximate wt.: 7½ lbs.
Comments: Made from the mid 1880's to the mid 1930's.
Estimated Value: **Excellent:**   **$800.00 - $2,000.00**
                  Very good: **$620.00 - $1,500.00**

Winchester Model 1886 Carbine

Similar to the Model 1886 with a 22" barrel.
Estimated Value: **Excellent:**   **$800.00 - $2,000.00**
                  Very good: **$640.00 - $1,600.00**

Winchester Model 53

Winchester Model 65

Winchester Model 94

Winchester Model 94 Trapper

Winchester Model 53
Similar to the Model 92 with a 6- or 7-shot magazine; 22" nickel steel barrel; choice of straight or pistol grip stock. Made from the mid 1920's to the early 1930's.
Estimated Value: Excellent: $825.00
                                    Very good: $660.00

Winchester Model 65
Similar to the Model 53 in 25-20 & 32-30 caliber; semi-pistol grip stock; other minor improvements. Made from the early 1930's to late 1940's.
Estimated Value: Excellent: $800.00
                                    Very good: $640.00

Winchester Model 65, 218 Bee
Similar to the Model 65 with peep sight & 24" barrel. Made from the late 1930's to late 1940's.
Estimated Value: Excellent: $1,000.00
                                    Very good: $ 800.00

Winchester Model 94
Caliber: 25-35, 30-30, 32 Special, 32-40, 38-55
Action: Lever action; exposed hammer; repeating
Magazine: 4- or 7-shot tubular
Barrel: 22", 26", round, octagon or half-octagon
Sights: Open rear, bead front
Stock & Forearm: Straight stock & forearm; saddle ring on some models
Approximate wt.: 6¾ lbs.
Comments: Made from 1894 to the late 1930's. Sometimes referred to as the "Klondike" model.
Estimated Value: Excellent: $475.00
                                    Very good: $380.00

Winchester Model 94 Carbine
Similar to the Model 94 with a 20" barrel; barrel band; saddle ring. 6-shot magazine. Add $200.00 for pre-World War II models. Add $400.00 for pre-1925 Models with saddle ring. Made to mid 1960's.
Estimated Value: Excellent: $275.00
                                    Very good: $225.00

Winchester Model 94 Standard
Caliber: 30-30
Action: Lever action, exposed hammer; repeating; Angle-eject feature added in 1984, listed as "Side eject" in 1986. Hammer stop safety added in 1992.
Magazine: 6-shot
Barrel: 20" round with barrel band
Sights: Hooded or post front, adjustable rear
Stock & Forearm: Plain or checkered walnut two piece straight grip stock & forearm; barrel band
Approximate wt.: 6½ lbs.
Comments: Made from the mid 1960's to date. Also made in calibers 44 mag., 45 Colt & 444 Marlin in the mid 1980's. 100th anniversary inscription in 1994.
Estimated Value: New (retail): $393.00
                                    Excellent: $295.00
                                    Very good: $235.00

Winchester Model 94 WinTuff
Same as the Model 94 Standard except: laminated stock of brown dyed hardwood; hammer stop; 100th anniversary inscription in 1994.
Estimated Value: New (retail): $404.00
                                    Excellent: $300.00
                                    Very good: $245.00

Winchester Model 94 Antique
Similar to the Model 94 Standard with case hardened, scroll design frame. Made from the late 1960's to 1984 in 30-30 caliber.
Estimated Value: Excellent: $275.00
                                    Very good: $220.00

Winchester Model 94 Trapper
Same as the Model 94 Standard except: 16" barrel; 44 Rem. mag. & 45 Colt added in the mid 1980's, 357 added in 1992. Magazine capacity is 5-shot in 30-30 & 9-shot in 357, 44, & 45; made from 1980 to present. Add 5% for 44 & 45 caliber. 100th anniversary inscription in 1994.
Estimated Value: New (retail): $363.00
                                    Excellent: $275.00
                                    Very good: $220.00

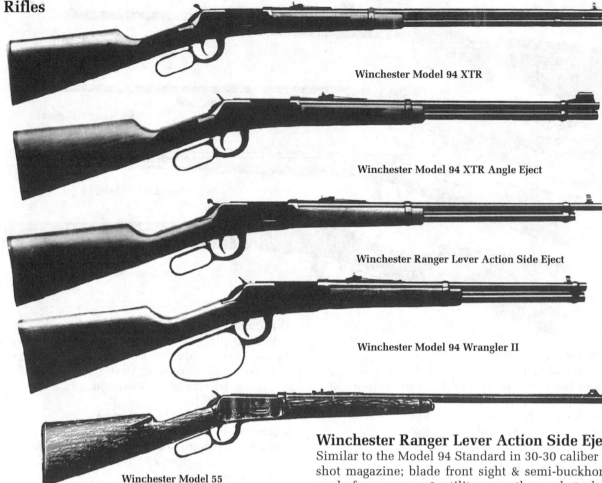

Winchester Model 94 XTR

Winchester Model 94 XTR Angle Eject

Winchester Ranger Lever Action Side Eject

Winchester Model 94 Wrangler II

Winchester Model 55

Winchester Model 94 XTR

Similar to the Model 94 Standard with higher grade wood, checkered stock & forearm. Made from 1979 to 1984 in 30-30 & 375 Win.; 375 Win. has recoil pad. Add 23% for 375 Win.

Estimated Value: Excellent: $240.00
                      Very good: $190.00

Winchester Model 94 XTR Angle Eject

Similar to the Model 94XTR except an "angle eject" feature was added in 1984; in 1986 Winchester called it "side eject." Made in calibers 30-30, 7x30 Waters, 307, 356 & 357 Win.; 7x30 Waters has 7-shot magazine & 24" barrel; other models have 6-shot magazines & 20" barrels; 307, 356 & 357 calibers made from 1984 to 1986; 30-30 & 7x30 Waters made from 1984 to 1987; add 10% for 7x30 Waters.

Estimated Value: Excellent: $275.00
                      Very good: $205.00

Winchester Model 94 Side Eject

Similar to the Model 94 Standard with "Side Eject" feature; cal. 30-30, 308, 356, 375 Win. & 7x30 Waters, 6-shot mag.; recoil pad; made from 1985 to date. 32 Win. Spec. added 1992 to 1994. Add 10% for checkered stock and forearm. Hammer stop safety added in 1992. 100th anniversary inscription in 1994.

Estimated Value: Excellent: $285.00
                      Very good: $230.00

Winchester Ranger Lever Action Side Eject

Similar to the Model 94 Standard in 30-30 caliber with 5-shot magazine; blade front sight & semi-buckhorn rear; made for economy & utility; smooth wood stock & forearm with walnut finish; made from the mid 1980's to present. 100th anniversary inscription in 1994.

Estimated Value: New (retail): $320.00
                      Excellent: $240.00
                      Very good: $195.00

Winchester Model 94 Classic Rifle or Carbine

Similar to the Model 94 Standard with select walnut stock; scroll engraving. Made from the late 1960's to early 1970's.

Estimated Value: Excellent: $230.00
                      Very good: $185.00

Winchester Model 94 Wrangler

Same as the Model 94 Trapper except: large loop-type finger lever; roll-engraved receiver; 32 Special caliber with 5-shot magazine; no angle eject feature; made from about 1980 to 1984.

Estimated Value: Excellent: $240.00
                      Very good: $195.00

Winchester Model 94 Wrangler II

Similar to the Model 94 Wrangler in 38-55 caliber; has angle eject feature. Made from about 1984 to 1986.

Estimated Value: Excellent: $250.00
                      Very good: $200.00

Winchester Model 55

Similar to the Model 94 with a 24" nickel steel barrel. Made from the mid 1920's to the early 1930's.

Estimated Value: Excellent: $690.00
                      Very good: $550.00

Winchester Model 64

Winchester Model 64 Deer

Winchester Model 64

Similar to the Model 94 & 55 with improvements; 20" or 26" barrel; available in 25-35, 30-30, 32, 219 Zipper (from 1938-41). Made from the early 1930's to the late 1950's. Add $350.00 for 219 Zipper caliber.

Estimated Value: Excellent: $475.00
                Very good: $400.00

Winchester Model 64 Deer

Similar to the Model 64 in 32 & 30-30 caliber; swivels; checkered pistol grip stock. Made from the mid 1930's to mid 1950's.

Estimated Value: Excellent: $500.00
                Very good: $400.00

Winchester Model 94 "Limited Edition" Centennial

Caliber: 30-30 Win.,

Action: Lever action; exposed hammer; repeating; side-eject; hammer stop safety;

Magazine: 5-shot (30-30); 9-shot (44) tubular

Barrel: 26"; half-round/half octagon; blued

Sights: Adjustable buckhorn rear, ramp front

Stock & Forearm: Checkered, straight, two-piece walnut stock and forearm; crescent steel butt plate and steel capped forearm

Approximate wt.: 8 lbs.

Comments: Introduced in 1994. 12,000 Grade I with engraving & 3,000 High Grade with more elaborate engraving; add 57% for High Grade.

Estimated Value: Excellent: $610.00
                Very good: $485.00

Winchester Model 95

Winchester Model 95 Carbine

Winchester Model 94 Big Bore

Winchester Model 95

Caliber: 30-40 Krag, 30-06, 30-30, 303, 35, 405

Action: Lever action; exposed hammer; repeating

Magazine: 4-shot & 5-shot box

Barrel: 24", 26", 28", octagon, round or half octagon

Sights: Open rear, bead front

Stock & Forearm: Plain wood straight stock & tapered lipped forearm. A limited number was available with a pistol grip.

Approximate wt.: 8½ lbs.

Comments: Made from about 1895 to the early 1930's. A few thousand early models were built with a flat receiver; add $200.00.

Estimated Value: Excellent: $1,000.00
                Very good: $ 800.00

Winchester Model 95 Carbine

Similar to the Model 95 with a 22" barrel.

Estimated Value: Excellent: $1,000.00
                Very good: $ 800.00

Winchester Model 1895 Musket

Similar to the Model 95 with a 28" or 30" round nickel steel barrel; full-length forearm; barrel bands; 30-40 gov't caliber. Add $300.00 for U.S. Gov't models.

Estimated Value: Excellent: $1,000.00
                Very good: $ 800.00

Winchester Model 94 Wrangler Large Loop Lever

Caliber: 30-30 Win., 44 Rem. mag.

Action: Lever action; exposed hammer; repeating; side-eject; hammer stop safety; large loop finger lever

Magazine: 5-shot (30-30); 9-shot (44) tubular

Barrel: 16"; round; blued

Sights: Open front adjustable rear

Stock & Forearm: Smooth walnut straight grip stock and forearm

Approximate wt.: 6 lbs.

Comments: Introduced in 1992. Add 6% for 44 Rem. mag. 100th anniversary inscription in 1994.

Estimated Value: New (retail): $384.00
                Excellent: $290.00
                Very good: $230.00

Winchester Model 94 Big Bore

Caliber: 307 Win., 356 Win.

Action: Lever action, repeating; exposed hammer; hammer stop safety

Magazine: 6-shot tubular

Barrel: 20"; round; blued

Sights: Adjustable rear, hooded ramp front

Stock & Forearm: Checkered American walnut, straight grip stock and forearm; barrel band

Approximate wt.: 6½ lbs.

Comments: Introduced in the mid 1990's.

Estimated Value: New (retail): $404.00
                Excellent: $305.00
                Very good: $245.00

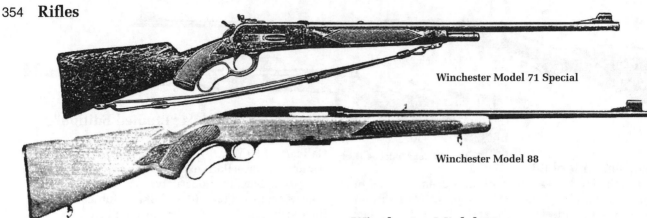

Winchester Model 71 Special

Winchester Model 88

Winchester Model 71
Caliber: 348 Win.
Action: Lever action; exposed hammer; repeating
Magazine: 4-shot tubular
Barrel: Blued; 20" or 24"
Sights: Open rear, hooded ramp front; peepsights available
Stock & Forearm: Plain or checkered walnut pistol grip stock & forearm; swivels available
Approximate wt.: 8 lbs.
Comments: Made from the mid 1930's to the late 1950's.
Estimated Value:　Excellent:　$650.00
　　　　　　　　　　Very good:　$500.00

Winchester Model 71 Special
Similar to the Model 71 with checkering & swivels.
Estimated Value:　Excellent:　$700.00
　　　　　　　　　　Very good:　$560.00

Winchester Model 88
Caliber: 243, 284, 308, 358
Action: Lever action; hammerless; repeating
Magazine: 4-shot box on late models; 5-shot box on early models; 3-shot box in 284 caliber
Barrel: 22"
Sights: Folding leaf rear, hooded ramp front
Stock & Forearm: Checkered walnut one-piece semi-pistol grip stock & forearm; barrel band
Approximate wt.: 7¼ lbs.
Comments: Made from the mid 1950's to mid 1970's.
Estimated Value:　Excellent:　$370.00
　　　　　　　　　　Very good:　$295.00

Winchester Model 88 Carbine
Similar to the Model 88 with a plain stock & forearm & 19" barrel. Made from the late 1960's to early 1970's.
Estimated Value:　Excellent:　$395.00
　　　　　　　　　　Very good:　$315.00

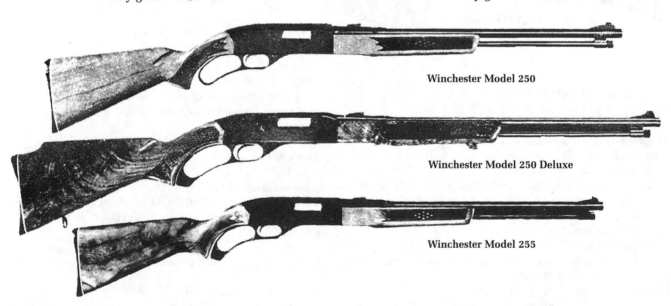

Winchester Model 250

Winchester Model 250 Deluxe

Winchester Model 255

Winchester Model 250
Caliber: 22 short, long, long rifle
Action: Lever action; hammerless; repeating
Magazine: Tubular; 15 long rifles, 17 longs, 21 shorts
Barrel: Blued; 20½"
Sights: Open rear, ramp front
Stock & Forearm: Plain or checkered walnut semi-pistol grip stock & forearm
Approximate wt.: 5 lbs.
Comments: Made from the early 1960's to mid 1970's.
Estimated Value:　Excellent:　$135.00
　　　　　　　　　　Very good:　$110.00

Winchester Model 250 Deluxe
Similar to the Model 250 with Monte Carlo stock & swivels.
Estimated Value:　Excellent:　$150.00
　　　　　　　　　　Very good:　$125.00

Winchester Model 255
Similar to the Model 250 in 22 magnum caliber; 11-shot magazine. Made from the mid 1960's to early 1970's.
Estimated Value:　Excellent:　$160.00
　　　　　　　　　　Very good:　$130.00

Winchester Model 9422

Winchester Model 9422 & 9422 XTR
Caliber: 22 short, long, or long rifle; 22 mag.
Action: Lever action; exposed hammer; repeating; hammer stop safety in 1992
Magazine: Tubular; 15 long rifles, 17 long, 21 shorts. 11 22 mag.
Barrel: 20"
Sights: Adjustable rear, hooded ramp front
Stock & Forearm: Plain or checkered wood straight grip stock & forearm; barrel band
Approximate wt.: 6¼ lbs.
Comments: Made from 1972 to date. 9422XTR made from late 1970's to late 1980's Add 4% for mag.
Estimated Value: New (retail): $407.00
                                 Excellent: $305.00
                                 Very good: $245.00

Winchester Model 9422XTR Classic Rifle
Similar to the Model 9422XTR with satin-finish walnut pistol grip stock & forearm, fluted comb & crescent steel buttplate; curved finger lever; longer forearm; 22½" barrel; 22 or 22 magnum caliber. Produced from 1986 to 1989.
Estimated Value: Excellent: $250.00
                                 Very good: $200.00

Winchester Model 9422 Win-Tuff & Win-Cam
Similar to the Model 9422 with laminated stock of brown dyed wood (Win-Tuff) or green & brown dyed wood (Win-Cam). Add 4% for mag. or Win-Cam.
Estimated Value: New (retail): $407.00
                                 Excellent: $305.00
                                 Very good: $245.00

Winchester Model 9422 High Grade
Caliber: 22 short, long, long rifle
Action: Lever action, repeating; exposed hammer; hammer stop safety
Magazine: Tubular; 21 shorts, 17 longs, or 15 long rifle
Barrel: 20½" round, blued
Sights: Adjustable rear, hooded ramp front
Stock & Forearm: Checkered walnut, straight grip stock and forearm; barrel band
Approximate wt.: 6 lbs.
Comments: Introduced in the mid 1990's, engraved receiver.
Estimated Value: New (retail): $489.00
                                 Excellent: $365.00
                                 Very good: $295.00

Winchester Model 9422 Trapper
Similar to the Model 9422 High Grade except: 16½" barrel; less magazine capacity; plain receiver; lesser quality stock and forearm; approximate wt: 5½ lbs. Introduced in the mid 1990's.
Estimated Value: New (retail): $407.00
                                 Excellent: $305.00
                                 Very good: $245.00

Winchester Model 150
Caliber: 22 short, long, long rifle
Action: Lever action; hammerless; repeating
Magazine: Tubular; 15 long rifles, 17 longs, 21 shorts
Barrel: Blued; 20½"
Sights: Open adjustable rear, blade front
Stock & Forearm: Straight stock & forearm; barrel band; alloy receiver
Approximate wt.: 5 lbs.
Comments: Made from the late 1960's to mid 1970's.
Estimated Value: Excellent: $130.00
                                 Very good: $105.00

Winchester Model 150

Winchester Model 06

Winchester Model 1890

Winchester Model 06
Caliber: 22 short, long, long rifle
Action: Slide action; exposed hammer; repeating
Magazine: Tubular; 11 long rifles, 12 longs, 15 shorts
Barrel: Blued; 20"
Sights: Open rear, bead front
Stock & Forearm: Plain wood straight stock, grooved or plain slide handle; nickel trimmed receiver & pistol grip stock available
Approximate wt.: 5 lbs.
Comments: Made from 1906 until the early 1930's.
Estimated Value: Excellent: $425.00
                                 Very good: $340.00

Winchester Model 1890
Caliber: 22 short, long, long rifle
Action: Slide action; exposed hammer; repeating
Magazine: Tubular; 11 long rifles, 12 longs, 15 shorts
Barrel: 24" octagon
Sights: Open, bead front
Stock & Forearm: Plain wood straight grip stock & grooved slid handle
Approximate wt.: 5¾ lbs.
Comments: Made from 1890 to the early 1930's.
Estimated Value: Excellent: $500.00
                                 Very good: $400.00

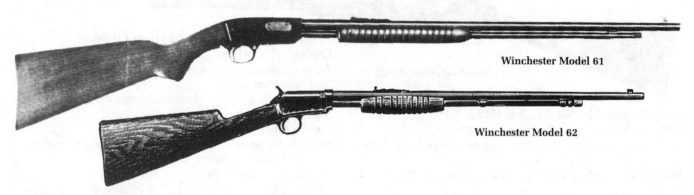

Winchester Model 61

Winchester Model 62

Winchester Model 61

Caliber: 22 short, long, long rifle
Action: Slide action; repeating
Magazine: Tubular; 14 long rifles, 16 longs, 20 shorts
Barrel: Blued; 24", round or octagon
Sights: Open rear, bead front
Stock & Forearm: Plain wood semi-pistol grip stock & grooved slide handle
Approximate wt.: 5½ lbs.
Comments: Made from the early 1930's to early 1960's.
Estimated Value: Excellent: $355.00
                   Very good: $285.00

Winchester Model 61 Magnum

Similar to the Model 61 in 22 magnum. Made in the early 1960's.

Estimated Value: Excellent: $400.00
                   Very good: $320.00

Winchester Model 62, 62A

Caliber: 22 short, long, long rifle
Action: Slide action; exposed hammer; repeating
Magazine: Tubular; 14 long rifles, 16 longs, 20 shorts
Barrel: Blued; 23"
Sights: Open rear, blade front
Stock & Forearm: Walnut straight grip stock & grooved slide handle
Approximate wt.: 5½ lbs.
Comments: Made from the early 1930's to the late 1950's. A gallery model was available chambered for 22 shot only. It became 62A in the 1940's with internal improvements.
Estimated Value: Excellent: $390.00
                   Very good: $310.00

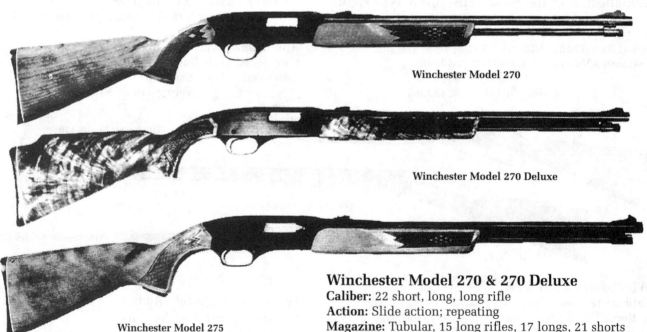

Winchester Model 270

Winchester Model 270 Deluxe

Winchester Model 275

Winchester Model 275 & 275 Deluxe

Similar to the Model 270 & 270 Deluxe in 22 magnum caliber.

Estimated Value: Excellent: $125.00
                   Very good: $ 90.00

Winchester Model 270 & 270 Deluxe

Caliber: 22 short, long, long rifle
Action: Slide action; repeating
Magazine: Tubular, 15 long rifles, 17 longs, 21 shorts
Barrel: 20½"
Sights: Open rear, ramp front
Stock & Forearm: Wanut pistol grip stock & slide handle; plastic available; later models checkered; Model 270 Deluxe has Monte Carlo stock.
Approximate wt.: 5 lbs.
Comments: Made from the mid 1960's to mid 1970's.
Estimated Value: Excellent: $120.00
                   Very good: $ 85.00

Winchester Model 03

Winchester Model 05

Winchester Model 07

Winchester Model 10

Winchester Model 03

Caliber: 22 short, long, long rifle
Action: Semi-automatic
Magazine: 10-shot tubular, loaded in stock
Barrel: Blued; 20"
Sights: Open rear, bead front
Stock & Forearm: Plain wood semi-pistol grip or straight stock; checkering on some models
Approximate wt.: 6 lbs.
Comments: Made from 1903 to the mid 1930's.
Estimated Value: Excellent: $300.00
                        Very good: $225.00

Winchester Model 05

Similar to the Model 03 in 32 Win. & 35 Win. caliber with a 5- or 10-shot detachable box magazine; 22" barrel. Made to about 1920.
Estimated Value: Excellent: $400.00
                        Very good: $320.00

Winchester Model 07

Caliber: 351
Action: Semi-automatic; hammerless
Magazine: 5- or 10-shot detachable box
Barrel: Blued; 20"
Sights: Open rear, bead front
Stock & Forearm: Semi-pistol grip stock & forearm; plain wood
Approximate wt.: 7½ lbs.
Comments: Made from 1907 to the late 1950's.
Estimated Value: Excellent: $450.00
                        Very good: $360.00

Winchester Model 10

Similar to the Model 07 except: 401 caliber; 4-shot magazine. Made until the mid 1930's.
Estimated Value: Excellent: $475.00
                        Very good: $380.00

Winchester Model 63

Winchester Model 74

Winchester Model 63

Caliber: 22 long rifle, high speed; 22 long rifle Super X
Action: Semi-automatic
Magazine: 10-shot tubular, load in stock
Barrel: Blued; 20", 23"
Sights: Open rear, bead front
Stock & Forearm: Plain wood pistol grip stock & forearm
Approximate wt.: 5½ lbs.
Comments: Made from the early 1930's to the late 1950's.
Estimated Value: Excellent: $425.00
                        Very good: $320.00

Winchester Model 74

Caliber: 22 long rifle only or 22 short only
Action: Semi-automatic
Magazine: Tubular; 14 long rifles, 20 shorts; in stock
Barrel: Blued; 24"
Sights: Open rear, bead front
Stock & Forearm: Plain wood one-piece semi-pistol grip stock & forearm
Approximate wt.: 6¼ lbs.
Comments: Made from the late 1930's to the mid 1950's.
Estimated Value: Excellent: $200.00
                        Very good: $150.00

Winchester Model 77

Winchester Model 100

Winchester Model 190

Winchester Model 490

Winchester Model 77

Caliber: 22 long rifle
Action: Semi-automatic
Magazine: 8-shot detachable
Barrel: Blued; 22"
Sights: Open rear, bead front
Stock & Forearm: Plain walnut one-piece semi-pistol grip stock & forearm
Approximate wt.: 5½ lbs.
Comments: Made from the mid 1950's to early 1960's.
Estimated Value: Excellent: $135.00
                       Very good: $105.00

Winchester Model 77 Tubular

Similar to the Model 77 with a 15-shot tubular magazine.
Estimated Value: Excellent: $140.00
                       Very good: $110.00

Winchester Model 100

Caliber: 243, 284, 308
Action: Semi-automatic, gas operated
Magazine: 4-shot clip; 10-shot clip in 284
Barrel: Blued; 19", 22"
Sights: Open rear, hooded ramp front
Stock & Forearm: Checkered walnut one-piece stock & forearm; swivels
Approximate wt.: 7 lbs.
Comments: Made from the early 1960's to mid 1970's.
Estimated Value: Excellent: $375.00
                       Very good: $300.00

Winchester Model 100 Carbine

Similar to the Model 100 with no checkering: 19" barrel; barrel bands.
Estimated Value: Excellent: $390.00
                       Very good: $310.00

Winchester Model 190

Caliber: 22 short, long , long rifle
Action: Semi-automatic; hammerless
Magazine: Tubular; 15 long rifles, 17 longs, 21 shorts
Barrel: 20½", 22"
Sights: Open rear, blade front
Stock & Forearm: Plain semi-pistol grip stock & forearm
Approximate wt.: 5 lbs.
Comments: 22 short dropped in the early 1970's; made from the mid 1960's to the late 1970's.
Estimated Value: Excellent: $100.00
                       Very good: $ 80.00

Winchester Model 190 Carbine

Similar to the Model 190 with a 20½" barrel; barrel band & swivels. Discontinued in the early 1970's.
Estimated Value: Excellent: $110.00
                       Very good: $ 85.00

Winchester Model 290

Caliber: 22 short, long, long rifle
Action: Semi-automatic
Magazine: Tubular; 15 longs, 17 long rifles, 21 shorts
Barrel: 20½"
Sights: Open rear, ramp front
Stock & Forearm: Checkered walnut pistol grip stock & forearm
Approximate wt.: 5 lbs.
Comments: Made from the mid 1960's to mid 1970's.
Estimated Value: Excellent: $115.00
                       Very good: $ 90.00

Winchester Model 490

Caliber: 22 long rifle
Action: Semi-automatic
Magazine: 5-, 10- or 15-shot clip
Barrel: Blued; 22"
Sights: Folding leaf rear, hooded ramp front
Stock & Forearm: Checkered walnut one-piece pistol grip stock & forearm
Approximate wt.: 6 lbs.
Comments: Made in the mid 1970's.
Estimated Value: Excellent: $165.00
                       Very good: $130.00

Handguns

AMT 360
American 362
Astra 362
Auto Mag 367
Bauer 367
Bayard 367
Beretta 368
Browning 376
Browning, FN 379
CZ 380
Charter Arms 382
Colt 385
Dardick 407
Desert Eagle 407
Detonics 409
Fiala 409

Glock 410
Great Western 411
Harrington & Richardson 411
Hartford 418
Heckler & Koch 419
High Standard 420
Iver Johnson 429
Japanese 434
Lignose 435
Llama 436
MAB 438
Mauser 440
Mitchell Arms 441
New England 442
North American Arms 443
Remington 443

Rossi 445
Ruger 446
Sauer 452
Savage 453
Sheridan 454
Smith & Wesson 454
Star 477
Sterling 481
Stevens 483
Steyr 485
Taurus 486
Thompson Center 490
Walther 490
Webley 493
Wesson 496

AMT

AMT Lightning Pistol
Caliber: 22 long rifle
Action: Semi-automatic, concealed hammer
Magazine: 10-shot clip
Barrel: 5" bull, 6½" tapered or bull, 8½" tapered or bull, 10" tapered or bull, 12½" tapered
Sights: Rear adjustable for windage
Finish: Stainless steel; rubber wrap-around grips
Length Overall: 9" (5" barrel)
Approximate wt.: 38 oz. (5" bull barrel)
Comments: Made from the mid to late 1980's. Add 5% for 12½" barrel.
Estimated Value: Excellent: $245.00
  Very good: $195.00

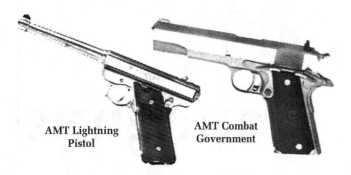

AMT Lightning Pistol   **AMT Combat Government**

AMT Combat & Standard Government
Caliber: 45 ACP
Action: Semi-automatic; exposed hammer; loaded chamber indicator; manual and grip safeties; adjustable target-type trigger
Magazine: 7-shot clip
Barrel: 5"
Sights: Fixed
Finish: Checkered walnut or neoprene wrap around grips; all stainless steel construction
Length Overall: 8½"
Approximate wt.: 39 oz.
Comments: Made from 1970's to present.
Estimated Value: New (retail): $490.00
  Excellent: $370.00
  Very good: $295.00

AMT Long Slide
Same as the AMT Combat Goverment except: 7" barrel; 10½" overall length; adjustable 3 dot sight system.
Estimated Value: New (retail): $596.00
  Excellent: $450.00
  Very good: $355.00

AMT Skipper
Same as the AMT Combat Goverment except: 4" barrel; 7½" overall length; 40 S&W caliber; approx. wt. 33 ozs.; adj. sights; discontinued in early 1990's.
Estimated Value: Excellent: $400.00
  Very good: $320.00

AMT Hardballer
Same as the AMT Combat Government except; adjustable combat-type sights; serrated matte slide rib; grooved front and backstraps.
Estimated Value: New (retail): $550.00
  Excellent: $415.00
  Very good: $330.00

AMT 380 Backup

AMT Backup & Backup II
Caliber: 380 ACP, 22 long rifle
Action: Semi-automatic; concealed hammer; manual and grip safeties; double action only model introduced in 1992 (without grip safety).
Magazine: 5-shot clip in 380 ACP; 8-shot in 22LR
Barrel: 2½"
Sights: Fixed
Finish: Smooth or checkered wood grips; all stainless steel construction; Lexon grips on later models
Length Overall: 5"
Approximate wt.: 18 oz.
Comments: Made from 1970's to present. Add 6% for double action only model (Backup); 22 cal. Discontinued in late 1980's.
Estimated Value: New (retail): $310.00
  Excellent: $235.00
  Very good: $185.00

AMT Backup Double Action

AMT Backup Double Action
Caliber: 38 Super, 9mm, 40 S&W, and 45ACP
Action: Semi-automatic; double action only; no manual safety
Magazine: 6-shot (38 Super or 9mm); 5-shot (40 S&W or 45ACP)
Barrel: 3"
Sights: Grooved slide type
Finish: Stainless steel, checkered fiberglass grips
Length Overall: 5¾"
Approximate wt.: 23 to 25 oz.
Comments: Introduced in the mid 1990's.
Estimated Value: New (retail): $450.00
  Excellent: $340.00
  Very good: $270.00

AMT "On Duty" DA

Caliber: 9mm, 40 S&W, 45ACP
Action: Semi-automatic; double action only with trigger disconnect thumb safety or decocker model
Magazine: 15-shot (9mm), 11-shot (40 S&W), 9-shot (45)
Barrel: 4½"
Sights: Fixed; 3 dot system
Finish: Anodized black matte; carbon fiber grips
Length Overall: 7½"
Approximate wt.: 32 oz.
Comments: Produced from 1992 to 1995. Add 8% for 45ACP.
Estimated Value: Excellent: $355.00
                        Very good: $285.00

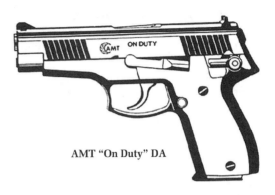

AMT "On Duty" DA

AMT Automag II

Caliber: 22 magnum
Action: Gas assisted, single action, semi-automatic
Magazine: 9-shot clip
Barrel: 3⅜", 4½", or 6"
Sights: Adjustable front and rear
Finish: Grooved carbon-fiber grips; stainless steel
Approximate wt.: 24 to 32 oz.
Length Overall: 6¾", 8", 9¼"
Comments: Introduced in the late 1980's; promoted as the "first and only production semi-automatic handgun in its caliber."
Estimated Value: New (retail): $406.00
                        Excellent: $305.00
                        Very good: $245.00

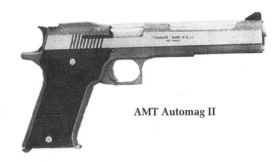

AMT Automag II

AMT Automag III

Caliber: 30 (M1 Carbine)
Action: Semi-automatic; exposed hammer
Magazine: 8-shot clip
Barrel: 6⅜"
Sights: Adjustable 3-dot system
Finish: Stainless steel; horizontally grooved carbon-fiber grips
Length Overall: 10½"
Approximate wt.: 43 oz.
Comments: Introduced in the early 1990's.
Estimated Value: New (retail): $470.00
                        Excellent: $350.00
                        Very good: $280.00

AMT Automag V

AMT Automag IV

Similar to the Automag III except: 45 Winchester magmum caliber; weight: 46 oz.; 7-shot clip; 6½" barrel; overall length 10½".
Estimated Value: New (retail): $700.00
                        Excellent: $525.00
                        Very good: $420.00

AMT Automag V

Similar to the Automag III except: gas venting system to reduce recoil; 50 caliber; weight 46 oz.; 5-shot clip. Introduced in 1994; dropped in 1996.
Estimated Value: Excellent: $675.00
                        Very good: $540.00

American

American Two Barrel Derringers

Caliber: 22 S, L, & LR; 22 WMR; 38 Spec.; about 60 different rifle & pistol calibers introduced in the 1980's
Action: Single action; exposed hammer; spur trigger; tip-up barrels; hammer block safety after late 1980's
Cylinder: None; chambers in barrels; 2-shot capacity
Barrel: 3" double barrel (superposed)
Sights: Fixed
Finish: Stainless steel; rose wood, walnut, or plastic grips
Length Overall: 5"
Approximate wt.: 15 oz., 11oz., or ultra light 7½ oz.
Comments: Made from about 1972 to 1974. Reintroduced in 1980. All stainless steel construction. Current models marked "American Derringer"; Prices vary according to caliber.

Estimated Value:		
New (retail):	$225.00 - $385.00
Excellent:	$170.00 - $300.00
Very good:	$135.00 - $240.00

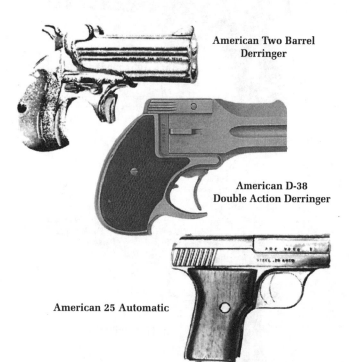

American Two Barrel Derringer

American D-38 Double Action Derringer

American 25 Automatic

American D-38 Double Action Derringer

Caliber: 22 long rifle, 22 magnum, 38 Special, 9mm Luger, 357 magnum, 40 S&W
Action: Double action only; hammerless; hammerblock thumb safety
Cylinder: None; chambers in barrels; 2-shot capacity
Barrel: 3" over and under
Sights: Fixed
Finish: Satin stainless steel or blued; with aluminum grip frame; rosewood, walnut, hardwood, or black plastic grips
Length Overall: 5"
Approximate wt.: 14 oz.
Comments: Introduced in 1980's.

Estimated Value:	New (retail):	$300.00 - $350.00
	Excellent:	$225.00 - $260.00
	Very good:	$180.00 - $210.00

American 25 Automatic

Caliber: 25 ACP; 250 mag. (after 1980)
Action: Semi-automatic; concealed hammer
Magazine: 8-shot clip; 7-shot in mag.
Barrel: 2"
Sights: Fixed
Finish: Blue or stainless steel; smooth rosewood or walnut grips
Length Overall: 4½"
Approximate wt.: 15½ lbs.
Comments: Made from about 1969 to 1974; reintroduced in 1980. Early models (1969 to 1974) are marked "American Firearms." Current models (after 1980) are marked "American Derringer." Add 25% for .250 mag. Discontinued in 1980's.

Estimated Value:	Blue	Stainless Steel
Excellent:	$150.00	$175.00
Very good:	$120.00	$140.00

American Baby Model

Similar to the 25 Automatic except slightly more compact, 6-shot clip. Produced from 1982 to 1985.

Estimated Value:	Excellent:	$140.00
	Very good:	$110.00

Astra

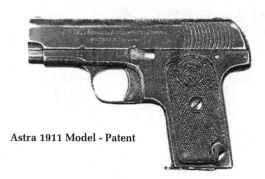

Astra 1911 Model - Patent

Astra 1911 Model - Patent

Caliber: 32 ACP (7.65 mm)
Action: Semi-automatic, concealed hammer
Magazine: 7-shot clip
Barrel: 3¼"
Sights: Fixed
Finish: Blued; checkered hard rubber grips
Length Overall: 5¾"
Approximate wt.: 29 oz.
Comments: A Spanish copy of the Browning blowback action, probably made of trade parts. Not made by Uneta Y Compania.

Estimated Value:	Excellent:	$160.00
	Very good:	$130.00

Astra 1915 Model - Patent

Astra 1915 Model - Patent
Caliber: 32 ACP (7.65 mm)
Action: Semi-automatic, concealed hammer
Magazine: 9-shot clip
Barrel: 3¼"
Sights: Fixed
Finish: Blued; checkered hard rubber grips
Length Overall: 5¾"
Approximate wt.: 29 oz.
Comments: A Spanish copy of the Browning blowback action, probably made of trade parts. Not made by Uneta Y Compania.
Estimated Value: Excellent: $140.00
                      Very good: $110.00

Astra 1924 Hope
Caliber: 25 ACP (6.35)
Action: Semi-automatic; concealed hammer
Magazine: 6-shot clip
Barrel: 2"
Sights: Fixed
Finish: Blued; checkered rubber grips
Length Overall: 4⅓"
Approximate wt.: 12 oz.
Comments: Some of these pistols have "HOPE" designation on barrel.
Estimated Value: Excellent: $160.00
                      Very good: $130.00

Astra 1916 Model - Patent
Caliber: 32 ACP (7.65 mm)
Action: Semi-automatic, concealed hammer
Magazine: 9-shot clip
Barrel: 4"
Sights: Fixed
Finish: Blued; checkered hard rubber or wood grips
Length Overall: 6½"
Approximate wt.: 32 oz.
Comments: A Spanish copy of the Browning blowback action, made under several trade names, probably of trade parts. Many were sold in the United States, Central America and South America. Not made by Uneta Y Compania.
Estimated Value: Excellent: $150.00
                      Very good: $120.00

Astra 1924 Hope

Astra Model 300
Caliber: 380 ACP (9 mm Kurz); 32ACP
Action: Semi-automatic; concealed hammer
Magazine: 7-shot clip
Barrel: 4¼"
Sights: Fixed
Finish: Blued; checkered rubber grips
Length Overall: 6½"
Approximate wt.: 21 oz.
Comments: This pistol was a shorter version of the Model 400 and production was started in 1922.
Estimated Value: Excellent: $250.00
                      Very good: $200.00

Astra Model 300

Astra Model 400

Astra Model 400
Caliber: 9mm Bayard long; 38 ACP, 9mm Steyr, 9mm Glisenti, 9mm Luger, 9mm Browning long cartridges can be used due to chamber design
Action: Semi-automatic; concealed hammer
Magazine: 9-shot clip
Barrel: 6"
Sights: Fixed
Finish: Blued; checkered rubber grips
Length Overall: 9"
Approximate wt.: 36 oz.
Comments: Made from 1921 until 1945 for both commercial and military use.
Estimated Value: Excellent: $325.00
                      Very good: $260.00

Astra 2000 Cub Pocket

Caliber: 22 short, 25 ACP (6.35 mm)
Action: Semi-automatic; exposed hammer
Magazine: 6-shot clip
Barrel: 2⅛"
Sights: Fixed
Finish: Blued; chrome and/or engraved, checkered grips
Length Overall: 4½"
Approximate wt.: 13 to 14 oz.
Comments: A well-made pistol of the post-World War II period. Importation to the United States was discontinued in 1968. Add $20.00 for chrome finish.
Estimated Value: Excellent: $180.00
                         Very good: $140.00

Astra Model 2000 Cub Pocket

Astra Camper Pocket

Same as Astra Cub (Model 2000) except: 22 caliber short only; 4" barrel which extends beyond front of slide; laterally adjustable rear sight. Discontinued in 1966. Add $10.00 for chrome finish.
Estimated Value: Excellent: $160.00
                         Very good: $110.00

Astra Camper Pocket

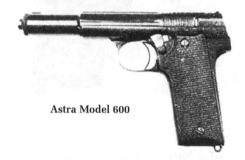

Astra Model 600

Astra Model 600

Caliber: 32 ACP (7.65 mm), 9mm Luger
Action: Semi-automatic; concealed hammer
Magazine: 10-shot clip in 32 caliber; 8-shot clip in 9mm
Barrel: 5¼"
Sights: Fixed
Finish: Blued; checkered rubber or wood grips
Length Overall: 8½"
Approximate wt.: 35 oz.
Comments: Made from 1944 to 1945 for military and police use. The 9mm was used as a substitute pistol in German military service, so some will have German acceptance marks.
Estimated Value: Excellent: $275.00
                         Very good: $220.00

Astra Model 800 Condor

Caliber: 9mm Parabellum
Action: Semi-automatic; exposed hammer
Magazine: 8-shot clip
Barrel: 5¼"
Sights: Fixed
Finish: Blued; checkered grips
Length Overall: 8¼"
Approximate wt.: 32 oz.
Comments: A post-war version of the Model 600 military pistol. It has a loaded chamber indicator.
Estimated Value: Excellent: $350.00
                         Very good: $280.00

Astra Model 800 Condor

Astra Model 200 Firecat

Caliber: 25 ACP (6.35mm)
Action: Semi-automatic; concealed hammer; grip safety
Magazine: 6-shot clip
Barrel: 2¼"
Sights: Fixed
Finish: Blued or chrome; plastic grips
Length Overall: 4½"
Approximate wt.: 13 oz.
Comments: A well-machined pistol made from early 1920 to present. It was imported to the United States from World War II until 1968. Add $10.00 for chrome finish.
Estimated Value: Excellent: $175.00
                         Very good: $140.00

Astra Model 200 Firecat

Astra Model 3000

Caliber: 22 long rifle, 32 ACP, 380ACP (9mm short)
Action: Semi-automatic; concealed hammer
Magazine: 10-shot clip in 22 caliber, 7-shot clip in 32 caliber; 6-shot clip in 380; clip
Barrel: 4"
Sights: Fixed
Finish: Blued; checkered grips
Length Overall: 6⅜"
Approximate wt.: 23 oz.
Comments: Made from about 1947 to 1956. Well-machined and well-finished commercially produced pistol. The 380 caliber has loaded chamber indicator.
Estimated Value: Excellent: $220.00
Very good: $175.00

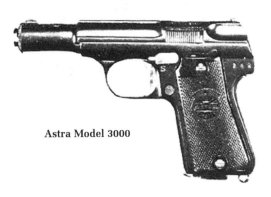

Astra Model 3000

Astra Model 4000 Falcon

Astra Model 4000 Falcon

Caliber: 22 long rifle, 32 ACP (7.65mm), 380 ACP (9mm short)
Action: Semi-automatic; exposed hammer
Magazine: 10-shot clip in 22 caliber, 8-shot clip in 32 caliber; 7-shot clip in 380 caliber
Barrel: 4¼"
Sights: Fixed
Finish: Blued; checkered grips
Length Overall: 6½"
Approximate wt.: 20 to 24 oz.
Comments: A conversion unit was available to fit the 32 caliber and 380 caliber pistols, so that 22 caliber long rifle ammunition could be used. Made from the mid 1950's to early 1980's.
Estimated Value: Excellent: $230.00
Very good: $185.00

Astra Model 5000 Constable

Astra Model 5000 Constable

Caliber: 22 long rifle, 32 ACP (7.65mm), (32 discontinued), 380 ACP
Action: Double action; semi-automatic; exposed hammer with round spur
Magazine: 10-shot clip in 22 caliber long rifle, 8-shot clip in 32 ACP; 7-shot clip in 380 ACP
Barrel: 3½"; 6" on Sport model
Sights: Fixed
Finish: Blued or chrome; grooved grips; checkered on late model; plastic or wood grips
Length Overall: 6⅝" to 9⅛"
Approximate wt.: 24 to 26 oz.
Comments: The barrel is rigidly mounted in the frame, all steel construction with hammer block safety. Add 40% for factory engraving; 7% for chrome finish; 4% for 22 cal.
Estimated Value: Excellent: $260.00
Very good: $210.00

Astra Model A-80, A-90

Caliber: 9mm Parabellum, 38 Super, 45 ACP
Action: Double action; semi-automatic; exposed hammer
Magazine: 14-shot clip in 9mm and 38 calibers; 8-shot clip in 45 ACP
Barrel: 3¾"
Sights: Fixed
Finish: Blued or chrome; checkered plastic grips
Length Overall: 7"
Approximate wt.: 40 oz.
Comments: Imported from 1982 to 1990; replaced by Model A-100 in 1990. Add 10% for chrome finish.
Estimated Value: Excellent: $375.00
Very good: $300.00

Astra Model A-100

Astra Model A-100

Similar to the Model A-80, A-90 except: caliber 9mm, 40 S&W, or 45ACP; re-engineered in 1993 incorporating increased magazine: 17-shot (9mm), 12-shot (40 S&W), or 9-shot (45ACP). Add 6% for nickel finish.
Estimated Value: New (retail): $445.00
Excellent: $335.00
Very good: $270.00

Astra Model 357 Magnum

Astra Model 357 Magnum
Caliber: 357 magnum, 38 special
Action: Double action
Cylinder: 6-shot, swing out
Barrel: 3", 4", 6", 8½" heavyweight with rib
Sights: Adjustable rear, fixed front
Finish: Blued; checkered walnut grips; stainless steel available after 1982
Length Overall: 8¼" to 13¾"
Approximate wt.: 38 to 42 oz.
Comments: All steel construction with wide spur hammer and grooved trigger. Currently made. Add 3% for 8½" barrel; 10% for stainless steel.
Estimated Value: Excellent: $250.00
                        Very good: $200.00

Astra Model 41, 44
Similar to the Model 357 except 41 magnum or 44 magnum caliber; 6" or 8½" barrel. Introduced in the early 1980's. Add $10.00 for 8½" barrel; Model 41 discontinued in mid 1980's.
Estimated Value: Excellent: $335.00
                        Very good: $270.00

Astra Model 45
Similar to the Model 357 except 45 Colt or 45 ACP caliber; 6" barrel. Produced from the early 1980's to 1987.
Estimated Value: Excellent: $260.00
                        Very good: $210.00

Astra Model A-70
Caliber: 9mm Parabellum, 40 S&W
Action: Single action; semi-automatic; exposed hammer
Magazine: 8-shot clip (9mm); 7-shot clip (40 S&W)
Barrel: 3½"
Sights: Fixed
Finish: Blued or nickel; checkered plastic or rubber grips
Length Overall: 6½"
Approximate wt.: 29 oz.
Comments: Introduced in 1992. Add 10% for nickel finish.
Estimated Value: New (retail): $359.00
                        Excellent: $270.00
                        Very good: $215.00

Astra Model A-75
Similar to the Model A-70 except: also caliber 45ACP; double action with decocker; ambidextrous magazine release; approximate wt.: 34 oz. Add 11% for 45ACP; add 7% for nickel finish. Introduced in 1993.
Estimated Value: New (retail): $416.00
                        Excellent: $315.00
                        Very good: $250.00

Astra Model A-75

Astra Cadix

Astra Cadix
Caliber: 22 short, long and long rifle, 38 Special
Action: Double action
Cylinder: Swing out 9-shot in 22 caliber; 5-shot in 38 Special
Barrel: 2", 4", and 6"
Sights: Adjustable rear on 4" and 6" barrel
Finish: Blued; checkered grips
Length Overall: 6½", 9", 11"
Approximate wt.: 25 to 27 oz.
Comments: Made from about 1960 to the late 1960's.
Estimated Value: Excellent: $140.00
                        Very good: $110.00

Auto Mag

Auto Mag

Caliber: 357 auto magnum or 44 auto magnum custom loaded or hand loaded cartridges (no commerical ammo available)

Action: Semi-automatic; exposed hammer; adjustable trigger

Magazine: 7-shot clip

Barrel: 6½" ventilated rib (44 auto mag.); 6½" or 8½" (.357 auto mag.); no rib on 8½" barrel

Sights: Ramp front sight & adjustable rear sight

Finish: Stainless steel; black polyurethane grips

Length Overall: 11½"

Approximate wt.: 60 oz.

Comments: The most potent autoloader made. Designed by Harry Sanford, it was made by different factories (Auto Mag Corp., TDE Corp., High Standard & etc.). Requires special ammunition made from the 308 Winchester, .243, or 7.62 NATO cases. Made from about 1970 to late 1970's. All stainless steel construction. Total production was rather small. First model called Pasadena Auto Mag. in .44 caliber only.

Auto Mag

Estimated Value:	Excellent:	$1,800.00 - $2,500.00
	Very good:	$1,500.00 - $2,000.00

Bauer

Bauer Stainless

Bauer Stainless

Caliber: 25ACP

Action: **Single-action** semi-automatic; concealed hammer

Magazine: 6-shot clip

Barrel: 2⅛"

Sights: Fixed

Finish: Heat treated stainless steel; plastic grips

Length Overall: 4"

Approximate wt.: 10 oz.

Comments: Manufactured in the United States from about 1972 to mid 1980's.

Estimated Value:	Excellent:	$135.00
	Very good:	$110.00

Bayard

Bayard Model 1908

Bayard Model 1923

Bayard Model 1908

Caliber: 25ACP (6.35 mm), 32ACP (7.65mm), 380ACP (9mm short)

Action: Semi-automatic; concealed hammer

Magazine: 6-shot clip

Barrel: 2¼"

Sights: Fixed

Finish: Blued; checkered grips

Length Overall: 5"

Approximate wt.: 15 to 17 oz.

Comments: Made from basic Pieper patents of the 1900's. All calibers appear the same from a side view. Commercially sold throughout the world; one of the most compact pistols made.

Estimated Value:	Excellent:	$190.00
	Very good:	$150.00

Bayard Model 1923 (25ACP)

Caliber: 25 ACP

Action: Semi-automatic; concealed hammer

Magazine: 6-shot clip

Barrel: 2⅛"

Sights: Fixed

Finish: Blued; checkered grips

Length Overall: 4⅓"

Approximate wt.: 12 oz.

Comments: A Belgian variation of the Browning. This model has better construction than the Model 1908.

Estimated Value:	Excellent:	$200.00
	Very good:	$160.00

Bayard Model 1923 (32, 380)
Caliber: 32 ACP (7.65mm), 380 ACP (9mm short)
Action: Semi-automatic; concealed hammer
Magazine: 6-shot clip
Barrel: 3⅜"
Sights: Fixed
Finish: Blued; checkered grips
Length Overall: 5¾"
Approximate wt.: 18 to 19 oz.
Comments: A Belgian variation of the Browning. Better construction than the 1908.
Estimated Value: Excellent: $225.00
                        Very good: $165.00

Bayard Model 1930
Caliber: 25 ACP (6.35mm)
Action: Semi-automatic; concealed hammer
Magazine: 6-shot clip
Barrel: 2"
Sights: Fixed
Finish: Blued; checkered grips
Length Overall: 4⅜"
Approximate wt.: 12 oz.
Comments: A modification of the Model 1923.
Estimated Value: Excellent: $200.00
                        Very good: $160.00

Beretta

Beretta Model 1915

Beretta Model 1919 Bantam

Beretta Model 1923

Beretta Model 1915
Caliber: 32 ACP (7.65mm)
Action: Semi-automatic; concealed hammer
Magazine: 8-shot clip
Barrel: 3¼"
Sights: Fixed
Finish: Blued; wood or metal grips
Length Overall: 5⅞"
Approximate wt.: 20 oz.
Comments: The earliest of the Beretta series used for military service during World War I as well as being sold commercially. Has rigid lanyard loop on left side. Grip safety was added in 1919. Made from about 1915 to 1924.
Estimated Value: Excellent: $275.00
                        Very good: $220.00

Beretta Model 1919 Bantam
Caliber: 25 ACP (6.35mm)
Action: Semi-automatic; concealed hammer
Magazine: 7-shot clip
Barrel: 2½"
Sights: Fixed
Finish: Blued; wood grips
Length Overall: 4½"
Approximate wt.: 14 oz.
Comments: Basic Beretta patent with addition of a grip safety. The front sight contour was changed prior to World War II. Importation to the United States was discontinued in 1956.
Estimated Value: Excellent: $200.00
                        Very good: $160.00

Beretta Model 1923
Caliber: 9mm Luger
Action: Semi-automatic; exposed hammer
Magazine: 9-shot clip
Barrel: 4"
Sights: Fixed
Finish: Blued; wood grips
Length Overall: 6½"
Approximate wt.: 30 oz.
Comments: Basically an Italian service pistol, but also sold commercially. A modified version of the 1915, 1919 patents. This was the first model produced with exposed hammer. Lanyard loop on left side.
Estimated Value: Excellent: $330.00
                        Very good: $265.00

Beretta Model 1931
Caliber: 32 ACP (7.65mm)
Action: Semi-automatic; concealed hammer
Magazine: 7-shot clip
Barrel: 3⁵⁄₁₆"
Sights: Fixed
Finish: Blued; wood grips
Length Overall: 5¾"
Approximate wt.: 22 oz.
Comments: A modified version of the Model 1923.
Estimated Value: Excellent: $275.00
 Very good: $220.00

Beretta Model 1931

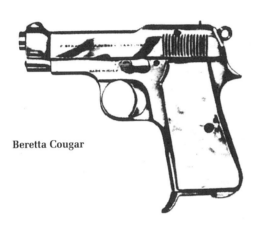

Beretta Cougar

Beretta Model 934 (1934)

Beretta Model 934 (1934) 380 & 935 (1935) 32
Caliber: 32 ACP (7.65mm), 380 ACP (9mm short)
Action: Semi-automatic; exposed hammer
Magazine: 8-shot clip in 32; and 7-shot clip in 380
Barrel: 3½"
Sights: Fixed
Finish: Blued; plastic grips
Length Overall: 6"
Approximate wt.: 22 to 24 oz.
Comments: Official pistol of the Italian Armed Forces
 from 1934 until 1951 in 380 caliber. Sold commer-
 cially and used by Italian police. Lanyard loop on
 left side. Model 935 was discontinued in 1958.
Estimated Value: Excellent: $290.00
 Very good: $230.00

Beretta Cougar
Caliber: 380 ACP (9mm short)
Action: Semi-automatic; exposed hammer
Magazine: 7-shot clip
Barrel: 3½"
Sights: Fixed
Finish: Blued or chrome; plastic grips
Length Overall: 6"
Approximate wt.: 22 oz.
Comments: A post-World War II version of the Model
 934 (1934). Those imported into the United States
 have the "Cougar" name on pistol. Some of the later
 models are marked "P.B. 1966." Add $10.00 for
 chrome.
Estimated Value: Excellent: $280.00
 Very good: $225.00

Beretta Model 948 Plinker
Caliber: 22 long rifle
Action: Semi-automatic; exposed hammer
Magazine: 7-shot clip
Barrel: 3½", 6"
Sights: Fixed
Finish: Blued; plastic grips
Length Overall: 6" or 8½"
Approximate wt.: 16 to 18 oz.
Comments: Made from 1948 to 1958. Similar to the
 1934/35 series except: 22 caliber; aluminum alloy
 frame. Replaced by the "Jaguar." The 6" barrel
 extends beyond the slide about 3".
Estimated Value: Excellent: $175.00
 Very good: $140.00

Beretta Model 935 (1935)

Beretta Model 70 Puma

Caliber: 32 ACP (7.65mm); 380 ACP
Action: Semi-automatic; exposed hammer
Magazine: 7-shot clip
Barrel: 3½"
Sights: Fixed
Finish: Blued; plastic wrap-around grip
Length Overall: 6½"
Approximate wt.: 15 oz.
Comments: Post-World War II (1946) version of the Model 935 (1935). Aluminum alloy frame was used to reduce weight. Those imported into the United States have "Puma" designation. Also made with steel frame. Discontinued. Add $15.00 for nickel finish. Made from 1960 to mid 1980's.
Estimated Value: Excellent: $250.00
                        Very good: $200.00

Beretta Model 70 Puma

Beretta Model 71 & 72 Jaguar

Beretta Model 70S

Caliber: 380 ACP (9mm short); 22 long rifle
Action: Semi-automatic; exposed hammer
Magazine: 7-shot clip in 380; 8-shot clip in 22
Barrel: 3½"
Sights: Fixed
Finish: Blued; 2-piece wrap-around plastic grip
Length Overall: 6¼"
Approximate wt.: 24 oz.
Comments: All steel compact pistol imported from Italy. Made from late 1970's to mid 1980's.
Estimated Value: Excellent: $235.00
                        Very good: $190.00

Beretta Model 70T

Beretta Model 70T

Caliber: 32 ACP (7,65mm)
Action: Semi-automatic; exposed hammer
Magazine: 9-shot clip
Barrel: 6"
Sights: Adjustable rear; blade front
Finish: Blued; plastic wrap-around grip
Length Overall: 9½"
Approximate wt.: 20 oz.
Comments: Imported from Italy from 1956 to 1968. Target length barrel extends beyond front of slide.
Estimated Value: Excellent: $230.00
                        Very good: $180.00

Beretta Model 101

Same as Model 70T except: 22 caliber long rifle; 10-shot clip. Made from 1960 to mid 1980's.
Estimated Value: Excellent: $220.00
                        Very good: $180.00

Beretta Models 71 & 72 Jaguar

Caliber: 22 long rifle
Action: Semi-automatic; exposed hammer
Magazine: 7-shot clip
Barrel: 3½" (Model 71) and 6" (Model 72)
Sights: Fixed
Finish: Blued; wrap-around plastic grip
Length Overall: 6¼" or 8¾"
Approximate wt.: 16-18 oz.
Comments: Importation to the United States started in 1956. The light weight was obtained by using aluminum alloy receiver. Similar in appearance to the Puma except the 6" barrel extends about 3" beyond the slide.
Estimated Value: Excellent: $225.00
                        Very good: $180.00

Beretta Model 949 Olympic

Beretta Model 949 Olympic, 949C

Caliber: 22 short, 22 long rifle
Action: Semi-automatic; exposed hammer
Magazine: 5-shot clip
Barrel: 8¾" with compensator muzzle brake
Sights: Rear adjustable for windage, front adjustable for elevation
Finish: Blued; checkered walnut grips with thumb rest
Length Overall: 12½"
Approximate wt.: 38 oz.
Comments: Also called the 949C, it was designed for use in Olympic rapid-fire matches & designed 949LR. Made from 1950's to mid 1960's.
Estimated Value: Excellent: $500.00
                        Very good: $400.00

Beretta Model 951 (1951)

Caliber: 9mm Parabellum (Luger)
Action: Semi-automatic; exposed hammer
Magazine: 8-shot clip
Barrel: 4½"
Sights: Fixed
Finish: Blued; plastic wrap-around grip
Length Overall: 8"
Approximate wt.: 31 oz.
Comments: First produced in 1950 & adopted by Italian Army & Navy. Basic 1934 model features except it has aluminum alloy receiver. Also known as Brigadier model.
Estimated Value: Excellent: $335.00
                                Very good: $270.00

Beretta Minx M2 & Model 950 B

Caliber: 22 short, 25 ACP
Action: Semi-automatic; exposed hammer
Magazine: 6-shot clip
Barrel: 2½"
Sights: Fixed
Finish: Blued or nickel; plastic grips; wood grips
Length Overall: 4½"
Approximate wt.: 10 oz.
Comments: Made from 1956 to present. Imported from 1956 to 1968. Aluminum alloy frame with a hinged barrel that tips up. Can be used as single shot by removing magazine & tipping up barrel to load. Reintroduced in 1979, manufactured in the United States. Add 17% for nickel finish.
Estimated Value: Excellent: $135.00
                                Very good: $100.00

Beretta Model 951 (1951)

Beretta Model 21 & 21 Bobcat

Caliber: 22 long rifle, 25 ACP
Action: Straight blowback, double action semi-automatic
Magazine: 7-shot clip (22 caliber); 8-shot clip (25ACP)
Barrel: 2½" tip up
Sights: Fixed
Finish: Blued; matte or nickel, alloy frame; wood or plastic grips
Length Overall: 5"
Approximate wt.: 12 oz.
Comments: Introduced in 1984. Add 5% for nickel finish (after 1987). Add 21% for engraving with wood grips; deduct 20% for matte finish.
Estimated Value: New (retail): $244.00
                                Excellent: $185.00
                                Very good: $145.00

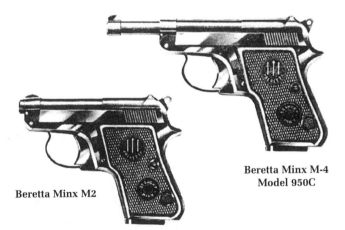

**Beretta Minx M-4
Model 950C**

Beretta Minx M2

Beretta Model 21

Beretta Tomcat

Beretta Minx M-4, Model 950C, 950 BS4

Same as Minx M-2, except: 4" barrel; overall length 6"; approximate weight 12 ozs. Add 10% for nickel finish.
Estimated Value: Excellent: $150.00
                                Very good: $110.00

Beretta Jetfire Model 950B

Same as Minx M-2, except: 25 ACP (6.35mm) caliber; 8-shot clip. Add 17% for nickel finish; Add 44% for engraved model with walnut grips; deduct 18% for matte finish with plastic grips.
Estimated Value: New (retail): $187.00
                                Excellent: $140.00
                                Very good: $112.00

Beretta Tomcat 3000 & 3032

Caliber: 22 long rifle, 32 (3032)
Action: Semi-automatic; double or single action, straight blow-back system with tip-up barrel; exposed hammer.
Magazine: 7-shot clip
Barrel: 2½" tip-up
Sights: Fixed blade front, drift adjustable rear
Finish: Matte or blued with plastic or wood grips
Length Overall: 5"
Approximate wt.: 15 oz.
Comments: Introduced in the mid 1990's. Add 20% for blued model with wood grips.
Estimated Value: New (retail): $240.00
                                Excellent: $180.00
                                Very good: $145.00

Beretta Model 76 Target

Caliber: 22 long rifle
Action: Semi-automatic; exposed hammer
Magazine: 10-shot clip
Barrel: 6"
Sights: Adjustable rear, blade front
Finish: Blued; 2-piece wrap around plastic or wood grip
Length Overall: 9½"
Approximate wt.: 35 oz.
Comments: Imported from Italy. Competition-type heavy barrel. Add 10% for wood grips. Made from 1965 to mid 1980's.

Estimated Value:	Excellent:	$350.00
	Very good:	$280.00

Beretta Model DA 380

Beretta Model 76 Target

Beretta Model 92SB

Caliber: 9mm Parabellum
Action: Semi-automatic; straight blowback; double action; exposed hammer
Magazine: 15-shot staggered clip
Barrel: 5"
Sights: Fixed
Finish: Blued; walnut or checkered plastic grips
Length Overall: 8½"
Approximate wt.: 34½ oz.
Comments: Made from the early 1980's to 1986. Add 3% for wood grips.

Estimated Value:	Excellent:	$450.00
	Very good:	$340.00

Beretta Model 92SB Compact

Similar to the Model 92SB except 4¼" barrel; 13-shot clip; weighs 31 oz. Add 3% for wood grips. Discontinued 1986.

Estimated Value:	Excellent:	$465.00
	Very good:	$375.00

Beretta Model DA 380

Caliber: 380 ACP (9mm short)
Action: Double action; semi-automatic; exposed round spur hammer
Magazine: 13-shot staggered clip
Barrel: 3¾"
Sights: Fixed
Finish: Blued; smooth walnut grips
Length Overall: 6½"
Approximate wt.: 23 oz.
Comments: This pistol features magazine release and safety release for either right or left hand.

Estimated Value:	Excellent:	$325.00
	Very good:	$260.00

Beretta Model 90

Caliber: 32 ACP (7.65mm short)
Action: Semi-automatic; straight blowback; double action; exposed hammer
Magazine: 8-shot clip
Barrel: 3½"
Sights: Fixed
Finish: Blued; contoured plastic grips
Length Overall: 6½"
Approximate wt.: 19 oz.
Comments: Discontinued in mid 1980's.

Estimated Value:	Excellent:	$300.00
	Very good:	$240.00

Beretta Model 92, 92S

Caliber: 9mm Parabellum
Action: Semi-automatic; double and single action
Magazine: 15-shot clip
Barrel: 5"
Sights: Fixed
Finish: Blued; plastic or smooth wood grips
Length Overall: 8½"
Approximate wt.: 33 oz.
Comments: Made from the late 1970's to early 1980's. Add 5% for wood grips. Loaded chamber indicator.

Estimated Value:	Excellent:	$410.00
	Very good:	$300.00

Beretta Model 90

Beretta Model 92

Beretta Model 92F & 92FS (after 1991)

Caliber: 9mm Parabellum

Action: Double action semi-automatic; locked breech; delayed blowback; exposed hammer; manual ambidextrous safety; large frame

Magazine: 15-shot staggered clip; 10-shot after Sept. 13, 1994

Barrel: 5"

Sights: Fixed blade front; square notched bar rear, dovetailed to slide; 3-dot sight system

Finish: Combat-style alloy frame and steel slide matte finish; or alloy frame and stainless steel; smooth or checkered plastic or wood grips

Length Overall: 8½"

Approximate wt.: 34 oz.

Comments: Similar to the Model 92SB with improved safety features and open slide design. Adopted as the official side arm of the U.S. Military in the mid 1980's. Made from 1986 to present. Add 3% for wood grips, 21% for stainless steel, 15% for tritium sights.

Estimated Value: New (retail): $626.00
Excellent: $470.00
Very good: $375.00

Beretta Model 92F

Beretta Model 92F and 92FS Compact

Similar to the Model 92F with a 4¼" barrel, 13-shot clip, weighs 31 oz. Add 3% for wood grips. Made from 1986 to present.

Estimated Value: New (retail): $626.00
Excellent: $470.00
Very good: $375.00

Beretta Model 92FS Compact Type M

Same as the Model 92FS Compact except: narrower grip, holding a single line 8-shot clip. The magazine release is not ambidextrous. Produced from the late 1980's to early 1990's.

Estimated Value: Excellent: $460.00
Very good: $365.00

Beretta Model 92F Compact

Beretta Model 96 and 96 Compact

Same as the Model 92FS except: 40 S&W caliber with 10-shot clip; the 96 Compact is the same as Model 92FS Compact except 40 S&W caliber with 9-shot clip. Introduced in 1992. Also available in stainless steel with wood or rubber grips. Add 15% for tritium sights.

Estimated Value: Excellent: $480.00
Very good: $385.00

Beretta Model 92G and 96G

Same as the Model 92FS except: hammer drop lever does not function as a traditional safety. When the lever is released after dropping the hammer, it returns to firing position. It can be fired (double action mode for first shot) by pulling the trigger. 96G is 40 S&W caliber with 10-shot clip. Add 2% for Model 96G.

Estimated Value: New (retail): $626.00
Excellent: $470.00
Very good: $375.00

Beretta Model 96

Beretta Model 92D/96D

Beretta Model 92DS and 96DS

Same as the Model 92FS except: double action only; bobbed hammer; hammer returns to the down position after each slide cycle; safety lever. 96DS is 40 S&W caliber with 10-shot clip. Add 4% for 96DS. Introduced in 1992. Add 16% for tritium sights.

Estimated Value: New (retail): $586.00
Excellent: $440.00
Very good: $350.00

Beretta Model 92D and 96D

Same as the Model 92DS and 96DS except: without a safety; the safety lever has been eliminated. Add 4% for Model 96D (40 cal.) Introduced in 1992. Add 16% for tritium sights.

Estimated Value: New (retail): $586.00
Excellent: $440.00
Very good: $350.00

Beretta Model 20

Beretta Model 20

Caliber: 25 ACP
Action: Straight blowback, recoil ejection, double action semi-automatic
Magazine: 8-shot clip
Barrel: 2½" tip-up
Sights: Fixed
Finish: Blued; alloy frame, plastic or walnut grips
Length Overall: 5"
Approximate wt.: 10½ oz.
Comments: Produced from 1984 to 1987.
Estimated Value: Excellent: $220.00
Very good: $175.00

Beretta Model 92FS Centurion

Same as the Model 92FS except: 4¼" barrel (as the 92FS Compact) but has the 15-shot clip (as the 92FS); 10-shot clip after 1995. Introduced in 1992. Add 15% for tritium sights.

Estimated Value: New (retail): $626.00
Excellent: $470.00
Very good: $375.00

Beretta Model 96 Centurion

Same as the Model 92FS Centurion except: 40 S&W caliber with 10-shot clip. Introduced in 1992. Add 14 % for tritium sights.

Estimated Value: New (retail): $643.00
Excellent: $480.00
Very good: $385.00

Beretta Model 96 Centurian

Beretta Cougar 8000

Beretta Cougar 8000 & 8040

Caliber: 9mm (8000), 40 S&W (8040)
Action: Semi-automatic, short recoil, rotating barrel; exposed hammer; Model D has no hammer spur and is double action only; Models F & G are single or double action
Magazine: 10-shot clip
Barrel: 3.6" rotating; chromium plated inside
Sights: 3-dot system with front and rear dovetailed to the slide
Finish: Matte black with checkered plastic grips
Length Overall: 7"
Approximate wt.: 32½ oz.
Comments: Introduced in the mid 1990's. Deduct 5% for Model D.
Estimated Value: New (retail): $699.00
Excellent: $525.00
Very good: $420.00

Beretta Model 81

Beretta Model 82
Caliber: 32 ACP (7.65mm)
Action: Semi-automatic; straight blowback; double action; exposed hammer; medium frame
Magazine: 9-shot clip
Barrel: 3¾"
Sights: Fixed
Finish: Blued or nickel, walnut grips
Length Overall: 6¾"
Approximate wt.: 17 oz.
Comments: Similar to the Model 81 with a more compact grip size. Add 15% for nickel finish.
Estimated Value: Excellent: $350.00
Very good: $275.00

Beretta Model 83 & 83 Cheeta
Similar to the Model 82 except: 380 caliber; 4" barrel; 7-shot in-line clip; checkered plastic or walnut grips; add 5% for walnut grips; add 8% for nickel.
Estimated Value: Excellent: $360.00
Very good: $290.00

Beretta Model 84 & 84 Cheeta
Similar to the Model 81 in 380 caliber (9mm short); 10- or 13-shot staggered clip; plastic grips; Add 6% for wood grips; 13% for nickel finish with wood grips.
Estimated Value: New (retail): $529.00
Excellent: $395.00
Very good: $320.00

Beretta Model 85 & 85 Cheeta
Similar to the Model 82 except: 380 caliber (9mm short); 8-shot in line clip; plastic grips; Add 20% for nickel; 7% for wood grips.
Estimated Value: New (retail): $499.00
Excellent: $375.00
Very good: $300.00

Beretta Model 86 & 86 Cheeta
Similar to the Model 85 except: tip-up barrel for loading without working the slide; wood grips.
Estimated Value: New (retail): $514.00
Excellent: $385.00
Very good: $310.00

Beretta Model 81
Caliber: 32 ACP
Action: Semi-automatic; double & single action
Magazine: 12-shot clip
Barrel: 3¾"
Sights: Fixed
Finish: Blued or nickel; plastic or smooth wood grips
Length Overall: 6¾"
Approximate wt.: 23½ oz.
Comments: Produced in the late 1970's to about 1984. Add 3% for wood grips; 15% for nickel finish.
Estimated Value: Excellent: $340.00
Very good: $270.00

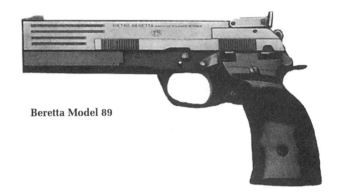

Beretta Model 89

Beretta Model 86

Beretta Model 87 & 87 Cheeta
Similar to the Model 85 except: 22 long rifle; 7-shot clip; Add 4% for 6" barrel & counterweight.
Estimated Value: New (retail): $493.00
Excellent: $370.00
Very good: $295.00

Beretta Model 89 & 89 Gold Standard
Caliber: 22 long rifle
Action: Single-action, semi-automatic; target pistol
Magazine: 8-shot clip
Barrel: 6"
Sights: Adjustable target sights
Finish: Blued; contoured walnut grips with thumb rest
Length Overall: 9½"
Approximate wt.: 41 oz.
Comments: Introduced in the late 1980's.
Estimated Value: New (retail): $736.00
Excellent: $555.00
Very good: $445.00

Browning

Browning Hi Power

Browning 25 Pocket
Caliber: 25 ACP (6.35mm)
Action: Semi-automatic; concealed hammer
Magazine: 6-shot clip
Barrel: 2⅛"
Sights: Fixed
Finish: Blued; hard rubber grips; nickel plated, lightweight, plastic pearl grips; Renaissance engraved Nacolac pearl grips available
Length Overall: 4"
Approximate wt.: 8 to 10 oz.
Comments: A post-World War II modification of the FN Browning Baby Automatic pistol, it was lightened & the grip safety removed. Imported into the U.S. from 1954 to 1968. Pistols imported into the U.S. & Canada usually do not have the FN trademark. Add 10% for nickel finish; Add 200% for nickel plated Renaissance engraved model (mint).
Estimated Value: Excellent: $275.00
                        Very good: $225.00

Browning Model 1910

Browning Model 1910 (1955)
Caliber: 380 ACP (9mm short), 32 ACP
Action: Semi-automatic; concealed hammer
Magazine: 6-shot clip
Barrel: 3½"
Sights: Fixed
Finish: Blued; hard rubber grips; Renaissance engraved, Nacolac pearl grips available
Length Overall: 6"
Approximate wt.: 21 oz.
Comments: Basic design of the 1900 model FN Browning, with the appearance streamlined & a grip safety added. Imported from 1954 to 1968. Pistols imported into the U.S. & Canada usually do not have the FN trademark. Add 200% for nickel plated Renaissance engraved model (mint).
Estimated Value: Excellent: $325.00
                        Very good: $275.00

Browning 9mm, Hi Power
Caliber: 9mm Parabellum; 40 S&W (added 1994)
Action: Semi-automatic; exposed hammer; single action
Magazine: 13-shot clip; 10-shot after 9-13-94
Barrel: 4⅝"
Sights: Fixed or adjustable rear sight
Finish: Blued; checkered walnut or molded Polymide grips; Renaissance engraved, Nacolac pearl grips available; chrome available 1982 with Packmayr grips; nickel available until 1986; Matte finish with molded grips available after 1985.
Length Overall: 7¾"
Approximate wt.: 34 oz.
Comments: Imported into the U.S. from 1954 to present. Pistols imported into the U. S. from Belgium usually do not have FN trademark. Add 10% for adjustable sights; 10% for nickel or chrome finish; 200% for nickel plated Renaissance engraved (mint).
Estimated Value: New (retail): $585.00
                        Excellent: $435.00
                        Very good: $350.00

Browning Hi Power Mark III
Similar to the Hi Power except: nonglare matte, or polished blue or silver chrome finish; low profile fixed or adj. sights; two-piece molded grips with thumb rest or walnut grips; Introduced in 1991. Add 3% for silver chrome finish; add 6% for walnut grips; add 9% for adjustable sights.
Estimated Value: New (retail): $551.00
                        Excellent: $410.00
                        Very good: $330.00

Browning Hi Power Practical
Similar to the Hi Power except: contrasting blue slide and silver-chrome frame; wrap-around Pachmayr grips; round serrated hammer; removable front sight; add 8% for adjustable sights.
Estimated Value: New (retail): $630.00
                        Excellent: $470.00
                        Very good: $375.00

Browning Renaissance Engraved Cased Set
Contains one each of the following:
   Browning 25 Automatic Pistol
   Browning Model 1910 380 Automatic Pistol
   Browning Model 1935 Hi Power Automatic Pistol
in a special walnut carrying case. Each pistol is nickel plated, Renaissance Engraved with Nacolac pearl grips. Imported into the U.S. from 1954 through 1968. Price includes walnut case.
Estimated Value: Mint condition (unused): $4,500.00

Browning Challenger

Browning Challenger III

Browning Challenger

Caliber: 22 long rifle
Action: Semi-automatic; concealed hammer
Magazine: 10-shot clip
Barrel: 4½" or 6¾"
Sights: Removable blade front, adjustable rear
Finish: Blued; checkered walnut grips; Gold model (gold inlaid) finely figured walnut grips; Renaissance engraved finely figured walnut grips
Length Overall: 9³⁄₁₆" or 11⁷⁄₁₆"
Approximate wt.: 36 or 38 oz.
Comments: Blued model made from 1963 to 1974. Gold and Renaissance models introduced in 1971. All steel construction. Add 100% for gold model; add 130% for nickel plated Renaissance engraved model (mint).
Estimated Value: Excellent: $340.00
Very good: $275.00

Browning Challenger II

Similar to the Challenger except 6¾" barrel only; made from about 1975 to mid 1980's. Impregnated wood grips.
Estimated Value: Excellent: $210.00
Very good: $170.00

Browning Challenger III

Caliber: 22 long rifle
Action: Semi-automatic; concealed hammer
Magazine: 10-shot clip
Barrel: 5½" bull barrel
Sights: Blade front, adjustable rear
Finish: Blued; smooth impregnated hardwood grips
Length Overall: 9½"
Approximate wt.: 35 oz.
Comments: Produced 1982 to 1986.
Estimated Value: Excellent: $215.00
Very good: $175.00

Browning Challenger III Sporter

Browning Challenger III Sporter

Similar to the Challenger III with 6¾" round barrel. Produced 1985 to 1987.
Estimated Value: Excellent: $200.00
Very good: $160.00

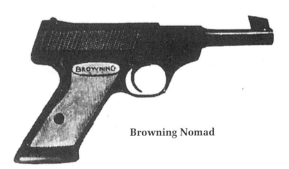

Browning Nomad

Browning Nomad

Caliber: 22 long rifle
Action: Semi-automatic; concealed hammer
Magazine: 10-shot clip
Barrel: 4½" or 6¾"
Sights: Removable blade front, adjustable rear sight
Finish: Blued; plastic grips
Length Overall: 9" and 11¼"
Approximate wt.: 26 to 28 oz.
Comments: Made from 1963 to 1973 with an alloy frame.
Estimated Value: Excellent: $250.00
Very good: $190.00

Browning Buck Mark 22 & Buck Mark Plus

Caliber: 22 long rifle
Action: Semi-automatic; blowback; concealed hammer
Magazine: 10-shot clip
Barrel: 5½" bull barrel with non-glare top
Sights: Adjustable rear, ramp front
Finish: Blued; matte except for lustre barrel sides; checkered black molded composite grips; Buck Mark Plus has deer head medallion; brass-plated trigger; laminated wood grips; nickel finish available after 1991
Length Overall: 9½"
Approximate wt.: 32 oz.
Comments: Introduced in 1985; Add 21% for Buck Mark Plus, 17% for nickel finish.
Estimated Value: New (retail): $257.00
                        Excellent: $195.00
                        Very good: $155.00

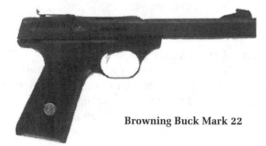

Browning Buck Mark 22

Browning Buck Mark Bullseye

Similar to the Browning Buck Mark 22 except: 7¼" round fluted barrel; approximate wt.: 36 oz.; rubber or rosewood grips; adjustable trigger pull; introduced in 1996. Add 28% for contoured rosewood grips (target model).
Estimated Value: New (retail): $377.00
                        Excellent: $280.00
                        Very good: $225.00

Browning Buck Mark Micro

Same as Buck Mark 22 except: 4" barrel; weighs 36 oz.; overall length 8". Add 17% for nickel finish, 21% for Buck Mark Micro Plus.
Estimated Value: New (retail): $257.00
                        Excellent: $195.00
                        Very good: $155.00

Browning Buck Mark 5.5 Field & Target

Similar to the Buck Mark 22 except: 5½" heavy round barrel; with a full length scope mount rib. Add 12% for Gold or nickel Target model.
Estimated Value: New (retail): $412.00
                        Excellent: $310.00
                        Very good: $250.00

Browning Buck Mark Silhouette & Unlimited

A silhouette-style pistol based on the Buck Mark design; 9⅞" bull barrel on the silhouette model. Unlimited has 14" barrel; hooded, adjustable sights mounted on a full length scope rib base; walnut grips; finger groove or smooth walnut forearm. Introduced in 1988. Add 23% for Unlimited model;
Estimated Value: New (retail): $435.00
                        Excellent: $325.00
                        Very good: $260.00

Browning Buck Mark Varmint

A varmint pistol based on the Buck Mark design; 9⅞" bull barrel; full-length scope base rib; no sights; walnut grips; walnut forearm is available. Introduced in 1988.
Estimated Value: New (retail): $391.00
                        Excellent: $290.00
                        Very good: $235.00

Browning Model BDM

Caliber: 9mm Luger
Action: Semi-automatic; short recoil; double action for first shot or selector switch for double action only for all shots
Magazine: 15-shot clip; 10-shot clip after Sept. 13, 1994
Barrel: 4¾"
Sights: Adjustable rear, low-profile removable blade front
Finish: Black matte; molded wrap-around grips
Length Overall: 7¾"
Approximate wt.: 31 oz.
Comments: Introduced in 1991.
Estimated Value: New (retail): $613.00
                        Excellent: $460.00
                        Very good: $370.00

Browning Model BDA

Caliber: 45 ACP, 9mm, 38 Super ACP
Action: Semi-automatic; exposed hammer; built-in safety block; double and single action
Magazine: 7-shot clip in 45 ACP; 9-shot clip in 9mm and 38 Super
Barrel: 4½"
Sights: Adjustable square notch rear, blade front
Finish: Blued; black checkered plastic grips
Length Overall: 7¾"
Approximate wt.: 29 oz.
Comments: Produced from late 1970's to 1980.
Estimated Value: Excellent: $390.00
                        Very good: $315.00

Browning Model BDA 380

Browning Model BDA 380

Caliber: 380 ACP
Action: Semi-automatic; exposed hammer; double action for first shot
Magazine: 13-shot staggered row clip; 10-shot after Sept. 13, 1994
Barrel: 3¾"
Sights: Adjustable square notch rear, blade front
Finish: Blued; smooth walnut grips, bronze medallion; nickel finish available after 1981
Length Overall: 6¾"
Approximate wt.: 32 oz.
Comments: Introduced in the late 1970's. Add 8% for nickel finish.
Estimated Value: New (retail): $564.00
                        Excellent: $424.00
                        Very good: $340.00

Browning
International
Medalist

Browning Medalist

Caliber: 22 long rifle
Action: Semi-automatic; concealed hammer
Magazine: 10-shot clip
Barrel: 6¾", ventilated rib
Sights: Removable blade front, adjustable micrometer rear
Finish: Blued; checkered walnut grips with thumb rest; Gold model (gold inlaid) finely figured and carved walnut grips with thumb rest, Renaissance Model engraved, finely figured and carved walnut grips with thumb rest
Length Overall: 11¾"
Approximate wt.: 45 oz.
Comments: All steel construction, made from 1963 to 1974. Gold model and Renaissance model introduced in 1971. Add 80% for Gold model; Add 120% for nickel plated Renaissance engraved model (mint). Price includes case and accessories.
Estimated Value: Excellent: $575.00
  Very good: $460.00

Browning International Medalist

Caliber: 22 long rifle
Action: Semi-automatic; hammerless
Magazine: 10-shot clip
Barrel: 5¹⁵⁄₁₆" heavy, counter weight
Sights: Fixed, non-reflective
Finish: Blued; wide walnut grips, adjustable hand stop
Length Overall: 11¾"
Approximate wt.: 46 oz.
Comments: A target pistol produced in early 1970's.
Estimated Value: Excellent: $550.00
  Very good: $440.00

Browning, FN

FN Browning Model 1900

Caliber: 32 ACP (7.65mm)
Action: Semi-automatic; concealed hammer
Magazine: 7-shot clip
Barrel: 4"
Sights: Fixed
Finish: Blued, hard rubber grips with FN trademark
Length Overall: 6¾"
Approximate wt.: 22 oz.
Comments: John Browning's first commercially successful pistol. This was the beginning for the 32 automatic cartridge, which is called 7.65 Browning pistol cartridge in the rest of the world. The 1900 was sold commercially throughout the world & was also used by police & military in countries such as Belgium, Russia, China & France. Made from 1900 to 1912.
Estimated Value: Excellent: $300.00
  Very good: $225.00

FN Browning Model 1903 Military

Caliber: 9mm Browning long
Action: Semi-automatic; concealed hammer
Magazine: 7-shot clip
Barrel: 5"
Sights: Fixed
Finish: Blued, hard rubber grips with FN trademark
Length Overall: 8"
Approximate wt.: 33 oz.
Comments: Made from 1903 to 1939. Lanyard ring on left grip.
Estimated Value: Excellent: $290.00
  Very good: $220.00

FN Browning
Model 1903 Military

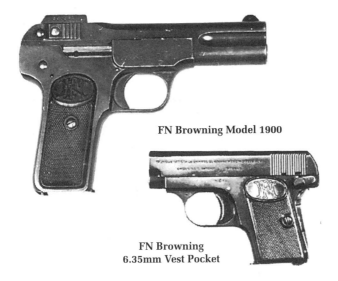

FN Browning Model 1900

FN Browning
6.35mm Vest Pocket

FN Browning 6.35mm Vest Pocket

Caliber: 25 ACP (6.35mm)
Action: Semi-automatic; concealed hammer; grip safety
Magazine: 6-shot clip
Barrel: 2"
Sights: Fixed
Finish: Blued; hard rubber grips with FN trademark
Length Overall: 4½"
Approximate wt.: 13 oz.
Comments: Made from 1905 to 1947.
Estimated Value: Excellent: $335.00
  Very good: $250.00

FN Browning
Model 1910

FN Browning Model 1922
Military and Police

FN Browning Model
1935 Hi Power

FN Browning Model 1910

Caliber: 32 ACP (7.65mm), 380 ACP (9mm short)
Action: Semi-automatic; concealed hammer
Magazine: 7-shot clip in 32 ACP, 6-short clip in 380
Barrel: 3½"
Sights: Fixed
Finish: Blued, hard rubber grips with FN trademark
Length Overall: 6"
Approximate wt.: 21 oz..
Comments: The basic design of the Model 1900 except it has streamlined appearance and grip safety.

| Estimated Value: | Excellent: | $275.00 |
| | Very good: | $225.00 |

FN Browning Baby

Caliber: 25 ACP (6.35mm)
Action: Semi-automatic; concealed hammer
Magazine: 6-shot clip
Barrel: 2⅛"
Sights: Fixed
Finish: Blued, hard rubber grips with FN trademark
Length Overall: 4"
Approximate wt.: 10 oz.
Comments: Introduced in 1940. All steel construction, similar to Browning 25 Pocket Automatic Pistol, imported into U. S. from 1954 to 1968.

| Estimated Value: | Excellent: | $360.00 |
| | Very good: | $275.00 |

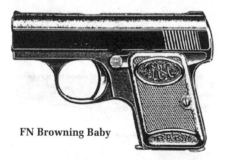

FN Browning Baby

FN Browning Model 1922 Military and Police

Caliber: 32 ACP (7.65mm), 380 ACP (9mm short)
Action: Semi-automatic; concealed hammer
Magazine: 9-shot clip in 32; 8-shot clip in 380
Barrel: 4½"
Sights: Fixed
Finish: Blued, hard rubber grips with FN trademark
Length Overall: 7"
Approximate wt.: 24 oz.
Comments: Identical to Model 1910 except it has longer grip frame, magazine and barrel. Lanyard ring on the left grip.

| Estimated Value: | Excellent: | $225.00 |
| | Very good: | $170.00 |

FN Browning Model 1935 Hi Power

Caliber: 9mm Parabellum
Action: Semi-automatic; exposed hammer
Magazine: 13-shot staggered line clip
Barrel: 4⅝"
Sights: Fixed or adjustable
Finish: Blued or parkerized; checkered walnut or plastic grips
Length Overall: 7¾"
Approximate wt.: 34 oz.
Comments: Production of this model by John Inglis Co. of Canada began in 1943. Some of these were produced with an alloy frame to reduce weight. Also during World War II Model 1935 was produced under German supervision for military use. The quality of the German pistol was poorer than those made before or after the war. A smaller version was also made from 1937 to 1940 with shorter barrel, slide & 10-shot clip.

Estimated Value:	FN	German (superv.)	Canadian
Excellent:	$450.00	$350.00	$390.00
Very good:	$340.00	$265.00	$300.00

CZ

CZ Model 22 (1922)

Caliber: 380 ACP (9mm short), 25 ACP
Action: Semi-automatic; exposed hammer with shielding on both sides
Magazine: 8-shot clip
Barrel: 3½"
Sights: Fixed
Finish: Blued
Length Overall: 6"
Approximate wt.: 22 oz.
Comments: Made in Czechoslovakia in the 1920's.

| Estimated Value: | Excellent: | $200.00 |
| | Very good: | $160.00 |

CZ Model 22 (1922)

CZ Model 1936 Pocket

Caliber: 25 ACP (6.5mm)
Action: Double action semi-automatic; slide does not cock hammer; (hammer is cocked and released by the trigger) shield exposed hammer
Magazine: 8-shot clip
Barrel: 2½"
Sights: Fixed
Finish: Blued; plastic grips
Length Overall: 4¾"
Approximate wt.: 14 oz.
Comments: Introduced in 1936. U.S. importation discontinued in 1968.
Estimated Value: Excellent: $180.00
                  Very good: $140.00

CZ Model 1945 Pocket

Same as CZ Model 1936 except for minor modifications. Introduced in the mid 1940's. U.S. importation discontinued in 1968.
Estimated Value: Excellent: $190.00
                  Very good: $145.00

CZ Model 38 (1938)

Caliber: 380 ACP (9mm short)
Action: Double action; semi-automatic
Magazine: 9-shot clip
Barrel: 3¾"
Sights: Fixed
Finish: Blued; plastic grips
Length Overall: 7"
Approximate wt.: 28 oz.
Comments: Imported from the late 1930's to mid 1940's.
Estimated Value: Excellent: $225.00
                  Very good: $180.00

CZ Model 50 (1950)

Caliber: 32 ACP (7.65mm)
Action: Semi-automatic; exposed hammer; double action
Magazine: 8-shot clip
Barrel: 3⅛"
Sights: Fixed
Finish: Blued; plastic grips
Length Overall: 6½"
Approximate wt.: 25 oz.
Comments: No longer imported into the U.S.
Estimated Value: Excellent: $210.00
                  Very good: $160.00

CZ "Duo" Pocket

Caliber: 25 ACP (6.35mm)
Action: Semi-automatic; concealed hammer
Magazine: 6-shot clip
Barrel: 2⅛"
Sights: Fixed
Finish: Blued; plastic grips
Length Overall: 4½"
Approximate wt.: 15 oz.
Comments: Imported from the mid 1920's to early 1960's.
Estimated Value: Excellent: $190.00
                  Very good: $150.00

CZ Model 27 (1927) Pocket

Caliber: 32 ACP (7.65mm)
Action: Semi-automatic; exposed hammer with shielding on both sides
Magazine: 8-shot clip
Barrel: 4"
Sights: Fixed
Finish: Blued; plastic grips
Length Overall: 6½"
Approximate wt.: 25 oz.
Comments: This pistol usually bears the CZ mark, but World War II version may have the name Bohmische Waffenfabrik on slide. Made from 1927 to 1951.
Estimated Value: Excellent: $200.00
                  Very good: $160.00

CZ Model 27 (1927)

CZ Model 38 (1938)

CZ Model 1945 Pocket

CZ Model 50 (1950)

CZ "Duo" Pocket

CZ Model 70

Caliber: 7.65mm (32)
Action: Semi-automatic; exposed hammer; double action
Magazine: 8-shot clip
Barrel: 3⅛"
Sights: Fixed
Finish: Blued; checkered plastic grips
Length Overall: 6½"
Approximate wt.: 25 oz.
Comments: Produced in Czechoslovakia.
Estimated Value: Excellent: $250.00
                       Very good: $190.00

CZ Model 75

Caliber: 9mm Parabellum
Action: Semi-automatic; selective double action; exposed hammer;
Magazine: 15-shot clip
Barrel: 4½"
Sights: Fixed
Finish: Blued; checkered plastic grips
Length Overall: 8"
Approximate wt.: 35 oz.
Comments: Produced in Czechoslovakia.
Estimated Value: Excellent: $400.00
                       Very good: $310.00

Charter Arms

Charter Arms
Model 79K

Charter Arms
Police Bulldog

Charter Arms Bulldog

Charter Arms Model 79K

Caliber: 380 Auto, 32 Auto
Action: Semi-automatic; double action; exposed hammer
Magazine: 7-shot clip
Barrel: 3½"
Sights: Adjustable
Finish: Stainless steel; checkered walnut grips
Length Overall: 6½"
Approximate wt.: 24½ oz.
Comments: Made from 1985 to 1987.
Estimated Value: Excellent: $295.00
                       Very good: $220.00

Charter Arms Model 40

Similar to the Model 79K in 22 long rifle caliber; 8-shot clip; weighs 21½ oz. Made from 1985 to 1987.
Estimated Value: Excellent: $250.00
                       Very good: $195.00

Charter Arms Explorer II

Charter Arms Explorer II

Caliber: 22 long rifle
Action: Semi-automatic
Magazine: 8-shot clip
Barrel: 6" or 10" interchangeable
Sights: Blade front, adjustable rear
Finish: Black, semi-gloss textured enamel; simulated walnut grips; extra clip storage in grip; also available in silvertone
Length Overall: 13½" with 6" barrel
Approximate wt.: 27 oz.
Comments: A survival pistol styled from the AR-7 rifle; produced from the late 1970's to 1986.
Estimated Value: Excellent: $100.00
                       Very good: $ 80.00

Charter Arms Police Bulldog

Caliber: 38 Special, 32 H&R Mag.
Action: Single and double action
Cylinder: 6-shot swing-out
Barrel: 2", 3½", 4"; tapered, bull, or shrouded barrel
Sights: Fixed
Finish: Blue or stainless steel; checked walnut bulldog grips, square butt grips or Neoprene grips
Length Overall: 8½"
Approximate wt.: 21 oz.
Comments: Produced from 1976 to early 1990's. Add 25% for stainless steel. Add 8% for barrel shroud.
Estimated Value: Excellent: $200.00
                       Very good: $160.00

Charter Arms Bulldog

Caliber: 44 Special, 357 magnum (357 mag. discontinued in mid 1980's)
Action: Single and double action; exposed regular or bobbed hammer
Cylinder: 5-shot swing-out
Barrel: 2½", 3", 4", 6" (4" & 6" discontinued in 1985)
Sights: Fixed
Finish: Blued; oil finished, checkered walnut bulldog grips or Neoprene grips; stainless steel added 1982
Length Overall: 7½" (3" barrel)
Approximate wt.: 19 oz.
Comments: Made from 1971 to early 1990's. Add 20% for stainless steel.
Estimated Value: Excellent: $200.00
                       Very good: $160.00

Charter Arms Target Bulldog

Similar to the Bulldog except: 4" barrel; shrouded ejector rod; adjustable rear sight. Made from the late 1970's to 1989. Add 5% for 44 Special.

Estimated Value: **Excellent:**   **$175.00**
                             Very good: **$140.00**

Charter Arms Bulldog Pug

Similar to the Bulldog except: 2½" barrel; 44 spec.; blued, nickel, or stainless steel; shrouded ejector rod. Produced from 1986 to 1994. Add 8% for nickel; add 20% for stainless steel.

Estimated Value: **Excellent:**   **$200.00**
                             Very good: **$160.00**

Charter Arms Undercoverette & Lady Blue .32

Caliber: 32 S&W long
Action: Single & double action
Cylinder: 6-shot, swing-out
Barrel: 2"
Sights: Fixed
Finish: Blued; oil finished, plain walnut grips
Length Overall: 6¼"
Approximate wt.: 16½ oz.
Comments: Made from 1970 to early 1990's; Also called Undercover.

Estimated Value: **Excellent:**   **$180.00**
                             Very good: **$140.00**

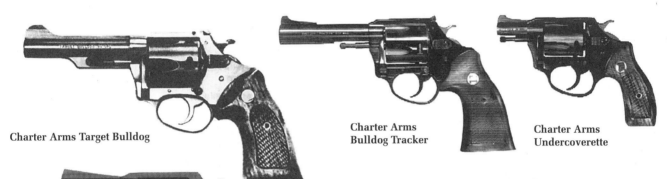

Charter Arms
Bulldog Tracker

Charter Arms
Undercoverette

Charter Arms Bulldog Tracker

Caliber: 357 magnum and 38 special
Action: Single & double action
Cylinder: 5-shot, swing-out
Barrel: 2½", 4", or 6" bull barrel (4" & 6" discontinued in 1989)
Sights: Adjustable rear, ramp front
Finish: Blued; checkered walnut square bull grips
Length Overall: 11"
Approximate wt.: 27½ oz.
Comments: Produced from 1980 to early 1990's.

Estimated Value: **Excellent:**   **$215.00**
                             Very good: **$175.00**

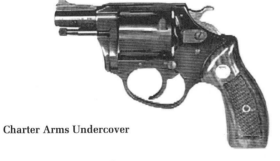

Charter Arms Target Bulldog

Charter Arms Bulldog Pug

Charter Arms Undercover

Charter Arms Pathfinder

Charter Arms Undercover

Caliber: 38 Special
Action: Single & double action
Cylinder: 5-shot, swing-out
Barrel: 2" or 3" (3" discontinued in 1990)
Sights: Fixed
Finish: Blued or nickel; oil finished, plain or hand checkered walnut grips or Neoprene grips; stainless steel added 1982; shrouded barrel after 1989
Length Overall: 6¼" or 7⅜"
Approximate wt.: 16 or 17 oz.
Comments: Made from 1965 to early 1990's; Add 5% for nickel (discontinued early 1980's); 25% for stainless steel.

Estimated Value: **Excellent:**   **$185.00**
                             Very good: **$145.00**

Charter Arms Pathfinder

Caliber: 22 long rifle, 22 magnum
Action: Single & double action
Cylinder: 6-shot, swing-out
Barrel: 2", 3" or 6" (3" & 6" only after 1987)
Sights: Adjustable rear and partridge-type front on serrated ramp
Finish: Blued; oil finished, plain or hand checkered walnut grips; stainless steel after 1982
Length Overall: 7⅛" (3" barrel)
Approximate wt.: 19 oz.
Comments: Made from 1970 to early 1990's. Add 25% for stainless steel; 10% for 6" barrel.

Estimated Value: **Excellent:**   **$200.00**
                             Very good: **$160.00**

Charter Arms Police Bulldog 44 Special
Caliber: 44 Special
Action: Single or double, exposed hammer
Cylinder: 5-shot, swing-out, simultaneous manual ejector
Barrel: 2½" or 3½" shrouded barrel with solid rib
Sights: Snag-free front; fixed or adjustable rear
Finish: Blued or stainless steel; bulldog checkered wood or neoprene grips
Length Overall: 7" or 8"
Approximate wt.: 23 oz.
Comments: Produced from 1990 to about 1993; add 2% for adjustable rear sight; add 12% for stainless steel.
Estimated Value: Excellent: $220.00
                                     Very good: $175.00

Charter Arms Police Bulldog

Charter Arms Police Bulldog 357 Magnum
Caliber: 357 magnum & 38 Special
Action: Single or double, exposed hammer
Cylinder: 5-shot, swing-out, simultaneous ejector
Barrel: 4" shrouded barrel
Sights: Ramp front, adjustable rear
Finish: Stainless steel; black neoprene grips
Length Overall: 8½"
Approximate wt.: 28 oz.
Comments: Produced from 1990 to about 1993.
Estimated Value: Excellent: $265.00
                                     Very good: $210.00

Charter Arms Bonnie & Clyde Set
Caliber: 32 magnum (Bonnie); 38 Special (Clyde)
Action: Single & double action; exposed hammer
Cylinder: 6-shot, swing-out; fluted
Barrel: 2" shrouded barrel marked "Bonnie – 32 mag." or "Clyde – 38 spec."
Sights: Ramp front; fixed rear
Finish: Blued with smooth wood grips
Length Overall: 6½"
Approximate wt.: 21 oz.
Comments: Each gun comes with a gun rug identified by name (Bonnie or Clyde). These guns are sold as a set. Produced from 1989 to about 1993.
Estimated Value: Excellent: $460.00 per set
                                     Very good: $365.00 per set

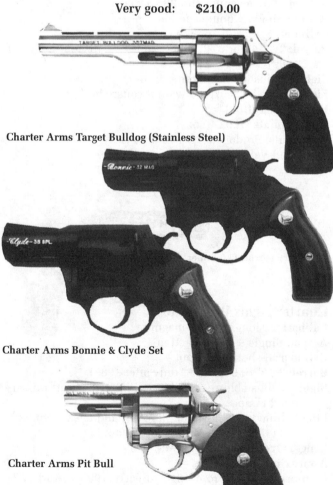

Charter Arms Target Bulldog (Stainless Steel)

Charter Arms Bonnie & Clyde Set

Charter Arms Pit Bull

Charter Arms Pit Bull
Caliber: 9mm
Action: Single & double, exposed hammer, regular or bobbed
Cylinder: 5-shot, swing-out, simultaneous ejector
Barrel: 2½", 3½" shrouded barrel
Sights: Fixed or adjustable
Finish: Blued or stainless steel; neoprene grips
Length Overall: 7" or 8"
Approximate wt.: 26 oz.
Comments: Produced from 1990 to about 1993; add 2% for adjustable sights; add 8% for stainless steel.
Estimated Value: Excellent: $245.00
                                     Very good: $200.00

Charter Arms Target Bulldog (Stainless Steel)
Caliber: 357 magnum & 38 Special; 44 Special; 9mm
Action: Single or double, exposed hammer
Cylinder: 5-shot, swing-out, simultaneous ejector
Barrel: 5½" shrouded barrel with ventilated rib
Sights: Ramp front; adjustable rear
Finish: Stainless steel with smooth wood target grips
Length Overall: 10"
Approximate wt.: 28 oz.
Comments: Produced from 1990 to about 1993.
Estimated Value: Excellent: $315.00
                                     Very good: $255.00

Charter Arms Pocket Target
Caliber: 22 short, long, long rifle
Action: Single & double action; exposed hammer
Cylinder: 6-shot, swing-out
Barrel: 3"
Sights: Adjustable snag-free rear, ramp front
Finish: Blued; plain grips or checkered walnut bulldog grips
Length Overall: 7⅛"
Approximate wt.: 19 oz.
Comments: Made from 1960's to 1970's.
Estimated Value: Excellent: $150.00
Very good: $120.00

Charter Arms Pocket Target

Charter Arms Police Undercover

Charter Arms Off Duty

Charter Arms Off Duty
Caliber: 38 Spec., 22 mag., 22LR
Action: Single & double; exposed hammer
Cylinder: 5-shot, swing-out, fluted; 6-shot in 22 cal.
Barrel: 2" (shrouded barrel after 1989)
Sights: Fixed
Finish: Flat black, nickel, or stainless steel; smooth or checkered walnut or Neoprene grips
Length Overall: 6½"
Approximate wt.: 16 oz.
Comments: Introduced in 1984. Add 20% for nickel; add 30% for stainless steel.
Estimated Value: New (retail): $199.00
Excellent: $150.00
Very good: $120.00

Charter Arms Police Undercover
Caliber: 32 H&R mag., 38 Spec.
Action: Single & double; exposed regular or bobbed hammer
Cylinder: 6-shot, swing-out, fluted
Barrel: 2" or 4" (shrouded barrel only after 1989)
Sights: Fixed
Finish: Blued, nickel, or stainless steel; checkered walnut or Neoprene grips
Length Overall: 6½"
Approximate wt.: 17½-20 oz.
Comments: Introduced in 1987. Add 6% for nickel; add 12% for stainless steel.
Estimated Value: New (retail): $238.00
Excellent: $180.00
Very good: $145.00

Colt

Colt Model 1900
Caliber: 38 ACP
Action: Semi-automatic; exposed spur hammer
Magazine: 7-shot clip
Barrel: 6"
Sights: Fixed
Finish: Blued; plain walnut grips
Length Overall: 9"
Approximate wt.: 35 oz.
Comments: Combination safety & rear sight. Rear sight is pressed down to block hammer from firing pin. One of the first automatic pistols made in the U.S. & first automatic pistol made by Colt. Made from 1900 to 1902. No slide lock.
Estimated Value: Excellent: $1,000.00
Very good: $ 800.00

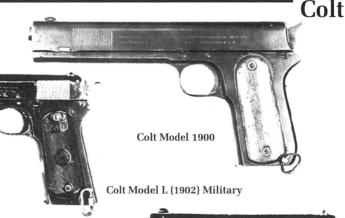

Colt Model 1900

Colt Model L (1902) Military

Colt Model L (1903) Pocket

Colt Model L (1902)
Similar to Colt Model 1900 except: no safety; round hammer; hard rubber grips. Made from 1902 to 1907.
Estimated Value: Excellent: $850.00
Very good: $650.00

Colt Model L (1902) Military
Same as Colt Model L (1902) except: longer grips (more square at bottom) with lanyard ring; 8-shot magazine; weighs 37 oz. Made from 1902 to 1928. Spur-type hammer after 1907.
Estimated Value: Excellent: $800.00
Very good: $640.00

Colt Model L (1903) Pocket
Caliber: 38 ACP
Action: Semi-automatic; exposed hammer
Magazine: 7-shot clip
Barrel: 4½"
Sights: Fixed
Finish: Blued; checkered hard rubber grips
Length Overall: 7½"
Approximate wt.: 31 oz.
Comments: Made from 1903 to 1927. Round-type hammer to 1908, then changed to spur-type hammer; no slide lock or safety.
Estimated Value: Excellent: $600.00
Very good: $475.00

Colt Model M (32) 1st Issue Pocket

Colt Model M (32) 2nd Issue Pocket

Colt Model M (32) 3rd Issue Pocket

Colt Model M (32) 3rd Issue Pocket

Similar to 2nd Issue Model M (32) except: safety disconnector, which prevents cartridge in chamber from being fired if magazine is removed. Made from 1926 to 1941.

Estimated Value: Excellent: $375.00
                     Very good: $300.00

Colt Model M (380) 1st Issue Pocket

Caliber: 380 ACP (9 mm short)
Action: Semi-automatic
Magazine: 7-shot clip
Barrel: 3¾"
Sights: Fixed
Finish: Blued or nickel; hard rubber or checkered walnut grips
Length Overall: 6¾"
Approximate wt.: 24 oz.
Comments: Made from 1908 to 1911. Slide lock safety and grip safety. Barrel lock bushing at muzzle.
Estimated Value: Excellent: $410.00
                      Very good: $325.00

Colt Model M (380) 2nd Issue Pocket

Similar to 1st Issue Model M (380) except: without barrel lock bushing and other minor changes. Made from 1911 to 1926. Add $200.00 for Military Model.

Estimated Value: Excellent: $375.00
                      Very good: $300.00

Colt Model M (380) 1st Issue Pocket

Colt Model M (380) 2nd Issue Pocket

Colt Model M (32) 1st Issue Pocket

Caliber: 32 ACP (7.65 mm short)
Action: Semi-automatic; concealed hammer
Magazine: 8-shot clip
Barrel: 3¾"
Sights: Fixed
Finish: Blued or nickel; hard rubber or checkered walnut grips
Length Overall: 6¾"
Approximate wt.: 25 oz.
Comments: Made from 1903 to 1911. Slide lock safety and grip safety. Barrel lock bushing at muzzle.
Estimated Value: Excellent: $400.00
                      Very good: $320.00

Colt Model M (32) 2nd Issue Pocket

Similar to 1st Issue Model M (32) except: without barrel lock bushing and other minor modifications. Made from 1911 to 1926. Add $200.00 for Military Model.

Estimated Value: Excellent: $350.00
                      Very good: $280.00

Colt Model M (380) 3rd Issue Pocket

Similar to 2nd Issue Model M (380) except: it has safety disconnector, which prevents cartridge in chamber from being fired if magazine is removed. Made from 1926 to 1941.

Estimated Value: Excellent: $380.00
                      Very good: $310.00

Colt Model 1905 Military

Colt Model 1905 Military

Caliber: 45 ACP
Action: Semi-automatic
Magazine: 7-shot clip
Barrel: 5"
Sights: Fixed
Finish: Blued; checkered walnut grips
Length Overall: 8½"
Approximate wt.: 34 oz.
Comments: Made from 1905 to 1912. Similar to Model 1902 38 caliber automatic pistol. First 45 caliber military automatic pistol made by Colt. Slide stop but no safety except some experimental models with short grip safety. Round hammer 1905 to 1908; after 1908 spur-type hammer. Approximately 5,000 produced. Some were fitted and equipped with a short-stock holster. These are scarce collectors items and valued much higher.
Estimated Value: Excellent: $1,200.00
                      Very good: $ 950.00

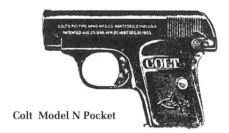

Colt Model N Pocket

Colt Model N Pocket
Caliber: 25 ACP
Action: Semi-automatic; concealed striker instead of hammer
Magazine: 6-shot clip
Barrel: 2"
Sights: Fixed
Finish: Blued or nickel; hard rubber or checkered walnut grips
Length Overall: 4½"
Approximate wt.: 14 oz.
Comments: Made from 1908 to 1941. Magazine safety disconnector added in 1916 (about serial number 141,000). All models have thumb safety & grip safety. Add $200.00 for Military Model; $50.00 for nickel finish.
Estimated Value: Excellent: $325.00
                  Very good: $245.00

Colt Government Model 1911
Caliber: 45 ACP
Action: Semi-automatic; exposed spur hammer
Magazine: 7-shot clip
Barrel: 5"
Sights: Fixed
Finish: Blued, nickel and parkerized or similar finish, checkered walnut grips
Length Overall: 8½"
Approximate wt.: 39 oz.
Comments: Slide lock, thumb safety and grip safety. Adopted as a military side arm in 1911 in U.S. Made from 1911 to present with some modifications. Changed to Model 1911 A1 in 1925. Military models are marked "U.S. Army," U.S. Navy," or "U.S. Marines" and "United States Property." Colt licensed other firms to produce this pistol during both World Wars. Check prices under manufacturer's name. Also check commercial model prices.
Estimated Value: Excellent: $500.00
                  Very good: $400.00

Colt Government Model 1911 A1
Same as Government Model 1911 except: the grip safety tang was lengthened (to stop the hammer bite on fleshy hands); the trigger was shortened (to allow stubby fingers better control); the back strap below the grip safety was arched (for better instinctive pointing); the sights were made larger & squared (to improve sight picture). Also the grips were made of checkered walnut or plastic. The 1911 A1 was made from 1925 to present. Changes started about serial number 650000 in military model. Also check prices for other manufacturer's & commercial models.
Estimated Value: Excellent: $475.00
                  Very good: $385.00

Colt Commercial Model 1911
Same as Government Model 1911 except: not marked with military markings. The letter "C" is used in serial numbers. Blued or nickel finish. Made from 1911 to 1926 then changed to 1911 A1 about serial number C130000.
Estimated Value: Excellent: $550.00
                  Very good: $425.00

Colt Commercial Model 1911 A1
Same as Government Model 1911 except it has same modifications as the Government Model 1911 A1. Made from 1925 to 1970.
Estimated Value: Excellent: $450.00
                  Very good: $350.00

Colt Government Model 1911

Colt Government Model 1911 A1

Colt Junior Pocket Model 0-6

Colt Junior Pocket Model 0-6
Caliber: 22 short, 25 ACP
Action: Semi-automatic; exposed round spur hammer
Magazine: 6-shot clip
Barrel: 2⅛"
Sights: Fixed
Finish: Blued; checkered walnut grips
Length Overall: 4½"
Approximate wt.: 13 to 14 oz.
Comments: Made in Spain by Astra (Uneta Y Compania, Guernice, Spain) for Colt as a replacement for the Model N which was discontinued in 1941. Imported from about 1957 to 1968. Colt advertised in 1984 that many of these guns made between 1957 and 1973 were unsafe due to the firing mechanism. Colt offered to modify the pistol free and advised owners of non-modified pistols to carry the pistol with an empty chamber.
Estimated Value: Excellent: $220.00
                  Very good: $175.00

Colt 1911 (North American Arms Co.)

Same general specifications as 1911 Colt except made by North American Arms Co., in World War I period. About 100 made; company marking and serial number on slide.

Estimated Value: Excellent: $6,000.00
                   Very good: $5,000.00

Colt 1911 (Remington UMC)

Colt Super 38

Same as Colt Commercial Model 1911 A1 except: caliber is 38 Super ACP; magazine is 9-shot clip. Made from about 1928 to 1970.

Estimated Value: Excellent: $500.00
                   Very good: $400.00

Colt Super 38 Match

Same as Colt Super except: adjustable rear sight; hand-honed action; match grade barrel. Made from about 1932 to 1940.

Estimated Value: Excellent: $800.00
                   Very good: $640.00

Colt National Match

Same as Colt Commercial Model 1911 A1 except: adjustable rear sight; hand-honed action; match grade barrel. Made from about 1932 to 1940.

Estimated Value: Excellent: $690.00
                   Very good: $550.00

Colt Service Model Ace

Similar to Colt National Match except: 22 caliber long rifle; 10-shot clip; weighs about 42 oz. It has a "floating chamber" that makes the recoil much greater than normal 22 caliber. Made from 1938 to mid 1940's. See Colt Ace (current).

Estimated Value: Excellent: $1,000.00
                   Very good: $ 800.00

Colt 1911 Springfield Armory N.R.A.

Same general specifications as 1911 Colt except approximately 200 were made prior to World War I and sold through the Director of Civilian Marksmanship and have N.R.A. markings on frame.

Estimated Value: Excellent: $3,000.00
                   Very good: $2,500.00

Colt 1911 (Springfield Armory)

Same general specifications as 1911 Colt except approximately 26,000 were produced. Eagle motif and flaming bomb on frame and slide. Made in World War I period.

Estimated Value: Excellent: $650.00
                   Very good: $500.00

Colt 1911 (Remington UMC)

Same general specifications as 1911 Colt except approximately 22,000 were produced in World War I period. Inspector stamps B or E.

Estimated Value: Excellent: $600.00
                   Very good: $450.00

Colt 1911 A1 (Singer Manufacturing Co.)

Same general specifications as 1911 A1 Colt except approximately 500 made; blued finished, slide marked S.M. Co., JKC inspector marking.

Estimated Value: Excellent: $3,200.00
                   Very good: $2,600.00

Colt 1911 A1 pistols were also produced during WWII by Union Switch & Signal Company, Remington Rand, Inc., and Ithaca Gun Company, Inc. Generally the estimated values of these pistols are about the same as the 1911 A1 pistol produced by Colt.

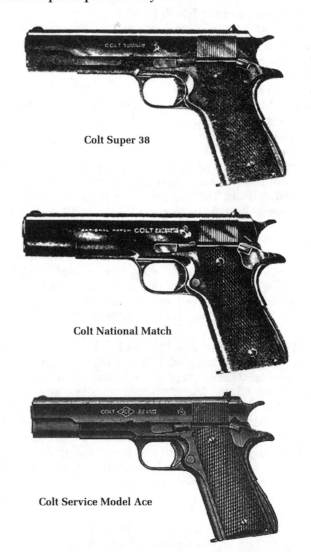

Colt Super 38

Colt National Match

Colt Service Model Ace

Colt Gold Cup National Match

Same as Colt Commercial Model 1911 A1 except: hand fitted slide; enlarged ejection port; adjustable rear sight; adjustable trigger stop; new bushing design; checkered walnut grips; match grade barrel; flat grip below safety like model 1911. Made from about 1957 to 1970.

Estimated Value: Excellent: $525.00
Very good: $420.00

Colt Gold Cup National Match III

Similar to Colt Gold Cup National Match except chambered for 38 Special mid-range wad cutter only. Operates with fixed barrel rather than locked breech. Made from 1960 to 1974.

Estimated Value: Excellent: $550.00
Very good: $450.00

Colt Gold Cup MK IV National Match (Series 70)

Caliber: 38 Special Mid-Range, 45 ACP
Action: Semi-automatic; exposed spur hammer
Magazine: 9-shot clip in 38; 7-shot in 45
Barrel: 5"
Sights: Adjustable rear for wind and elevation
Finish: Blued; checkered walnut grips with gold medallion
Length Overall: 8¾"
Approximate wt.: 39 oz.
Comments: Arched or flat housing below grip safety. Adjustable trigger stop, hand-fitted slide, and improved barrel bushing. Made from about 1970 to mid 1980's.

Estimated Value: Excellent: $475.00
Very good: $380.00

**Colt Gold Cup National Match
MK IV Series 80**

Colt Gold Cup National Match MK IV/Series 80

Similar to the Gold Cup MK IV National Match (Series 70) with internal improvements. Introduced in 1983; 45 caliber only; stainless steel model introduced in 1985. Add 8% for stainless steel; 14% for polished stainless steel.

Estimated Value: New (retail): $937.00
Excellent: $750.00
Very good: $600.00

**Colt Government
Model MK IV/Series 70**

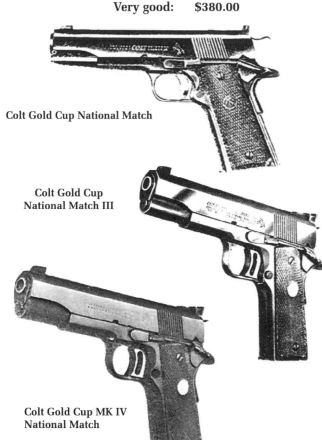

Colt Gold Cup National Match

**Colt Gold Cup
National Match III**

**Colt Gold Cup MK IV
National Match**

Colt Government Model MK IV / Series 70

Caliber: 9mm Parabellum, 38 Super ACP, 45 ACP
Action: Semi-automatic; exposed spur hammer
Magazine: 9-shot clip in 9mm & 38; 7-shot in 45
Barrel: 5"
Sights: Fixed
Finish: Blued or nickel; smooth or checkered walnut grips
Length Overall: 8½"
Approximate wt.: 38 to 39 oz.
Comments: Made from about 1970 to mid 1980's. Add $15.00 for 38 Super; $5.00 for 9mm; $25.00 for nickel finish.

Estimated Value: Excellent: $375.00
Very good: $300.00

Colt Government Model MK IV/Series 80

Similar to the MK IV Series 70 with internal improvements. Introduced in 1983. Calibers 9mm., 38 Super, & 45ACP; Add 8% for nickel finish (discontinued); add 8% for stainless steel; 17% for polished stainless steel; 45ACP and 38 Super Cals. only after 1995.

Estimated Value: New (retail): $735.00
Excellent: $550.00
Very good: $440.00

Colt Combat Government Model/80

Similar to the Government MK IV/Series 80 with undercut front sight, outline rear sight, Colt Pachmayr grips and other slight variations. Produced 1984 to 1987.

Estimated Value: **Excellent:**   **$500.00**
                        Very good: **$400.00**

Colt 380 Government MK IV Series 80

A "scaled down" version of the Colt Government Model MK IV Series 80 in 380ACP caliber; with round spur hammer; 3¼" barrel, weighs 21¾ oz., overall length 6⅛". Introduced in 1984. Add 7% for stainless steel; add 14% for nickel.

Estimated Value: **New (retail):**   **$462.00**
                        Excellent: **$345.00**
                        Very good: **$275.00**

Colt 380 Government
MK IV Series 80

Colt 380 Government
Pocketlite

Colt 380 Government Pocketlite

Similar to the 380 Government Model, MK IV Series 80 with alloy receiver. Weighs 15 oz. Add 7% for stainless steel.

Estimated Value: **New (retail):**   **$462.00**
                        Excellent: **$345.00**
                        Very good: **$275.00**

Colt MK IV Series 80 Officer's ACP

Caliber: 45 ACP
Action: Semi-automatic; exposed round spur hammer
Magazine: 6-shot clip
Barrel: 3½"
Sights: Fixed with dovetail rear
Finish: Non-glare matte blue; blue or stainless steel (1986); checkered wood grips; polished stainless steel (1988)
Length Overall: 7¼"
Approximate wt.: 24 oz. (lightweight); 34 oz. (steel)
Comments: A compact 45 ACP pistol about 1¼" shorter than the regular Colt Government models. Available in lightweight aluminum alloy or steel models. Add 8% for stainless steel. Add 15% for polished stainless steel.

Estimated Value: **New (retail):**   **$735.00**
                        Excellent: **$550.00**
                        Very good: **$440.00**

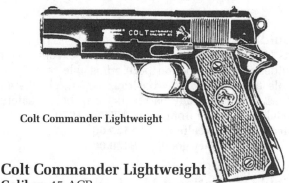

Colt Commander Lightweight

Colt Commander Lightweight

Caliber: 45 ACP
Action: Semi-automatic; exposed round spur hammer
Magazine: 7-shot clip
Barrel: 4¼"
Sights: Fixed
Finish: Blued; checkered or smooth walnut grips
Length Overall: 7¾"
Approximate wt.: 27 oz.
Comments: Same design as Gov. 1911 A1 model except shorter and lighter; rounded hammer. Aluminum alloy receiver and frame. Made from 1949 to mid 1980's. An all-steel model was introduced in 1971 known as Combat Commander.

Estimated Value: **Excellent:**   **$350.00**
                        Very good: **$280.00**

Colt Combat Commander LW MK IV Series 80

Similar to the Lightweight Commander with internal improvements. Introduced in 1983. Caliber 45ACP; blued.

Estimated Value: **New (retail):**   **$735.00**
                        Excellent: **$550.00**
                        Very good: **$440.00**

Colt Combat Commander

Colt Combat Commander

Caliber: 9mm Parabellum, 38 Super ACP, 45 ACP
Action: Semi-automatic; exposed round hammer
Magazine: 9-shot clip in 9mm and 38 Super; 7-shot clip in 45 ACP
Barrel: 4¼"
Sights: Fixed
Finish: Blued or nickel (in 45 caliber only); checkered walnut grips
Length Overall: 7⅞"
Approximate wt.: 37 oz.
Comments: Same design as Government 1911 A1 model except: shorter and lighter; rounded hammer; made from about 1971 to mid 1980's with all steel frame and flat or arched mainspring housing. Add $5.00 for 9mm; $20.00 for nickel finish.

Estimated Value: **Excellent:**   **$400.00**
                        Very good: **$320.00**

**Colt Combat Commander
MK IV Series 80**

Colt Combat Commander MK IV Series 80

Similar to the Combat Commander with internal improvements; introduced in 1983. Calibers 9mm, 38 Super, & 45ACP; add 8% for nickel finish; add 8% for stainless steel finish (introduced in 1990). 9mm dropped in 1995.

Estimated Value: New (retail): $735.00
                   Excellent: $550.00
                   Very good: $440.00

Colt 1991 A1 MK IV Series 80

Colt 1991 A1 MK IV Series 80

Caliber: 45 ACP
Action: Semi-automatic; exposed spur or round spur hammer; single action
Magazine: 7-shot clip (5 & 4½" barrel models); 6-shot clip (3½" compact model)
Barrel: 3½" (compact model); 4½" (combat model); 5" (regular model)
Sights: Hi profile; fixed
Finish: Parkerized matte; stainless steel matte (1994); black composition grips
Length Overall: 7¼", 7¾", & 8½"
Approximate wt.: 34, 36, & 38 oz.
Comments: A modern version of the 1911 GI service 45 in three sizes; regular model introduced in 1991; combat and compact models introduced in 1994. Add 10% for stainless steel.
Estimated Value: New (retail): $538.00
                       Excellent: $400.00
                       Very good: $320.00

Colt MK IV Series 80 Mustang 380

Caliber: 380 ACP
Action: Semi-automatic; exposed round spur hammer
Magazine: 5-shot clip
Barrel: 2¾"
Sights: Fixed, with dovetail rear
Finish: Blued; nickel, electroless nickel or stainless steel; composition grips
Length Overall: 5½"
Approximate wt.: 18½ oz.
Comments: A small, compact pistol introduced in 1986. Add 12% for nickel and 7% for electroless nickel. Add 7% for stainless steel.
Estimated Value: New (retail): $462.00
                       Excellent: $345.00
                       Very good: $275.00

Colt MK IV Series 80 Mustang Plus II

Similar to the Mustang 380 but combines the full grip length of the Colt Government Model with the shorter compact barrel and slide of the Mustang. Introduced in 1988. Add 7% for stainless steel (added in 1990).
Estimated Value: New (retail): $462.00
                       Excellent: $345.00
                       Very good: $275.00

Colt MK IV Series 80 Mustang Pocketlite

Similar to the MK IV Series 80 Mustang 380 with an alloy receiver; weighs 12½ oz. Introduced in 1988. Add 7% for stainless steel or nickel.
Estimated Value: New (retail): $462.00
                       Excellent: $345.00
                       Very good: $275.00

Colt MK IV Series 80 Mustang 380

Colt MK IV Series 80 Mustang Plus II

Colt Delta Elite

Colt Delta Elite, MK IV Series 80
Caliber: 10mm
Action: Semi-automatic; exposed round hammer; long trigger
Magazine: 7-shot clip
Barrel: 5"
Sights: Fixed, white dot
Finish: Blued; black Neoprene "pebbled" wrap-around combat-style grips with Colt Delta medallion; stainless steel available late 1980's
Length Overall: 8½"
Approximate wt.: 38 oz.
Comments: Redesigned and re-engineered Colt Government for the 10mm cartridge. Introduced in 1987. Add 8% for stainless steel; 28% for Gold Cup model.
Estimated Value: New (retail): $807.00
Excellent: $605.00
Very good: $485.00

Colt Double Eagle Series 90
Caliber: 45ACP, 10mm, 9mm; 38 Super (added in 1992)
Action: Double action semi-automatic with exposed combat style rounded hammer. A decocking lever allows the hammer to be decocked with a round in the chamber without using the trigger. The firing pin remains locked during this sequence.
Magazine: 8-shot clip
Barrel: 5"
Sights: Fixed, white dot; adjustable sights available
Finish: Matte stainless steel; checkered Xenoy grips.
Length Overall: 8½"
Approximate wt.: 39 oz.
Comments: Introduced in 1990. Add 3% for 10mm; add 4% for adjustable sights. 45ACP only after 1995.
Estimated Value: New (retail): $727.00
Excellent: $545.00
Very good: $435.00

Colt Double Eagle Officer's Model
Similar to the Double Eagle with 3½" barrel, stainless steel or blued finish.
Estimated Value: New (retail): $727.00
Excellent: $545.00
Very good: $435.00

Colt Double Eagle Combat Commander
Similar to the Double Eagle in 45ACP or 40 S&W caliber; 4¼" barrel.
Estimated Value: New (retail): $727.00
Excellent: $545.00
Very good: $435.00

Colt Combat Elite
Caliber: 45ACP; 38 Super (added in 1993)
Action: Semi-automatic; exposed round combat hammer
Magazine: 7-shot clip
Barrel: 5"
Sights: Fixed, white dot sights
Finish: Matte stainless steel receiver with blue carbon steel slide & internal working parts; black Neoprene "pebbled" wrap-around combat-style grips
Length Overall: 8½"
Approximate wt.: 38 oz.
Comments: Introduced in 1990; designed for combat-style match shooters.
Estimated Value: New (retail): $895.00
Excellent: $670.00
Very good: $540.00

Colt Combat Elite

Colt Double Eagle Series 90

Colt Double Eagle Officer's Model

Colt Ace Target

Caliber: 22 long rifle
Action: Semi-automatic
Magazine: 10-shot clip
Barrel: 4¾"
Sights: Adjustable rear sight
Finish: Blued; checkered walnut or plastic grips
Length Overall: 8¼"
Approximate wt.: 38 oz.
Comments: Similar in appearance to the 1911 A1 with same safety features. Made from about 1931 to 1941.
Estimated Value: Excellent: $850.00
                       Very good: $675.00

Colt Ace Target

Colt Ace (Later)

Caliber: 22 long rifle
Action: Semi-automatic; exposed spur hammer
Magazine: 10-shot clip
Barrel: 5"
Sights: Fixed rear, ramp-style front
Finish: Blued; checkered walnut grips
Length Overall: 8⅜"
Approximate wt.: 42 oz.
Comments: A full-size automatic similar to the Colt Government MK IV/Series in 22 long rifle. Produced from 1979 to mid 1980's. Also see Colt Service Model Ace.
Estimated Value: Excellent: $400.00
                       Very good: $320.00

Colt Woodsman Sport Model
(1st Issue)

Colt Woodsman Sport Model (1st Issue)

Caliber: 22 long rifle
Action: Semi-automatic; concealed hammer
Magazine: 10-shot clip
Barrel: 4½" tapered barrel
Sights: Adjustable
Finish: Blued; checkered walnut grips
Length Overall: 8½"
Approximate wt.: 27 oz.
Comments: Same as Colt Woodsman Target Model (2nd Issue) except shorter. Made from about 1933 to late 1940's.
Estimated Value: Excellent: $400.00
                       Very good: $320.00

Colt Woodsman Target Model (1st Issue)

Caliber: 22 long rifle (regular velocity)
Action: Semi-automatic; concealed hammer
Magazine: 10-shot clip
Barrel: 6½"
Sights: Adjustable
Finish: Blued; checkered walnut grips
Length Overall: 10½"
Approximate wt.: 28 oz.
Comments: This model was not strong enough for Hi-speed cartridges, until a strong heat treated housing was produced about serial number 83790. Thumb safety only. Made from about 1915 to 1932.
Estimated Value: Excellent: $390.00
                       Very good: $310.00

Colt Woodsman Target Model
(1st Issue)

Colt Woodsman Target Model (2nd Issue)

Same as Colt Woodsman Target Model 1st Issue except heavier tapered barrel and stronger housing for using either the 22 long rifle regular or Hi-speed cartridges. Made from about 1932 to 1945. Approximate wt. is 29 oz.

Estimated Value: Excellent: $425.00
Very good: $350.00

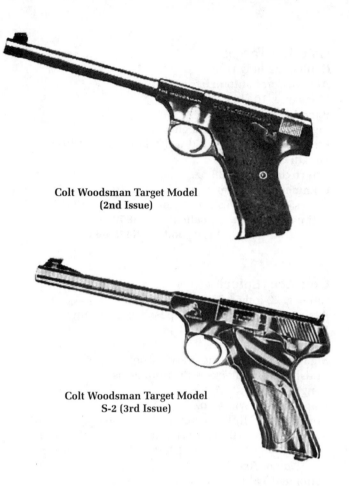

**Colt Woodsman Target Model
(2nd Issue)**

Colt Woodsman Target Model S-2 (3rd Issue)

Same as Colt Woodsman Target Model (2nd Issue) except longer grips with thumb rest, larger thumb safety; slide stop; magazine disconnector; slide stays open when magazine is empty; checkered walnut or plastic grips. Approximate wt. is 32 oz. Made from 1948 to late 1970's.

Estimated Value: Excellent: $350.00
Very good: $280.00

**Colt Woodsman Target Model
S-2 (3rd Issue)**

Colt Woodsman Sport Model S-1 (2nd Issue)

Same as Colt Woodsman Target Model S-2 (3rd Issue) except 4½" barrel, 9" overall length; approximate weight is 30 oz. Made from about 1948 to late 1970's.

Estimated Value: Excellent: $320.00
Very good: $255.00

Colt Model S-4 Targetsman

Similar to Colt Woodsman Target Model (3rd Issue) except cheaper made adjustable rear sight and lacks automatic slide stop. Made from about 1959 to late 1970's.

Estimated Value: Excellent: $250.00
Very good: $200.00

Colt 22 Semi-Auto

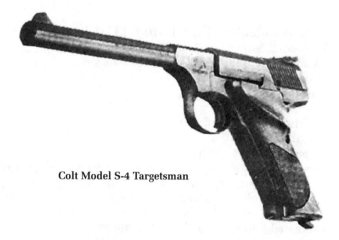

**Colt Woodsman Sport Model S-1
(2nd Issue)**

Colt 22 Semi-Auto

Caliber: 22 long rifle
Action: Semi-automatic; concealed hammer; factory adjusted trigger travel on target model
Magazine: 10-shot clip
Barrel: 4½" or 6" (target model); bull barrel with ventilated sighting rib; counter bored at muzzle; elevated scope mount on target model
Sights: Fixed; adjustable rear and removable front on target model
Finish: Matte stainless steel; black composite monogrip
Length Overall: 8⅝" or 10⅝"
Approximate wt.: 33½ oz. to 40½ oz.
Comments: Introduced in the mid 1990's; add 50% for target model (adjustable trigger travel, 6" bull barrel, adjustable sights, target ventilated rib and scope mount rail).

Estimated Value: New (retail): $248.00
Excellent: $185.00
Very good: $150.00

Colt Model S-4 Targetsman

Colt Woodsman Match Target (1st Issue)
Caliber: 22 long rifle
Action: Semi-automatic; concealed hammer
Magazine: 10-shot clip
Barrel: 6½"; slightly tapered with flat sides
Sights: Adjustable rear
Finish: Blued; checkered walnut, one-piece grip with extended sides
Length Overall: 11"
Approximate wt.: 36 oz.
Comments: Made from about 1938 to 1942.
Estimated Value: Excellent: $600.00
Very good: $475.00

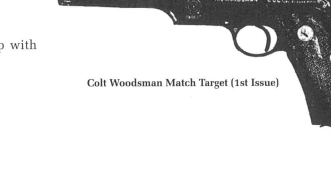
Colt Woodsman Match Target (1st Issue)

Colt Woodsman
Match Target Model S-3

Colt Woodsman Match Target Model S-3
Caliber: 22 long rifle
Action: Semi-automatic; concealed hammer
Magazine: 10-shot clip
Barrel: 4½", 6"
Sights: Adjustable rear
Finish: Blued; checkered walnut grips with thumb rest
Length Overall: 9", 10½"
Approximate wt.: 36 to 39 oz.
Comments: Made from about 1948 to late 1970's. Flat sided weight added to full-length of barrel. It has a slide stop and magazine safety.
Estimated Value: Excellent: $350.00
Very good: $290.00

Colt Huntsman Model S-5
Caliber: 22 long rifle
Action: Semi-automatic; concealed hammer
Magazine: 10-shot clip
Barrel: 4½", 6"
Sights: Fixed
Finish: Blued; checkered walnut grips
Length Overall: 9", 10½"
Approximate wt.: 31 to 32 oz.
Comments: Made from about 1955 to 1970's.
Estimated Value: Excellent: $260.00
Very good: $210.00

Colt Challenger Model
Caliber: 22 long rifle
Action: Semi-automatic; concealed hammer
Magazine: 10-shot clip
Barrel: 4½", 6"
Sights: Fixed
Finish: Blued; checkered plastic grips
Length Overall: 9", 10½"
Approximate wt.: 30 to 32 oz. (depending on length)
Comments: Same basic design as Colt Woodsman Target Model (3rd Issue) except slide doesn't stay open when magazine is empty; no magazine safety. Made from about 1950 to 1955.
Estimated Value: Excellent: $250.00
Very good: $200.00

Colt Challenger Model

Colt Huntsman Model S-5

Colt Lightning Model

Caliber: 38 centerfire, 41 centerfire
Action: Single or double action
Cylinder: 6-shot; ⅔ fluted; side load; loading gate
Barrel: 2½", 3½", 4½", 6"
Sights: Fixed
Finish: Blued or nickel; hard rubber birds-head grips
Length Overall: 7½" to 11"
Approximate wt.: 26 to 30 oz.
Comments: Made from about 1877 to 1912 with and without side rod ejector. This was the first double action revolver made by Colt.
Estimated Value: Excellent: $700.00
                      Very good: $575.00

Colt Double Action Philippine Model

Same as Colt Double Action Army Model except larger trigger guard and trigger. It was made originally for the Army in Alaska but was sent to the Philippines instead.
Estimated Value: Excellent: $700.00
                      Very good: $560.00

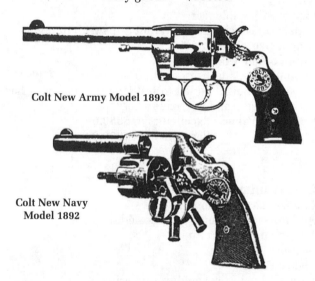

Colt New Army Model 1892

Colt New Navy
Model 1892

Colt New Army Model 1892

Caliber: 38 Colt short & long, 41 Colt short & long, 38 Special added in 1904, 32-30 added in 1905
Action: Single or double action
Cylinder: 6-shot; ⅔ fluted; swing out; simultaneous hand ejector
Barrel: 3", 4½", 6"
Sights: Fixed
Finish: Blued or nickel; hard rubber or walnut grips
Length Overall: 8¼" to 11¼"
Approximate wt.: 29 to 32 oz.
Comments: Made from 1892 to 1908. Lanyard swivel attached to butt in 1901. All calibers on 41 caliber frame.
Estimated Value: Excellent: $500.00
                      Very good: $400.00

Colt New Navy Model 1892

Similar to Colt New Army Model 1892 except has double cylinder notches and locking bolt. Sometimes called New Army 2nd issue.
Estimated Value: Excellent: $550.00
                      Very good: $440.00

Colt Double Action Army Model

Caliber: 38-40, 44-40, 45 Colt
Action: Single or double action
Cylinder: 6-shot; ⅔ fluted; side load
Barrel: 3½" and 4" without side rod ejector; 4¾", 5½" and 7½" with the side rod ejector
Sights: Fixed
Finish: Blued or nickel; hard rubber or checkered walnut grips
Length Overall: 8½" to 12½"
Approximate wt.: 35 to 39 oz.
Comments: Made from about 1877 to 1910. Lanyard loop in butt; also called "Double Action Frontier."
Estimated Value: Excellent: $675.00
                      Very good: $540.00

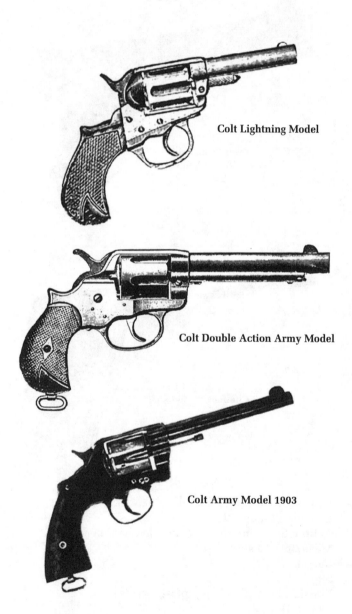

Colt Lightning Model

Colt Double Action Army Model

Colt Army Model 1903

Colt Army Model 1903

Same as Colt New Army Model 1892 except modified grip design (smaller and shaped better); bore is slightly smaller in each caliber to increase accuracy.
Estimated Value: Excellent: $575.00
                      Very good: $460.00

Colt New Pocket

Caliber: 32 short & long Colt
Action: Single or double action
Cylinder: 6-shot; swing out; simultaneous ejector
Barrel: 2½", 3½", 6"
Sights: Fixed
Finish: Blued or nickel; hard rubber grips
Length Overall: 6½" to 10½"
Approximate wt.: 15 to 18 oz.
Comments: Made from about 1895 to 1905.
Estimated Value: Excellent: $325.00
                       Very good: $260.00

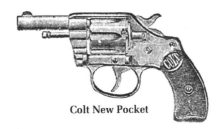

Colt New Pocket

Colt Pocket Positive

Similar to the New Pocket with the positive locking system of the Police Positive; 32 short and long S&W cartridges or 32 Colt Police Positive. Made from the early 1900's to just prior to World War II.
Estimated Value: Excellent: $300.00
                       Very good: $240.00

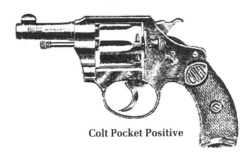

Colt Pocket Positive

Colt New Police

Caliber: 32 Colt short & long, 32 Colt New Police (S&W long)
Action: Single or double action
Cylinder: 6-shot; swing out; simultaneous ejector
Barrel: 2½", 4", 6"
Sights: Fixed
Finish: Blued or nickel; hard rubber grips
Length Overall: 6½" to 10½"
Approximate wt.: 16 to 18 oz.
Comments: Built on same frame as New Pocket except larger grips. Made from about 1896 to 1905.
Estimated Value: Excellent: $350.00
                       Very good: $290.00

Colt New Police

Colt New Police Target

Same as Colt New Police except: 6" barrel only; blued finish and target sights. This is a target version of the New Police Model, made from 1896 to 1905.
Estimated Value: Excellent: $425.00
                       Very good: $350.00

Colt Bisley Model

Caliber: 32 long centerfire, 32-20 WCF, 38 long Colt CF, 38-40 WCF, 41 long Colt CF, 44 S&W Russian, 44-40 WCF, 45 Colt, 455 Eley
Action: Single action
Cylinder: 6-shot; half flute; side load
Barrel: 4¾", 5½", 7½" with side rod ejector
Sights: Fixed
Finish: Blued with case-hardened frame and hammer; checkered hard rubber grips
Length Overall: 10¼" to 13"
Approximate wt.: 36 to 40 oz.
Comments: Developed from the original Single Action Army Revolver by changing the trigger, hammer and grips. Made from 1897 to 1912.
Estimated Value: Excellent: $700.00
                       Very good: $560.00

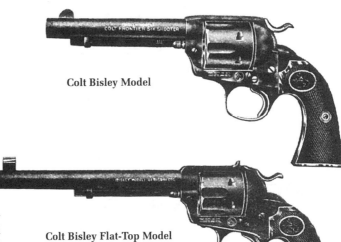

Colt Bisley Model

Colt Bisley Flat-Top Model

Colt Bisley Flat-Top Model

Similar to Colt Bisley Model except frame over the cylinder has a flat top; the longer barrel models were referred to as target models; wood and ivory grips as well as hard rubber; target adjustable sights or regular fixed sights. Short barrel models sometimes referred to as the Pocket Bisley. It usually had fixed sights and no side rod ejector.
Estimated Value: Excellent: $1,000.00
                       Very good: $ 800.00

Colt New Service

Caliber: 38 special, 357 magnum (introduced about 1936), 38-40, 44-40, 44 Russian, 44 Special, 45 ACP, 45 Colt, 450 Eley, 455 Eley and 476 Eley
Action: Single or double action
Cylinder: 6-shot; swing out; simultaneous ejector
Barrel: 4", 5", 6" in 357 and 38 Special; 4½", 5½", 7½" in other calibers; 4½" in 45 ACP (Model 1917 Revolver made for U.S. government during World War II)
Sights: Fixed
Finish: Blued or nickel; checkered walnut grips
Length Overall: 9¼" to 12¾"
Approximate wt.: 39 to 44 oz.
Comments: Made from about 1898 to 1942. The above calibers were made sometime during this period.
Estimated Value: Excellent: $600.00
                        Very good: $475.00

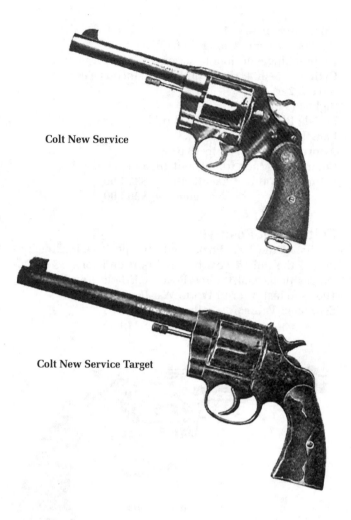

Colt New Service

Colt New Service Target

Colt New Service Target

Caliber: Originally made for 44 Russian, 450 Eley, 455 Eley and 476 Eley. Later calibers were made for 44 Special, 45 Colt and 45 ACP
Action: Single or double action
Cylinder: 6-shot; swing out; simultaneous ejector
Barrel: 6" and 7"
Sights: Adjustable target sights
Finish: Blued; checkered walnut grips
Length Overall: 11¼" to 12¾"
Approximate wt.: 40 to 42 oz.
Comments: A target version of the New Service revolver with hand-finished action. Made from about 1900 to 1939.
Estimated Value: Excellent: $900.00
                        Very good: $750.00

Colt Police Positive

Colt Police Positive

Caliber: 32 short and long Colt (discontinued in 1915), 32 Colt New Police (32 S&W long), 38 New Police (38 S&W long)
Action: Single or double action
Cylinder: 6-shot; swing out; simultaneous ejector
Barrel: 2½", 4", 5", and 6"
Sights: Fixed
Finish: Blued or nickel; hard rubber or checkered walnut grips
Length Overall: 6½" to 10½"
Approximate wt.: 18 to 22 oz.
Comments: This is an improved version of the New Police with the Positive Lock feature which prevents the firing pin from contacting the cartridge until the trigger is pulled. Made from 1905 to 1943.
Estimated Value: Excellent: $300.00
                        Very good: $250.00

Colt Police Positive Target

Colt Police Positive Target

Same as Colt Police Positive except 22 caliber long rifle from 1910 to 1932 and 22 long rifle regular or hi-speed after 1932, 22 Winchester rim fire from 1910 to 1935; blued finish; 6" barrel only; adjustable target sights; checkered walnut grips. Approximate wt. is 22 to 26 oz.
Estimated Value: Excellent: $400.00
                        Very good: $320.00

Colt Marine Corps Model 1905

Colt Marine Corps Model 1905
Caliber: 38 Colt short and long
Action: Single or double action
Cylinder: 6-shot; ⅔ fluted; swing out; simultaneous hand ejector
Barrel: 6"
Sights: Fixed
Finish: Blued or nickel; hard rubber or walnut grips
Length Overall: 10½"
Approximate wt.: 32 oz.
Comments: Made from 1905 to 1908. Lanyard ring in butt; grip is smaller and more rounded at the butt than the Army or Navy Models. Sometimes called Model 1907.
Estimated Value: Excellent: $750.00
                       Very good: $570.00

Colt Police Positive Special
Caliber: 32-20 (discontinued in 1942), 32 New Police (S&W long), 38 Special
Action: Single or double action
Cylinder: 6-shot; swing out; simultaneous ejector
Barrel: 4", 5", 6"
Sights: Fixed
Finish: Blued or nickel; checkered rubber, plastic or walnut grips
Length Overall: 8¾" to 10¾"
Approximate wt.: 23 to 28 oz.
Comments: Made from about 1907 to 1970's.
Estimated Value: Excellent: $275.00
                       Very good: $220.00

Colt Police Positive Special

**Colt Officers Model Target
(1st Issue)**

Colt Officers Model Target (1st Issue)
Caliber: 38 special
Action: Single or double action
Cylinder: 6-shot; ⅔ fluted; swing out; simultaneous ejector
Barrel: 6"
Sights: Adjustable
Finish: Blued; checkered walnut grips
Length Overall: 10½"
Approximate wt.: 34 oz.
Comments: Hand-finished action. Made from about 1904 to 1908.
Estimated Value: Excellent: $475.00
                       Very good: $380.00

Colt Camp Perry (1st Issue)
Caliber: 22 short, long, long rifle
Action: Single
Cylinder: 1-shot; swing-out flat steel block instead of cylinder with rod ejector
Barrel: 10"
Sights: Adjustable front for elevation & adjustable rear for windage
Finish: Blued; checkered walnut grips with medallion
Length Overall: 14"
Approximate wt.: 35 oz.
Comments: Built on Officers Model frame. Made from about 1926 to 1934.
Estimated Value: Excellent: $800.00
                       Very good: $640.00

**Colt Camp Perry
(2nd Issue)**

Colt Camp Perry (2nd Issue)
Same as 1st Issue except: 8" barrel (heavier); shorter hammer fall; overall length 12"; approximate wt. 34 oz., chamber is recessed for cartridge head to make it safe to use 22 long rifle Hi-Speed cartridges. Made from about 1934 to 1941.
Estimated Value: Excellent: $850.00
                       Very good: $680.00

Colt New Service Model 1909

Caliber: 32-20, 38 Special, 38-40, 42 Colt short & long, 44 Russian, 44-40, 45 Colt
Action: Single or double action
Cylinder: 6-shot; ⅔ fluted; swing out; simultaneous hand ejector
Barrel: 4", 4½", 5", 6"
Sights: Fixed
Finish: Blued or nickel; hard rubber or walnut grips
Length Overall: 9¼" to 11¼"
Approximate wt.: 32 to 34 oz.
Comments: Made from 1909 to 1928. Adopted by U.S. armed forces from 1909 to 1911 (Automatic became standard sidearm). Also called "Army Special."

Estimated Value:		
	Excellent:	$400.00
	Very good:	$320.00

Colt New Service Model 1909

Colt Officers Model Target
(2nd Issue)

Colt Army Model 1917

Colt Army Model 1917

Caliber: 45 ACP or 45 ACP rim cartridges
Action: Single or double action
Cylinder: 6-shot; fluted; swing out; simultaneous hand ejector; used semi-circular clips to hold rimless case of 45 ACP
Barrel: 5½" round tapered
Sights: Fixed
Finish: Blued; oiled-finished walnut grips
Length Overall: 10¾"
Approximate wt.: 40 oz.
Comments: Made from about 1917 to 1928.

Estimated Value:		
	Excellent:	$450.00
	Very good:	$375.00

Colt Bankers Special

Caliber: 22 short, long, long rifle (Regular or Hi-Speed); 38 New Police (S&W long)
Action: Single or double action
Cylinder: 6-shot; swing out; simultaneous ejector
Barrel: 2"
Sights: Fixed
Finish: Blued; checkered walnut grips
Length Overall: 6½"
Approximate wt.: 19 to 23 oz.
Comments: Same as Police Positive except 2" barrel only & rounded grip after 1933. Made from about 1928 to 1940.

Estimated Value:	22 Cal.	38 Cal.
Excellent:	$800.00	$500.00
Very good:	$600.00	$375.00

Colt Officers Model Target (2nd Issue)

Caliber: 22 long rifle (regular) 1930-32; 22 long rifle (Hi-speed) 1932-49; 32 Police Positive 1932-42; 38 Special 1908-49
Action: Single or double action
Cylinder: 6-shot; ⅔ fluted; swing out; simultaneous hand ejector
Barrel: 6" in 22 caliber & 32 Police Positive; 4", 4½", 5", 6" & 7½" in 38 Special
Sights: Adjustable rear
Finish: Blued; checkered walnut grips
Length Overall: 9¼" to 12¾"
Approximate wt.: 32 to 40 oz.
Comments: Hand-finished action, tapered barrel. Made from about 1908 to 1949.

Estimated Value:		
	Excellent:	$375.00
	Very good:	$285.00

Colt Bankers Special

Colt Shooting Master

Caliber: 38 Special, 357 magnum (introduced in 1936), 44 Special, 45 ACP, 45 Colt
Action: Single or double action
Cylinder: 6-shot; swing out; simultaneous ejector
Barrel: 6"
Sights: Adjustable target sight
Finish: Blued; checkered walnut grips
Length Overall: 11¼"
Approximate wt.: 42 to 44 oz.
Comments: A deluxe target revolver based on the New Service revolver. Made from about 1932 to 1940.

Estimated Value: Excellent: $600.00
　　　　　　　　　Very good: $460.00

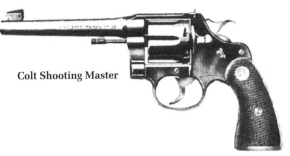

Colt Shooting Master

Colt Official Police (Model E-1)

Caliber: 22 long rifle (regular) introduced in 1930; 22 long rifle (Hi-Speed) introduced in 1932; 32-30 made from about 1928 to 1942; 38 Special made from 1928 to 1969; 41 long Colt made from 1928 to 1930
Action: Single or double action
Cylinder: 6-shot; fluted; swing out; simultaneous ejector
Barrel: 4" & 6" in 22 caliber; 4", 5" & 6" in 32-20; 2", 4", 5" & 6" in 41 caliber
Sights: Fixed
Finish: Blued or nickel; checkered walnut or plastic grips
Length Overall: 7¼" to 11¼"
Approximate wt.: 30 to 38 oz.
Comments: 41 caliber frame in all calibers. A refined version of the New Service Model 1909 which was discontinued in 1928. Made from about 1928 to 1970.

Estimated Value: Excellent: $300.00
　　　　　　　　　Very good: $225.00

Colt Commando

Similar to Colt Official Police (Model E-1) except made to government specifications in 38 Special only; sandblasted blue finish; produced for the government during WW II. Made from 1942 to 1945.

Estimated Value: Excellent: $325.00
　　　　　　　　　Very good: $245.00

Colt Detective Special

Colt Commando Special

Colt Detective Special

Caliber: 32 New Police (S&W long), 38 Special
Action: Single or double action
Cylinder: 6-shot; swing out; simultaneous ejector
Barrel: 2" & 3"
Sights: Fixed
Finish: Blued or nickel; checkered walnut grips with rounded or square butt
Length Overall: 6¾" to 7¾"
Approximate wt.: 21 oz.
Comments: Made from about 1926 to 1987. Available with or without hammer shroud. Add 10% for nickel finish.

Estimated Value: Excellent: $350.00
　　　　　　　　　Very good: $280.00

Colt Commando Special

Similar to the Detective Special with matte finish & rubber grips. Produced 1984 to 1987.

Estimated Value: Excellent: $260.00
　　　　　　　　　Very good: $210.00

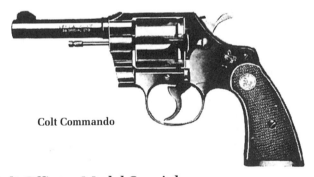

Colt Commando

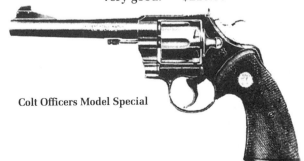

Colt Officers Model Special

Colt Officers Model Special

Caliber: 22 long rifle (regular & Hi-Speed); 38 Special
Action: Single or double action
Cylinder: 6-shot, ⅔ fluted; swing out; simultaneous ejector
Barrel: 6"
Sights: Adjustable for windage & elevation
Finish: Blued; checkered plastic grips
Length Overall: 11¼"
Approximate wt.: 42 oz. in 22 caliber, 38 oz. in 38 caliber
Comments: Replaced the Officers Model Target (2nd issue) as target arm; heavier non-tapered barrel & redesigned hammer. Made from 1949 to 1953.

Estimated Value: Excellent: $300.00
　　　　　　　　　Very good: $225.00

Colt Cobra Model D-3
Caliber: 22 S, L, LR; 32 New Police ; 38 Special
Action: Single or double action
Cylinder: 6-shot, ⅔ fluted; swing out; simultaneous ejector
Barrel: 2", 3", 4" & 5"
Sights: Fixed
Finish: Blued or nickel; checkered walnut grips
Length Overall: 6⅝" to 9⅝"
Approximate wt.: 16 to 22 oz.
Comments: Frame is made of a light alloy, but cylinder is steel. Made from 1950 to late 1970. Add 10% for nickel finish.
Estimated Value: Excellent: $260.00
                       Very good: $210.00

Colt Cobra Model D-3

Colt Agent Model D-4
Caliber: 38 Special
Action: Single or double action
Cylinder: 6-shot, swing out; simultaneous ejector
Barrel: 2"
Sights: Fixed
Finish: Blued; checkered walnut grips
Length Overall: 6¾"
Approximate wt.: 14 oz.
Comments: Frame made of lightweight alloy. Made from 1955 to late 1970's. Also available with hammer shroud.
Estimated Value: Excellent: $240.00
                       Very good: $195.00

Colt Agent Light Weight
Similar to the Detective Special with matte finish; 2" barrel; approx. wt. is 17 oz.; produced in the mid 1980's.
Estimated Value: Excellent: $250.00
                       Very good: $200.00

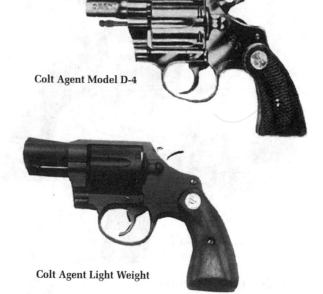

Colt Agent Model D-4

Colt Agent Light Weight

Colt Air Crewman Special
Caliber: 38 Special
Action: Single or double action
Cylinder: 6-shot, swing out; simultaneous ejector; aluminum alloy
Barrel: 2"
Sights: Fixed
Finish: Blued; checkered walnut grips
Length Overall: 6¾"
Approximate wt.: 14 oz.
Comments: A rare lightweight special revolver developed by Colt at the request of U.S. Air Force during the Korean War. They were recalled in 1960.
Estimated Value: Excellent: $1,000.00
                       Very good: $800.00

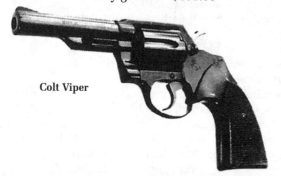

Colt Viper

Colt Viper
Caliber: 38 Special
Action: Single or double action
Cylinder: 6-shot, swing out
Barrel: 4"
Sights: Fixed rear, ramp front
Finish: Blued or nickel; checkered walnut wrap-around grips
Length Overall: 8⅝"
Approximate wt.: 20 oz.
Comments: Lightweight aluminum alloy frame, shrouded ejector rod. Made in the late 1970's. Add $20.00 for nickel model.
Estimated Value: Excellent: $235.00
                       Very good: $190.00

Colt Border Patrol
Caliber: 38 Special
Action: Single or double action
Cylinder: 6-shot, swing out; simultaneous ejector
Barrel: 4"
Sights: Fixed; Baughman quick draw front sight
Finish: Blued; checkered walnut grips
Length Overall: 8¾"
Approximate wt.: 34 oz.
Comments: In 1952 about 400 were produced for a branch of the U.S. Treasury Dept. The barrel is marked on the left side "Colt Border Patrol."
Estimated Value: Excellent: $1,200.00
                       Very good: $1,000.00

Colt Officers Model Match

Caliber: 22 long rifle, 38 Special
Action: Single or double action
Cylinder: 6-shot; swing out; simultaneous ejector; ⅔ fluted
Barrel: 6"
Sights: Adjustable for windage & elevation
Finish: Blued; checkered walnut grips
Length Overall: 11¼"
Approximate wt.: 22 caliber, 42 oz; 38 caliber, 38 oz.
Comments: Has heavy tapered barrel & wide hammer spur. Made from about 1953 to 1970.
Estimated Value: **Excellent:** $320.00
                 Very good: $240.00

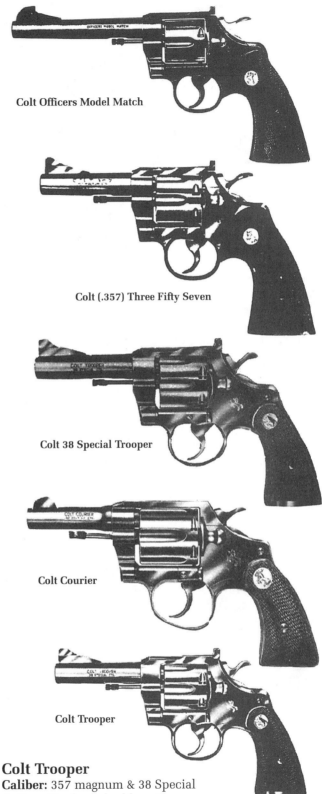

Colt Officers Model Match

Colt (.357) Three Fifty Seven

Colt 38 Special Trooper

Colt Courier

Colt Trooper

Colt (.357) Three Fifty Seven

Caliber: 357 magnum & 38 Special
Action: Single or double action
Cylinder: 6-shot; swing out; simultaneous ejector
Barrel: 4" & 6"
Sights: Adjustable rear sight
Finish: Blued; checkered walnut grips
Length Overall: 9¼" & 11¼"
Approximate wt.: 36 to 39 oz.
Comments: Made from about 1953 to 1962. It was replaced by Trooper Model.
Estimated Value: **Excellent:** $300.00
                 Very good: $240.00

Colt 38 Special Trooper

Caliber: 22, 38 Special
Action: Single or double action
Cylinder: 6-shot; swing out; simultaneous ejector;
Barrel: 4" & 6"
Sights: Adjustable rear & quick draw front
Finish: Blued or nickel; checkered walnut square butt grips
Length Overall: 9¼" & 11¼"
Approximate wt.: 36 to 43 oz.
Comments: Made from about 1953 to 1962.
Estimated Value: **Excellent:** $275.00
                 Very good: $210.00

Colt Courier

Caliber: 22 short, long, long rifle, 32 New Police (S&W long)
Action: Single or double action
Cylinder: 6-shot; swing out; simultaneous ejector; made of lightweight alloy
Barrel: 3"
Sights: Fixed
Finish: Dual tone blue; checkered plastic grips
Length Overall: 7½"
Approximate wt.: 14 to 20 oz.
Comments: Frame & cylinder made of lightweight alloy. Made in 1954 & 1955 only.
Estimated Value: **Excellent:** $725.00
                 Very good: $550.00

Colt Trooper

Caliber: 357 magnum & 38 Special
Action: Single or double action
Cylinder: 6-shot; swing out; simultaneous ejector
Barrel: 4" or 6"
Sights: Adjustable rear & quick draw front
Finish: Blued or nickel; checkered walnut, square butt grips
Length Overall: 9¼" to 11¼"
Approximate wt.: 34 to 38 oz.
Comments: Made from about 1953 to 1969.
Estimated Value: **Excellent:** $270.00
                 Very good: $215.00

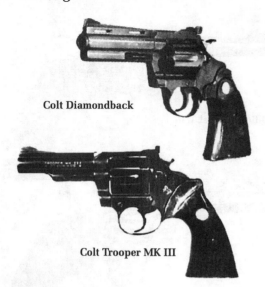

Colt Diamondback

Colt Trooper MK III

Colt Trooper MK III

Caliber: 357 magnum & 38 Special; 22 long rifle & 22 WMR added in 1979

Action: Single or double action

Cylinder: 6-shot; swing out; simultaneous ejector

Barrel: 4", 6", 8" in 1980

Sights: Adjustable rear

Finish: Blued or nickel; checkered walnut grips; non-glare electroless plating available after 1981 (Colt-guard)

Length Overall: 9½", 11¼" & 13½"

Approximate wt.: 39 to 42 oz.

Comments: Made from about 1969 to mid 1980's; wide target-type trigger & hammer. Add $20.00 for nickel; $7.00 for 8" barrel.

Estimated Value: Excellent: $280.00
**   Very good: $225.00**

Colt Trooper MK V

Colt Trooper MK V

Caliber: 357 magnum & 38 Special

Action: Single or double action; exposed hammer

Cylinder: 6-shot; swing out; simultaneous ejector

Barrel: 4" or 6" ventilated rib

Sights: Red insert front, adjustable rear

Finish: Blued, nickel or non-glare electroless plating (Colt-guard); checkered walnut grips

Length Overall: 9½" to 11½"

Approximate wt.: 39 to 45 oz.

Comments: A medium frame revolver with inner & outer improvements on the Trooper MK III. Produced 1982 to 1987. Add 9% for nickel finish.

Estimated Value: Excellent: $290.00
**   Very good: $230.00**

Colt Diamondback

Caliber: 22, 22 long rifle, 38 Special

Action: Single or double

Cylinder: 6-shot; swing out; simultaneous ejector

Barrel: 2½", 4", 6" ventilated rib; 2½" dropped in late 1970's

Sights: Adjustable rear

Finish: Blued or nickel; checkered walnut square butt grips

Length Overall: 7½", 9"

Approximate wt.: 26 to 32 oz.

Comments: Made from 1967 to 1987. Add 10% for nickel finish.

Estimated Value: Excellent: $375.00
**   Very good: $300.00**

Colt Lawman MK III

Colt Lawman MK III

Caliber: 357 magnum & 38 Special

Action: Single or double action

Cylinder: 6-shot; swing out; simultaneous ejector

Barrel: 2" or 4"

Sights: Fixed

Finish: Blued or nickel; checkered walnut grips; non-glare electroless plating available after 1981 (Colt-guard)

Length Overall: 7¼", 9¼"

Approximate wt.: 36 to 39 oz.

Comments: Made in 1970's & early 1980's. Add 10% for nickel.

Estimated Value: Excellent: $250.00
**   Very good: $200.00**

Colt Lawman MK V

Colt Lawman MK V

Similar to the Trooper MK V except: 2" or 4" solid rib barrel; fixed sights. Add 10% for nickel finish. Discontinued in mid 1980's.

Estimated Value: Excellent: $270.00
**   Very good: $215.00**

Colt King Cobra

Caliber: 357 magnum; 38 Special
Action: Single or double action
Cylinder: 6-shot; swing out; simultaneous ejector
Barrel: 2½", 4", 6" or 8"; 4" or 6" after 1995
Sights: Red ramp front with white outline adjustable rear
Finish: Blued, matte stainless steel or bright polished stainless steel. Black rubber combat grips
Length Overall: 8", 9", 11" or 13"; 9" or 11" after 1995
Approximate wt.: 36, 42, 46 or 48 oz.; 42 to 46 oz. (1995)
Comments: Introduced in 1989. It has a full-length contoured ejector rod housing & a solid barrel rib. Stainless steel only after 1995.
Estimated Value: New (retail): $455.00
                    Excellent: $340.00
                    Very good: $275.00

Colt Model I-3 Python, New Police Python, Python

Caliber: 357 magnum, 38 Special; 22 long rifle & 22 WMR available in 1981 only
Action: Single or double action
Cylinder: 6-shot; swing out; simultaneous ejector
Barrel: 2½", 3", 4", 6" or 8" after 1980; ventilated rib
Sights: Blade front, adjustable rear (for windage & elevation). Red insert in front sight in 1980's
Finish: Blued or nickel; checkered walnut target grips; also rubber grips in 1980's; non-glare electroless plating & stainless steel in 1980's
Length Overall: 7¼" to 13¼"
Approximate wt.: 39 to 44 oz.
Comments: Made from about 1955 to present. Add 16% for black stainless steel; add 11% for stainless steel; add 4% for nickel finish (discontinued).
Estimated Value: New (retail): $815.00
                    Excellent: $610.00
                    Very good: $490.00

Colt Official Police MK III

Caliber: 38 Special
Action: Single or double
Cylinder: 6-shot; swing out; simultaneous ejector
Barrel: 4", 5", 6"
Sights: Fixed
Finish: Blued; checkered walnut square butt grips
Length Overall: 9¼", 10¼", 11¼"
Approximate wt.: 34 to 36 oz.
Comments: Made from about 1970 to late 1970's.
Estimated Value: Excellent: $280.00
                    Very good: $225.00

Colt Official Police MK III

Colt Peacekeeper

Caliber: 357 magnum & 38 Special
Action: Single or double action
Cylinder: 6-shot; swing out; simultaneous ejector
Barrel: 4" or 6" with ventilated rib & short ejector shroud
Sights: Red insert front & white outline adjustable rear
Finish: Non-glare matte blue combat finish with Colt rubber combat grips
Length Overall: 9" or 11"
Approximate wt.: 38 or 42 oz.
Comments: A medium frame 357 magnum introduced in the mid 1980's & discontinued 1988.
Estimated Value: Excellent: $270.00
                    Very good: $215.00

Colt Peacekeeper

Colt Model Python

Colt Anaconda

Caliber: 44 mag., 44 Special; 45 Colt (added in 1994)
Action: Single or double action
Cylinder: 6-shot; swing out; simultaneous ejector
Barrel: 4", 6" or 8"; ventilated rib
Sights: Red ramp front, white outline adjustable rear
Finish: Matte stainless steel; rubber combat grips
Length Overall: 9" to 13¼"
Approximate wt.: 47 to 59 oz.
Comments: Introduced 1992.
Estimated Value: New (retail): $612.00
                    Excellent: $460.00
                    Very good: $365.00

Colt Realtree Anaconda

Same as the Anaconda except: 44 magnum caliber or 44 Special; 8" barrel; grey camo finish on exposed metal (Realtree); combat style or Hogue monogrip; scope and scope mounts optional; add 35% for scope and mounts; introduced in the mid 1990's.
Estimated Value: New (retail): $740.00
                    Excellent: $560.00
                    Very good: $445.00

Colt .38 SF-VI

Caliber: 38 Special
Action: Single or double action; exposed hammer
Cylinder: 6-shot; swing out; simultaneous ejector; fluted
Barrel: 2" or 4"; ejector rod shroud
Sights: Ramp front, grooved frame rear
Finish: Blued or stainless steel; black Neopreme round butt grips
Length Overall: 7" or 9"
Approximate wt.: 21 to 25oz.
Comments: A smooth action similar to the Python; introduced in 1994.
Estimated Value: New (retail): $408.00
                    Excellent: $300.00
                    Very good: $240.00

Colt Single Action Army

Caliber: 357 magnum, 38 Special, 44 Special, 45 Colt
Action: Single action
Cylinder: 6-shot; side load; loading gate; under barrel ejector rod
Barrel: 4¾", 5½", & 7½"
Sights: Fixed
Finish: Blued with case-hardened frame; composite rubber grips; nickel with checkered walnut grips
Length Overall: 10⅛" to 12⅞"
Approximate wt.: 37 or 43 oz.
Comments: A revival of the Single Action Army Revolver, which was discontinued in 1941. The serial numbers start at 1001 SA. The letters SA were added to the serial numbers when production was resumed. Made from about 1955 to mid 1980's. Add 4% for a 7½" barrel; add 12% for nickel.
Estimated Value: Excellent: $575.00
                     Very good: $470.00

Colt New Frontier, Single Action Army

This is the same handgun as the Colt Single Action Army revolver except frame is flat topped; finish is high polished; ramp front sight & adjustable rear sight (wind & elevation); blued & case-hardened finish; smooth walnut grips. This is a target version of the SA Army, made from about 1961 to mid 1980's in 44-40, 44 Spec., & 45 Colt caliber only. Add $20.00 for 7½" barrel.
Estimated Value: Excellent: $600.00
                     Very good: $480.00

**Colt New Frontier,
Single Action Army**

Colt Frontier Scout

Caliber: 22 & 22 WRF (interchangeable cylinder)
Action: Single action
Cylinder: 6-shot side load; loading gate; under barrel ejector rod
Barrel: 4¾" or 9½" (Buntline Scout)
Sights: Fixed
Finish: Blued or nickel; plastic or wood grips
Length Overall: 9⁵⁄₁₆" to 14¼"
Approximate wt.: 24 to 34 oz.
Comments: Single Action Army replica ¾ scale size in 22 caliber. Made with bright alloy frame & blued steel frame from about 1958 to 1972. Add $10.00 for interchangeable cylinder; $10.00 for nickel finish; $10.00 for Buntline Scout.
Estimated Value: Excellent: $260.00
                     Very good: $210.00

Colt Single Action Buntline Special

Colt New Frontier Buntline Special

Same as the Colt New Frontier (1961 Model) except: 45 caliber only; 12" barrel; 17½" overall; weighs 42 oz. Made from 1962 to 1967.
Estimated Value: Excellent: $535.00
                     Very good: $430.00

Colt Single Action Buntline Special

This is basically the same revolver as the Colt Single Action Army Revolver (1955 Model) except it is 45 Colt caliber only. The barrel is 12"; the gun has an overall length of 17½"; weighs about 42 oz. It was made from about 1957 until 1975. Available again in 1980. Add 15% for nickel finish. 44 Special available after 1981.
Estimated Value: Excellent: $490.00
                     Very good: $395.00

**Colt Peacemaker 22
Single Action**

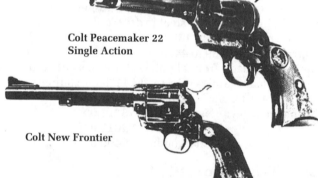

Colt New Frontier

Colt Peacemaker 22 Single Action

Caliber: 22, 22 WRF when equipped with dual cylinder
Action: Single
Cylinder: 6-shot side load; loading gate; under barrel ejector rod
Barrel: 4¾", 6" & 7½"
Sights: Fixed
Finish: Blued barrel & cylinder; case-hardened frame; black composite rubber grips
Length Overall: 9⁵⁄₁₆" to 12¾"
Approximate wt.: 29 to 33 oz.
Comments: All steel, 22 caliber version of the 45 caliber Peacemaker. Made from 1972 to late 1970's. Add $6.00 for 7½" barrel.
Estimated Value: Excellent: $235.00
                     Very good: $190.00

Colt New Frontier

Same as the Colt Peacemaker 22 SA except equipped with a ramp front sight & adj. rear sight; flat top frame. Reintroduced in 1982 to 1986.
Estimated Value: Excellent: $250.00
                     Very good: $200.00

Dardick

Dardick Magazine Pistol

Dardick Magazine Pistol

David Dardick developed a handgun, which resembles an automatic pistol, around a new type of cartridge called the "tround." The tround has a triangular case made of plastic. For the 38 caliber, the primer, powder, & bullets are loaded into the tround. The 22 caliber cartridges are simply placed in a plastic tround to adapt them to the feeding system. The firing pin position is changed to rimfire by manually turning a screw in the frame. Therefore, the basic gun will shoot 22 caliber or 38 caliber by changing the barrel. The feeding system used a three-legged star wheel which moves from magazine to firing position & dumps rounds through opening on right side. The feeding system is moved 120° with each pull of the trigger. The magazine is loaded by placing trounds in singly or by using 10-shot stripper clips. Production was started in 1959 in Hamden, Connecticut & ceased in 1960. All facilities, guns, & parts were auctioned to Numrich Arms in 1960. Approximately 40 guns were produced. The gun was made in three models & a rifle conversion kit. All models were made with two barrels (22 and 38 caliber).

Dardick 1100 - 11 shot
Dardick 1500 - 15 shot
Dardick 2000 - 20 shot

All models could be converted to a rifle by removing the barrel & fitting the frame into the rifle conversion kit.

Estimated Value:

	Pistol with 22 & 38 caliber barrels
Excellent:	$500.00
Very good:	$375.00

	Pistol with 22 & 38 caliber barrels & rifle conversion kit
Excellent:	$1,200.00
Very good:	$ 960.00

Desert Eagle (Magnum Research, Inc.)

Desert Eagle, Mark I & Mark VII

Caliber: 357 mag. (in early 1980's); 44 mag. (in 1986); 41 mag. (in 1989); 50 Action Express mag. (1992) (6" barrel only)

Action: Gas operated semi-automatic; single action (double action in 1992); exposed hammer; rotating locking bolt

Magazine: 9-shot clip (357 mag.); 8-shot clip (41 & 44 mag.); 7-shot clip (50 mag.)

Barrel: 6" standard; 10" or 14" available

Sights: Combat-style or target-style with adjustable rear

Finish: Black oxide; satin nickel; bright nickel; or blued; wrap-around rubber grips; alloy or stainless steel frame

Length Overall: 10½", 14½", or 18½"

Approximate wt.: 48 to 59 oz. (alloy frame); 58 to 70 oz. (steel or stainless steel)

Comments: Add 58% for 50 mag.; add 14% for 44 mag.; add 14% for 41 mag; add 6% for stainless steel frame; add 20% for 10" or 14" barrel.

Estimated Value:
New (retail): $789.00
Excellent: $590.00
Very good: $475.00

Desert Eagle

Magnum Research Desert Eagle Mark XIX System

Caliber: 357 magnum; 44 magnum; 50AE

Action: Gas operated semi-automatic; double action; exposed hammer; rotating locking bolt

Magazine: 9-shot clip (357); 8-shot clip (44); 7-shot clip (50)

Barrel: 6" or 10"

Sights: Adjustable rear, ramp front

Finish: Black oxide; other finishes available; alloy, steel, or stainless steel frame

Length Overall: 10½" or 14½"

Approximate wt.: 48 to 60 oz.

Comments: Introduced in 1996; the XIX System consists of a basic platform to which different caliber barrel, slide, and clip can be attached to provide different calibers with the same pistol. Add 7% for 50 caliber; add 3% for 44 caliber; priced for 357 caliber pistol; add 5% for 10" barrel.

Estimated Value:

New (retail):	$979.00
Excellent:	$735.00
Very good:	$590.00

**Magnum Research
Desert Eagle Mark XIX System**

Magnum Research Baby Eagle

Caliber: 9 mm, 41AE, 40 S&W

Action: Semi-automatic, single or double action; exposed hammer; decocking safety

Magazine: 10-shot clip

Barrel: 3½" or 3¾"

Sights: Combat style

Finish: Black oxide; other finishes available

Length Overall: 7" to 8¼"

Approximate wt.: 38 oz.

Comments: Introduced in 1992.

Estimated Value:

New (retail):	$569.00
Excellent:	$425.00
Very good:	$340.00

**Magnum Research
Baby Eagle**

**Magnum Research
Mountain Eagle**

Magnum Research Mountain Eagle

Caliber: 22 long rifle

Action: Semi-automatic, single action

Magazine: 15-shot clip, 10-shot after September 1994

Barrel: 4½", 6", or 8"; polymer and steel barrel

Sights: Adjustable rear, ramp front

Finish: Black oxide; black, one-piece injection molded grips

Length Overall: 8½" to 12¼"

Approximate wt.: 19 to 23 oz.

Comments: Introduced in 1992; add 40% for target model (8" barrel); add 20% for 6" barrel.

Estimated Value:

New (retail):	$199.00
Excellent:	$150.00
Very good:	$120.00

Magnum Research Lone Eagle SSP-91

Caliber: Almost any caliber from 22 long rifle to 444 Marlin available

Action: Single shot, interchangeable actions of different calibers can be snapped into place on the high-tech polymer stock assembly

Magazine: None, single shot

Barrel: 10"

Sights: Adjustable rear, ramp front

Finish: Black oxide; other finishes available; polymer stock and action bed

Length Overall: 15⅛"

Approximate wt.: 65 to 72 oz.

Comments: Introduced in 1992. Barreled action assemblies approximately $290.00 for each caliber in black oxide finish. Priced for stock assembly and one barreled action assembly.

Estimated Value:

New (retail):	$408.00
Excellent:	$310.00
Very good:	$245.00

**Magnum Research
Lone Eagle SSP-91**

Detonics

Detonics Mark I, Combat Master MC-1
Caliber: 45 ACP; 9 mm; 38 Super ACP
Action: Semi-automatic; exposed hammer; single action; thumb safety
Magazine: 6-shot clip
Barrel: 3¼"
Sights: Fixed; some models have adjustable sights
Finish: Polished blue, matte blue; walnut grips
Length Overall: 6¾"
Approximate wt.: 29 oz.
Comments: A lightweight compact combat pistol made from the late 1970's to early 1990's.
Estimated Value: Excellent: $690.00
                       Very good: $550.00

Detonics Mark V, Combat Master
Similar to the Mark I except matte stainless steel finish. Discontinued 1985.
Estimated Value: Excellent: $600.00
                       Very good: $480.00

Detonics Mark VI, Combat Master
Similar to the Mark V with polished stainless steel finish. Discontinued early 1990's.
Estimated Value: Excellent: $595.00
                       Very good: $475.00

Detonics Scoremaster
Similar to the Combat Master with a 5" or 6" barrel, 7 or 8-shot clip; 45 ACP or 451 Detonics magnum. Add 4% for 6" barrel. Discontinued in early 1990's.
Estimated Value: Excellent: $880.00
                       Very good: $700.00

Detonics Service Master
Similar to the Combat Master except slightly longer and heavier, Millett sights, dull finish. Discontinued in mid 1980's.
Estimated Value: Excellent: $550.00
                       Very good: $445.00

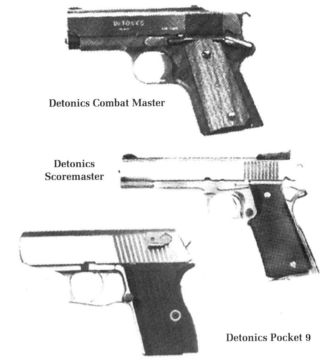

Detonics Combat Master

Detonics Scoremaster

Detonics Pocket 9

Detonics Pocket 9
Caliber: 9 mm
Action: Double and single action, blowback; semi-automatic
Magazine: 6-shot clip
Barrel: 3"
Sights: Fixed
Finish: Matte finish stainless steel, hooked and serrated trigger guard
Length Overall: 5¾"
Approximate wt.: 26 oz.
Comments: Produced in the mid 1980's.
Estimated Value: Excellent: $400.00
                       Very good: $320.00

Fiala

Fiala Single Shot Magazine Pistol

Fiala Single Shot Magazine Pistol
Caliber: 22 short, long, long rifle
Action: Hand operated slide action to chamber cartridge, cock striker & eject empty case
Magazine: 10-shot clip
Barrel: 3", 7½", 20"
Sights: Target sight (adjustable rear sight)
Finish: Blued; plain wood grips
Length Overall: 6¾", 11¼" or 23¾"
Approximate wt.: 27 to 44 oz.
Comments: Produced from about 1920 to 1923. A rare American pistol which had the appearance of an automatic pistol. A shoulder stock was supplied for use with the 20" barrel.

Estimated Value:	Pistol with 3" & 7½" barrel	Pistol with all 3 barrels & shoulder stock
Excellent:	$425.00	$850.00
Very good:	$350.00	$680.00

Glock

Glock 17, 17L, 19
Caliber: 9mm Luger
Action: Recoil operated semi-automatic; double action only; concealed hammer
Magazine: 17 shot clip (17 & 17L); 15-shot clip (19); or an optional 19 or 17- shot clip; 10-shot clips in USA after 9-13-94
Barrel: 4" (19); 4½" (17); 6" (17L)
Sights: Fixed (service model) or adjustable rear (sport model)
Finish: Space-age polymer & machined steel
Length Overall: 7½" (17); 9" (17L); 7" (19)
Approximate wt.: 23 oz. (17L); 21 oz. (19)
Comments: Introduced in 1983. Standard sidearm of Austrian Armed Forces 1985. The 17L has cut away slide top with ported barrel. Add 30% for 17L; add 5% for adjustable sights.
Estimated Value: New (retail): $606.00
Excellent: $455.00
Very good: $365.00

Glock 17

Glock 20

Glock 20 & 21
Similar to the Glock 19 except: Calibers 10mm (15-shot Glock 20) and 45ACP (13-shot Glock 21); 10-shot clips in USA after 9-13-94; 4½" barrels; add 5% for adjustable sights.
Estimated Value: New (retail): $658.00
Excellent: $495.00
Very good: $395.00

Glock 22 & 23
Similar to the Glock 20 & 21 except: 40 S&W caliber; Glock 22 has 13- shot clip with 4½" barrel and Glock 23 has 15-shot clip with 4" barrel. 10-shot clips after 9-13-94, add 5% for adjustable sights
Estimated Value: New (retail): $606.00
Excellent: $455.00
Very good: $365.00

Glock 24

Glock 24 & 24C
Similar to the 17L with 6" barrel except: ported or unported barrel; in 40 S & W caliber; approximate wt.: 27 oz.; add 5% for adjustable sights; add 6% for ported barrel (24C); 10-shot clip in USA. Introduced in 1994.
Estimated Value: New (retail): $790.00
Excellent: $595.00
Very good: $475.00

Glock 26 & 27
Caliber: 9mm Luger (26); 40 S & W (27)
Action: Recoil operated semi-automatic; double action only; concealed hammer
Magazine: 10-shot clip (26); 9-shot clip (27)
Barrel: 3½"
Sights: Fixed or adjustable
Finish: Space age polymer and machined steel
Length Overall: 6¼"
Approximate wt.: 20 oz.
Comments: Introduced in the mid 1990's; add 5% for adjustable sights.
Estimated Value: New (retail): $459.00
Excellent: $345.00
Very good: $275.00

Great Western

Great Western Frontier

Great Western Double Barrel Derringer
Caliber: 38 Special; 38 S & W
Action: Single, double barrel; tip up to eject & load
Cylinder: None; barrels chambered for cartridges
Barrel: Superposed 3" double
Sights: Fixed
Finish: Blued; checkered plastic grips
Length Overall: 4⅞"
Approximate wt.: 14 oz.
Comments: Replica of the Remington Double Derringer. Made from about 1952 to 1962.
Estimated Value: Excellent: $200.00
                       Very good: $175.00

Great Western Frontier
Caliber: 22 short, long, long rifle, 32-20; 357 magnum, 38 Special, 44-40; 44 magnum, 44 Special, 45 Colt
Action: Single, hand ejector
Cylinder: 6-shot; fluted
Barrel: 4¾", 5½", 7½" round barrel with ejector housing under barrel
Sights: Blade front; groove in top strap for rear sight
Finish: Blued; imitation stag grips
Length Overall: 10⅜" to 13⅛"
Approximate wt.: 38 to 42 oz.
Comments: Replica of the Colt Single Action revolver. Made from about 1951 to 1962. Values of these revolvers vary due to the poor quality of the early models. After 1955 they were also available in unassembled kit form. Values for factory-made models.
Estimated Value: Excellent: $350.00
                       Very good: $300.00

Harrington & Richardson

H & R Self Loading 25
Caliber: 25 ACP
Action: Semi-automatic; concealed hammer
Magazine: 6-shot clip; simultaneous ejector
Barrel: 2"
Sights: None
Finish: Blued; hard rubber grips
Length Overall: 4½"
Approximate wt.: 13 oz.
Comments: Approx. 20,000 made from about 1912 to 1915.
Estimated Value: Excellent: $280.00
                       Very good: $225.00

H & R Self Loading 25

H & R Self Loading 32

H & R Self Loading 32
Caliber: 32 ACP
Action: Semi-automatic; concealed hammer; grip safety
Magazine: 8-shot clip
Barrel: 3½"
Sights: Fixed
Finish: Blued; hard rubber grips
Length Overall: 6½"
Approximate wt.: 22 oz.
Comments: A modified Webley & Scott design. Approx. 40,000 produced from about 1916 to 1939.
Estimated Value: Excellent: $275.00
                       Very good: $220.00

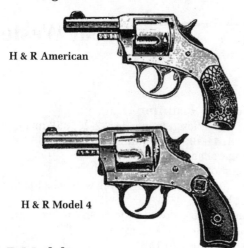

H & R American

H & R Model 4

H & R Model 4
Caliber: 32 S&W, 32 S&W long, 38 S&W
Action: Double & single; exposed hammer; solid frame; side load
Cylinder: 6-shot in 32 caliber, 5-shot in 38 caliber, removable cylinder
Barrel: 2½", 4½" or 6" hexagon barrel
Sights: Fixed
Finish: Blued or nickel; hard rubber grips
Length Overall: 6½" to 10"
Approximate wt.: 14 to 18 oz.
Comments: Made from about 1904 to 1941.
Estimated Value: Excellent: $100.00
                       Very good: $ 75.00

H & R Model 5
Similar to the Model 4 except: 32 S&W caliber only; smaller frame and cylinder (5 shot); weighs 10 to 12 oz. Produced from about 1905 to 1939.
Estimated Value: Excellent: $90.00
                       Very good: $70.00

H & R Model 6
Similar to the Model 5 except: 22 short, long, long rifle; 7-shot cylinder; minor change in shape of top of frame at rear of cylinder. Made from about 1906 to 1941.
Estimated Value: Excellent: $100.00
                       Very good: $ 75.00

H & R Trapper Model
Same as Model 6 except 6" barrel, checkered square butt walnut grips. Made from about 1924 to 1942.
Estimated Value: Excellent: $120.00
                       Very good: $ 95.00

H & R Hunter Model (1926)
Same as Trapper Model except 10" barrel, weighs 18 oz. Made from about 1926 to 1930.
Estimated Value: Excellent: $125.00
                       Very good: $100.00

H & R Hunter Model (1930)
Similar to Hunter Model (1926) except: larger frame; 9-shot safety cylinder (recessed chambers); weighs 26 oz. Made from about 1930 to 1941.
Estimated Value: Excellent: $125.00
                       Very good: $100.00

H & R American
Caliber: S&W, 32 S&W long; 38 S&W
Action: Single or double; exposed hammer; solid frame; side load
Cylinder: 6-shot in 32 caliber; 5-shot in 38 caliber; removable cylinder
Barrel: 2½", 4½" or 6" hexagon barrel
Sights: Fixed
Finish: Blued or nickel; hard rubber round butt grips
Length Overall: 6½" to 9¾"
Approximate wt.: 14 to 16 oz.
Comments: Made from about 1883 to 1941.
Estimated Value: Excellent: $105.00
                       Very good: $ 85.00

H & R Young American
Caliber: 22 short, long, long rifle, 32 S&W short
Action: Single or double; exposed hammer; solid frame; side load
Cylinder: 7-shot in 22 caliber; 5-shot in 32 caliber; removable cylinder
Barrel: 2", 4½" or 6" hexagon barrel
Sights: Fixed
Finish: Blued or nickel; hard rubber round butt grips
Length Overall: 5½" to 9¾"
Approximate wt.: 10 to 12 oz.
Comments: Made from about 1885 to 1941.
Estimated Value: Excellent: $100.00
                       Very good: $ 75.00

H & R Vest Pocket
Same as H & R Young American except 1⅛" barrel only; double action only; no spur on hammer; approximate weight 8 oz. Produced from about 1891 to 1941.
Estimated Value: Excellent: $90.00
                       Very good: $70.00

H & R Young American

H & R Model 6

H & R Trapper Model

H & R Automatic Ejecting Revolver

Caliber: 32 S&W, 32 S&W long; 38 S&W
Action: Single or double; exposed hammer; hinged frame; top break
Cylinder: 6-shot in 32 caliber; 5-shot in 38 caliber; simultaneous automatic ejector
Barrel: 3¼", 4", 5" or 6" round barrel with rib
Sights: Fixed
Finish: Blued or nickel; hard rubber round butt grips
Length Overall: 7¼" to 10"
Approximate wt.: 15 to 18 oz.
Comments: Made from about 1891 to 1941.
Estimated Value: Excellent: $125.00
Very good: $100.00

H & R Automatic
Ejecting Revolver

H & R Model 50

Same as Automatic Ejecting Revolver except: double action only; concealed hammer; frame completely encloses hammer area. Made from about 1899 to 1941.
Estimated Value: Excellent: $150.00
Very good: $125.00

H & R Model 50

H & R Premier

Caliber: 22 short, long, long rifle, 32 S&W
Action: Single or double; exposed hammer; small hinged frame; top break
Cylinder: 7-shot in 22 caliber; 5-shot in 32 caliber; simultaneous automatic ejector
Barrel: 2", 3", 4", 5" or 6" round ribbed barrel
Sights: Fixed
Finish: Blued or nickel; hard rubber round butt grips
Length Overall: 5¾" to 9¾"
Approximate wt.: 12 to 16 oz.
Comments: Made from about 1895 to 1941.
Estimated Value: Excellent: $140.00
Very good: $110.00

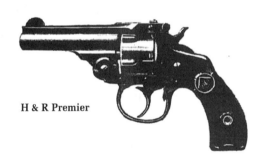

H & R Premier

H & R Model 40

Same as Premier except double action only; concealed hammer; frame completely encloses hammer area. Made from about 1899 to 1941.
Estimated Value: Excellent: $150.00
Very good: $115.00

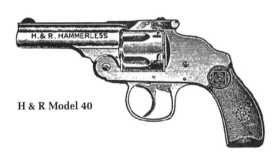

H & R Model 40

H & R Model 944

H & R Model 944

Caliber: 22 short, long, long rifle, 22 WRF
Action: Single or double; exposed hammer; heavy hinged frame; top break
Cylinder: 9-shot; simultaneous automatic ejector
Barrel: 6" round ribbed barrel
Sights: Fixed
Finish: Blued; checkered square butt walnut grips
Length Overall: 10"
Approximate wt.: 24 oz.
Comments: Produced from about 1925 to 1930.
Estimated Value: Excellent: $140.00
Very good: $115.00

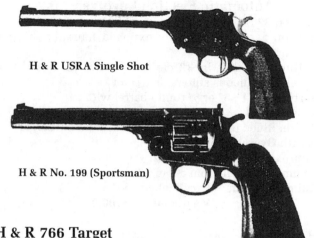

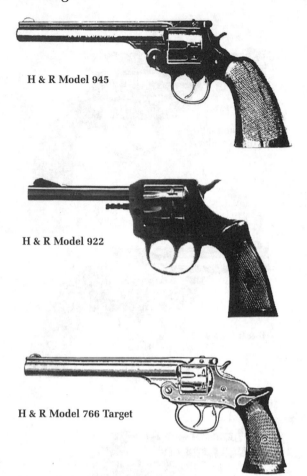

H & R Model 945

H & R Model 922

H & R Model 766 Target

H & R USRA Single Shot

H & R No. 199 (Sportsman)

H & R Model 945

Same as Model 944 except safety cylinder (recessed chambers). Made from about 1929 to 1941.

Estimated Value: Excellent: $135.00
                        Very good: $110.00

H & R Model 955

Same as Model 945 except: 10" barrel; approximate weight is 28 oz. Made from about 1929 to 1941.

Estimated Value: Excellent: $130.00
                        Very good: $115.00

H & R Model 922

Caliber: 22 short, long, long rifle
Action: Single or double; exposed hammer; solid frame; side load
Cylinder: 9-shot removable cylinder
Barrel: 4", 6" or 10" octagon barrel in early models, later models had 2½", 4" or 6" round barrel
Sights: Fixed
Finish: Blued; checkered walnut grips on early models; plastic grips on later models
Length Overall: 8¼" to 14¼"
Approximate wt.: 20 to 26 oz.
Comments: Maded from about 1929 to 1970's.
Estimated Value: Excellent: $110.00
                        Very good: $ 90.00

H & R Model 923

Same as Model 922 except nickel finish. Made from about 1930 to late 1970's.

Estimated Value: Excellent: $105.00
                        Very good: $ 95.00

H & R 766 Target

Caliber: 22 short, long, long rifle, 22 WRF
Action: Single or double; exposed hammer; small hinged frame; top break
Cylinder: 7-shot; simultaneous automatic ejector
Barrel: 6" round barrel
Sights: Fixed
Finish: Blued; checkered square butt walnut grips
Length Overall: 10"
Approximate wt.: 16 oz.
Comments: Made from about 1926 to 1936.
Estimated Value: Excellent: $140.00
                        Very good: $105.00

H & R Ultra Sportsman

Caliber: 22 short, long, long rifle, 22 WRF
Action: Single or double; exposed hammer; top break
Cylinder: 9-shot; simultaneous automatic ejector
Barrel: 6" round barrel
Sights: Adjustable target sights
Finish: Blued; checkered square butt walnut grips
Length Overall: 10"
Approximate wt.: 30 oz.
Comments: Heavy frame; short cylinder; wide hammer spur. Made from about 1928 to 1938.
Estimated Value: Excellent: $175.00
                        Very good: $140.00

H & R USRA Single Shot

Same as Ultra Sportsman except single shot only (no cylinder); cartridge chamber in barrel; barrel fills in cylinder space; 7", 8", or 10" barrrel lengths; approximate weight is 29 to 31 oz. Made from about 1928 to 1943.

Estimated Value: Excellent: $330.00
                        Very good: $250.00

H & R No. 199 (Sportsman)

Caliber: 22 short, long, long rifle
Action: Single or double; exposed hammer; hinged frame; top break
Cylinder: 9-shot; simultaneous automatic ejector
Barrel: 6" round barrel, ribbed
Sights: Adjustable target
Finish: Blued; checkered square butt walnut grips
Length Overall: 11"
Approximate wt.: 27 oz.
Comments: Maded from about 1931 to 1951.
Estimated Value: Excellent: $135.00
                        Very good: $110.00

H & R Defender 38

Similar to No. 199 Sportsman Model except: 38 S & W caliber; 4" or 6" barrel; fixed sights, plastic grips. Made from about 1933 to 1946.

Estimated Value: Excellent: $150.00
Very good: $120.00

H & R Model 299 New Defender

Similar to No. 199 Sportsman Model except 2" barrel; 6¼" overall length. Made from about 1936 to 1941.

Estimated Value: Excellent: $150.00
Very good: $125.00

H & R No. 999 (Deluxe Sportsman)

Same as H&R No.199 (Sportsman) except: redesigned hammer & barrel rib; Made from 1951 to 1986. 32 caliber (6-shot) with 4" barrel available after 1978. Produced in 22 caliber in early 1990's.

Estimated Value: New (retail): $252.00
Excellent: $190.00
Very good: $150.00

H & R Model 999
(Deluxe Sportsman)

H & R Model 299 New Defender

H & R Bobby Model 15

Caliber: 32 S&W, 32 S&W long, 38 S&W
Action: Single or double; exposed hammer; hinged frame; top break
Cylinder: 6-shot in 32 caliber, 5-shot in 38 caliber; simultaneous automatic ejector
Barrel: 4" round, ribbed
Sights: Fixed
Finish: Blued; checkered square butt walnut grips
Length Overall: 9"
Approximate wt.: 23 lbs.
Comments: Made from about 1941 to 1943.
Estimated Value: Excellent: $125.00
Very good: $100.00

H & R Model 732 Guardsman

H & R Model 929 Side-Kick

H & R Model 632

H & R Model 929 & 930 Side-Kick

Caliber: 22 short, long, long rifle
Action: Single or double; exposed hammer; solid frame
Cylinder: 9-shot swing out; simultaneous manual ejector
Barrel: 2½", 4" or 6" round, ribbed
Sights: 2½" has fixed sights; 4" & 6" have windage adjustable rear sights
Finish: Blued; checkered plastic grips; walnut grips available after 1982
Length Overall: 6¾" to 10¼"
Approximate wt.: 22 to 28 oz.
Comments: Made from about 1956 to 1986. Reintroduced in 1990's with 4" barrel. Add $15.00 for walnut grips. Model 930 has nickel finish. Add 10% for nickel finish.
Estimated Value: New (retail): $179.00
Excellent: $130.00
Very good: $100.00

H & R Model 632 & 633

Caliber: 32 S&W, 32 S&W long
Action: Single or double; exposed hammer; solid frame
Cylinder: 6-shot
Barrel: 2½" or 4" round
Sights: Fixed
Finish: Blued or nickel (633); checkered tenite grips
Length Overall: 6¾" to 8¼"
Approximate wt.: 19 to 21 oz.
Comments: 2½" barrel model has round butt grips. Made from abt. 1946 to 1986. Model 633 has nickel finish. Add 10% for nickel finish.
Estimated Value: Excellent: $95.00
Very good: $75.00

H & R Model 732 & 733 Guardsman

Caliber: 32 S&W, 32 S&W long
Action: Single or double; exposed hammer; solid frame
Cylinder: 6-shot swing out; simultaneous manual ejector
Barrel: 2½" or 4" round
Sights: Fixed
Finish: Blued or nickel; checkered plastic grips; walnut grips available after 1982
Length Overall: 6¾" to 8¼"
Approximate wt.: 23 to 26 oz.
Comments: Made from abt. 1958 to 1986. Add 10% for walnut grips. Model 733 has nickel finish. Add 10% for nickel finish.
Estimated Value: Excellent: $110.00
Very good: $ 90.00

H & R Model 622 & 623

Caliber: 22 short, long, long rifle
Action: Single or double; exposed hammer; solid frame; side load
Cylinder: 6-shot removable
Barrel: 2½", 4", 6" round
Sights: Fixed
Finish: Blued or nickel; checkered plastic grips
Length Overall: 6¾" to 10¼"
Approximate wt.: 24 to 28 oz.
Comments: Made from about 1957 to 1986. Model 623 has nickel finish. Add 10% for nickel finish.
Estimated Value: Excellent: $90.00
Very good: $75.00

H & R Model 622

H & R Model 642

Similar to the Model 622 in 22 WMR caliber; 2½" or 4" barrel. Discontinued in 1983.
Estimated Value: Excellent: $100.00
Very good: $ 80.00

H & R Model 939 & 940 Ultra Sidekick

Caliber: 22 short, long, long rifle
Action: Single or double; exposed hammer; solid frame
Cylinder: 9-shot swing out; simultaneous manual ejector
Barrel: 6" ventilated rib target barrel; bull barrel on 940
Sights: Ramp front; adjustable rear sight
Finish: Blued; checkered walnut grips with thumb rest
Length Overall: 10½"
Approximate wt.: 33 oz.
Comments: Made from about 1958 to 1980's. Reintroduced in 1990's as 939 Premier.
Estimated Value: New (retail): $189.00
Excellent: $140.00
Very good: $110.00

H & R Model 903

Similar to the Model 939 with a solid heavy flat side barrel & adjustable sights. Produced from 1980 to 1984.
Estimated Value: Excellent: $125.00
Very good: $105.00

H & R Model 603

Similar to the Model 903 in 22 magnum. Made from the early to mid 1980's.
Estimated Value: Excellent: $135.00
Very good: $115.00

H & R Model 904 & 905

Similar to the Model 903 with a 4" or 6" heavy round barrel. Blue satin finish available after 1982. Model 905 has nickel finish. Add 10% for nickel finish.
Estimated Value: Excellent: $130.00
Very good: $100.00

H & R Maddel 604

Similar to the Model 904 in 22 magnum.
Estimated Value: Excellent: $140.00
Very good: $115.00

H & R Model 900 & 901

Caliber: 22 short, long, long rifle
Action: Single or double; exposed hammer; solid frame; side load
Cylinder: 9-shot removable
Barrel: 2½", 4" or 6"
Sights: Fixed
Finish: Blued; checkered plastic grips
Length Overall: 6½" to 10"
Approximate wt.: 23 to 26 oz.
Comments: Made from about 1962 to 1973. Model 901 has nickel finish. Add 10% for nickel finish.
Estimated Value: Excellent: $100.00
Very good: $ 80.00

H & R Model 900

H & R Model 939 Ultra Sidekick

H & R Model 925 Defender

Caliber: 38 S&W
Action: Single or double; exposed hammer; hinged frame; top break
Cylinder: 5-shot; simultaneous automatic ejector
Barrel: 2½" round, ribbed
Sights: Fixed front sight; adjustable rear sight
Finish: Blued; one-piece wrap-around grip
Length Overall: 6¾"
Approximate wt.: 22 oz.
Comments: Made from about 1964 to late 1970's.
Estimated Value: Excellent: $125.00
Very good: $100.00

H & R Model 949
Forty-Niner

H & R Model 926

H & R Model 926
Caliber: 38 S&W; 22 S, L, LR
Action: Single or double; exposed hammer; hinged frame; top break
Cylinder: 5-shot in 38 cal.; 9-shot in 22 cal.
Barrel: 4"
Sights: Adjustable rear sight
Finish: Blued; checkered plastic square butt grips
Length Overall: 8¼"
Approximate wt.: 31 oz.
Comments: Made from abt. 1972 to late 1970's.
Estimated Value: Excellent: $130.00
                       Very good: $110.00

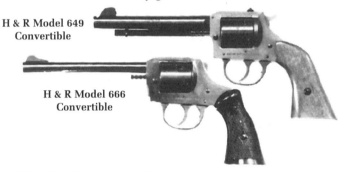

H & R Model 649
Convertible

H & R Model 666
Convertible

H & R Model 666 Convertible
Caliber: 22 short, long, long rifle, 22 magnum (WMR) with extra interchangeable cylinder
Action: Single or double; exposed hammer; solid frame; side load
Cylinder: 6-shot removable; extra interchangeable cylinder so either cartridge can be used
Barrel: 6" round
Sights: Fixed
Finish: Blued; black cycolac, square butt grips
Length Overall: 10¼"
Approximate wt.: 28 oz.
Comments: Made from about 1975 to late 1970's.
Estimated Value: Excellent: $115.00
                       Very good: $ 85.00

H & R Model 676 Convertible
Similar to Model 649 Convertible except: 4½", 5½", 7½" or 12" barrel; blued barrel with antique color case hardened frame; finger rest at back of trigger guard. Discontinued early 1980's. Add 12% for 12" barrel.
Estimated Value: Excellent: $120.00
                       Very good: $ 95.00

H & R Model 686 Convertible
Similar to the Model 676 with ramp front sight, adjustable rear sight. Add $20.00 for 12" barrel.
Estimated Value: Excellent: $135.00
                       Very good: $100.00

H & R Model 949 & 950 Forty-Niner
Caliber: 22 short, long, long rifle
Action: Single or double; exposed hammer; solid frame; side load & ejection
Cylinder: 9-shot
Barrel: 5½" or 7½"round
Sights: Blade front; adjustable rear sights
Finish: Blued; smooth walnut, one-piece, western style grips; case colored frame
Length Overall: 10¼" to 12¼"
Approximate wt.: 36 oz. to 38 oz.
Comments: Made from about 1959 to 1986. Reintroduced in 1990's. Model 950 has nickel finish. Add 10% for nickel finish.
Estimated Value: New (retail): $189.00
                       Excellent: $140.00
                       Very good: $115.00

H & R Model 976
Similar to 949 with 7½" barrel, case-hardened frame. Add $20.00 for nickel finish. Discontinued early 1980's.
Estimated Value: Excellent: $115.00
                       Very good: $ 95.00

H & R Model 649 & 650 Convertible
Caliber: 22 short, long, long rifle, 22 magnum (WMR) with extra interchangeable cylinder
Action: Single or double; exposed hammer; solid frame; side load & ejection
Cylinder: 6-shot removable cylinder; single manual ejector; extra interchangeable cylinder
Barrel: 5½" or 7½" round barrel; ejector rod housing under barrel
Sights: Blade front; adjustable rear sights
Finish: Blued barrel; satin finish frame; smooth western-style walnut grips
Length Overall: 10¼"
Approximate wt.: 32 oz.
Comments: Western style; made from about 1975 to 1986. Model 650 has nickel finish. Add 10% for nickel finish.
Estimated Value: Excellent: $125.00
                       Very good: $ 95.00

H & R Model 532

H & R Model 532
Caliber: 32 H&R magnum
Action: Single or double
Cylinder: 5-shot pull-pin removable
Barrel: 2¼", 4" round
Sights: Fixed
Finish: Blued; smooth walnut grips
Length Overall: 6¾" to 8¼"
Approximate wt.: 20 to 25 oz.
Comments: Introduced in 1984 for the new H&R magnum caliber. Discontinued 1986.
Estimated Value: Excellent: $100.00
                       Very good: $ 80.00

H & R Model 504

H & R Model 829

H & R Model 504

Caliber: 32 H&R magnum
Action: Single or double; swing-out cylinder; exposed hammer
Cylinder: 5-shot swing out
Barrel: 3", 4", 6" target bull
Sights: Blade front; rear adjustable for windage & elevation
Finish: Blued; smooth walnut grips, round or square butt
Length Overall: 7½" to 10"
Approximate wt.: 29 to 35 oz.
Comments: Introduced in 1984 for the new H&R magnum caliber. Discontinued 1986.
Estimated Value: Excellent: $150.00
                       Very good: $120.00

H & R Model 586

H & R Model 586

Caliber: 32 H&R magnum
Action: Single or double; side loading & ejection
Cylinder: 5-shot removable
Barrel: 4½", 5½", 7½", 10" round
Sights: Ramp & blade front, rear adjustable for windage & elevation
Finish: Blued; case-hardened frame; hardwood grips
Length Overall: 10¼" (5½" barrel)
Approximate wt.: 30 to 38 oz.
Comments: Introduced in 1984 for the new 32 H&R magnum caliber. Discontinued 1986.
Estimated Value: Excellent: $145.00
                       Very good: $110.00

H & R Model 829 & 830

Caliber: 22 long rifle
Action: Single or double; exposed hammer
Cylinder: 9-shot swing out
Barrel: 3" bull barrel
Sights: Ramp front, adjustable rear
Finish: Blued or nickel; smooth walnut grips
Length Overall: 7¼"
Approximate wt.: 27 oz.
Comments: Produced from 1981 to 1984. Model 830 has nickel finish. Add 10% for nickel finish.
Estimated Value: Excellent: $125.00
                       Very good: $ 95.00

H & R Model 826

Similar to the Model 829 in 22 magnum caliber.
Estimated Value: Excellent: $135.00
                       Very good: $110.00

H & R Model 832 & 833

Similar to the Model 829 in 32 caliber. Made from 1982 to 1984. Model 833 has nickel finish. Add 10% for nickel finish.
Estimated Value: Excellent: $130.00
                       Very good: $105.00

Hartford

Hartford Automatic Target

Hartford Automatic Target

Caliber: 22 long rifle
Action: Semi-automatic; concealed hammer
Magazine: 10-shot clip
Barrel: 6¾"
Sights: Fixed front; rear sight dovetailed in slide
Finish: Blued; black rubber grips
Length Overall: 10¾"
Approximate wt.: 32 oz.
Comments: Made from about 1929 to 1930. Similar in appearance to Colt Woodsman & Hi Standard Model B Automatic Pistol. Rights & properties of Hartford Arms were sold to High Standard Mfg. Co. in 1932.
Estimated Value: Excellent: $425.00
                       Very good: $350.00

Hartford Single Shot

Caliber: 22 long rifle
Action: Single action, hand operated, concealed hammer
Magazine: None; single shot
Barrel: 6¾"
Sights: Fixed front; rear sight dovetailed in slide
Finish: Matte finish on slide & frame; blued barrel; black rubber or walnut grips
Length Overall: 10¾"
Approximate wt.: 37 oz.
Comments: Made from about 1929 to 1930.
Estimated Value: Excellent: $450.00
                       Very good: $355.00

Hartford Repeating Pistol

Caliber: 22 long rifle
Action: Manual operation of slide after each shot to eject cartridge & feed another cartridge from magazine to chamber; concealed hammer
Magazine: 10-shot clip
Barrel: 6¾"
Sights: Fixed front; rear sight dovetailed in slide
Finish: Blued; black rubber grips
Length Overall: 10¾"
Approximate wt.: 31 oz.
Comments: Made from about 1929 to 1930.
Estimated Value: Excellent: $400.00
                       Very good: $300.00

Heckler & Koch

H& K Model P7 (M-8, M-10, M-13, & K-3)
Caliber: 9mm Parabellum (M-8 & M13); 380 ACP (K-3) added in 1988; 40 S&W (M-10) added in 1991
Action: Recoil operated semi-automatic; concealed hammer; contains a unique system of cocking by squeezing front of grips, uncocking by releasing; also double action
Magazine: 8-shot clip (M-8 & K-3); 10-shot clip (M-10); 13-shot clip (M-13); 10-shot clip after Sept. 13, 1994
Barrel: 4⅛"
Sights: Fixed
Finish: Blued or nickel; black grips
Length Overall: 6½"
Approximate wt.: 33½ oz.
Comments: Made in West Germany. Introduced in 1982; add 19% for M-10; add 21% for M-13.
Estimated Value: New (retail): $1,187.00
                       Excellent: $ 890.00
                       Very good: $ 715.00

Heckler & Koch Model P9S

H & K Model P9S
Caliber: 9mm Parabellum; 45 ACP
Action: Semi-automatic; concealed hammer; cocking lever
Magazine: 9-shot clip (9mm); 7-shot clip in 45 ACP
Barrel: 4"
Sights: Fixed; blade front, square notch rear
Finish: Blued; black plastic grips; wood combat grips available
Length Overall: 7½"
Approximate wt.: 28 to 31 oz.
Comments: Made in West Germany. Discontinued in 1989.
Estimated Value: Excellent: $975.00
                       Very good: $780.00

H & K Model P9S Competition
Similar to the Model P9S Target with both 4" & 5½" barrels, 2 slides, wood competition grips and plastic grips, all packed in a special case. 9mm only.
Estimated Value: Excellent: $1,150.00
                       Very good: $ 920.00

H & K Model P9S Target
Similar to the Model P9S with adjustable trigger, trigger stop & adjustable rear sight; 5½" barrel available.
Estimated Value: Excellent: $1,035.00
                       Very good: $ 830.00

H & K Model HK4
Caliber: 380; Conversion kits available for calibers 38, 25 and 22 long rifle
Action: Semi-automatic; double action; exposed hammer spur
Magazine: 7-shot clip
Barrel: 3⅜"
Sights: Fixed; blade front, notch rear; non-reflective
Finish: Blued; black plactic grips; grip extension on clip
Length Overall: 6"
Approximate wt.: 17 oz.
Comments: Discontinued in mid 1980's. Add 60% for all three conversion kits.
Estimated Value: Excellent: $320.00
                       Very good: $240.00

Heckler & Koch Model HK4

H & K Model VP70Z
Caliber: 9mm
Action: Semi-automatic; blow back, recoil operated; double action only; hammerless
Magazine: Double stacked 18-shot clip
Barrel: 4½"
Sights: Fixed; ramp front, notched rear
Finish: Blued; black plastic grips; solid plastic receiver
Length Overall: 8"
Approximate wt.: 29 oz.
Comments: A pistol with few moving parts, designed for the outdoorsman. Discontinued in mid 1980's.
Estimated Value: Excellent: $350.00
                       Very good: $280.00

H & K Model USP 9, USP 40 & USP 45
Caliber: 9mm (USP 9), 40 S&W (USP 40); 45ACP (USP)45
Action: Semi-automatic; double action & single action or double action only; manual safety, decocking lever, or no decocking lever; about 10 variations of actions to select from; exposed or bobbed hammer
Magazine: 13-shot clip (USP 40); 15-shot clip (USP 9); 10-shot clip after Sept. 13, 1994
Barrel: 4⅛" steel barrel; 6"
Sights: Fixed 3-dot sight system; tritium sights optional
Finish: One piece milled steel slide; "HE" finish to resist corrosion; metal reinforced polymer frame and integral non-slip grip with stippling and cross hatched grooves; stainless steel availabe in 1996.
Length Overall: 7¾"
Approximate wt.: 26 to 28 oz.
Comments: Introduced in 1993. Add 7% for stainless steel; add 10% for cal. 45ACP
Estimated Value: New (retail): $636.00
                       Excellent: $475.00
                       Very good: $380.00

High Standard

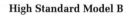

High Standard Model B

High Standard Model B
Caliber: 22 long rifle
Action: Semi-automatic; concealed hammer; thumb safety
Magazine: 10-shot clip
Barrel: 4½" or 6¾"
Sights: Fixed
Finish: Blued; hard rubber grips
Length Overall: 8½" and 10¾"
Approximate wt.: 30 to 34 oz.
Comments: Produced from about 1931 to 1942.
Estimated Value: **Excellent:** **$300.00**
    Very good: **$240.00**

High Standard Model HB
Same as Model B except exposed hammer & no thumb safety. Made from about 1932 to 1942.
Estimated Value: **Excellent:** **$315.00**
    Very good: **$250.00**

High Standard Model A
Caliber: 22 long rifle
Action: Semi-automatic; concealed hammer; thumb safety
Magazine: 10-shot clip
Barrel: 4½" or 6¾"
Sights: Adjustable target sights
Finish: Blued; checkered walnut grips
Length Overall: 9¼" & 11¼"
Approximate wt.: 34 to 36 oz.
Comments: Made from about 1937 to 1942.
Estimated Value: **Excellent:** **$320.00**
    Very good: **$260.00**

High Standard Model HA
Same as Model A except exposed hammer spur & no thumb safety.
Estimated Value: **Excellent:** **$340.00**
    Very good: **$275.00**

High Standard Model D
Same as Model A except heavier barrel; approximate weight is 37 to 40 oz., depending on barrel length.
Estimated Value: **Excellent:** **$350.00**
    Very good: **$290.00**

High Standard Model HD
Same as Model D except exposed hammer spur & no thumb safety.
Estimated Value: **Excellent:** **$360.00**
    Very good: **$300.00**

High Standard Model HDM or HD Military
Same as Model HD except it has thumb safety. Made from about 1941 to 1947, stamped "U.S. Property."
Estimated Value: **Excellent:** **$350.00**
    Very good: **$280.00**

High Standard Model SB
Same as Model B except 6¾" smooth bore for shooting 22 long rifle shot cartridges.
Estimated Value: **Excellent:** **$290.00**
    Very good: **$225.00**

High Standard Model C
Same as Model B except chambered for 22 short cartridges. Made from about 1932 to 1942.
Estimated Value: **Excellent:** **$300.00**
    Very good: **$240.00**

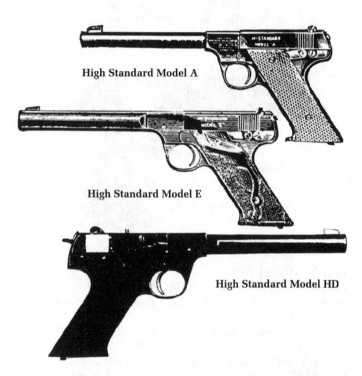

High Standard Model A

High Standard Model E

High Standard Model HD

High Standard Model HD Military (Postwar)
Same as Model HDM except it is not stamped "U.S. Property." Made from about 1946 to 1951 (post-World War II model).
Estimated Value: **Excellent:** **$300.00**
    Very good: **$240.00**

High Standard Model E
Similar to Model A except extra heavy barrel; thumb rest grips. Approximate weight is 39 to 42 oz.
Estimated Value: **Excellent:** **$325.00**
    Very good: **$265.00**

High Standard Model HE
Same as Model E except exposed hammer spur & no thumb safety.
Estimated Value: **Excellent:** **$375.00**
    Very good: **$315.00**

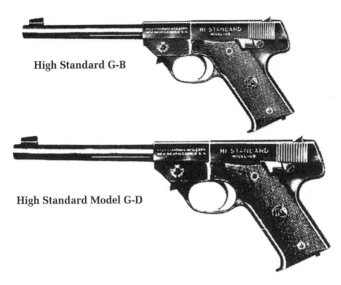

High Standard G-B

High Standard Model G-D

High Standard Model G-B
Caliber: 22 long rifle
Action: Semi-automatic; concealed hammer; takedown model; interchangeable barrels; thumb safety
Magazine: 10-shot clip
Barrel: 4½" or 6¾"
Sights: Fixed
Finish: Blued; checkered plastic grips
Length Overall: 8½" & 10¾"
Approximate wt.: 34 to 36 oz.
Comments: Made from about 1948 to 1951. Add 25% if pistol has both barrels.
Estimated Value: **Excellent:**   **$250.00**
                     Very good: **$200.00**

High Standard Model G-D
Same as Model G-B except: adjustable target sights; checkered walnut grips; approximate weight is 38 to 40 oz.; length overall about 9¼" to 11½". Add 25% if pistol has both barrels.
Estimated Value: **Excellent:**   **$275.00**
                     Very good: **$225.00**

High Standard Model G-E
Same as Model G-D except: heavy barrel; thumb rest; walnut grips; approximate weight is 42 to 44 oz. Add 25% if pistol has both barrels. Made from late 1940's to early 1950's
Estimated Value: **Excellent:**   **$300.00**
                     Very good: **$240.00**

High Standard Model G-380

High Standard Olympic 1st Model
Same as Model G-E except 22 short caliber; light alloy slide; made from about 1950 to 1951; approximate weight is 38 to 40 oz. Add 20% if pistol has both barrels.
Estimated Value: **Excellent:**   **$295.00**
                     Very good: **$235.00**

High Standard Olympic 2nd Model
Same as Olympic 1st Model except: thumb safety located at center top of left grip; plastic grips with thumb rest; produced from about 1951 to 1958. Add 20% if pistol has both barrels.
Estimated Value: **Excellent:**   **$325.00**
                     Very good: **$260.00**

High Standard Olympic 1st Model

High Standard Olympic 2nd Model

High Standard Model G-380
Caliber: 380 ACP
Action: Semi-automatic; exposed hammer spur; thumb safety; barrel takedown model
Magazine: 6-shot clip; bottom release
Barrel: 5"
Sights: Fixed; blade front & notched rear
Finish: Blued; checkered plastic grips
Length Overall: 9"
Approximate wt.: 40 oz.
Comments: First of the barrel takedown models produced by High Standard. Made from about 1944 to 1950.
Estimated Value: **Excellent:**   **$350.00**
                     Very good: **$280.00**

High Standard Olympic ISU

High Standard Olympic ISU
Caliber: 22 short
Action: Semi-automatic; concealed hammer; wide target trigger; anti-backlash trigger adjustment
Magazine: 10-shot clip
Barrel: 5½" bull barrel (1963 to 1966); 8" tapered barrel (1958 to 1964); 6¾" tapered barrel (1958 to present); integral stabilizer & 2 removable weights
Sights: Ramp front; adjustable rear
Finish: Blued; checkered walnut grips with thumb rests
Length Overall: 11¼" (6¾" barrel)
Approximate wt.: 40 to 41 oz.
Comments: Meets International Shooting Union Regulations; left or right hand grips; regular Hi-Standard style grip or the squared military style grip; military style has rear sight frame mounted. Made from about 1958 to late 1970's.
Estimated Value: Excellent: $400.00
Very good: $320.00

High Standard Olympic Military
Caliber: 22 short
Action: Semi-automatic; concealed hammer
Magazine: 5-shot clip
Barrel: 5½" bull barrel
Sights: Adjustable rear, ramp front; drilled and tapped for scope mount
Finish: Blued aluminum alloy slide and carbon steel frame
Length Overall: 11½"
Approximate wt.: 44 oz.
Comments: Reintroduced in the 1990's.
Estimated Value: New (retail) $536.00
Excellent: $400.00
Very good: $320.00

High Standard Olympic RF (Rapid Fire)
Similar to the Olympic Military except: matte finish; 4" barrel; integral muzzle brake and forward mounted compensator; ventilated rib; adjustable trigger; special international grips; introduced in 1996.
Estimated Value: New (retail) $1,995.00
Excellent: $1,450.00
Very good: $1,200.00

High Standard Sport-King 1st Model
Caliber: 22 long rifle
Action: Semi-automatic; concealed hammer; takedown model with interchangeable barrel; thumb safety at top center of left grip
Magazine: 10-shot clip
Barrel: 4½" &/or 6¾"
Sights: Fixed
Finish: Blued; checkered plastic grips with thumb rest
Length Overall: 9", 11¼"
Approximate wt.: 36 to 39 oz.
Comments: Made from about 1951 to 1958. Add 25% for pistol with both barrels.
Estimated Value: Excellent: $215.00
Very good: $175.00

High Standard Sport-King 2nd Model
Similar to Sport-King 1st Model except: made from about 1958 to 1965; interior changes; interchangeable barrels; blue or nickel finish; weighs 39 to 42 oz. Add $15.00 for nickel finish. Reintroduced in early 1980's to 1985 and again in 1990's. Slightly different grip style. Add 25% for both barrels.
Estimated Value: New (retail): $300.00
Excellent $225.00
Very good: $180.00

High Standard Lightweight Sport-King
Same as Sport-King 1st Model except: made from about 1954 to 1965; aluminum alloy frame; weighs 28 to 30 oz. Add 25% for pistol with both barrels.
Estimated Value: Excellent: $220.00
Very good: $175.00

High Standard Flite-King 1st Model
Same as Sport-King 1st Model except: made from about 1953 to 1958; aluminum alloy frame and slide; weighs 24 to 26 oz.; 22 short caliber only. Add 25% for pistol with both barrels.
Estimated Value: Excellent: $220.00
Very good: $175.00

High Standard Sport-King 1st Model

High Standard Sport-King 2nd Model

High Standard Flite-King 1st Model

High Standard Flite-King 2nd Model
Same as Sport-King 1st Model Automatic except: made from about 1958 to 1965; all steel construction; 22 long rifle caliber only. Add 25% for pistol with both barrels.
Estimated Value: Excellent: $230.00
                   Very good: $185.00

High Standard Field-King
Same as Sport-King 1st Model except: adjustable target sights; 6¾" heavy barrel; weighs about 44 oz.
Estimated Value: Excellent: $250.00
                   Very good: $200.00

High Standard Field-King

High Standard Supermatic Series
Caliber: 22 long rifle
Action: Semi-automatic; concealed hammer; thumb safety; takedown model with interchangeable barrels
Magazine: 10-shot clip
Barrel: 4½", 5½", 6¾" 7¼", 8", 10"
Sights: Ramp front, adjustable rear
Finish: Blued; checkered plastic or checkered wood grips with or without thumb rest
Length Overall: 9¼" to 14¾"
Approximate wt.: 40 to 46 oz.
Comments: The 5¼" barrels are heavy (bull) barrels & the 7¼" barrels are heavy (bull) fluted barrels.

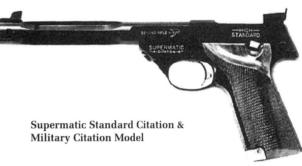
Supermatic Standard Citation &
Military Citation Model

Standard Supermatic Model manufactured from about 1951 to 1958; 4¼" & 6¾" interchangeable barrels. Add 25% for pistols with both barrels.
Estimated Value: Excellent: $250.00
                   Very good: $200.00

Supermatic Tournament Model made from about 1958 to 1963; 5½" bull barrel &/ or 6¾" regular barrel with stabilizer & 2 removable weights; adjustable trigger pull. Add 20% for pistol with both barrels. Reintroduced in 1990's.
Estimated Value: New (retail): $400.00
                   Excellent: $300.00
                   Very good: $240.00

Supermatic Citation, Military or Citation II made from about 1965 to 1985; 5½" heavy (bull) or 7¼" heavy fluted barrel with military grip or standard grip. 5½" or 7¼" slabbed barrel in 1984 (Citation II). Dropped in 1984; reintroduced in 1990's with 5½" barrel.
Estimated Value:: New (retail): $416.00
                   Excellent: $315.00
                   Very good: $250.00

High Standard Citation MS (Metallic Silhouette)
Same as the Supermatic Citation except: 10" barrel; matte blue finish; RPM sights; approximate wt.: 49 oz.; length overall: 14"; introduced in 1996.
Estimated Value: New (retail) $695.00
                   Excellent: $520.00
                   Very good: $420.00

Supermatic Trophy Citation made from about 1959 to 1966; 5½" bull barrel or 7¼" heavy fluted barrel.
Estimated Value: Excellent: $350.00
                   Very good: $280.00

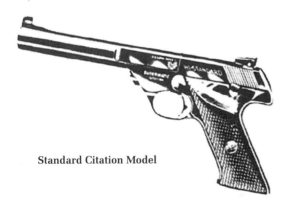
Standard Citation Model

Supermatic Trophy Military Model

Supermatic Citation Model made from about 1959 to 1966; 5½" bull barrel &/or 6¾", 8" or 10" tapered barrel with stabilizer & 2 removable weights; adjustable trigger pull.
Estimated Value: Excellent: $350.00
                   Very good: $280.00

Supermatic Trophy Military Model manufactured from about 1965 to 1985; 5½" bull barrel or 7¼" fluted barrel with square military-style grip; adjustable trigger pull. Add 20% for both barrels.
Estimated Value: Excellent: $360.00
                   Very good: $290.00

High Standard Dura-Matic

Caliber: 22 long rifle
Action: Semi-automatic; concealed hammer; takedown interchangeable barrels model
Magazine: 10-shot clip
Barrel: 4½", 6½"
Sights: Fixed
Finish: Blued; checkered plastic grips
Length Overall: 8⅞", 10⅞"
Approximate wt.: 33 to 35 oz.
Comments: Manufactured from about 1954 to 1969.
Estimated Value: Excellent: $200.00
                        Very good: $160.00

High Standard Dura-Matic

High Standard Plinker

Caliber: 22 long rifle
Action: Semi-automatic; concealed hammer
Magazine: 10-shot clip
Barrel: 4½", 6½"
Sights: Fixed
Finish: Blued; checkered plastic grips
Length Overall: 9" to 11"
Approximate wt.: 28 to 30 oz.
Comments: Made from about 1971 to 1974.
Estimated Value: Excellent: $175.00
                        Very good: $140.00

High Standard Plinker

High Supermatic Trophy

Caliber: 22 long rifle
Action: Semi-automatic; concealed hammer; adjustable trigger pull
Magazine: 10-shot clip
Barrel: 5½" or 7¼"; bull or fluted barrel
Sights: Adjustable; drilled and tapped for scope mount
Finish: Blued; checkered wood grips
Length Overall: 9½" or 11¼"
Approximate wt.: 44 oz.
Comments: Reintroduced in the 1990's; add 4% for 7¼" barrel.
Estimated Value: New (retail): $516.00
                        Excellent: $390.00
                        Very good: $310.00

High Standard Sharpshooter and Survival Pack

Caliber: 22 long rifle
Action: Semi-automatic; concealed hammer
Magazine: 10-shot clip
Barrel: 5½" bull barrel
Sights: Ramp front; adjustable rear
Finish: Blued; checkered walnut grips; nickel available after 1982
Length Overall: 10¼"
Approximate wt.: 42 oz.
Comments: Made from abt. 1971 to 1985. A survival pack consisting of a nickel pistol; extra magazine & canvas case after 1982. Add 25% for complete pack.
Estimated Value: Excellent: $275.00
                        Very good: $220.00

High Standard Sharpshooter

High Standard Victor

Caliber: 22 long rifle
Action: Semi-automatic; concealed hammer; interchangeable barrel
Magazine: 10-shot clip
Barrel: 4½" or 5½" with solid or aluminum ventilated rib & barrel weights
Sights: Ramp front; adjustable rear
Finish: Blued; checkered walnut grips with thumb rest; later models have some parts gold plated
Length Overall: 8¾", 9¾"
Approximate wt.: 38 to 42 oz.
Comments: Hi-Standard type grip or square military type grip. Made from about 1972 to 1985. Reintroduced in the 1990's.
Estimated Value: New (retail)   **$532.00**
                               Excellent: **$400.00**
                               Very good: **$320.00**

High Standard Victor

High Standard 10-X

Caliber: 22 long rifle
Action: Semi-automatic; concealed hammer; adjustable target trigger
Magazine: 10-shot clip; 2 extra (standard)
Barrel: 5½" bull barrel
Sights: Blade front, adjustable rear mounted independent of slide
Finish: Non-reflective blue; checkered walnut military grip; components hand picked & fitted by gunsmith; gunsmith's initials located under left grip
Length Overall: 10¼"
Approximate wt.: 42 oz.
Comments: A custom competition gun. Made in 1980's & 1990's.
Estimated Value: New (retail)   **$870.00**
                               Excellent: **$650.00**
                               Very good: **$520.00**

High Standard 10-X

High Standard Sentinel

Caliber: 22 short, long, long rifle
Action: Single or double; solid frame
Cylinder: 9-shot swing out; simultaneous manual ejector
Barrel: 3", 4", 6"
Sights: Fixed
Finish: Blued or nickel; checkered plastic grips
Length Overall: 8" to 11"
Approximate wt.: 18 to 24 oz.
Comments: Made from about 1954 to 1974; aluminum alloy frame.
Estimated Value: Excellent: **$130.00**
                               Very good: **$105.00**

High Standard Sentinel

High Standard Sentinel Deluxe

Same as Sentinel Revolver except adjustable rear sight; checkered square butt walnut grips; wide trigger; 4" or 6" only; made from about 1965 to 1974.
Estimated Value: Excellent: **$135.00**
                               Very good: **$110.00**

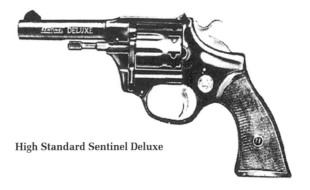

High Standard Sentinel Deluxe

High Standard Sentinel Imperial

Same as Sentinel revolver except ramp front sight; black or nickel finish; checkered square butt walnut grips. Made from about 1961 to 1965.

Estimated Value:	Excellent:	$140.00
	Very good:	$115.00

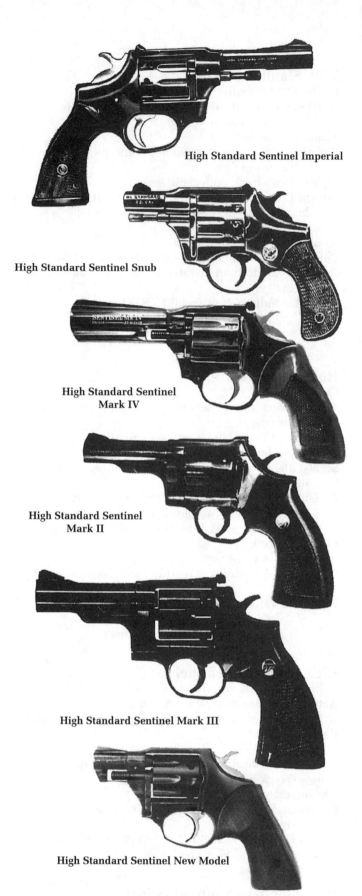

High Standard Sentinel Imperial

High Standard Sentinel Snub

Same as Sentinel revolver except 2⅜" barrel only; overall length 7½"; weighs 15 oz.; checkered plastic bird's head grip (round butt). Made from about 1956 to 1974. Some were made in pink, turquoise & gold colored finish as well as blue & nickel.

Estimated Value:	Excellent:	$165.00
	Very good:	$130.00

High Standard Sentinel Snub

High Standard Sentinel Mark I

Caliber: 22 short, long, long rifle
Action: Single or double; solid frame
Cylinder: 9-shot swing out; simultaneous manual ejector
Barrel: 2", 4"
Sights: Ramp front; fixed or adjustable rear
Finish: Blued or nickel; smooth walnut grips
Length Overall: 7", 9"
Approximate wt.: 28 to 30 oz.
Comments: A completely redesigned & improved all steel version of the 22 caliber Sentinel. Made from about 1974 to late 1970's. Add $10.00 for nickel finish; $10.00 for adjustable rear sight.

Estimated Value:	Excellent:	$175.00
	Very good:	$140.00

High Standard Sentinel
Mark IV

High Standard Sentinel
Mark II

High Standard Sentinel Mark IV

Same as Sentinel Mark I except 22 magnum only. Add $10.00 for nickel finish or adjustable rear sight.

Estimated Value:	Excellent:	$180.00
	Very good:	$145.00

High Standard Sentinel Mark II

Caliber: 38 Special, 357 magnum
Action: Single or double; solid frame
Cylinder: 6-shot swing out; simultaneous manual ejector
Barrel: 2½", 4", 6"
Sights: Fixed rear; ramp front
Finish: Blued; checkered walnut grips
Length Overall: 7½" to 11"
Approximate wt.: 38 to 40 oz.
Comments: Heavy-duty all steel revolver. Made from about 1974 to late 1970's.

Estimated Value:	Excellent:	$195.00
	Very good:	$155.00

High Standard Sentinel Mark III

High Standard Sentinel New Model

High Standard Sentinel Mark III

Same as Sentinel Mark II except deluxe trophy blue finish; checkered walnut wrap-around grips; checkered back strap; adjustable rear sight.

Estimated Value:	Excellent:	$205.00
	Very good:	$165.00

High Standard Sentinel New Model

Similar to the Sentinel with 22 caliber cylinder & interchangeable 22 magnum cylinder. Available with 2" or 4" barrel. Reintroduced in 1982 to 1985. Add $20.00 for extra cylinder.

Estimated Value:	Excellent:	$190.00
	Very good:	$155.00

High Standard Longhorn

Caliber: 22 short, long, long rifle
Action: Single or double; solid frame
Cylinder: 9-shot swing out; simultaneous manual ejector
Barrel: 4½" or 5½" (1961 to 1966); 9½" (1971 to present); dummy ejector housing under barrel
Sights: Blade front; fixed or adjustable rear
Finish: Blued; plastic grips; walnut grips on 9½" barrel model
Length Overall: 10", 11", 15"
Approximate wt.: 26 to 32 oz.
Comments: Aluminum alloy frame (about 1961 to 1971). Steel frame (about 1971 to 1985).
Estimated Value: Excellent: $195.00
Very good: $160.00

High Standard Longhorn Combination

Similar to Longhorn revolver except extra interchangeable cylinder in 22 magnum caliber; 9½" barrel only; smooth walnut grips. Made from about 1971 to 1985.
Estimated Value: Excellent: $225.00
Very good: $180.00

High Standard Kit Gun

Caliber: 22 short, long, long rifle
Action: Single or double; solid frame
Cylinder: 9-shot swing out; simultaneous manual ejector
Barrel: 4"
Sights: Ramp front; adjustable rear
Finish: Blued; checkered walnut grips
Length Overall: 9"
Approximate wt.: 19 oz.
Comments: Aluminum alloy frame. Made from about 1970 to 1973.
Estimated Value: Excellent: $140.00
Very good: $115.00

High Standard Double Nine

Caliber: 22 short, long, long rifle
Action: Single or double; solid frame
Cylinder 9-shot swing out; simultaneous manual ejector
Barrel: 5½"; dummy ejector housing under barrel
Sights: Blade front; fixed or adjustable rear
Finish: Blued or nickel; plastic grips
Length Overall: 11"
Approximate wt.: 28 oz.
Comments: Aluminum alloy frame (about 1958 to 1971); a western style of the Sentinel revolvers. Steel frame from about 1971 to 1985. Add $10.00 for nickel finish.
Estimated Value: Excellent: $190.00
Very good: $150.00

High Standard Double Nine Combination

Same as Double Nine revolver except: extra interchangeable cylinder in 22 magnum caliber; smooth walnut grip; made from about 1971 to 1985; steel frame; weighs 32 oz. Add $10.00 for nickel finish.
Estimated Value: Excellent: $205.00
Very good: $165.00

High Standard Natchez

Similar to Double Nine revolver except 4½" barrel only; 10" overall length; weighs 32 oz.; blued finish only; plastic ivory bird's head grips. Made from about 1961 to 1966.
Estimated Value: Excellent: $160.00
Very good: $130.00

High Standard Posse

Similar to Double Nine revolver except 3½" barrel without dummy ejector housing; 9" overall length; weighs 24 oz.; brass trigger guard & grip frame; blued finish only; smooth walnut grips. Made from about 1961 to 1966.
Estimated Value: Excellent: $150.00
Very good: $120.00

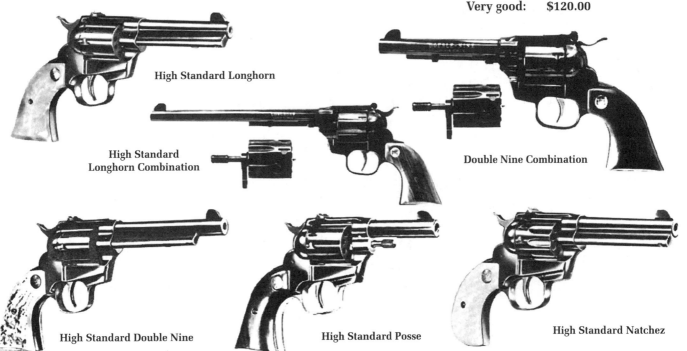

High Standard Longhorn

High Standard Longhorn Combination

Double Nine Combination

High Standard Double Nine

High Standard Posse

High Standard Natchez

High Standard Hombre

Caliber: 22 short, long, long rifle
Action: Single or double; solid frame
Cylinder: 9-shot swing out; simultaneous ejector
Barrel: 4½"
Sights: Blade front; adjustable rear
Finish: Blued or nickel; smooth walnut grip
Length Overall: 10"
Approximate wt.: 26 oz.
Comments: Steel frame; manufactured from about 1972 to 1974. Add $5.00 for nickel finish.
Estimated Value: Excellent: $150.00
                       Very good: $120.00

High Standard Durango

Caliber: 22 short, long, long rifle
Action: Single or double; solid frame
Cylinder: 9-shot swing out; simultaneous ejector
Barrel: 4½", 5½"; dummy ejector housing under barrel
Sights: Blade front; adjustable rear
Finish: Blued or nickel; smooth walnut grip
Length Overall: 10", 11"
Approximate wt.: 25 to 27 oz.
Comments: Made from about 1972 to 1975.
Estimated Value: Excellent: $165.00
                       Very good: $135.00

High Standard High Sierra Combination

Caliber: 22 short, long, long rifle & 22 magnum
Action: Single or double; solid frame
Cylinder: 9-shot swing out; two interchangeable cylinders (22 cal. and 22 mag. cal.)
Barrel: 7" octagonal
Sights: Blade front; adjustable rear
Finish: Blued; smooth walnut grip
Length Overall: 12½"
Comments: Steel frame; gold plated trigger guard & backstrap. Made from about 1973 to 1985.
Estimated Value: Excellent: $220.00
                       Very good: $175.00

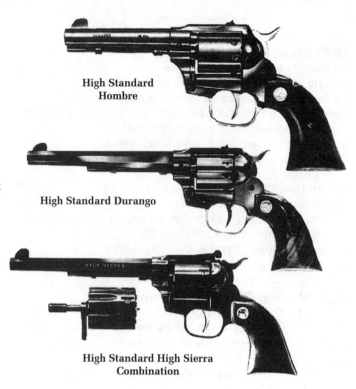

High Standard
Hombre

High Standard Durango

High Standard High Sierra
Combination

High Standard Camp Gun

Caliber: 22 short, long, long rifle and 22 magnum
Action: Single or double; solid frame; simultaneous ejector
Cylinder: 9-shot swing out
Barrel: 6"
Sights: Ramp front; adjustable rear
Finish: Blued; checkered walnut grip
Length Overall: 11"
Approximate wt.: 28 oz.
Comments: Made from about 1975 to late 1970's. Add $10.00 for 22 magnum caliber. Reintroduced in 1982 to 1985.
Estimated Value: Excellent: $200.00
                       Very good: $160.00

High Standard Crusader

Caliber: 44 magnum, 45 Colt, 357 magnum
Action: Single or double
Cylinder: 6-shot
Barrel: 4½" in 44 or 45; 6½" in 44, 45 or 357; 8⅜" in 44, 45 or 357
Sights: Adjustable rear, ramp blade front;
Finish: Blued; shrouded ejector rod; smooth walnut grips in 44; checkered walnut grips in 45 & 357
Length Overall: 9⅞" to 14"
Approximate wt.: 43 to 52 oz.
Comments: A large frame handgun made from about the late 1970's to early 1980's. Add $5.00 for 6½" barrel; add $12.00 for 8⅜" barrel.
Estimated Value: Excellent: $325.00
                       Very good: $260.00

High Standard Crusader Medium Frame

Similar to the Crusader in 357 magnum only; 4½" or 6½" barrel; weight is 40 to 42 oz.; a smaller version of the Crusader. Add $7.00 for 6½" barrel.
Estimated Value: Excellent: $300.00
                       Very good: $240.00

High Standard Camp Gun

High Standard Crusader

High Standard
Crusader Medium Frame

High Standard Derringer

Caliber: 22 short, long, long rifle (1962 to present); 22 magnum rim fire (1963 to present)

Action: Double; concealed hammer; hammer block safety; front of trigger guard cut away

Cylinder: None; 2-shot chambers in barrels

Barrel: 3½" double barrel (superposed); duel ejection; cartridge chamber in each barrel

Sights: Fixed

Finish: Blued or nickel; plastic grips (1962 to present); gold plated presentation model in walnut case (1965 to 1966). Electroless nickel finish and walnut grips after 1982.

Length Overall: 5"

Approximate wt.: 11 oz.

Comments: Steel barrels; aluminum alloy frame. Made from about 1962 to 1985.

High Standard
22 Caliber Derringer

Estimated Value:	Blued	Nickel	Electro. Nickel
Excellent:	$150.00	$170.00	$190.00
Very Good:	$130.00	$135.00	$150.00

Gold presentation models with case in unused condition: (with consecutive numbers)
1-derringer $350.00
2-derringer $800.00

Iver Johnson

Iver Johnson X300 Pony & PO 380

Caliber: 380 ACP

Action: Single action; semi-automatic; exposed hammer

Magazine: 6-shot clip

Barrel: 3"

Sights: Adjustable rear, blade front

Finish: Blued, nickel or military; checkered or smooth walnut grips; stainless steel in 1990 only

Length Overall: 6"

Approximate wt.: 20 oz.

Comments: Add 5% for nickel finish; add 15% for stainless steel; made 1984 to 1990.

Estimated Value:	Excellent:	$230.00
	Very good:	$185.00

Iver Johnson X300 Pony

Iver Johnson Model TP22

Iver Johnson Safety Hammer

Iver Johnson Model TP22 & TP25

Caliber: 22 long rifle (TP22); 25 ACP (TP25)

Action: Double action; semi-automatic; exposed hammer

Magazine: 7-shot clip

Barrel: 3"

Sights: Fixed

Finish: Blued, nickel; plastic grips; finger extension on clip

Length Overall: 5½"

Approximate wt.: 15 oz.

Comments: Made from 1982 to 1991. Add 8% for nickel.

Estimated Value:	Excellent:	$155.00
	Very good:	$125.00

Iver Johnson Trailsman

Caliber: 22 long rifle

Action: Semi-automatic, concealed hammer

Magazine: Clip

Barrel: 4½" or 6"

Sights: Fixed

Finish: Blued; checkered plastic or smooth hardwood grips

Length Overall: 9" to 11"

Approximate wt.: 28 to 30 oz.

Comments: Produced from 1984 to 1987. Add 10% for HiPolish with hardwood grips.

Estimated Value:	Excellent:	$150.00
	Very good:	$120.00

Iver Johnson Safety Hammer

Caliber: 22 S, L, & LR; 32 S&W; 32 S&W long; & 38 S&W

Action: Single or double; exposed hammer; hinged frame; top break style; simultaneous ejector; heavier frame on 32 & 38 caliber

Cylinder: 7-shot in 22 caliber; 6-shot in 32 caliber; 5-shot in 38 caliber

Barrel: 2", 3", 3¼", 4", 5", 6"; round barrel with solid rib

Sights: Fixed

Finish: Blued or nickel; rubber or wood grips; round or square butt

Length Overall: 6¾" to 10¾" depending on barrel length

Approximate wt.: 14 to 21 oz. depending on caliber & barrel length

Comments: Made from about 1892 to 1950 with some improvements & minor changes.

Estimated Value:	Excellent:	$130.00
	Very good:	$105.00

Iver Johnson
Safety Hammerless

Iver Johnson Safety Hammerless

Same as Safety Hammer model except side plates of frame extended to enclose hammer; double action only; concealed hammer. Made from about 1895 to 1950.

Estimated Value: Excellent: $135.00
                    Very good: $110.00

Iver Johnson Model 1900

Caliber: 22 short, long, long rifle, 32 S&W, 32S&W long, 38 S&W

Action: Single or double; exposed hammer; solid frame; side load

Cylinder: 7-shot in 22 caliber; 6-shot in 32 caliber; 5-shot in 38 caliber; removable cylinder

Barrel: 2½", 4½", 6"; octagon barrel

Sights: Fixed

Finish: Blued or nickel; hard rubber grips

Length Overall: 7" to 10¾" depending on barrel length

Approximate wt.: 11 to 19 oz.

Comments: Made from about 1900 to mid 1940's.

Estimated Value: Excellent: $120.00
                    Very good: $ 95.00

Iver Johnson Model 1900 Target

Same as Model 1900 except 22 caliber only; 6" or 9" barrel length; length overall 10¾" to 13¾"; approximate weight is 22 to 26 oz.; checkered walnut grips; blued finish only. Made from about 1925 to 1942.

Estimated Value: Excellent: $130.00
                    Very good: $105.00

Iver Johnson Target 9-Shot Revolver

Similar to Model 1900 Target except 9-shot cylinder; 6" or 10" barrel; 10¾" to 14¾" length overall; weighs 24 to 28 oz. Introduced about 1929 & discontinued in mid 1940's.

Estimated Value: Excellent: $125.00
                    Very good: $100.00

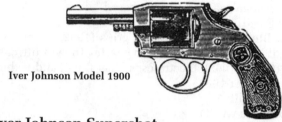

Iver Johnson Model 1900

Iver Johnson Supershot

Caliber: 22 short, long, long rifle

Action: Single or double; exposed hammer; hinged frame; top break style; simultaneous ejector

Cylinder: 7-shot; 9-shot

Barrel: 6"; round barrel with solid rib on top

Sights: Fixed

Finish: Blued; checkered walnut grips (one piece)

Length Overall: 10¾"

Approximate wt.: 25 oz.

Comments: Some have adjustable finger rest behind trigger guard. Made from about 1929 to 1950.

Estimated Value: Excellent: $140.00
                    Very good: $115.00

Iver Johnson Sealed Eight Supershot

Similar to Supershot Revolver except: 8-shot cylinder recessed for cartridge head; 10" barrel length; 10¾" to 14¾" overall length; adjustable rear sight. Made from about 1931 to 1957.

Estimated Value: Excellent: $150.00
                    Very good: $120.00

Iver Johnson Sealed Eight Target

Caliber: 22 short, long, long rifle

Action: Single or double; exposed hammer; solid frame; side load

Cylinder: 8-shot; cylinder recessed for cartridge head; removable

Barrel: 6", 10"; octagon barrel

Sights: Fixed

Finish: Blued; checkered walnut grips (one piece)

Length Overall: 10¾"; 14¾"

Approximate wt.: 24 to 28 oz.

Comments: Made from about 1931 to 1957.

Estimated Value: Excellent: $135.00
                    Very good: $110.00

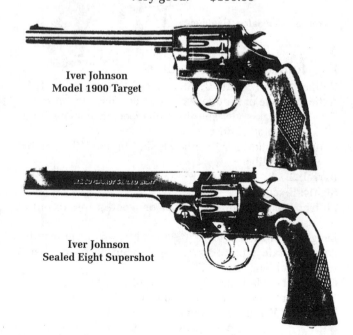

Iver Johnson
Model 1900 Target

Iver Johnson
Sealed Eight Supershot

Iver Johnson Sealed Eight Target

Iver Johnson Sealed Eight Protector

Caliber: 22 short, long, long rifle
Action: Single or double; exposed hammer; hinged frame; top break style; simultaneous ejector
Cylinder: 8-shot; cylinder recessed for cartridge head
Barrel: 2½"
Sights: Fixed
Finish: Blued; checkered walnut grips
Length Overall: 7½"
Approximate wt.: 20 oz.
Comments: Some had adjustable finger rest behind trigger guards. Made from about 1933 to late 1940's.
Estimated Value: Excellent: $150.00
**   Very good: $120.00**

Iver Johnson
Sealed Eight Protector

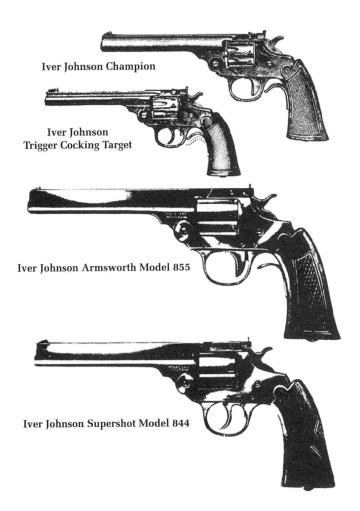
Iver Johnson Champion

Iver Johnson
Trigger Cocking Target

Iver Johnson Armsworth Model 855

Iver Johnson Supershot Model 844

Iver Johnson Champion

Caliber: 22 short, long, long rifle
Action: Single; exposed hammer; hinged frame; top break style; simultaneous ejector
Cylinder: 8-shot; cylinder recessed for cartridge head
Barrel: 6"
Sights: Adjustable target sights
Finish: Blued; checkered walnut grips (one piece)
Length Overall: 10¾"
Approximate wt.: 28 oz.
Comments: Made from about 1938 to 1948. Adjustable finger rest behind trigger guards.
Estimated Value: Excellent: $160.00
**   Very good: $130.00**

Iver Johnson Trigger Cocking Target

Same as Champion Revolver except the trigger cocks the hammer on the first pull, then releases the hammer to fire the revolver on the second pull. Made from about 1940 to 1947.
Estimated Value: Excellent: $170.00
**   Very good: $140.00**

Iver Johnson Armsworth Model 855

Caliber: 22 short, long, long rifle
Action: Single; exposed hammer; hinged frame; top break style; simultaneous ejector
Cylinder: 8-shot; cylinder recessed for cartridge head
Barrel: 6"
Sights: Adjustable front and rear sights
Finish: Blued; checkered walnut grips (one piece)
Length Overall: 10¾"
Approximate wt.: 30 oz.
Comments: Adjustable finger rest behind trigger guards. Made from about 1954 to 1957.
Estimated Value: Excellent: $145.00
**   Very good: $115.00**

Iver Johnson Supershot Model 844

Similar to Armsworth Model 855 except double & single action; 4½" or 6" barrel lengths; 9¼" to 10¾" overall length. Introduced about 1955, discontinued about 1957.
Estimated Value: Excellent: $150.00
**   Very good: $120.00**

Iver Johnson Model 55S Cadet

Iver Johnson Model 55S Cadet

Caliber: 22 short, long, long rifle, 32, 38
Action: Single or double; solid frame; exposed hammer; side load
Cylinder: 8-shot in 22 caliber; 5-shot in 32 & 38 caliber; removable cylinder
Barrel: 2½"
Sights: Fixed
Finish: Blued; plastic round butt grips
Length Overall: 7"
Approximate wt.: 24 oz.
Comments: Made from about 1954 to 1961.
Estimated Value: Excellent: $125.00
**   Very good: $100.00**

Iver Johnson Model 55 S-A Cadet
Similar to Model 55S Cadet except addition of loading gate about 1962; also in calibers 22 WMR and 38 Special. Made from about 1962 to late 1970's.
Estimated Value: Excellent: $120.00
　　　　　　　　　Very good: $ 95.00

Iver Johnson Model 55
Caliber: 22 short, long, long rifle
Action: Single or double; exposed hammer; solid frame; side load
Cylinder: 8-shot; chambers recessed for cartridge head; removable cylinder; unfluted cylinder
Barrel: 4½", 6"
Sights: Fixed
Finish: Blued; checkered walnut grips
Length Overall: 9¼" to 10¾"
Approximate wt.: 22 to 24 oz.
Comments: Made from about 1955 to 1961.
Estimated Value: Excellent: $110.00
　　　　　　　　　Very good: $ 85.00

Iver Johnson Model 55A Target
Same as Model 55 Revolver except: fluted cylinder; loading gate; checkered plastic grips. Introduced about 1962. Made to late 1970's.
Estimated Value: Excellent: $120.00
　　　　　　　　　Very good: $ 95.00

Iver Johnson Model 57
Same as Model 55 Revolver except: adjustable front and rear sights; checkered plastic grips. Made from about 1955 to 1961.
Estimated Value: Excellent: $125.00
　　　　　　　　　Very good: $100.00

Iver Johnson Model 57A Target
Same as Model 55 Revolver except: fluted cylinder; adjustable front and rear sights; checkered plastic grips; loading gate. Produced about 1962 to mid 1970's.
Estimated Value: Excellent: $130.00
　　　　　　　　　Very good: $105.00

Iver Johnson
Model 55 S-A Cadet

Iver Johnson Model 50A Sidewinder

Iver Johnson Model 50A Sidewinder
Caliber: 22 short, long, long rifle
Action: Single or double; exposed hammer; solid frame; side load with loading gates; removable cylinder
Cylinder: 8-shot; recessed chambers
Barrel: 4½", 6"; ejector rod under barrel
Sights: Fixed or adjustable
Finish: Blued; plastic grips
Length Overall: 9¾", 11¼"
Approximate wt.: 32 oz.
Comments: Frontier-style double action revolver. Made from about 1961 to late 1970's. Add 20% for adjustable sights.
Estimated Value: Excellent: $120.00
　　　　　　　　　Very good: $ 95.00

Iver Johnson Model 50A Sidewinder Convertible
Same as Model 50A Sidewinder except: extra interchangeable cylinder for 22 mag. (WMR). Add 10% for adjustable sights.
Estimated Value: Excellent: $130.00
　　　　　　　　　Very good: $105.00

Iver Johnson Model 66 Trailsman
Caliber: 22 short, long, long rifle; 32 S&W; 38 S&W
Action: Single or double; exposed hammer; hinged frame; top break style; simultaneous manual ejector under barrel; rebounding type hammer
Cylinder: 8-shot in 22 caliber; 5-shot in 32 & 38 caliber; recessed chambers
Barrel: 2¾", 6", rib on top of barrel
Sights: Adjustable
Finish: Blued; checkered walnut or plastic grip; round butt on 2¾" barrel; square butt on 6" barrel
Length Overall: 7", 11"
Approximate wt.: 28 to 32 oz.
Comments: 2¾" barrel model from about 1961 to 1971; 6" barrel made from about 1958 to 1975.
Estimated Value: Excellent: $120.00
　　　　　　　　　Very good: $ 95.00

Iver Johnson Model 57A Target

Iver Johnson
Model 66 Trailsman

Iver Johnson Model 67 Viking

Same as Model 66 Trailsman except: hammer safety device; 4½" or 6" barrel lengths. Made from about 1964 to 1975.

Estimated Value: Excellent: $135.00
Very good: $110.00

Iver Johnson Model 67S Viking

Same as Model 67 except: 2¾" barrel lengths; overall length 7"; approximate weight is 25 oz.

Estimated Value: Excellent: $140.00
Very good: $115.00

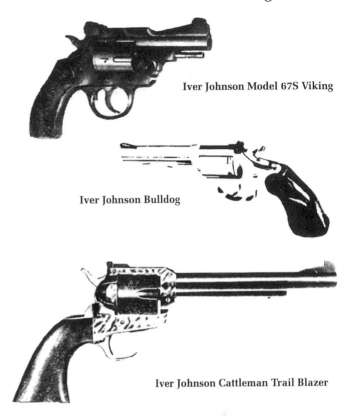

Iver Johnson Model 67S Viking

Iver Johnson Bulldog

Iver Johnson Bulldog

Caliber: 22 short, long, long rifle; 38 Special
Action: Single or double; exposed hammer; solid frame; side load with loading gate
Cylinder: 8-shot in 22 caliber; 5-shot in 38 caliber recessed chambers
Barrel: 2½", 4", heavy duty ribbed
Sights: Adjustable
Finish: Blued; plastic grips; round or square butt
Length Overall: 6½", 9"
Approximate wt.: 26 to 30 oz.
Comments: Made from about 1974 to late 1970's. Add $2.00 for 4" barrel; $10.00 for 38 caliber.

Estimated Value: Excellent: $125.00
Very good: $100.00

Iver Johnson Cattleman Trail Blazer

Iver Johnson Cattleman Trail Blazer

Caliber: 22 short, long, long rifle; 22 magnum (WMR)
Action: Single action; solid frame; exposed hammer; side load with loading gate
Cylinder: 6-shot; 2 interchangeable cylinders
Barrel: 5½", 6", manual ejector rod under barrel
Sights: Ramp front; adjustable rear
Finish: Blued; case-hardened frame, brass backstrap & trigger guard; smooth walnut grip
Length Overall: 11¼" to 12¼"
Approximate wt.: 38 to 40 oz.
Comments: Made from about 1974 to late 1970's. Price includes both cylinders.

Estimated Value: Excellent: $195.00
Very good: $155.00

Iver Johnson Cattleman Magnum

Caliber: 357 mag. & 38 Spec.; 45 long Colt; 44 mag. & 44 Spec.
Action: Single; solid frame; exposed hammer; side load with loading gate
Cylinder: 6-shot
Barrel: 4¾", 5½", 7½" (357 mag. & 44 LC); 4¾", 6", 7½" (44 mag.); manual ejector rod under barrel
Sights: fixed
Finish: Blued; case-hardened frame, brass backstrap and trigger guard; smooth walnut grip
Length Overall: 10½" to 13¼"
Approximate wt.: 38 to 46 oz.
Comments: Made from about 1974 to early 1980's. Add 12% for 44 mag.

Estimated Value: Excellent: $210.00
Very good: $170.00

Iver Johnson Cattleman Buckhorn Magnum

Same as Cattleman Magnum except: ramp front sight & adj. rear sight. Add 10% for 12" barrel; 10% for 44 mag.

Estimated Value: Excellent: $220.00
Very good: $175.00

Iver Johnson Cattleman Buckhorn Buntline

Same as Cattleman Buckhorn Magnum except: 18" barrel length only; grip backstrap is cut for shoulder stock attachment; smooth walnut attachable shoulder stock; overall length without shoulder stock 24" & with shoulder stock 36½"; approximate wt. is 56 oz. without shoulder stock; shoulder stock wt. is approximately 30 oz. Prices include stock. Add 8% for 44 mag.

Estimated Value: Excellent: $375.00
Very good: $305.00

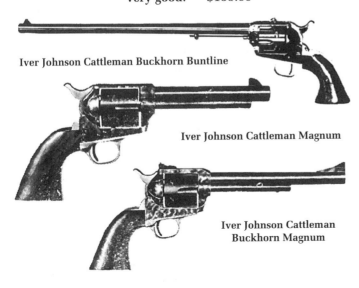

Iver Johnson Cattleman Buckhorn Buntline

Iver Johnson Cattleman Magnum

Iver Johnson Cattleman Buckhorn Magnum

Iver Johnson Sportsman

Iver Johnson Rookie
Caliber: 38 Special
Action: Single or double
Cylinder: 5-shot; fluted
Barrel: 4"
Sights: Fixed
Finish: Blued or nickel; plastic grips
Length Overall: 9"
Approximate wt.: 29 oz.
Comments: Made from the mid to late 1970's.
Estimated Value: Excellent: $140.00
                       Very good: $115.00

Iver Johnson Deluxe Target
Similar to the Sportsman with adjustable sights.
Estimated Value: Excellent: $135.00
                       Very good: $110.00

Iver Johnson Sportsman
Similar to the Rookie in 22 long rifle caliber; 4¾" or 6" barrel; blued finish; made in the mid 1970's.
Estimated Value: Excellent: $130.00
                       Very good: $105.00

Japanese

Type 26 Japanese

Type 26 Japanese
Caliber: 9mm rimmed pistol
Action: Double only; top break; hammer without cocking spur
Magazine: 6-shot; automatic ejector
Barrel: 4¾"
Sights: Blade front; "V" notch rear
Finish: Blued; checkered one-piece round grip
Length Overall: 9½"
Approximate wt.: 32 oz.
Comments: Made from about 1893 to 1914.
Estimated Value: Excellent: $270.00
                       Very good: $215.00

1904 Nambu Japanese
Caliber: 8mm bottle-necked Japanese
Action: Semi-automatic; grip safety below trigger guard
Magazine: 8-shot chip
Barrel: 4¾"
Sights: Barley corn front; notched tangent rear
Finish: Blued; checkered wood grips
Length Overall: 8¾"
Approximate wt.: 32 oz.
Comments: Made from about 1904 to 1925. Usually has a slot cut in rear of grip to accommodate shoulder stock holster. Add 10% for shoulder stock holster.
Estimated Value: Excellent: $865.00
                       Very good: $690.00

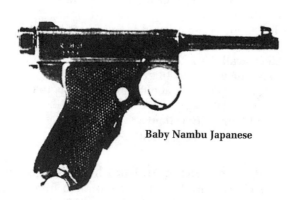

Baby Nambu Japanese

Nambu Type 14 Japanese
Caliber: 8mm bottle-necked Japanese
Action: Semi-automatic; manual safety
Magazine: 8-shot chip
Barrel: 4¾"
Sights: Barley corn front; undercut notch rear
Finish: Blued; grooved wood grips
Length Overall: 9"
Approximate wt.: 32 oz.
Comments: A modified form of the 1904 Nambu introduced about 1925 & produced until about 1945.
Estimated Value: Excellent: $430.00
                       Very good: $345.00

Baby Nambu Japanese
Caliber: 7mm bottle-necked Japanese cartridge
Action: Semi-automatic; grip safety below trigger guard
Magazine: 7-shot chip
Barrel: 3¼"
Sights: Barley corn front; "V" notch rear
Finish: Blued; checkered wood grips
Length Overall: 7¼"
Approximate wt.: 24 oz.
Comments: This is a smaller version of the 1904 Nambu.
Estimated Value: Excellent: $1,500.00
                       Very good: $1,200.00

Modified Nambu Type 14 Japanese

Similar to Nambu Type 14 except it has enlarged trigger guard to allow use of heavy gloves & a spring mounted in lower front of grip to hold magazine more securely.

Estimated Value: **Excellent:** $460.00
  Very good: $370.00

Type 94 Japanese

Caliber: 8mm bottle-necked Japanese
Action: Semi-automatic
Magazine: 6-shot clip
Barrel: 3¾"
Sights: Barley corn front; square notch rear
Finish: Blued; checkered grips
Length Overall: 7¼"
Approximate wt.: 28 oz.
Comments: Made from about 1934 to 1945. Made for export but was used as a service pistol during World War II. Most show evidence of poor manufacture.

Estimated Value: **Excellent:** $325.00
  Very good: $260.00

Type 57 New Nambu Japanese

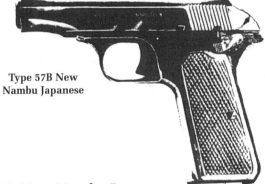

Type 57B New Nambu Japanese

Type 57 New Nambu Japanese

Caliber: 9mm Parabellum; 45 ACP
Action: Semi-automatic; recoil operated
Magazine: 8-shot clip
Barrel: 4½"
Sights: Fixed
Finish: Blued; checkered grips
Length Overall: 7¾"
Approximate wt.: 28 oz.
Comments: A modified copy of the U.S. 1911 A1 produced by the firm of Shin Chuo Kogyo K.K. since World War II. Magazine catch at bottom of grip; doesn't have the grip safety.

Estimated Value: **Excellent:** $215.00
  Very good: $175.00

Type 57B New Nambu Japanese

Caliber: 32 ACP (7.65mm Browning)
Action: Semi-automatic; blowback operated
Magazine: 8-shot clip
Barrel: 3"
Sights: Fixed
Finish: Blued; checkered grips
Length Overall: 6¼"
Approximate wt.: 20 oz.
Comments: A modified copy of the Browning M1910 pistol produced by the firm of Shin Chuo Kogyo K.K. after World War II.

Estimated Value: **Excellent:** $190.00
  Very good: $150.00

Lignose

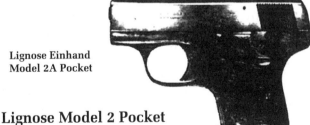

Lignose Einhand Model 2A Pocket

Lignose Model 2 Pocket

Lignose Model 2 Pocket

Caliber: 25 ACP (6.35mm)
Action: Semi-automatic; concealed hammer, thumb safety at top rear of left grip
Magazine: 6-shot clip
Barrel: 2⅛"
Sights: Fixed
Finish: Blued; checkered hard rubber grips
Length Overall: 4¾"
Approximate wt.: 15 oz.
Comments: Operation principle based on the 1906 Browning 25 caliber automatic pocket pistol; production started about 1920. Made in Germany. Early models marked "Bergmann."

Estimated Value: **Excellent:** $270.00
  Very good: $215.00

Lignose Einhand Model 2A Pocket

Similar specifications as Model 2 except designed for one-hand operation, hence the name Einhand (one hand). Slide can be retracted to load & cock hammer, by using the trigger finger to pull back the front part of the trigger guard.

Estimated Value: **Excellent:** $300.00
  Very good: $240.00

Lignose Einhand Model 3A Pocket

Same as Model 2A except longer grip & uses 9-shot clip.

Estimated Value: **Excellent:** $325.00
  Very good: $260.00

Llama

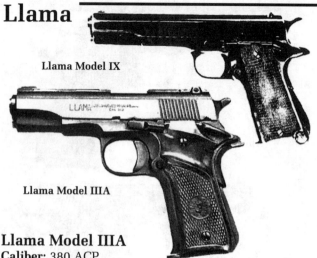

Llama Model IX

Llama Model IIIA

Llama Model IIIA

Caliber: 380 ACP

Action: Semi-automatic; manual & grip safety; exposed hammer

Magazine: 7-shot clip

Barrel: 3¹¹⁄₁₆"

Sights: Partridge front; adjustable rear

Finish: Blued, chrome, chrome engraved; plastic or polymer grips

Length Overall: 6¼"

Approximate wt.: 24 oz.

Comments: Made from about 1951 to present. Ventilated rib on top of slide. Add 18% for chrome; $50.00 for engraving.

Estimated Value: New (retail) $249.00
                        Excellent: $185.00
                        Very good: $150.00

Llama Model VIII

Caliber: 9mm Luger, 38 Super ACP

Action: Semi-automatic; manual & grip safety; exposed hammer

Magazine: 9-shot clip

Barrel: 5"

Sights: Fixed front; adjustable rear

Finish: Blued, chrome, chrome engraved; checkered wood or simulated pearl grips

Length Overall: 8½"

Approximate wt.: 39 oz.

Comments: Made from about 1953 to late 1970's. Add 15% for chrome; 30% for engraved.

Estimated Value: Excellent: $275.00
                        Very good: $220.00

Llama Model XI

Caliber: 9mm Luger

Action: Semi-automatic; manual safety; no grip safety; round exposed hammer

Magazine: 8-shot clip

Barrel: 4⅞"

Sights: Fixed

Finish: Blued, chrome; checkered plastic grips with modified thumb rest

Length Overall: 8"

Approximate wt.: 34 oz.

Comments: Made from about 1951 to late 1970's, with some minor modifications. Add 15% for chrome.

Estimated Value: Excellent: $250.00
                        Very good: $190.00

Llama Model IX

Caliber: 45 ACP

Action: Semi-automatic; locked breech; exposed hammer; manual safety

Magazine: 7-shot clip

Barrel: 5"

Sights: Fixed

Finish: Blued, checkered walnut grips

Length Overall: 8½"

Approximate wt.: 39 oz.

Comments: Made from about 1936 to 1952.

Estimated Value: Excellent: $215.00
                        Very good: $170.00

Llama Model IXA

Similar to Model IX except ventilated rib on slide; modified & improved version; also in chrome & chrome engraved finish. Made from about 1952 to late 1970's. Add 15% for chrome; 30% for chrome engraved.

Estimated Value: Excellent: $225.00
                        Very good: $170.00

Llama Standard Automatic Large Frame

Similar to the Model VIII and IXA except plain slide. Add 25% for chrome finish.

Estimated Value: Excellent: $225.00
                        Very good: $180.00

Llama Model I

Caliber: 32 ACP (7.65mm)

Action: Semi-automatic; blowback-type; exposed hammer

Magazine: 8-shot clip

Barrel: 4"

Sights: Fixed

Finish: Blued, wood grips

Length Overall: 6½"

Approximate wt.: 25 oz.

Comments: Made from about 1935 to 1941.

Estimated Value: Excellent: $175.00
                        Very good: $140.00

Llama Model II

Similar to the Model I except 7-shot clip; caliber 380 ACP (9mm short). Made from about 1935 to 1941.

Estimated Value: Excellent: $185.00
                        Very good: $150.00

Llama Model III

A modified version of the Model II. Made from about 1947 to 1954.

Estimated Value: Excellent: $190.00
                        Very good: $155.00

Llama Model XI

Llama Model XV

Caliber: 22 long rifle
Action: Semi-automatic; blowback-type; exposed hammer; grip & manual safety.
Magazine: 9-shot clip
Barrel: 3¹¹⁄₁₆"
Sights: Partridge type, fixed
Finish: Blued, chrome, chrome engraved; checkered wood grips
Length Overall: 6¼"
Approximate wt.: 18 oz.
Comments: A smaller version of the 1911 A1 Colt 45 ACP. Made from about 1955 to late 1970's. Add 15% for chrome; 30% for engraved.
Estimated Value: Excellent: $210.00
                      Very good: $170.00

Llama Model XA

Same as Model XV except caliber 32 ACP; 8-shot clip. Add 15% for chrome.
Estimated Value: Excellent: $225.00
                      Very good: $180.00

Llama Standard Automatic Small Frame

Similar to the Model XV, XA & IIIA except: 22 LR & 380 calibers; plain slide. Add 35% for chrome finish.
Estimated Value: Excellent: $185.00
                      Very good: $150.00

Llama Standard Automatic
Compact & Mini-Max

Similar to the Large Frame Model but scaled down; 9mm, 40 S & W, or 45ACP caliber; walnut or teakwood grips; 7 or 10-shot clip; 34 to 37 oz.; 4" barrel. Introduced in 1987. Add 12% for chrome finish; add 18% for stainless steel.
Estimated Value: New (retail): $367.00
                      Excellent: $275.00
                      Very good: $220.00

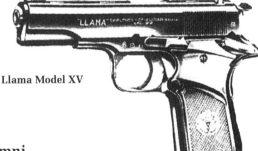

Llama Model XV

Llama Omni

Caliber: 9mm Parabellum, 45 Auto
Action: Semi-automatic; double action; exposed hammer
Magazine: 13-shot clip in 9mm; 7-shot clip in 45
Barrel: 5"
Sights: Ramp blade front; adjustable rear
Finish: Blued; checkered plastic grips
Length Overall: 7½"
Approximate wt.: 30 oz.
Comments: Produced 1982 to 1988.
Estimated Value: Excellent: $350.00
                      Very good: $275.00

Llama Model XVII

Llama M-82 DA

Caliber: 9mm
Action: Double action; semi-automatic
Magazine: 15-shot clip
Barrel: 4¼"
Sights: Fixed front, adjustable rear
Finish: Blued, matte black polymer grips
Length Overall: 7¾"
Approximate wt.: 39 oz.
Comments: Produced in late 1980's & early 1990's.
Estimated Value: Excellent: $730.00
                      Very good: $585.00

Llama Model XVII

Caliber: 22 short
Action: Semi-automatic; exposed hammer with round spur; manual safety
Magazine: 6-shot clip
Barrel: 2⅜"
Sights: Fixed
Finish: Blued, chrome; plastic grips
Length Overall: 4½"
Approximate wt.: 14 oz.
Comments: No longer imported into U.S.A. because of 1968 gun control law. Also known as Executive Model. Add 10% for chrome.
Estimated Value: Excellent: $215.00
                      Very good: $180.00

Llama Model XVIII

Same as Model XVII except 32 ACP caliber only; no longer imported into U.S.A. Add 10% for chrome.
Estimated Value: Excellent: $200.00
                      Very good: $165.00

Llama Max-I

Caliber: 45ACP
Action: Semi-automatic; exposed spur hammer; grip safety; single action
Magazine: 7-shot clip
Barrel: 4¼" (Compact Model); 5½" (Large Frame Model)
Sights: Fixed; 3-dot combat style
Finish: Non-glare combat matte; satin finish chrome; smooth rubber grips
Length Overall: 7⅞" (Compact Model); 8½" (Large Frame Model)
Approximate wt.: 34 to 36 oz.
Comments: Introduced in the early 1990's. Add 14% for chrome. Add 40% for compensator model.
Estimated Value: New (retail): $350.00
                      Excellent: $265.00
                      Very good: $210.00

Llama Martial

Caliber: 22 short, long, long rifle; 38 Special
Action: Double action; solid frame; simultaneous ejector
Cylinder: 6-shot swing out with thumb latch on left side of frame
Barrel: 6" in 22 caliber; 4" and 6" in 38 Special; ventilated rib
Sights: Target sights
Finish: Blued, chrome, chrome engraved; checkered wood or simulated pearl grips
Length Overall: 9¼" to 11¼"
Approximate wt.: 35 to 40 oz.
Comments: Made from about 1969 to late 1970's. Add 10% for chrome; 15% for engraved.
Estimated Value: Excellent: $200.00
                     Very good: $160.00

Llama Martial

Llama Comanche I

Caliber: 22 short, long, long rifle
Action: Double; simultaneous hand ejector; solid frame
Cylinder: 6-shot swing out with thumb latch on left side of frame
Barrel: 6" with ventilated rib
Sights: Ramp front; adjustable rear
Finish: Blued; checkered walnut target grips
Length Overall: 9¼"
Approximate wt.: 36 oz.
Comments: Made from about 1978 to mid 1980's. Add 10% for chrome.
Estimated Value: Excellent: $250.00
                     Very good: $200.00

Llama Comanche II

Similar to the Comanche I in 38 Special with a 4" or 6" barrel. Produced from 1973 to 1980's.
Estimated Value: Excellent: $220.00
                     Very good: $175.00

Llama Comanche III

Similar to the Comanche II in 357 magnum caliber. Add 17% for satin chrome finish.
Estimated Value: Excellent: $255.00
                     Very good: $200.00

Llama Super Comanche, Super Comanche IV

A heavier version of the Comanche in 44 mag.; 6" barrel; 8½" barrel available after early 1980's.
Estimated Value: Excellent: $340.00
                     Very good: $275.00

Llama Super Comanche V

Similar to the Super Comanche IV except 357 caliber. This heavy frame revolver has 4", 6", & 8½" barrel. Produced in 1980's & early 1990's.
Estimated Value: Excellent: $325.00
                     Very good: $260.00

Llama Commanche II

MAB

MAB Model A

Caliber: 25 ACP (6.35mm)
Action: Semi-automatic; concealed hammer; manual safety; blowback design
Magazine: 6-shot clip
Barrel: 2½"
Sights: Fixed front; no rear
Finish: Blued; checkered hard rubber or plastic grips
Length Overall: 4½"
Approximate wt.: 18 oz.
Comments: Resembles Browning Model 1906 vest pocket pistol. Production started about 1924, imported into U.S.A. as WAC Model A or Le Defendeur. Importation stopped in 1968.
Estimated Value: Excellent: $200.00
                     Very good: $160.00

MAB Model B

Similar to Model A except top part of front section of slide cut away for empty cartridges to eject at top. Made from about 1932 to 1966 (never imported into U.S.A.).
Estimated Value: Excellent: $210.00
                     Very good: $170.00

MAB Model C
Caliber: 32 ACP, 380 ACP
Action: Semi-automatic; concealed hammer; grip safety & manual safety
Magazine: 7-shot clip in 32 ACP; 6-shot clip in 380 ACP
Barrel: 3¼"
Sights: Fixed
Finish: Blued; checkered hard rubber grips
Length Overall: 6¼"
Approximate wt.: 23 oz.
Comments: Production started about 1933. Importation into U.S.A. stopped in 1968.
Estimated Value: Excellent: $215.00
Very good: $175.00

MAB Model E
Caliber: 25 ACP (6.35mm)
Action: Semi-automatic; concealed hammer; manual safety & grip safety
Magazine: 10-shot clip
Barrel: 4"
Sights: Fixed
Finish: Blued; checkered plastic grips
Length Overall: 7"
Approximate wt.: 24 oz.
Comments: Production started about 1949; importation into U.S.A. discontinued in 1968. Imported into U.S.A. as WAC Model E.
Estimated Value: Excellent: $210.00
Very good: $170.00

MAB Model F
Caliber: 22 long rifle
Action: Semi-automatic; concealed hammer; manual safety; blowback design
Magazine: 9-shot clip
Barrel: 4½", 6", 7"
Sights: Fixed
Finish: Blued; checkered grips
Length Overall: 8½" to 11"
Approximate wt.: 23 oz.
Comments: Production began in 1950. Imported into U.S.A. under WAC trademark. Importation stopped in 1968.
Estimated Value: Excellent: $215.00
Very good: $175.00

MAB Model E

MAB Model D
Caliber: 32 ACP, 380 ACP
Action: Semi-automatic; concealed hammer; grip safety & manual safety
Magazine: 9-shot clip in 32 ACP, 8-shot clip in 380 ACP
Barrel: 4"
Sights: Fixed
Finish: Blued; checkered hard rubber grips
Length Overall: 7"
Approximate wt.: 25 oz.
Comments: Imported into U.S.A. as WAC Model D or MAB Le Gendarme; manufacture started about 1932; importation discontinued in 1968.
Estimated Value: Excellent: $220.00
Very good: $180.00

MAB Model R

MAB Model P-15
Caliber: 9mm Parabellum
Action: Semi-automatic; exposed hammer with round spur; recoil operated with locking breech; manual safety
Magazine: 8-shot clip; 15-shot staggered row clip
Barrel: 4½"
Sights: Blade front; notch rear
Finish: Blued; checkered grips
Length Overall: 8"
Approximate wt.: 25 oz.
Comments: Bears a resemblance to the Browning Model 1935.
Estimated Value: Excellent: $325.00
Very good: $260.00

MAB Model R
Caliber: 22 long rifle; 32 ACP, 380 ACP, 9mm Parabellum
Action: Semi-automatic; exposed hammer; manual safety
Magazine: 9-shot clip in 22 caliber; 8-shot clip in 32 ACP; 7-shot clip in 380 ACP, 7- or 14-shot clip in 9mm
Barrel: 4½" or 7½" (22); 4" in other calibers
Sights: Fixed
Finish: Blued; checkered grips
Length Overall: 7" to 10½"
Approximate wt.: 25 oz.
Comments: This model was never imported into U.S.A.
Estimated Value: Excellent: $230.00
Very good: $190.00

Mauser

Mauser WTP Model 1 Vest Pocket
Caliber: 25 ACP
Action: Semi-automatic; concealed hammer
Magazine: 6-shot clip
Barrel: 2⅜"
Sights: Fixed
Finish: Blued; hard rubber grips
Length Overall: 4¼"
Approximate wt.: 12 oz.
Comments: Made from about 1923 to 1939.
Estimated Value: Excellent: $325.00
                     Very good: $260.00

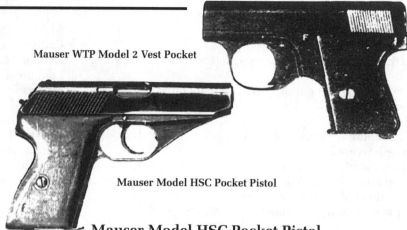

Mauser WTP Model 2 Vest Pocket

Mauser Model HSC Pocket Pistol

Mauser WTP Model 2 Vest Pocket
Similar to the Model 1 except: curved back strap & trigger guard; smaller size (2" barrel, about 4" overall length); approximate weight is 10 oz. Made from about 1939 to 1942 & from about 1950 to present. Importation into U.S.A. discontinued in 1968.
Estimated Value: Excellent: $315.00
                     Very good: $250.00

Mauser Automatic Pocket
Caliber: 25 ACP, 32 ACP
Action: Semi-automatic; concealed hammer
Magazine: 9-shot clip in 25 ACP, 8-shot clip in 32 ACP
Barrel: 3" on 25 ACP; 3½" on 32 ACP
Sights: Fixed
Finish: Blued; checkered walnut or hard rubber grips
Length Overall: 5½" on 25 ACP; 6" on 32 ACP
Approximate wt.: 22 oz.
Comments: 25 ACP model made from about 1910 to 1939. 32 ACP model made from about 1914 to 1934.
Estimated Value: Excellent: $250.00
                     Very good: $200.00

Mauser Model 1934 Pocket

Mauser Model 1934 Pocket
Similar to Automatic Pocket Pistol except larger one-piece wooden wrap-around grip which covered the back strap. Made from about 1934 to 1939. 32 ACP only.
Estimated Value: Excellent: $265.00
                     Very good: $215.00

Mauser Model HSC Pocket Pistol
Caliber: 32 ACP, 380 ACP
Action: Semi-automatic; double action; exposed hammer
Magazine: 8-shot clip
Barrel: 3⅜"
Sights: Fixed
Finish: Blued or nickel; checkered wood grips
Length Overall: 6¼"
Approximate wt.: 21 oz.
Comments: Made from about 1938 to World War II and from about 1968 to late 1980's. Add 5% for nickel finish.
Estimated Value: Excellent: $360.00
                     Very good: $290.00

Mauser Military Model (Broomhandle Mauser)
Caliber: 7.63 Mauser; 9mm Parabellum (during World War I marked with a large figure "9" cut in the wood grip), 9mm Mauser
Action: Semi-automatic; exposed hammer; selective fire introduced in 1930 – selective lever on "N" operated as normal semi-automatic & on "R" operated as a machine pistol with fully automatic fire
Magazine: 5- to 10-shot box magazine standard; 5- to 20-shot magazine on selective fire models
Barrel: 5½" standard; also manufactured with other barrel lengths
Sights: Adjustable for elevation
Finish: Blued; checkered wood, serrated wood, carved wood, smooth wood, or hard rubber grips
Length Overall: 12" with 5½" barrel
Approximate wt.: 43 oz. with 5½" barrel
Comments: Made from about 1896 to 1918 and from about 1922 to 1937 with minor changes & improvements. Also produced with a shoulder stock holster (wood).
Estimated Value: Excellent: $1,500.00 - $7,500.00
                     Very good: $ 850.00 - $4,000.00

Mauser Military Model
(Broomhandle Mauser)

Mitchell Arms
(Mitchell High Standard)

Mitchell Arms Citation II & Trophy II

Caliber: 22 long rifle

Action: Single action semi-automatic; push button barrel change; concealed hammer; thumb safety

Magazine: 10-shot clip

Barrel: 5½" or 7¼" fluted

Sights: Ramp front; adjustable rear on frame-mounted bridge

Finish: Stainless steel; checkered walnut grips with thumb rest

Length Overall: 10¼" to 12½"

Approximate wt.: 42 to 44 oz.

Comments: Made in mid 1990's; based on the High Standard Supermatic Series. Add 6% for the Trophy II Model.

Estimated Value:	Excellent:	$350.00
	Very good:	$280.00

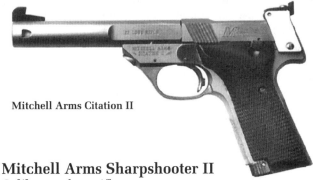

Mitchell Arms Citation II

Mitchell Arms Olympic ISU II

Caliber: 22 long rifle; 22 short (not interchangeable)

Action: Single action semi-automatic; concealed hammer; adjustable trigger; changeable barrel button

Magazine: 10-shot clip

Barrel: 6¾" tapered; integral stabilizer and two removable weights

Sights: Ramp front; frame mounted bridge for adjustable rear sight; drilled and tapped for scope mount

Finish: Stainless steel; checkered grips with thumb rest; stippled front and rear grip frame

Length Overall: 11¼"

Approximate wt.: 40 oz.

Comments: Made in mid 1990's; see High Standard Olympic ISU.

Estimated Value:	Excellent:	$450.00
	Very good:	$360.00

Mitchell Arms Sharpshooter II

Caliber: 22 long rifle

Action: Single action semi-automatic; push button barrel change; concealed hammer; thumb safety

Magazine: 10-shot clip

Barrel: 5½" bull barrel

Sights: Ramp front; adjustable rear

Finish: Stainless steel; checkered walnut grips

Length Overall: 10¼"

Approximate wt.: 42 oz.

Comments: Made in mid 1990's.

Estimated Value:	Excellent:	$285.00
	Very good:	$225.00

Mitchell Arms Sport King II

Caliber: 22 long rifle

Action: Single action semi-automatic; push button barrel change; concealed hammer; thumb safety

Magazine: 10-shot clip

Barrel: 4½" or 6¾"

Sights: Ramp front; adjustable rear

Finish: Stainless steel; checkered plastic grips

Length Overall: 9" or 11¼"

Approximate wt.: 36 to 39 oz.

Comments: Made in mid 1990's.

Estimated Value:	Excellent:	$235.00
	Very good:	$190.00

Mitchell Arms Victor II

Mitchell Arms Victor II

Caliber: 22 long rifle

Action: Single action semi-automatic; push button barrel change; concealed hammer; thumb safety

Magazine: 10-shot clip

Barrel: 4½" or 5½"; ventilated rib, solid rib, or Weaver rib

Sights: Adjustable target sights

Finish: Stainless steel; checkered walnut grips with thumb rest; stippled grip frame in front and rear; gold plated trigger, safety, magazine release, slide lock, and gold filled markings

Length Overall: 9" or 11¼"

Approximate wt.: 36 to 39 oz.

Comments: Made in mid 1990's. Same as the High Standard Victor; add 5% for solid rib model; add 14% for Weaver rib model.

Estimated Value:	Excellent:	$425.00
	Very good:	$340.00

Mitchell Arms Signature Series '94 (Standard Model)

Caliber: 45ACP
Action: Single action semi-automatic; exposed target-style skeleton round spur hammer; grip safety and manual thumb safety
Magazine: 8-shot clip; beveled magazine well
Barrel: 5"; low profile rib on slide
Sights: Fixed or adjustable
Finish: Blued steel or stainless steel; checkered walnut grips; stippled grip frame
Length Overall: 8½"
Approximate wt.: 40 oz.
Comments: Add 8% for adjustable sights; add 6% for stainless steel. Made in mid 1990's.

Estimated Value:	Excellent:	$395.00
	Very good:	$320.00

Mitchell Arms Signature Series '94 (Wide Body)

Same as Standard Model except: wider grip frame to accommodate the staggered 13-shot clip; smooth walnut grips; add 6% for adjustable sights; add 5% for stainless steel finish.

Estimated Value:	Excellent:	$510.00
	Very good:	$405.00

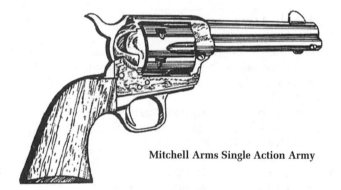

Mitchell Arms Single Action Army

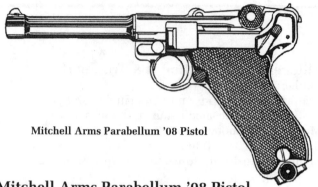

Mitchell Arms Parabellum '08 Pistol

Mitchell Arms Parabellum '08 Pistol

Caliber: 9mm Luger
Action: Single action semi-automatic; patterned after the German 9mm Luger pistol
Magazine: 7-shot clip
Barrel: 5"; round
Sights: Fixed
Finish: Stainless steel, checkered grips
Length Overall: 10"
Approximate wt.: 36 oz.
Comments: Made in mid 1990's.

Estimated Value:	Excellent:	$520.00
	Very good:	$415.00

Mitchell Arms Single Action Army

Caliber: 357 magnum and 38 Special; 45 Colt
Action: Single action ; exposed hammer; side load
Cylinder: 6-shot with loading gate
Barrel: 4¾"; 5½", or 7½"; ejector rod
Sights: Fixed; blade front, notched rear
Finish: Blued or nickel; walnut grips
Length Overall: 10"
Approximate wt.: 36 oz.
Comments: Patterned after the Colt Single Action Army Revolver. Add 10% for nickel finish. Add 38% for extra cylinder in 45 ACP. Made in mid 1990's.

Estimated Value:	Excellent:	$300.00
	Very good:	$240.00

New England

New England Standard Revolver-22

Caliber: 22 short, long, or long rifle; 22 Win. magnum
Action: Single or double; exposed hammer; solid frame
Cylinder: 9-shot 22 short, long, or long rifle; 6-shot in 22 magnum; swing-out, simultaneous manual ejector
Barrel: 2½" or 4"
Sights: Blade front; fixed rear (groove in frame)
Finish: Blued or nickel; hardwood, walnut finish smooth grips
Length Overall: 7" (2½" barrel), 8½" (4" barrel)
Approximate wt.: 26 oz.
Comments: Introduced in 1989. Add 10% for nickel finish.

Estimated Value:	New (retail):	$136.00
	Excellent:	$105.00
	Very good:	$ 80.00

New England Standard Revolver-32 H&R Magnum

New England Standard Revolver-32 H&R Magnum

Same as the Standard Revolver-22 except 32 H&R magnum caliber only; 5-shot cylinder; approximate wt: 25 oz. Introduced in 1989. Add 10% for nickel finish.

Estimated Value:	New (retail):	$136.00
	Excellent:	$105.00
	Very good:	$ 80.00

New England Ultra Revolver

Caliber: 22 S, L, or LR; 22 Win. mag.; 32 H&R mag

Action: Single or double; exposed hammer; swing out cylinder

Cylinder: 9-shot; (22 S, L, or LR); 6-shot (22 mag.); 5-shot (32 H&R mag.); simultaneous manual ejector

Barrel: 3" or 6"; with solid rib

Sights: Blade front; adjustable rear

Finish: Blued; hardwood, walnut finish smooth grips

Length Overall: 7⅝" (3" barrel); 10⅝" (6" barrel)

Approximate wt.: 31 to 36 oz.

Comments: Introduced in 1990. Add 5% for 32 mag.

Estimated Value:	New (retail):	$189.00
	Excellent:	$140.00
	Very good:	$115.00

New England
Ultra Revolver

New England Lady Ultra

Caliber: 32 H&R mag

Action: Single or double; exposed hammer; solid frame

Cylinder: 5-shot swing out; simultaneous ejector

Barrel: 3" solid rib

Sights: Blade front; adjustable rear

Finish: Blued; smooth wood grips

Length Overall: 7¼"

Approximate wt.: 31 oz.

Comments: Introduced in the early 1990's.

Estimated Value:	New (retail):	$195.00
	Excellent:	$140.00
	Very good:	$115.00

North American Arms

North American Arms (Mini Revolver)

Caliber: 22 short; 22 long rifle (1976); 22 mag. (1978)

Action: Single action; exposed hammer; spur trigger; solid frame

Cylinder: 5-shot; removable cylinder; available with two cylinders (22 long rifle and 22 mag.)

Barrel: 1⅛"; 1⅝"; 2½"; 4"

Sights: Blade front; fixed rear

Finish: Stainless steel; polycarbonate round butt (bird head) grips

Length Overall: 4" to 8", depending on barrel length & caliber

Approximate wt.: 4 to 6 oz.

Comments: Made from about 1975 to present. Add 12% for 22 mag.; 30% for revolver with both cylinders; add 65% for 4" barrel.

Estimated Value:	New (retail):	$157.00
	Excellent:	$118.00
	Very good:	$ 95.00

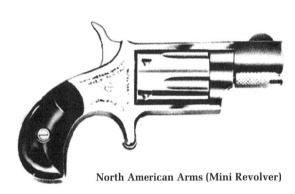

North American Arms (Mini Revolver)

Remington

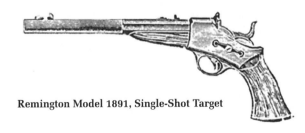

Remington Model 1891, Single-Shot Target

Remington Model 1891, Single-Shot Target

Caliber: 22, 25, 32RF, 32 S&W CF

Action: Single

Cylinder: None; single-shot with rolling breech block for rim fire or center fire calibers

Barrel: 8", 10", 12"; half-octagon

Sights: Dovetail, German silver front & adjustable "V" notch rifle rear

Finish: Blued barrel; case-hardened frame; oil finished walnut grips & fore-end

Length Overall: 12" to 16" depending on barrel length

Approximate wt.: 40 to 45 oz.

Comments: Made from about 1891 to 1900 in light target calibers. Serial number on side of frame under grip. Less than 200 made.

Estimated Value:	Excellent:	$1,200.00
	Very good:	$ 900.00

Remington 41 Caliber Double Derringer

Caliber: 41 caliber rim fire
Action: Single; visible hammer with safety position; sheath trigger; manual extractor
Cylinder: None; 2-shot double barrels
Barrel: 3" superposed double barrels; ribbed top barrel; barrels swing up to load & extract cartridges
Sights: Blade front; groove in frame rear
Finish: Blued or nickel plated; plain or engraved; round butt grips made of metal, walnut, rosewood, hard rubber, ivory or pearl
Length Overall: 4⅞"
Approximate wt.: 11 oz.
Comments: Approximately 132,000 were produced from about 1866 to 1935. Serial numbers were repeated on these pistols, so the best way to estimate the age of a pistol is by the markings. They were marked as follows:
1866-1869: no extractors; left side of barrel E. REMINGTON & SONS, ILION, N.Y.; right side of barrel ELLIOT'S PATENT DEC. 12, 1865
1869-1880: left side of barrel - ELLIOT'S PATENT DEC. 12 1865; right side of barrel - E. REMINGTON & SONS, ILION, N.Y.
1880-1888: barrel rib top - E. REMINGTON & SONS, ILION N.Y. ELLIOT'S PATENT DEC. 12th 1865
1888-1910: barrel rib top - REMINGTON ARMS CO. ILION N.Y.
1910-1935: barrel rib top - REMINGTON ARMS U.M.C. CO. ILION, N.Y.
In 1934 the Double Derringer was called Model No. 95.
Estimated Values:

Plain models	Excellent:	$500.00 - $1,000.00
	Very good:	$400.00 - $ 800.00
Presentation models	Excellent:	$650.00 - $1,200.00
	Very good:	$450.00 - $1,000.00

Remington 41 Caliber
Double Derringer

Remington Model 1901, De-Luxe (S-S) Target

Caliber: 22 short, long, long rifle, 44 Russian CF
Action: Single
Cylinder: None; single-shot with rolling breech block for rim fire or center fire calibers
Barrel: 9" round; 10" half-octagon
Sights: Ivory bead front; adjustable "V" rear
Finish: Blued barrel & frame; checkered walnut grips & fore-end
Length Overall: 13" to 14"
Approximate wt.: 36 to 44 oz.
Comments: Made from about 1901 to 1909. Approximately 1,000 produced.
Estimated Value: Excellent: $1,000.00
                    Very good: $ 800.00

Remington Model 1901,
De-Luxe (S-S) Target

Remington Model XP-100 Long Range

Caliber: 221 Remington "Fire Ball"
Action: Bolt action; single shot; thumb safety
Cylinder: None
Barrel: 10½" round steel with ventilated rib
Sights: Blade front; adjustable rear
Finish: Blued with bright polished bolt & handle; brown checkered nylon (Zytel) one-piece grip & fore-end. Fore-end has cavity for adding balance weights
Length Overall: 16¾"
Approximate wt.: 60 oz.
Comments: Made from about 1963 to 1986. Receiver is drilled & tapped for scope mount.
Estimated Value: Excellent: $300.00
                    Very good: $240.00

Remington Model XP-100
Long Range

Remington Model XP-100 Silhouette

Similar to the Model XP-100 Long Range except: 10½" or 14½" plain barrel; 7mm Benchrest Rem. caliber; walnut or Zytel (nylon) stock; adj. sights; produced from 1980 to present.

 Estimated Value: New (retail): $625.00
                     Excellent: $460.00
                     Very good: $375.00

Remington Model XP-100
Silhouette

Remington Model XP-100 Varmint Special

Similar to the XP-100 Silhouette in 223 Rem. caliber. Zytel (nylon) stock; Introduced in 1988.
Estimated Value: Excellent: $340.00
                    Very good: $275.00

Remington Model XP-100 Hunter
Caliber: 223 Rem., 7mm-08 Rem., 35 Rem.
Action: Bolt action; single shot
Cylinder: None
Barrel: 14½" plain; drilled & tapped for scope
Sights: None
Finish: Blued; laminated wood, one-piece stock
Length Overall: 21"
Approximate wt.: 4½lbs.
Comments: Introduced in 1993.
Estimated Value: New (retail): $548.00
                    Excellent: $410.00
                    Very good: $330.00

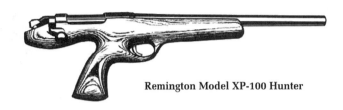
Remington Model XP-100 Hunter

Remington Experimental 45 Caliber
An estimated value hasn't been placed on this pistol since it is not known how many were produced or how they were marked. They were similar to the Remington Model 51 Automatic Pistol except: in 45 caliber, larger, & had an exposed spur hammer. They were made for the U.S. Government test purposes about 1917.

Remington US Model 1911 and 1911 A1
These were pistols made by Remington, on the Colt Patent, for the U.S. Government during World War I & World War II. See "Colt Government Model 1911 and 1911 A1" for prices.

Remington Model 51
Caliber: 32 ACP, 380 ACP
Action: Semi-automatic; concealed hammer
Magazine: 8-shot clip in 32 caliber; 7-shot clip in 380 caliber
Barrel: 3¼"
Sights: Fixed
Finish: Blued; hard rubber grips
Length Overall: 6⅝"
Approximate wt.: 20 oz.
Comments: Made from about 1920 to 1934. Approximately 69,000 were produced in 32 and 380 calibers.
Estimated Value: Excellent: $400.00
                    Very good: $320.00

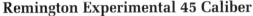

Rossi

Rossi Model M68 & M88
Caliber: 38 Special
Action: Double or single; exposed hammer
Cylinder: 5-shot fluted, swing out
Barrel: 2" or 3"; partially shrouded ejector rod
Sights: Fixed; ramp front, low profile rear
Finish: Blued or nickel (M68); stainless steel (M-88); checkered wood or rubber combat style grips
Length Overall: 6½" to 7½"
Approximate wt.: 21 to 23 oz.
Comments: Introduced in the 1980's. Add 4% for nickel finish; add 18% for stainless steel.
Estimated Value: New (retail): $225.00
                    Excellent: $170.00
                    Very good: $135.00

Rossi Model M68 & M88

Rossi Model M515 & M518
Caliber: 22 mag. (M515); 22 short, long, and long rifle (M518)
Action: Double or single; exposed hammer
Cylinder: 6-shot fluted, swing out
Barrel: 4"; partially shrouded ejector rod; solid rib
Sights: Ramp front with red insert; adjustable rear
Finish: All stainless steel; checkered wood or wrap around rubber combat grips
Length Overall: 9"
Approximate wt.: 30 oz.
Comments: Introduced in 1994. Add 6% for 22 magnum (M515).
Estimated Value: New (retail): $275.00
                    Excellent: $205.00
                    Very good: $165.00

Rossi Model M720 & M720 Hammerless
Caliber: 44 Special
Action: Double or single on exposed hammer model; double only on shrouded hammer model
Cylinder: 5-shot fluted, swing out
Barrel: 3"; shrouded ejector rod; solid rib
Sights: Ramp front with red insert; adjustable rear; fixed square notch rear on hammerless model
Finish: Stainless steel; rubber wrap around combat grips
Length Overall: 8"
Approximate wt.: 28 oz.
Comments: Hammerless model introduced in 1994.
Estimated Value: New (retail): $312.00
                    Excellent: $235.00
                    Very good: $190.00

Rossi Model M851

Caliber: 38 Special
Action: Double or single; exposed hammer
Cylinder: 6-shot, swing out
Barrel: 4"; shrouded ejector rod; ventilated rib
Sights: Ramp front with red insert; adjustable rear
Finish: Stainless steel; checkered wood grips
Length Overall: 9"
Approximate wt.: 35 oz.
Comments: Introduced in the late 1980's.
Estimated Value: New (retail): $270.00
                  Excellent: $205.00
                  Very good: $165.00

Rossi Model M851

Rossi Model M971

Rossi Model M971

Caliber: 357 magnum and 38 Special
Action: Double or single; exposed hammer
Cylinder: 6-shot, swing out
Barrel: 2½", 4", or 6", shrouded ejector rod; solid rib
Sights: Ramp front with red insert; adjustable rear
Finish: Blued (4" only); stainless steel in all barrel lengths; checkered wood or rubber combat grips
Length Overall: 8¼", 9¼", or 11¼"
Approximate wt.: 22, 36, or 41 oz.
Comments: Add 12% for stainless steel.
Estimated Value: New (retail): $290.00
                  Excellent: $218.00
                  Very good: $175.00

Ruger

Ruger Standard Automatic

Caliber: 22 long rifle
Action: Semi-automatic; concealed hammer; thumb safety
Magazine: 9-shot clip
Barrel: 4¾" or 6"; tapered round barrel
Sights: Partridge-type front; dovetail rear
Finish: Blued; checkered walnut or hard rubber grips
Length Overall: 8¾", 10"
Approximate wt.: 36 to 38 oz.
Comments: Made from about 1949 to 1982. (Sturm Ruger Company was formed about 1949.) Red eagle insignia on grip used until 1951, then changed to black eagle insignia, after death of Alex Sturm. Add 130% for red eagle insignia on grip (pre-1951).
Estimated Value: Excellent: $175.00
                  Very good: $140.00

Ruger Mark I Target

Similar to Ruger Standard Automatic except adjustable sights; 6⅞" tapered barrel only. Made from about 1950 to 1982.
Estimated Value: Excellent: $180.00
                  Very good: $140.00

Ruger Standard Automatic

Ruger Mark I Target

Ruger Mark I Bull Barrel Target

Similar to Ruger Mark I Target Pistol except barrel length 5½"; overall length 9½"; untapered heavier barrel. Made from about 1963 to 1982.
Estimated Value: Excellent: $185.00
                  Very good: $145.00

Ruger Mark II Standard Automatic

Similar to the Standard Automatic except: blued or stainless steel; internal improvements; 10-shot clip; slight difference in rear receiver design; 4¾" or 6" round tapered barrel. Introduced in 1982. Add 31% for stainless steel.
Estimated Value: New (retail): $252.00
                  Excellent: $190.00
                  Very good: $150.00

Ruger Mark II Target

Similar to the Mark II Standard Automatic with adjustable sights. 5½", 6⅞, or 10" tapered barrel. Introduced in 1982. Add 28% for stainless steel.
Estimated Value: New (retail): $311.00
                  Excellent: $230.00
                  Very good: $185.00

Ruger Mark I Bull Barrel Target

Ruger Mark II Bull Barrel Target
Similar to the Mark II Target with 5½" or 6⅞" bull barrel. Introduced in 1982. Also 10" bull barrel introduced in 1983. Add 20% for stainless steel.

Estimated Value:	New (retail):	$357.00
	Excellent:	$265.00
	Very good:	$215.00

Ruger Mark II Government
Similar to the Mark II Bull Barrel with a 6⅞" bull barrel. Add 20% for stainless steel.

Estimated Value:	New (retail):	$357.00
	Excellent:	$265.00
	Very good:	$215.00

Ruger 22/45
Similar to the Mark II 22 models except: 4¾" and 5¼" tapered barrel or 5½" bull barrel; 400 series stainless steel; approximate wt.: 28 to 35 oz.; injection moulded grip and trigger guard; frame of Zytel, a fiberglass reinforced composite; the grip angle and magazine latch almost identical to the Colt 1911 Model 45 ACP; fixed or adjustable sights; add 18% for 5¼" or 5½" barrel with adjustable sights.

Estimated Value:	New (retail):	$280.00
	Excellent:	$210.00
	Very good:	$170.00

Important safety warning to owners of Ruger P85 made between 1987 and 1990. If the firing pin is broken, these pistols may fire when the safety/decock lever is depressed. Contact Sturm, Ruger, and Company, Prescott, Arizona 1-(800)-424-1886 to schedule factory modification.

Ruger Model P85
Caliber: 9mm
Action: Double action, recoil operated semi-automatic, ambidextrous safety
Magazine: 15-shot, staggered detachable
Barrel: 4½"
Sights: Fixed
Finish: Blued or stainless steel; grooved plastic grips with Ruger insignia
Length Overall: 8"
Approximate wt.: 32 oz.
Comments: A compact combat pistol; made from 1987 to 1990. Add 10% for extra magazine & high impact molded case. Add 12% for stainless steel.

Estimated Value:	Excellent:	$285.00
	Very good:	$230.00

Ruger Model P85 Mk II
Same as the Model P85 except: new features and field-tested refinements, such as changes to the safety mechanism to prevent firing during decocking, even in the event of a broken firing pin. Introduced in 1990. Add 10% for stainless steel. Discontinued in 1993.

Estimated Value:	Excellent:	$310.00
	Very good:	$245.00

Ruger Model P85

Ruger Model P89
Similar to the Model P85 MK II except: decocking lever or regular safety. Introduced in 1991. Also available in double action only with spurless hammer. Add 10% for stainless steel.

Estimated Value:	New (retail):	$410.00
	Excellent:	$310.00
	Very good:	$245.00

Ruger Model P90
Similar to the Model P85 MK II except: 45ACP; 7-shot clip; regular safety or decocking lever; stainless steel only. Introduced 1992.

Estimated Value:	New (retail):	$489.00
	Excellent:	$365.00
	Very good:	$295.00

Ruger Model P91
Similar to the Model P85 MK II except: 40 S&W; 11-shot clip; stainless steel only; no external safety lever; decocking lever or double action only; double action only has spurless hammer.

Estimated Value:	New (retail):	$489.00
	Excellent:	$365.00
	Very good:	$295.00

Ruger Model P93
Similar to the Model P91 except: 15-shot clip; 9mm; 4" barrel; also in stainless steel with decocking lever or double action only; double action only has spurless hammer. Introduced in 1993.

Estimated Value:	New (retail):	$520.00
	Excellent:	$390.00
	Very good:	$310.00

Ruger Model P94
Similar to the Model P93 except: 4½" barrel; overall length 7½"; approximate wt.: 33 oz.; 9mm 15-shot or 40 S&W 11-shot; all stainless steel; slightly larger than the Model P93; fixed white dot sights; it has a tilting barrel link as in the Colt M1911A1; available in following models: double action with regular safety; decocking lever; and double action only spurless hammer.

Estimated Value:	New (retail):	$520.00
	Excellent:	$390.00
	Very good:	$310.00

Ruger GP-100 Double-Action Revolver

Caliber: 357 mag. or 38 Special
Action: Double & single; solid frame; exposed hammer
Cylinder: 6-shot; swing out; simultaneous ejector
Barrel: 3", 4", or 6" heavy barrel with ejector rod shroud
Sights: Fixed or changeable front; fixed or adjustable rear
Finish: Blued or stainless steel; with a cushioned grip system. A newly designed skeleton-type grip frame is used. The grips are rubber with polished wood inserts.
Length Overall: 8⅜" or 11⅜"
Approximate wt.: 36 to 46 ozs.
Comments: Introduced in 1986. Add 8% for stainless steel. Add 4% for adjustable sights.
Estimated Value: New (retail): $440.00
                       Excellent: $330.00
                       Very good: $265.00

Ruger Model SP 101

Caliber: 9mm; 357 mag. & 38 Spl.; 32 H&R; 22 S, L, or LR
Action: Single & double; exposed hammer; or spurless hammer
Cylinder: 5-shot (9mm, 357 mag. &38 Spl.); 6-shot (22 & 32 H&R caliber); swing-out
Barrel: 2" or 3¹⁄₁₆" (38 Special); 2" or 4" (22 caliber); shrouded ejector rod
Sights: Ramp front; fixed rear; 22 has adjustable rear
Finish: Stainless steel except grips & sights; rubber grips with polished inserts
Length Overall: 7½" to 9½"
Approximate wt.: 25 to 27 ozs. (38 Spl, 9mm & 357 mag.); 32 oz. (22 & 32 H&R)
Comments: Introduced in 1990.
Estimated Value: New (retail): $443.00
                       Excellent: $335.00
                       Very good: $265.00

Ruger GP-100 Double-Action Revolver

In 1982 Ruger announced the production of a Single Action Conversion Kit that could be fitted on any "Old Model" Ruger Single Action revolver. This innovation, fitted at the factory, would give the old model a "transfer bar" type mechanism by replacing a few key parts in the revolver. This would provide a safer handling single action. Unless it can be verified that the conversion has been made at the factory, all "Old Model" Single Action revolvers should be handled as such with caution.

Ruger Single-Six

Caliber: 22 short, long, long rifle, 22 WMR (after 1959)
Action: Single; solid frame with loading gate
Cylinder: 6-shot half fluted; flat loading gate from 1954 to 1957 then changed to fit the contour of the frame
Barrel: 4⅝", 5½", 6½", 9½"; ejector rod under barrel
Sights: Blade front; rear sight dovetailed & can be tapped to left or right
Finish: Blued; checkered hard rubber or smooth walnut grips
Length Overall: 10", 10⅞", 11⅞", 14⅞"
Approximate wt.: 32 to 36 oz.
Comments: The grip frame is made of aluminum alloy & the frame is made of chrome molybdenum steel; produced from about 1953 to 1973. Add $150.00 for flat loading gate.
Estimated Value: Excellent: $200.00
                       Very good: $160.00

Ruger Lightweight Single-Six

Same as Ruger Single-Six except: made in 22 short, long & long rifle only; 4⅝" barrel; 10" overall length; weighs 23 oz.; cylinder & frame made of lightweight alloy. Produced from about 1956 to 1958.
Estimated Value: Excellent: $225.00
                       Very good: $180.00

Ruger Convertible Single-Six

Same as Ruger Single-Six revolver except: furnished with two cylinders – one chambered for 22 & the other chambered for 22 WMR. Manufactured from about 1961 to 1973. Prices for guns with both cylinders.
Estimated Value: Excellent: $220.00
                       Very good: $175.00

Ruger Convertible Super Single-Six Convertible

Same as Ruger Single-six revolver except: ramp front sight; adjustable rear sight with protective ribs on frame to protect rear sight. Made from about 1964 to 1973. Priced for gun with both cylinders.
Estimated Value: Excellent: $225.00
                       Very good: $180.00

Ruger Single-Six

Ruger New Model Super Single-Six Convertible

Similar to Ruger Convertible Super Single-Six except: adj. sights; improved version featuring wide trigger; heavy stronger lock words; transfer bar firing pin protector; new interlocking mechanism; other improvements. Made from about 1973 to present. 22 LR and 22 WMR cylinders.

Estimated Value:	New (retail):	$393.00
	Excellent:	$295.00
	Very good:	$235.00

Ruger New Model Super Single-Six Convertible Stainless Steel

Same as Ruger New Model Super Single-Six Convertible Revolver except: all stainless steel construction except sights (blued). 5½" or 6½" barrel only. Made from about 1976 to present. Priced for gun with both cylinders.

Estimated Value:	New (retail):	$393.00
	Excellent:	$295.00
	Very good:	$235.00

Ruger New Model Super Single-Six Convertible

Ruger New Model Super Single-Six Convertible Stainless Steel

Ruger New Model Single-Six 32 Mag

Ruger Blackhawk 357 Convertible

Ruger Vaquero

Caliber: 45 long Colt (1993); 44-40 (1994); 44 mag. (1994)
Action: Single; solid frame with loading gate
Cylinder: 6-shot; fluted
Barrel: 4⅝", 5½", or 7½" in 45 long Colt and 44-40 calibers; 5½", or 7½" in 44 mag.; ejector rod
Sights: Fixed; blade front and groove in frame for rear
Finish: Blued with color case finish on frame or high gloss stainless steel; smooth rosewood grips
Length Overall: 10¼" to 13⅛"
Approximate wt.: 39 to 41 oz.
Comments: Introduced in 1993. Blued or stainless steel same price. Add 8% for simulated ivory grips.

Estimated Value:	New (retail):	$434.00
	Excellent:	$325.00
	Very good:	$260.00

Ruger New Model Super Single-Six 32 Mag.

Caliber: 32 H&R; also handles 32 S&W & 32 S&W long
Action: Single; solid frame with loading gate
Cylinder: 6-shot; heavy fluted cylinder
Barrel: 4¾", 5½", 6½" or 9½"; ejector rod
Sights: Ramp front, adjustable rear
Finish: Blued; smooth walnut grips
Length Overall: 9⅞" to 14⅞"
Approximate wt.: 32 to 36 oz.
Comments: Introduced in 1986 to bridge the gap between the 22 caliber & 38 caliber revolvers.

Estimated Value:	New (retail):	$313.00
	Excellent:	$235.00
	Very good:	$190.00

Ruger Blackhawk 357 Magnum

Caliber: 357 magnum & 38 Special interchangeably
Action: Single; solid frame with loading gate
Cylinder: 6-shot
Barrel: 4⅝", 6½"; round barrel with ejector rod under barrel
Sights: Ramp front; adjustable rear sight
Finish: Blued; checkered hard rubber or smooth walnut wood grips
Length Overall: 10⅛"; 12"
Approximate wt.: 35 to 40 oz.
Comments: Made from about 1955 to 1973. In 1961 the frame was modified to a heavier frame with integral ribs on top to protect rear sight and slight grip alterations to improve the comfort of the "hold."

Estimated Value:	Pre-1961	Post-1961
Excellent:	$200.00	$230.00
Very good:	$150.00	$185.00

Ruger Blackhawk 357 Convertible

Same as Ruger Blackhawk 357 Magnum Revolver except fitted with extra interchangeable cylinder for 9mm Parabellum cartridges. Manufactured from about 1967 to 1973.

Estimated Value:	Excellent:	$240.00
	Very good:	$190.00

Ruger New Model Blackhawk

Similar to Ruger Blackhawk 357 except: improved version featuring wide trigger; stronger lock works; transfer bar firing pin protector; new interlocking mechanism; other improvements. Made from about 1973 to present in 30 carbine, 357 mag., 41 mag. & 45 long Colt.

Estimated Value:	New (retail):	$360.00
	Excellent:	$270.00
	Very good:	$215.00

Ruger Stainless Steel New Model Blackhawk 357

Same as Ruger New Model Blackhawk except: Stainless steel construction except sights (blued). Made from about 1976 to present.

Estimated Value:	New (retail):	$443.00
	Excellent:	$330.00
	Very good:	$265.00

Ruger New Model Blackhawk Convertible

Same as Ruger New Model Blackhawk except: fitted with extra interchangeable cylinder for 357 magnum & 9mm Parabellum cartridges from about 1973 to present; 45 Colt & 45 ACP cartridges from about 1973 to 1984; blued finish.

Estimated Value:	New (retail):	$380.00
	Excellent:	$285.00
	Very good:	$225.00

Ruger Super Blackhawk 44 Magnum

Ruger Super Blackhawk 44 Mag.

Caliber: 44 mag. & 44 S&W Special(interchangeably)
Action: Single; solid frame with loading gate
Cylinder: 6-shot; heavy non-fluted cylinder
Barrel: 7½"; ejector rod
Sights: Ramp front; adjustable rear sight
Finish: Blued; smooth walnut wood grips; square back trigger guard
Length Overall: 13⅜"
Approximate wt.: 48 oz.
Comments: Produced from about 1959 to 1973.

Estimated Value:	Excellent:	$250.00
	Very good:	$200.00

Ruger New Model Super Blackhawk 44 Mag.

Similar to Super Blackhawk 44 Mag. except: improved version, featuring stronger lock works; transfer bar firing pin protector; new interlocking mechanism; blued or stainless steel; 5½", 7½" or 10½" barrel; other improvements. Made from about 1973 to present. Add 10% for stainless steel.

Estimated Value:	New (retail):	$413.00
	Excellent:	$310.00
	Very good:	$245.00

Ruger New Model Blackhawk

Ruger Stainless Steel New Model Blackhawk 357

Ruger Blackhawk 44 Magnum

Caliber: 44 magnum & 44 S&W Special interchangeably
Action: Single; solid frame with loading gate
Cylinder: 6-shot; heavy fluted cylinder
Barrel: 6½"; ejector rod under barrel
Sights: Ramp front; adjustable rear sight
Finish: Blued; smooth walnut grips
Length Overall: 12½"
Approximate wt.: 40 oz.
Comments: Produced from about 1956 to 1962.

Estimated Value:	Excellent:	$300.00
	Very good:	$250.00

Ruger Blackhawk 41 Magnum

Caliber: 41 magnum
Action: Single; solid frame with loading gate
Cylinder: 6-shot
Barrel: 4⅝", 6½" with ejector rod
Sights: Ramp front; adjustable rear sight
Finish: Blued; smooth walnut grips
Length Overall: 10¾"; 12⅛"
Approximate wt.: 35 to 38 oz.
Comments: Produced from about 1965 to 1973.

Estimated Value:	Excellent:	$240.00
	Very good:	$190.00

Ruger Blackhawk 30 Caliber

Caliber: 30 U.S. Carbine (M1)
Action: Single; solid frame with loading gate
Cylinder: 6-shot
Barrel: 7½" with ejector rod
Sights: Ramp front; adjustable rear sight
Finish: Blued; smooth walnut wood grips
Length Overall: 13⅛"
Approximate wt.: 39 oz.
Comments: Made from about 1968 to 1973. A good companion handgun for the M1 carbine (30 caliber).

Estimated Value:	Excellent:	$230.00
	Very good:	$185.00

Ruger Blackhawk 30 Caliber

Ruger Blackhawk 45 Caliber

Caliber: 45 long Colt
Action: Single; solid frame with loading gate
Cylinder: 6-shot
Barrel: 4⅝", 7½" round barrel with ejector rod under barrel
Sights: Ramp front; adjustable rear sight
Finish: Blued; smooth walnut grips
Length Overall: 10⅛"; 13⅛"
Approximate wt.: 38 to 40 oz.
Comments: Made from about 1970 to 1973. Replaced by New Model Blackhawk in 1973.
Estimated Value: Excellent: $220.00
                      Very good: $175.00

Ruger Redhawk

Caliber: 357 mag.; 41 mag.; 44 mag.
Action: Double & single; solid frame; exposed hammer
Cylinder: 6-shot swing out; simultaneous ejector
Barrel: 5½", 7½", shrouded ejector rod under barrel
Sights: Adjustable rear, blade front
Finish: Stainless steel; blued model added in 1986; checkered or smooth walnut grips
Length Overall: 11", 13"
Approximate wt.: 52 oz.
Comments: A heavy frame 44 mag. revolver introduced in 1979. 357 mag. & 41 mag. added in 1984. Add 13% for stainless steel; 8% for scope rings; 357 mag. dropped in 1986. 41 mag. dropped in 1992.
Estimated Value: New (retail): $547.00
                      Excellent: $410.00
                      Very good: $325.00

Ruger Super Redhawk

Caliber: 44 magnum & .44 Special
Action: Double & single
Cylinder: 6-shot swing out; simultaneous ejector; fluted cylinder
Barrel: 7½" or 9½"
Sights: Ramp front base with interchangeable insert sight blades; adjustable white outline square notch rear
Finish: Stainless steel; cushioned grip system. A skeleton-type grip frame features rubber panels with Goncalo Alves panel inserts.
Length Overall: 13" or 15"
Approximate wt.: 56 oz.
Comments: Introduced in 1987.
Estimated Value: New (retail): $589.00
                      Excellent: $440.00
                      Very good: $355.00

Ruger Police Service-Six

Ruger Blackhawk 45 Caliber Convertible

Same as Blackhawk 45 Caliber revolver except: fitted with extra interchangeable cylinder for 45 ACP cartridges. Made from about 1970 to 1973. Replaced by New Model Blackhawk in 1973.
Estimated Value: Excellent: $250.00
                      Very good: $200.00

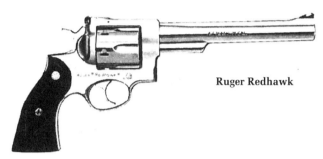

Ruger Redhawk

**Ruger Security-Six
357 Magnum**

Ruger Security-Six 357 Mag.

Caliber: 357 magnum, 38 Special
Action: Double & single; solid frame; exposed hammer
Cylinder: 6-shot; simultaneous ejector
Barrel: 2¾", 4", 6"
Sights: Adjustable
Finish: Blued or stainless steel; square butt, checkered walnut grips
Length Overall: 8", 9¼" 11"
Approximate wt.: 32 to 35 oz.
Comments: Made from 1972 to mid 1980's. A solid frame revolver with swing-out cylinder. Stainless steel model made from about 1975 to mid 1980's. Add 9% for stainless steel.
Estimated Value: Excellent: $225.00
                      Very good: $180.00

Ruger Speed-Six

Similar to Security-Six 357 Magnum revolver except: round butt style grips & in calibers 9mm Parabellum, 38 Special & 357 magnum. Fixed sights only. Made from about 1975 to 1989. Add $16.00 for 9mm; add 9% for stainless steel. 9mm dropped in mid 1980's.
Estimated Value: Excellent: $220.00
                      Very good: $165.00

Ruger Service-Six & Police Service-Six

Similar to Speed-Six revolver except: square butt style grips. Made from about 1976 to 1989. Add 8% for 9mm; add 8% for stainless steel. 9mm dropped in mid 1980's. Called Police Service-Six after 1987.
Estimated Value: Excellent: $215.00
                      Very good: $160.00

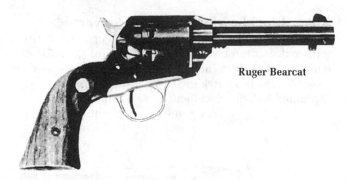

Ruger Bearcat

Ruger Hawkeye Single Shot

Caliber: 256 mag.
Action: Single action; single shot
Cylinder: None; rotate breech block to load the chamber, which is part of the barrel
Barrel: 8½"; chamber in barrel; under barrel ejector rod
Sights: Adjustable target sights
Finish: Blued; smooth walnut grips
Length Overall: 14½"
Approximate wt.: 44 oz.
Comments: The Hawkeye is built on the Ruger 44 mag. frame & resembles a revolver in appearance. Made from about 1963 to 1966.
Estimated Value: Excellent: $1000.00
Very good: $ 800.00

Ruger New Bearcat (Convertible)

Caliber: 22 short, long or long rifle; 22WMR
Action: Single; solid frame with loading gate
Cylinder: 6-shot; non-fluted, roll-engraved; each gun is fitted with two cylinders (regular 22 and 22 mag.)
Barrel: 4" round with ejector rod
Sights: Fixed; blade front; groove in frame for rear
Finish: Blued or high gloss stainless steel; smooth walnut grips
Length Overall: 9¼"
Approximate wt.: 28 oz.
Comments: All steel construction; reintroduced in 1994; add 9% for stainless steel.
Estimated Value: New (retail): $298.00
Excellent: $225.00
Very good: $180.00

Ruger New Model Bisley

Caliber: 22 long rifle or 32 H&R mag. in small frame; 357 mag., 41 mag., 44 mag. or 45 long Colt in large frame
Action: Single; solid frame with loading gate
Cylinder: 6-shot fluted or non-fluted cylinder with or without roll engraving
Barrel: 6½" small frame, 7½" large frame; ejector rod under barrel
Sights: Ramp front, adjustable or fixed rear
Finish: Blued; smooth wood grips
Length Overall: 11½" frame, 13" large frame
Approximate wt.: 41 oz. small frame, 48 oz. large frame
Comments: Introduced in 1985 & 1986. Based on the Ruger single action design with a longer, different-angle grip similar to the old Colt Bisley revolvers.

	Small Frame	Large Frame
Estimated Value:		
New (retail):	$360.00	$430.00
Excellent:	$270.00	$325.00
Very good:	$215.00	$260.00

Ruger Bearcat

Caliber: 22 short, long or long rifle
Action: Single; solid frame with loading gate
Cylinder: 6-shot; non-fluted, engraved
Barrel: 4" round with ejector rod
Sights: Fixed
Finish: Blued; smooth walnut grips
Length Overall: 8⅞"
Approximate wt.: 17 oz.
Comments: Alloy frame; coil springs & non-fluted engraved cylinder. Manufactured from about 1958 to 1972.
Estimated Value: Excellent: $300.00
Very good: $225.00

Ruger Super Bearcat

Same as Ruger Bearcat revolver except all steel construction & made from about 1971 to 1975.
Estimated Value: Excellent: $275.00
Very good: $220.00

Sauer

Sauer 1913 (Old Model)

Sauer 1930 Model

Sauer 1913 (Old Model)

Caliber: 32 ACP (7.65mm); 25 ACP (6.35mm)
Action: Semi-automatic; concealed hammer
Magazine: 7-shot clip
Barrel: 3"
Sights: Fixed
Finish: Blued; checkered hard rubber grips
Length Overall: 5⅞"
Approximate wt.: 32 oz.
Comments: Made from about 1913 to 1930.
Estimated Value: Excellent: $250.00
Very good: $200.00

Sauer 1930 Model

Similar to Sauer 1913 (Old Model) except improved version with main difference being the improved grip design which provides a better hold; some models made with indicator pins to show when they were cocked; some models made with alloy slide & receiver (approximately 15 oz.) Made from about 1930 to 1938.
Estimated Value: Excellent: $265.00
Very good: $210.00

Sauer WTM Pocket
Caliber: 25ACP (6.35mm)
Action: Semi-automatic; concealed hammer
Magazine: 6-shot clip
Barrel: 2½"
Sights: Fixed
Finish: Blued; checkered hard rubber grips
Length Overall: 4⅛"
Approximate wt.: 18 oz.
Comments: Made from about 1924 to 1928. Fluted slide with top ejection port.
Estimated Value: Excellent: $240.00
                       Very good: $195.00

Sauer 1938 Model (Model H)

Sauer 1928 Model Pocket
Similar to Sauer WTM Pocket Pistol except: smaller in size, 2" barrel & about 3⅞" overall length. Made from about 1928 to 1938.
Estimated Value: Excellent: $250.00
                       Very good: $200.00

Sauer 1938 Model (Model H)
Caliber: 32ACP (7.65mm); 380ACP; 22 LR
Action: Semi-automatic; double action; concealed hammer; lever on left side permitted hammer to be cocked or uncocked by the thumb; also could be fired by pulling trigger in double action style
Magazine: 7-shot clip
Barrel: 3¼"
Sights: Fixed
Finish: Blued; checkered plastic grips
Length Overall: 6¼"
Approximate wt.: 26 oz.
Comments: Some models made with alloy slide (approximately 18 oz. in weight); wartime models (WWII) inferior to earlier models. Made from about 1938 to 1944. Add 25% for 22 caliber.

Estimated Value:	pre-War models	Wartime models
Excellent:	$300.00	$220.00
Very good:	$240.00	$175.00

Savage

Savage Model 1905 Military Type
Caliber: 45ACP
Action: Semi-automatic; blowback design, grip safety; exposed cocking lever
Magazine: 8-shot clip
Barrel: 5¼"
Sights: Fixed
Finish: Blued, checkered walnut grips
Length Overall: 9"
Approximate wt.: 36 oz.
Comments: Approximately 200 were produced from about 1908 to 1911 & sold to U.S. Government Ordnance Dept. for tests, but lost to competition.
Estimated Value: Excellent: $2,400.00
                       Very good: $1,950.00

Savage Model 1907

Savage Model 1915

Savage Model 1907
Caliber: 32ACP, 380ACP (after 1912)
Action: Semi-automatic; exposed rounded or spur cocking lever
Magazine: 10-shot in 32 caliber, 9-shot in 380 caliber
Barrel: 3¾" in 32 caliber; 9-shot in 380 caliber
Sights: Fixed
Finish: Blued, metal, hard rubber or wood grips
Length Overall: 6½" (32 caliber); 7" (380 caliber)
Approximate wt.: 20 oz.
Comments: Manufactured from about 1908 to 1920, with improvements & some changes in 1909, 1914 & 1918. Some military models with lanyard loop were made of the 1912 variety & sold from 1915 to 1917.
Estimated Value: Excellent: $280.00
                       Very good: $225.00

Savage Model 1915
Caliber: 32ACP, 380ACP
Action: Semi-automatic; concealed hammer
Magazine: 10-shot in 32 caliber, 9-shot in 380 caliber
Barrel: 3¾" (caliber); 4¼" (380 caliber)
Sights: Fixed
Finish: Blued; hard rubber grips
Length Overall: 6½" (32 caliber), 7" (380 caliber)
Approximate wt.: 22 oz.
Comments: Manufactured from about 1915 to 1917. Approximately 6,500 were produced in 32 caliber & approximately 2,350 were produced in 380 caliber.
Estimated Value: Excellent: $300.00
                       Very good: $240.00

Savage Model 1917

Caliber: 32 ACP, 380 ACP

Action: Semi-automatic; exposed spur cocking lever; thumb safety

Magazine: 10-shot clip in 32; 9-shot clip in 380, wider magazine than previous models to allow for cartridges to be staggered in a double row

Barrel: 3¾" in 32; 7" in 380

Sights: Fixed

Finish: Blued; hard rubber grips

Length Overall: 6½" in 32, 7" in 380

Approximate wt.: 24 oz.

Comments: Made from about 1918 to 1928. Approximately 28,000 made in 32 caliber & 126,000 in 380 caliber. Wide frame & flared grips & the slide has small verticle gripping serrations.

Estimated Value: Excellent: $320.00

Very good: $260.00

Savage Model 1917

Savage Model 101 Single Shot

Savage Model 101 Single Shot

Caliber: 22 short, long, long rifle

Action: Single; single shot

Cylinder: None; the false cylinder is the chamber part of the barrel

Barrel: 5½" alloy steel; swings out to load; ejector rod under barrel

Sights: Blade front; notched-bar rear

Finish: Blued barrel; painted one-piece aluminum alloy frame; compressed impregnated wood grips

Length Overall: 9½"

Approximate wt.: 20 oz.

Comments: A single shot pistol built to resemble a single action frontier revolver. Made from about 1960 to 1968.

Estimated Value: Excellent: $160.00

Very good: $130.00

Sheridan

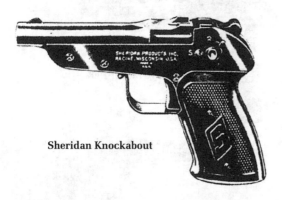

Sheridan Knockabout

Sheridan Knockabout

Caliber: 22 short, long, long rifle

Action: Single; exposed hammer

Magazine: None; single shot

Barrel: 5½"; tip up barrel

Sights: Fixed

Finish: Blued; checkered plastic grips

Length Overall: 6¾"

Approximate wt.: 21 oz.

Comments: An inexpensive single shot pistol which resembles an automatic pistol. Made from about 1953 to 1962. Approximately 20,000 produced.

Estimated Value: Excellent: $150.00

Very good: $115.00

Smith & Wesson

Smith & Wesson 1891 Single Shot Target Pistol

Caliber: 22 short, long, long rifle

Action: Single; exposed hammer; hinged frame (top break); single shot

Cylinder: None

Barrel: 10"

Sights: Adjustable target

Finish: Blued; hard rubber square butt grips

Length Overall: 13½"

Approximate wt.: 25 oz.

Comments: Made from about 1905 to 1909.

Estimated Value: Excellent: $450.00

Very good: $375.00

Smith & Wesson 1891 Single Shot Target Pistol

Smith & Wesson Perfected Single Shot

Similar to Model 1891 Single Shot except: double & single action; checkered square butt walnut grips; made from about 1909 to 1923; the U.S. Olympic team of 1920 used this pistol, therefore it is sometimes designated "Olympic Model." Add $125.00 for Olympic Models.

Estimated Value: Excellent: $475.00

Very good: $390.00

Smith & Wesson Straightline

Caliber: 22 short, long, long rifle
Action: Single; exposed striker (hammer); single shot
Magazine: None
Barrel: 10"; cartridge chamber in barrel; barrel pivots to left to eject & load
Sights: Target sights
Finish: Blued; walnut grips
Length Overall: 11½"
Approximate wt.: 35 oz.
Comments: Pistol resembles automatic pistol in appearance; sold with metal case, screwdriver & cleaning rod. Made from about 1925 to 1937. Add $100.00 for original case & accessories.

Estimated Value: Excellent: $1,000.00
Very good: $ 800.00

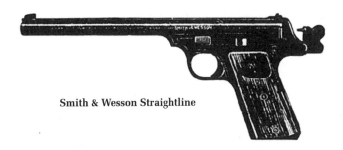

Smith & Wesson Straightline

Smith & Wesson
Model 32 Automatic

Smith & Wesson Model 39

Smith & Wesson
Model 59

Smith & Wesson Model 39

Caliber: 9mm (Parabellum) Luger
Action: Semi-automatic; double action; exposed hammer; thumb safety
Magazine: 8-shot clip
Barrel: 4"
Sights: Ramp front; rear adjustable for windage
Finish: Blued or nickel; checkered walnut grips
Length Overall: 7½"
Approximate wt.: 28 oz.
Comments: Made from about 1954 to 1982. Normally pistol has aluminum alloy frame; approximately 925 pistols were produced with steel frames sometime prior to 1966. Add $25.00 for nickel finish. Replaced by S&W Model 439.

	Alloy Frame	Steel Frame
Estimated Value: Excellent:	$375.00	$1,050.00
Very good:	$300.00	$ 850.00

Smith & Wesson Model 32 Automatic

Caliber: 32 ACP
Action: Semi-automatic; concealed hammer; grip safety located in front of grip below trigger guard
Magazine: 7-shot clip
Barrel: 3½"; barrel is fixed to the frame; the slide fits into guides on the barrel
Sights: Fixed
Finish: Blued; smooth walnut grips
Length Overall: 6½"
Approximate wt.: 24 oz.
Comments: Serial numbers are a separate series beginning at number 1. Approximately 958 produced from about 1924 to 1937.

Estimated Value: Excellent: $1,250.00
Very good: $1,000.00

Smith & Wesson Model 35 Automatic

Caliber: 35 S&W automatic
Action: Semi-automatic; concealed hammer; grip safety located in front of grip below trigger guard; manual safety at rear of left grip
Magazine: 7-shot clip
Barrel: 3½"; barrel hinged to rear of frame
Sights: Fixed
Finish: Blued or nickel; smooth walnut grips
Length Overall: 6½"
Approximate wt.: 22 oz.
Comments: Serial numbers are a separate series beginning at number 1. Approximately 8,350 were produced from about 1913 to 1921.

Estimated Value: Excellent: $650.00
Very good: $520.00

Smith & Wesson Model 59

Caliber: 9mm (Parabellum) Luger
Action: Semi-automatic; double action; exposed hammer; thumb safety
Magazine: 14-shot staggered column clip
Barrel: 4"
Sights: Ramp front; rear adjustable for windage
Finish: Blued or nickel; checkered molded nylon grips
Length Overall: 7½"
Approximate wt.: 28 oz.
Comments: Similar to Model 39 except: straight back grip; grip is wider to accommodate the staggered column magazine. Made from about 1973 to 1982. Add 8% for nickel. Replaced by S&W Model 459.

Estimated Value: Excellent: $350.00
Very good: $280.00

Smith & Wesson Model 52, 38 Master

Caliber: 38 Special (mid-range wadcutter only)
Action: Single action; semi-automatic; exposed hammer;
     thumb safety
Magazine: 5-shot clip
Barrel: 5"
Sights: Adjustable rear sight & ramp front
Finish: Blued; checkered walnut grips
Length Overall: 8⅞"
Approximate wt.: 42 oz.
Comments: Made from about 1961 to 1993.
Estimated Value: Excellent: $665.00
                       Very good: $535.00

Smith & Wesson Model 439

Caliber: 9mm (Parabellum) Luger
Action: Semi-automatic; double action; exposed ham-
     mer; thumb safety
Magazine: 8-shot clip
Barrel: 4"
Sights: Serrated ramp front; rear adjustable or fixed
Finish: Blued or nickel; checkered walnut grips with
     S&W monogram
Length Overall: 7½"
Approximate wt.: 30 oz.
Comments: The frame is constructed of aluminum alloy.
     It is similar to the Model 39 except with improved
     extraction system. Made from about 1981 to 1989.
     Add 8% for nickel finish.
Estimated Value: Excellent: $370.00
                       Very good: $295.00

Smith & Wesson Model 539

Similar to the Model 439 except the frame is constructed
of steel & the weight is about 36 oz.; made from about
1981 to mid 1980's. Add 8% for nickel finish.
Estimated Value: Excellent: $375.00
                       Very good: $300.00

Smith & Wesson Model 639

Similar to the Model 439 except satin stainless steel finish. Approx. wt. is 36 oz. Add 4% for adjustable rear
sight. Made from 1984 to 1989.
Estimated Value: Excellent: $415.00
                       Very good: $330.00

Smith & Wesson Model 459

Smith & Wesson Model 439

Smith & Wesson Model 459

Caliber: 9mm (Parabellum) Luger
Action: Semi-automatic; double action
Magazine: 14-shot staggered clip
Barrel: 4"
Sights: Serrated ramp front sight; rear adjustable for
     windage & elevation or fixed
Finish: Blued or nickel; checkered high-impact molded
     nylon grips
Length Overall: 7½"
Approximate wt.: 30 oz.
Comments: The frame is constructed of aluminum alloy;
     the grip back is straight; the grip is thick to accom-
     modate the staggered column magazine; it has an
     improved extraction system. Nickel finish discon-
     tinued late 1980's. Add 4% for adjustable rear sight.
     Made from 1981 to 1989.
Estimated Value: Excellent: $400.00
                       Very good: $320.00

Smith & Wesson Model 559

Similar to the Model 459 except the frame is steel & the
weight is approximately 40 oz. Made from about 1981 to
mid 1980's. Add 7% for nickel finish.
Estimated Value: Excellent: $390.00
                       Very good: $310.00

Smith & Wesson Model 659

Similar to the Model 459 except satin stainless steel finish. Approx. wt. is 40 oz. Add 4% for adjustable rear
sight. Made 1984 to 1989.
Estimated Value: Excellent: $425.00
                       Very good: $350.00

Smith & Wesson Model 645

Caliber: 45 ACP
Action: Double action; semi-automatic; exposed hammer
Magazine: 8-shot clip
Barrel: 5"
Sights: Red-ramp front, fixed white-outline rear
Finish: Stainless steel; checkered high-impact
     molded nylon grips
Length Overall: 8⅝"
Approximate wt.: 38 oz.
Comments: Made from the mid 1980's to 1989.
Estimated Value: Excellent: $465.00
                       Very good: $370.00

Smith & Wesson Model 52

Smith & Wesson Model 645

Smith & Wesson Model 745

Caliber: 45ACP
Action: Single action; semi-automatic; adjustable trigger stop
Magazine: 8-shot clip
Barrel: 5"
Sights: Ramp front, square notch rear, adjustable for windage
Finish: Stainless steel frame; blued carbon steel slide, hammer, trigger, sights; checkered walnut grips
Length Overall: 8⅝"
Approximate wt.: 38¾ oz.
Comments: Introduced in 1987. Discontinued in 1990.
Estimated Value: Excellent: $550.00
Very good: $440.00

Smith & Wesson Model 469

Caliber: 9mm (Parabellum) Luger
Action: Double action; semi-automatic; exposed bobbed hammer
Magazine: 12-shot clip
Barrel: 3½"
Sights: Serrated ramp front, square notch rear
Finish: Blued; pebble grain molded Debrin grips; aluminum alloy frame
Length Overall: 6⅞"
Approximate wt.: 26 oz.
Comments: Made 1984 to 1989.
Estimated Value: Excellent: $360.00
Very good: $290.00

Smith & Wesson Model 669

Same as the model 469 except barrel & slide are stainless steel. Made from mid 1980's to 1989.
Estimated Value: Excellent: $390.00
Very good: $310.00

Smith & Wesson Model 3904

Caliber: 9mm
Action: Double action, semi-automatic with exposed hammer & ambidextrous safety
Magazine: 8-shot clip
Barrel: 4"
Sights: Post front with white dot, fixed or micrometer adjustable rear with 2 white dots
Finish: Blued; aluminum alloy frame, carbon steel slide; Debrin one-piece wrap-around grips with curved back strap.
Length Overall: 7½"
Approximate wt.: 28 oz.
Comments: Made from 1989 to 1991. Add 5% for adjustable rear sight.
Estimated Value: Excellent: $400.00
Very good: $320.00

Smith & Wesson Model 3906

Same as the Model 3904 except stainless steel. Add 4½% for adjustable rear sight.
Estimated Value: Excellent: $450.00
Very good: $360.00

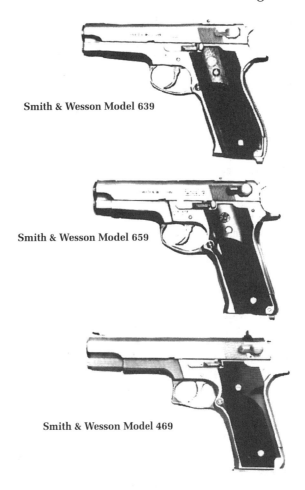

Smith & Wesson Model 639

Smith & Wesson Model 659

Smith & Wesson Model 469

Smith & Wesson Model 1006

Caliber: 10mm
Action: Double action; semi-automatic, exposed hammer, ambidextrous safety
Magazine: 9-shot clip
Barrel: 5"
Sights: Post front with white dot, fixed rear with 2 white dots or adjustable rear with white dots
Finish: Stainless steel, Debrin one-piece wrap-around grips with straight back strap
Length Overall: 8½"
Approximate wt.: 38 oz.
Comments: Produced from 1990 to 1993. Add 4% for adjustable rear sight.
Estimated Value: Excellent: $575.00
Very good: $470.00

Smith & Wesson Model 3904

Smith & Wesson Model 5903
Caliber: 9mm Luger Parabellum
Action: Double action, semi-automatic, ambidextrous safety, exposed hammer
Magazine: 15-shot clip; 10-shot clip after 9-13-94
Barrel: 4"
Sights: Post front with white dot, fixed or micrometer adjustable rear with 2 white dots
Finish: Stainless steel slide with aluminum alloy frame; Debrin one-piece wrap-around grips; curved back strap
Length Overall: 7½"
Approximate wt.: 29 ozs.
Comments: Introduced in 1990. Add 5% for adjustable rear sight.

Estimated Value:	New (retail):	$690.00
	Excellent:	$515.00
	Very good:	$415.00

Smith & Wesson Model 5904
Same as the Model 5903 except: blued finish; carbon steel slide. Approximate weight 27 oz. Introduced in 1989. Add 5% for adjustable rear sight.

Estimated Value:	New (retail):	$642.00
	Excellent:	$480.00
	Very good:	$385.00

Smith & Wesson Model 5906
Same as the Model 5903 except: stainless steel slide & frame; approx. wt. 38 oz.; Add 5% for adj. rear sight. Add 15% for fixed night sights. Introduced in 1989.

Estimated Value:	New (retail):	$707.00
	Excellent:	$530.00
	Very good:	$425.00

Smith & Wesson Model 5906

Smith & Wesson Model 5926
Similar to the Model 5903 except: fixed sights only; stainless steel slide and frame; no safety lever, it uses a decocking lever to lower the hammer from the cocked position (this permits the pistol to be fired double action without moving a safety lever); Produced from 1991 to 1993.

Estimated Value	Excellent:	$520.00
	Very good:	$420.00

Smith & Wesson Model 5946
Same as the Model 5926 except: no decocking lever; it can only be fired double action for each shot; the hammer is bobbed. Introduced in 1991.

Estimated Value:	New (retail):	$707.00
	Excellent:	$530.00
	Very good:	$425.00

Smith & Wesson Model 3914

Smith & Wesson Model 3913
(Lady Smith)

Smith & Wesson Model 3913 & 3913 LS
Caliber: 9mm Luger Parabellum
Action: Double action, semi-automatic with bobbed hammer & ambidextrous safety
Magazine: 8-shot clip
Barrel: 3½"
Sights: Post front with white dot front sight, fixed rear with 2 white dots
Finish: Stainless steel slide; black Debrin one-piece wrap-around grips
Length Overall: 6¾"
Approximate wt.: 25 oz.
Comments: Introduced in 1989. A small, compact double action 9mm automatic specially designed for the female shooters; add 3% for 3913 LS.

Estimated Value:	New (retail):	$622.00
	Excellent:	$470.00
	Very good:	$375.00

Smith & Wesson Model 3914
Similar to the Model 3913 (lady smith) except: blued finish carbon steel slide and alloy frame with gray Debrin one-piece wrap-around grips. Produced 1989 to 1993.

Estimated Value:	Excellent:	$420.00
	Very good:	$335.00

Smith & Wesson Models 3953 & 3954
Same as the Models 3913 and 3914 except: double action only for each shot; no safety lever; Model 3953 has stainless steel slide and alloy frame. Model 3954 has blued finish with carbon steel slide and alloy frame. Add 11% for stainless steel slide (Model 3953). Introduced in 1991. Model 3954 discontinued in 1993.

Estimated Value:	New (retail):	$622.00
	Excellent:	$465.00
	Very good:	$370.00

Smith & Wesson Model 6904

Caliber: 9mm Luger Parabellum
Action: Double action, semi-automatic; exposed bobbed hammer; ambidextrous safety
Magazine: 12-shot clip; 10-shot after Sept. 13, 1994
Barrel: 3½"
Sights: Post front with white dot; fixed rear with 2 white dots
Finish: Blued, carbon steel slide with aluminum alloy frame; Debrin one-piece wrap-around grips with curved backstrap
Length Overall: 6⅞"
Approximate wt.: 27 oz.
Comments: Introduced in 1989.
Estimated Value: New (retail): $614.00
Excellent: $460.00
Very good: $370.00

Smith & Wesson Model 6906

Same as the Model 6904 except stainless steel slide with aluminum alloy frame. Introduced in 1989. Add 16% for night sights (1992).
Estimated Value: New (retail): $677.00
Excellent: $510.00
Very good: $400.00

Smith & Wesson Model 6946

Same as the Model 6906 except: double action only for each shot; no safety lever; introduced in 1991.
Estimated Value: New (retail): $677.00
Excellent: $510.00
Very good: $400.00

Smith & Wesson Model 1066

Similar to the Model 6906 except: 4¼" barrel; overall length is approximately 7¾"; fixed sights.
Estimated Value: Excellent: $550.00
Very good: $440.00

Smith & Wesson Model 1076

Same as the Model 1066 except: decocking lever; no safety lever.
Estimated Value: Excellent: $565.00
Very good: $450.00

Smith & Wesson Model 1086

Same as the Model 1066 except: double action only for all shots; bobbed hammer; no decocking lever; no safety lever.
Estimated Value: Excellent: $550.00
Very good: $440.00

Smith & Wesson Model 4006

Smith & Wesson Model 6906

Smith & Wesson Model 4006

Caliber: 40 S&W
Action: Double action, semi-automatic; exposed hammer; ambidextrous safety
Magazine: 11-shot clip; 10-shot after 9-13-94
Barrel: 4"
Sights: Post with white dot front; fixed or adjustable rear with two white dots
Finish: Stainless steel slide and frame; Debrin one-piece wrap-around straight backstrap grips
Length Overall: 7½"
Approximate wt.: 30 oz.
Comments: Introduced in 1990. Add 4% for adjustable sights. Add 15% for fixed night sights (1992).
Estimated Value: New (retail): $745.00
Excellent: $560.00
Very good: $450.00

Smith & Wesson Model 4026

Same as the Model 4006 except: it has a decocking lever to lower the hammer; no safety lever.
Estimated Value: Excellent: $540.00
Very good: $435.00

Smith & Wesson Model 4046

Same as the Model 4006 except: double action only for each shot; no safety lever; bobbed hammer; add 15% for fixed night sights. Introduced in 1991.
Estimated Value: New (retail): $745.00
Excellent: $560.00
Very good: $450.00

Smith & Wesson Models 4003 & 4004

Same as the Model 4006 except: Model 4003 has aluminum alloy frame and stainless steel slide; Model 4004 has aluminum alloy frame and carbon steel slide with blued finish. Add 7% for stainless steel slide (4003). Model 4004 discontinued in 1995.
Estimated Value: Excellent: $480.00
Very good: $385.00

Smith & Wesson Models 4043 & 4044

Same as the Models 4003 and 4004 except: double action only with bobbed hammer; no safety lever. Introduced in 1992. 4044 discontinued in 1995.
Estimated Value: New (retail): $727.00
Excellent: $545.00
Very good: $440.00

Smith & Wesson Model 4053 & 4054

Same as Models 4043 and 4044 except: more compact; 3½" barrel; approximately 7" overall. Introduced in 1992; model 4054 discontinued 1995.

Estimated Value: New (retail): $722.00
Excellent: $540.00
Very good: $435.00

Smith & Wesson Model 4013 & 4014

Same as the Model 4003 & 4004 except: more compact; 3½" barrel; overall length is approximately 7"; Model 4013 has stainless steel slide and alloy frame; Model 4014 has blued finish with carbon steel slide and alloy frame. Introduced in 1992.

Estimated Value: New (retail): $722.00
Excellent: $540.00
Very good: $435.00

Smith & Wesson Model 4516

Caliber: 45ACP
Action: Double action, semi-automatic, exposed hammer; ambidextrous safety
Magazine: 7-shot clip
Barrel: 3¾"
Sights: Post front with white dot; fixed rear with two white dots
Finish: Stainless steel frame and slide with Debrin one-piece wrap around grips
Length Overall: 7¼"
Approximate wt.: 35 oz.
Comments: A compact 45 automatic; introduced in 1989.

Estimated Value: New (retail): $774.00
Excellent: $580.00
Very good: $465.00

Smith & Wesson
Model 908

Smith & Wesson
Model 909, 910

Smith & Wesson Model 4506

Smith & Wesson Model 4506

Caliber: 45ACP
Action: Double action, semi-automatic; exposed hammer, ambidextrous safety
Magazine: 8-shot clip
Barrel: 5"
Sights: Post front with white dot; fixed or micrometer adjustable rear with two white dots
Finish: Stainless steel frame and slide with Debrin one-piece wrap-around grips
Length Overall: 8½"
Approximate wt.: 39 oz.
Comments: Introduced in 1989. Add 4% for adjustable rear sight.

Estimated Value: New (retail): $774.00
Excellent: $580.00
Very good: $465.00

Smith & Wesson Model 4576

Same as the Model 4506 except: more compact; 4¼" barrel; approximate overall length is 7¾"; decocking lever; no safety lever.

Estimated Value: Excellent: $570.00
Very good: $455.00

Smith & Wesson Model 4566

Same as the Model 4506 except: 4¼" barrel; approximate overall length 7¾"; more compact; introduced in 1990.

Estimated Value: New (retail): $774.00
Excellent: $580.00
Very good: $465.00

Smith & Wesson Model 4586

Same as the Model 4576 except: double action only for all shots; no decocking lever; no safety lever. Introduced in 1991.

Estimated Value: New (retail): $774.00
Excellent: $580.00
Very good: $465.00

Smith & Wesson Model 908, 909, 910

Caliber: 9mm
Action: Double action, semi-automatic; 908 has bobbed hammer, 909 & 910 have exposed hammer
Magazine: 8-shot clip (908), 9-shot clip (909), 10-shot staggered clip (910)
Barrel: 3½" (908), 4" (909 & 910)
Sights: Fixed white dot
Finish: Blued; carbon steel slide and alloy frame; 908 has straight back strap; 909 & 910 have curved back strap
Length Overall: 6⅞" (908); 7⅜" (909 & 910)
Approximate wt.: 30 oz.
Comments: 908 introduced in 1996; 909 & 910 introduced in the early 1990's.

Estimated Value: New (retail): $443.00
Excellent: $330.00
Very good: $265.00

Smith & Wesson Model 915

Caliber: 9mm
Action: Double or single; exposed hammer
Magazine: 15-shot clip
Barrel: 4"
Sights: Fixed
Finish: Blued; carbon steel slide and alloy frame; checkered composite straight-back strap grips
Length Overall: 7½"
Approximate wt.: 29 oz.
Comments: Produced in the early 1990's.
Estimated Value: Excellent: $350.00
                         Very good: $280.00

Smith & Wesson Model 411

Similar to the Model 915 except: 40 S&W caliber; 11-shot clip; approximate wt.: 30 oz. Produced in the early 1990's.
Estimated Value: Excellent: $395.00
                         Very good: $315.00

Smith & Wesson Model 410

Caliber: 40 S & W
Action: Double action, semi-automatic; exposed hammer
Magazine: 10-shot clip
Barrel: 4"
Sights: Fixed white dot
Finish: Blued; carbon steel slide and alloy frame; straight back strap
Length Overall: 7½"
Approximate wt.: 30 oz.
Comments: Introduced in 1996.
Estimated Value: New (retail): $490.00
                         Excellent: $365.00
                         Very good: $295.00

Smith & Wesson Model 915

Smith & Wesson Model 410

Smith & Wesson Model 457

Smith & Wesson Model 457

Caliber: 45ACP
Action: Double action, semi-automatic, bobbed hammer
Magazine: 7-shot clip
Barrel: 3¾"
Sights: Fixed white dot
Finish: Matte blue; alloy frame and carbon steel slide; straight back strap grip
Length Overall: 7¼"
Approximate wt.: 30 oz.
Comments: Introduced in 1996.
Estimated Value: New (retail): $490.00
                         Excellent: $365.00
                         Very good: $295.00

Smith & Wesson Model 41

Caliber: 22 short or 22 long rifle (not interchangeable)
Action: Single action; semi-automatic; concealed hammer; thumb safety
Magazine: 12-shot clip; 10-shot after 9-13-94
Barrel: 5½" heavy barrel or 7" regular barrel
Sights: Adjustable micrometer rear; Partridge front
Finish: Blued; checkered walnut grips with thumb rest
Length Overall: 8⅝" to 10½"
Approximate wt.: 40 to 44 oz.
Comments: Made from about 1957 to present. Made for 22 long rifle only at present.
Estimated Value: New (retail): $753.00
                         Excellent: $565.00
                         Very good: $450.00

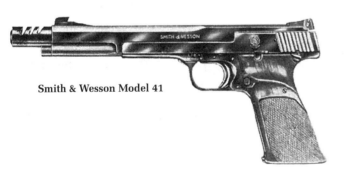

Smith & Wesson Model 41

Smith & Wesson Model 46

Similar to Model 41 except: 22 long rifle caliber only; plastic grips with thumb rest. Made from about 1957 to 1966.
Estimated Value: Excellent: $480.00
                         Very good: $385.00

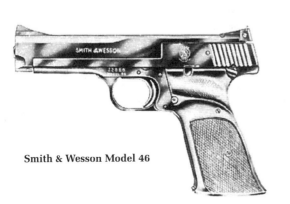

Smith & Wesson Model 46

Smith & Wesson Model 2213 & 2214

Caliber: 22 long rifle
Action: Single action, semi-automatic; concealed hammer
Magazine: 8-shot clip
Barrel: 3"
Sights: Fixed sights with white dots
Finish: Model 2213 has stainless steel slide with alloy frame. Model 2214 is blued carbon steel slide with alloy frame.
Length Overall: 7"
Approximate wt.: 18 oz.
Comments: Introduced in 1991. Add 17% for stainless steel (2213).
Estimated Value: New (retail): $269.00
　　　　　　　　 Excellent: $200.00
　　　　　　　　 Very good: $160.00

Smith & Wesson Model 61 Escort

Caliber: 22 long rifle
Action: Semi-automatic; concealed hammer; thumb safety
Magazine: 5-shot clip
Barrel: 2⅛"
Sights: Fixed
Finish: Blued or nickel; checkered plastic grips
Length Overall: 4¾"
Approximate wt.: 14 oz.
Comments: Made from about 1970 to 1973. Add $15.00 for nickel finish.
Estimated Value: Excellent: $275.00
　　　　　　　　 Very good: $220.00

Smith & Wesson Model 422

Caliber: 22 long rifle
Action: Single action; semi-auto.; concealed hammer.
Magazine: 12-shot clip; 10-shot clip after 9-13-94
Barrel: 4½" or 6" barrel
Sights: Fixed sights; adjustable sights on target model
Finish: Blued; aluminum frame, carbon steel slide; plastic grips on field; checkered walnut on target
Length Overall: 7½" or 9"
Approximate wt.: 22 to 23 oz.
Comments: Introduced in 1987; add 25% for target sights.
Estimated Value: New (retail): $235.00
　　　　　　　　 Excellent: $175.00
　　　　　　　　 Very good: $140.00

Smith & Wesson Model 622

Same as the Model 422 except stainless steel slide & aluminum alloy frame. Introduced in 1990. Add 20% for target sights. Add 9% for ventilated rib.
Estimated Value: New (retail): $284.00
　　　　　　　　 Excellent: $215.00
　　　　　　　　 Very good: $170.00

Smith & Wesson Model 2206

Same as the Model 422 except: stainless steel slide & frame; 6" barrel. Introduced in 1990. Add 12% for target model.
Estimated Value: New (retail): $385.00
　　　　　　　　 Excellent: $290.00
　　　　　　　　 Very good: $230.00

Smith & Wesson SW380

Smith & Wesson Sigma Series SW380

Caliber: 380ACP
Action: Double action only, semi-automatic; concealed hammer
Magazine: 6-shot clip
Barrel: 3"
Sights: Post front, gutter type rear
Finish: Blued; one piece grip and polymer frame
Length Overall: 6"
Approximate wt.: 14 oz.
Comments: Introduced in 1995, a small, lightweight concealable pistol.
Estimated Value: New (retail): $308.00
　　　　　　　　 Excellent: $230.00
　　　　　　　　 Very good: $185.00

Smith & Wesson Sigma Series SW9C & SW40C

Caliber: 9mm (SW9C) or 40 S & W (SW40C)
Action: Double action only, semi-automatic; concealed hammer
Magazine: 10-shot clip
Barrel: 4"
Sights: White dot, optional night sights
Finish: Blued; one piece grip and polymer frame
Length Overall: 7⅜"
Approximate wt.: 26 oz.
Comments: Introduced in 1994.
Estimated Value: New (retail): $593.00
　　　　　　　　 Excellent: $445.00
　　　　　　　　 Very good: $355.00

Smith & Wesson SW9C　　　Smith & Wesson SW9F

Smith & Wesson Sigma Series SW9F & SW40F

Caliber: 9mm (SW9F) or 40 S & W (SW40F)
Action: Double action only, semi-automatic; concealed hammer
Magazine: 10-shot clip
Barrel: 4½"
Sights: White dot, optional night sights
Finish: Matte blue; one piece grip and polymer frame; carbon steel slide
Length Overall: 7⅜"
Approximate wt.: 26 oz.
Comments: Introduced in the early 1990's.
Estimated Value: New (retail): $593.00
　　　　　　　　 Excellent: $445.00
　　　　　　　　 Very good: $355.00

Smith & Wesson No. 3
New Model Double Action

Smith & Wesson No. 3
Single Action New Model

Smith & Wesson 32 Double Action

Caliber: 32 S&W center fire
Action: Single & double; exposed hammer; hinged frame (top break)
Cylinder: 5-shot; simultaneous ejector
Barrel: 3" 1880-1882; 3", 3½", 6", 8", 10" 1882-1909; 3", 3½", 6" 1909-1919
Sights: Fixed
Finish: Blued or nickel; round butt, hard rubber grips
Length Overall: 7¼" to 14¼"
Approximate wt.: 23 to 28 oz.
Comments: Made from about 1880 to 1919 in five modifications or issues; rear of trigger guard is square.

Estimated Value:

Issue	Dates	Quantity	Excellent	Very Good
1st	1880	Less than 100	$2,500.00	$2,000.00
2nd	1880-1882	22,000	$ 230.00	$ 200.00
3rd	1882-1889	21,200	$ 235.00	$ 205.00
4th	1889-1909	239,500	$ 180.00	$ 150.00
5th	1909-1919	44,600	$ 200.00	$ 175.00

Smith & Wesson No. 3 Single Action New Model

Caliber: 44 S&W Russian center fire
Action: Single; exposed hammer; hinged frame (top break); simultaneous automatic ejector
Cylinder: 6-shot
Barrel: 4", 5", 6", 6½", 7½" or ribbed
Sights: Fixed or target
Finish: Blued or nickel; round butt, hard rubber or checkered walnut grips
Length Overall: 9" to 13"
Approximate wt.: 36 to 40 oz.
Comments: An improved version of the S&W Russian single action revolver. Approximately 36,000 were manufactured from about 1878 to 1908. Sometimes called Single Action Russian Model.
Estimated Value: Excellent: $900.00
Very good: $720.00

Smith & Wesson No. 3 New Model Double Action

Same as No. 3 Single Action New Model except: double & single action; 4", 5", 6" & 6½" barrel; overall length 9" to 11½"; sometimes listed as S&W 1881 Navy Revolver; rear of trigger guard is square. Made from about 1881 to 1908.
Estimated Value: Excellent: $500.00
Very good: $400.00

Smith & Wesson Double Action 44 Wesson Favorite

Similar to No. 3 Single Action New Model except: double & single action; 5" barrel only; lighter barrel & frame. Made from about 1882 to 1883 (approximately 1,200 produced).
Estimated Value: Excellent: $1,800.00
Very good: $1,200.00

Smith & Wesson 38 Double Action

Caliber: 38 S&W
Action: Single & double; exposed hammer; hinged frame; top break; back of trigger guard squared
Cylinder: 5-shot; simultaneous ejector
Barrel: 3¼", 4", 5", 6"
Sights: Fixed
Finish: Blued or nickel; round butt; hard rubber grips
Length Overall: 7½" to 10¼"
Approximate wt.: 20 to 24 oz.
Comments: Made from about 1880 to 1910 with some improvements & minor changes.
Estimated Value: Excellent: $450.00
Very good: $360.00

Smith & Wesson Safety Model Double Action

Caliber: 32 S&W, 38 S&W
Action: Double only; concealed hammer with frame enclosing it; hinged frame; top break style; grip safety on rear of grip frame
Cylinder: 5-shot; simultaneous ejector
Barrel: 2", 3", or 3½" in 32 caliber; 2", 3¼", 4", 5", or 6" in 38 caliber; rib on top
Sights: Fixed
Finish: Blued or nickel; hard rubber or checkered walnut grips
Length Overall: 5¾" to 9¾"
Approximate wt.: 15 to 20 oz.
Comments: Sometimes listed as the Safety Hammerless, New Department Model. Made from about 1887 to 1941. About five changes & improvements were made from 1887 to 1940.
Estimated Value: Excellent: $400.00
Very good: $320.00

Smith & Wesson Perfected 38

Caliber: 38 S&W center fire
Action: Single & double; exposed hammer; hinged frame (top break; but also has side latch)
Cylinder: 5-shot; simultaneous ejector
Barrel: 3¼", 4", 5", & 6"
Sights: Fixed
Finish: Blued or nickel; round butt, hard rubber grip
Length Overall: 7½" to 10¼"
Approximate wt.: 24 to 30 oz.
Comments: Similar to earlier 38 double action revolvers except: heavier frame; a side latch along with the top latch; improved lock work. Approximately 58,400 were produced from about 1909 to 1920.
Estimated Value: Excellent: $410.00
Very good: $325.00

Smith & Wesson Single Action Target

Caliber: 32-44 S&W, 38-44 S&W
Action: Single; exposed hammer; hinged frame (top break)
Cylinder: 6-shot; simultaneous ejector
Barrel: 6½"
Sights: Target
Finish: Blued or nickel; round butt; hard rubber or checkered walnut grips
Length Overall: 11"
Approximate wt.: 38 to 40 oz.
Comments: One of the first handguns to prove that a short-barrel arm could be a really accurate weapon. Made from 1887 to 1910.
Estimated Value: Excellent: $700.00
Very good: $560.00

Smith & Wesson No. 3 Single Action Frontier

Caliber: 44-40 Winchester rifle cartridge
Action: Single; exposed hammer; hinged frame (top break)
Cylinder: 6-shot; simultaneous automatic ejector
Barrel: 4", 5" & 6½"
Sights: Fixed or target
Finish: Blued or nickel; round butt, hard rubber or checkered walnut grips
Length Overall: 8½" to 11"
Approximate wt.: 38 to 42 oz.
Comments: Approximately 2,000 manufactured from about 1885 to 1908.
Estimated Value: Excellent: $1,100.00
Very good: $ 900.00

Smith & Wesson Double Action Frontier

Similar to No. 3 Single Action Frontier except: double & single action; rear of trigger guard is square. Made from about 1886 to 1908 (approximately 15,000 were produced).
Estimated Value: Excellent: $650.00
Very good: $500.00

Smith & Wesson
1891 Single Action

Smith & Wesson
Military & Police
Winchester 32-20

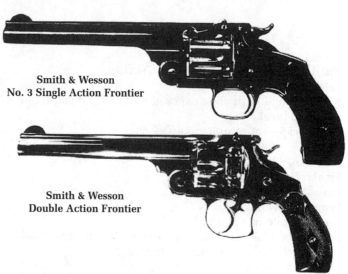

Smith & Wesson
No. 3 Single Action Frontier

Smith & Wesson
Double Action Frontier

Smith & Wesson 1891 Single Action

Caliber: 38 S&W center fire
Action: Single; exposed hammer; hinged frame (top break)
Cylinder: 5-shot; simultaneous ejector
Barrel: 3¼", 4", 5" & 6"
Sights: Fixed
Finish: Blued or nickel; round butt, hard rubber grips
Length Overall: 6¾" to 9½"
Approximate wt.: 34 to 38 oz. (depending on barrel length)
Comments: This revolver was also available with an accessory single shot target barrel in 22 caliber, 32 caliber or 38 caliber; & 6", 8" & 10" lengths. Made from 1891 to 1911.

Estimated Value:	Revolver	Revolver and single shot barrel
Excellent:	$560.00	$950.00
Very good:	$450.00	$825.00

Smith & Wesson 1899 Hand Ejector

Caliber: 38 long Colt
Action: Double & single; exposed hammer; solid frame
Cylinder: 6-shot; swing out; simultaneous manual ejector; cylinder release on side of frame
Barrel: 4", 5", 6" or 6½"
Sights: Fixed
Finish: Blued or nickel; checkered hard rubber or walnut round butt grips
Length Overall: 9" to 11½"
Approximate wt.: 22 to 25 oz.
Comments: Made for police, Army, Navy & commercial use; forerunner of the military & police models. Made from about 1899 to 1902 (approximately 21,000 produced). Army & Navy versions have lanyard swivel in butt & 6" or 6½" barrel lengths.
Estimated Value: Excellent: $550.00
Very good: $440.00

Smith & Wesson Military & Police Winchester 32-20

Similar to Model 1899 except: caliber 32-20 only; some improvements & changes over the years produced from about 1899 to 1940.
Estimated Value: Excellent: $350.00
Very good: $280.00

Smith & Wesson Model M Hand Ejector
Caliber: 22 short, long, long rifle
Action: Double & single; exposed hammer; solid frame.
Cylinder: 9-shot; swing out, simultaneous manual ejector
Barrel: 2¼" (1902 to 1911); 3", 3½" (1906 to 1911) or 6" (1911 to 1921)
Sights: Fixed or adjustable (available after 1911)
Finish: Blued or nickel; checkered hard rubber round butt grips (1902 to 1911); checkered hard rubber square butt grips (1911 to 1921)
Length Overall: 5¾" to 10½"
Approximate wt.: 10 to 14 oz.
Comments: Cylinder latch release on left side of frame 1902 to 1906; cylinder latch under barrel 1906 to 1921. Made from about 1902 to 1921, sometimes called Lady Smith.
Estimated Value: Excellent: $725.00
                       Very good: $600.00

Smith & Wesson Model
M Hand Ejector

Smith & Wesson Model 1 Hand Ejector
Caliber: 32 S&W long
Action: single & double; exposed hammer; first Smith & Wesson solid frame revolver; longer top strap over cylinder than later models
Cylinder: 6-shot; swing out; simultaneous manual ejector
Barrel: 3¼", 4¼", or 6"
Sights: Fixed
Finish: Blued or nickel; round butt; hard rubber grips
Length Overall: 8" to 10¾"
Approximate wt.: 20 to 24 oz.
Comments: First model produced by Smith & Wesson with solid frame. Made from about 1896 to 1903.
Estimated Value: Excellent: $450.00
                       Very good: $360.00

Smith & Wesson Model
30 Hand Ejector

Smith & Wesson Model 30 Hand Ejector
Caliber: 32 S&W & 32 S&W long
Action: Single & double; exposed hammer; solid frame
Cylinder: 6-shot swing out; simultaneous manual ejector; cylinder release on left side of frame
Barrel: 2" (1949 to 1975); 3", 4", 6"
Sights: Fixed
Finish: Blued or nickel; checkered hard rubber or checkered walnut round butt grips
Length Overall: 6" to 10"
Approximate wt.: 16 to 20 oz.
Comments: Made from about 1903 to 1975 with many improvements & minor changes over the years.
Estimated Value: Excellent: $250.00
                       Very good: $200.00

Smith & Wesson Mexican Model
Caliber: 38 S&W center fire
Action: Single; exposed hammer; hinged frame (top break); spur trigger
Cylinder: 5-shot; simultaneous ejector
Barrel: 3¼", 4", 5" & 6"
Sights: Fixed
Finish: Blued or nickel; round butt, hard rubber grips
Length Overall: 7¾" to 10½"
Approximate wt.: 34 to 38 oz.
Comments: Similar to Model 1891 except: it has a spur trigger; doesn't have half-cock notch on the hammer. Approximately 2,000 manufactured from about 1891 to 1911.
Estimated Value: Excellent: $1,200.00
                       Very good: $ 900.00

Smith & Wesson New Century Triple Lock
Caliber: 44 S&W Special, 450 Eley, 45 Colt or 455 Mark II British
Action: Single & double; exposed hammer; solid frame
Cylinder: 6-shot swing out; simultaneous hand ejector; called triple lock because of lock on cylinder crane as well as the usual locks under barrel & at rear of cylinder
Barrel: 4", 5", 6½", 7½" tapered round
Sights: Fixed
Finish: Blued or nickel; checkered square butt walnut grips
Length Overall: 9¼" to 12¾"
Approximate wt.: 36 to 41 oz.
Comments: Approximately 20,000 made from about 1908 to 1915; about 5,000 of these were made for the British Army.
Estimated Value: Excellent: $675.00
                       Very good: $575.00

Smith & Wesson 44 Hand Ejector
Similar to New Century Triple Lock except: cylinder crane lock eliminated; 44 Smith & Wesson Special, 44 Smith & Wesson Russian or 45 Colt calibers; 45 Colt caliber made in 6½" barrel only; other calibers in 4", 5", 6" lengths. Made from about 1915 to 1937.
Estimated Value: Excellent: $550.00
                       Very good: $440.00

Smith & Wesson 22/32 Target
Caliber: 22 short, long, long rifle
Action: Single & double; exposed hammer; solid frame
Cylinder: 6-shot swing out; recessed chamber (1935 to 1953); cylinder release on left side of frame
Barrel: 6"
Sights: Adjustable target sights
Finish: Blued; checkered square butt walnut grips
Length Overall: 10½"
Approximate wt.: 24 oz.
Comments: Frame design similar to Model 30 hand ejector model. Made about 1911 to 1953.

Estimated Value:	Excellent:	$310.00
	Very good:	$250.00

Smith & Wesson Model
22/32 Target

Smith & Wesson 22/32 1935 Kit Gun
Same as 22/32 Target except: 4" barrel; overall length 8"; weighs about 21 oz.; round butt grips. Made from about 1935 to 1953.

Estimated Value:	Excellent:	$290.00
	Very good:	$230.00

Smith & Wesson Model 35 22/32 Target
Similar to 22/32 target except: newer type adjustable rear sight; S&W magna-type target grips; weighs about 25 oz. Made from about 1953 to 1974.

Estimated Value:	Excellent:	$275.00
	Very good:	$220.00

Smith & Wesson Model 34 1953 22/32 Kit Gun
Similar to 22/32 Kit Gun except: 2" or 4" barrel; round or square butt grips; blued or nickel finish. Made from about 1953 to 1992. Nickel finish discontinued late 1980's.

Estimated Value:	Excellent:	$270.00
	Very good:	$210.00

Smith & Wesson Model 51
1960 22/32 Kit Gun

Smith & Wesson Model 43
1955 22/32 Kit Gun

Smith & Wesson Model 43 1955 22/32 Kit Gun
Same as Model 34 1953 22/32 Kit Gun except: 3½" barrel only; lighter alloy frame; weighs approximately 15 oz.; square butt grips. Made from about 1954 to 1974.

Estimated Value:	Excellent:	$260.00
	Very good:	$210.00

Smith & Wesson Model 51 1960 22/32 Kit Gun
Same as Model 43 1953 22/32 Kit Gun except: chambered for 22 magnum only; all steel construction; weighs approximately 24 oz. Made from about 1960 to 1974.

Estimated Value:	Excellent:	$275.00
	Very good:	$220.00

Smith & Wesson 1917 Army
Caliber: 45 auto rim cartridge; 45 ACP (by using two 3 round steel half moon clips to hold the cartridge heads)
Action: Single & double; exposed hammer; solid frame
Cylinder: 6-shot swing out; simultaneous manual ejector; release on left side of frame
Barrel: 5½"
Sights: Fixed
Finish: Blued; smooth or checkered square butt walnut grips
Length Overall: 10¾"
Approximate wt.: 37 oz.
Comments: Approximately 175,000 made for U.S. Government from about 1917 to 1919. Then made for commercial sale from about 1919 to 1941. U.S. Government models had a dull blue finish & smooth grips.

Estimated Value:	Military	Commercial
Excellent:	$350.00	$400.00
Very good:	$275.00	$325.00

Smith & Wesson Model 22 1950 Army
Similar to 1917 Army except: made after World War II; minor changes. Made from about 1950 to 1967.

Estimated Value:	Excellent:	$295.00
	Very good:	$235.00

Smith & Wesson 1926 Model 44 Military
Caliber: 44 S&W Special
Action: Single & double; exposed hammer
Cylinder: 6-shot swing out; simultaneous manual ejector; cylinder release on left side of frame
Barrel: 3¼", 4", 5", 6½"
Sights: Fixed
Finish: Blued or nickel; checkered square butt walnut grips
Length Overall: 9¼" to 11¾"
Approximate wt.: 40 oz.
Comments: Made from about 1926 to 1941.
Estimated Value: Excellent: $500.00
Very good: $400.00

Smith & Wesson 1926 Model 44 Target
Same as 1926 Model Military except: 6½" barrel only; adjustable target sights; blued finish only. Made from about 1926 to 1941.
Estimated Value: Excellent: $520.00
Very good: $420.00

Smith & Wesson Model 21 1950 44 Military
Similar to 1926 Model Military revolver except: made after World War II; minor changes. Made from about 1950 to 1967.
Estimated Value: Excellent: $320.00
Very good: $255.00

Smith & Wesson Model 24 1950 44 Target
Similar to 1926 Model 44 Target except: 4" or 6½" barrel; made after World War II; minor changes; ribbed barrel. Made from about 1950 to 1967. A limited edition of 7,500 were made in mid 1980's.
Estimated Value: Excellent: $350.00
Very good: $280.00

Smith & Wesson Model 624 44 Special
Similar to the Model 24, 1950 44 Target Revolver except stainless steel. Produced only in the mid 1980's. Add 3% for 6½" barrel.
Estimated Value: Excellent: $400.00
Very good: $320.00

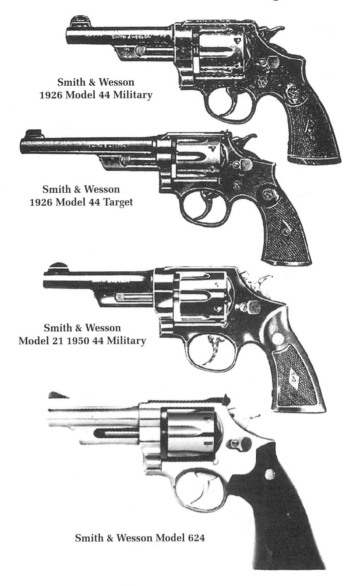

Smith & Wesson
1926 Model 44 Military

Smith & Wesson
1926 Model 44 Target

Smith & Wesson
Model 21 1950 44 Military

Smith & Wesson Model 624

Smith & Wesson
Model 24 1950 44 Target

Smith & Wesson
Model 25 1955 Target

Smith & Wesson Model 25 45 Colt
Caliber: 45 Colt
Action: Single & double; exposed hammer; solid frame
Cylinder: 6-shot swing out; simultaneous manual ejector; cylinder release on left side
Barrel: 4", 6", 8⅜"
Sights: Red ramp front; micrometer click rear adjustable for windage & elevation
Finish: Blued or nickel; checkered Goncolo Alves target grips
Length Overall: 9⅜" to 13¾"
Approximate wt.: 44 to 52 oz.
Comments: This revolver is built on the large N frame. Made from about 1955 to 1992. Add 3% for 8⅜" barrel, add 9% for presentation box. Nickel finish discontinued late 1980's.
Estimated Value: Excellent: $320.00
Very good: $260.00

Smith & Wesson Model 25 1955 Target
Similar to the Model 25 except 6" barrel only; blued finish only; 45 ACP caliber; ⅛" plain partridge front sight; add 9% for presentation box.
Estimated Value: Excellent: $325.00
Very good: $260.00

Smith & Wesson Model 20 Heavy Duty
Caliber: 38 Special
Action: Single & double; exposed hammer; solid frame
Cylinder: 6-shot swing out; simultaneous ejector; release on left side of frame
Barrel: 4", 5", 6½"
Sights: Fixed
Finish: Blued or nickel; checkered square butt walnut grips
Length Overall: 9⅜" to 11⅞"
Approximate wt.: 38 to 41 oz.
Comments: Made from about 1930 to 1967.
Estimated Value: Excellent: $350.00
Very good: $280.00

Smith & Wesson Model 20
Heavy Duty

Smith & Wesson Model 23 Outdoorsman Revolver
Similar to Model 20 Heavy Duty except; target version; 6½" barrel only; ribbed barrel after 1950; approximately 42 oz. wt.; blued finish; adjustable target sights. Made from about 1930 to 1967.
Estimated Value: Excellent: $400.00
Very good: $320.00

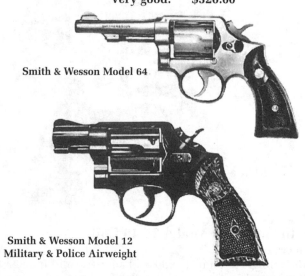

Smith & Wesson Model 64

Smith & Wesson Model 12
Military & Police Airweight

Smith & Wesson Model 64 Military & Police
Same as Model 10 Military & Police except: satin finish stainless steel. Made from about 1972 to present.
Estimated Value: New (retail): $415.00
Excellent: $315.00
Very good: $250.00

Smith & Wesson Model 12 Military & Police Airweight
Same as Model 10 Military & Police except: light alloy frame; 2" or 4" barrel; approx. wt. 28 oz. Made from about 1952 to late 1980's.
Estimated Value: Excellent: $260.00
Very good: $210.00

Smith & Wesson K-32 Target
Similar to S&W 38 Military & Police Target except: caliber 32 S&W; 32 S&W long; & 32 Colt New Police; heavy barrel; approx. wt. 34 oz. Made from about 1940 to 1941.
Estimated Value: Excellent: $675.00
Very good: $540.00

Smith & Wesson Military & Police
Caliber: 38 Special
Action: Single & double; exposed hammer; solid frame
Cylinder: 6-shot swing out; simultaneous ejector; release on left side of frame
Barrel: 2" (after 1933); 4", 5", 6" 6½" (1902-1915)
Sights: Fixed
Finish: Blued or nickel; checkered hard rubber or checkered walnut round or square butt grips
Length Overall: 7" to 11½"
Approximate wt.: 26 to 32 oz.
Comments: Made from about 1902 to 1942 with improvements & minor changes. Basic frame is known as S&W K frame. Add 5% for nickel finish. Also known as 1902 Model & 1905 Model M&P.
Estimated Value: Excellent: $265.00
Very good: $210.00

Smith & Wesson Model 10 Military & Police
Caliber: 38 Special
Action: Double & single; exposed hammer; solid frame
Cylinder: 6-shot swing out: simultaneous manual ejector
Barrel: 2", 3" or 4"
Sights: Fixed
Finish: Blued or nickel: square or round butt checkered walnut grips
Length Overall: 7" to 9½"
Approximate wt.: 28 to 34 oz.
Comments: Made from about 1948 to present. Add 4% for nickel finish; blued only in the 1990's.
Estimated Value: New (retail): $383.00
Excellent: $285.00
Very good: $230.00

Smith & Wesson Victory Model
Same as Model 10 Military & Police except: sand blasted or brushed parkerized finish; 4" barrel; smooth square butt grips with lanyard ring; made from about 1941 to 1946 for the U.S. Government during World War II; 38 Special caliber; Some 38-200 caliber with 5" barrel were made for the British Forces.
Estimated Value: Excellent: $325.00
Very good: $265.00

Smith & Wesson 38 Military & Police Target
Same as Model 10 Military & Police except: 6" barrel only; approximate wt. is 33 oz.; checkered walnut grips; adjustable target sights. Made from about 1924 to 1941.
Estimated Value: Excellent: $275.00
Very good: $220.00

Smith & Wesson
Model 13 M&P

Smith & Wesson Model 13 M&P

Similar to the Model 10 Military & Police except 357 mag. caliber & 3" or 4" heavy barrel.

Estimated Value: New (retail): $394.00
Excellent: $295.00
Very good: $235.00

Smith & Wesson Model 65 M&P

Similar to the Model 13 except: satin stainless steel finish; 3"or 4" barrel.

Estimated Value: New (retail): $427.00
Excellent: $320.00
Very good: $255.00

Smith & Wesson Model 65 Lady Smith

Similar to the Model 65 M&P except: 3" barrel; round butt rosewood grips; includes soft side Lady Smith case; glass bead finished stainless steel. Introduced in 1992.

Estimated Value: New (retail): $461.00
Excellent: $345.00
Very good: $275.00

Smith & Wesson
Model 27 357 Mag.

Smith & Wesson Model 28
Highway Patrolman

Smith & Wesson Model 27 357 Mag.

Caliber: 357 mag. & 38 Special
Action: Single & double; exposed hammer; solid frame
Cylinder: 6-shot swing out; simultaneous manual ejector
Barrel: 3½", 5", 6", 6½", 8⅜" ribbed
Sights: ramp front, adjustable rear
Finish: Blued or nickel; checkered walnut grips
Length Overall: 7⅞" to 14¼"
Approximate wt.: 42 to 49 oz.
Comments: Made from about 1935 to mid 1990's. Made from 1935 to 1938 on special orders. Add 2% for 8⅜" barrel. Presently made in 6" barrel. Add $40.00 for Presentation Box.

Estimated Value: Excellent: $365.00
Very good: $290.00

Smith & Wesson Model 28 Highway Patrolman

Similar to Model 27 357 Mag. except: 4" or 6" barrel; ramp front sight & adj. rear sight; blued finish. Made from about 1954 to late 1980's. Add 10% for target grips.

Estimated Value: Excellent: $285.00
Very good: $225.00

Smith & Wesson Model 31
Regulation Police

Smith & Wesson Model 32 Terrier

Smith & Wesson Model 31 Regulation Police

Caliber: 32 S&W Long, 32 Colt New Police
Action: Single & double; exposed hammer; solid frame
Cylinder: 6-shot swing out; simultaneous manual ejector; release on left side of frame
Barrel: 2" (1949 to present); 3", 3¼", 4", 4¼", 6"
Sights: Fixed
Finish: Blued or nickel; checkered square butt walnut grips
Length Overall: 6½" to 10½"
Approximate wt.: 17 to 20 oz.
Comments: Made from about 1917 to 1992. Nickel finish discontinued in early 1980's.

Estimated Value: Excellent: $295.00
Very good: $235.00

Smith & Wesson Regulation Police Target

Similar to Smith & Wesson Model 31 Regulation Police except: 6" barrel only; adjustable target sights; blued finish. Made from abt. 1917 to 1940.

Estimated Value: Excellent: $260.00
Very good: $210.00

Smith & Wesson Model 33 Regulation Police Revolver

Same as S&W Model 31 Regulation Police except: 38 caliber S&W & 38 Colt New Police; 5-shot cylinder. Made from about 1917 to 1974.

Estimated Value: Excellent: $250.00
Very good: $200.00

Smith & Wesson Model 32 Terrier

Similar to Model 33 Regulation Police except: 2" barrel only; 6½" overall length. Made from about 1936 to 1974.

Estimated Value: Excellent: $235.00
Very good: $185.00

Smith & Wesson Model K-22 Outdoorsman
Caliber: 22 short, long, long rifle
Action: Single & double; exposed hammer; solid frame
Cylinder: 6-shot swing out; simultaneous manual ejector
Barrel: 6"
Sights: Fixed or target sights
Finish: Blued or nickel; checkered walnut grips
Length Overall: 11½"
Approximate wt.: 35 oz.
Comments: Made from abt. 1931 to 1942.
Estimated Value: Excellent: $320.00
                    Very good: $250.00

Smith & Wesson K-22
Outdoorsman

Smith & Wesson
Model 14 Single Action

Smith & Wesson
Model 16 K-32 Masterpiece

Smith & Wesson K-22 Masterpiece
Same as K-22 Outdoorsman except: improved version; better adjustable rear sight; short cocking action; antibacklash trigger; made from about 1942 to 1947.
Estimated Value: Excellent: $300.00
                    Very good: $240.00

Smith & Wesson Model 14 K-38 Masterpiece
Caliber: 38 Special
Action: Single or double; or single action only; exposed hammer; solid frame
Cylinder: 6-shot swing out; simultaneous manual ejector; release on left side of frame
Barrel: 6" or 8⅜"; 6" only after mid 1980's
Sights: Partridge front; click adjustable rear
Finish: Blued; checkered square butt walnut grips
Length Overall: 11⅛" or 13½"
Approximate wt.: 36 to 38 oz.
Comments: Made from about 1947 to present. Add $10.00 for 8⅜" barrel; $40.00 for target accessories.
Estimated Value: New (retail): $465.00
                    Excellent: $350.00
                    Very good: $280.00

Smith & Wesson Model 14 Single Action
Similar to the Model 14 K-38 Masterpiece except: single action; 6" barrel only.
Estimated Value: Excellent: $300.00
                    Very good: $240.00

Smith & Wesson Model 16 K-32 Masterpiece
Same as Model 14 K-38 Masterpiece except: 32 S&W long & 32 Colt Police caliber; 6" barrel only; double & single action. Made from about 1947 to 1974.
Estimated Value: Excellent: $295.00
                    Very good: $240.00

Smith & Wesson Model 14
K-38 Masterpiece

Smith & Wesson Model 15
38 Combat Masterpiece
Same as Model 14 K-38 Masterpiece except: 2", 4", 6" or 8⅜" barrel; approximate wt. is 30 oz. to 39 oz.; quick draw front sight; blued or nickel finish; double & single action. Made from about 1950 to present. Add 7% for nickel finish (discontinued late 1980's); 3% for 8⅜" barrel (discontinued 1989). 4" barrel only after 1990.
Estimated Value: New (retail): $419.00
                    Excellent: $315.00
                    Very good: $250.00

Smith & Wesson Model 67
38 Combat Masterpiece
Same as Model 15 38 combat Masterpiece except: 4" barrel only; satin finish stainless steel construction. Made from about 1972 to present.
Estimated Value: New (retail): $467.00
                    Excellent: $350.00
                    Very good: $280.00

Smith & Wesson Model 19
357 Combat Magnum
Same as Model 15 38 Combat Masterpiece except: 2½", 4" or 6" barrel; caliber 357 magnum or 38 Special; round or square butt. Made from about 1956 to present. Add 2% for square butt target stocks, 6% for target sights.
Estimated Value: New (retail): $416.00
                    Excellent: $310.00
                    Very good: $250.00

Smith & Wesson Model 66 357 Combat Magnum
Same as Model 19 357 Combat Magnum except: satin finish stainless steel. Produced from about 1972 to present. Add 12% for target accessories; 2% for target sights.
Estimated Value: New (retail): $466.00
                    Excellent: $350.00
                    Very good: $280.00

Smith & Wesson 17
K-22 Masterpiece

Smith & Wesson
Model 36 Chiefs Special

Smith & Wesson
Model 37 Airweight

Smith & Wesson
Model 60 Chiefs
Special Stainless

Smith & Wesson
Model 38 Bodyguard
Airweight

Smith & Wesson Model 49
Bodyguard

Smith & Wesson Model 649
Bodyguard

Smith & Wesson Model 17 K-22 Masterpiece

Same as Model 14 K-38 Masterpiece except: 22 short, long, long rifle caliber; 4", 6" or 8⅜" barrel. Made from about 1947 to 1996; approx. wt. 40 ozs. Add 3% for 8⅜" barrel; 9% for target trigger & hammer. Full-length ejector housing added in 1989.

Estimated Value: Excellent: $300.00
                  Very good: $240.00

Smith & Wesson Model 18 Combat Masterpiece

Same as Model 17 K-22 Masterpiece except: 4" barrel; length overall 9⅛"; approx. wt. 38 ozs. Made from 1950 to mid 1980's. Add 10% for target trigger & hammer.

Estimated Value: Excellent: $270.00
                  Very good: $215.00

Smith & Wesson Model 36 Chiefs Special

Caliber: 38 Special
Action: Single & double; exposed hammer; solid frame
Cylinder: 5-shot swing out; simultaneous manual ejector
Barrel: 2" or 3"
Sights: Fixed
Finish: Blued or nickel; round or square butt, checkered walnut grips
Length Overall: 6½" to 7¾"
Approximate wt.: 19 to 20 ozs.
Comments: Made from about 1950 to date. Add 4% for nickel finish.

Estimated Value: New (retail): $377.00
                  Excellent: $285.00
                  Very good: $225.00

Smith & Wesson Model 37 & 637 Airweight Chiefs Special

Same as Model 36 Chiefs Special except: light alloy frame; approximate weight is 13 to 14 oz. Made from about 1954 to present. Add 4% for nickel finish or stainless steel (637).

Estimated Value: New (retail): $412.00
                  Excellent: $310.00
                  Very good: $250.00

Smith & Wesson Model 60 Chiefs Special Stainless

Same as Model 36 Chiefs special except: satin finish stainless steel; round butt grip; approximate wt. 20 ozs. Made from about 1965 to present.

Estimated Value: New (retail): $458.00
                  Excellent: $345.00
                  Very good: $275.00

Smith & Wesson Model 38 Bodyguard Airweight

Same as Model 36 Chiefs Special except: light alloy frame; shrouded hammer; approximate weight 15 ozs.; 2" barrel only. Produced from about 1955 to present. Add 3% for nickel finish.

Estimated Value: New (retail): $444.00
                  Excellent: $335.00
                  Very good: $265.00

Smith & Wesson Model 49 Bodyguard

Same as Model 38 Bodyguard Airweight except: steel frame; approximate weight is 21 oz. Made from about 1959 to present. Nickel finish discontinued late 1980's.

Estimated Value: New (retail): $409.00
                  Excellent: $310.00
                  Very good: $245.00

Smith & Wesson Model 649 Bodyguard

Same as the Model 49 Bodyguard except: stainless steel.

Estimated Value: New (retail): $469.00
                  Excellent: $350.00
                  Very good: $285.00

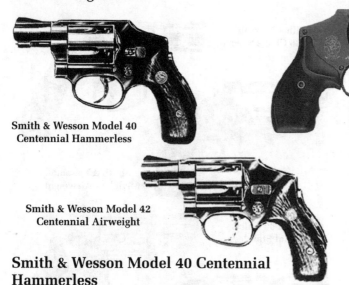

Smith & Wesson Model 40
Centennial Hammerless

Smith & Wesson Model 42
Centennial Airweight

Smith & Wesson Model 642
Centennial Airweight

Smith & Wesson Model 40 Centennial Hammerless

Same as Model 36 Chiefs Special except: concealed hammer; frame extends over hammer area; 2" barrel; double action only; grip safety located on rear of grip. Made from about 1952 to 1974.

Estimated Value: Excellent: $290.00
                   Very good: $230.00

Smith & Wesson Model 42 Centennial Airweight

Same as Model 40 Centennial except: light alloy frame; approximate wt. is 13 oz. Made from about 1954 to 1974.

Estimated Value: Excellent: $300.00
                   Very good: $240.00

Smith & Wesson Model 940 Centennial

Caliber: 9mm
Action: Double action only; enclosed hammer; no grip safety
Cylinder: 5-shot swing out; simultaneous manual ejector
Barrel: 2" or 3"
Sights: Fixed; ramp front, square notch rear
Finish: Stainless steel; round butt combat grips
Length Overall: 6½" to 7½"
Approximate wt.: 23 to 24 oz.
Comments: Introduced in 1991; 2" barrel only after 1993.

Estimated Value: New (retail) $470.00
                   Excellent: $350.00
                   Very good: $285.00

Smith & Wesson Model 442 Centennial Airweight

Caliber: 38 Special
Action: Double action only; enclosed hammer; no grip safety; alloy frame
Cylinder: 5-shot swing out; simultaneous manual ejector
Barrel: 2"
Sights: Fixed; ramp front, square notch rear
Finish: Blued or nickel; round butt grips
Length Overall: 6½"
Approximate wt.: 16 oz.
Comments: Introduced in the 1990's; Add 3% for nickel finish.

Estimated Value: New (retail): $427.00
                   Excellent: $320.00
                   Very good: $255.00

Smith & Wesson Model 642 Centennial Airweight

Similar to the Model 442 Centennial Airweight except: stainless steel; 2" or 3" barrel; approximate wt.: 16 or 17 oz.

Estimated Value: New (retail) $442.00
                   Excellent: $330.00
                   Very good: $265.00

Smith & Wesson Model 642 LS (Lady Smith)

Same as the Model 642 Centennial Airweight except: 2" barrel; price includes softside carrying case.

Estimated Value: New (retail): $471.00
                   Excellent: $350.00
                   Very good: $285.00

Smith & Wesson Model 57 41 Mag.

Caliber: 41 magnum
Action: Single & double; exposed hammer; solid frame
Cylinder: 6-shot swing out; simultaneous manual ejector; release on left side of frame
Barrel: 4", 6", or 8⅜"
Sights: Ramp front, adjustable rear
Finish: Blued or nickel (discontinued late 1980's); checkered walnut grips
Length Overall: 9⅜" to 13¾"
Approximate wt.: 38 to 42 oz.
Comments: Made from about 1964 to 1993. Add 4% for 8⅜" barrel; $40.00 for presentation box.

Estimated Value: Excellent: $335.00
                   Very good: $265.00

Smith & Wesson Model 657 41 Mag.

Similar to the Model 57 41 Mag. except: stainless steel. Introduced in the mid 1980's. Add 4% for 8⅜" barrel.

Estimated Value: New (retail): $528.00
                   Excellent: $395.00
                   Very good: $320.00

Smith & Wesson Model 58 Military & Police

Similar to Model 57 41 magnum except: 4" barrel only; fixed sights; no rib on barrel. Made from about 1964 to late 1970's. Add $10.00 for nickel finish.

Estimated Value: Excellent: $300.00
                   Very good: $240.00

Smith & Wesson Model 58
Military Police

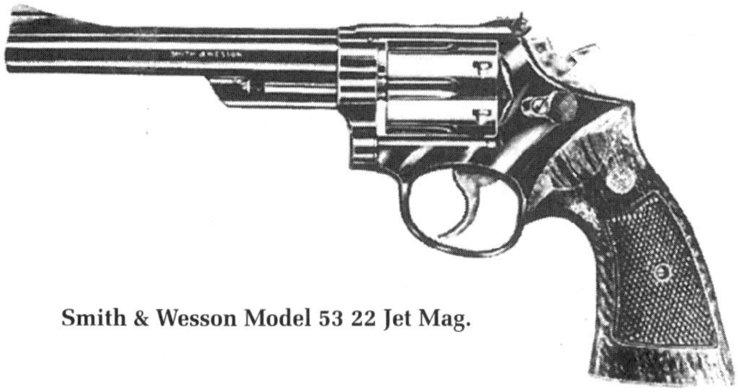

Smith & Wesson Model 53 22 Jet Mag.

Smith & Wesson Model 53 22 Jet Mag.

Caliber: 22 Rem. Jet center fire or 22 S, L, or LR by using chamber inserts & repositioning floating firing pin on hammer
Action: Single & double; exposed hammer; solid frame
Cylinder: 6-shot swing out; simultaneous manual ejector;
Barrel: 4", 6", or 8⅜"
Sights: Ramp front; adjustable rear
Finish: Blued; checkered walnut target grips
Length Overall: 9¼" to 13⅝"
Approximate wt.: 38 to 42 oz.
Comments: Made from about 1961 to 1974. Could be fitted with regular 22 caliber cylinder. Add $100.00 for extra cylinder.

Estimated Value:	**Excellent:**	**$575.00**
	Very good:	**$460.00**

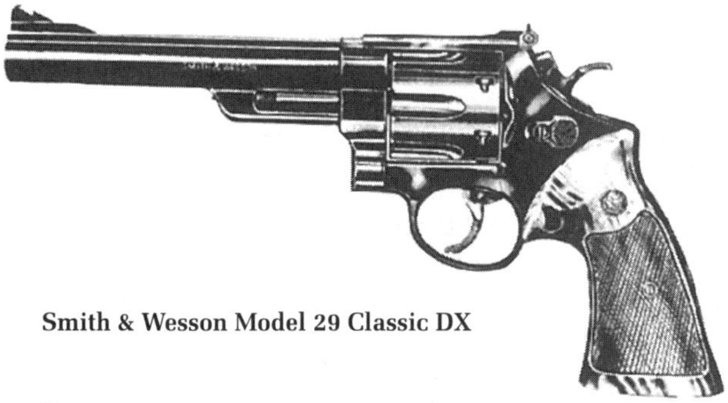

Smith & Wesson Model 29 Classic DX

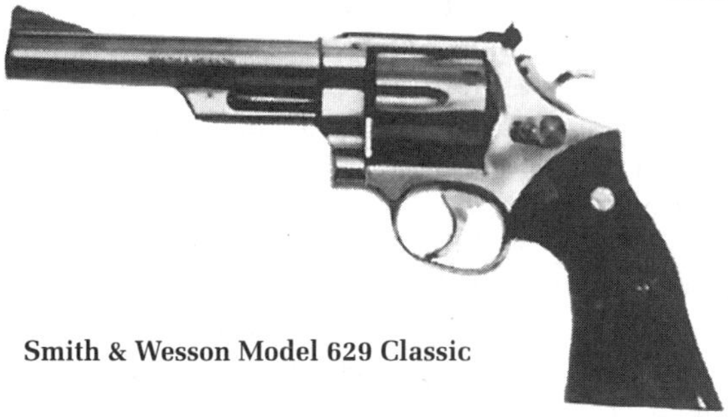

Smith & Wesson Model 629 Classic

Smith & Wesson Model 629 Classic

Similar to the Model 29 Classic 44 Mag. except: stainless steel construction. Add 3% for 8⅜" barrel. Introduced in 1990.

Estimated Value:	**New (retail):**	**$629.00**
	Excellent:	**$470.00**
	Very good:	**$375.00**

Smith & Wesson Model 29 Classic DX

Similar to the Model 29 Classic 44 mag. except: combat grips. Add 2% for 8⅝" barrel. Produced in early 1990s

Estimated Value:	**Excellent:**	**$535.00**
	Very good:	**$425.00**

Smith & Wesson Model 629 Classic DX

Similar to the Model 29 Classic DX except: stainless steel. Add 3% for 8⅝" barrel. Introduced in 1990.

Estimated Value:	**New (retail):**	**$811.00**
	Excellent:	**$610.00**
	Very good:	**$485.00**

Smith & Wesson Model 29 44 Magnum

Caliber: 44 magnum & 44 Special
Action: Single & Double; exposed hammer; solid frame
Cylinder: 6-shot swing out; simultaneous manual ejector; release on left side of frame
Barrel: 4", 6", 8⅝", or 10⅝" ribbed; 6" or 8⅜" only after early 1990's
Sights: Ramp front; adjustable rear
Finish: Blued or nickel: checkered wood grips
Length Overall: 9⅜" to 13¾"
Approximate wt.: 44 to 49 oz.
Comments: Made from about 1956 to present. Add 2% for 8⅜" or nickel finish; Add 11% for 10⅝" barrel; Add $40.00 for presentation box.

Estimated Value:	**New (retail):**	**$554.00**
	Excellent:	**$415.00**
	Very good:	**$330.00**

Smith & Wesson Model 29 Classic 44 Magnum

Similar to the Model 29 44 Magnum except: 5", 6", or 8⅝" barrel; full lug barrel; interchangeable front sight. Add 2% for 8⅝" barrel. Produced in early 1990's.

Estimated Value:	**Excellent:**	**$445.00**
	Very good:	**$355.00**

Smith & Wesson Model 629 44 Mag.

Same as the Model 29 44 mag. except: satin stainless steel finish. Add 3% for 8⅜" barrel; Add $40.00 for presentation box. 10⅝" barrel not available.

Estimated Value:	**New (retail):**	**$587.00**
	Excellent:	**$435.00**
	Very good:	**$350.00**

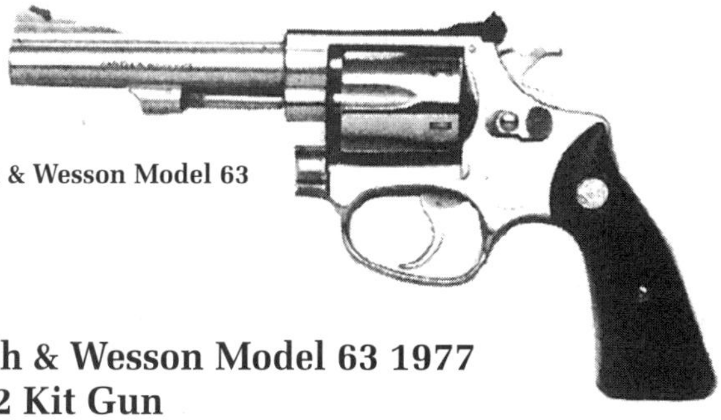

Smith & Wesson Model 63

Smith & Wesson Model 63 1977 22/32 Kit Gun

Caliber: 22 S, L, or LR
Action: Single & double; exposed hammer
Cylinder: 6-shot swing out
Barrel: 2" or 4"
Sights: Adj. micrometer square notch rear, red ramp front
Finish: Satin stainless steel; checkered walnut grips
Length Overall: 9⅜"
Approximate wt.: 24½ oz.
Comments: Made from 1977 to present.

Estimated Value:	**New (retail):**	**$460.00**
	Excellent:	**$345.00**
	Very good:	**$275.00**

Smith & Wesson Model 581 Distinguished Service Mag.

Caliber: 357 mag. & 38 Special
Action: Single & double; exposed hammer; solid frame
Cylinder: 6-shot swing out; simultaneous manual ejector;
Barrel: 4" or 6" heavy barrel with full-length ejector rod shroud. 4" barrel only after mid 1980's.
Sights: Serrated ramp front, fixed rear
Finish: Blued or nickel; checkered walnut magna service grips
Length Overall: 9¾" to 11¾"
Approximate wt.: 42 to 44 oz.
Comments: Smith & Wesson's new "L" frame revolver. It is slightly larger than the K frame which permits it to accommodate a sturdier cylinder. Introduced in 1982. Nickel finish discontinued late 1980's.
Estimated Value: Excellent: $290.00
Very good: $230.00

Smith & Wesson Model 681 Distinguished Service Mag.

Similar to the Model 581 except: satin stainless steel finish; 4 " barrel only.
Estimated Value: Excellent: $310.00
Very good: $245.00

Smith & Wesson Model 547
Military & Police

Smith & Wesson Model 547 Military & Police

Caliber: 9mm Parabellum
Action: Single & double; exposed hammer; solid frame
Cylinder: 6-shot swing out; simultaneous manual ejector; release on left side of frame
Barrel: 3" or 4" heavy barrel
Sights: Fixed rear, serrated ramp front
Finish: Blued; checkered walnut round butt grips with 3" barrel & square butt with 4" barrel
Length Overall: 8¼" to 9¼"
Approximate wt.: 32 to 34 oz.
Comments: A 9mm revolver built on a K frame that features a unique new extraction system for positive extraction of the 9mm cartridge. Made from about 1981 to mid 1980's.
Estimated Value: Excellent: $275.00
Very good: $220.00

Smith & Wesson Model 625

Caliber: 45ACP
Action: Single & double; exposed hammer; solid frame
Cylinder: 6-shot swing out; simultaneous manual ejector
Barrel: 3", 4", 5"; full-length ejector housing under barrel
Sights: Serrated black ramp front & micrometer adjustable rear
Finish: Stainless steel; Pachmayr Gripper round butt grips
Length Overall: 8⅜", 9⅜", 10⅜"
Approximate wt.: 41, 43, & 46 oz.
Comments: Introduced in 1989. 5" barrel only after 1991.
Estimated Value: New (retail): $597.00
Excellent: $440.00
Very good: $355.00

Smith & Wesson Model 586
Distinguished Combat Mag.

Smith & Wesson Model 586 Distinguished Combat Magnum

Caliber: 357 mag. & 38 Special
Action: Single & double; exposed hammer; solid frame
Cylinder: 6-shot swing out; simultaneous manual ejector; cylinder release on left side
Barrel: 4", 6" or 8⅜" heavy barrel with a full-length ejector shroud; 8⅜" barrel discontinued 1991
Sights: Red ramp front, micrometer click rear adjustable for windage & elevation
Finish: Blue or nickel; checkered Goncalo Alves grips
Length Overall: 9¾" to 13¾"
Approximate wt.: 42 to 46 oz.
Comments: S & W's new "L" frame revolver; slightly larger than the K frame which permits it to accommodate a sturdier cylinder; introduced in 1982. Add 3% for nickel finish; 9% for adjustable front sight; 5% for 8⅜" barrel.
Estimated Value: New (retail): $461.00
Excellent: $345.00
Very good: $275.00

Smith & Wesson Model 686 Distinguished Combat Magnum

Similar to the Model 586 except: satin stainless steel. Add 2% for target grips; 7% for adjustable front sight; 5% for 8⅜" barrel. Also available with 2½" barrel.
Estimated Value: New (retail): $481.00
Excellent: $360.00
Very good: $285.00

Smith & Wesson Model 686 Plus
Caliber: 357 magnum or 38 Special
Action: Double or single action
Cylinder: 7-shot
Barrel: 2½", 4", or 6", full lug
Sights: Red ramp front, adjustable blade rear
Finish: Stainless steel; Hogue rubber grip
Length Overall: 7½", 9½", or 12"
Approximate wt.: 35 to 45 oz.
Comments: Introduced in 1996.
Estimated Value: New (retail) $498.00
                       Excellent: $375.00
                       Very good: $300.00

Smith & Wesson Model 60
357 Mag Chiefs Special

Smith & Wesson Model 686 Plus

Smith & Wesson Model 36
Lady Smith

Smith & Wesson Model 60
Lady Smith

Smith & Wesson Model 60
357 Mag Chiefs Special
Caliber: 357 magnum or 38 Special
Action: Double or single action; exposed hammer
Cylinder: 5-shot; swing out
Barrel: 2⅛" or 3"
Sights: Black ramp front, fixed notch rear
Finish: Stainless steel; Uncle Mike's combat grip
Length Overall: 6⁵⁄₁₆"
Approximate wt.: 24 oz.
Comments: Introduced in 1996 (357 caliber).
Estimated Value: New (retail): $431.00
                       Excellent: $325.00
                       Very good: $260.00

Smith & Wesson Model 617 K-22 Masterpiece

Smith & Wesson Model 36 Lady Smith
Caliber: 38 special
Action: Single & double action with exposed hammer; solid frame
Cylinder: 5-shot swing out; simultaneous manual ejector
Barrel: 2", 3" heavy barrel
Sights: Serrated front; fixed notch rear
Finish: Blued; 2" barrel has smooth wood grips; 3" heavy barrel has smooth wood combat-style grips
Length Overall: 6¼" (2" barrel); 7⅜" (3" barrel)
Approximate wt.: 20 oz. (2" barrel); 23 oz. (3" barrel)
Comments: Introduced in 1989.
Estimated Value: New (retail): $408.00
                       Excellent: $305.00
                       Very good: $245.00

Smith & Wesson Model 60 Lady Smith
Same as the Model 36 Lady Smith except: all stainless steel; 2" barrel. Introduced in 1989.
Estimated Value: New (retail): $461.00
                       Excellent: $345.00
                       Very good: $275.00

Smith & Wesson Model 617 K-22 Masterpiece
Caliber: 22 short, long, & long rifle
Action: Single & double action; exposed hammer; solid frame
Cylinder: 6-shot swing out; simultaneous manual ejector
Barrel: 4", 6", 8⅜"; full-length ejector shroud
Sights: Ramp front & micrometer adjustable rear
Finish: Stainless steel; square butt Goncalo Alves grips
Length Overall: 9⅛", 11⅛", 13½"
Approximate wt.: 42, 48, 54 oz.
Comments: Introduced in 1990. Add 3% for 8⅜" barrel; add 6% for target trigger & hammer.
Estimated Value: New (retail): $460.00
                       Excellent: $345.00
                       Very good: $280.00

Smith & Wesson Model 648
Same as the Model 617 except: 6" barrel, 22 mag caliber. Produced in early 1990's.
Estimated Value: Excellent: $350.00
                       Very good: $280.00

Smith & Wesson Model 17 K-22 Masterpiece

Caliber: 22 short, long, long rifle
Action: Double or single action; exposed hammer; solid frame
Cylinder: 10-shot; swing out
Barrel: 6", carbon steel
Sights: Ramp front, adjustable rear
Finish: Blued; Hogue rubber grips
Length Overall: 11⅛"
Approximate wt.: 42 oz.
Comments: Introduced in 1996.
Estimated Value: New (retail): $490.00
                        Excellent: $370.00
                        Very good: $295.00

Smith & Wesson Model 17
K-22 Masterpiece

Smith & Wesson Model 650 Service Kit Gun

Smith & Wesson Model 640 Centennial

Caliber: 38 Special
Action: Double action only; concealed hammer; solid frame
Cylinder: 5-shot swing out; simultaneous manual ejector
Barrel: 2" or 3"
Sights: Ramp front; fixed square notch rear
Finish: Stainless steel with smooth Goncalo Alves round butt grips
Length Overall: 6¼"
Approximate wt.: 20 oz.
Comments: Introduced in 1990.
Estimated Value: New (retail): $474.00
                        Excellent: $360.00
                        Very good: $285.00

Smith & Wesson Model 650 Service Kit Gun

Caliber: 22 magnum
Action: Single & double action, exposed hammer
Cylinder: 6-shot swing out, simultaneous ejector
Barrel: 3" heavy barrel
Sights: Serrated ramp front, fixed square notch rear
Finish: Satin stainless steel; checkered walnut round butt grips
Length Overall: 7"
Approximate wt.: 23½ oz.
Comments: A "J" frame revolver produced in mid 1980's.
Estimated Value: Excellent: $320.00
                        Very good: $250.00

Smith & Wesson Model 16

Smith & Wesson Model 651 Kit Gun

Smith & Wesson Model 16

Caliber: 32 mag. & 32 S&W
Action: Single & double; exposed hammer; solid frame
Cylinder: 6-shot swing out; simultaneous manual ejector
Barrel: 4", 6", 8⅜"; full-length ejector rod housing.
Sights: Ramp front sight; S&W micrometer adj. rear
Finish: Blued with square butt Goncalo Alves combat style grips
Length Overall: 9⅛" (4 barrel); 11⅛" (6" barrel); 13½" (8⅜" barrel)
Approximate wt.: 42, 47, & 54 oz.
Comments: Produced from 1989 to 1994. Add 3% for 6" barrel; add 4% for 8⅜" barrel; add 7% for target trigger & target hammer. 6" barrel only after 1991.
Estimated Value: Excellent: $315.00
                        Very good: $250.00

Smith & Wesson Model 651 Kit Gun

Caliber: 22 mag.
Action: Double & single, exposed hammer
Clynder: 6-shot swing out, simultaneous ejector
Barrel: 4"
Sights: Red ramp front, adjustable micrometer click rear
Finish: Satin stainless steel; checkered walnut square butt grips
Length Overall: 8⅜"
Approximate wt.: 24½ oz.
Comments: A "J" frame revolver produced from the mid 1980's to present.
Estimated Value: New (retail): $460.00
                        Excellent: $345.00
                        Very good: $275.00

Star Model 1919 Pocket
Caliber: 25 ACP (6.35mm)
Action: Semi-automatic; exposed hammer
Magazine: 8-shot clip
Barrel: 2⅝"
Sights: Fixed
Finish: Blued; checkered walnut grips
Length Overall: 4⅞"
Approximate wt.: 16 oz.
Comments: Made from about 1919 to 1934. Distinguished by the safety at the top rear of the slide.
Estimated Value: **Excellent:**   **$245.00**
                       Very good: **$195.00**

Star Model 1919 Pocket

Star Model CO Pocket
Improved version of the 1919 Model; safety in front of left grip rather than top rear of slide; plastic grips; some engraved nickel plated models produced. Made from about 1934 to 1957. Add $20.00 for engraved nickel model.
Estimated Value: **Excellent:**   **$220.00**
                       Very good: **$175.00**

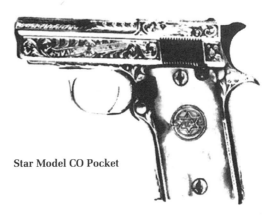
Star Model CO Pocket

Star Model H
Similar to Model CO pistol except: caliber 32 ACP; 9-shot clip; approximate wt. is 20 oz. Made from about 1934 to 1941.
Estimated Value: **Excellent:**   **$180.00**
                       Very good: **$145.00**

Star Model HN
Same as Model H except: caliber 380 ACP; 6-shot clip.
Estimated Value: **Excellent:**   **$190.00**
                       Very good: **$150.00**

Star Model H

Star Model E Pocket
Caliber: 25 ACP (6.35mm)
Action: Semi-automatic; exposed hammer
Magazine: 6-shot clip
Barrel: 2"
Sights: Fixed
Finish: Blued; checkered grips
Length Overall: 4"
Approximate wt.: 10 oz.
Comments: Small compact pocket pistol; safety located in front of left grip; no longer in production.
Estimated Value: **Excellent:**   **$195.00**
                       Very good: **$155.00**

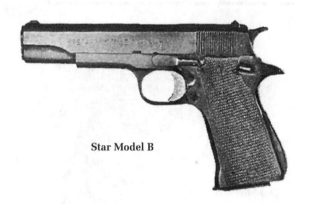

Star Model B

Star Model B Super

Caliber: 9mm Parabellum
Action: Semi-automatic; exposed hammer
Magazine: 8-shot clip
Barrel: 5"
Sights: Blade front; fixed rear
Finish: Blued; all steel
Length Overall: 8¾"
Approximate wt.: 38 oz.
Comments: Imported from 1970's to early 1990's; an improved version of the Model B with loaded chamber indicator; refined takedown & re-assembly system; a high visability white dot sighting system. Add 9% for nickel finish.
Estimated Value: Excellent: $270.00
Very good: $215.00

Star Model F & FR

Caliber: 22 long rifle
Action: Semi-automatic; exposed hammer; manual safety at top rear of left grip
Magazine: 10-shot clip
Barrel: 4¼" (regular); 6" & 7" on Sport & Target models
Sights: Fixed; adjustable on Sport & Target models
Finish: Blued, chromed or chromed engraved; plastic grips
Length Overall: 7¼" to 10"
Approximate wt.: 24 to 32 oz..
Comments: Model F made from about 1942 to 1968. Model FR is improved version made from about 1968 to late 1970's. Add $10.00 for chrome model.
Estimated Value: Excellent: $175.00
Very good: $140.00

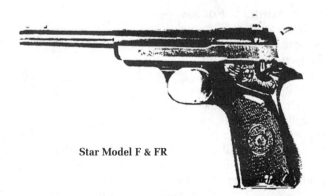

Star Model F & FR

Star Model A & AS

Caliber: 9mm Luger, 9mm Bergman, 9mm Largo, 38 Super auto
Action: Semi-automatic; exposed hammer
Magazine: 8-shot clip
Barrel: 5"
Sights: Fixed
Finish: Blued; checkered walnut grips
Length Overall: 8"
Approximate wt.: 35 oz.
Comments: This handgun resembles the 1911 A1 Colt. Made from about 1924 to late 1970's.
Estimated Value: Excellent: $215.00
Very good: $175.00

Star Model B

Similar to Model A except: barrel lengths 4¼" or 6½"; caliber 9mm Parabellum only. Made from about 1924 to 1976.
Estimated Value: Excellent: $230.00
Very good: $185.00

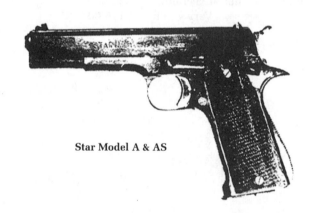

Star Model A & AS

Star Model I (Police Model)

Caliber: 32 ACP
Action: Semi-automatic; exposed hammer
Magazine: 9-shot clip
Barrel: 4¾"
Sights: Fixed
Finish: Blued; plastic grips
Length Overall: 7½"
Approximate wt.: 25 oz.
Comments: Made from about 1934 to 1945; never imported to U.S.A.
Estimated Value: Excellent: $175.00
Very good: $140.00

Star Model IN

Same as Model I except: caliber 380 ACP; 8-shot clip.
Estimated Value: Excellent: $200.00
Very good: $160.00

Star Model Super Star

Star Model M (Military)
Caliber: 380 ACP; 9mm Luger; 9mm Bergmann, 38 ACP, 45 ACP
Action: Semi-automatic; exposed hammer; manual safety
Magazine: 7-shot clip in 45 caliber, 8-shot clip in all other calibers
Barrel: 5"
Sights: Fixed
Finish: Blued; checkered grips
Length Overall: 8½"
Approximate wt.: 36 oz.
Comments: A modified version of the U.S. Government Colt 1911 45 automatic, made from about 1935. Not imported into U.S.A.
Estimated Value: Excellent: $215.00
Very good: $175.00

Star Model Super Star
Same as Model M except: 38 Super ACP, 9mm Parabellum & 38 ACP only; addition of disarming bolt; improved sights; magazine safety; indicator for number of unfired cartridges. Made from about 1942 to 1954.
Estimated Value: Excellent: $245.00
Very good: $195.00

Star Model 31P & 31PK
Caliber: 9mm Parabellum, 40 S&W
Action: Double action, semi-automatic; exposed hammer; ambidextrous safety & decocking lever
Magazine: 15-shot clip
Barrel: 3¾"
Sights: Blade front; adjustable rear
Finish: 31P has all-steel construction in blued or Starvel finish; 31PK has alloy frame in blued finish only
Length Overall: 7¾"
Approximate wt.: 39½ oz. (31P) 30 oz. (31PK)
Comments: Imported from 1990 to 1995. Add 6% for all-weather Starvel finish, 10% for 40 S&W.
Estimated Value: Excellent: $300.00
Very good: $335.00

Star Megastar
Caliber: 10 mm, 45 ACP
Action: Double action, semi-automatic; exposed hammer; ambidextrous safety
Magazine: 12-shot clip, 10-shot in USA after 9-13-94
Barrel: 4½"
Sights: Combat-style triple dot system; fully adjustable rear sight
Finish: All-steel blued or all-weather Starvel finish; rubber grips
Length Overall: 8½"
Approximate wt.: 47½ oz.
Comments: Imported from 1992 to 1995. Add 5% for Starvel finish.
Estimated Value: Excellent: $490.00
Very good: $390.00

Star Firestar M-40, M-43, & M-45
Caliber: 9mm (M43); 40 S&W (M-40); 45 ACP (M-45)
Action: Double action, semi-automatic; exposed hammer; ambidextrous safety
Magazine: 7-shot clip (M-43), 6-shot in 40 or 45 caliber
Barrel: 3½"
Sights: Combat-style triple dot system; fully adjustable rear sight
Finish: All-steel blued or all-weather Starvel finish
Length Overall: 6½"
Approximate wt.: 30½ oz.
Comments: Introduced in 1990. Add 6% for Starvel finish. Add 5% for 40 caliber; add 9% for 45 caliber.
Estimated Value: New (retail): $469.00
Excellent: $350.00
Very good: $280.00

Star Firestar

Star Model 31P

Star Model S

Caliber: 38 ACP
Action: Semi-automatic; exposed hammer; thumb safety
Magazine: 7-shot clip
Barrel: 4"
Sights: Fixed
Finish: Blued or chromed; engraved; plastic grips
Length Overall: 6½"
Approximate wt.: 20 oz.
Comments: A scaled-down modification of the Colt 1911 45 Automatic. Imported from about 1941 to 1968.
Estimated Value: Excellent: $215.00
                        Very good: $175.00

Star Model SI

Same as Model S except: caliber 32 ACP; 8-shot clip.
Estimated Value: Excellent: $205.00
                        Very good: $165.00

Star Model Super S

Same as Model S except: addition of disarming bolt; improved luminous sights; magazine safety; indicator for number of unfired cartridges. Discontinued in 1954.
Estimated Value: Excellent: $240.00
                        Very good: $190.00

Star Model Super SI

Same as Model Super S except: 32 ACP; 8-shot clip.
Estimated Value: Excellent: $220.00
                        Very good: $175.00

Star Model Super S

Star Model Super SI

Star Model Super SM

Caliber: 380 ACP
Action: Semi-automatic; exposed hammer; thumb safety
Magazine: 9-shot clip
Barrel: 4"
Sights: Blade front; rear adjustable for windage
Finish: Blued or chrome; checkered wood grips
Length Overall: 6¾"
Approximate wt.: 21 oz.
Comments: Made from about 1970 to late 1970's. Add 4% for chrome model.
Estimated Value: Excellent: $260.00
                        Very good: $210.00

Star Model DK (Starfire)

Caliber: 380 ACP
Action: Semi-automatic; exposed hammer; thumb safety
Magazine: 6-shot clip
Barrel: 5"
Sights: Fixed
Finish: Blued; checkered plastic grips
Length Overall: 5½"
Approximate wt.: 16 oz.
Comments: Imported from about 1958 to the late 1960's.
Estimated Value: Excellent: $260.00
                        Very good: $210.00

Star Model HK (Lancer)

Star Model CU (Starlet)

Caliber: 25 ACP
Action: Semi-automatic; exposed hammer
Magazine: 8-shot clip
Barrel: 2⅜"
Sights: Fixed
Finish: Blued or chromed slide; black, gray, gold, blue or green receiver; checkered plastic grips
Length Overall: 4¾"
Approximate wt.: 12 oz.
Comments: Imported from about 1957 to 1968. Manual safety catch at top rear of left grip. Alloy frame.
Estimated Value: Excellent: $200.00
                        Very good: $160.00

Star Model HK (Lancer)

Basically same as Model CU Starlet except: caliber 22 long rifle; 3" barrel; 5½" overall length. Imported from the mid 1950's to the late 1960's.
Estimated Value: Excellent: $195.00
                        Very good: $155.00

Star Model Super SM

Star Model 28

Caliber: 9mm Parabellum
Action: Semi-automatic; double action; exposed hammer
Magazine: 15-shot clip
Barrel: 4¼"
Sights: Notched partridge front, adjustable rear
Finish: Blued; checkered plastic grips
Length Overall: 8"
Approximate wt.: 40 oz.
Comments: Imported from 1982 to 1985.
Estimated Value: Excellent: $335.00
Very good: $270.00

Star Model 30PK

An improved version of the Model 28 with alloy frame & slightly shorter; 15-shot clip; combat-style trigger guard.
Estimated Value: Excellent: $410.00
Very good: $325.00

Star Model 30 M

Similar to the Model 30PK with steel frame & better sight plane.
Estimated Value: Excellent: $430.00
Very good: $345.00

Star Model BKS, BKM

Caliber: 9mm Parabellum
Action: Semi-automatic; exposed hammer; manual thumb safety
Magazine: 8-shot clip
Barrel: 4½"
Sights: Fixed
Finish: Blued; chrome; checkered walnut grips
Length Overall: 7¼"
Approximate wt.: 26 oz.
Comments: Imported from about 1970 to early 1990's. Alloy frame; resembles Colt 1911. Add 4% for chrome model.
Estimated Value: Excellent: $315.00
Very good: $250.00

Star Model BM

Similar to the Model BKM without alloy frame, weighs 35 oz. Add $15.00 for chrome finish; add 13% for Starvel weather resistant finish.
Estimated Value: Excellent: $300.00
Very good: $240.00

Star Model PD

Star Model PD

Caliber: 45 ACP
Action: Semi-automatic; exposed hammer
Magazine: 6-shot clip
Barrel: 4"
Sights: Ramp front; adjustable rear
Finish: Blued; chrome available until early 1980's; checkered wood grips; Starvel weather resistant finish available 1990.
Length Overall: 7"
Approximate wt.: 25 oz.
Comments: Imported from about 1975 to early 1990's. Add 3% for chrome model; add 10% for Starvel finish.
Estimated Value: Excellent: $365.00
Very good: $290.00

Star Model BM

Star Model BKS

Sterling

Sterling Model 283

Caliber: 22 long rifle
Action: Semi-automatic; exposed hammer; adjustable trigger & a rear lock safety
Magazine: 10-shot clip
Barrel: 4½", 6" or 8" heavy bull barrel
Sights: Blade front; click adjustable rear
Finish: Blued; checkered plastic grips
Length Overall: 9", 10½" or 12½"
Approximate wt.: 36 to 40 oz.
Comments: All steel construction. Made from about 1970 to 1972. Also known as Target 30 Model.
Estimated Value: Excellent: $160.00
Very good: $130.00

Sterling Model 283

Sterling Model 284
Same as Model 283 automatic pistol except: lighter tapered barrel, also know as Target 300L Model. Made from about 1970 to 1972.

Estimated Value:	Excellent:	$165.00
	Very good:	$135.00

Sterling Model 285
Same as Model 283 automatic pistol except: ramp front sight, fixed rear sight; made in 4½" heavy barrel only; non-adjustable trigger. Made from about 1970 to 1972. Also known as Husky Model.

Estimated Value:	Excellent:	$175.00
	Very good:	$140.00

Sterling Model 286
Same as Model 283 automatic pistol except: ramp front sight, fixed rear sight; made in 4½" & 6" tapered barrel only; non-adjustable trigger. Also known as Trapper Model. Made from about 1970 to 1972.

Estimated Value:	Excellent:	$155.00
	Very good:	$125.00

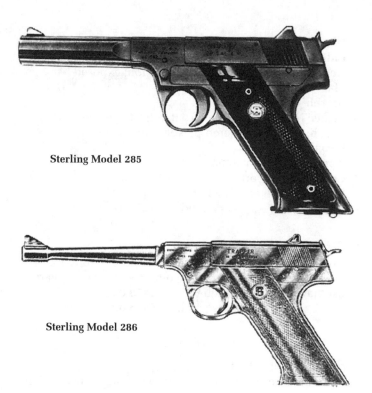

Sterling Model 285

Sterling Model 286

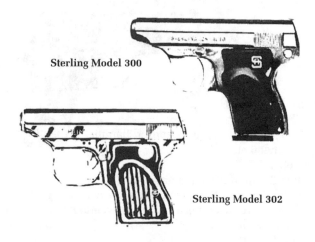

Sterling Model 300

Sterling Model 302

Sterling Model 400 Automatic Pistol
Caliber: 380 ACP
Action: Semi-automatic; double action; exposed hammer; safety locks firing pin
Magazine: 6-shot clip
Barrel: 3½"
Sights: Ramp front, adjustable rear
Finish: Blued or nickel; checkered grips
Length Overall: 6½"
Approximate wt.: 24 oz.
Comments: All steel construction. Made from about 1973 to late 1970's. Replaced by Mark II 400. Add 10% for nickel finish.

Estimated Value:	Excellent:	$210.00
	Very good:	$170.00

Sterling MK II 400 & MK II400S
Similar to 400 except streamlined & lightweight, also 32 ACP. Add 5% for nickel finish; 15% for stainless steel (400S MK II).

Estimated Value:	Excellent:	$195.00
	Very good:	$160.00

Sterling Model 300 & 300S
Caliber: 25 ACP
Action: Semi-automatic blowback action; concealed hammer
Magazine: 6-shot clip
Barrel: 2½"
Sights: None
Finish: Blued, nickel or stainless steel (after 1975) with cycolac grips
Length Overall: 4½"
Approximate wt.: 13 oz.
Comments: All steel construction. Made from about 1972 to mid 1980's. Add 10% for nickel finish; 20% for stainless steel.

Estimated Value:	Excellent:	$100.00
	Very good:	$ 80.00

Sterling Model 302 & 302S
Same as Model 300 Automatic Pistol except caliber 22 long rifle. Model 302S is stainless steel; add 20% for stainless steel.

Estimated Value:	Excellent:	$120.00
	Very good:	$ 95.00

Sterling Model MK II 400

Sterling Model 402
Similar to Model 400 automatic pistol except: caliber 22 long rifle, 8-shot clip magazine. Made from about 1973 to 1975. Add $10.00 for nickel finish.
Estimated Value: Excellent: $190.00
Very good: $150.00

Sterling Model 402 MK II, 402S MK II
Similar to the Model 400 MK II in 32 ACP caliber. Model 402S MK II is stainless steel; add 15%.
Estimated Value: Excellent: $215.00
Very good: $170.00

Sterling Model 400S
Similar to Model 400 except constructed of stainless steel. Made from about 1976 to late 1970's.
Estimated Value: Excellent: $235.00
Very good: $185.00

Sterling Model X Caliber
Caliber: 22 S, L, & LR; 22 mag.; 357 mag.; 44 mag.
Action: Single action; single shot
Magazine: None
Barrel: 8" or 20" heavy octagonal; a caliber change is made by changing barrel
Sights: Ramp front, adjustable rear; tapped for scope mounts
Finish: Blued; smooth wood, finger-grooved grips & small lipped forearm
Length Overall: 13" with 8" barrel
Approximate wt.: 54 to 62 oz.
Comments: A silhouette-style single shot pistol with interchangeable barrels for caliber change. Add 50% for each additional barrel.
Estimated Value: Excellent: $200.00
Very good: $160.00

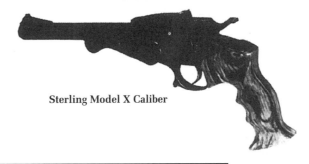

Sterling Model X Caliber

Stevens

Stevens Tip-Up Pocket
Caliber: 22 short, 30 RF (to 1902)
Action: Single with sheath trigger (spur)
Cylinder: None; single shot with tip-up barrel
Barrel: 3½"; part octagon
Sights: Blade front; notch in frame rear
Finish: Blued barrel; nickel plated frame to 1912; blued frame after 1912; varnished walnut square butt grips
Length Overall: 6¼"
Approximate wt.: 10 oz.
Comments: Made from about 1888 to 1915. Marked "J Stevens A. & T. Co."
Estimated Value: Excellent: $250.00
Very good: $200.00

Stevens Tip-Up Pocket

Stevens Diamond Target

Stevens Diamond Target
Caliber: 22 RF long rifle (black power 1888 to 1912); 22 long rifle (smokeless powder 1912 to 1915)
Action: Single; sheath trigger (spur)
Cylinder: None; single shot with tip-up
Barrel: 6", 10"; part octagon
Sights: Globe or bead front; peep or adjustable rear
Finish: Blued barrel; nickel plated iron frame to 1912; varnished long walnut square grips
Length Overall: 9½" to 13½"
Approximate wt.: 10 to 13 oz.
Comments: Made from about 1888 to 1915. Marked "J. Stevens A. & T. Co." Approximately 132,000 produced.
Estimated Value: Excellent: $240.00
Very good: $195.00

Stevens Hunter's Pet
Caliber: 22 long rifle, 25 RF, 32 RF, 38 long RF, 44 long RF, 38-40, 44-40, 38-35, 44-50, 24 gauge
Action: Single with sheath trigger (spur)
Cylinder: None; single shot with pivoted barrel
Barrel: 18", 20", 22" or 24" octagon & half octagon
Sights: Adjustable for elevation; also some had Steven's Vernier peep sight attached to back strap
Finish: Blued barrel; nickel plated frame & detachable skeleton stock; smooth, varnished walnut, square butt grips
Length Overall: 22" to 28"
Approximate wt.: 5¾ lbs.
Comments: Serial numbers in 4,000 to 13,000 range. Approximately 8,000 produced from about 1888 to 1907.
Estimated Value: Excellent: $475.00
Very good: $380.00

Stevens Lord Gallery
Caliber: 22 long rifle, 25 RF (smokeless powder)
Action: Single; tip-up barrel
Magazine: None; single shot
Barrel: Octagon breech; 6", 8" , 10"
Sights: Bead front; stepped elevator rear
Finish: Blued barrel; plated frame; varnished walnut grips with base butt cap; blued frame after 1912
Length Overall: 9¼" to 13¼"
Approximate wt.: 24 to 28 oz.
Comments: Made from about 1907 to 1915. Marked "J Stevens A. & T. Co."
Estimated Value: Excellent: $250.00
                       Very good: $200.00

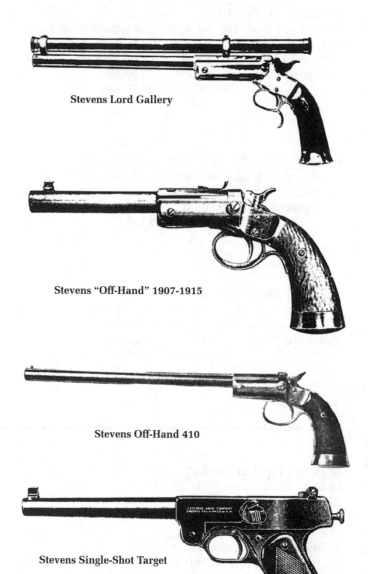

Stevens Lord Gallery

Stevens "Off-Hand" 1907-1915

Stevens Off-Hand 410

Stevens Single-Shot Target

Stevens "Off-Hand" 1907-1915
Caliber: 22 long rifle, 25 RF, smokeless powder
Action: Single, tip-up barrel
Cylinder: None; single shot
Barrel: Octagon breech; 6", 8", 10"
Sights: Bead front; stepped elevator rear
Finish: Blued barrel; plated frame; varnished walnut grips with base butt cap; blued frame after 1912
Length Overall: 9¼" to 13¼"
Approximate wt.: 24 to 28 oz.
Comments: Made from about 1907 to 1915. Marked "J. Stevens A. & T. Co."
Estimated Value: Excellent: $295.00
                       Very good: $235.00

Stevens Off-Hand 1923-1939
Caliber: 22 long rifle
Action: Single; tip-up barrel
Cylinder: None; single shot
Barrel: Octagon breech; 6", 8", 20",12¼"
Sights: Bead front; rear adjustable for elevation
Finish: Blued barrel & frame, also plated frame; walnut grips with butt cap
Length Overall: 9¼" to 15½"
Approximate wt.: 24 to 34 oz.
Comments: Made from about mid 1920's to late 1930's.
Estimated Value: Excellent: $290.00
                       Very good: $230.00

Stevens Off-Hand 410
Caliber: 410 gauge (2½")
Action: Single; tip-up barrel
Cylinder: None; single shot
Barrel: Octagon breech; choked 8" or 12¼" barrel
Sights: Shotgun front sight
Finish: Blued barrel & frame, also plated frame; walnut grips with butt cap
Length Overall: 11¼" to 15½"
Approximate wt.: 23 to 25 oz.
Comments: Made from about 1925 to 1935. Marked "J Stevens Arms Company."
Estimated Value: Excellent: $300.00
                       Very good: $240.00

Stevens Single-Shot Target
Caliber: 22 long rifle
Action: Single; tip up barrel; round knurled cocking piece
Cylinder: None; single shot
Barrel: Round, 8"
Sights: Partridge front; adjustable windage rear
Finish: Blued (blackish blue color); black composition checkered grips
Length Overall: 11½"
Approximate wt.: 37 oz.
Comments: A single shot target pistol with configuration of an automatic pistol. Made from about 1919 to 1942. Approximately 10,000 produced. The 1919 pistols had serial numbers from 1 to approximately 5,000 range with "Pat. App'd For" on barrel. After 1920 marked "Pat'd April 27, 1920." All pistols marked "J. Stevens Arms Company."
Estimated Value: Excellent: $310.00
                       Very good: $245.00

Steyr

Roth-Steyr Self-Loading Pistol
Caliber: 8mm Roth-Steyr
Action: Semi-automatic concealed striker; locked breech design uses rotation of barrel by cam action to unlock barrel when fired; the striker is cocked by the recoil, but the trigger action has to pull it further back before it will release to fire
Magazine: 10-shot non-detachable; usually loaded by a charger from the top
Barrel: 5⅛"
Sights: Fixed
Finish: Blued; checkered wood grips
Length Overall: 9⅛"
Approximate wt.: 36 lbs.
Comments: Adopted by the Austro-Hungarian Cavalry in 1907. This is one of the earliest forms of successful locked-breech pistols.
Estimated Value: Excellent: $220.00
Very good: $175.00

Steyr Model 1909 Pocket Automatic Pistol
Caliber: 32 ACP
Action: Semi-automatic; concealed hammer; blowback action; early models have no extractor (empty case is blown out by gas after the breech-block is pushed open by firing); barrel can be tipped down for cleaning, using as single shot pistol, or for removing unfired cartridge
Magazine: 7-shot clip
Barrel: 3½"
Sights: Fixed
Finish: Blued; checkered wood grips
Length Overall: 6½"
Approximate wt.: 23 oz.
Comments: Made in both Austria & Belgium. The Austrian variety was a finer pistol from the standpoint of manufacture & reliability. Add $30.00 for later model with extractor.
Estimated Value: Excellent: $215.00
Very good: $170.00

Steyr-Solothurn Pocket Model Automatic Pistol
Similar to the Steyr model 1909 except: a modified version; uses extractors to remove empty cases; production started abt. 1934 from Solothurn factory in Switzerland.
Estimated Value: Excellent: $225.00
Very good: $180.00

Steyr Vest Pocket (Baby) Automatic

Steyr Vest Pocket (Baby) Automatic Pistol
Caliber: 25 ACP
Action: Semi-automatic; concealed hammer; blowback action; early models have no extractor (empty case is blown out by gas after the breech block is pushed open by firing); barrel can be tipped down for cleaning, using as a single shot pistol or for removing unfired cartridges
Magazine: 6-shot clip
Barrel: 2"
Sights: Fixed
Finish: Blued; hard rubber checkered grips
Length Overall: 4½"
Approximate wt.: 12 oz.
Comments: First manufactured about 1908. Add $10.00 for later model with extractor.
Estimated Value: Excellent: $225.00
Very good: $180.00

Steyr Model 1912 Military
Caliber: 9mm Steyr
Action: Semi-automatic; exposed hammer; short recoil; locked breech action (barrel rotates to unlock breech when gun is fired)
Magazine: 8-shot non-detachable; loaded from top singly or by using a strip clip
Barrel: 5"
Sights: Fixed
Finish: Blued; checkered wood grips
Length Overall: 8½"
Approximate wt.: 33 oz.
Comments: Made from about 1911 until after World War I; also referred to as Model 1911 or Steyr-Hahn; adopted by the Austro-Hungarian Army in 1912.
Estimated Value: Excellent: $320.00
Very good: $260.00

Steyr Nazi-Proofed
Same as Steyr Model 1912 except: converted to fire the 9mm Luger cartridge during World War II & marked "P-08" on left side of slide.
Estimated Value: Excellent: $325.00
Very good: $260.00

Steyr Model GB
Caliber: 9mm Parabellum
Action: Gas delayed blowback action, semi-automatic, double action
Magazine: 18-shot clip
Barrel: 5½"
Sights: Fixed
Finish: Black crinkled with blued slide; plastic checkered grips & trigger guard
Length Overall: 8½"
Approximate wt.: 39 oz.
Comments: Imported in the mid 1980's.
Estimated Value: Excellent: $445.00
Very good: $335.00

Taurus

Taurus Model PT-58

Taurus Model 58, PT-58

Caliber: 380 ACP
Action: Semi-automatic; double action; exposed round spur hammer
Magazine: 12-shot staggered clip; 10-shot after 9-13-94
Barrel: 4"
Sights: Blade front, notched bar rear
Finish: Blue, stainless steel, or satin nickel; smooth walnut grips
Length Overall: 7"
Approximate wt.: 30 oz.
Comments: Made in Brazil; introduced in 1988; add 5% for satin nickel finish; Add 10% for stainless steel.
Estimated Value: New (retail): $429.00
Excellent: $320.00
Very good: $260.00

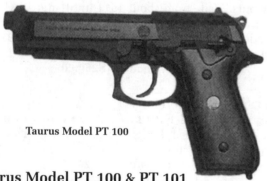

Taurus Model PT 100

Taurus Model PT 100 & PT 101

Caliber: 40 S&W
Action: Double action only; semi-automatic; ambidextrous safety
Magazine: 11-shot clip; 10-shot after 9-13-94
Barrel: 5"
Sights: Fixed (PT 100); adj. rear, 3-dot combat (PT 101)
Finish: Blued, satin nickel, or satin stainless steel; Brazilian hardwood grips
Length Overall: 8½"
Approximate wt.: 34 oz.
Comments: Introduced in 1992. Add 8% for nickel; add 10% for stainless steel; add 11% for adjustable sights.
Estimated Value: New (retail): $469.00
Excellent: $350.00
Very good: $280.00

Taurus Model PT 92AF & PT 99AF

Caliber: 9mm Parabellum
Action: Semi-automatic, double action; exposed round spur hammer
Magazine: 15-shot clip; 10-shot after 9-13-94
Barrel: 5"
Sights: Blade front, notched bar rear (PT92AF); blade front, micrometer adjustable rear (PT99AF)
Finish: Blued or satin nickel; smooth walnut grips; stainless steel available after 1992.
Length Overall: 8½"
Approximate wt.: 34 oz.
Comments: Made in Brazil. Add 8% for satin nickel; add 8% for adj. sights; add 14% for stainless steel.
Estimated Value: New (retail): $449.00
Excellent: $350.00
Very good: $270.00

Taurus Model 92 AFC

Taurus Model 92 AFC

A compact version of the Model PT 92AF; 4" barrel; 13-shot clip; 10-shot after 9-13-94. Add 8% for nickel finish; add 14% for stainless steel.
Estimated Value: New (retail): $449.00
Excellent: $335.00
Very good: $270.00

Taurus Model PT 940 & PT 945

Caliber: 40 S & W (PT 940); 45ACP (PT 945)
Action: Semi-automatic; double action; exposed round spur hammer; last shot hold-open; manual ambidextrous hammer-drop safety
Magazine: 9-shot clip (PT 940); 8-shot clip (PT 945)
Barrel: 4½"
Sights: Fixed; 3-dot combat
Finish: Blued or stainless steel; hardwood or Santoprene II grips
Length Overall: 7½"
Approximate wt.: 30 oz.
Comments: Introduced in mid 1990's. Made in Brazil; add 10% for stainless steel.
Estimated Value: New (retail): $453.00
Excellent: $340.00
Very good: $275.00

Taurus Model 73 & 741

Caliber: 32 H&R magnum
Action: Single and double action; exposed hammer
Cylinder: 6-shot, swing out; simultaneous ejector
Barrel: 3" or 4" heavy barrel
Sights: Fixed or adj. sights
Finish: Blue, satin nickel, or stainless steel
Length Overall: 7¾" or 8¾"
Approximate wt.: 20 oz.
Comments: Produced in Brazil. Add 10% for satin nickel; add 35% for stainless steel.
Estimated Value: Excellent: $190.00
　　　　　　　　　 Very good: $150.00

Taurus Model 94

Taurus Model 76 & 761

Similar to the Model 73 & 741 except: blued finish only, 6" barrel.
Estimated Value: Excellent: $245.00
　　　　　　　　　 Very good: $195.00

Taurus Model 65

Caliber: 357 mag. & 38 Spl.
Action: Single and double action; exposed hammer
Cylinder: 6-shot swing out, simultaneous ejector
Barrel: 2½" or 4" heavy barrel
Sights: Fixed; ramp front, square notch rear
Finish: Royal blue or satin nickel; checkered walnut grips
Length Overall: 8½" or 9½"
Approximate wt.: 34 oz.
Comments: Currently produced in Brazil. Add 5% for satin nickel finish. Add 24% for stainless steel.
Estimated Value: New (retail): $290.00
　　　　　　　　　 Excellent: $218.00
　　　　　　　　　 Very good: $175.00

Taurus Model 66

Similar to the Model 65 except: 2½", 4", & 6" barrel lengths; serrated ramp front sight & micrometer adjustable rear; blued, satin nickel or stainless steel; checkered walnut target grip on 6"; add 5% for satin nickel finish; add 24% for stainless steel.
Estimated Value: New (retail): $318.00
　　　　　　　　　 Excellent: $240.00
　　　　　　　　　 Very good: $190.00

Taurus Model 669 & 689

Same as the Model 66 except: 4" or 6" barrel; full ejector rod shroud; blued or stainless steel only; introduced in 1988. Add 24% for stainless steel. 689 has ventilated rib (add 4%).
Estimated Value: New (retail): $327.00
　　　　　　　　　 Excellent: $245.00
　　　　　　　　　 Very good: $195.00

Taurus Model 94 & 941

Caliber: 22 short, long, & long rifle (Model 94); 22 magnum (Model 941)
Action: Single and double; exposed hammer
Cylinder: 9-shot (Model 94); 8-shot (Model 941)
Barrel: 3" or 4" heavy, solid rib; Model 941 has ejector shroud under barrel; 5" barrel added in 1996.
Sights: Fixed; ramp front, adjustable rear
Finish: Blued or stainless steel; checkered hardwood grips
Length Overall: 8¼" or 9¼"
Approximate wt.: 24 to 28 oz.
Comments: Made in Brazil; add 8% for Model 941; add 16% for stainless steel.
Estimated Value: New (retail): $293.00
　　　　　　　　　 Excellent: $220.00
　　　　　　　　　 Very good: $175.00

Taurus Model 65

Taurus Model 66

Taurus Model PT 22 & PT 25

Caliber: 22 long rifle (PT 22); 25ACP (PT 25)
Action: Double action only; semi-automatic; tip-up barrel
Magazine: 9-shot clip (PT 22), 8-shot clip (PT 25)
Barrel: 2¾" tip-up
Sights: Fixed
Finish: Blued or nickel; smooth Brazilian hardwood grips
Length Overall: 5¼"
Approximate wt.: 12¼ oz.
Comments: Introduced in 1992. Add 5% for nickel.
Estimated Value: New (retail): $187.00
          Excellent: $140.00
          Very good: $115.00

Taurus Model PT 22/PT 25

Taurus Model PT 908

Caliber: 9mm Parabellum
Action: Semi-automatic; double action; exposed round spur hammer; last shot hold-open; manual hammer-drop safety
Magazine: 8-shot clip
Barrel: 3¾"
Sights: Fixed; 3-dot combat
Finish: Blued or stainless steel; rubber grips
Length Overall: 7"
Approximate wt.: 30 oz.
Comments: Introduced in 1993. Made in Brazil; add 9% for stainless steel.
Estimated Value: New (retail): $435.00
          Excellent: $325.00
          Very good: $260.00

Taurus Model PT 908

Taurus Model 605

Taurus Model 605

Caliber: 357 magnum & 38 Special
Action: Double or single action; exposed hammer
Cylinder: 5-shot swing out
Barrel: 2¼" or 3" heavy, solid rib
Sights: Fixed; notched rear and serrated ramp front
Finish: Blued or stainless steel; Santoprene I grip
Length Overall: 7½" to 8¼"
Approximate wt.: 25 to 30 oz.
Comments: Introduced in the mid 1990's; add 20% for stainless steel.
Estimated Value: New (retail): $262.00
          Excellent: $195.00
          Very good: $160.00

Taurus Model 605 CH

Same as Model 605 except: spurless hammer; 2¼" barrel only; add 20% for stainless steel; double action only.
Estimated Value: New (retail): $262.00
          Excellent: $195.00
          Very good: $160.00

Taurus Model 607

Caliber: 357 magnum & 38 Special
Action: Double or single action; exposed hammer
Cylinder: 7-shot; swing out
Barrel: 4" heavy, solid rib; 6½" heavy, ventilated rib; integral compensator
Sights: Adjustable rear and serrated ramp front
Finish: Blued or stainless steel; Santoprene I grip
Length Overall: 9½" to 11½"
Approximate wt.: 30 to 32 oz.
Comments: Introduced in the mid 1990's; add 15% for stainless steel; add 4% for ventilated rib.
Estimated Value: New (retail): $425.00
          Excellent: $320.00
          Very good: $255.00

Taurus Model 608

Same as Model 607 except: 8-shot cylinder; introduced in 1996; add 15% for stainless steel; add 4% for ventilated rib.
Estimated Value: New (retail): $425.00
          Excellent: $320.00
          Very good: $255.00

Taurus Model 80, 82

Taurus Model 80 & 82
Caliber: 38 Spl.
Action: Single or double action; exposed hammer
Cylinder: 6-shot swing out; simultaneous ejector
Barrel: 3" or 4"; standard barrel (80); heavy barrel (82)
Sights: Fixed
Finish: Blued, satin nickel, or stainless steel; checkered walnut grips
Length Overall: 8⅛" or 9⅛"
Approximate wt.: 30 oz. (80); 34 oz. (82)
Comments: Made in Brazil. Add 6½% for satin nickel finish. Add 20% for stainless steel.
Estimated Value: New (retail): $252.00
                        Excellent: $190.00
                        Very good: $150.00

Taurus Model 83
Similar to the Model 82 except: 4" heavy barrel only; ramp front sight & micrometer adjustable rear sight. Add 5% for satin nickel finish. Add 18% for stainless steel.
Estimated Value: New (retail): $265.00
                        Excellent: $200.00
                        Very good: $160.00

Taurus Model 86 Target

Taurus Model 86 & 96 Target
Caliber: 38 Spl. (86); 22 S, L, or LR (96)
Action: Single or double; exposed hammer
Cylinder: 6-shot swing out; simultaneous ejector
Barrel: 6"
Sights: Partridge-type front; micrometer adjustable rear
Finish: Blued; checkered walnut target grip
Length Overall: 11¼"
Approximate wt.: 34 oz.
Comments: Produced in Brazil. Model 86 dropped in mid 1990's.
Estimated Value: New (retail): $358.00
                        Excellent: $270.00
                        Very good: $215.00

Taurus Model 85
Caliber: 38 Spl.
Action: Single or double action; exposed hammer
Cylinder: 5-shot swing out, simultaneous ejector
Barrel: 2" or 3" heavy barrel
Sights: Fixed; serrated ramp front, notch rear
Finish: Royal blue, satin nickel, or stainless steel
Length Overall: 6½" or 7½"
Approximate wt.: 21 oz.
Comments: Produced in Brazil. Add 7% for satin nickel finish. Add 22% for stainless steel.
Estimated Value: New (retail): $239.00
                        Excellent: $180.00
                        Very good: $145.00

Taurus Model 85 CH
Same as the Model 85 except: 2" barrel; spurless hammer; double action only. Add 22% for stainless steel.
Estimated Value: New (retail): $239.00
                        Excellent: $180.00
                        Very good: $145.00

Taurus Model 85

Taurus Model 431 & 441
Caliber: 44 Special
Action: Single or double; exposed hammer
Cylinder: 5-shot swing-out
Barrel: 3" or 4" (Model 431); 3", 4", or 6" (Model 441); heavy solid rib and ejector shroud
Sights: Fixed (Model 431); Partridge front, adjustable rear (Model 441)
Finish: Blued or stainless steel; checkered hardwood grips
Length Overall: 8¼" or 11¼"
Approximate wt.: 34 to 40 oz.
Comments: Made in Brazil; add 9% for Model 441 (adj. sights); add 24% for stainless steel.
Estimated Value: New (retail): $286.00
                        Excellent: $215.00
                        Very good: $172.00

Taurus Model 44
Caliber: 44 magnum or 44 Special
Action: Single or double; exposed hammer
Cylinder: 6-shot swing-out
Barrel: 4", 6½", or 8⅜"; heavy solid rib on 4"; ventilated rib on other models
Sights: Ramp front, adjustable rear
Finish: Blued or stainless steel; hardwood grips
Length Overall: 9¾" or 14"
Approximate wt.: 44 to 57 oz.
Comments: Made in Brazil; add 5% for 6½" or 8⅜" barrel; add 15% for stainless steel. Introduced in 1994.
Estimated Value: New (retail): $425.00
                        Excellent: $320.00
                        Very good: $255.00

Thompson Center

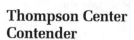

Thompson Center Contender

Thompson Center Contender

Caliber: 22 S, L, or LR to 45-70 Gov't.;
over the years approximately 35 to 40 calibers were made including some wildcat calibers. Presently made in 18 calibers: 22 long rifle, 22 Win. mag., 22 Hornet, 222 Rem., 223 Rem., 270 Rem., 7mm TCU, 7x30 Waters, 30-30 Win., 32-20 Win., 357 mag., 357 Rem. maximum, 35 Rem., 10mm auto, 44 mag., 445 Super mag.; 45-70 Gov't., & 45 Colt/410 gauge

Action: Single action with adj. trigger; the frame will accommodate any caliber barrel & the hammer adjusts to rim fire or center fire ammunition

Cylinder: None; single shot

Barrel: 8¾" (discontinued in the early 1980's), 10" & 14" (introduced in the late 1970's), 16¼" (introduced in 1990). Octagon or round; regular or bull barrel; plain or ventilated rib; the 45 Colt/410 gauge barrel has a removable internal choke to use for 410 gauge shot shells. Blued or stainless steel

Sights: Ramp front; adj. rear; vent. rib has fixed sights

Finish: Blued or stainless steel frame; checkered or smooth walnut grip & fore-end

Length Overall: 12½" to 20"

Approximate wt.: 38 to 60 oz.

Comments: Made from abt. 1967 to present. Add 3% for internal choke or vent. rib. Add 4% for 16" barrel. Add 3% for stainless steel barrel. Add 6% for stainless steel barrel & frame.

Estimated Value:　New (retail):　$473.00
　　　　　　　　　　Excellent:　　　$355.00
　　　　　　　　　　Very good:　　　$285.00

Thompson Center Contender Armour Alloy II

Similar to the Contender except the parts & barrels are not interchangeable with the standard model Contender. It has a special Armour Alloy II non-glare satin finish. Made in the following calibers: 22 long rifle, 223 Rem., 357 magnum, 357 Rem. maximum, 44 magnum, 7mm TCU, 7x30 Waters, 30-30 Win., 35 Rem., 45 Colt/410 gauge. The 45 Colt/410 gauge has a removable internal choke to use with regular 410 gauge shot shells in 10" bull barrel or ventilated rib barrel. All other calibers use 10" bull barrel or 14" bull barrel. Introduced in 1986 & discontinued in 1990. Add 5% for ventilated rib with internal choke. Add 3% for 14" barrel.

Estimated Value:　Excellent:　　　$300.00
　　　　　　　　　　Very good:　　　$240.00

Thompson Center Contender Hunter

Caliber: 223 Rem.; 7x30 Waters; 30-30 Win.; 375 Win.; 35 Rem.; 44 mag.; 45-70 Gov't.

Action: Single action; adjustable trigger; break open

Cylinder: None; single shot

Barrel: 12" or 14" round; T/C Muzzle Tamer to reduce muzzle jump & recoil; blued or stainless steel

Sights: 2.5x T/C scope with lighted duplex reticle

Finish: Blued or stainless steel frame; smooth walnut grip & fore-end; grip has rubber insert to cushion recoil; QD swivels & nylon sling

Length Overall: 16"

Approximate wt.: 65 oz.

Comments: Introduced in 1990. Add 2% for stainless steel barrel; add 4% for stainless steel barrel & frame.

Estimated Value:　New (retail):　$798.00
　　　　　　　　　　Excellent:　　　$600.00
　　　　　　　　　　Very good:　　　$480.00

Walther

Walther Model 1 Vest Pocket

Caliber: 25 ACP

Action: Semi-automatic; concealed hammer

Magazine: 6-shot clip

Barrel: 2"

Sights: Fixed

Finish: Blued; checkered hard rubber grips

Length Overall: 4¼"

Approximate wt.: 10 oz.

Comments: Top section of slide is cut away from behind top sight to breech block face. Made from about 1908 to 1912.

Estimated Value:　Excellent:　　　$330.00
　　　　　　　　　　Very good:　　　$265.00

Walther Model 2 Vest Pocket

Similar to Model 1 except: slide fully encloses the barrel; ejector port right side of slide; overall length is 4¼"; approximate wt. is 12 oz. Made from about 1909 to 1915.

Estimated Value:　Excellent:　　　$345.00
　　　　　　　　　　Very good:　　　$275.00

Walther Model 3 Pocket

Caliber: 32 ACP

Action: Semi-automatic; concealed hammer

Magazine: 6-shot clip

Barrel: 2⅝"

Sights: Fixed

Finish: Blued; checkered hard rubber grips

Length Overall: 5"

Approximate wt.: 17 oz.

Comments: Made from about 1910 to 1918; ejector port on left side of slide.

Estimated Value:　Excellent:　　　$400.00
　　　　　　　　　　Very good:　　　$320.00

Walther Model 4 Pocket

Similar to Model 3 except: larger in overall size; 3½" barrel; 6" overall; longer grip; 8-shot clip; a slide extension connected to forward end of the slide. Made from about 1910 to 1918.

Estimated Value: Excellent: $300.00
Very good: $240.00

Walther Model 5 Vest Pocket Pistol

Similar to Model 2 except: improved version with a better finish. Made from about 1913 to 1920.

Estimated Value: Excellent: $350.00
Very good: $280.00

Walther Model 6

Caliber: 9mm Parabellum
Action: Semi-automatic; concealed hammer
Magazine: 8-shot clip
Barrel: 4¾"
Sights: Fixed
Finish: Blued; hard rubber grips
Length Overall: 8¼"
Approximate wt.: 33 oz.
Comments: Made from about 1915 to 1917; ejection port on right side of slide.

Estimated Value: Excellent: $600.00
Very good: $480.00

Walther Model 7 Pocket

Caliber: 25 ACP
Action: Semi-automatic; concealed hammer
Magazine: 8-shot clip
Barrel: 3"
Sights: Fixed
Finish: Blued; checkered hard rubber grips
Length Overall: 5¼"
Approximate wt.: 13 oz.
Comments: Introduced in 1917, discontinued in 1918. Ejection port on right side of slide.

Estimated Value: Excellent: $375.00
Very good: $300.00

Walther Model 8 Pocket

Caliber: 25 ACP
Action: Semi-automatic; concealed hammer
Magazine: 8-shot clip
Barrel: 2⅞"
Sights: Fixed
Finish: Blued; checkered plastic grips
Length Overall: 5⅛"
Approximate wt.: 13 oz.
Comments: Made from about 1920 to 1945. Earlier models had takedown catch but later models used trigger guard as slide lock; a variety of special styles were made such as nickel or gold plated, engraved finishes with pearl or ivory grips. Special plated & engraved styles worth more.

Estimated Value: Excellent: $335.00
Very good: $265.00

Walther Model 8 Lightweight Pocket

Same as Model 8 except: aluminum alloy used for frame, making it lighter; approximate wt. is 9 oz.

Estimated Value: Excellent: $340.00
Very good: $270.00

Walther Model 9 Vest Pocket

Caliber: 25 ACP
Action: Semi-automatic; concealed hammer
Magazine: 6-shot clip
Barrel: 2"
Sights: Fixed
Finish: Blued; checkered plastic grips
Length Overall: 4"
Approximate wt.: 9½ oz.
Comments: Made from about 1921 to 1945; a variety of special styles were made such as nickel or gold plated engraved finishes with pearl or ivory grips; top section of slide from front sight to breech block face is cut away. Special plated & engraved styles worth more.

Estimated Value: Excellent: $350.00
Very good: $280.00

Walther Model 4 Pocket

Walther Model 5 Vest Pocket Pistol

Walther Model 7 Pocket

Walther Model 9 Vest Pocket

Walther Model PP

Walther Model PP

Caliber: 22 long rifle, 25 ACP, 32 ACP or 380 ACP
Action: Semi-automatic; double action; exposed hammer; thumb safety that drops the hammer on blocked firing pin
Magazine: 8-shot clip
Barrel: 3¾"
Sights: Fixed
Finish: Blued; checkered plastic or checkered wood grips; steel back strap
Length Overall: 6⁹⁄₁₆"
Approximate wt.: 24 oz.
Comments: Made from about 1929 to 1945; also nickel, silver & gold plated engraved models with ivory & pearl grips were produced; first commercially successful double action automatic pistol; initially made in 32 ACP but later made in 22, 25 & 380 calibers; the center fire calibers were made with & without a signal pin to indicate a round in the chamber; World War II models had poorer finish & workmanship. Special plated & engraved models worth more.

Estimated Value:	Regular Model	WWII Model
Excellent:	$470.00	$360.00
Very good:	$360.00	$270.00

Walther Model PPK

Same as Model PP except: 3¼" barrel; 5¹⁵⁄₁₆" overall length; 7-shot magazine; approximate wt. is 19 oz.; one piece wrap-around grip. Made from about 1931 to 1945.

Estimated Value:	Regular Model	WWII Model
Excellent:	$460.00	$350.00
Very good:	$350.00	$265.00

Walther Model PPK

Walther Models PP & PPK Lightweight

Same as Models PP & PPK except lighter in weight due to aluminum alloy frame.

Estimated Value:	Excellent:	$450.00
	Very good:	$360.00

Walther Model PPK/S (West German)

Same as Model PPK except: larger size to meet U.S.A. Treasury Dept. specifications in 1968; uses the slide & barrel of PPK Model mounted on the PP Model frame; overall length of about 6"; 8-shot magazine.

Estimated Value:	Excellent:	$410.00
	Very good:	$330.00

Walther Model PP (West German)

Same as pre-World War II Model PP except produced in West Germany from about 1955 to present. Add 50% for 32 or 380 ACP.

Estimated Value:	New (retail):	$999.00
	Excellent:	$750.00
	Very good:	$600.00

Walther Model PPK Auto

Same as pre-World War II Model PPK except produced in West Germany from about 1955 to date. Importation into U.S.A. discontinued in 1968 due to restrictions imposed by the U.S. Treasury Dept.

Estimated Value:	Excellent:	$500.00
	Very good:	$400.00

Walther Model PPK Lightweight

Same as Model PPK except: lighter in weight due to use of aluminum alloy frame & not made in 380 caliber. Importation discontinued in 1968.

Estimated Value:	Excellent:	$450.00
	Very good:	$340.00

Walther Model PPK American

Similar to the Model PPK except manufactured in the United States in blue or stainless steel. Introduced in 1986.

Estimated Value:	New (retail):	$540.00
	Excellent:	$405.00
	Very good:	$325.00

Walther Model PPK/S American

Caliber: 380 ACP
Action: Semi-automatic; double action; exposed hammer
Magazine: 7-shot clip
Barrel: 3¼"
Sights: Fixed
Finish: Blued or stainless steel; plastic grips
Length Overall: 6"
Approximate wt.: 23 oz.
Comments: An American-built model of the Walther PPK/S, introduced in the late 1970's.

Estimated Value:	New (retail):	$540.00
	Excellent:	$405.00
	Very good:	$325.00

Walther Model P-5

Walther Model P-5 (West German)

Caliber: 9mm Parabellum
Action: Semi-automatic; double action; exposed hammer
Magazine: 8-shot clip
Barrel: 3½" or 3"
Sights: Adjustable rear, blade front
Finish: Blued; plastic grips
Length Overall: 7"
Approximate wt.: 28 oz.
Comments: Introduced in 1980.

Estimated Value:	New (retail):	$900.00
	Excellent:	$675.00
	Very good:	$540.00

Walther Model HP

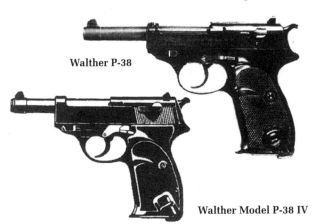

Walther P-38

Walther Model P-38 IV

Walther Model HP
Caliber: 9mm Parabellum
Action: Semi-automatic; double action; exposed hammer
Magazine: 8-shot clip
Barrel: 5"
Sights: Fixed
Finish: Blued; checkered walnut or plastic grips
Length Overall: 8⅜"
Approximate wt.: 35 oz.
Comments: Well-made pistol, produced from about 1937 to 1945.

Estimated Value:	Excellent:	$950.00
	Very good:	$760.00

Walther P-38 Military
Similar to Model HP except: modified version of the Model HP adopted as the Offical German service arm in 1938 & produced until about 1945. A poorer quality mass-produced military pistol; some of the wartime models were of very loose fit & very rough finish.

Estimated Value:	Excellent:	$500.00
	Very good:	$400.00

Walther P-38 (West German)
Same as P-38 Military Model except: improved workmanship; use of aluminum alloy in construction of frame; calibers 22 long rifle, 30 Luger & 9mm Parabellum; approximate wt. is 28 oz.; add 11% for 22 caliber.

Estimated Value:	Excellent:	$620.00
	Very good:	$495.00

Walther Model P-38 IV
Similar to the P-38 with strengthened slide, no dust cover & steel reinforced frame; adjustable rear sight.

Estimated Value:	Excellent:	$520.00
	Very good:	$415.00

Walther Model P-38 K
Similar to the Model P-38 IV with a 2¾" barrel.

Estimated Value:	Excellent:	$475.00
	Very good:	$345.00

Walther Model P88 (West German)
Caliber: 9mm Parabellum
Action: Double action, semi-automatic; exposed hammer
Magazine: 15-shot clip; 10-shot clip in USA after 9-13-94
Barrel: 4"
Sights: Rear adjustable for windage & elevation
Finish: Blued, non reflective matte finish; alloy frame; black plastic grips
Length Overall: 7⅜"
Approximate wt.: 31½" oz.
Comments: A combat-style handgun designed for ambidextrous use. Introduced in 1987. Produced in West Germany.

Estimated Value:	New (retail):	$900.00
	Excellent:	$675.00
	Very good:	$540.00

Walther Model TPH
Caliber: 22 long rifle; 25 ACP
Action: Semi-automatic, exposed hammer
Magazine: 6-shot clip, with finger rest
Barrel: 2¼"
Sights: Fixed
Finish: Blue or Stainless steel; black plastic grips
Length Overall: 5⅜"
Approximate wt.: 14 oz.
Comments: A scaled-down version of the Model PP-PPK series in 22 long rifle; 25 ACP added in 1992. Introduced in the late 1980's.

Estimated Value:	New (retail):	$440.00
	Excellent:	$330.00
	Very good:	$265.00

Webley

Webley 1906 Model Vest Pocket
Caliber: 25 ACP
Action: Semi-automatic; exposed hammer; grip safety in front of grip
Magazine: 6-shot clip
Barrel: 2⅛"
Sights: None
Finish: Blued; checkered hard rubber grips
Length Overall: 4¾"
Approximate wt.: 12 oz.
Comments: Made from about 1906 to 1940.

Estimated Value:	Excellent:	$200.00
	Very good:	$160.00

Welby 1906 Model Vest Pocket

Webley & Scott 1909 Model Vest Pocket
Similar to 1906 except: ejection port in top of slide; concealed hammer; has fixed front & rear sights mounted on slide. Made from about 1909 to 1940.

Estimated Value:	Excellent:	$220.00
	Very good:	$175.00

Webley & Scott 9mm Military & Police

Caliber: 9mm Browning long
Action: Semi-automatic; exposed hammer; grip safety
Magazine: 8-shot clip
Barrel: 5¼"
Sights: Fixed
Finish: Blued; checkered plastic grips
Length Overall: 8"
Approximate wt.: 32 oz.
Comments: Made from about 1909 to 1930.
Estimated Value: Excellent: $500.00
                       Very good: $375.00

Webley & Scott 9mm Military & Police

Webley & Scott Mark I

Caliber: 455 Webley self-loading
Action: Semi-automatic; exposed hammer; grip safety
Magazine: 7-shot clip
Barrel: 5"
Sights: Fixed front; movable rear
Finish: Blued; checkered hard rubber or checkered walnut grips
Length Overall: 8½"
Approximate wt.: 39 oz.
Comments: Adopted by British Royal Navy & Marines in 1913. Made from about 1911 to 1931.
Estimated Value: Excellent: $360.00
                       Very good: $285.00

Webley & Scott Mark I No. 2

Similar to Mark I except: a slightly different version with fitted shoulder stock & adjustable rear sight; issued to the British Royal Flying Corps in 1915. Prices for gun with shoulder stock.
Estimated Value: Excellent: $750.00
                       Very good: $560.00

Webley & Scott 38

Similar to Mark I except: a smaller modified version with concealed hammer; 8-shot magazine; 38 ACP caliber. Made from about 1910 to 1930.
Estimated Value: Excellent: $300.00
                       Very good: $225.00

Webley & Scott 1909 Model
Single Shot Target

Webley & Scott 1909 Model Single Shot Target

Caliber: 22 short, long, long rifle
Action: Single action; exposed hammer; hinged frame; tip-up barrel; trigger guard also barrel release
Cylinder: None; single shot; chamber in barrel
Barrel: 10" round
Sights: Fixed; later models have adjustable rear sight
Finish: Blued; hard rubber or wood grips
Length Overall: 15"
Approximate wt.: 35 oz..
Comments: Target pistol. Made from about 1909 to 1965 with improvements.
Estimated Value: Excellent: $260.00
                       Very good: $210.00

Webley & Scott 1906 Model Police

Caliber: 32 ACP; 380 ACP
Action: Semi-automatic; exposed hammer
Magazine: 8-shot clip in 32 ACP, 7-shot clip in 380 ACP
Barrel: 3½"
Sights: Fixed; police version has rear sight & civilian model has a groove for rear sight
Finish: Blued; checkered hard rubber grips
Length Overall: 6¼"
Approximate wt.: 20 oz.
Comments: Made from about 1905 to 1940; with or without grip safety.
Estimated Value: Excellent: $200.00
                       Very good: $150.00

Webley & Scott 1911 Model Single Shot

Caliber: 22 short, long, long rifle
Action: Manually operated slide to chamber cartridge; exposed hammer
Magazine: None; single shot
Barrel: 4½" or 9"
Sights: Adjustable
Finish: Blued; checkered hard rubber grips
Length Overall: 6¼" to 10¾"
Approximate wt.: 20 to 24 oz.
Comments: Has the appearance of automatic pistol; built on the 32 caliber frame; made for police training arm; some had removable wooden shoulder stocks. Made from about 1925 to 1927 with only a few hundred being produced.
Estimated Value: Excellent: $400.00
                       Very good: $300.00

Webley & Scott Match Invader Single Shot Target

Similar to 1909 Model Single Shot Target except: also in caliber 32 S&W long, 38S&W or 38 Special; approximate wt. is 33 oz. Made from about 1952 to 1965.
Estimated Value: Excellent: $200.00
                       Very good: $150.00

Webley & Scott Mark III Government Model
Caliber: 450, 455 or 476 Webley
Action: Single or double; exposed hammer; hinged frame; top break; simultaneous ejector
Cylinder: 6-shot
Barrel: 4", 6", 7½"
Sights: Fixed, also adjustable rear
Finish: Blued; hard rubber or wood grips
Length Overall: 9¼" to 12¾"
Approximate wt.: 36 to 40 oz.
Comments: Made from about 1896 to 1928.
Estimated Value: Excellent: $220.00
                       Very good: $175.00

Webley & Scott Pocket Model Hammerless
Caliber: 32 S&W
Action: Double action; concealed hammer; hinged frame; top break; simultaneous ejector
Cylinder: 6-shot
Barrel: 3½"
Sights: Fixed
Finish: Blued; hard rubber or wood grips
Length Overall: 6½"
Approximate wt.: 18 oz.
Comments: The hammer is enclosed by the frame. Made from about 1898 to 1940.
Estimated Value: Excellent: $200.00
                       Very good: $160.00

Webley & Scott Police & Civilian Pocket
Similar to Pocket Model Hammerless except: exposed hammer; double & single action. Made from about 1901 to 1940.
Estimated Value: Excellent: $190.00
                       Very good: $145.00

Webley Mark IV Police Model
Caliber: 38 S&W
Action: Single or double; exposed hammer; hinged frame; top break; simultaneous ejector
Cylinder: 6-shot
Barrel: 4", 5", 6"
Sights: Fixed or adjustable
Finish: Blued; checkered walnut or plastic grips
Length Overall: 8⅛" to 10⅛"
Approximate wt.: 24 to 29 oz.
Comments: Made from about 1927 to present.
Estimated Value: Excellent: $195.00
                       Very good: $150.00

Webley Mark IV War Model
Similar to Mark IV Police Model except: made during World War II (from about 1940 to 1945); poor finish & fitting.
Estimated Value: Excellent: $200.00
                       Very good: $150.00

Webley Mark IV Pocket Model
Similar to Mark IV Police Model except: calibers 32 S&W, 32 S&W long or 38 S&W; barrel length 3"; approximate wt. is 24 oz.; overall length is 7⅛".
Estimated Value: Excellent: $210.00
                       Very good: $165.00

Webley & Scott Mark III Police
Caliber: 38 S&W
Action: Single or double; exposed hammer; hinged frame; top break simultaneous ejector
Cylinder: 6-shot
Barrel: 3", 4", 5"
Sights: Fixed or adjustable rear
Finish: Blued; checkered hard rubber or walnut grips
Length Overall: 8¼" to 10¼"
Approximate wt.: 19 to 22 oz.
Comments: Made from about 1897 to 1945.
Estimated Value: Excellent: $200.00
                       Very good: $160.00

Webley & Scott
Mark III Government Model

Webley Mark IV
Pocket Model

Webley Mark IV
Police Model

Webley Mark IV Target Model
Similar to Mark IV Police Model except: caliber 22 short, long, long rifle only; adjustable rear sight; barrel length 6"; approximate wt. is 32 oz. Made from about 1931 to 1968.
Estimated Value: Excellent: $250.00
                       Very good: $190.00

Webley Mark VI British Service
Caliber: 455 Webley
Action: Single or double; hinged frame; top break; simultaneous ejector
Cylinder: 6-shot
Barrel: 4", 6", 7½"
Sights: Fixed
Finish: Blued; checkered hard rubber or wood grips
Length Overall: 9¼" to 12¾"
Approximate wt.: 34 to 39 oz.
Comments: Made from about 1915 to 1928.
Estimated Value: Excellent: $220.00
                       Very good: $170.00

Webley Police Mark VI Target
Similar to Mark VI British except: caliber 22 short, long, long rifle; barrel length 6" only; target sights; approximate wt. is 40 oz.
Estimated Value: Excellent: $225.00
                       Very good: $180.00

Wesson

Dan Wesson Model 12

Dan Wesson Model 11

Dan Wesson Model 14

Dan Wesson Model 11

Caliber: 357 magnum or 38 Special (interchangeable)
Action: Double or single; exposed hammer; simultaneous ejector
Cylinder: 6-shot; swing out
Barrel: 2½", 4", 6"; interchangeable barrels
Sights: Ramp front; fixed rear
Finish: Blued; one-piece changeable walnut grip
Length Overall: 7¾" to 11¼"
Approximate wt.: 36 to 40 oz.
Comments: Made from about 1970 to 1974. Barrels and barrel cover (shroud) can be changed quickly by means of a recessed barrel nut; also one-piece grip readily changeable to option styles.
Estimated Value: Excellent: $200.00
Very good: $160.00

Dan Wesson Model 12

Same as Model 11 except target model with adjustable rear sight.
Estimated Value: Excellent: $215.00
Very good: $170.00

Dan Wesson Model 14, 14-2, & 714

Caliber: 357 mag. or 38 Special (interchangeable)
Action: Double or single; exposed hammer
Cylinder: 6-shot; swing out
Barrel: 2½", 4", 6"; interchangeable barrels
Sights: Ramp front; fixed rear
Finish: Blued; one-piece walnut grip; satin blue available; 714 stainless steel
Length Overall: 7¾" to 13¼"
Approximate wt.: 36 to 42 oz.
Comments: Made from about 1973 to present. A modified version of the Model 22. Price increases with barrel length. Add 15% for stainless steel (714).
Estimated Value: Excellent: $200.00 - $210.00
Very good: $160.00 - $170.00

Dan Wesson Model 15

Similar to the Model 14 except adjustable rear sight. Made from about 1973 to 1976.
Estimated Value: Excellent: $210.00
Very good: $170.00

Dan Wesson Pistol Pack

A carrying case containing revolver, 2, 3, or 4 interchangeable barrels (2½", 4", 6", 8"), interchangeable grips, additional colored sight blades. Model Nos. beginning with the digit 7 are stainless steel

	Excellent	VG
Model 8-2 (3 barrels)	$350.00	$275.00
Model 708 (3 barrels)	$390.00	$310.00
Model 9-2	$460.00	$370.00
Model 709	$515.00	$412.00
Model 9-2V	$535.00	$430.00
Model 709-V	$590.00	$475.00
Model 9-2VH	$600.00	$480.00
Model 709-VH	$665.00	$530.00
Model 14-2 (3 barrels)	$350.00	$275.00
Model 14-2B	$325.00	$260.00
Model 714	$390.00	$310.00
Model 15-2	$460.00	$370.00
Model 715	$515.00	$410.00
Model 15-2H	$340.00	$275.00
Model 15-2V	$535.00	$430.00
Model 715-V	$590.00	$475.00
Model 15-2VH	$600.00	$480.00
Model 715-VH	$665.00	$530.00
Model 22	$475.00	$380.00
Model 22M	$475.00	$380.00
Model 722	$540.00	$435.00
Model 722M	$540.00	$430.00
Model 22-V	$550.00	$440.00
Model 722-V	$620.00	$495.00
Model 22M-V	$550.00	$440.00
Model 722M-V	$610.00	$490.00
Model 22-VH	$620.00	$495.00
Model 722-VH	$690.00	$550.00
Model 22M-VH	$620.00	$495.00
Model 722M-VH	$690.00	$550.00
Model 41-V	$465.00	$370.00
Model 741-V	$515.00	$410.00
Model 41-VH	$500.00	$400.00
Model 741-VH	$550.00	$440.00
Model 44V	$490.00	$395.00
Model 744V	$545.00	$435.00
Model 44-VH	$530.00	$425.00
Model 744-VH	$610.00	$490.00
Model 32	$460.00	$370.00
Model 32-V	$535.00	$430.00
Model 32-VH	$615.00	$490.00
Model 732	$515.00	$415.00
Model 732-V	$590.00	$475.00
Model 732-VH	$670.00	$535.00
Model 45-V	$530.00	$425.00
Model 45-VH	$565.00	$450.00
Model 745-V	$610.00	$490.00
Model 745-VH	$650.00	$520.00

Dan Wesson Model 8-2 & 708
Similar to Model 14 except 38 caliber only. Add $15.00 for bright blue finish (8-2B) (discontinued 1987); 15% for stainless steel (708).

Estimated Value: Excellent: $200.00 - $210.00
Very good: $160.00 - $170.00

Dan Wesson Model 15-2 & 715
Caliber: 357 magnum or 38 Special (interchangeable)
Action: Double or single; exposed hammer
Cylinder: 6-shot; swing out; simultaneous ejector
Barrel: 2½", 4", 6", 8", 10", 12" 15" interchangeable barrels
Sights: Interchangeable colored front sight blade; adjustable rear sight with white outline
Finish: Blued; checkered wood target grips; 715 is stainless steel
Length Overall: 7¾" to 13¼"
Approximate wt.: 32 to 42 oz.
Comments: Made from about 1975 to present. Price increases with barrel length. Add 9% for stainless steel (715).

Estimated Value: Excellent: $250.00 - $295.00
Very good: $200.00 - $235.00

Dan Wesson Model 9-2 & 709
Similar to Model 15-2 except 38 caliber only. No 12" or 15" barrel. Add 9% for stainless steel (709).

Estimated Value: Excellent: $250.00 - $290.00
Very good: $200.00 - $230.00

Dan Wesson Model 9-2V & 709-V
Similar to Model 9-2 with ventilated rib. Price increased with barrel length. Add 12% for stainless steel (709-V).

Estimated Value: Excellent: $270.00 - $315.00
Very good: $215.00 - $250.00

Dan Wesson Model 9-2VH & 709-VH
Similar to Model 9-2 with heavier bull barrel & ventilated rib. Prices increases with barrel length. Add 10% for stainless steel (709-VH).

Estimated Value: Excellent: $290.00 - $350.00
Very good: $230.00 - $280.00

Dan Wesson Model 9-2

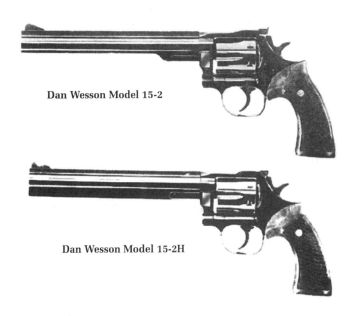

Dan Wesson Model 15-2

Dan Wesson Model 15-2H

Dan Wesson Model 15-2H
Same as Model 15-2 except it has a heavier bull barrel. A special order item after 1981.

Estimated Value: Excellent: $260.00
Very good: $195.00

Dan Wesson Model 15-2V & 715-V
Same as Model 15-2 except it has ventilated rib. Add 9% for stainless steel (715-V).

Estimated Value: Excellent: $270.00 - $320.00
Very good: $215.00 - $255.00

Dan Wesson Model 15-2V

Dan Wesson Model 15-2VH

Dan Wesson Model 15-2VH & 715-VH
Same as Model 15-2 except: heavier bull barrel with ventilated rib. Add 12% for stainless steel (715-VH).

Estimated Value: Excellent: $295.00 - $340.00
Very good: $235.00 - $270.00

Dan Wesson Model 22 & 722

Similar to the Model 15-2 except: 22 caliber. Introduced in the late 1970's. Not available with 10", 12", or 15" barrel. Price increases with barrel length. Add 12% for stainless steel (722).

Estimated Value: Excellent: $260.00 - $285.00
                   Very good: $210.00 - $225.00

Dan Wesson Model 22M & 722M

Similar to the Model 22 except: 22 mag. caliber. Add 10% for stainless steel finish (722M).

Estimated Value: Excellent: $260.00 - $285.00
                   Very good: $210.00 - $225.00

Dan Wesson Model 22M-V & 722M-V

Similar to the Model 22-V except: 22 mag. caliber. Add 10% for stainless steel finish (722M-V).

Estimated Value: Excellent: $280.00 - $305.00
                   Very good: $220.00 - $245.00

Dan Wesson Model 22M-VH & 722M-VH

Similar to the Model 22-VH except: 22 mag. caliber. Add 10% for stainless steel finish (722M-VH).

Estimated Value: Excellent: $300.00 - $320.00
                   Very good: $240.00 - $255.00

Dan Wesson Model 22V & 722-V

Similar to the Model 22 except: ventilated rib. Price increases with barrel length. Add 12% for stainless steel (722-V).

Estimated Value: Excellent: $300.00 - $310.00
                   Very good: $240.00 - $250.00

Dan Wesson Model 22V

Dan Wesson Model 22-VH & 722-VH

Similar to the Model 22 with heavier bull barrel & ventilated rib. Price increases with barrel length. Add 10% for stainless steel (722-VH).

Estimated Value: Excellent: $305.00 - $330.00
                   Very good: $240.00 - $265.00

Dan Wesson Model 32 & 732

Similar to the Model 15-2 except: 32 mag. caliber; 2½", 4", 6", or 8" barrel. Introduced in the mid 1980's. Add 9% for stainless steel (732).

Estimated Value: Excellent: $250.00 - $275.00
                   Very good: $200.00 - $220.00

Dan Wesson Model 32-V & 732-V

Similar to the Model 32 with ventilated rib. Add 9% for stainless steel (732-V).

Estimated Value: Excellent: $270.00 - $300.00
                   Very good: $215.00 - $240.00

Dan Wesson Model 32-VH & 732-VH

Similar to the Model 32 with ventilated rib, heavy barrel. Add 9% for stainless steel (732-VH).

Estimated Value: Excellent: $295.00 - $315.00
                   Very good: $235.00 - $255.00

Dan Wesson Model 40-V & 740-V 357 Super Magnum

Caliber: 357 Maximum
Action: Double & single; exposed hammer
Cylinder: 6-shot; swing out; fluted
Barrel: 4",6", 8", or 10"; interchangeable barrels; ventilated rib
Sights: Interchangeable colored front sight blade, adjustable interchangeable rear
Finish: Blued; smooth grips; stainless steel   (740-V)
Length Overall: 14½" with 8" barrel
Approximate wt.: 59 to 62 oz.
Comments: Introduced in the mid 1980's. Comes with an extra barrel. Price increases with barrel length. Add 13% for stainless steel.

Estimated Value: Excellent: $366.00 - $415.00
                   Very good: $293.00 - $330.00

Dan Wesson Model 40-V8S & 740-V8S

Similar to the Model 40-V except: slotted barrel shroud; 8" barrel only; extra barrel included; weighs 64 oz. Add 10% for stainless steel (740-V8S).

Estimated Value: Excellent: $430.00
                   Very good: $340.00

Dan Wesson Model 40-VH & 740-VH

Similar to the Model 40-V with heavy barrel; extra barrel included. Add $60.00 for stainless steel (740-VH).

Estimated Value: Excellent: $380.00 - $430.00
                   Very good: $300.00 - $345.00

Dan Wesson Model 375V Super Mag.

Similar to the Model 40V except: 375 mag. caliber.

Estimated Value: Excellent: $375.00 - $410.00
                            Very good: $300.00 - $325.00

Dan Wesson Model 375-V8S Super Mag.

Similar to the Model 375 V except: slotted barrel shroud and 8" barrel.

Estimated Value: Excellent: $400.00
                            Very good: $320.00

Dan Wesson Model 375V Super Mag

Dan Wesson Model 375-VH Super Mag.

Similar to the Model 375 V except: ventilated rib shroud & heavy barrel.

Estimated Value: Excellent: $380.00 - $430.00
                            Very good: $305.00 - $345.00

Dan Wesson Model 44-V

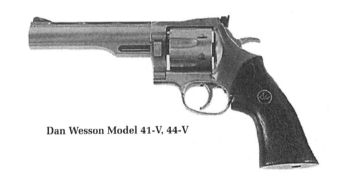

Dan Wesson Model 41-V, 44-V

Dan Wesson Model 44-V & 744-V

Caliber: 44 mag. & 44 Special (jacketed only)
Action: Single & double, exposed hammer, wide hammer & trigger
Cylinder: 6-shot; swing out; simultaneous ejector
Barrel: 4", 6", 8", 10" interchangeable barrel; ventilated rib
Sights: Interchangeable colored front sight blade, adjustable rear with white outline
Finish: Blued; smooth or checkered walnut grips with thumb flute; stainless steel (744-V)
Length Overall: 12" with 6" barrel
Approximate wt.: 48 to 63 oz.
Comments: Introduced in the early 1980's. Price increases with barrel length. Add 17% for stainless steel (744-V).

Estimated Value: Excellent: $325.00 - $355.00
                            Very good: $260.00 - $285.00

Dan Wesson Model 41-V & 741-V

Similar to the Model 44V except: 41 mag. caliber. Add 12% for stainless steel finish (741-V).

Estimated Value: Excellent: $310.00 - $335.00
                            Very good: $250.00 - $270.00

Dan Wesson Model 44-VH & 744-VH

Similar to the Model 44 V except: heavier bull barrel. Price increases with barrel length. Add 16% for stainless steel (744-VH).

Estimated Value: Excellent: $340.00 - $370.00
                            Very good: $270.00 - $300.00

Dan Wesson Model 41-VH & 741-VH

Similar to the Model 44VH in 41 magnum caliber. Add 11% for stainless steel finish (741-VH).

Estimated Value: Excellent: $325.00 - $360.00
                            Very good: $260.00 - $285.00

Dan Wesson Model 45-V & 745-V

Caliber: 45 Colt
Action: Single & double, exposed hammer, wide hammer & trigger
Cylinder: 6-shot; swing out; simultaneous ejector
Barrel: 4", 6", 8", or 10" ventilated rib shroud
Sights: Interchangeable colored front sight blade
Finish: Blued; smooth walnut grips; stainless steel (745-V)
Length Overall: 12" with 6" barrel
Approximate wt.: 48 to 63 oz.
Comments: Introduced in 1988. Price increases with barrel length. Add 17% for stainless steel (745-V).

Estimated Value:	Excellent:	$325.00 - $350.00
	Very good:	$260.00 - $280.00

Dan Wesson Model 45-V

Dan Wesson Model 445V & 7445V

Caliber: 445 Supermag
Action: Double or single; exposed hammer
Cylinder: 6-shot swing-out
Barrel: 4", 6", 8", or 10"; interchangeable; ventilated rib shroud
Sights: Interchangeable colored blade front; adjustable rear
Finish: Blued or stainless steel (7445V); smooth wood grips
Length Overall: 10" to 16"
Approximate wt.: 50 to 64 oz.
Comments: Introduced in the early 1990's; add 15% for stainless steel; add 3% per inch of barrel length over 4".

Estimated Value:	Excellent:	$390.00
	Very good:	$310.00

Dan Wesson Model 445VH & 7445VH

Same as the Model 445V & 7445V except: ventilated heavy rib shroud.

Estimated Value:	Excellent:	$405.00
	Very good:	$325.00

Dan Wesson Model FB 44 & FB 744

Caliber: 44 magnum and 44 Special
Action: Double or single; exposed hammer
Cylinder: 6-shot swing-out
Barrel: 4", 5", 6", or 8"; fixed
Sights: Red ramp front, adjustable rear
Finish: Blued or brushed stainless steel (FB 744); Hogue finger grooved rubber grips
Length Overall: 9¾" to 13¾"
Approximate wt.: 50 to 66 oz.
Comments: Introduced in the early 1990's; add 10% for stainless steel (FB 744); add 1% per inch for barrel length over 4".

Estimated Value:	Excellent:	$300.00
	Very good:	$240.00

Dan Wesson Model 45-VH & 745-VH

Similar to the Model 45-V with heavier bull barrel. Price increases with barrel length. Add 17% for stainless steel (745-VH).

Estimated Value:	Excellent:	$340.00 - $370.00
	Very good:	$270.00 - $300.00

Dan Wesson Model 445V

Dan Wesson Model FB44

Dan Wesson Model FB-14 & FB-714

Caliber: 357 magnum and 38 Special
Action: Double or single; exposed hammer
Cylinder: 6-shot swing-out
Barrel: 2½" or 4"; fixed
Sights: Fixed
Finish: Blued or stainless steel (FB-714); smooth wood grips
Length Overall: 8¼" to 9¾"
Approximate wt.: 36 to 40 oz.
Comments: Introduced in the early 1990's; add 8% for stainless steel (FB-714); add 2% for 4" barrel.
Estimated Value: Excellent: $185.00
Very good: $150.00

Dan Wesson Model FB-14

Dan Wesson Model FB-15 & FB-715

Same as the Model FB-14 & FB-714 except: 3", 4", 5", or 6" barrel; adjustable rear sight; add 8% for stainless steel (FB-715); add 2% per inch of barrel length over 3".
Estimated Value: Excellent: $195.00
Very good: $155.00

Dan Wesson Model 738P

Dan Wesson Model 738P

Caliber: 38 Special +P
Action: Double or single; exposed hammer
Cylinder: 5-shot swing-out
Barrel: 2" fixed
Sights: Fixed
Finish: Stainless steel, wood or rubber grips
Length Overall: 6½"
Approximate wt.: 24½ oz.
Comments: Made in the early to mid 1990's.
Estimated Value: Excellent: $215.00
Very good: $170.00

COLLECTOR BOOKS

Informing Today's Collector

For over two decades we have been keeping collectors informed on trends and values in all fields of antiques and collectibles.

DOLLS, FIGURES & TEDDY BEARS

4707	A Decade of **Barbie** Dolls & Collectibles, 1981–1991, Summers	$19.95
4631	**Barbie** Doll Boom, 1986–1995, Augustyniak	$18.95
2079	**Barbie** Doll Fashions, Volume I, Eames	$24.95
3957	**Barbie** Exclusives, Rana	$18.95
4632	**Barbie** Exclusives, Book II, Rana	$18.95
4557	**Barbie**, The First 30 Years, Deutsch	$24.95
4657	**Barbie** Years, 1959–1995, Olds	$16.95
3310	**Black Dolls**, 1820–1991, Perkins	$17.95
3873	**Black Dolls**, Book II, Perkins	$17.95
1529	Collector's Encyclopedia of **Barbie** Dolls, DeWein	$19.95
4506	Collector's Guide to **Dolls in Uniform**, Bourgeois	$18.95
3727	Collector's Guide to **Ideal Dolls**, Izen	$18.95
3728	Collector's Guide to Miniature **Teddy Bears**, Powell	$17.95
3967	Collector's Guide to **Trolls**, Peterson	$19.95
4571	**Liddle Kiddles**, Identification & Value Guide, Langford	$18.95
4645	**Madame Alexander** Dolls Price Guide #21, Smith	$9.95
3733	**Modern Collector's** Dolls, Sixth Series, Smith	$24.95
3991	**Modern Collector's** Dolls, Seventh Series, Smith	$24.95
4647	**Modern Collector's** Dolls, Eighth Series, Smith	$24.95
4640	Patricia Smith's **Doll Values**, Antique to Modern, 12th Edition	$12.95
3826	Story of **Barbie**, Westenhouser	$19.95
1513	**Teddy Bears & Steiff** Animals, Mandel	$9.95
1817	**Teddy Bears & Steiff** Animals, 2nd Series, Mandel	$19.95
2084	**Teddy Bears, Annalee's & Steiff** Animals, 3rd Series, Mandel	$19.95
1808	Wonder of **Barbie**, Manos	$9.95
1430	World of **Barbie** Dolls, Manos	$9.95

FURNITURE

1457	American **Oak** Furniture, McNerney	$9.95
3716	American **Oak** Furniture, Book II, McNerney	$12.95
1118	Antique **Oak** Furniture, Hill	$7.95
2132	Collector's Encyclopedia of **American** Furniture, Vol. I, Swedberg	$24.95
2271	Collector's Encyclopedia of **American** Furniture, Vol. II, Swedberg	$24.95
3720	Collector's Encyclopedia of **American** Furniture, Vol. III, Swedberg	$24.95
3878	Collector's Guide to **Oak** Furniture, George	$12.95
1755	Furniture of the **Depression Era**, Swedberg	$19.95
3906	**Heywood-Wakefield** Modern Furniture, Rouland	$18.95
1885	**Victorian** Furniture, Our American Heritage, McNerney	$9.95
3829	**Victorian** Furniture, Our American Heritage, Book II, McNerney	$9.95
3869	**Victorian** Furniture books, 2 volume set, McNerney	$19.90

JEWELRY, HATPINS, WATCHES & PURSES

1712	Antique & Collector's **Thimbles** & Accessories, Mathis	$19.95
1748	Antique **Purses**, Revised Second Ed., Holiner	$19.95
1278	Art Nouveau & Art Deco **Jewelry**, Baker	$9.95
4558	**Christmas Pins**, Past and Present, Gallina	$18.95
3875	Collecting Antique **Stickpins**, Kerins	$16.95
3722	Collector's Ency. of **Compacts, Carryalls & Face Powder Boxes**, Mueller	$24.95
4655	Complete Price Guide to **Watches**, #16, Shugart	$26.95
1716	Fifty Years of Collectible **Fashion Jewelry**, 1925-1975, Baker	$19.95
1424	**Hatpins** & Hatpin Holders, Baker	$9.95
4570	Ladies' **Compacts**, Gerson	$24.95
1181	100 Years of Collectible **Jewelry**, 1850-1950, Baker	$9.95
2348	20th Century Fashionable Plastic **Jewelry**, Baker	$19.95
3830	Vintage **Vanity Bags & Purses**, Gerson	$24.95

TOYS, MARBLES & CHRISTMAS COLLECTIBLES

3427	**Advertising Character** Collectibles, Dotz	$17.95
2333	Antique & Collector's **Marbles**, 3rd Ed., Grist	$9.95
3827	Antique & Collector's **Toys**, 1870–1950, Longest	$24.95
3956	Baby Boomer **Games**, Identification & Value Guide, Polizzi	$24.95
3717	**Christmas** Collectibles, 2nd Edition, Whitmyer	$24.95
1752	**Christmas** Ornaments, Lights & Decorations, Johnson	$19.95
4649	Classic Plastic **Model Kits**, Polizzi	$24.95

4559	Collectible **Action Figures**, 2nd Ed., Manos	$17.95
3874	Collectible Coca-Cola Toy **Trucks**, deCourtivron	$24.95
2338	Collector's Encyclopedia of **Disneyana**, Longest, Stern	$24.95
4639	Collector's Guide to **Diecast Toys & Scale Models**, Johnson	$19.95
4651	Collector's Guide to **Tinker Toys**, Strange	$18.95
4566	Collector's Guide to **Tootsietoys**, 2nd Ed., Richter	$19.95
3436	Grist's Big Book of **Marbles**	$19.95
3970	Grist's Machine-Made & Contemporary **Marbles**, 2nd Ed.	$9.95
4569	**Howdy Doody**, Collector's Reference and Trivia Guide, Koch	$16.95
4723	**Matchbox®** Toys, 1948 to 1993, Johnson, 2nd Ed	$18.95
3823	**Mego** Toys, An Illustrated Value Guide, Chrouch	15.95
1540	**Modern Toys** 1930–1980, Baker	$19.95
3888	**Motorcycle** Toys, Antique & Contemporary, Gentry/Downs	$18.95
4728	Schroeder's Collectible **Toys**, Antique to Modern Price Guide, 3rd Ed.	$17.95
1886	Stern's Guide to **Disney** Collectibles	$14.95
2139	Stern's Guide to **Disney** Collectibles, 2nd Series	$14.95
3975	Stern's Guide to **Disney** Collectibles, 3rd Series	$18.95
2028	**Toys**, Antique & Collectible, Longest	$14.95
3979	**Zany Characters** of the Ad World, Lamphier	$16.95

INDIANS, GUNS, KNIVES, TOOLS, PRIMITIVES

1868	Antique **Tools**, Our American Heritage, McNerney	$9.95
2015	Archaic **Indian** Points & Knives, Edler	$14.95
1426	**Arrowheads** & Projectile Points, Hothem	$7.95
4633	**Big Little Books**, Jacobs	$18.95
2279	**Indian** Artifacts of the Midwest, Hothem	$14.95
3885	**Indian** Artifacts of the Midwest, Book II, Hothem	$16.95
1964	**Indian** Axes & Related Stone Artifacts, Hothem	$14.95
2023	**Keen Kutter** Collectibles, Heuring	$14.95
4724	Modern **Guns**, Identification & Values, 11th Ed., Quertermous	$12.95
4505	Standard Guide to **Razors**, Ritchie & Stewart	$9.95
4730	Standard **Knife** Collector's Guide, 3rd Ed., Ritchie & Stewart	$12.95

PAPER COLLECTIBLES & BOOKS

4633	**Big Little Books**, Jacobs	$18.95
1441	Collector's Guide to **Post Cards**, Wood	$9.95
2081	Guide to Collecting **Cookbooks**, Allen	$14.95
4648	Huxford's **Old Book** Value Guide, 8th Ed.	$19.95
2080	Price Guide to **Cookbooks & Recipe Leaflets**, Dickinson	$9.95
2346	**Sheet Music** Reference & Price Guide, 2nd Ed., Pafik & Guiheen	$18.95
4654	**Victorian Trading Cards**, Historical Reference & Value Guide, Cheadle	$19.95

GLASSWARE

1006	**Cambridge Glass** Reprint 1930–1934	$14.95
1007	**Cambridge Glass** Reprint 1949–1953	$14.95
4561	Collectible **Drinking Glasses**, Chase & Kelly	$17.95
4642	Collectible **Glass Shoes**, Wheatley	$19.95
4553	Coll. **Glassware** from the 40's, 50's & 60's, 3rd Ed., Florence	$19.95
2352	Collector's Encyclopedia of **Akro Agate Glassware**, Florence	$14.95
1810	Collector's Encyclopedia of **American Art Glass**, Shuman	$29.95
3312	Collector's Encyclopedia of **Children's Dishes**, Whitmyer	$19.95
4552	Collector's Encyclopedia of **Depression Glass**, 12th Ed., Florence	$19.95
1664	Collector's Encyclopedia of **Heisey Glass**, 1925–1938, Bredehoft	$24.95
3905	Collector's Encyclopedia of **Milk Glass**, Newbound	$24.95
1523	Colors In **Cambridge Glass**, National Cambridge Society	$19.95
4564	**Crackle Glass**, Weitman	$19.95
2275	**Czechoslovakian Glass** and Collectibles, Barta/Rose	$16.95
4714	**Czechoslovakian Glass** and Collectibles, Book II, Barta/Rose	$16.95
4716	**Elegant Glassware** of the Depression Era, 7th Ed., Florence	$19.95
1380	Encylopedia of **Pattern Glass**, McClain	$12.95
3981	Ever's Standard **Cut Glass** Value Guide	$12.95
4659	**Fenton** Art Glass, 1907–1939, Whitmyer	$24.95
3725	**Fostoria**, Pressed, Blown & Hand Molded Shapes, Kerr	$24.95
3883	**Fostoria Stemware**, The Crystal for America, Long & Seate	$24.95
3318	**Glass Animals** of the Depression Era, Garmon & Spencer	$19.95
4644	**Imperial Carnival Glass**, Burns	$18.95

COLLECTOR BOOKS
Informing Today's Collector

3886	**Kitchen Glassware** of the Depression Years, 5th Ed., Florence	$19.95
2394	**Oil Lamps II**, Glass Kerosene Lamps, Thuro	$24.95
4725	Pocket Guide to **Depression Glass**, 10th Ed., Florence	$9.95
4634	Standard Encyclopedia of **Carnival Glass**, 5th Ed., Edwards	$24.95
4635	Standard **Carnival Glass** Price Guide, 10th Ed.	$9.95
3974	Standard Encyclopedia of **Opalescent Glass**, Edwards	$19.95
4731	**Stemware Identification**, Featuring Cordials with Values, Florence	$24.95
3326	**Very Rare Glassware** of the Depression Years, 3rd Series, Florence	$24.95
3909	**Very Rare Glassware** of the Depression Years, 4th Series, Florence	$24.95
4732	**Very Rare Glassware** of the Depression Years, 5th Series, Florence	$24.95
4656	**Westmoreland Glass**, Wilson	$24.95
2224	World of **Salt Shakers**, 2nd Ed., Lechner	$24.95

POTTERY

4630	**American Limoges**, Limoges	$24.95
1312	**Blue & White Stoneware**, McNerney	$9.95
1958	So. Potteries **Blue Ridge Dinnerware**, 3rd Ed., Newbound	$14.95
1959	**Blue Willow**, 2nd Ed., Gaston	$14.95
3816	Collectible **Vernon Kilns**, Nelson	$24.95
3311	Collecting **Yellow Ware** – Id. & Value Guide, McAllister	$16.95
1373	Collector's Encyclopedia of **American Dinnerware**, Cunningham	$24.95
3815	Collector's Encyclopedia of **Blue Ridge Dinnerware**, Newbound	$19.95
4658	Collector's Encyclopedia of **Brush-McCoy Pottery**, Huxford	$24.95
2272	Collector's Encyclopedia of **California Pottery**, Chipman	$24.95
3811	Collector's Encyclopedia of **Colorado Pottery**, Carlton	$24.95
2133	Collector's Encyclopedia of **Cookie Jars**, Roerig	$24.95
3723	Collector's Encyclopedia of **Cookie Jars**, Volume II, Roerig	$24.95
3429	Collector's Encyclopedia of **Cowan Pottery**, Saloff	$24.95
4638	Collector's Encyclopedia of **Dakota Potteries**, Dommel	$24.95
2209	Collector's Encyclopedia of **Fiesta**, 7th Ed., Huxford	$19.95
4718	Collector's Encyclopedia of **Figural Planters & Vases**, Newbound	$19.95
3961	Collector's Encyclopedia of **Early Noritake**, Alden	$24.95
1439	Collector's Encyclopedia of **Flow Blue China**, Gaston	$19.95
3812	Collector's Encyclopedia of **Flow Blue China**, 2nd Ed., Gaston	$24.95
3813	Collector's Encyclopedia of **Hall China**, 2nd Ed., Whitmyer	$24.95
3431	Collector's Encyclopedia of **Homer Laughlin China**, Jasper	$24.95
1276	Collector's Encyclopedia of **Hull Pottery**, Roberts	$19.95
4573	Collector's Encyclopedia of **Knowles, Taylor & Knowles**, Gaston	$24.95
3962	Collector's Encyclopedia of **Lefton China**, DeLozier	$19.95
2210	Collector's Encyclopedia of **Limoges Porcelain**, 2nd Ed., Gaston	$24.95
2334	Collector's Encyclopedia of **Majolica Pottery**, Katz-Marks	$19.95
1358	Collector's Encyclopedia of **McCoy Pottery**, Huxford	$19.95
3963	Collector's Encyclopedia of **Metlox Potteries**, Gibbs Jr.	$24.95
3313	Collector's Encyclopedia of **Niloak**, Gifford	$19.95
3837	Collector's Encyclopedia of **Nippon Porcelain I**, Van Patten	$24.95
2089	Collector's Ency. of **Nippon Porcelain**, 2nd Series, Van Patten	$24.95
1665	Collector's Ency. of **Nippon Porcelain**, 3rd Series, Van Patten	$24.95
3836	**Nippon Porcelain** Price Guide, Van Patten	$9.95
1447	Collector's Encyclopedia of **Noritake**, Van Patten	$19.95
3432	Collector's Encyclopedia of **Noritake**, 2nd Series, Van Patten	$24.95
1037	Collector's Encyclopedia of **Occupied Japan**, Vol. I, Florence	$14.95
1038	Collector's Encyclopedia of **Occupied Japan**, Vol. II, Florence	$14.95
2088	Collector's Encyclopedia of **Occupied Japan**, Vol. III, Florence	$14.95
2019	Collector's Encyclopedia of **Occupied Japan**, Vol. IV, Florence	$14.95
2335	Collector's Encyclopedia of **Occupied Japan**, Vol. V, Florence	$14.95
3964	Collector's Encyclopedia of **Pickard China**, Reed	$24.95
1311	Collector's Encyclopedia of **R.S. Prussia**, 1st Series, Gaston	$24.95
1715	Collector's Encyclopedia of **R.S. Prussia**, 2nd Series, Gaston	$24.95
3726	Collector's Encyclopedia of **R.S. Prussia**, 3rd Series, Gaston	$24.95
3877	Collector's Encyclopedia of **R.S. Prussia**, 4th Series, Gaston	$24.95
1034	Collector's Encyclopedia of **Roseville Pottery**, Huxford	$19.95
1035	Collector's Encyclopedia of **Roseville Pottery**, 2nd Ed., Huxford	$19.95
3357	**Roseville** Price Guide No. 10	$9.95
3965	Collector's Encyclopedia of **Sascha Brastoff**, Conti, Bethany & Seay	$24.95
3314	Collector's Encyclopedia of **Van Briggle** Art Pottery, Sasicki	$24.95
4563	Collector's Encyclopedia of **Wall Pockets**, Newbound	$19.95
2111	Collector's Encyclopedia of **Weller Pottery**, Huxford	$29.95
3452	Coll. Guide to **Country Stoneware & Pottery**, Raycraft	$11.95
2077	Coll. Guide to **Country Stoneware & Pottery**, 2nd Series, Raycraft	$14.95
3434	Coll. Guide to **Hull Pottery**, The Dinnerware Line, Gick-Burke	$16.95

3876	Collector's Guide to **Lu-Ray Pastels**, Meehan	$18.95
3814	Collector's Guide to **Made in Japan** Ceramics, White	$18.95
4646	Collector's Guide to **Made in Japan** Ceramics, Book II, White	$18.95
4565	Collector's Guide to **Rockingham**, The Enduring Ware, Brewer	$14.95
2339	Collector's Guide to **Shawnee Pottery**, Vanderbilt	$19.95
1425	**Cookie Jars**, Westfall	$9.95
3440	**Cookie Jars**, Book II, Westfall	$19.95
3435	Debolt's Dictionary of **American Pottery Marks**	$17.95
2379	Lehner's Ency. of **U.S. Marks** on Pottery, Porcelain & China	$24.95
4722	**McCoy Pottery**, Collector's Reference & Value Guide, Hanson/Nissen	$19.95
3825	**Puritan Pottery**, Morris	$24.95
4726	**Red Wing Art Pottery**, 1920s–1960s, Dollen	$19.95
1670	**Red Wing Collectibles**, DePasquale	$9.95
1440	**Red Wing Stoneware**, DePasquale	$9.95
3738	**Shawnee Pottery**, Mangus	$24.95
4629	Turn of the Century **American Dinnerware**, 1880s–1920s, Jasper	$24.95
4572	**Wall Pockets** of the Past, Perkins	$17.95
3327	**Watt Pottery** – Identification & Value Guide, Morris	$19.95

OTHER COLLECTIBLES

4704	Antique & Collectible **Buttons**, Wisniewski	$19.95
2269	Antique **Brass & Copper** Collectibles, Gaston	$16.95
1880	Antique **Iron**, McNerney	$9.95
3872	Antique **Tins**, Dodge	$24.95
1714	**Black** Collectibles, Gibbs	$19.95
1128	**Bottle** Pricing Guide, 3rd Ed., Cleveland	$7.95
4636	**Celluloid Collectibles**, Dunn	$14.95
3959	**Cereal Box** Bonanza, The 1950's, Bruce	$19.95
3718	Collectible **Aluminum**, Grist	$16.95
3445	Collectible **Cats**, An Identification & Value Guide, Fyke	$18.95
4560	Collectible **Cats**, An Identification & Value Guide, Book II, Fyke	$19.95
1634	Collector's Ency. of Figural & Novelty **Salt & Pepper Shakers**, Davern	$19.95
2020	Collector's Ency. of Figural & Novelty **Salt & Pepper Shakers**, Vol. II, Davern	$19.95
2018	Collector's Encyclopedia of **Granite Ware**, Greguire	$24.95
3430	Collector's Encyclopedia of **Granite Ware**, Book II, Greguire	$24.95
4705	Collector's Guide to **Antique Radios**, 4th Ed., Bunis	$18.95
1916	Collector's Guide to **Art Deco**, Gaston	$14.95
3880	Collector's Guide to **Cigarette Lighters**, Flanagan	$17.95
4637	Collector's Guide to **Cigarette Lighters**, Book II, Flanagan	$17.95
1537	Collector's Guide to **Country Baskets**, Raycraft	$9.95
3966	Collector's Guide to **Inkwells**, Identification & Values, Badders	$18.95
3881	Collector's Guide to **Novelty Radios**, Bunis/Breed	$18.95
4652	Collector's Guide to **Transistor Radios**, 2nd Ed., Bunis	$16.95
4653	Collector's Guide to **TV Memorabilia**, 1960s–1970s, Davis/Morgan	$24.95
2276	**Decoys**, Kangas	$24.95
1629	**Doorstops**, Identification & Values, Bertoia	$9.95
4567	Figural **Napkin Rings**, Gottschalk & Whitson	$18.95
3968	**Fishing Lure** Collectibles, Murphy/Edmisten	$24.95
3817	**Flea Market Trader**, 10th Ed., Huxford	$12.95
3976	Foremost Guide to **Uncle Sam** Collectibles, Czulewicz	$24.95
4641	**Garage Sale & Flea Market Annual**, 4th Ed.	$19.95
3819	**General Store Collectibles**, Wilson	$24.95
4643	**Great American West** Collectibles, Wilson	$24.95
2215	Goldstein's **Coca-Cola** Collectibles	$16.95
3884	Huxford's Collectible **Advertising**, 2nd Ed.	$24.95
2216	**Kitchen Antiques**, 1790–1940, McNerney	$14.95
3321	Ornamental & Figural **Nutcrackers**, Rittenhouse	$16.95
2026	**Railroad** Collectibles, 4th Ed., Baker	$14.95
1632	**Salt & Pepper Shakers**, Guarnaccia	$9.95
1888	**Salt & Pepper Shakers** II, Identification & Value Guide, Book II, Guarnaccia	$14.95
2220	**Salt & Pepper Shakers** III, Guarnaccia	$14.95
3443	**Salt & Pepper Shakers** IV, Guarnaccia	$18.95
4555	**Schroeder's Antiques Price Guide**, 14th Ed., Huxford	$12.95
2096	**Silverplated Flatware**, Revised 4th Edition, Hagan	$14.95
1922	Standard **Old Bottle** Price Guide, Sellari	$14.95
4708	Summers' Guide to **Coca-Cola**	$19.95
3892	**Toy & Miniature Sewing Machines**, Thomas	$18.95
3828	Value Guide to **Advertising Memorabilia**, Summers	$18.95
3977	Value Guide to **Gas Station** Memorabilia, Summers & Priddy	$24.95
3444	**Wanted to Buy**, 5th Edition	$9.95

This is only a partial listing of the books on antiques that are available from Collector Books. All books are well illustrated and contain current values. Most of these books are available from your local bookseller, antique dealer, or public library. If you are unable to locate certain titles in your area, you may order by mail from COLLECTOR BOOKS, P.O. Box 3009, Paducah, KY 42001-3009 ... tomers with Visa or MasterCard may phone in orders from 7:00–4:00 CST, Monday–Friday, Toll Free 1-800-626-5420. Add $2.00 for postage for the fir... ...0 for each additional book. Include item number, title, and price when ordering. Allow 14 to 21 days for delivery.

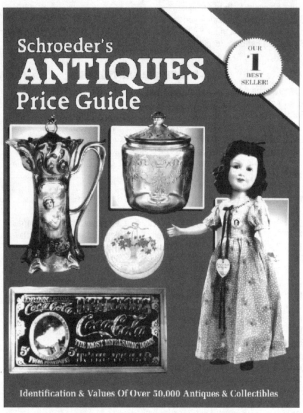